ROYAL
DUTCH
AIR
LINES
H-NKLM
SEE TWICE AS MUCH OF
EUROPE
IN HALF THE TIME

KLM
AMSTERDAM-BATAVIA
DRIEMAAL PER WEEK

BLUE SKIES, ORANGE WINGS

The Global Reach of Dutch Aviation in War and Peace, 1914–1945

BLUE SKIES,

Ryan K. Noppen

ORANGE WINGS

The Global Reach of Dutch Aviation in War and Peace, 1914–1945

Wm. B. Eerdmans Publishing Co.
Grand Rapids, Michigan / Cambridge, U.K.

Published 2016 by
Wm. B. Eerdmans Publishing Co.
2140 Oak Industrial Drive N.E., Grand Rapids, Michigan 49505 /
P.O. Box 163, Cambridge CB3 9PU U.K.

Printed in the United States of America

22 21 20 19 18 17 16 7 6 5 4 3 2 1

Library of Congress Cataloging-in-Publication Data

Noppen, Ryan, author.
Blue skies, orange wings : the global reach of Dutch aviation in war and peace, 1914-1945 / Ryan K. Noppen.
pages cm
Includes bibliographical references and index.
ISBN 978-0-8028-4870-3 (cloth : alk. paper)
1. Aeronautics — Netherlands — History — 20th century.
I. Title.
TL526.N4N67 2016
387.709492'09041 — dc23
2015029836

www.eerdmans.com

CONTENTS

FOREWORD

“Being able to live on air is hard work” was a popular phrase used by Albert Plesman, the first president of KLM Royal Dutch Airlines. In 1919, the former lieutenant aviator was a driving force behind the First Aviation Exhibition, Amsterdam, with more than half a million visitors learning about the transnational phenomenon for the first time. In that same year, he was one of the co-founders of the International Air Travel Association (IATA), before joining KLM. Today, KLM is the oldest airline in the world still operating under its original name —uninterruptedly since its foundation in 1919—from Schiphol Amsterdam Airport.

In 1916, Schiphol started as a small military airfield—barely passable during wet periods. Here, the Dutch army operated a handful of aircraft and pilots. Nevertheless, General C. J. Snijders, Commander-in-Chief of the Dutch land and naval forces, played a crucial role in the development of aviation in the Netherlands. In 1913, he founded the Luchtvaartafdeeling (LVA, Aviation Group), later renamed the Royal Dutch Airforce, becoming a major advocate of civil aviation.

“Skeptics . . . will not further the cause of aviation,” lieutenant aviator Marius Hofstee assured the readers of the brochure entitled “The Future of Aviation in the Netherlands,” which was published in 1918. Sure enough, no skepticism existed. Referring to the legend, the Flying Dutchman became reality.

“I was very fortunate to be born at precisely the right time. If I had started off a few years earlier, I would have risked breaking my neck performing the first primitive test flights. Had I waited another two years, the required technological know-how would have been beyond me,” is how Anthony Fokker looked back on his decision to be an aviator. Fokker developed into a very successful aircraft manufacturer, with factories in Germany, the Netherlands, and the United States.

Ryan Noppen has managed to present these developments taking place between 1914 and 1945 in a highly readable format. Courage and vision have made the Netherlands a key player in global aviation ever since the beginning of the period described by Noppen. He tells the fascinating story of all those resourceful Flying Dutchmen in *Blue Skies, Orange Wings: The Global Reach of Dutch Aviation in War and Peace, 1914-1945*, an attractive, visual piece of work which goes beyond the initial pioneering phase of Dutch aviation. Plesman referred to the relationship between man and machine clearly and concisely: “The Ocean of the Air Unites all People.”

PROF. JAN PETER BALKENENDE, PH.D.
Former Prime Minister of the
Kingdom of the Netherlands

FOREWORD

Ryan Noppen's book about the global reach of Dutch aviation from 1914 to 1945 is another illustration of former President Clinton's remark that the Netherlands is a small country with a big footprint in the world. In the First World War, Dutch airplane designer Anthony Fokker worked on the German side, while his compatriot Frits Koolhoven worked for the British. Fokker's Triplane became famous as the German Red Baron's plane, and even inspired Charles Schulz's immortal dog Snoopy. In this time and era of Boeings and Airbuses, many will have forgotten that in the Roaring Twenties, Fokker planes were the dominant passenger planes in the United States before Donald Douglas introduced his DC-2 and DC-3. This book reads like an adventure story about an age when flying was still a new and thrilling, but also a dangerous experience, an experience culminating in World War II, when planes became destructive instruments of war.

While the Dutch developed their national air forces in the Netherlands and in their former colony the Netherlands East Indies, now Indonesia, they became the world's pioneers in passenger travel when Albert Plesman established KLM Royal Dutch Airlines in 1919. He started a passenger service in Europe which became a frontrunner with the Fokker F.III, the first plane designed specifically for passenger transport. Plesman expanded his network worldwide by flying passengers to Java in the Netherlands East Indies, in this way initiating one of the first passenger services to Asia and so giving a new meaning to the 17th century legend of the Flying Dutchman. While the Dutch had been able against all odds to stay neutral in the First World War, they were not so lucky in the Second. Many people may be aware of the ruthless destruction of Rotterdam by Göring's Luftwaffe bombers, but it is perhaps less known that thanks to the brave actions of the Dutch military and naval air forces, and in particular Dutch anti-aircraft gunners, 328 German planes (mainly Junkers 52, used by German paratroopers in the first airborne operation in World War II) were destroyed. This serious loss of Junkers 52 transports for airborne operations would affect Hitler's planned invasion of Great Britain in the fall of 1940.

In *Blue Skies, Orange Wings* (orange is the national color of the Netherlands, as soccer and speed skating fans will know) Ryan Noppen presents a thorough image of Dutch aviation in a time of fast changes in air transport. The book is illustrated with many, sometimes rare pictures and drawings of the main players and planes concerned, and interspersed with their personal testimonies. For example, Fokker's rascally adventure of illegally taking more than one hundred Fokker D.VII fighters and other Fokkers by train from a chaotic and dangerous postwar Germany to the Netherlands is highlighted.

These planes became the basis of his airplane industry. I found the author's detailed description of Fokker's entry into the American market particularly intriguing. Fokker entered the USA with his planes and started production there at a time when America was still behind Europe in developing an aerial civil transport and cargo transcontinental network. American general Billy Mitchell, Henry Ford, Juan Trippe of Pan American, Major Carl Spaatz, Fokker's personal friend Donald Douglas, and Elliott Roosevelt, President Roosevelt's son—they all play important roles in the chapter "The Dutch Immigrate to America." In a chapter titled "East Indiamen of the Air," no doubt a reference to the Dutch East Company, Noppen paints a fascinating picture of KLM Royal Dutch Airlines' pioneering of prestigious travel to Asia in the 1930s. While many Fokker airplanes played a key role in the exploration of difficult-to-access parts of the world like the North and South Poles, the Netherlands more slowly than surely developed its air forces in the Netherlands and the Netherlands East Indies. Because of the Dutch government's false hopes to stay out of the next war, both air forces were not equipped to fight the enormous forces of Nazi Germany and the Japanese Empire when these attacked in 1940 and 1942. But with the planes that the pilots had—mainly Dutch, American, and English—they fought heroically up to the end of the war in both the European and Asia-Pacific theatres. To defend the Netherlands East Indies following the Japanese attack on Pearl Harbor, Dutch pilots mostly flew mediocre, outclassed American fighters and bombers like the Curtiss Hawk and Brewster Buffalo fighters, and Glenn Martin bombers that were ultimately no match for the numerically superior Japanese planes like the Mitsubishi Zeros.

All in all, this books presents a fascinating view on the Dutch role in both military and civil aviation in Europe, the U.S., and Asia during and in between the two terrible wars that affected the world in the twentieth century. The author's insight into the Dutch military and political perspective on aviation, to which two Dutch companies, KLM Royal Dutch Airlines and Fokker, added a global vision, adds to the value of this book for non-Dutch readers.

Klaas van der Tempel
MA History, Leyden University
Consul General of the Netherlands in Chicago

ACKNOWLEDGMENTS

There are many people I owe thanks to for assisting me in the research, image collecting, and writing of this book. My first thanks go to George Harper, William Spoelhof, and Conrad Bult, all of whom actively encouraged me to put a rough idea to pen and paper. Second, I wish to thank William Eerdmans for taking on my proposal and overseeing its transition from rough outlines into a beautiful illustrated tome; not to mention our civilized business meetings where progress was discussed over a number of *borreltjes* of Jenever.

The following is a list of individuals who were kind enough to provide me with photographs of surviving Dutch aircraft from museums and other sites throughout the world: Andy Davey, aircraft photographer; Antonio Jesus Muñoz Garcia, of the Museo de Aeronáutica y Astronáutica del Ejercito del Aire en Madrid; Erin Hansen, of the Brisbane Airport Corporation Pty Limited; Kylie Jennings, of the Broome Historical Society Museum; Peter de Jong, fellow Dutch aviation author; Max Kaegi, of the Swiss Aircraft Museum at Duebendorf, Switzerland; Kai Mecklin, director of the Finnish Air Force Museum; Park M. Morrison, of the Owls Head Transportation Museum; Don Parsons, aircraft photographer; Tony Podmore of the Shuttleworth Collection; Clark Seaborn, patron of the Western Canada Aviation Museum; Per Arvid Tellemann and Anders Utgård, of the Norwegian Aviation Museum; Thamara Vervuurt, of Het Curaçaosch Museum; Max Wenden, professional Antarctic pilot; and András Zboray, of Fliegel Jezerniczky Expeditions. Thanks also go to professional artist Frank Speyers, who offered advice on the color profile drawings I drafted for this book.

Next come those who assisted me in my research: Christina Douglass and Brett Stolle of the Museum of the United States Air Force; former Collectiebeheer Dirk de Graaf of the Aviodrome and his research assistant Erik Ruitenberg as well as the current Collectiebeheer of the Aviodrome, Will Porrio; Robert Heesterbeek, of the Militair Luchtvaart Museum; B. D. D. "Duy" Huynh, of the Netherlands Institute for Military History; Thomas James of Moundsville, West Virginia, for giving me a tour of the old Fokker factory at Glen Dale, West Virginia; and Harry van der Meer, curator of the Koolhoven Society. Thanks also go to Dr. Conrad Kiewiet De Jonge, ML-KNIL bomber pilot and veteran of the Second World War, who kindly shared his personal journal and photograph collection with me.

Special thanks go to the prolific author and aviation specialist R. E. G. Davies, of the National Air and Space Museum, who shared his vast knowledge and research collections with me as well as edited the initial drafts of this book. Special thanks also go to Colonel Douglas C.

Dildy (USAF, ret.) for our frequent talks on Dutch military aviation as well as his research and editorial assistance. I also wish to thank Rev. William and Althea Buursma for their willing help with the Dutch language whenever I ran into translation difficulties.

Finally, I owe a great deal of thanks to my family: warm thanks to Hans, Astrid, Daniel, and Barbara Noppen for putting me up, for sending me books and articles on Dutch aviation, and for the nice family dinners in Den Haag; warm thanks to Maarten, Ellie, and Chris Noppen, as well as Jeroen Noppen, for hosting me in Rotterdam and for the wonderful meals at Chez Maarten and Hotel New York; warm thanks to David, Fiona, and Finula Op't Holt for putting me up in London and introducing me to some fine Twickingham pubs. Warm thanks (and treats) go to my furry boys Wolfie and Chester who were with me every late night I was busily working away on this book and for their assistance with my research, whether it be falling asleep on an open notebook or chewing the cover off my first edition of Anthony Fokker's autobiography. Warm thanks to my brother Kevin, who made sure I did not spend too many weekend evenings working away on this tome; last but not least, the warmest thanks go to my mom and dad, who have always supported my efforts with the greatest love, patience, and care—for reading me books on planes, trains, and automobiles when I was a kid—for watching my furry boys while I was away on research trips—for the constant stream of baked goods . . . and the occasional sanity-preserving bottle of Tangueray —to both of you this book is lovingly dedicated.

INTRODUCTION

In a bit of historical irony, the very first Fokker F.VII trimotor — the most iconic Dutch aircraft of the interwar years and the world's first purpose-designed commercial aircraft built in numbers—sits not in a museum in the Netherlands but in the Henry Ford Museum in Dearborn, Michigan, far from Amsterdam where it was assembled in the Fokker factory in 1925. The airplane was purchased by Henry Ford after it flew in the Ford Reliability Air Tour, a series of air races across much of the American Midwest, sponsored by Ford, to promote the safety of flight to the American public—and to promote the new aviation division of Ford's massive motor car company. This F.VIIa/3m eventually became a piece of Ford's growing collection of historical artifacts.

Six decades later, when I was a boy, my parents took my brother and me to the Henry Ford Museum. I imagine we all saw the Fokker trimotor, but admittedly I do not remember it making much of an impression. I was too busy looking at all the cars, trucks, and trains in the museum (my early love of vehicles probably came from Richard Scarry's children's classic *Cars and Trucks and Things That Go*, which I insisted my parents read to me every other night before bedtime). It did not dawn on me until much later that perhaps the most important surviving aircraft in Dutch aviation history sat only two hours away from where I grew up in Kalamazoo, Michigan.

As time went on I became more and more interested in aviation and its history, studying it in graduate school, working with it in the defense industry, and reading about it in my spare time. After visiting the Militair Luchtvaart Museum in Soesterberg, the Netherlands, in 2004, I became increasingly interested in the aviation history of my ancestral homeland. The tenacity with which pilots of the Militair Luchtvaart fought the Luftwaffe during the *Meidagen* (literally "May Days," referring to May 10-14, 1940—the German invasion of the Netherlands) particularly impressed me. Additionally, the aerial empire established by the Dutch national airline KLM in the 1920s and 1930s was a remarkable achievement. I also learned of the role Dutch aviation played in my family's history, going well beyond the beautiful two-tone blue 747s of KLM that brought my great-aunt and great-uncle to visit when I was a child or carried me over to Europe in my college years for my first in-depth international travels. I was told stories of how great-aunts and great-uncles visited Schiphol in their childhood to see the aircraft of KLM, of flights taken over the East Indies in the Fokker trimotors of the Dutch colonial airline KNILM by relatives and ancestors, and of German paratroopers coming down in the village of Valkenburg, north of The Hague, and setting up machine gun nests near where my great-grandparents and their parents lived and worked.

These are but a few personal examples of how aviation in the Netherlands impacted people's lives. Dutch aviation had a worldwide impact and was a very tangible development in the modernization of society in the Netherlands in the twentieth century. This book is a survey of that development.

Early on in my research I found that the bookshops and *antiquariaats* of Amsterdam, The Hague, Rotterdam, and Delft were filled with books on Dutch aviation . . . not surprisingly, written in Dutch. I quickly discovered that there was no comparable account in the English language; and that is the void this book is intended to fill. The "Golden Age" of Dutch aviation roughly spans the first half of the twentieth century. This period saw a massive leap in aviation technology, spurred on by military necessity because of the world wars. It saw the rapid transition of commercial flight from thrill-seeking passengers riding in the open cockpits of biplanes, flying more for the experience than to get from one place to another, to relatively modern airliners providing regularly scheduled flights and the development of aspects of modern air travel that are still with us today: in-flight meals, beverage service, stewards and stewardesses to look after passengers' needs, cushy reclining seats, and (sigh) surcharges for overweight luggage.

Anyone familiar with the history of the Netherlands knows of the *Gouden Eeuw*, or Golden Age, of the seventeenth century; this was the age of Rembrandt and Vermeer but also the period that saw the Netherlands create a worldwide empire, dominate seaborne trade, and hold its own against the military superpowers of Spain, England, and France. In the interwar years of the twentieth century, KLM created a successful airline whose routes spanned the globe and reached all corners of the Dutch Empire. KLM was a model airline that successfully sought the proper balance between sound financial management—taking full advantage of the latest technical innovations—and superior service to its patrons. As a result, by 1939 it was the second-largest airline in Europe (surpassed only by Deutsche Lufthansa), beating out the major airlines of France and Great Britain. The Dutch domestic aero industry was also innovative and very successful during this period, selling aircraft throughout the world. Its success is attested by this fact: more Fokker-built airliners were flying in the United States in the late 1920s than those of any American aero manufacturer. The number of Fokker aircraft used on record-breaking and major exploratory flights is unmatched. Finally, the combat aircraft produced in the Netherlands and the tenacity of Dutch military pilots played an important role in the defense of the Netherlands in 1940 and the East Indies in 1941-1942. While the Netherlands was no longer a formidable military power, its airmen nevertheless demonstrated that they were very capable of giving the Axis powers a bloody nose. Thus, just as the Netherlands played a disproportionate role on the world stage during its *Gouden Eeuw*, so too did Dutch aviation play a leading role in the "Golden Age" of aviation.

Now when I go back to the Henry Ford Museum, I am still just as fascinated by the cars, trucks, and trains as I was as a child. However, I now find myself spending much more time looking over Tony Fokker's first trimotor airliner; this airplane was the first to fly to the North Pole and laid the groundwork for a Dutch domination of the civil airliner trade in the 1920s. In a sense, it is a testament to the impact the Netherlands had on world aviation that this important aircraft should reside far from its Amsterdam birthplace . . . and an interesting coincidence that the first place this author traveled to begin the research for this book was only a two-hour drive from his home.

ABBREVIATIONS AND FOREIGN TERMS

ABBREVIATIONS

KLM – Koninklijke Luchtvaart Maatschappij: Royal Dutch Airlines (1919-present)
KNIL – Koninklijk Nederlands-Indisch Leger: Royal Netherlands East Indies Army
KNILM – Koninklijke Nederlandsch-Indische Luchtvaart Maatschappij: Royal Netherlands East Indian Airways (1928-1947)
LA-KNIL – Luchtvaartafdeling van het Koninklijk Nederlands-Indisch Leger: Aviation Service of the Royal Netherlands East Indies Army (1921-1939)
LVA – Luchtvaartafdeeling: (Army) Aviation Service (1913-1938)
ML – Wapen der Militair Luchtvaart: Military Aviation Arm (1938-1940)
MLD – Marine-Luchtvaartdienst: Navy Aviation Service (1917-present)
ML-KNIL – Militair Luchtvaart van het Koninklijk Nederlands-Indisch Leger: Military Aviation of the Royal Netherlands East Indies Army (1939-1950)
PVA-KNIL – Proefvliegafdeling van het Koninklijk Nederlands-Indisch Leger: Test Flight Service of the Royal Netherlands East Indies Army (1915-1921)
RAAF – Royal Australian Air Force (1921-present)
RAF – Royal Air Force (1918-present)
USAAC – United States Army Air Corps (1926-1941)
USAAF – United States Army Air Force (1941-1947)

TERMS *(all Dutch unless otherwise noted):*

Afdeling: squadron
Bombardeervliegtuigafdeling (BomVA): Bombardment Squadron
Fallschirmjäger *(German):* paratroopers
Groepen Vliegtuigen (GVT): aircraft group (MLD term)
Jachtgroep (JG): Fighter Group
Jachtvliegtuigafdeling (JaVA): fighter squadron
Koninklijke Landmacht (KL): Royal Netherlands Army
Koninklijke Marine (KM): Royal Netherlands Navy
Luchtvaartbrigade (ML): Aviation Brigade
Luchtvaartregiment (LVR): Aviation Regiment
Luftlande *(German):* air-landing troops
Luftwaffe: German air force (1935-1945)
Meidagen: "May Days" – term for the days of the German invasion, May 10-14, 1940
Patrouille: flight (ML-KNIL term)
Strategische Verkenningsvliegtuigafdeling (StratVerVA): Strategic Reconnaissance Squadron
Verkenningsafdeling (VerVA): reconnaissance squadron (ML-KNIL term)
Verkenningsgroep (VG): Reconnaissance Group
Vliegtuiggroep (VLG): Aircraft Group (ML-KNIL term)

A group of Farman pusher biplanes lined up for an air race on the beach at Scheveningen on March 6, 1916. This race was organized as a publicity stunt to demonstrate the potential of the military's air arm to the Dutch public. [Militair Luchtvaart Museum, Soesterberg]

Chapter One

THE FIRST WORLD WAR

Flying Dutchmen

The rise of Dutch aviation came not out of an interest in flight as a sport, which had happened particularly in the United States and France, but rather out of the early flames of World War I. The possibility of an impending war involving the great powers of Europe rumbled in the distance across the continent for several years leading up to 1914. Traditional colonial and industrial powers such as Great Britain and France were eager to maintain their supremacy on the world scene against the rising colonial and industrial power of the newly unified German Reich. Older empires, such as Russia, Austria-Hungary, and the Ottoman Empire, struggled for survival against the growing industrial might of Western Europe. And then there were other countries, such as the newly formed kingdom of Italy, which had its own imperial agenda; Belgium, with its huge Congo territory; and the kingdom of the Netherlands, a traditional colonial power that simply sought to maintain its place in the world. The Netherlands had no interest in becoming involved in a major European war: involvement on either side of the conflict might risk invasion or the loss of the empire. The nation had not fought any great power since the Napoleonic Wars, and at the beginning of the twentieth century its army and navy were in great need of modernization.

In terms of foreign policy, the Dutch government held the British in low regard because of British action against Dutch settlers in South Africa during the Boer War at the turn of the century. The Netherlands was in no position to come to the aid of the Boers against the might of the British Empire; but its relationship with Germany improved because the Germans helped to supply the Boers with munitions and supplies via German East Africa and Southwest Africa. Foreign relations with Germany took a downturn in 1906, however, when the Dutch government learned about the Schleiffen Plan.

While the great powers of Europe were establishing a system of alliances at the end of the nineteenth and the beginning of the twentieth centuries, most nations had devised intricate plans that would be implemented upon the outbreak of war. Developed in 1905 by the German chief of the general staff, Alfred von Schleiffen, the Schleiffen Plan called for German armies, in the event of a war with France, to sweep through southern Holland, Belgium, and northern France to encircle the French armies stationed along the German border and to rapidly capture Paris. The plan was revised six years later by Schleiffen's successor, Helmuth von Moltke, who decided that the violation of Dutch territory would bring more harm to Germany than good. The Dutch government did not learn about this, and thus from 1906 to

As an engineer by military training, General Cornelis Jacobus Snijders recognized the potential offered by aircraft in modern warfare and played an important role in the creation of the LVA. During the war, Snijders was made the supreme commander of the Dutch army and navy and was given the unenviable task of preparing the Dutch armed forces for war while at the same time not antagonizing either side of the conflict by maintaining strict neutrality.

1914, the Netherlands began to strengthen its military defenses. This was meant to act as a deterrent to nations who considered them a weakened power and an easy target for invasion. The Dutch military air service was born out of this atmosphere of rearmament.

Proponents of military aviation in the Netherlands before World War I had a strong ally in the supreme commander of land and sea forces (Opperbevelhebber van Land- en Zeemacht), General Cornelis Jacobus Snijders, who had a great interest in aviation and believed that it would play an important role in future conflicts. He became the head of the Nederlandsche Vereeniging voor Luchtvaart (NVvL), the Dutch Association for Aviation, in 1907, and in 1911 he began to push for the creation of a military air service. Bureaucratic squabbling kept this from being created for another two years, but on April 16, 1913, Queen Wilhelmina signed Order in Council #29, and on July 1, 1913, the Luchtvaartafdeeling (LVA), the Army Air Service, was born. The navy also operated aircraft, but it did not formally establish its air arm, the Marine Luchtvaartdienst (MLD), until August 21, 1917.

The first officer selected to command the LVA was Captain H. Walaardt Sacré, a member of the NVvL who had also been a student of Snijders at the Koninklijke Militaire Academie. As an early member of the NVvL, Sacré had an excellent knowledge of the state of European aviation before 1913. He had been sent to Germany to study the use and tactics of balloons, and also to France, where he learned how to pilot an airship. The LVA had three other professional pilots at its beginning: Lieutenant Floris A. Van Heyst, the first test pilot of the LVA and one of its first instructors; Lieutenant W. C. J. Versteegh, who later became the commandant of the LVA's flight school and was responsible for training the first generation of Dutch military pilots; and Lieutenant L. A. Coblijn. It had only one aircraft, which the LVA rented from its designer, Marinus van Meel. The aircraft, named *De Brik* ("the brig"), was van Meel's improved version of a Farman biplane. The Netherlands had no domestic aircraft industry at that time, and it had to look abroad to find aircraft for its fledgling air service.[1]

In May 1913, Sacré and Van Heyst went to France to examine the products of the French aero industry, which at the time was the most advanced in the world. After a thorough search and a testing of a number of aircraft, Sacré selected the Farman HF.20 pusher biplane as the first standard aircraft of the LVA and purchased three of them. Farman had established itself as one of the world's leading aircraft manufacturers. Farman aircraft of the 20 Series were widely used during the first year of World War I and were purchased by the French, British, Russian, Romanian, Belgian, Italian, and Dutch air forces. The three HF-20s that Sacré purchased for the LVA were delivered to the military airfield at Soesterberg in September 1913. Van Heyst and the other pilots found the Farmans to have suitable performance, and they ordered six of the slightly improved HF.22 biplanes before the outbreak of the war. On June 13, 1914, another improved "Brik" from van Meel was added to the LVA. When large-scale hostilities broke out, this brought the total number of LVA aircraft to nine: four Farman HF.22s (only four of the six ordered from Farman had been delivered), three HF-20s, and two "Brikken."

It is interesting that, when World War I began, the two Dutch aircraft designers who would later become the two greatest aircraft manufacturers in the Netherlands were working abroad for opposing sides of the conflict. Sytse Frederick Willem ("Frits") Koolhoven, who flew the *Heidevogel*, the first aircraft of his own design on July 29, 1910, moved to France in 1911 and later to Great Britain in 1913, and worked for several aviation firms. Anthony Herman Gerard Fokker, who built his first aircraft, the

Spin, in a zeppelin hangar in Baden Baden in 1910, established his own company in Schwerin, Germany, a town to the east of Hamburg, in 1913, and was building aircraft for Die Fliegertruppen des deutschen Kaiserreiches (Imperial German Army Air Service), known during the war as Die Deutsche Luftstreitkräfte.[2]

The Fight to Remain Neutral

At the beginning of the Great War, the Netherlands declared itself to be strictly neutral. On August 3, 1914, Queen Wilhelmina made the following decree:

> We, Wilhelmina, by the grace of God, Queen of the Netherlands, Princess of Orange-Nassau, etc.
>
> Considering that it is necessary to prevent foreign armies from obtaining information concerning our preparations for war. . . .
>
> Having approved and undertaken to order that the crossing of the land frontiers by airships not belonging to the Netherlands land or sea forces is prohibited for so long as the conditions named under paragraph 1 of Article 1 of the law of May 23, 1899 (Staatsblad, No. 128) exist.[3]

Strict neutrality called for the defense of all its borders—aerial as well as territorial land borders and nautical borders. The airplane was a relatively new invention, and its full military potential had not yet been defined. Other nations had previously experimented with aircraft in battle on only a few occasions; most of the great pow-

Major Hendrik Walaardt Sacré was the LVA's first commanding officer and led the service through the years of the First World War. During the war Walaardt Sacré pushed for the creation of a modern air force by encouraging domestic industry to produce aircraft, evaluating and putting modern interned aircraft into service, and pushing the government for more funding and to attempt to purchase modern aircraft abroad. [Militair Luchtvaart Museum, Soesterberg]

ABOVE *The first aircraft acquired by the LVA was a domestic machine nicknamed the "Brik" (brick) produced by early Dutch aviation pioneer Marinus van Meel (left). Van Meel was hired to train the LVA's first pilots. The LVA's early pilots were trained on the Brik and a second larger Brik but van Meel never built another aircraft for the LVA, closing his business after he was mobilized into the army after the outbreak of the First World War.* [Militair Luchtvaart Museum, Soesterberg]

RIGHT *Lieutenant Floris A. Van Heyst in van Meel's Brik. The first test pilot of the LVA and one of its first instructors, Van Heyst, along with Jan Versteegh, trained most of the LVA's first pilots throughout the First World War. Van Heyst returned to the air service in the late 1930s to become the last commandant of the LVA and went on to command the Luchtvaartbrigade in the newly formed Militair Luchtvaart, or ML, until the end of the German invasion of the Netherlands in May 1940.* [Militair Luchtvaart Museum, Soesterberg]

FÉDÉRATION AÉRONAUTIQUE INTERNATIONALE.

ÖSTERREICH.
AUTRICHE. Nr. 40

Die unterzeichnete von der **Fédération Aéronautique Internationale für Österreich** anerkannte Sportmacht bescheinigt, daß	Nous soussignés, pouvoir sportif reconnu par la **Fédération Aéronautique Internationale pour l'Autriche,** certifions que

Herr / Monsieur Leutnant d. k. holl. Landarmee William Carel Johan Versteegh
geb. in / né à Solo, Java am / le 19. Mai 1886

nach Erfüllung aller von der **F. A. I.** verlangten Bedingungen diplomiert wurde als	ayant rempli toutes les conditions imposées par la **F. A. I.** a été breveté

Aviatischer Pilot – Aviateur

WIEN, am / le 2. November 1911

ÖSTERREICHISCHER AÉRO-CLUB

Präsident: / Le Président:
Schriftführer: / Le Secrétaire:

Unterschrift des Inhabers:

ers had taken careful notes on the various uses of aircraft and had laid the foundations of air industries that would greatly expand throughout the war. The Netherlands, on the other hand, staggered far behind other European nations on the aeronautical front. The Dutch had only four aircraft at their disposal when the war began, with another six on order. Germany had fifty-eight times as many aircraft, France had thirty-five times as many, and even Belgium had six times as many. This numerical disadvantage was not because of Dutch lack of interest in military aviation; rather, it was the result of the bureaucratic squabbling of a government that had mixed views on the war and on Holland's military preparedness or lack thereof. During the war the Dutch were to struggle with the issue of neutrality, because both sides of the conflict made ever-increasing demands on and threats to the nation's sovereignty. In the end, the Netherlands succeeded in maintaining its neutrality and developed two military air services to the best of its ability. Throughout World War I and immediately after it, the strict neutrality pursued by the Netherlands was frequently threatened by the actions of aircraft from belligerent nations and by Dutch attempts to acquire aircraft for its military air services.[4]

When the war began, the Netherlands was caught between two bellicose and threatening great powers. At various times both Germany and Great Britain sought to push the Netherlands into the war—each on its own side. In some instances the British wanted the Netherlands to tie down more German forces on yet another front, and they also wanted to obtain the Dutch merchant fleet either through alliance or capture. For the first two years of the war Germany was less belligerent because the Netherlands provided an important avenue through which trade could still take place outside the British blockade of the Central Powers' ports. Beginning in 1917, however, Germany took a more threatening approach. The Dutch government then recognized the designs that both powers had on the nation and decided to play a diplomatic

Left *Johan Carel Willem Versteegh was trained as a pilot in 1911 at the flying school of Igo Etrich, the designer of the early Taube monoplane, at Wiener Neustadt in Austria-Hungary. As one of the LVA's first pilots, he became the most skilled Dutch pilot during the First World War, flying almost every aircraft acquired during the conflict, and he was made the commander of the LVA's flying school at Soesterberg airfield. His jovial nature coupled with his insistence on precision flying earned him the nickname of Baas Versteegh among his pilots.* [Militair Luchtvaart Museum, Soesterberg]

Above *Versteegh's first flight certificate.* [Militair Luchtvaart Museum, Soesterberg]

Queen Wilhelmina entering the Ridderzaal in the Binnenhof complex on Prinsjesdag for the annual opening of the Dutch Parliament in The Hague. The Queen took a much more militant view of neutrality than did the parliamentary cabinet, particularly when it came to the matter of the British blockade zone around Germany. Although she worried about a German invasion of the Netherlands at the beginning of the war, Queen Wilhelmina saw the British blockade as a greater threat to Dutch sovereignty.

game that would maintain a careful balance in order to maintain Dutch territorial and imperial integrity.

There was a consensus among the Dutch leadership about adhering to neutrality, but opinions differed as to how exactly to define neutrality. Cort van der Linden, the minister-president, tended to favor Germany and was thus known in British diplomatic circles as "Caught unter den Linden." John Loudon, the Dutch foreign minister, maintained pro-Allied sympathies. The government realized early on that, if the Netherlands were to side with Germany, it could result in the loss of Dutch imperial possessions overseas. Maritime and imperial trade was vital to the Dutch economy, so they could not take the risk of losing the empire and the merchant fleet. On the other hand, if the nation were to side with Britain, it could lead to the eventual occupation of the Netherlands by the German army. Even though the Dutch army numbered 450,000 toward the end of World War I, it did not possess enough ammunition for a protracted conflict, nor did it have a significant amount of modern artillery, steel helmets, gas masks, or other military necessities. Furthermore, the military's plan for the defense of the nation called for a *waterlinie* (water line), which would result in the inundation of much of the eastern part of the nation to protect the territory around Amsterdam, Rotterdam, and The Hague. Neither alliance—with Germany or Great Britain—offered any benefits to the nation, so Queen Wilhelmina and the government decided to attempt a policy of strict neutrality between themselves and the belligerent nations.[5]

The Dutch declaration originally called for all belligerents to respect the borders of Dutch territories, and it demanded that the nation should not support in any way one side of the conflict over the other. This kind of neutrality was defined as "academic neutrality" and was for the most part successfully maintained throughout the first two years of the war; however, this strict observance of neutrality could not be maintained during the last two years of the war. The German declaration of Unrestricted Submarine Warfare in 1917 led to the confiscation of Dutch merchant vessels in Allied ports by the Al-

A veteran diplomat who had worked in China, Great Britain, France, and the United States, John Loudon served as foreign minister in Cort van der Linden's cabinet. Loudon insisted upon rigid neutrality although he personally supported the Allied cause. This neutral rigidity brought him into frequent conflict with Cort van der Linden, Gen. Snijders, and Queen Wilhelmina, especially during the Allied confiscation of Dutch merchant shipping in the spring of 1918.

Adrianus Pieter Cort van der Linden was Prime Minister of the Netherlands from 1913 to 1918. Although he was personally pro-German (earning him the nickname "Caught unter den Linden" by his detractors), he insisted upon the strictest definition of neutrality, believing that neither side in the war offered any immediate benefit to the nation.

lied nations in 1917 and 1918, and it led to an increasing amount of smuggling across the borders. Neutrality of any kind, however, required a constant vigil along all the nation's borders, and the introduction of aerial warfare meant that the skies over the Netherlands would have to be patrolled. Aerial warfare added a new dimension to the battlefield, and it also created a new border, which had to be guarded. The Dutch, with their miniscule air service, were ill prepared to defend the neutrality of their airspace in 1914; but throughout the war the Dutch air services would expand and meet face to face with the larger and better-equipped air services of their belligerent neighbors.[6]

Despite having difficulties with all the major powers, Dutch foreign relations with Germany for most of the war were less problematic and more productive than those with the Allies. The Dutch were dependent on Germany for the majority of its coal supply and military assistance. The Germans, on the other hand, relied on the Netherlands as a source for imported goods and resources, and the Netherlands itself provided a land buffer between Germany and Great Britain. Both nations benefited from Dutch neutrality. Memories of British cruelty toward the Dutch Boers during the Boer War were still fresh to many Dutchmen; furthermore, the British frequently violated Dutch neutrality by sending their aircraft through Dutch airspace to attack German targets beyond. As early as September 12, 1914, a British aircraft bombed Maastricht; the Dutch towns of Zierikzee, Goes, Axel, and Sas van Gent were also bombed, resulting in damage and some fatalities. When fragments of the bombs were examined and found to be British, the Dutch government lodged a protest. The British responded by paying nearly 30,000 florins to the victims of the bombing raids.

Gifts from Above

As the war progressed and as more belligerent aircraft violated Dutch airspace, the Dutch military realized that its small air force would not be enough to protect its airspace. Obtaining aircraft during the war was to be the most difficult task for Walaardt Sacré, but he approached the problem with creative energy. Since the Dutch domes-

Queen Wilhelmina believed the Netherlands should maintain a modern and well-equipped military, but her desire for such was often thwarted by budget-minded politicians. Nevertheless she frequently visited her troops and encouraged them to maintain a high state of readiness.

tic aero industry was still in its infancy and was not able at the time to build up-to-date aircraft, the Netherlands utilized an alternative source for modern aircraft for its aerial arsenal. Ironically, some of the best aircraft obtained for the LVA's wartime inventory almost literally dropped from the sky. According to international law of the time, any belligerent troops who violated the territory of a neutral power would be interned within the neutral state in question for the duration of hostilities. This law applied to belligerent naval vessels, and it came to be applied to belligerent aircraft during World War I. The Dutch interned their first aircraft on August 17, 1914; by the end of the conflict, 107 belligerent aircraft had been interned in the Netherlands. Aircraft that either landed in Dutch territory because of mechanical failure or had strayed into Dutch airspace and were forced down by Dutch aircraft or antiaircraft fire were interned by the Dutch military. Interned aircraft that were potentially useful were given Dutch registration and incorporated into the LVA or MLD, while less useful interned aircraft were returned to their nations of origin at the end of the war. The Dutch frequently purchased those aircraft that they kept from the nations that originally owned them—in order to smooth over any diplomatic issues that might arise.

Both the LVA and MLD faced a logistical nightmare of servicing such a diverse body of aircraft, but the planes did give Dutch pilots a chance to test some of the latest examples of aviation technology.[7] German aircraft interned included a variety of Albatros and D.F.W. two-seat reconnaissance aircraft; Albatros, Pfalz, and Fokker fighters; a Gotha G.IV bomber; and a number of floatplanes. British aircraft included Airco DH.9 and Avro 504 two-seaters; Sopwith 1½ Strutter, Pup, and Camel fighters; and a Handley-Page 0/400 bomber. Only five French aircraft, including a SPAD S.VII, and one each of Belgian and American aircraft were interned. The Dutch air services could not take full advantage of the interned aircraft until the last two years of the war, because that was the period in which most of the aircraft interned landed on Dutch soil. Although Dutch pilots had virtually no combat experience during the war, they acquired a great deal of experience in dealing with the various types of aircraft from many nations and consequently became some of the most skilled pilots in the world.

A crater left in a street in Maastricht following the accidental British bombing on September 12, 1914. These Dutch civilians received a foretaste of aerial bombardment very early in the war.

Spyker Airplanes

Although the LVA and MLD acquired many aircraft via internment during World War I, this was hardly a dependable or regulated way to obtain equipment. Early in the war, Walaardt Sacré approached French manufacturers for aircraft; but the French army refused to allow any aircraft that were desperately needed at the front to be sold to a neutral power. During the first two years of the war,

Inside one of the workshops at Soesterberg. Two interned German observation aircraft are in the foreground, the cockpit nacelle of a Farman HF.22 is on the far right, and a Gotha G.IV bomber sits behind them with its wings removed. LVA mechanics worked hard to make interned aircraft airworthy despite the challenge of having to deal with such a variety of engines, parts, and construction techniques. [Militair Luchtvaart Museum, Soesterberg]

German Pfalz D.IIIa fighter interned at Schoondijke on June 12, 1918.

British Sopwith 1F.1 Camel fighter interned at Groede on October 7, 1918.

German Hannover Cl.IIIa ground attack aircraft interned at Axel on April 15, 1918.

British Handley-Page 0/400 bomber interned at Valkennisse on January 17, 1918. [Militair Luchtvaart Museum, Soesterberg]

Sacré was able to obtain only twenty-seven Gnome-Rhone 80-horsepower rotary engines from the French. The German air authority also turned down early Dutch appeals for aircraft. Meanwhile, another Dutchman was planning his own aircraft factory inside the Netherlands.

Henri Wijnmalen, a renowned pilot who had achieved a world altitude record in 1910 and was an associate of Dutch aircraft designer Frits Koolhoven, petitioned the Dutch military authorities to help him establish his own domestic aircraft firm. He argued that a Dutch aircraft factory could eventually make the Netherlands independent of foreign manufacturers, thus saving the LVA money and offering it the ability to receive aircraft in a more timely manner. Sacré encouraged the establishment of Dutch aero firms, but he was skeptical that Wijnmalen's firm alone would be able to meet the LVA's needs, and he thought that Wijnmalen's production expectations were naively optimistic. Nevertheless, Wijnmalen's factory, the NV Nederlandse Vliegtuigenfabriek, was established in June 1914, and Wijnmalen was able to acquire the rights from Farman to license the production of its HF-20. Throughout 1914 and 1915, Wijnmalen failed to meet his promised production and delivery schedules, much to the annoyance of Walaardt Sacré. In 1915, Wijnmalen became the director of the Industrieele Maatschappij Trompenburg, an automobile manufacturer that produced the Spyker line of motorcars; he merged that firm with his aircraft company to form the Nederlandsche Automobiel en Vliegtuigfabriek Trompenburg. Between 1915 and 1916, the Trompenburg factory produced eleven license-built Farman HF.22s for the LVA and the navy. By 1916, however, the various Farman 20-Series aircraft were completely outclassed, and this called for either a new domestic design or new foreign designs. The Farman 20-Series aircraft were not intended as fighters and were successful only in reconnaissance and training roles. The HF.20 was powered by a Gnome 7A seven-cylinder rotary engine, which produced 80 horsepower. It had a maximum speed of only 65 miles per hour and could not support a heavy machine gun. Madsen light machine guns were mounted in the cockpits of Dutch Farman Series 20 aircraft, but this gun was not as effective as those mounted on German aircraft.[8]

On February 2, 1917, Captain A. Poillon, U.S. military attaché of the American legation to The Hague, submitted a report on airplanes and airplane motors in the Neth-

As was the case with other nations, the Netherlands turned to its automobile industry to produce aircraft during the war. The Nederlandsche Automobiel en Vliegtuigfabriek Trompenburg, manufacturer of Spyker autos, began to manufacture domestically designed aircraft. Here is a line-up of Spyker autos of the royal family in front of Centraal Station in Amsterdam.

In 1913, Captain Walaardt Sacré, Lts. van Heyst and Versteegh, and head of the LVA's technical service engineer Hugo Adrianus Vreeburg traveled to France and purchased three Farman HF.20 pusher biplanes. Further HF.22s were ordered and during the war the NV Nederlandse Vliegtuigenfabriek of Henri Wijnmalen produced eleven HF.22s for the LVA and three for the navy between June 1915 and April 1916. Barely able to support the weight of a machine gun and two crew members, the aircraft could not be considered a combat aircraft but did serve successfully in the training role. At far left is a cockpit nacelle of an HF.22 showing the crew seats and fuel tank.

BELOW LEFT *This replica of an LVA Farman HF.22 is on display in the Nationaal Militair Museum in Soest, the Netherlands.* [Militair Luchtvaart Museum, Soesterberg]

Farman HF.22
length: 26 ft 10¾ in (8.2 m)
wingspan: 50 ft 10½ in (15.5 m)
engine: 80 hp Gnome Rhone rotary
maximum speed: 62.1 mph (100 km/h)
endurance: 3 hours
crew: 2

Sytse Frederick Willem "Frits" Koolhoven was born in Bloemendaal in 1886 and was trained as a mechanical engineer in technical schools in Liege and Antwerp. After learning to fly from René Hanriot in France, he worked briefly in the Netherlands before moving to Great Britain to work as a design engineer at Deperdussin's British factory at the end of 1911. He later went to work for Sir W. G. Armstrong Whitworth & Co. Ltd. and was the company's head aircraft designer when the First World War began.

One of the founding fathers of Dutch aviation, Henri Wijnmalen dropped out of medical school in order to learn to fly. After training under Louis Bleriot and Henry Farman, he was awarded his flight certificate in August 1910 and later that year captured the world's altitude record at 2,780 meters. Eventually returning to the Netherlands, he became the director of the new aviation division of the Nederlandsche Automobiel en Vliegtuigfabriek Trompenburg. Here he speaks with Duchess Marie of Mecklenburg, the mother of Prince Hendrik of the Netherlands.

erlands. He wrote: "At the present the aviation section of the Netherlands Army is working with a Henry Farman machine of which they have twenty-eight (28). They still seem to favor the Henry Farman machine. They claim, except for its speed, it fulfills all their requirements."[9] At the time this evaluation did not reflect the true feelings of Dutch pilots and air officers. Indeed, they wanted a real fighter plane, and Walaardt Sacré tried to get one for them. Already in 1915, after lengthy negotiations with the French government, the Dutch Ministry of Defense was able to order five Nieuport 11 fighters and five Caudron G-III reconnaissance aircraft, which were meant to replace the Farmans. The French, with heightened wartime demands of their own, were slow to fulfill the order of a nation that refused to side with the Allied cause; thus the delivery of the aircraft was continuously delayed. Although Trompenburg-Spyker had a virtual monopoly on the sale of aircraft to the LVA and the navy, especially in view of foreign reluctance to sell aircraft to the Dutch, Wijnmalen realized that his license-produced HF.22s were obsolescent at best.

In 1916, Trompenburg-Spyker had completed a design for a new, domestically built fighter that would have an 80-horsepower rotary engine. The resulting aircraft was the Spyker V.I, a rather basic design, yet with a streamlined engine cowling; the plane was designed by Fransman Vannehard, who also happened to be Henri Wijnmalen's personal chauffeur. That first domestically developed Dutch fighter made its first flight on March 31, 1917, under the controls of van Heyst, the chief test pilot. It was an improvement over the Farman machines because its design was far more aerodynamic, and it had a top speed of 83 mph (138 km/h). Nonetheless, by the standards of other aircraft on the western front, it was still underpowered. The Dutch produced only one example of this aircraft because it did not perform very well against the foreign aircraft that were being interned at that time, and it was rejected by the Ministry of Defense and LVA. But, even though it was not put into production, the Spyker V.I had demonstrated that the Netherlands was now capable of building its own aircraft.[10]

During 1916 and early 1917, Sacré had petitioned Trompenburg-Spyker to copy and produce an existing fighter, particularly the Sopwith Pup, from one of the belligerent powers. Wijnmalen refused to consider the option because he believed that the Spyker V.I would be put into immediate production for the LVA. When no order for that airplane came, Sacré and Wijnmalen were stuck in difficult positions: one wanted a high-performance fighter, and the other was unable to provide one. On February 26, 1917, however, a Nieuport 11 fighter of the British Royal Naval Air Service made a forced landing at Cadzand in Zeeland. It was taken to Soesterberg, where it was repaired and made operational. Sacré summoned Wijnmalen to Soesterberg to inspect the aircraft, and the LVA commander suggested that Trompenburg-Spyker should copy it and put it into production.

Since the Nieuport 11s ordered from France in 1915 had yet to be delivered, this was the perfect opportunity for the Dutch to obtain the fighter their pilots longed for; and because the military authorities had just rejected the Spyker V.I, Wijnmalen was willing to accommodate Sacré's request. On January 30, 1918, the first Spyker-Nieuport 11 was completed. But it was found to be so structurally weak that it was not put into service; and this was the case with the following twelve that rolled off the assembly line at Trompenburg-Spyker. As it turned out, the five Nieuport 11s that the Dutch had ordered from the French in 1915 arrived in the Netherlands on June 24, 1918; but those were also unusable because they had been in storage for almost three years. The only Spyker design to go into series production and be used by the LVA and the MLD was the Spyker V.2, also designed by

The Spyker V.I earned the title of the first fighter aircraft to be designed and constructed in the Netherlands. After a request for a fighter from the Ministry of War in 1916, Spyker built the very pedestrian-looking design with the exception of a streamlined cowling over its 80 hp engine. Its development took a long time and did not have a successful sustained flight until March 1917. Two months later it was tested against a Sopwith Pup fighter and the British aircraft outclassed the V.I in almost every regard. The LVA declined to order any V.Is from Spyker. [Militair Luchtvaart Museum, Soesterberg]

Nieuport-Spyker XI
length: 19 ft ¼ in (5.8 m)
wingspan: 24 ft 5¾ in (7.46 m)
engine: 80 hp Thulin rotary
maximum speed: 96.3 mph (155 km/h)
ceiling: 14,763.78 ft (4,500 m)
endurance: 1.5 hours
crew: 1

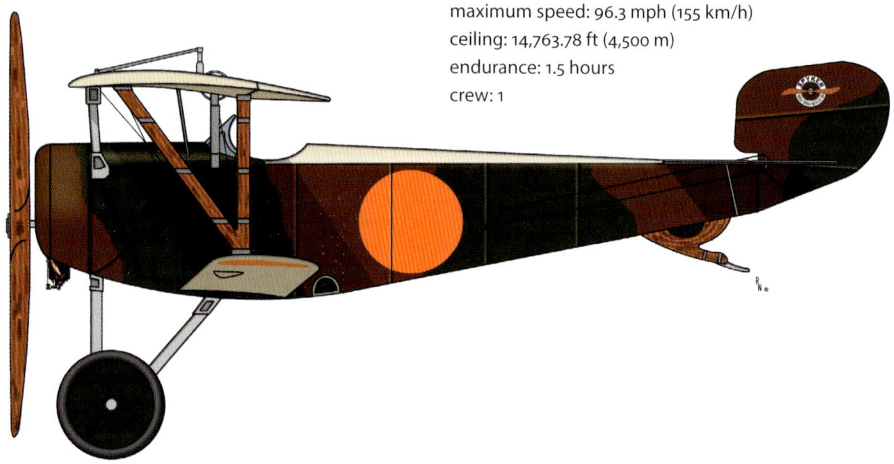

On February 26, 1917, a Nieuport 11 of the British Royal Naval Air Service was interned and repaired by the LVA. Henri Wijnmalen obtained it so that Spyker could build copies. When the first Nieuport-Spyker was finally flown on January 30, 1918, the aircraft was clearly underpowered and its construction proved to be poor and weak. Walaardt Sacré refused to endanger the lives of his pilots in these sub-par machines and the 12 that were built were never used operationally. [Militair Luchtvaart Museum, Soesterberg]

Fransman Vannehard. It was a two-seat trainer that used the same Thulin 90-horsepower motor that the V.I had. The V.2 was adequate for training purposes, and Trompenburg-Spyker received an order for fifty-eight of the machines from the LVA and an order of eighteen from the MLD. The V.2 would serve for several years with both air services, and it was not retired until 1926.[11]

The primary problem the Dutch aero industry faced with respect to the production of competitive aircraft during World War I was the lack of higher-powered aero engines. In the intense air battles over the western front, air superiority could be decided simply by the introduction of a new aircraft design or by using higher-powered engines. As Trompenburg began construction of Nieuport Spyker XIs and was testing the Spyker V.I, the best engine the Dutch military had in its inventory was the 80-horsepower Gnome seven-cylinder rotary engine. Meanwhile, the standard engine for German aircraft at this point was the Mercedes D IIIa six-cylinder, liquid-cooled inline engine with 160 horsepower; the British S.E.5 used a Wolseley W4 Viper eight-cylinder, liquid-cooled in-line engine with 200 horsepower; and the French SPAD S. VII used a Hispano-Suiza 8 Ac eight-cylinder, liquid-cooled in-line engine with 175 horsepower. It is true that both sides were still using and designing aircraft with 80- and 110-horsepower rotary engines, but these were specified designs that took advantage of the lightness of the rotaries.

During the war the Dutch aero industry did not have the ability to purchase in-line engines with greater horsepower, nor did it have the design expertise to make the fullest use of the lighter-weight rotaries. Early in 1917, Poillon noted that "Mr. Wynmalen, the managing director and one of the early fliers himself, who is in charge of all the construction, states that he experimented with all the motors on... interned machines, and others, which the Government has purchased for trial, and in his opinion the finest motor to-day used on the continent or anywhere for that matter, is the German 6-cylinder vertical motor Mercedes."[12] Without access to better engines or innovative designs, the Dutch aero industry always remained a year or two behind that of the Germans, British, and French.

Shopping Abroad

The Dutch authorities also looked to other neutral nations as potential sources for aircraft and aero engines. The navy was the primary recipient of these aircraft. In 1916 a group of navy officers traveled to the United States to examine naval aircraft. The aero industry in the United States during World War I was a technological backwater compared to the nation's great automobile industry. Nevertheless, the Dutch navy was eager to purchase floatplanes, and its representatives purchased two Glenn Martin R and four Glenn Martin S floatplanes. Those planes arrived in the Netherlands late in 1916, where they were assembled and kept in a hangar at Schellingwoude. Then, in January 1917, Sacré sent van Heyst and Hugo Adrianus Vreeburg, head of the LVA's technical service, to Sweden to inspect the suitability of products of the Swedish aero industry; they were to order engines and aircraft if those could be made available. The Enoch Thulins Aeroplanfabrik of Landskrona was able to supply both engines and aircraft to the Netherlands, and Van Heyst and Vreeburg returned after having placed an order for ninety Thulin 80-horsepower rotary engines for the LVA. Van Heyst was not particularly impressed with the aircraft Thulin had to offer, but a purchasing commission from the MLD was less fussy. The MLD ordered twelve Type K monoplane fighters (rough copies of the Morane-Saulnier monoplane fighter) and three Type KA monoplane trainers from Thulin. These aircraft arrived throughout 1917 and 1918. Powered by a Thulin Type A 90-horsepower rotary engine, they had a maximum speed of roughly 90 mph, a maximum ceiling of roughly 9,000 ft, and an endurance of an hour and a half. They were armed with Madsen machine guns or a combination of a Madsen machine gun and a Madsen 20mm cannon. But these aircraft were obsolete before their arrival in the Netherlands. The Swedish aero industry, like its

Thulin K
length: 21 ft 4 in (6.50 m)
wingspan: 29 ft 10¼ in (9.10 m)
engine: 90 hp Thulin A rotary
maximum speed: 94 mph (150 km/h)
armament: one synchronized machine gun
crew: 1

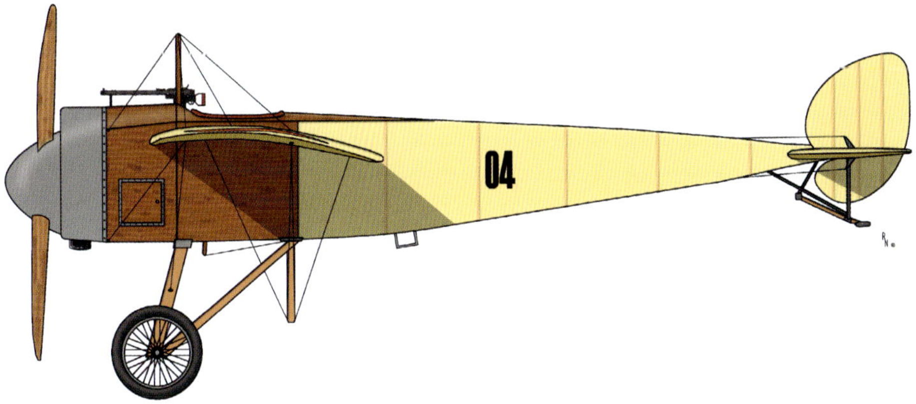

The Swedish aero firm of Enoch Thulins Aeroplanfabrik of Landskrona became a source of fighter aircraft for the newly formed Marine Luchtvaartdient or MLD in 1917. Sweden was one of the few neutral countries from which the Dutch could purchase aero engines and aircraft. The MLD ordered 12 Thulin Type K monoplane fighters which were delivered in late 1917 into 1918. Roughly based on the Morane-Saulnier Type N fighter of 1915, the Thulin Type K was obsolete but came equipped with synchronized machine guns. [Militair Luchtvaart Museum, Soesterberg]

"The Idealist," begins the caption on this German cartoon. "America is for the freedom of the seas... meanwhile it takes the liberty to steal German ships." When the United States entered the war in April 1917, not only did it confiscate German merchant ships interned in its ports, but the following April confiscated neutral Dutch ships as well. The Dutch were furious with President Woodrow Wilson, who had pushed so strongly for the rights of neutrals prior to April 1917, for his violation of neutral sovereignty. This marked the lowest point in Dutch-American relations in history and Queen Wilhelmina considered breaking off diplomatic relations with the United States.

Dutch counterpart, was also producing copies of foreign aircraft with copied engines, but the resulting airplanes were obsolete by the time they took to the skies. However, the MLD needed all the aircraft they could obtain because of the increasing neutrality violations along the Dutch coast, and in a closed belligerent market, neutral beggars could not be choosers. In this atmosphere, the MLD also purchased from Sweden ten Thulin Type LA biplane trainers, whose design was based on the design of the German Albatros B.II reconnaissance aircraft and was powered by the same 90-horsepower rotary engine as the Type K fighter. As with the Type K, the military effectiveness of these machines was limited because they were not received until November 1918, the month of the armistice.[13]

With increasing violations of airspace and the lack of availability of adequate fighter aircraft in 1917, the preservation of strict neutrality by the Dutch military grew more difficult as the war trudged on. On the night of April 29, 1917, Zierikzee in Zeeland was again bombed by a British airplane. The British claimed that the incident was an accident and paid the Dutch government £92,000; but a family of three was killed. April 1917 also witnessed the entry of the United States into the war. The difficulties that the LVA and the MLD experienced because of this event were the result of threats at sea rather than in the air.

Before the United States entered the war, the Dutch government viewed it as largely representing the interests of the neutral powers. But once in the war, the United States ceased giving consideration to the interest of neutrals and took a much more bellicose attitude toward the Dutch government. Beginning in the early summer of 1917, the British government seized a number of Dutch merchant ships in British ports. By the fall there was speculation that the British and Americans might seize all Dutch merchant vessels anchored in Allied ports. The Allied governments eventually justified these seizures by referring to the law of *angary*, an old maritime practice that allowed belligerents to seize and use neutral vessels with compensation. If the Dutch government was to actively oppose the seizure of its vessels, it would surely mean war with the Allies, and the threat of invasion might become a reality. Thus, the U.S. entry into the war meant that the Dutch military needed more aircraft to prepare for a potential Allied invasion.[14]

In March 1917, Sacré sent Lieutenant J. G. C. Duinker to Germany to negotiate the purchase of ten Albatros D.III fighters. Sacré had done his research, and since the Albatros was the best fighter over the western front at the time, he hoped that these new German fighters would form the nucleus of a modern fighter force. After protracted negotiations, the Germans refused to sell any of their precious Albatroses to the Dutch, especially in the middle of what the British referred to as "Bloody April," when the Albatros had had its maximum effect over the front and had secured air superiority for the Luftstreitkräfte. Duinker then traveled to the Fokker works, which was producing mediocre biplane designs at the time; but the German Air Authority was reluctant to part with even aircraft it considered "second line."

In August 1917, Duinker returned to Berlin, this time accompanied by Versteegh, to again negotiate the purchase of German aircraft for the LVA. This time the German Air Authority relented, perhaps because of the threatening attitude the British and the Americans were beginning to take toward the Dutch, and in October the GAA allowed the sale of ten Fokker D.III fighters. The payment requested by the German army for these aircraft was 5,000 one-year-old horses; this was an awkward currency, but the Germans were in desperate need of transport animals. While in Germany, Versteegh tested the D.III; although "second line" by German standards, it was a vast improvement over the aging Farmans back at Soesterberg. Although this transaction could technically be considered a breach of neutrality in its strictest definition, the Dutch were desperate for any modern aircraft that they could acquire, especially with the Allies making threats on Dutch seaborne commerce. The Fokker D.IIIs fighters were the first true fighters used by the LVA. Put into service in the early fall of 1916, the D.III had a 160-horsepower Oberursal UR.III rotary engine, had a maximum speed of 100 mph, and was armed with two LMG 08/15 machine guns (though the D.IIIs that arrived in the Netherlands were not equipped with machine guns or synchronizing mechanisms). Versteegh returned to Germany in March 1918 and visited the Rumpler-Werke at Johannisthal. He test-flew several aircraft and was able to order forty Rumpler C.VIII two-seat reconnaissance biplanes. The first was delivered to Soesterberg on April 25, and the remaining ones arrived throughout the rest of the year. Thus did the LVA finally secure a number of modern foreign aircraft.[15]

On March 20, 1918, the British and the Americans seized Dutch merchant vessels that were anchored in their ports. Queen Wilhelmina was outraged by this action, and she canceled all soldiers' leaves. The intensifying war at sea was damaging the vital seaborne link between the Netherlands and its most important overseas colony, the Dutch East Indies. To demonstrate Dutch resolve and her contempt for the Allied seizures, the Queen decided to send a small convoy, escorted by a warship, to the Dutch East Indies. Some of the convoy's cargo was for the maintenance of the small military air presence in the colony. The Dutch had not overlooked the potential usefulness of military aircraft in the East Indies. On May 30, 1914, the Proefvliegafdeling van het Koninklijk Nederlands Indisch Leger (PVA-KNIL), the Flight Test Squadron of the Royal Dutch East Indies Army, was established without having any aircraft at its immediate disposal. The KNIL leadership decided that it would first experiment with floatplanes in the multi-island colony before purchasing land-based aircraft. There was a high degree of skepticism that aircraft made of canvas and wood could sustain the rigors of the tropical climate, and the KNIL did not want to invest heavily in runways, hangars, and workshops for an unproven technology.

Floatplanes were the ideal test instruments because alighting areas at sea cost nothing to build. Since no orders could be placed in Europe, and the British blockade of the North Sea complicated shipments from the Netherlands, Lieutenant General Johan Pieter Michielsen, the commander of the KNIL, sent a committee to the United States in 1915 to select and purchase floatplanes. The

The best fighter aircraft in service at the beginning of 1917 was the German Albatros D.III and Walaardt Sacré wanted it for his country's pilots. In March 1917, Walaardt Sacré sent Second Lieutenant J. G. C. Duinker to the Albatros works at Johannistal to negotiate the purchase of ten Albatros D.IIIs for the LVA. The timing of the visit was poor, however, as the Germans were in the process of reclaiming air superiority over the western front. Amid claims that every Albatros fighter was needed immediately at the front, the deal fell through. [Militair Luchtvaart Museum, Soesterberg]

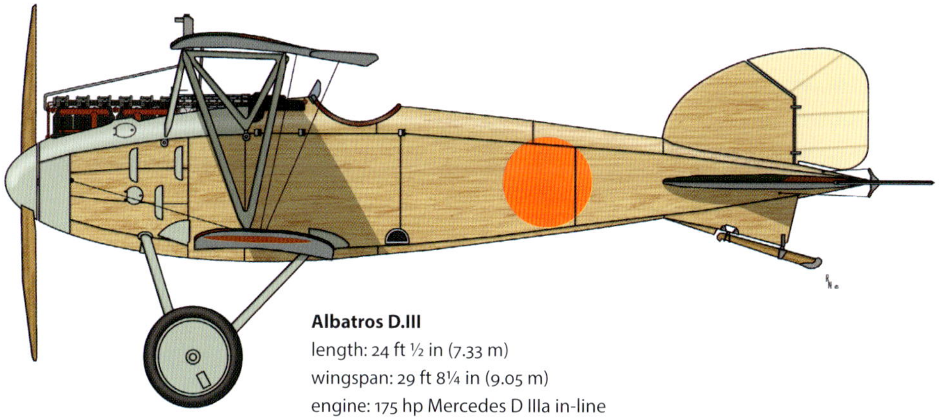

Albatros D.III
length: 24 ft ½ in (7.33 m)
wingspan: 29 ft 8¼ in (9.05 m)
engine: 175 hp Mercedes D IIIa in-line
maximum speed: 103 mph (165 km/h)
ceiling: 18,044 ft (5,500 m)
endurance: 2 hours
armament: two synchronized Spandau LMG 08/15 machine guns
crew: 1

Fokker D.III
length: 20 ft 8 in (6.3 m)
wingspan: 29 ft 8¼ in (9.05 m)
engine: 160 hp Oberursel U.III rotary
maximum speed: 99.4 mph (160 km/h)
ceiling: 13,123.36 ft (4,000 m)
endurance: 1.5 hours
crew: 1

Rumpler C.VIII
length: 25 ft 11 in (7.9 m)
wingspan: 40 ft 1 in (12.22 m)
engine: 180 hp Argus in-line
maximum speed: 105.6 mph (170 km/h)
crew: 2

Lts. Duinker and Versteegh returned to Germany in the autumn of 1917 and were allowed by the German military authorities to visit the Fokker works at Schwerin and were able to arrange the purchase of ten Fokker D.III fighters. Although the D.IIIs were delivered unarmed, they were used as advanced fighter trainers. Versteegh returned to Germany in the spring of 1918 where he recommended the purchase of the Rumpler C.VIII observation aircraft. His request was granted by the LVA and an order for 40 C.VIIIs was placed. The Rumplers were used extensively throughout 1919 but most were grounded in 1920 due to several in-flight fires. [Militair Luchtvaart Museum, Soesterberg]

committee returned to the East Indies in the fall 1915 with two Glenn Martin TA floatplanes, the best that could be obtained from the American aero industry. Lieutenant Hein ter Poorten made the first PVA-KNIL flight at the new floatplane base at Tanjong Priok in one of the Glenn Martins on November 6, 1915. The performance of this aircraft was limited by its 140-horsepower Hall Scott engine, which did not perform well in the tropical climate. The replacement of the heavy floats with locally built landing gear allowed for a better performance, but engine failure was the cause of the crash of one of the Glenn Martins on February 14, 1916, which wounded Lt. ter Poorten and killed his high-ranking passenger, none other than Lt. Gen. Michielsen. The PVA-KNIL purchased six Glenn Martin TT floatplanes and then eight Glenn Martin R floatplanes in 1917. The PVA-KNIL and its pilots did not believe that these were the most suitable aircraft for the East Indies, but they were the only floatplanes that could be purchased. When the United States entered the war in the spring of 1917, supplies for their easily worn-out engines could no longer be obtained. The PVA-KNIL would have to wait until the end of the war to finally obtain good aircraft.

Back in the Netherlands, however, the MLD had extensively tested an interned Friedrichshafen FF.33 floatplane and determined that its robust construction, coupled with its reliable 150-horsepower Benz engine, made it an ideal candidate for service in the East Indies. In the spring of 1918, the MLD decided to ship one of its Friedrichshafen FF.33s, as well as an interned Rumpler 6B2 floatplane, in the convoy that was being sent to the East Indies. The Dutch government informed the British about its plan to send an armed convoy to the East Indies, implying that as the convoy was escorted by a warship of the Dutch navy, any aggressive action made by the British blockading forces would be seen as an assault on Dutch sovereignty.

That summer, the Holland America Line's SS *Noordam* accompanied by a collier, the auxiliary cruiser *Tabanan*, and the cruiser *Hertog Hendrik*, made their way to the East Indies despite the protests of the British. This was a risky show of saber rattling in the face of the mighty Royal British Navy, particularly with two ex-German aircraft as part of the cargo manifest; but it worked. Thus ended another showdown between the Dutch and the British. The Friedrichshafen FF.33 performed so well in the East Indies that in October the navy ordered eighteen of the type for use in the colony. But the war ended before any additional Friedrichshafens were delivered to the MLD.[16]

Lieutenant Hein ter Poorten about to make the first flight for the Proefvliegafdeling-KNIL in an American-built Glenn Martin TA floatplane on November 6, 1915. Ter Poorten rose through the ranks of the East Indies army over the years and was its commander at the outbreak of World War II in the Pacific. [Militair Luchtvaart Museum, Soesterberg]

Domestic Difficulties

Back in Europe in the summer of 1918, the defense of Dutch airspace became the subject of intensified diplomatic tensions between Germany and the Netherlands. German diplomats approached the Dutch government with a series of complaints regarding numerous viola-

On May 29, 1917, a German Rumpler 6B2 floatplane landed near Westkapelle and was interned. It was taken over by the MLD and given the serial number U1. It, along with an interned Freidrichshafen FF.33J, was shipped in an armed convoy to the East Indies in the summer of 1918. These were the first aircraft to represent the MLD in the colony. [Militair Luchtvaart Museum, Soesterberg]

tions of Dutch airspace by British aircraft. These were flying through Dutch airspace in order to attack German U-boat bases along the Belgian and German coast and then returning to Britain through Dutch airspace before German aircraft could take to the skies to pursue them. German General Erich Ludendorff demanded that the Dutch government make a stronger protest to the British than they had up to that point. If the Dutch were to take a stronger posture toward the British regarding airspace violations than with the Germans, this would in effect be a visible end to their neutrality. The Dutch countered the German complaints by declaring that its military lacked the equipment necessary to strictly defend its airspace. Furthermore, German aircraft also violated Dutch airspace. Between March 15 and May 28, 1918, there were twenty-seven violations, of which five were by Allied aircraft while nineteen were by German aircraft. Gen. Ludendorff disregarded this disparity and insisted that British aircraft assembled for attacks in Dutch airspace and then escaped via the same route, thus avoiding German antiaircraft fire.

In correspondence with Gen. Snijders on July 20, 1918—and after examining the testimony given by a captured British flier to the German military authorities—the Dutch foreign minister Loudon said he believed that not all British aerial violations were unintentional. The Kaiser considered sending military antiaircraft equipment to the Dutch; but this idea was rejected when he was reminded that the equipment could be used against German aircraft as well. Gen. Ludendorff considered an invasion of the Netherlands for some time. Fortunately for the Dutch, he realized that he could not spare any troops from the intense fighting on the western front, and he left the matter to be resolved peacefully by the diplomats. Germany's envoy to The Hague, Friedrich Rosen, suggested to Reichskanzler Georg von Hertling that cooperation with and assisting the Dutch could be an inconspicuous way to supervise aircraft observation and defense in the Netherlands. Moreover, Maj. von Schweinitz, the German military attaché in The Hague, considered Gen. Snijders to be *deutschfreundlich*. The Dutch government's claim was that the inability to effectively guard its aerial borders was primarily caused by a lack of sufficient numbers of modern aircraft. The Germans finally acknowledged that, but after the major spring offensives had ground to a halt in France, they were in no position to offer any aircraft to the Dutch.[17]

With veiled threats of war from both sides, the Dutch government pushed the domestic industry to meet its demands for more effective and up-to-date aircraft. Discussions began already in 1917 about a new domestic type to replace the Spyker V.I. The government ordered large quantities of the Spyker V.3—a somewhat improved version of the V.I, having a more powerful license-built 130-horsepower Clerget engine—before the end of the war. The V.3 had a top speed of 108 mph and had two machine guns, but it still could not match the performance of any of the front-line aircraft of the belligerent powers. Besides, the prototype was not flown until after the war ended. Walaardt Sacré was frustrated by Trompenburg-Spyker's seeming inability to produce a competitive fighter in a timely manner, and he hoped to promote domestic competition and improve the inventory of the

LVA by eliminating Trompenburg-Spyker's monopoly on domestic aircraft production. He gave the Goedkoop furniture firm of Amsterdam an interned SPAD VII to examine, with the intention of copying it and putting it into production. The war ended before the firm could begin the project. In terms of overall output, the Dutch domestic air industry, compared to that of the other nations involved in the conflict, had a rather poor showing in total aircraft produced: fewer than fifty.[18]

One of the greatest problems facing the Dutch aero industry during World War I was the lack of experienced aircraft designers. Frits Koolhoven left the Netherlands for Great Britain before the war to become the chief engineer of the British Deperdussin Syndicate, a French company that designed high-speed monoplanes. After Deperdussin's bankruptcy in Britain in 1913, Koolhoven was invited to design aircraft for the industrial concern of W. G. Armstrong, Whitworth and Company, of Newcastle-upon-Tyne. His first design to be produced in quantity was the Armstrong Whitworth F.K.3, an improved version of the Royal Aircraft Factory's B.E.2 two-seater multirole reconnaissance plane. Production began in 1915, and about five hundred F.K.3s were ordered. Although the F.K.3 was a better design, the British government–sponsored Royal Aircraft Factory was given a much greater contract for the B.E.2, of which roughly 3,500 were built. But Koolhoven's F.K.8 two-seater reconnaissance airplane attracted more publicity and thus more sales. The F.K.8 was a much more streamlined aircraft: the camera was mounted internally rather than on the outside, and this caused considerably less drag. It was also powered by a more powerful 160-horsepower Beardmore in-line engine, offering the same amount of horsepower as contemporary German two-seaters. At least 1,652 F.K.8s were ordered, and the first service model came off the Armstrong Whitworth line at the end of 1916. The aircraft was capable of performing a multitude of roles: bombing, reconnaissance, photography, strafing, artillery spotting, and even dropping supplies to troops in the field.[19]

In Great Britain, Koolhoven's F.K.3 and F.K.8 gave him

The LVA requested Wijnmalen to develop a trainer around the Thulin engine and the result was the Spyker V.2. The trainer flew for the first time on April 9, 1918, and the LVA was pleased enough with its performance that it ordered 58 of the type. Only three V.2s were completed in 1918, the rest being delivered in 1919. Both the LVA and MLD used the V.2 as a trainer until 1926 when it was replaced with improved Fokker trainers. [Militair Luchtvaart Museum, Soesterberg]

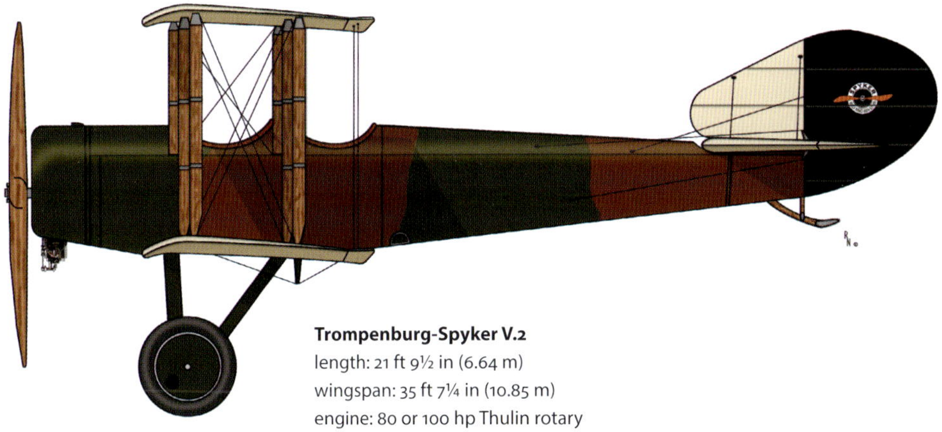

Trompenburg-Spyker V.2
length: 21 ft 9½ in (6.64 m)
wingspan: 35 ft 7¼ in (10.85 m)
engine: 80 or 100 hp Thulin rotary
maximum speed: 83.9 mph (135 km/h)
crew: 2

On November 18, 1917, a French SPAD S.VII fighter was interned and made airworthy at Soesterberg. Tired of delays and poor construction at Trompenburg-Spyker, Walaardt Sacré took the SPAD to the Goedkoop furniture firm in Amsterdam and asked its personnel to examine the aircraft to see if they could copy it for production. The main problem with this project was where to procure in-line engines for production aircraft and the war ended before any serious work could be undertaken by Goedkoop. [Militair Luchtvaart Museum, Soesterberg]

a reputation for designing and building sound and reliable aircraft. But some of his other designs for Armstrong Whitworth were of a totally different character. Early in the war, some British aerial theorists contemplated the idea of a large destroyer aircraft that would mount multiple guns in nacelles detached from the fuselage. One of the culminations of this idea was Koolhoven's F.K.6 "Zeppelin Destroyer," a large triplane aircraft powered by a single Rolls Royce 220-horsepower Eagle engine. The wings sat directly behind the engine, and the cockpit was situated in the middle of the fuselage, on each side of which was a gunner's nacelle mounted on the center wing. Observers would sit in these nacelles and operate machine guns or cannons. The method behind this unmaneuverable madness was that the pilot would fly the aircraft alongside or behind a zeppelin, enabling both the observers and gunners the opportunity to shoot the airship down with ease via a rotatable gun mount. (This aircraft was designed before the British began to produce a machine-gun synchronization device.) By the middle of the war, when the first prototype of the F.K.6 was tested, aviators quickly realized that this lumbering giant would not be effective in combat, and no orders were forthcoming. But this was not the only example of Koolhoven's eccentric wartime designs.

In March 1917, Armstrong Whitworth tested the F.K.10, a two-seater quadruplane designed by Koolhoven. When it was tested, the aircraft had good maneuverability but was slow; it suffered from multiple maintenance problems; and pilots were wary of the unorthodox quadruplane design. A government order for fifty F.K.10s was canceled because of the aircraft's poor performance, and only a few were built. Evidently, more wings did not necessarily guarantee better performance; but Koolhoven remained convinced that they would. After the F.K.10, he designed the F.K.11, which had fifteen 18-inch-wide wings; but it never left the drawing board. Koolhoven could certainly not be charged with a lack of creativity. In 1917 he transferred to the British Aerial Transport (BAT) company, where he was offered the position of chief designer for the firm. He remained at BAT

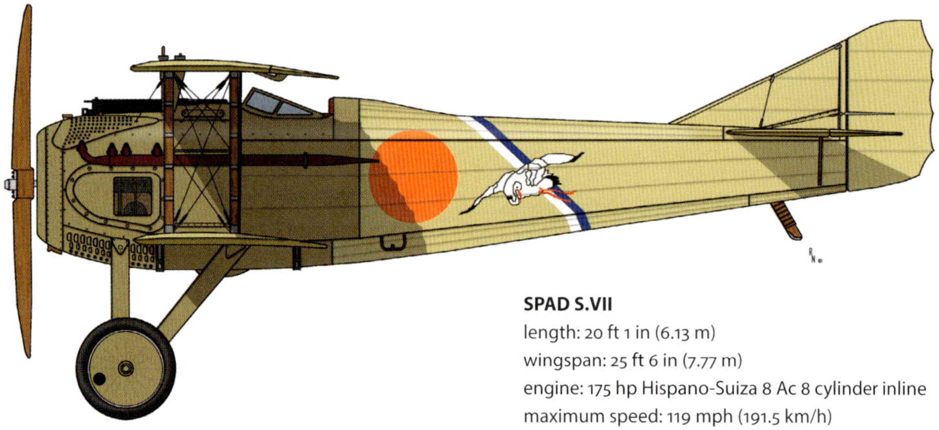

SPAD S.VII
length: 20 ft 1 in (6.13 m)
wingspan: 25 ft 6 in (7.77 m)
engine: 175 hp Hispano-Suiza 8 Ac 8 cylinder inline
maximum speed: 119 mph (191.5 km/h)
ceiling: 18,000 ft (5,485 m)
endurance: 2 hours
armament: one .303 cal. Vickers machine gun
crew: 1

working on high-performance fighter designs until the end of the war.[20]

The "Fokker Scourge"

By the fall of 1918, the German army was withdrawing eastward, and it appeared that the long struggle of the Dutch for neutrality was almost at a close. Then a rapid series of events occurred at the very end of the war that almost brought about the collapse of the Dutch nation. On October 26, a mutiny swept through several units of the Dutch army, and revolutionaries took to the streets. Snijders was blamed by elements within the government for the mutiny and was dismissed on November 9, 1918. The day after the November 11 armistice, in a humanitarian action, the Dutch military allowed sick and wounded German soldiers to cross the province of Limburg into Germany. The Allies, perceiving this as an indication that the Netherlands could not effectively maintain its neutrality and that the Dutch government did indeed have pro-German leanings, made threats that Allied armies might pursue the Germans across Limburg whether the Dutch government allowed them to or not. Furthermore, at the time of the armistice, the Belgian government sought to take advantage of the Allies' displeasure with the Netherlands by making demands for Dutch territory as war reparations. The Netherlands also had to deal with two unexpected guests who showed up on its doorstep out of the chaos and internal unrest of postwar Germany. The first was Kaiser Wilhelm II, whom the Dutch government allowed to take refuge in the Netherlands on November 10. The second came several weeks after the armistice: he was the Dutch-born German aircraft designer and industrialist Anthony Herman Gerard Fokker.[21]

The name Fokker is easily recognized by scholars and enthusiasts of aircraft of World War I: the period of his rise to prominence in the world of aviation paralleled the development of military aviation in the Netherlands. Although Fokker had little to do with aviation in the Netherlands during the war, some of his wartime

The most successful aircraft Koolhoven designed in Great Britain during the war was the Armstrong Whitworth F.K.8. Nicknamed the "Big Ack" it was a rugged two-seater that could serve in bombing, reconnaissance, ground attack, and artillery spotting roles. In a competition to replace the B.E.2, the F.K.8 was beaten out by the Royal Aircraft Factory's inferior R.E.8 but over 1,650 "Big Acks" were produced and served in Western Europe, the Balkans, and the Middle East from mid-1916 to the end of the war. [Photo AVIODROME Luchtfotografie, Lelystad, Holland]

Armstrong Whitworth F.K.8
length: 31 ft 5 in (9.58 m)
wingspan: 43 ft 6 in (13.26 m)
engine: Beardmore 160 hp in-line
maximum speed: 95 mph (153 km/h)
armament: one synchronized .303 cal. Vickers machine gun, one .303 cal. Lewis gun
crew: 2

Above *Frits Koolhoven had a passion for the unconventional and this began to manifest itself in some of his designs for Armstrong Whitworth. The F.K.6 single-engine "Zeppelin Destroyer," with its two gunners' nacelles in the wings, was an unwieldy machine whose purpose was made obsolete with the advent of fighters armed with synchronized machine guns.*

Below *The F.K.10 two-seater quadruplane was Koolhoven's response to the triplane craze in 1917. In practice, the F.K.10's performance was worse than a conventional Sopwith 1½ Strutter two-seater biplane and the project was canceled.* [Photo AVIODROME Luchtfotografie, Lelystad, Holland]

innovations dictated the course of the war in the air and were echoed in his later postwar designs. "Tony" Fokker was a hero to the German pilots who perfected and admired his innovative machines in the skies over the various fronts of the war. To the Allies, however, he was a treacherous neutral who had thrown in his lot with the Germans and had on his hands the blood of many an Allied pilot who fell to his killing machines. To some, he was an opportunist and a self-promoter; to others, he was an innovator and a genius. To himself, Fokker was a self-educated and self-made man who simply had a great passion for flight.

Fokker was born on April 6, 1890, in Kediri, Java. His father owned a successful coffee plantation in the East Indies, but he returned with his family to Haarlem to give his son and daughter a proper education. Anthony did not take well to structured education. According to his autobiography, "classes were boring, teachers stupid; I seemed almost heroically dumb." By all accounts, he was not a very good student and was frequently getting into trouble with his instructors. Nonetheless, he proved to be very adept at building and mechanics, creating his own electric railway, stationary steam engines, and a canoe. Fokker summed up his own appreciation for his informal and practical approach to education in this way: "The modern boy, who has all these toys bought for him, is very badly off, in my opinion. The whole fun is in making them. When parents buy elaborate toys for their children, they are doing them a disservice. It would be better to give them scraps of material, and let their ingenuity do the rest." It was this hands-on practical ingenuity that led Fokker to produce some of the best aircraft of World War I.[22]

Fokker was already an established aircraft manufacturer with a factory in Schwerin in Germany in 1914. He had been designing and flying his own airplanes since 1910, after he had learned some basic automotive and aeronautical skills in German technical schools. One might wonder why Fokker, a Dutch neutral, ended up building aircraft for the Imperial German Air Service, the Luftstreitkrafte. Fokker later commented:

> As I have moved about the world I have heard some criticism leveled at me because I threw my lot in with the Germans. Certain Allied spokesmen have said that I should have joined with them. Such critics disregarded the fact that my own country had seen fit to prefer French planes to my own; England and Italy had scarcely acknowledged my advances; Russia had proved too corrupt a soil for me to take root, while Germany alone had welcomed me, if not with open arms, at least warmly enough.[23]

Fokker's first significant contribution to the war in the air was a synchronization interrupter device that would allow the bullets of a machine gun to pass through but not hit the rotating blades of a propeller. After examining a captured French aircraft with a primitive bullet-deflection device on April 19, 1915, Fokker and his engineers returned forty-eight hours later with a synchronization device installed with a machine gun on one of his airplanes. The airplane Fokker selected was his M.5K, a lightweight and maneuverable monoplane that was based on earlier French Morane Saulnier types. Fokker successfully tested it before the German crown prince and high-ranking army officers. The soon-to-be ace Oswald Boelcke then shot down several enemy planes, and Fokker's aircraft and its new device were ordered into mass production. The M.5K was redesignated as the Eindecker I, or E.I. Considered the first successful fighter aircraft in history, the Eindeckers began to take a devastating toll on the morale of Allied pilots in the summer of 1915. From the fall of 1915 to the early spring of 1916, they achieved air superiority for the Germans over the western front; in fact, this period was eventually referred to as the "Fokker Scourge" by the British, who called their aircraft "Fokker fodder."

German aces Oswald Boelcke, Max Immelmann, and Ernst Udet honed their aerial hunting skills in Eindeckers during this period. However, some of the actual physical results of the "Fokker Scourge" did not match the proportions of the legend that eventually formed around it. Few Eindeckers were actually produced, and the majority of their victims were relatively defenseless

LEFT *Shown here in traditional Dutch clothing with his sister, Anthony H. G. Fokker became fascinated with aviation in his youth and, after dropping out of school, was sent by his father to Germany for a technical education. Fokker had a non-academic hands-on approach to design and testing which was to characterize his methodology in aviation for the rest of his career, claiming that improvements could be made based upon the "feel" of an aircraft in flight rather than from studies conducted by "experts."*

BELOW *He never lost his boyish charm, his disregard for expert scientific design methods, or his love of enjoying life, evident here during his early days as an aero manufacturer in Germany.* [Photo AVIODROME Luchtfotografie, Lelystad, Holland]

observation aircraft. What cannot be denied, however, is the effect that the "Fokker Scourge" had on the Germans and the Allies alike: it gave the Germans air superiority; it was a significant morale boost to the German war effort; and it significantly damaged the morale of Allied airmen. Indeed, it changed the course of aerial warfare. An order from British High Command on January 14, 1916, highlighted the superiority of the Fokker Eindecker:

> [It is] a hard and fast rule that a machine proceeding on a reconnaissance must be escorted by at least three other fighting machines. These machines must fly in close formation and a reconnaissance should not be continued if any of the machines become detached. . . . Flying in close formation must be practised by all pilots.[24]

On one occasion, a reconnaissance plane was accompanied by twelve fighters. The "Fokker Scourge" made Anthony Fokker a legend, his name a household word.[25]

By the summer of 1916, Fokker's Eindecker had become outclassed by a series of streamlined Albatros biplanes. Fokker designed a number of biplanes, but none of them proved to be better than those of his other German competitors. A year would pass before one of Fokker's fighter designs again captured the attention of the leadership of the Luftstreitkräfte. During the interlude, Fokker and his lead designer, Reinhold Platz, examined two refinements in design that would become hallmarks of Fokker aircraft for a number of years. The first feature was a cantilever wing: thick and heavy spars ran through the wing, to which ribs were attached; a cover was placed over the spars and ribs, and the spars bore the load, allowing the wing to accommodate stress without external bracings. The cantilever wing was much stronger than truss-like biplane designs, which required several sets of struts and cables, all of which caused drag.

The second design feature that Fokker and Platz incorporated into their future designs was the use of a plywood veneer to cover the ribs of aircraft wings. Fokker became aware of this innovation through contact with Villehad Forssman, an eccentric Swedish inventor who

When the First World War began, Tony Fokker (right) was only 24 but he was already a successful industrialist. Before the war he founded the Fokker Aeroplanbau GmbH in Schwerin, Germany (above). The company's main product was the Fokker M.5 unarmed reconnaissance monoplane, an improved version of the Morane-Saulnier Type H made out of welded steel tubes powered by a license-built 80 hp Gnôme rotary engine. The welded steel fuselage was the creation of Tony and his employee Reinhold Platz, an expert welder who like Tony took a hands-on approach to design that emphasized strength through simplicity. German and Austro-Hungarian military orders came in for the M.5 and the M.8, a two-seat version of the M.5. [Photo AVIODROME Luchtfotografie, Lelystad, Holland]

In 1915, the name Fokker sent a chill to the bones of Allied fliers. The cause was Fokker's introduction of an aircraft armed with a machine gun synchronized to fire between the moving blades of a propeller.

ABOVE *The pilot simply had to aim his aircraft at the target and 600 rounds per minute could be fired at the enemy.* [Photo AVIODROME Luchtfotografie, Lelystad, Holland]

RIGHT TOP *Inspired by a captured French bullet-deflection device, the Fokker Stangensteurerung, or synchronizing gear, was a set of cams and push rods that stopped the fire of a machine gun when a propeller blade passed in front of the gun's barrel. The mechanism was pefected by firing bullets through a plywood disk with the outline of a propeller drawn on it until the proper tempo was reached where not a single bullet passed through the propeller outline.*

RIGHT BOTTOM *Fokker mounted the Stangensteurerung into one of his M.5K monoplanes and the result was the world's first fighter aircraft.*

Fokker E.III
length: 23 ft 11.25 in (7.3 m)
wingspan: 30 ft 10.5 in (9.41 m)
power plant: 100 hp Oberursel UI 9-cylinder rotary
maximum speed: 87.5 mph (140 km/h)
ceiling: 11,483 ft (3,500 m)
endurance: 1.5 hours
armament: one synchronized Spandau LMG 08/15 machine gun
crew: 1

The term "Eindecker" came to refer to the E.I, E.II, E.III, and E.IV series of Fokker monoplane fighters, which were armed with one or two machine guns and equipped with the Stangensteuerung, and manufactured in 1915 and 1916. The fall of 1915 and early winter of 1916, during which the Eindeckers began to patrol over the western front in numbers, came to be known as the "Fokker Scourge" to Allied airmen, who were suddenly outmatched in the air, tactically and technologically. Allied reconnaissance aircraft became known as "Fokker Fodder." The Allies tried in vain to replicate Fokker's Stangensteuerung, but it would not be until the fall of 1916 that the first Allied fighters with synchronized machine guns made their appearance in numbers.

ABOVE *The replica E.III shown here is part of the Museum of Flight's collection in Seattle, Washington.*

RIGHT *The world's only surviving Eindecker is this E.III on display without its fabric coverings in the London Science Museum* [photo courtesy of Mr. David Op't Holt]. *It was captured intact by the British on April 8, 1916, when its pilot landed behind enemy lines by mistake.*

created the largest aircraft design of the war, the Poll Giant triplane. A plywood veneer over a wing frame was lighter and more durable than a fabric cover. Platz took Forssman's plywood wing veneer and applied it to his cantilever wing design: the result was a light but strong wing that did not require the external bracings of previous designs. Fokker and Platz tested these refinements in the V.I biplane prototype, and Fokker was extremely pleased with the strength of the wing and the increased maneuverability that its lightness allowed for. But the V.I was underpowered because of its 100-horsepower engine, and it attracted little military interest.

Finally, in the summer of 1917, Fokker's fortunes changed when the Luftstreitkräfte called for a triplane that could match the perceived threat of Britain's Sopwith triplane. Using their knack for practical engineering and improving on other innovations, Fokker and Platz produced the Dr.I triplane, which could outmaneuver nearly all Allied aircraft. It was not an easy machine to fly: the initial series production was plagued by poor quality control, and the aircraft required the skill of an experienced pilot. Nonetheless, several experienced German pilots brought the Dr.I into the limelight, the most notable being Manfred von Richthofen. Fokker and Richthofen were personal friends, and Richthofen had great praise for the triplane. The "Red Baron" flew to his death in a bright red Dr.I in April 1918, just after his eightieth kill. Only three hundred twenty Dr.I's were produced, but the image of the Red Baron and his red Fokker triplane added to Fokker's fame and mystique.[26]

If the Dr.I triplane further publicized the Fokker name via the image of the Red Baron, then it was Fokker's next and arguably best design of the war that gave substantial physical evidence to his skills as an innovative aircraft builder. In January 1918, the Luftstreitkräfte held a competition at Adlershof for a new fighter design that could effectively contend with a new generation of Allied fighters, such as the French SPADs, the British S.E.5s, and the Sopwith Camels. For the competition, Platz designed the V.11 biplane according to Fokker's specifications. It would become the best fighter of the war. Fokker and

The Fokker Eindecker fighters produced the first fighter aces in aviation history.

ABOVE *On January 12, 1916, Oswald Boelcke became the first German pilot to receive the Orden Pour le Mérite, more commonly known as the Blue Max, after shooting down nine enemy aircraft.*

RIGHT *Fellow Eindecker fighter ace Max Immelmann received the Blue Max four days later. Not only did these two pilots create the mystique of the fighter ace but they also created stratagems and tactics including the Dicta Boelcke and the Immelmann Turn still practiced by fighter pilots in the modern day.*

Fokker Dr.I
length: 18 ft 11 in (5.77 m)
wingspan: 23 ft 7.5 in (7.19 m)
power plant: 110 hp Oberursel UR.II rotary or Thulin-built Le Rhone 9-cylinder rotary
maximum speed: 103 mph (165 km/h)
ceiling: 19,685 ft (6,000 m)
endurance: 1.5 hours
armament: two synchronized Spandau LMG 08/15 machine guns
crew: 1

After examining a captured Sopwith Triplane, Fokker returned to Schwerin and, with the assistance of Reinhold Platz, designed and built the Fokker Dr.I triplane. It became the first Fokker production aircraft to feature a thick cantilever wing, implemented to reduce excess drag caused by extra struts and cables and to generate additional lift. When introduced in the late summer of 1917, the Dr.I could outclimb and outmaneuver any Allied aircraft in the air. Numerous kills racked up by a handful of expert pilots gave the Dr.I larger-than-life propaganda value and brought Tony Fokker back into the aviation limelight. No complete Fokker Dr.I survives but many replicas have been built over time. The one shown here is part of the Aviodrome's collection in Lelystad, the Netherlands. [Photo AVIODROME Luchtfotografie, Lelystad, Holland]

Platz again used the cantilever wing, first used in series production in the Dr.I. Prior to the fighter's official testing at the Adlershof competition, Fokker had Richthofen test the V.11.

After some faults were corrected, Richthofen praised the aircraft and encouraged his fellow pilots to test it. It won the Adlershof competition against thirty other entries and was ordered into immediate production as the Fokker D.VII. When it entered service in the spring of 1918, it soared over the western front with a vengeance. The Allies, who had been enjoying numerical and qualitative air superiority since the end of 1917 and the beginning of 1918, were shocked by the high performance of the new German fighter. It possessed a good speed, sturdiness, maneuverability, a fast rate of climb, and good high-altitude performance. During the summer of 1918, even though outnumbered nearly three to one, the German Luftstreitkräfte, with its new Fokker D.VIIs, achieved local air superiority in areas throughout the western front. In the month of August 1918 alone, just three months before the end of the war, German pilots and their Fokker D.VIIs shot down 565 enemy aircraft.[27]

In the fall of 1918, while Allied pilots were still reeling from the full wrath of the Fokker D.VII over the western front, the pilots of the Netherlands, on October 15, finally had their first encounter with the fighter. A D.VII of the German Seefront Staffel experienced engine trouble and landed within Dutch territory. On November 13, two days after the armistice, five more D.VIIs landed in the Netherlands. Two of those five aircraft were cannibalized for spare parts, while the other three were given Dutch serial numbers. That fortuitous receipt of D.VIIs gave the Netherlands its first taste of high-performance Fokker aircraft. With the exception of the ten D.IIIs from 1917, Fokker's high-performance aircraft were unobtainable for the Dutch during the war. The approaching armistice changed this situation dramatically, and the relationship between Fokker and Dutch aviation was about to begin.

The warrior is armed with his weapon: Tony Fokker demonstrating a Dr.I prototype before General Fritz von Lossberg as fighter ace Manfred von Richthofen gazes on. Richthofen's red Dr.I triplane became the most well-known aircraft of the First World War. Although Richthofen scored only 19 out of his 80 kills in the Dr.I, the mystique of the Red Baron and his red triplane remains one of the most enduring images of the First World War in popular culture, from film, to books, and even to Snoopy. [Photo AVIODROME Luchtfotografie, Lelystad, Holland]

One advantage that Tony Fokker had over rival German aero manufacturers was that he had developed good rapport and friendships with several influential German pilots. As a skilled pilot himself he could instantly relate to their critiques and recommendations, especially to the "feel" of an aircraft in flight. Collaboration with Oswald Boelcke and Max Immelmann helped to ensure the acceptance of the Eindeckers. Frequently Tony invited his pilot friends to test his new designs, making changes based upon their suggestions. Recommendations from Richthofen were implemented in the Dr.I and the D.VII. The endorsement of the Red Baron almost alone secured the acceptance and production of the D.VII. Here Tony Fokker poses behind the wheel with Manfred von Richthofen standing in the back seat. [Photo AVIODROME Luchtfotografie, Lelystad, Holland]

Refining design concepts from Hugo Junkers and Villehad Forssmann, Fokker developed a plywood-covered cantilever wing, first used in production on the Dr.I, which at the time was superior to what his rivals were manufacturing. Reinhold Platz, head of Fokker's prototype department, had a talent for speedily transferring these new ideas from drawing board into finished prototype. Using the cantilever wing and the usual welded steel tube fuselage, Fokker, Platz, and the company's engineering department developed a new protoype, the V.11, which was to become the D.VII. Platz is shown here on the far right in front of the V.11. [Photo AVIODROME Luchtfotografie, Lelystad, Holland]

Left *The Fokker V.11 (D.VII) biplane was judged by Manfred von Richthofen as the best new aircraft at the Aldershof Fighter Competition in January 1918. The fighter had excellent maneuverability, climb, and good speed, and its controls were very forgiving for less-experienced pilots. Furthermore, it could outperform Allied aircraft that had more powerful engines. It was said the D.VII made a novice a good pilot and a good pilot an ace. The D.VII was ordered into immediate production, and several other firms, including Fokker's predominant rival, Albatros, were ordered to manufacture the fighter.*

Below *This D.VII is preserved in the Royal Air Force Museum in Hendon, United Kingdom.*

Fokker D.VII
length: 22 ft 11.5 in (7 m)
wingspan: 29 ft 3.5 in (8.9 m)
power plant: 160 hp Mercedes D.III 6-cylinder in-line
maximum speed: 124 mph (200 km/h)
maximum ceiling: 19,685 ft (6,000 m)
endurance: 1.5 hours
armament: two synchronized Spandau LMG 08/15 machine guns
crew: 1

A second fighter competition was held in April 1918 at Aldershof, where Fokker unveiled his new V.26 prototype parasol monoplane. The cantilevered wing was of plywood construction, and the ailerons were tapered into the trailing edge of the wing. Powered by the 110-hp Oberursel UR.II rotary, the aircraft was maneuverable and was fast in takeoffs, climbs, and dives. The D.VIII entered combat in the last weeks of the war and turned out to be a nasty surprise to the Allied airmen who encountered it. Here ace Friedrich Altemeier stands in front of his D.VIII. (The rings painted on the fuselage are the logo of the Krupp works, where Altemeier was employed before the war.) [Museum of the United States Air Force]

Fokker D.VIII
length: 19 ft 4 in (5.87 m)
wingspan: 27 ft 6.75 in (8.4 m)
power plant: 110 hp Oberursel UR.II rotary
maximum speed: 127.5 mph (204 km/h)
ceiling: 20,670 ft (6,300 m)
endurance: 1.5 hours
armament: two synchronized Spandau LMG 08/15 machine guns
crew: 1

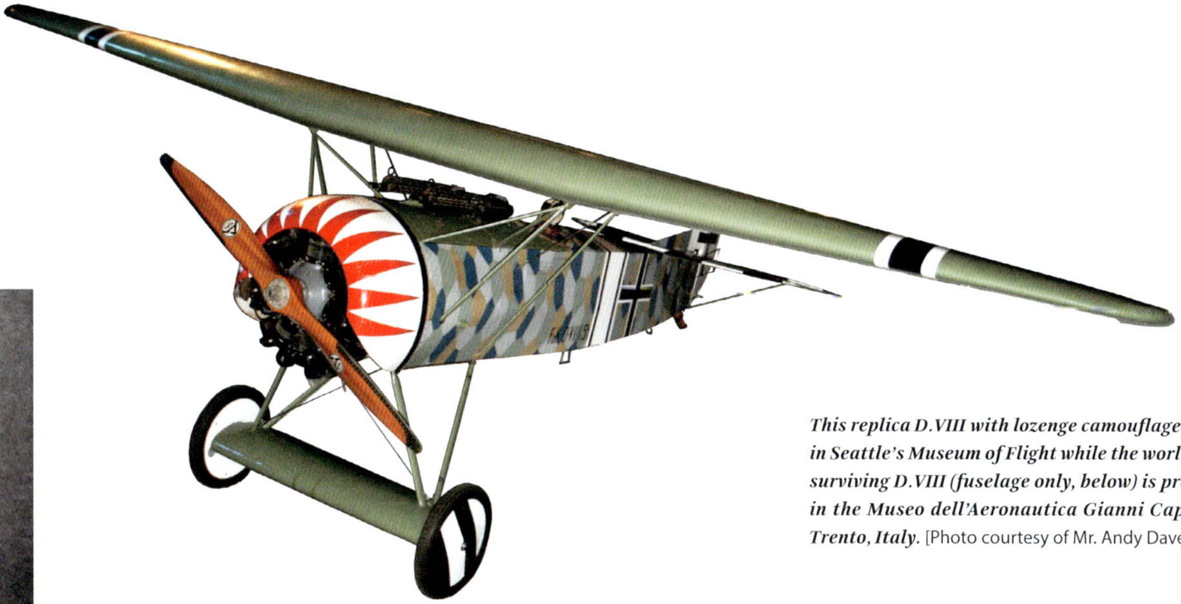

This replica D.VIII with lozenge camouflage resides in Seattle's Museum of Flight while the world's only surviving D.VIII (fuselage only, below) is preserved in the Museo dell'Aeronautica Gianni Caproni in Trento, Italy. [Photo courtesy of Mr. Andy Davey]

In his book on German aviation during the war, Deutschlands Krieg in der Luft, *the commander of the German Luftstreitkräfte General der Cavalerie Ernst Wilhem von Hoeppner made detailed reference to only two aircraft: the Fokker E.III and D.VII fighters. He recognized the E.III as being the first true fighter aircraft and the impact it had on the enemy. Hoeppner was particularly proud of the D.VII and its overall superiority to Allied fighters during the final months of the war. German successes over the western front began with a revolutionary Fokker fighter and ended with another.*

PH-ACJ
CF 893.

Chapter Two

THE POSTWAR ASCENT

THE END OF THE WAR?

As the war was coming to a close in the fall of 1918, the neutrality that the Dutch had so rigorously defended since August 1914 almost came to an abrupt and disastrous end. In August 1918, the Allies launched the Hundred Days Offensive, which pushed the German lines further and further east through France and Belgium until the armistice. As the German army fell back toward the German border, the Dutch high command worried that German troops might cross through the province of Limburg, the narrow part of the Netherlands that stretches between Belgium and Germany, or, on the other hand, that the Allies might march through the province while on their way to Germany. Gen. Snijders canceled all leaves on October 23 and put the Dutch army on alert in Limburg.

Snijders's suspicions were confirmed: in early November seventy thousand German soldiers, as they were passing through Belgium, approached the Dutch border and requested transit through Limburg to return to Germany. Many of these soldiers were wounded, and therefore the minister of foreign affairs, Dr. Herman Adriaan van Karnebeek, ruled that granting them safe passage through Limburg would be a humanitarian action as long as they were unarmed once they entered Dutch territory. One of the countries to take offense at this ruling was Belgium, which had viewed the Dutch as behind-the-scenes allies of the Germans during the war anyway, even though the Netherlands had provided considerable resources and aid to Belgian refugees. Because of supposed Dutch support for Germany during the war, the breach of neutrality in the Limburg episode, and the sanctuary offered to the Kaiser, the Belgians demanded the territories of Limburg, Dutch Flanders, and the Schelde River estuary. The French and the British gave some consideration to the Belgian demands. With the Queen and country refusing to surrender the Kaiser or Dutch sovereign territory to the Allies, who were already negatively inclined toward the Dutch, the Netherlands alone faced the possibility of a military showdown with Belgium—and possibly with other Allied nations.[1]

If the German Empire and its allies had not been able to stop the menacing onslaught of the Allied powers during four years of war, there was no chance that the Dutch could contain an Allied military incursion or blockade. This was especially true of the Luchtvaartafdeeling (LVA), the Army Air Service, which was in no position to offer an effective defense of Dutch skies after the armistice. Like the army, the LVA had been demobilized at the time of the armistice, so its personnel would have to be recalled to duty, and more pilots and ground crews would have

Beginning before the November 11 armistice was declared, thousands of German soldiers, disarmed by the Dutch, marched through the Dutch province of Limburg in hopes of making their way back to Germany without surrendering to the Allies. This incident also infuriated the Allies, particularly the Belgians, who believed that the Dutch had tacitly supported the Germans throughout the war.

A postcard showing the Belgian lion versus the Dutch lion, referring to the Dutch keeping the Schelde Estuary closed to Antwerp in time of war. [Conrad Bult Collection]

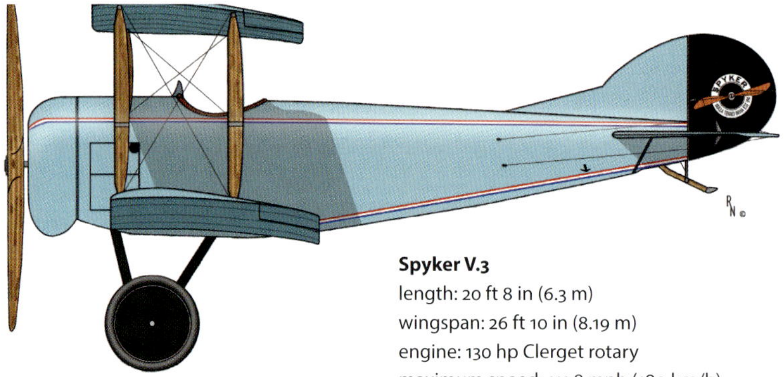

Spyker V.3
length: 20 ft 8 in (6.3 m)
wingspan: 26 ft 10 in (8.19 m)
engine: 130 hp Clerget rotary
maximum speed: 111.8 mph (180 km/h)
crew: 1

The best aircraft designed in the Netherlands during World War I, the Spyker V.3 single-seat fighter had significantly better performance than its predecessor, the V.1. But, after it made its maiden flight in July 1919, the Dutch government deemed its purchase unnecessary because thousands of surplus fighters had suddenly become available across Europe at war's end. Only the Spyker V.3 prototype was built, but it received good publicity at the ELTA, since it was flown in several competitions by Lt. Versteegh.

to be recruited. Although the Trompenburg works had promised a new fighter, the prototype of the Spyker V.3 was not even ready by 1919. The LVA had only a motley collection of obsolescent aircraft that were domestically produced and a handful of interned aircraft that could be used in combat. Although the Dutch interned 107 land-based aircraft during the war, only 73 were made airworthy; furthermore, in the event of war, most of these lacked spare parts. The only armed fighters that the Dutch could put into the air were twenty Nieuport-Spyker XIs armed with Lewis guns mounted on the top wing, five Nieuport-17s, which arrived from France in June 1918, and the few airworthy British, French, and German fighters that had been interned. The Fokker D.IIIs that had been purchased from Germany in 1917 were not delivered with synchronized machine guns, and the Dutch industry was not yet capable of producing the synchronization mechanism in sufficient numbers. In terms of ground-attack and reconnaissance aircraft, the LVA had forty Rumpler C.VIIIs, but these were not popular among Dutch pilots. The Rumplers were prone to have defective fuel lines; indeed, on several occasions the lines burst, spilling fuel onto the engine, with fatal results. The Spyker V.2s were underpowered and considered obsolete even before they left the factory floor.

At the height of the crises of early 1919, the LVA was in a desperate state. In stark contrast, the Belgian Aviation Militaire had modern Allied aircraft at its disposal and, most important, four years of combat experience behind it. Belgian pilots flew modern SPAD XIIIs, Hanriot HD-1s, and Sopwith Camels. In addition, there were a number of aces among their ranks, notably Willy Coppens, who had shot down thirty-four observation balloons and three aircraft during the war. No Dutch pilot of the LVA could claim combat experience: not a single intruding aircraft had been shot down by a Dutch plane during the four years of war.

The Return of the Prodigal Son

The armistice may have brought quiet to the western front, but it proved to be a time of crisis for Anthony Fokker. The German Empire had crumbled around him. A mutiny had begun among the sailors of the German High Seas Fleet on November 4, and within a few days the nation imploded as workers formed their own soviets and refused to continue with the war. Several days before the armistice was declared, chaos erupted at Fokker's Schwerin works when the revolutionary currents drifted into the town, as told by Fokker:

> The Revolution, which had broken out on November 9, two days before the Armistice, was full upon us, and we existed solely at the mercy of irresponsible dictators. For a time, we could not dismiss workmen without the consent of local authorities. Each section of the factory was run by a soviet of workmen. Finally, they were convinced that industry was rapidly going to rack and ruin by that uneconomic method of operation. Nevertheless, things went from bad to worse. We feared that we would not escape with our lives. Revolutionary guards circulated through our factories.
>
> They looted the banks and stole all current funds. Several manufacturers in Schwerin were killed outright when they showed opposition. Telegraph, telephone, and mail service was destroyed. No one knew what was happening throughout Germany. There was no police protection of any kind. I was called before the council of workers, holding forth in an arsenal, and told that I must produce more money or be shot.[2]

Fokker told the revolutionaries that his money was in Berlin and that he would have to go to his house in Schwerin to make the arrangements for it to be transferred. The revolutionaries sent him home with two guards to watch him. In the middle of the night, dressed in the clothes of his landlady's son, he crept out of his house past the guards. He ran down the street where his friend Bernard de Waal was waiting with a motorcycle:

> In an instant I was in the saddle and roaring out of Schwerin, headed for a village thirty miles away on the main railroad line. Through the night, afraid to show a light, I raced at forty miles an hour, fearful that at any moment I would hit something and break my neck, or run into a Revolutionary patrol.
>
> Arriving at the village, I hid the motorcycle in a deserted garden and quietly made my way to the railroad station. Not daring to enter the station itself, for fear of being recognized and seized, I waited on the other side of the tracks until a freight pulled in. Quickly, I scrambled aboard. After it had left the station behind, I walked back over the roofs to the caboose.[3]

When the freight train reached Berlin, Fokker hid out with a friend for fear of being recognized.

Revolutionary sailors marching past the Imperial Stadtschloß in Berlin. Fokker's factory in Schwerin was occupied by revolutionary sailors at war's end, and for a while Tony Fokker feared for his life. With Germany imploding around him, Fokker decided to escape to the Netherlands and continue his aviation activities there.

Tony Fokker hired a former German ace and gave him a D.VII to demonstrate to the military authorities of the Scandinavian countries in the summer of 1919. Spectators on the ground in Copenhagen and Stockholm were impressed by the pilot's skill and the performance of the aircraft, but no sales of surplus D.VIIs were forthcoming, since the former ace pilot was more interested in putting on shows and enjoying the nightlife. Disgusted, Fokker dispensed with his services. That pilot was Hermann Göring, future head of the German Luftwaffe and right-hand man to Adolf Hitler. Here Göring poses with Tony Fokker in 1918. [San Diego Air and Space Museum]

The unstable political and social situation in Germany, combined with the Allied ban on German military aircraft production, spelled the beginning of the end of Fokker's business ventures in Schwerin. Fokker himself was very shaken by the revolutionary movements, the Spartacist uprisings, and the street violence in postarmistice Germany. He wanted to return to the Netherlands as soon as possible. He did not plan to return as an empty-handed war refugee; he intended to start a new aviation company in the Netherlands and to take as many aircraft and pieces of equipment from the Schwerin works as he could manage. Thus began what Fokker later referred to as the "Great Smuggling Plot." The first obstacle Fokker faced was that not all of the aircraft parked at Schwerin belonged to him; a number had already been purchased by the German military. Fokker's office manager in Berlin approached the Reichsverwertungsamt (the state valuation bureau, which oversaw the sales of surplus war matériel), and he sent one of its officers to Schwerin to deal with Fokker. That officer was the last commander of Richthofen's "Flying Circus" and also a pilot whom Tony Fokker knew: Lieutenant Hermann Göring. The sympathetic young officer reached an agreement whereby Fokker could buy back the aircraft and engines belonging to the German military for a low price. Once the ownership issue was settled, a number of Tony's loyal German workers hid the remaining aircraft at Schwerin throughout the surrounding countryside, out of sight of the Inter-Allied Aeronautical Control Commission, which was supervising the demolition of the Luftstreitkräfte's aircraft and the dismantling of the German military aviation industry.

The next major obstacle was how to transport the Fokker aircraft across Germany and then across the border into the Netherlands without being intercepted by the Allies or the German government. Railway wagons were painstakingly assembled at Schwerin by Wilhelm Hahn, the chief of Fokker's transportation department. This was not an easy feat, since Germany's railways were in poor shape and somewhat disorganized from four years of war and the current civil unrest. Railway officials were bribed to obtain the wagons and to form sixty-car trains, which would be too long to be kept on sidings en route to the Netherlands, meaning that their movement would be expedited because they could not sit on the mainline for long, thus avoiding rigorous inspections.

> Trainmasters all along the way had been "seen," of course, so the tracks to the border were greased. Even more important was the bribing of the stationmasters on both sides of the frontier, and the small army of German customs officials. Fortunately for us, the Revolution and the depreciation of money had so reduced their circumstances that they proved more open to corruption than usual. Then, too, the German officials were naturally not in sympathy with obeying the Allied demands, and were willing to close their eyes if they thought they could do so in safety. As far as the smaller officials were concerned, it became comparatively easy to pay our way, once they were assured of the connivance of the men higher up. . . . Much of the bribing—this was specifically true in Holland—was not done by money at all. In the case of a minor official, usually a model of the Fokker plane was asked for. This demand seemed unlimited, and Hahn declared that he could accomplish as much with one airplane model as with a hundred guilders. Sewing machines and bicycles were other favorite bribes, and even today when I return to Holland, customs officials whom I have never met, stop me to say that their wives are still using the sewing machines I gave them back in 1919. . . .[4]

After the route to the Netherlands had been laid on a roadbed of bribes, the first of six trains chugged out of Schwerin and crossed the Dutch border without incident on March 18, 1919. Eventually all six trains made it across the border and were taken to a railyard near the Amsterdam Petroleum Harbor:

> Just before the transport rolled into Saltzbergen, a report was flashed to the Allied and German patrol that a large smuggling attempt was being made at a railroad station a short way down the border. Hahn had actually organized this smuggling party as a blind and it, by prearrangement of course, abandoned the bait when the patrol had been thrown off the scent. With the coast clear, our transport steamed on. . . .
>
> The Allied patrol never did catch on, for each time they were sent on a wild goose chase. Each time we allowed them a little capture and they never dreamed of the far greater loot which was at that moment steaming across the border into safety. The last transport which rolled across the line contained nearly thirty flat cars, loaded with airplanes, covered with tarpaulins on which was boldly printed the name of "FOKKER FLUGZEUGWERKE" and "SCHWERIN," because we had run out of anonymous covers. The airplanes we hadn't dared put on before, because their shape could not be disguised.[5]

In all, Fokker and his fellow conspirators managed to smuggle one hundred twenty D.VII fighters, sixty C.I two-seat reconnaissance planes, twenty D.VIII fighters, more than four hundred engines, and a variety of machine tools and aircraft parts. Now that his hidden stash of aeronautical contraband was safely in Amsterdam, the

Fokker did not escape from Germany empty-handed. Through widespread bribery and clandestine preparations, Fokker organized the movement of six trainloads of his Schwerin factory's aircraft, engines, and factory equipment across Germany and into the Netherlands in the spring of 1919. Fokker's "Great Smuggling Plot" allowed him to set up shop in his homeland with relative ease, and that led to the founding of his Dutch company, Nederlandse Vliegtuigenfabriek NV.

A flight of Fokker C.I reconnaissance aircraft of the LVA. The C.I was simply a lengthened version of the D.VII fighter and demonstrated Fokker's ability to creatively adapt his designs for different roles. [San Diego Air and Space Museum]

real challenge for Fokker began: What could he do with more than two hundred aircraft and more than four hundred aero engines?

After he had arrived in the Netherlands, Fokker learned of a deal that had been concluded between Spyker and the Dutch Ministry of Defense for the purchase of ninety-eight V.3 fighters and one hundred eighteen V.4 reconnaissance aircraft. Spyker had already produced a number of V.2 trainers for the LVA and the Marine Luchtvaartdienst (MLD), the Marine Aviation Service, but progress on the development of a new fighter and a new reconnaissance aircraft was proceeding at a snail's pace. The V.3 did not make its first flight until June 18, 1919, well after the Treaty of Versailles had been signed; and the V.4 was not even off the drawing board. When the V.3 made its first test flights, its performance was good but not exceptional, leaving the LVA frustrated with the contract with Trompenburg and its slow pace of production. Recognizing the LVA's displeasure with the Spyker aircraft and Trompenburg's nervousness over whether the company could complete the LVA's order on time, Fokker approached Henri Wijnmalen with an offer: Fokker would buy out Trompenburg's contract with the LVA and deliver D.VIIs and C.Is to its air arm, thus disposing of a number of aircraft he had brought with him from Germany:

> First I tried to sell my planes to the government direct, but all their appropriations were tied up in the Spyker contract. It was indicated, however, that the government would gladly buy my planes, if some way could be devised to get out of the earlier agreement. Further investigation disclosed that the Spyker firm, finding itself in a blind alley, was looking for a guide. They faced the loss of millions. I suggested a solution.
>
> My German planes, having once been figured as a total loss, could almost be counted as so much velvet. The price which the Dutch Government had contracted to pay for the Spyker planes was very high. Therefore, it was possible to make a deal whereby the Spyker firm could write off its losses and I could, at the same time, obtain a suitable price for my planes, while the government would spend no more money than it originally planned to do. Thus I hoped to turn my planes from frozen assets into good Dutch guilders.[6]

But Wijnmalen was in no mood to hand over an easy profit to Fokker: that would help to establish the newcomer as a competitor to Trompenburg's near monopoly on land-based aircraft production in the Netherlands. Almost a year later, in April 1920, after months of negotiations, the Dutch government bought out Trompenburg's

Part of the collection of the Militair Luchtvaart Museum in Soesterberg, this original D.VII is painted in the early colors of the LVA. [Nationaal Militair Museum in Soest]

contract and ordered twenty D.VIIs and sixty C.Is directly from Fokker, most still sporting their German lozenge camouflage. The Fokker C.I was a reconnaissance version of the D.VII fighter, powered by the same BMW IIIa engine that the fighter had, but with a lengthened fuselage to accommodate an observer and a rear machine-gun mounting. It was ordered by the Luftstreitkräfte, but the war ended before any could be put into service. For LVA pilots, switching from their Spyker V.2s to the Fokker C.Is was like trading in a minibus for a Porsche: even with a crew of two, the C.I performed like a fighter and was well loved by its pilots. Interestingly, this German-built aircraft would, along with the D.VII, be the longest-serving type in the LVA's inventory; the last operational C.I was retired in 1938. The LVA became the first air force to put a Fokker two-seat reconnaissance aircraft into service.

While negotiations between Fokker, Trompenburg, and the Dutch military were underway, the British lodged a complaint with the Dutch government. The Vickers company, which was also negotiating with the Dutch military over the sale of leftover aircraft from the war, found out about the Fokker smuggling plot and Fokker's negotiations with Trompenburg. Knowing that the Dutch military was inclined to purchase the Fokker aircraft, Vickers lobbied the British government, and the British ambassador to the Netherlands warned the Dutch minister of war that any purchase of Fokker aircraft would be considered an "unfriendly act" by the British government. Since there was still a pressing need for modern aircraft, this threat went unheeded. To cloak the source of the aircraft he was selling to the LVA, and to cover up his previous German connections, Fokker decided to start a new Dutch aircraft company. With the help of a number of high-placed Dutch businessmen and family connections, Fokker founded the Nederlandse Vliegtuigenfabriek (NV) on July 21, 1919. Although he was a director of the new company, Tony Fokker made sure that his name was not part of the company's title, nor was he even present when the company was registered.

Fortunately for the LVA, Allied concern over Fokker's smuggled aircraft and his presence in the Netherlands was waning even before Fokker founded his new company. Weary of further conflict, the Allies focused their attention on structuring a postwar world. The threats that seemed so imminent at the close of the war evaporated after the Treaty of Versailles. Due to Belgium's stubborn refusal to compromise during the Versailles negotiations, the British turned away from supporting Belgian demands for Dutch territory. The pressing need for aircraft and the Dutch pursuit of strict neutrality was

ABOVE *The British firm of Vickers was in the middle of negotiations for the sale of surplus aircraft to the Dutch government when Tony Fokker returned to the Netherlands with his trainloads of aircraft. The British protested the presence of Fokker in the Netherlands and also warned that any Dutch purchase of Fokker aircraft would be seen as an "unfriendly act." The Dutch ignored the British warnings, partly because Fokker's aircraft were superior to the ones being offered by Vickers.*

LEFT *A group of LVA and MLD pilots were visited by Prince Hendrik at the end of the war. Seated in front are Major Hendrik Walaardt Sacré, Prince Hendrik, and Lieutenant. F. A. van Heyst. Several of these pilots had notable careers: Willem Versteegh (25th from left), who would train many pilots of the LVA and go on to be president of KNILM; Simon Thomas (23rd from left), who bravely served as commander of the Waalhaven air base during the* Meidagen, *or "May Days," during the German invasion of May 1940; G. A. Koppen (7th from right), who would make a groundbreaking flight to the East Indies in 1927; finally, an obscure lieutenant, Albert Plesman (4th from left), who went on to build the Koninklijke Luchtvaart Maatschappij (KLM).* [Militair Luchtvaart Museum, Soesterberg]

finally over. As a result, a substantial number of the best military aircraft in the world, along with their designer, ended up in the Netherlands just when the tensions of the war years and the armistice's immediate aftermath in the following months had dissipated.[7]

The Shadow of the D.VII

While Anthony Fokker tried to keep a low profile in his homeland during 1919, the D.VIIs manufactured during the war continued to support his formidable reputation as a designer of rugged, high-performance aircraft that were known throughout the world. As the armistice came into effect on November 11, 1918, the deadly formations of Fokker D.VIIs that the German industry desperately produced during the last months of the war were grounded in the West. Many became the prized possessions of the Allied air services; furthermore, they were thought of so highly and still feared by the Allies that all existing models were to be confiscated from the Germans. In fact, it was the only aircraft to be mentioned specifically in the terms of the armistice. The British and the French simply let the fighters go to the scrap heap or sold them to other nations; they had plenty of surplus aircraft from their own domestic manufacturers. Belgium, however, put thirty-five D.VIIs into service in 1919; they served as escort fighters during the Belgian army's tour-of-occupation duty in Germany following the war. It must have seemed ironic to Germans to see their former fighters patrolling over them, aircraft that were still in German camouflage with Belgian markings painted on them. The United States put its one hundred forty-two D.VIIs to good use, many as advanced fighter trainers. Since that nation had not designed high-performance aircraft of its own during the war, it appreciated the information gathered from flight tests of the D.VIIs. During the Transcontinental Reliability and Endurance Test of 1919, the official report on the performance of a D.VII stated that the "simple cheap construction of the Fokker and its peculiar wing section are both radical depar-

One of the first D.VIIs handed over to the French at the Villacoublay airfield after the November 11 armistice. When Allied pilots flew the D.VII for themselves, they realized how great the aircraft was, and the air forces of Belgium and the United States shamelessly put them into postwar service, in some cases still with their German lozenge camouflage. [Museum of the United States Air Force]

tures in airplane design, and designers will do well in the future to consider this machine and its very ingenious construction."[8] This evaluation came to be the general American opinion of Fokker aircraft that were produced in the 1920s, and it hinted at a promising future of Fokker airplanes in the United States.

If the skies over the western front were quiet after the armistice, the same could certainly not be said for those territories of the eastern front, which had been occupied by Germany and Austria-Hungary since the beginning of 1918. The area fell into chaos immediately after the armistice was declared. The new nations of Hungary, Czechoslovakia, Poland, and the Soviet Union all began fighting to secure their borders, and they incorporated Fokker D.VIIs of the former Central Powers into their new air arms. During the war, Fokker had sold aircraft to the Austro-Hungarian k.u.k. Luftfahrtruppe, and in 1918 he introduced one of his D.VII derivatives, the V.22, which was equipped with a 200-horsepower Austro-Daimler engine, to the Austro-Hungarian air authorities. They decided to put the plane into production at the Ungarische Allgemeine Maschinenfabrik (AG or MAG); the Austrians also ordered D.VII airframes from Fokker's Schwerin works to be fitted with 225-horsepower Austro-Daimler engines by MAG. Several Austrian D.VIIs were completed by MAG before the war ended, but most were finished after the armistice. They were used by the short-lived Hungarian Soviet Republic in fighting against invading Czechoslovakian and Romanian forces in 1919. Czechoslovakia obtained only three D.VIIs, two of them during the dissolution of Austria-Hungary in October 1918, and another that was captured when a Hungarian D.VII made an emergency landing in Czechoslovakian territory during the border fighting of 1919.[9]

The D.VII saw significant action along the old eastern front, from the 1918 armistice until the end of the Russian Civil War. The re-created nation of Poland was quick to place the D.VII in its infant air service. In the chaotic early months of 1919, the Poles confiscated about ten D.VIIs in territory acquired from Germany. After the Treaty of Versailles, when the new borders of Germany and Poland were established, the Poles illegally acquired about twenty D.VIIs from German sources, with German pilots flying the planes over the Polish border rather than handing them over to the Inter-Allied Aeronautical Control Commission. The Poles also purchased twenty D.VIIs from the French, who had a surplus of grounded ex-German fighters. The Poles used their D.VIIs primarily in their war against Soviet Russian forces. This war of aggression on the part of the Soviet Russians had made them the outcasts of Europe. Having been almost completely dependent on the Allies for aircraft during the czarist years of World War I, and having a small domestic aviation industry itself, the Soviet Union was desperate for modern aircraft in its fight for survival.

In 1920, after Tony Fokker had failed to find a market in Europe for the surplus D.VIIs he had smuggled out of Germany, disposing of his remaining fighters for a profit seemed to be a forlorn hope. But no other nation in the world was openly selling aviation matériel to the Soviets, thus presenting Fokker with a desperate customer for his leftover stock. He did sell fifty D.VIIs and 3 C.Is to the Soviets in 1922, and the D.VII became the primary fighter of the fledgling Red Air Force. Thus began a clandestine

A group of pilots from the No. 15 Squadron of the Polish air force in front of a Fokker D.VII in the spring of 1920, during the Polish-Soviet War. [Photo AVIODROME Luchtfotografie, Lelystad, Holland]

relationship between the profit-minded capitalist, the "Flying Dutchman," and the radical communists of the Soviet Union.[10]

The ELTA

With the Great War over and the immediate postwar crises averted, the domestic aviation industry situation in the Netherlands was uncertain. During the war the LVA and the MLD strove long and hard to obtain a handful of modern aircraft from foreign manufacturers; and the government heavily subsidized a domestic industry to design and build aircraft. With the great powers disarming, thousands of surplus high-performance aircraft were suddenly available all across Europe, and they were better and cheaper than those being manufactured at home. The Treaty of Versailles and the making of the peace would eventually lead to the demise of numerous aviation companies and subsidiary industries throughout Europe, including those in the Netherlands, which were less developed than many of those on the rest of the Continent and thus vulnerable to competition with the latter.

Albert Plesman, as a lieutenant in the LVA, photographed in his flying suit in the observer's seat of a DH.9. Although clearly not the best pilot in the LVA, he was energetic and an excellent organizer who believed that aviation could fulfill a civil purpose in postwar Holland. After the war ended, he began to plan the ELTA. Plesman would go on to play a major role in the development of Dutch aviation, serving as the forceful first director of KLM. [Photo AVIODROME Luchtfotografie, Lelystad, Holland]

Lieutenants Marius Hofstee and Albert Plesman, the planners of the Eerste Luchtverkeer Tentoonstelling Amsterdam (First Aviation Exhibition Amsterdam, or ELTA).

Before the war, there had been little civil application of aviation beyond pleasure and competitive flights; now manufacturers were forced to look for practical commercial applications for their airplanes and airships. Even before the war ended, two forward-thinking officers in the LVA recognized the challenges and prospects of aviation in the forthcoming postwar world. The first was Lieutenant M. J. L. Hofstee, who wrote an essay in 1918 entitled "Travel by Aircraft in the Future," which speculated on the potential benefits of postwar commercial aviation. The second officer was Lieutenant Albert Plesman, who read Hofstee's essay and decided to act on it.

Plesman had begun his service in the LVA in October 1915 as an observer in one of the Farman HF.20 biplanes. In March 1917 he began his flight training to become a pilot under Willem Versteegh. Plesman was not the most talented pilot; in fact, Versteegh later observed that he had earned his wings only "by the grace of God." But what he lacked in piloting prowess he more than made up for in his organizational skills, foresight, and energetic drive. He frequently visited the workshops at Soesterberg and learned as much as he could about aero engines and the other mechanical aspects of flight. He also organized athletic classes for the officers at the base and became the chairman of the officers' casino. On one occasion he complained to Versteegh that he had too little to do, so the instructor gave the energetic lieutenant command of a squadron of DH.9s. Greatly impressed by the performance of this modern British aircraft, Plesman lamented that the Dutch aviation industry was not yet producing competitive aircraft. He had the foresight to realize that the future of aviation in the postwar world would be in civil transport, best summed up in one of his mottos: "Dit vliegen, dat een hel geweest is, kan een hemel worden" ("This flying, which has been hell, can become heaven").

As the war was coming to a close in the autumn of 1918, Plesman came up with the idea of having a large aviation exhibition in Amsterdam the following year. He took his idea to Major Walaardt Sacré, commander of the LVA, who approved it; Lt. Hofstee also volunteered his services. Sacré arranged for Plesman to meet with the

Ministry of War. There the lieutenant argued that his idea of an exposition would increase the Dutch public's awareness of flight and the civil potential of air transport; it would simultaneously show off the products of the Dutch aviation industry to foreign observers; and it might obtain foreign contracts for aircraft parts built by Dutch manufacturers. The Ministry of War agreed that such an exhibition would be beneficial not only for the Dutch aviation industry, but also from a diplomatic viewpoint: the invitation to Great Britain, France, and Italy to display their aircraft would help to improve foreign relations with those nations, relationships that had soured during the war and immediately after. However, this precluded the participation of any aircraft made by German or Austrian manufacturers, not exactly making the exhibition representative of what the entire Continent had to offer.

Eventually, several major Dutch business interests and government ministries offered their support to the exhibition, and a number of notable Dutch officials joined the planning committee, including Gen. Snijders and the chairman of the Koninklijke Nederlandsche Vereeniging voor Luchtvaart (Royal Netherlands Aeronautical Association) and former minister of war (and future prime minister) Hendrikus Colijn. The exhibition, officially titled the Eerste Luchtverkeer Tentoonstelling Amsterdam (First Aviation Exhibition Amsterdam), or ELTA, opened its doors to the public on August 1, 1919.[11]

The ELTA was a significant accomplishment for the Netherlands, not only because it was the world's first major aviation exhibition held after the end of the war, but also because it was held in a neutral nation that had been on poor terms with the British, French, and Americans. Plesman and his colleagues did not want the Netherlands to be left behind in the wake of aeronautical development in the former great belligerent nations. By seeing the aircraft of the Allied nations, Plesman hoped to inspire an enthusiasm for flight among the Dutch that would expand the future role that the Netherlands would play in the aeronautical world. Since the primary emphasis of the exhibition was the potential benefits of air transport, the aircraft that drew the most attention from the

A large restaurant was built adjacent to the main landing ground at the ELTA so that visitors could wine and dine as they observed the aircraft taking off and landing.

ABOVE *Gen. Snijders (far left) and Albert Plesman (7th from right) with the Italian delegation standing around an Ansaldo SVA.10 at the ELTA. The Italian government gave the SVA.10 to the LVA as a gift of good will.*

RIGHT *ELTA poster* [Photo AVIODROME Luchtfotografie, Lelystad, Holland]

The Dutch aero manufacturers display at the ELTA featuring the products of the Nederlandsche Automobiel en Vliegtuigenfabriek Trompenburg and Nederlandsche Vliegtuigenfabriek; (from left to right) the Spyker V.3 prototype, a Spyker V.2 trainer, and the Fokker V.39 prototype (a sports plane based on the D.VIII fighter but powered by a 50 hp Gnôme rotary engine).

crowds were the larger aircraft, such as the British Blackburn Kangaroo, the giant Italian Caproni Ca.48 triplane (a converted bomber/airliner), the British Handley Page V/1500, also a converted bomber/airliner, and the British Vickers F.B.28 Vimy Commercial airliner. On days when weather permitted, those who could afford the fare were able to take to the skies as passengers; most of those rides were offered in two-seaters, such as the Avro 504Ks or in Fokker C.Is.[12]

One airliner in particular drew great attention because it was designed by the Dutchman Frits Koolhoven, who unveiled the world's first purpose-designed airliner to the crowds at ELTA. The BAT F.K.26 was a biplane built of wood and fabric with a four-seat passenger cabin located directly behind the Rolls Royce 350-horsepower engine. According to Koolhoven, he showed his airliner design to the BAT management on the day of the armistice in 1918, because he had already concluded that the demand of the aeronautical industry would shift from a military to a civilian emphasis after the war. Designing and manufacturing such a purely civilian aircraft, however, was a risky business venture in the aftermath of the war. In a world about to be flooded with thousands of surplus military aircraft of all shapes and sizes, and—more important—at bargain prices, it would be difficult to sell

ABOVE RIGHT AND RIGHT *The world's first purpose-designed commercial airliner was the BAT F.K.26, the brainchild of Frits Koolhoven. He rightly believed that there would be little commercial success in flying passengers in the open cockpits of surplus military aircraft. The F.K.26 was unveiled to the world at the ELTA. Only four were built and only one was sold to an airline. Like the F.K.23 Bantam, the F.K.26 displayed Koolhoven's ability to design and build innovative aircraft; unfortunately, they came at a time when there was no market for them.*

FAR RIGHT *Frits Koolhoven (3rd from right) stands in front of an F.K.26 alongside Robert Noorduyn (4th from left), another Dutch aviation engineer who worked as a draftsman for BAT. Noorduyn went to work for Fokker during most of the 1920s and later founded his own company, Noorduyn Aviation, in Montreal in 1935.*

a purpose-built airliner at full price to emerging airline operators, who could simply purchase a cheap surplus bomber and place wicker chairs inside the fuselage. The F.K.26 embodied Frits Koolhoven's correct foresight into the future of air travel, but it came along at the wrong time. Just when the ELTA had convinced the Dutch public that air travel could be viable, Fokker was already waiting with a more modern airliner when the Koninklijke Luchtvaart Maatschappij (KLM) began shopping for aircraft in 1920. Either way, one of the world's first airliners came from the drawing board of a Dutchman.[13]

The Nederlandsche Automobiel en Vliegtuigenfabriek Trompenburg showed off its Spyker V.2 trainer and V.3 fighter. The newly formed Van Berkel's Patent Company in Rotterdam sent its prototype of a license-produced Hansa Brandenburg W.12 floatplane, which had just been put into production for the MLD. Frits Koolhoven also showed off his superb BAT F.K.23 Bantam fighter. This was one of the first fighter planes to be powered by a radial engine, but the end of the war eliminated its chance of mass production. Even Fokker was impressed to the extent that he commented to Koolhoven that the F.K.23 would have made a significant impact in the air had the war continued.

Below *Designed by Frits Koolhoven, the BAT F.K.23 Bantam was a streamlined and advanced fighter developed during the last year of World War I. The Bantam showed much promise but the experimental 170-horsepower A.B.C. Wasp radial engine encountered regular problems. The war ended before a more suitable engine could be fitted, and no military orders were forthcoming. The color profile is the lone BAT F.K.23, which was bought for evaluation by the United States Purchasing Mission in 1919, and is the only known Koolhoven-designed aircraft to have flown in the United States.*

Below Left *This surviving BAT F.K.23 is preserved in the Aviodrome collection in Lelystad, the Netherlands.*

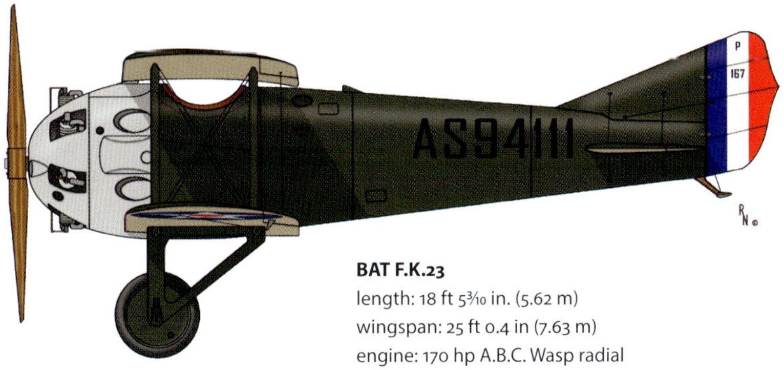

BAT F.K.23
length: 18 ft 5³⁄₁₀ in. (5.62 m)
wingspan: 25 ft 0.4 in (7.63 m)
engine: 170 hp A.B.C. Wasp radial
maximum speed: 133.6 mph (215 km/h)
crew: 1

ABOVE RIGHT ***A souvenir toy from the ELTA.*** [Militair Luchtmacht Museum, Soesterberg]

RIGHT ***Lieutenant Albert Plesman and Queen Wilhelmina observing the ELTA festivities. The royal family was very supportive of aviation efforts in the Netherlands.***

In addition to the aircraft, there were many military pilots from the represented countries who attended the ELTA, including celebrities such as Frenchman René Fonck, the top-scoring Allied ace of the war with seventy-five kills; Italian Arturo Ferrarin, a decorated fighter pilot who flew from Rome to Tokyo in 1920; and Sir John Alcock, who, along with his navigator, Arthur Whitten Brown, made the first nonstop transatlantic flight on June 14-15, 1919, in a Vickers Vimy bomber. The best military flier among the Dutch was Lieutenant Willem Versteegh, who performed a number of impressive maneuvers in the prototype Spyker V.3. On August 27, Queen Wilhelmina and Prince Hendrik attended the show and were greatly impressed with what they saw. Royal interest in aviation was certainly welcomed by Plesman and the other ELTA organizers and participants.[14]

THE KONINKLIJKE LUCHTVAART MAATSCHAPPIJ

When the dust on the ELTA fairgrounds had settled and the last visitor had gone home in September 1919, the seeds planted at the exhibition were already beginning to germinate. The skies over Amsterdam were not as busy as they had been in the previous weeks, but the drone of an aircraft overhead was about to become a routine rather than exceptional sound. During the closing months of the war, the Koninklijke Nederlandsche Vereeniging voor Luchtvaart (Royal Dutch Association for Air Travel) had already created a commission to investigate the possibilities of air transport in postwar Europe. A number of small air transport companies formed immediately in the wake of the ELTA. Lts. Hofstee and Plesman were each involved in two of these early airlines.

Hofstee and several other promoters formed the Internationale Lucht Vervoer Onderneming (International Air Transport Company), or ILVO, in Amsterdam immediately after the ELTA; they acquired the Spyker V.3 prototype, a Fokker Dr.I triplane, and a number of other war-surplus combat aircraft of German, British, and Austrian origin. They also considered purchasing the all-metal

Junkers F 13 monoplane airliner. But like many other air transport companies that were formed in the years immediately after the war, ILVO went bankrupt after less than a year. The only Dutch airline to survive and thrive was the one to which Alfred Plesman would be linked for the rest of his life. Even before the ELTA closed its gates, a number of its backers—including the Nederlandsche Handelmaatschappij, the Rotterdamsche en Twentsche Bank, the investment firm of Lippmann, Rosenthal and Company, and the Bataafsche Petroleum Maatschappij—had concluded that there was enough interest in air travel in the Netherlands to establish an airline. Upon the recommendation of the Royal Dutch Association for Air Travel, the Dutch government had already decided that Amsterdam would be the location for the nation's primary airport, and they selected the military aerodrome at Schiphol as the site.

On September 17, 1919, Albert Plesman, who had already been pushing for the formation of a Dutch airline, was asked by the ELTA backers to be the administrator of their new airline. The airline's board of directors admired his passion and drive, but they also recognized that the lieutenant was not an experienced businessman. Therefore, they required him to report to the board on a regular basis, thus ensuring that the airline would be run economically. Queen Wilhelmina had been impressed enough by the state of Dutch aviation from what she had seen at the ELTA that she allowed the new airline to carry the title *Koninklijke* ("Royal") at the head of its name. On October 7, 1919, the NV Koninklijke Luchtvaart Maatschappij voor Nederland en Koloniën, or KLM Royal Dutch Airlines ("for the Netherlands and its Colonies"), was founded in The Hague, supported by private shareholders and the Dutch government.[15]

In these early days of flight, weather was a critical factor because the aircraft of the time offered no protection against the cold, and thus no commercial flights were scheduled during the winter. This allowed Plesman several months to organize the airline between the founding of KLM in the fall of 1919 and the spring of 1920. The immediate problem was that he had just taken over an

The first brochure issued by KLM. [R. E. G. Davies Collection]

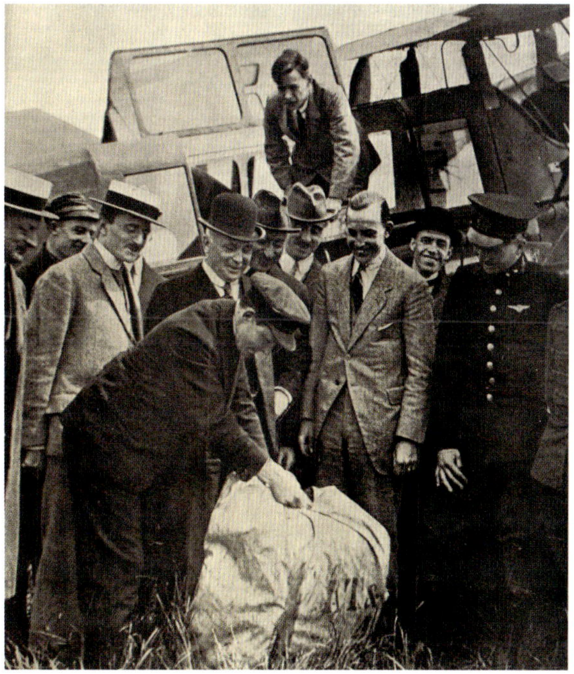

The first commercial flight of the Koninklijke Luchtvaart Maatschappij on May 17, 1920, was unique in that the airline had not yet purchased any aircraft. This first flight was between Amsterdam and London in an Airco DH.16 commercial aircraft, which Albert Plesman had leased (along with its British pilot, Jerry Shaw) from the British airline Aircraft Transport and Travel Limited. This picture shows the arrival of that first flight at Schiphol Airport in Amsterdam. Tony Fokker is opening the mailbag.

Airco DH.16
length: 31 ft 9 in (9.68 m)
wingspan: 46 ft 5¾ in (14.17 m)
engine: 450 hp Napier Lion 12-cylinder in-line
maximum speed: 136 mph (219 km/h)
range: 425 miles (684 km)
crew: 1
passengers: 4

airline that did not possess a single aircraft. As shown at the ELTA, there were only a handful of civilian airliners in existence, and most of those were rudimentary military conversions. Several infant airlines had already begun operations in Europe with such aircraft in the summer and fall of 1919; but this hardly seemed like a suitable solution to Plesman. In KLM's operations he wished to emphasize that air travel could be comfortable and routine rather than an adventure only for the daring. Nevertheless, with the spring having arrived and a business to begin—and having shopped in a new market with few options—Plesman settled on the Airco DH.16 airliner, a civilian conversion of the DH.9 reconnaissance bomber, which Plesman had flown during the war. He chartered a DH.16, owned by the British airline Aircraft Transport and Travel, along with its pilot, H. "Jerry" Shaw, to make KLM's first flight on May 17, 1920. Shaw took off from

One of the first aircraft used for KLM was the Airco DH.9 light bomber, which had been first flown by the British Royal Flying Corps in late 1917. The observer's cockpit was converted into a freight compartment or turned into seating space for up to two passengers, hardly an ideal arrangement since passengers had to wear flight gear and suits and were exposed to the same elements as the pilot. This photo shows Albert Plesman and Dutch postal officials in front of one of the DH.9Cs leased by KLM from Aircraft Transport and Travel Limited. The profile on the facing page shows one of the DH.9Cs purchased by KLM in 1920.

Airco DH.9C
length: 30 ft 5 in (9.27 m)
wingspan: 42 ft 4⅝ in (12.92 m)
engine: 230 hp Armstrong Siddeley Puma in-line
maximum speed: 113 mph (182 km/h)
crew: 2

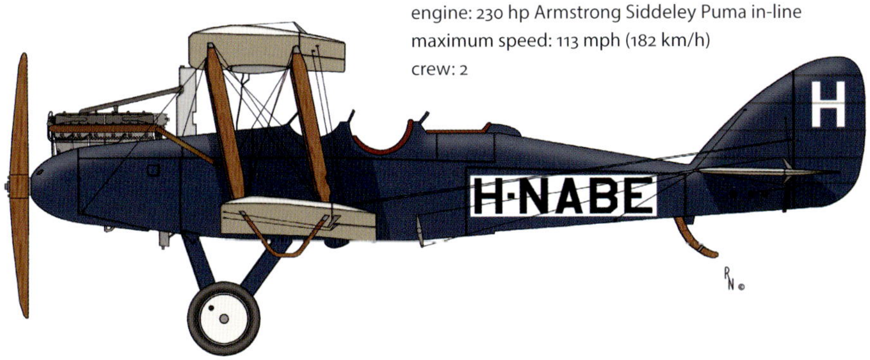

London's Hounslow aerodrome and landed two-and-a-half hours later at the Schiphol aerodrome outside Amsterdam. When Shaw arrived, he was welcomed by Plesman, Tony Fokker, and other dignitaries, and the event drew a great deal of public attention. Shaw flew back to London the following day, thus beginning KLM's first regular air route.

In a touch of irony, the new national airline of the Netherlands had inaugurated its service with a British aircraft chartered from a rival airline and flown by a British pilot. Additionally, Plesman started KLM service to Bremen and Hamburg using aircraft and pilots chartered from Deutsche Luft Reederei, as well as a route to Copenhagen in conjunction with the Danish airline Det Danske Luftfartselskab (DDL). The irony did not seem to bother Plesman in the least, and he was so optimistic that further business would be forthcoming that he ordered two Airco DH.9s, the first aircraft to be officially part of KLM's fleet. Nevertheless, he realized that his expanding airline needed dedicated commercial aircraft that offered passengers a higher degree of comfort than a windy, frigid open cockpit. Tony Fokker was aware of KLM's dilemma and approached Plesman in 1920 with a new aircraft that might fulfill the desires of both men.[16]

Fokker's First Transport

Fokker and Reinhold Platz had begun design work at the Schwerin works on the company's first purpose-built commercial airliner only a few weeks after the armistice. Well before the war came to its abrupt close, the duo had realized that the future of postwar aviation would most likely be found in the civil transport market. They gave the project they were designing the designation V.45, and it embodied the innovations that Fokker used in his best fighters from the last year of the war while, in a typically Fokker practical sense, utilizing materials already available. The V.45 was a high-wing monoplane design, using experience gathered during the development and construction of the highly maneuverable D.VIII fighter. The plywood-covered wooden cantilever wing derived itself from the upper wing of the D.VII fighter, along with the protruding ailerons. The result was an airliner that maneuvered like a fighter plane. The power plant they selected was the 185-horsepower BMW IIIa in-line engine, the same one used in later models of the D.VII. The lightweight rectangular steel-welded fuselage frame was another Fokker hallmark: it would be used extensively in the first and second generations of Fokker's civil airliner designs.

One of the first purpose-designed civil transports, the Fokker F.II was designed under the supervision of Reinhold Platz, using the design features that he had honed during World War I: the welded-steel-tube fuselage and the large wooden cantilevered wing. Work on the plane began in December 1918, and its first flight was made in October of the following year. The aircraft's first customer was KLM, which purchased two. The airline's pilot, W. G. R. Hinchliffe, recommended the plane, claiming that it performed like a fighter aircraft. Fokker (above) poses in front of the prototype of the F.II. [Photo AVIODROME Luchtfotografie, Lelystad, Holland]

The first airliner that Tony Fokker demonstrated to Albert Plesman and KLM had a rather embarrassing entrance into the Netherlands. Fokker's friend Bernard de Waal flew the F.II airliner from Schwerin but had to make a forced landing in Friesland. The landing gear broke during the landing and the aircraft had to be transported to Amsterdam by rail and barge before it was repaired in the Fokker workshops. [Photo AVIODROME Luchtfotografie, Lelystad, Holland]

The V.45 had an open cockpit with two seats, one for the pilot and one for a navigator or a daring passenger. Behind the cockpit was an enclosed cabin with windows on both sides, two seats facing forward and two seats facing aft. In October 1919, the V.45 prototype made its first takeoff, and several subsequent flights demonstrated that it was a strong and agile aircraft. The test pilot for Platz and Fokker, Adolf Parge, even attempted to perform a loop, but that proved to be a little too ambitious. Nevertheless, Tony was convinced that he had an excellent machine and was confident that he could sell the airliner to KLM. However, there was one major obstacle to overcome before he could demonstrate the V.45, now christened the F.II, to the KLM leadership. The Allies forbade the export of German-built aircraft, and Fokker's Schwerin works, still in operation and where the F.II was built, was a German company. Thus Fokker had to smuggle his own aircraft out of Germany into the Netherlands, something at which he had become something of a professional.[17]

In the spring of 1920, Fokker sent his friend and pilot Bernard de Waal to Schwerin to fly the F.II to the Netherlands. So as not to violate the Allied-imposed export ban, de Waal had to pretend that the aircraft was stolen. While Platz, who knew of the scheme, left the "scene of the crime," three loyal company employees prepared the aircraft for its flight. On March 20, 1920, de Waal took off for the Netherlands. After two forced landings in Germany and an encounter with two German policemen, he made a final forced landing in a field in Friesland, the impact of which broke the undercarriage. De Waal telephoned Fokker, and the latter drove to Friesland to pick up his friend. At least the aircraft was now on Dutch soil, and it was soon transported by rail and barge to Amsterdam. Once the aircraft was repaired, it was turned over to KLM pilot and former RAF ace Walter G. R. Hinchliffe, who praised the plane's fighterlike maneuverability, though he thought that the plane was underpowered. Nevertheless, Plesman was impressed enough to order two F.IIs, the first Dutch-designed aircraft to be used by KLM. This purchase not only heralded the beginning of a lengthy period of business between KLM and Fokker, but also the beginning of a frequently strained relationship between Plesman and Fokker.

Tony Fokker had neglected to tell Plesman that the F.IIs destined for KLM service had not been built in the Netherlands but rather in his old factory in Schwerin, Germany. Plesman realized that the authorities in Allied nations might refuse to do business with a Dutch airline that operated German aircraft. The F.IIs built for KLM arrived in the Netherlands in September 1920, and one of those airliners made a flight to London on September 30. Plesman, who was aboard as one of the passengers, was not sure how the British would react to the German-built airplane, with Dutch registration, when it landed in England. At the worst, Plesman feared, his new airliner might be confiscated by the authorities.

On the contrary, the aircraft was widely admired and praised on its arrival. Either the authorities did not know, or they chose to ignore, the origins of this spectacular new airplane. Regardless of this pleasant outcome, Plesman was reluctant to fully trust Fokker ever again. To increase the airliner's speed, KLM replaced the BMW engines with 240-horsepower Armstrong Siddeley Puma in-line engines. This was another Fokker design hallmark: the ability of the company's aircraft to accommodate a variety of engines. The F.II also demonstrated Fokker's prowess as a salesman: though only a handful of F.IIs were built in Schwerin, Fokker sold the license-manufacturing rights of the aircraft to Deutsche Aero Lloyd AG, which in turn built more than twenty of the airliners for its own service and its successor airline, Deutsche Luft Hansa.[18]

Flying in Comfort

Even before KLM's Fokker F.IIs had begun operational service, Albert Plesman consulted Tony Fokker about suggested improvements that could be made to the F.II. Rather than simply making them, Fokker and Platz designed a successor aircraft and constructed a mock-up in Fokker's Amsterdam shops only weeks after the F.II had made its first flight. Platz, who now supervised production at the Schwerin works, took the new design back to Germany, where he and his construction team assembled a prototype within only a month. The fuselage and wing of the new Fokker F.III were similar to those of the F.II. The main difference between the two airliners was the radical design of the F.IIIs cockpit and engine housing. Plesman's chief complaints about his new F.IIs were that the pilot's view was limited—being partially obstructed

Tony Fokker sits in the cockpit of his F.III with the side panel removed to show its interior layout. The Fokker F.III was essentially an improved F.II with higher speed and improved passenger comfort. Whereas the fifth passenger in the F.II had to sit in the open cockpit alongside the pilot, Platz designed a comfortable cabin, appointed with armchairs, carpet, curtains, and a table with an ashtray, that could accommodate all five passengers. To improve the pilot's line of sight, Fokker placed the pilot's seat alongside the engine, which was off-centered, an arrangement disliked by pilots because they sweated on the side next to the engine and froze on the open side of the cockpit. [Photo AVIODROME Luchtfotografie, Lelystad, Holland]

F.II in the Aviodrome's collection.

Fokker F.II
length: 38 ft 2 in (11.63 m)
wingspan: 52 ft 10 in (16.1 m)
engine: 185 hp BMW IIIa
cruising speed: 74.5 mph (119.9 km/h)
range: 745 miles (1,199 km)
crew: 1-2
passengers: 4-5

by the wing—and that the fifth passenger seat next to the pilot in the cockpit was completely unsuitable because of its exposed position. Fokker's radical solution to these problems was to put the cockpit alongside the engine, which was offset four inches from the center to compensate for the added width of the nose.

On paper, this seemed to be an ideal solution to Tony: the engine-cockpit pairing saved space, while the view for the pilot was dramatically improved, especially when a small section of the wing above the pilot was removed, allowing the pilot's seat to be raised. In practice, however, pilots were not enthusiastic about the engine arrangement. They enjoyed the improved view but not the cramped cockpit or the noise and the heat of the engine located alongside. The stubby engine-cockpit area also resulted in directional stability problems, but this was eventually corrected through trial-and-error adjustments. The prototype F.III took to the air for the first time on November 20, 1920, with KLM pilot Hinchliffe at the controls. After the adjustments and despite the awkward cockpit arrangement, Fokker had again created an airliner that could perform like a fighter. On one occasion, Fokker arranged a "dogfight" between an F.III piloted by Hinchliffe and an LVA Fokker C.I to show off the high-performance features of the airliner to the public.

The reason for the rapid development of the F.III was that KLM placed an order for it late in October 1920, before the prototype had even been tested in the sky. KLM initially ordered eight and eventually purchased six more. The first ones came from Schwerin, until production was transferred to the Netherlands at the end of 1921, when aircraft production at Schwerin ceased altogether. This time Albert Plesman knew for certain where his aircraft were coming from, but a new hiccup in the KLM-Fokker relationship developed during its purchase. Plesman claimed that Fokker had promised that he would buy back the F.IIs he had recently sold to KLM if the airline purchased the new F.IIIs; but later, after the sales contract had been signed, Fokker claimed that he had made no such promise. Plesman always wanted the best possible aircraft for the lowest price possible, while Fokker

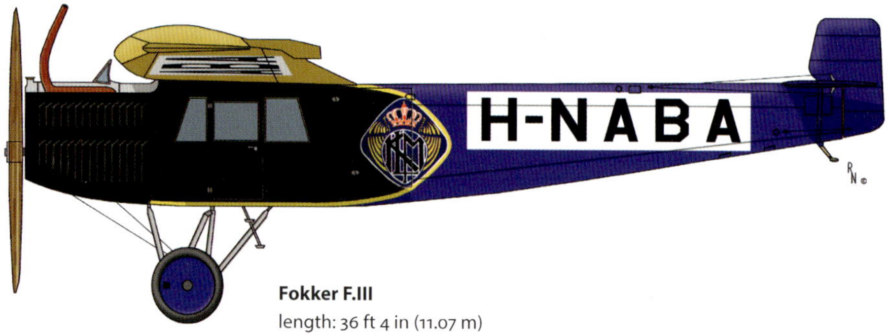

Fokker F.III
length: 36 ft 4 in (11.07 m)
wingspan: 58 ft 8 in (17.88 m)
engine: 230 hp Armstrong Siddeley Puma in-line and other engines
cruising speed: 84 mph (135.2 km/h)
range: 620 miles (998 km)
crew: 1
passengers: 5

A lineup of F.IIIs under production at Schwerin. The F.III was the last Fokker airliner to be manufactured in Germany. Production shifted to his factory in the Netherlands in 1921. [Photo AVIODROME Luchtfotografie, Lelystad, Holland]

was a shrewd businessman who often took a haphazard approach to design and development, and he expected his buyers to cover his research-and-development costs.

This was to continue to be the modus operandi of the relationship between these two giants in Dutch aviation, much to Plesman's chagrin in KLM's early days, because the Dutch government, which still subsidized the airline at that time, required it to purchase aircraft from domestic manufacturers. Nevertheless, Fokker's airliners gave KLM a modern and progressive image. KLM's F.IIIs made their first flight when the 1921 flying schedule began on April 14. The feature that most impressed the public, who dubbed the aircraft the "Limousine," was the richly appointed cabin with a three-person settee facing aft and two leather armchairs facing forward. The F.III was clearly purpose-built for passenger travel, unlike the converted bombers and reconnaissance planes other airlines were using. This quality, combined with the punctuality of its schedule, allowed KLM to set a new standard among Europe's developing airlines.[19]

The F.III was unveiled to the world at the Salon d'Aeronautique in November 1921. Fokker made sure that the display booth was registered under the new name of his company, the Nederlandsche Vliegtuigenfabriek (NV), which was an attempt to dissociate his name from the new business. He also wanted to hide the fact that the F.III, as well as a glider that had been converted from a D.VIII airframe that was on display, had been built in Germany, since German products were banned from the Salon. He tried to keep a low profile at the exhibition, but he was eventually recognized and soon became the main focus of attention for the media, curious onlookers, and angry crowds. Many in Paris, from the lowliest drunkard on the street to the highest government official, still saw Tony Fokker as the leading designer of aircraft for the "Boche." French aviation circles were reminded that Fokker's fighters had persistently outperformed their French counterparts on the battlefront. Although he was threatened to the extent that the French government had even sent secret-service operatives to protect him, Tony relished the worldwide attention that he and his aircraft were receiving. A group of French aircraft builders and pilots, headed by the war ace René Fonck, began a media slander campaign against the Nederlandsche Vliegtuigenfabriek and Fokker personally, and they petitioned to have his aircraft removed from the Salon. At times there was outright hostility toward the Dutchman on the floor of the Salon, as Fokker himself recounts:

> On the fourth day of the show, I was walking idly around when I met Commander White, of the American Legation, whom I knew very well. He asked me if I would accompany him and explain various technical matters. Everything went well until we were standing under the wing of a large ship and I started to explain the working of the first oleo shock absorber landing gear. It was

Prince Hendrik pulls away the chocks from KLM's first flight of the 1921 season on April 14. As pilots were exposed to the elements in early passenger aircraft, travel was suspended in the winter months in the first years of airline travel. This initial flight of 1921 was also KLM's first use of its new Fokker F.III aircraft.

Plush interior of a Fokker F.III's passenger cabin

Early KLM brochures featuring the F.III [R. E. G. Davies Collection]

one of the features of the exposition. To make it clear to Commander White, I drew a pencil from my pocket and started to sketch the system. I heard a big shout behind me.

"Here is Fokker, a spy copying our designs."

It was the inventor, Henri Potez, with three huskies, ready to beat me up, and there is no doubt a number of others would have gladly joined and helped him.

I retorted in French that I did not know how to copy designs, that I had not had five years' practice as the French had, beginning with my synchronizing gears. (!!)

One hot word led to another. We were just about to fight when one of the secret service agents jumped between us. The other took me by the arm and whispered that I must escape immediately. A crowd had gathered and half a hundred people pursued me, but I managed to slip out a side door after eluding them, picked up my Cadillac and went for a spin in the Bois.[20]

Not all the French pilots were so ill-tempered. In an honorable esprit de corps, the French ace Charles Nungesser held a dinner and reception for Fokker while he was in Paris. Despite his wartime activities, most of the public grew to admire Tony Fokker and his state-of-the-art machines.

While he may not have received a warm welcome in Paris, the opposite can be said for his arrival in the United States in 1921. He traveled across the Atlantic to demonstrate the new nature of European air travel with an F.III, the *Halve Moon* ("Half Moon"), named after the ship Henry Hudson sailed during his voyage of discovery in the New World on behalf of the Dutch in the early seventeenth century. On July 20, at Hazelhurst Airfield near Mineola on Long Island, veteran American pilot Bert Acosta took the F.III *Halve Moon* into the air and dazzled the crowds below with a very surprising performance for such a large airplane of that time. Over the next several days, Acosta made a number of flights over New York and Washington, D.C., demonstrating the speed and comfort that air travel could offer to businessmen and government officials. The *New York Times* reported: "One passenger commented: 'Sitting in perfect comfort, we had a wonderful view of the country, and it seemed hard to believe we were in an airplane. We could talk, move about the cabin, and, as we experimented, even write.'"[21]

The F.III attracted a great deal of public attention and was dubbed the "Rolls-Royce of the Air" by the American media. Yet, despite this glowing review and the warm receptions wherever it landed, the *Halve Moon* did not generate any orders in the United States. The American public had not yet fully embraced commercial flight as a regular mode of transportation, and there was no immediate market for the Dutch airliner. In spite of this American setback, the F.III sold very well on the European market, where infant airlines recognized its superiority to the war-surplus aircraft widely in use.

By 1921, with the advent of aircraft with enclosed passenger cabins, flying was described more as a typical mode of transportation than as an adventurous undertaking in spartan surroundings. Commercial flight was still in its infancy, but it was not too early to charge for baggage. Passengers were allowed thirty pounds of personal luggage without fee, but were charged extra per pound beyond that limit. By the summer of 1923, KLM's F.IIs and F.IIIs offered service from Amsterdam to Rotterdam, London, Hamburg, Copenhagen, Brussels, and Paris. The airline had an excellent safety record, but the unreliable nature of early aircraft engines compelled the

Albert Plesman showing one of KLM's F.IIIs to King Albert of Belgium. [Photo AVIODROME Luchtfotografie, Lelystad, Holland]

airline—and other airlines of the time—to offer accident insurance to its travelers in the event of death, permanent dismemberment, and temporary dismemberment. Nevertheless, KLM could count on the skill and professionalism of its pilots when problems arose. This was best exemplified on October 19, 1923, when the engine of an F.III en route to London, piloted by Captain Ivan Smirnoff, began to fail because of a cracked cylinder. A former fighter ace in the imperial Russian air service during World War I, Smirnoff calmly brought the plane down on a sandbar in the English Channel, amid screams of panic from his passengers. Although the seas were rising, Smirnoff calmed his passengers until a passing ship lowered a boat to collect the stranded fliers. This event aside, the F.III kept its reputation as a safe and efficient aircraft, and Fokker sold a number of them to German, Russian, Hungarian, and Swiss airlines.

Ivan Vasielivich Smirnoff, a Russian fighter ace during World War I, was one of KLM's first and best pilots, and served the airline until his retirement in 1950.

The Foundation of the Aerial Empire

Already by 1924, KLM was interested in larger airliners that could carry more passengers, and Fokker's answer was the F.VII. But the original F.VII did not begin as a project of Tony Fokker or Reinhold Platz. It was designed by another German engineer who had recently been hired by Fokker, Walter Rethel, the former chief designer of the Kondor Flugzeugwerke during the war. (After his tenure with the Fokker Company, Rethel went to Messerschmitt and designed the fighter that Germany produced in the largest numbers during World War II, the Bf 109.) Rethel used Fokker's formula of a welded-steel tube and canvas fuselage and a wooden cantilever wing; but he designed a much larger and rather ungainly-looking wing. The cockpit returned to the customary position behind the engine; the cabin had a seating capacity of eight passengers; and he selected a Rolls Royce Eagle IX in-line engine as the power plant. It was not the most attractive airplane, but it performed extremely well during its first flight on April 23, 1924. Later, Tony Fokker claimed to have performed a loop in the prototype. Plesman was impressed with the new airliner, and he purchased for KLM all five of the F.VIIs produced. He believed that he now had an aircraft with which he could test an idea that he had had in the back of his mind ever since KLM began operations: the possibility of an air route from Amsterdam to the Dutch East Indies, halfway around the world.

On September 1, 1924, the F.VII prototype was sold to the Comité Vliegtocht Nederland-Indië (the Netherlands-Indies Flying Expedition Committee), which, along with the Dutch East Indies government, had been cam-

With demand for air travel increasing, Plesman requested a new aircraft from Fokker in December 1923 that could accommodate more passengers and fly a longer distance. Not only did Plesman want a new aircraft with greater passenger capacity; he also wanted one that would have the range to fly to the East Indies in order to demonstrate that regular air service between the Netherlands and its largest colony would be possible. The first East Indies flight began on October 1, 1924, when the prototype F.VII (H-NACC) flew from Amsterdam to Batavia, arriving on November 24. [Photo AVIODROME Luchtfotografie, Lelystad, Holland]

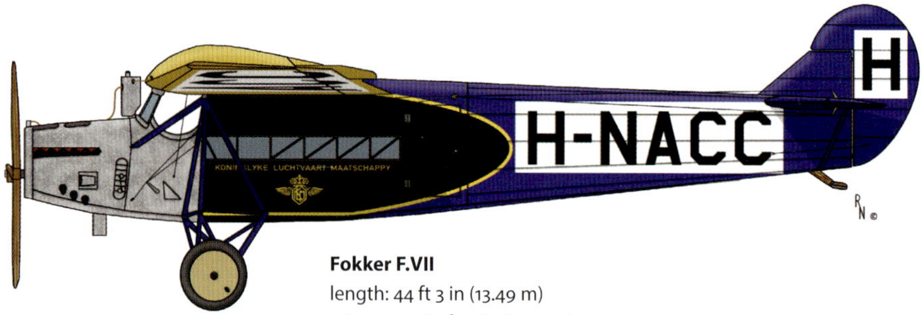

Fokker F.VII
length: 44 ft 3 in (13.49 m)
wingspan: 69 ft 11 in (21.31 m)
engine: 450 hp Napier Lion in-line
cruising speed: 109 mph (175.4 km/h)
passengers: 8

paigning for a proving flight from Amsterdam to Batavia, hoping that the end result would be the establishment of a regular KLM air route to that archipelago. KLM pilot Abraham Nicholaas Jan Thomassen à Thuessink van der Hoop was selected to fly the F.VII, along with Lieutenant H. van Weerden Poelman, of the LVA, and KLM flight engineer P. A. van den Broeke. Alterations to the aircraft began immediately. The passenger seats were removed and an enlarged fuel tank was installed to provide a fuel capacity of 224 gallons. Larger wheels were installed to the undercarriage to make landings on rough airstrips easier on the aircraft. Many spare parts, including a propeller, were loaded aboard. Since the F.VII would be flying over very remote areas of the world, the crew had to be prepared to make emergency repairs on the spot—by themselves.

On October 1, 1924, with all preparations in place, the F.VII, bearing the registration H-NACC in KLM livery, took off for the Far East. Only two days into the flight, however, the engine failed, and van der Hoop had to make a forced landing near the town of Philippopel (now Plovdiv) in Bulgaria. The undercarriage collapsed and the wing was damaged; fortunately, both could be repaired by the well-trained crew. But the more serious problem was that the engine was not reparable and had to be replaced. The local peasants who crowded around the F.VII made van der Hoop and his crew feel welcome, but they were frustrated that none of the locals could speak French, German, or English, let alone Dutch. Finally a schoolmaster who knew German appeared on the scene. He was the first useful contact the fliers had in this remote and relatively backward land.

According to van der Hoop:

> After an introductory ceremony, shaking hands and detailed information about our well-being, I began to ask again about a phone. He listened carefully and thoughtfully and told us that the only phone in the village was located twenty minutes away in a sentry box on the railway. Additionally, we were not allowed to use it, as it was intended only for official calls. I tried to tell him that in all civilized countries aircraft accidents had a priority on all

telephone and telegraph lines. He scratched his beard thoughtfully for a long time, but finally I got him walking in the desired direction, with all the speed of a constable in a quiet neighborhood.

We reached the railway via a rickety wooden bridge over the Maritza. We found a small guardhouse divided into two small rooms. It served as a guardhouse for a few men of a kind of Bulgarian Gendarmerie; they proved very suitable men to us later for guarding the aircraft, their good services having been demonstrated. In the other room was a phone, a prehistoric device the size of a mailbox with handles, bells, wires and doors on all sides, like a precious reliquary. A Bulgarian soldier sat there on guard. My good schoolmaster began to explain the case at length. The soldier listened with interest. So as to show his good spirit, he gave me a swig of water from a large stone jar. Using the telephone was indeed strictly prohibited; there was a wire around the phone, and the guard did not have the authority to break it.

I was desperate and decided to take drastic measures as my last resort. With some sweet talk I took the schoolmaster, and began an enthusiastic discussion about the wonderful weather and the beauty of the Bulgarian countryside, and when this man sank into a deep daydream, I slipped back inside. I did not have Bulgarian money, but as in most cases, I had a small amount of gold English pounds in my pocket. I let a gold coin sparkle in my hand. The result was unexpected; the soldier pulled a huge knife, and growing pale, I think the man wants to perform a summary execution for the attempted bribery of an official in the performance of his duty. His action proved to be very innocent; with one stroke of the knife the wire disappeared from the phone, and the line is free.[22]

After a number of attempted calls through the primitive Bulgarian telephone network, van der Hoop was finally able to get a message through to the Dutch consul in Philippopel and explain his predicament.

After the crew spent the night in the aircraft's cabin, the Dutch consul from Philippopel arrived the next day and drove the fliers into the town. Van der Hoop was able to speak with the Dutch ambassador, Jonkheer De Brauw, who told the pilot that he had already sent a message to Plesman in Amsterdam to report the aircraft's mishap. He had requested assistance from the Bulgarian authorities, who were prompt to reply. A military pilot and the chief of the technical service at Sofia airport flew in and examined the aircraft but both were pessimistic about repairing it on site. Rural Bulgaria offered little in the way of modern aviation facilities. The nation was banned from having an air force by the Treaty of Neuilly because of

ABOVE *Bulgarian villagers inspect the Fokker F.VII shortly after engine failure had forced pilot van der Hoop to make a landing that broke the undercarriage on KLM's first flight to the East Indies.*

BELOW *The arrival of the F.VII's new engine, donated by the Dutch magazine* Het Leven. *It arrived special delivery—by ox cart!*

Above *A hero's welcome for the East Indies fliers at Schiphol. Albert Plesman (far left) offers a toast to (in order) van den Broeke, van der Hoop, and van Weerden Poelman. Tony Fokker and Gen. Snijders (far right) were also present to welcome the fliers home. This long-distance aeronautical achievement would soon become a regular operation for KLM.* [Photo AVIODROME Luchtfotografie, Lelystad, Holland]

Top and Above *The arrival of the F.VII in the East Indies was widely celebrated, and van der Hoop, van Weerden Poelman, and van den Broeke were the toast of the colony.*

Bulgaria's alliance with the Central Powers during World War I. A new engine would have to be shipped from the Netherlands. But there was one problem with this: the Comité Vliegtocht Nederland-Indië had not budgeted for an engine replacement and had no funds with which to purchase a spare.[23]

But help came in an unexpected way. On October 13, Pieter Guilonard, the head of KLM's technical department, arrived in Sofia aboard the Orient Express and brought good tidings to the fliers. The plight of van der Hoop and his crew had been widely covered in the media in the Netherlands, and the Dutch magazine *Het Leven* had advertised a subscription campaign among its readers to raise enough money to purchase a new engine. The campaign had proved popular and within a few weeks, despite several problems getting an aircraft engine across Eastern European borders (problems that were also alleviated via a bribe here and there), a new Rolls Royce Eagle engine and a technical crew from the Netherlands arrived in Philoppopel. Guilonard and his crew fully used their technical talents in making all the necessary repairs on the spot where the H-NACC had been forced to land. On November 2, van der Hoop and his crew were airborne once again, finally arriving in Batavia on November 24. Despite their misadventures in Bulgaria, van der Hoop and his crew proved that commercial flights between Amsterdam and Batavia were not only possible but could eventually be inaugurated, as the performance of commercial aircraft continued to improve.

Koolhoven's Giant White Elephant

In 1924, when KLM's daytime flights were operating with a great degree of regularity and success, Albert Plesman pondered the benefits that could be reaped by nighttime flying. If KLM could attract customers who wished to travel late in the day or who wished to sleep during their flight, night flying could increase the volume of KLM's scheduled services and add revenue. Before this could happen, the hazards of nighttime flying had to be overcome. The primary threat to night flights was the risk of an engine failure: it was difficult enough to land a powerless aircraft during the day, but at night it was nearly impossible. Plesman decided that a three-engine aircraft would be required to assure safe night flights, and he requested designs from Fokker and the NV Nationale Vliegtuig Industrie (NVI) in The Hague. NVI was founded in April 1922 with support from Walaardt Sacré and the British Vickers firm. NVI was the first to respond and submitted a trimotor monoplane designed by Frits Koolhoven. After the failure of BAT to sell his F.K.23 fighter and F.K.26 transport, Frits Koolhoven returned to the Netherlands and worked for Spyker for a few years, designing automobiles. In 1922 he went to work as chief designer for the new NVI. Plesman was reasonably impressed, and construction began late in 1924, with NVI covering the development and building costs of the F.K.33. It reflected some of the eccentric design tendencies for which Frits Koolhoven was becoming known. Construction took place at NVI's factory in The Hague, and the components were eventually shipped to the Waalhaven airport in Rotterdam for completion.

The F.K.33 was the largest aircraft built in the Netherlands up to that time. It was a high-wing monoplane with two Armstrong Siddeley Puma 230-horsepower engines suspended under the wing. An enclosed cabin had wicker seats for ten passengers. The third Puma engine—in an unusual move—was mounted on top of the wing in a pusher configuration, with a four-bladed propeller. This high position and the general large size of the aircraft made it impossible to house in any of the existing hangars in the Netherlands. The engines had no cowlings and were completely exposed. Initially underestimating the size of the completed aircraft, its builders and the ground crew at Waalhaven had to take the hangar doors off their tracks and remove the upper engine so that the airplane could actually be removed from the hangar. From then on the airliner was nicknamed *Dikke Dirk* ("Fat Dirk").

KLM pilots Gerrit Geysendorffer and Nieuwenhuis began making test flights in the F.K.33 in September 1925.

The first trimotor airliner purchased by KLM surprisingly did not come from Tony Fokker, but rather from Frits Koolhoven's workshops at the Nationale Vliegtuig Industrie (NVI). At its own expense, NVI and Koolhoven went to work designing a three-engine airliner that could carry ten passengers for KLM. After much expense, the F.K.33 was first flown in 1925. KLM pilots were not particularly fond of its flight characteristics and derisively nicknamed the plane "Dikke Dirk." Its awkward engine arrangement, its poor performance, and the sudden availability of much more refined (and less expensive) trimotors from Fokker meant that KLM purchased only the prototype. [R. E. G. Davies Collection]

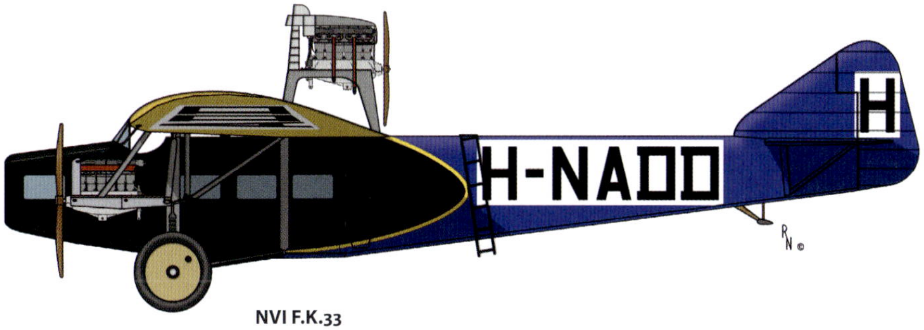

NVI F.K.33
length: 57 ft 3 in (17.45 m)
wingspan: 81 ft 6.3 in (24.85 m)
engines: three 230 hp Armstrong Siddelely Puma in-lines
maximum speed: 118.1 mph (190 km/h)
passengers: 10

NVI was not the only small aero manufacturer in the Netherlands in the interwar years. One of the most unique Dutch aircraft designs of this period was a purpose-built cargo aircraft ordered by KLM from the short-lived aircraft division of the Dutch railway engine and carriage manufacturer Werkspoor NV (Koninklijke Nederlandsche Fabriek van Werktuigen en Spoorwegmaterieel) in 1927. The Werkspoor Jumbo was a biplane designed by early Dutch aviation engineer Joop Carley and was delivered to KLM in 1931. It hauled freight for two years before it was used as a trainer until it was destroyed at Schiphol Airport during the Luftwaffe bombardment on May 10, 1940. Only one Jumbo was built, and although it did not prove commercially successful at the time, it foreshadowed the later development of large cargo aircraft and air freight services. [Wikimedia Commons]

The weight of the upper engine over the center of the fuselage made the aircraft difficult to keep level in flight. Koolhoven corrected this problem by adding four feet to the nose and storing luggage inside, thus causing the aircraft's weight to be more evenly distributed. Once all its other teething troubles were solved, the F..K.33 began commercial service with KLM at the end of 1925, making roundtrip flights out of Amsterdam to London, Paris, and Malmo. But this unique aircraft did not stay in KLM's service long: in July 1927, KLM sold it to an advertising firm in Hamburg, which then installed lights on the underside of the wing for use as a nocturnal flying billboard. KLM was so quick to dispose of the aircraft because it required frequent and extensive maintenance, which limited its revenue schedule. The engine mounted on top of the wing was aerodynamically inefficient, resulting in a low speed. The failure of the F.K.33 played a significant role in NVI closing its doors in 1926 due to lack of sales. Frits Koolhoven, who was let go from NVI due to disagreements with the management in 1925 and was himself tired of working for companies that failed or went bankrupt, founded his own company, NV Vliegtuigenfabriek Koolhoven, in the former NVI facilities at the Waalhaven Aerodrome outside of Rotterdam in 1926. In the end, the main reason that KLM withdrew the F.K.33 from service and sought no further orders from NVI was that Anthony Fokker had developed a more efficient trimotor design that had caught Plesman's eye. *Dikke Dirk* may have been the first trimotor airliner in the Netherlands, but it was Fokker's design that would focus the attention of the world's airliner market on the Netherlands.[24]

The First Fokker Trimotors

Like Koolhoven, Fokker had received a request from Plesman for a trimotor design that KLM could use for night flights. At the time, Fokker was busy with the F.VII and thus did not give his immediate attention to the request. But only five F.VIIs were produced, and Tony was not completely happy with the design; he thought it could be improved. Walter Rethel left the firm early in 1925, and Reinhold Platz redesigned the F.VII, most noticeably the wing. Platz removed the ungainly-shaped ailerons and replaced them with inset tapered ones that created a more aerodynamically defined wing, very similar to the one used for the D.VIII fighter. The new F.VIIa was initially powered by 400-horsepower Packard Liberty engines, which were cheap and readily available because there was a surplus of them from the war. Platz also designed a removable engine mount that could accommodate a variety of aero engines. This was beneficial for sales promotions, because the purchaser could customize the aircraft regarding his choice of engine.

The prototype F.VIIa first flew on March 12, 1925, solely as a company undertaking. Fokker correctly foresaw that KLM and other airlines would purchase the new aircraft. KLM purchased the first production version of the F.VIIa and ordered ten more, which the airline received between

Fokker F.VIIa
length: 47 ft 11 in (14.61 m)
wingspan: 64 ft 2 in (19.56 m)
power plant: 480 hp Bristol Jupiter radial
cruising speed: 100 mph (160.9 km/h)
range: 560 miles (901 km)
passengers: 8

Platz and a new team of young engineers recently hired by Fokker believed that they could make several improvements to the F.VII that would culminate in a better aircraft. Fokker and Platz saw the F.VII design as a prototype for a new production-series aircraft, something that Plesman wanted for KLM. The resulting F.VIIa had a number of aerodynamic refinements, the most notable being inset ailerons. Plesman was pleased with the new F.VIIa and ordered eleven for KLM. The aircraft to the right (with its interior shown above) has been preserved at the Aviodrome Museum. Another F.VIIa, in early Swiss Air colors (above right), is preserved in the Verkehrshaus der Schweiz in Luzern, Switzerland.

Perhaps the most well-known Fokker airliner, the F.VIIa/3m / F.VIIb/3m trimotor (the only difference between the two designations was that the F.VIIb/3m had a slightly larger wing than the F.VIIa/3m) was the most successful and numerous production series of Fokker airliners prior to the Cold War years. They became the standard airliner for KLM and a number of airlines throughout the world in the late 1920s and early 1930s. Over one hundred fifty F.VII/3ms were built, and they were seen as the standard airliner of the late 1920s. [Museum of the United States Air Force]

Fokker F.VIIb/3m
length: 47 ft 11 in (14.61 m)
wingspan: 71 ft 2 in (21.69 m)
power plant: three 300 hp Wright J-5 Whirlwind radials
cruising speed: 106 mph (170.6 km/h)
range: 530 miles (853 km)
passengers: 8

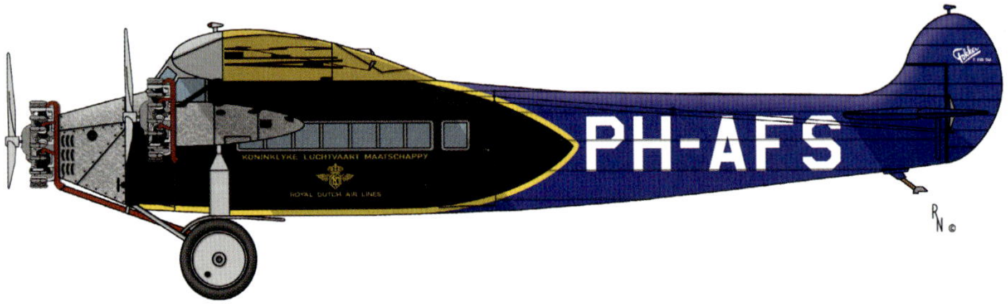

late 1925 and 1927. Plesman immediately fell in love with the aircraft: it offered a seat-mile cost ratio that was only 25 percent that of the F.III.

In the summer of 1925, Fokker had already decided to compete in the Ford Reliability Tour in the United States in September and October of that year with his F.VIIa. The emphasis of this contest was aircraft reliability, so Fokker concluded that the addition of two extra engines under the wings of the F.VIIa would make his airliner three times more reliable. Two Wright Wirlwind J4 engines were hastily installed under the wings to complement the one in the nose, and the first test flight was made on September 4. The aircraft handled well, and it was quickly disassembled and shipped to the United States—just in time to participate in the reliability tour. Interestingly, what would become Fokker's most successful commercial design was the product of rapid improvisation. Although the tour was not meant to be a race, Fokker made sure that his new F.VIIa/3m was the first aircraft to arrive at as many stops as possible. Its revolutionary trimotor layout, coupled with Fokker's flying and publicity skills, captured the attention of the American public, and American orders for the new airliner were rapidly forthcoming; European orders were quick to follow. (The full story of the F.VII/3m's impact on American and world aviation is in the next two chapters.)

Fokker built only eighteen of the F.VIIa/3m trimotors. They were replaced in production by the improved F.VIIb/3m: the only difference between the two models was that the "b" version had a larger wing. The F.VIIa/3ms were sold to the LVA, American and Italian airlines, and individual purchasers. One of the F.VIIa/3ms ordered by the LVA was made available to Lieutenant George Alexander Koppen, an LVA pilot who wished to make a return flight from Amsterdam to Batavia. The flight was supported by the Comité Vliegtocht Nederland-Indië and by Plesman, who was interested in the possibility of a KLM air route to the Far East now that a new reliable airliner was available. Lt. Koppen and his crew took off from Schiphol in their Fokker trimotor (named the *Postduif*) on October 1, 1927, and returned twenty-two days later.

That uneventful flight was a major publicity boost

for Dutch promoters of regular flights to the East Indies, and the crew provided important information about the terrain and weather conditions along the route. The F.VIIb/3m came to be recognized not only as a symbol of the modern equipment operated by KLM in the late 1920s but also as the ultimate representative of the 1920s generation of airliner design. Fokker received orders from KLM and a number of other airlines, but his factory was unable to keep up with the growing demand. He decided that the best way to remedy this situation was to sell license-manufacturing rights of the trimotor to foreign aero firms. The demands of airlines could thus be efficiently met, and Fokker would receive a profit from ninety-six licensed sales in Poland, Great Britain, Czechoslovakia, Belgium, and Italy.

The impact that the Fokker trimotor had on aviation in Europe during the late 1920s and early 1930s can be summed up this way: in 1932, the British Ministry of Aviation reported that, of all the trimotor designs being used on the Continent, 56 percent were Fokkers, and the remaining 44 percent were composed of twelve other types.[25]

New Routes and New Aircraft

The Amsterdam-to-Batavia flights of van der Hoop and Koppen advanced the possibility of a regular air route between the motherland and its distant colony. The establishment of regular commercial air service within the colony in 1928 further pushed for a regular Far Eastern service. The Koninklijke Nederlandsch-Indische Luchtvaart Maatschappij (KNILM) was founded by a group of investors from the colony on July 16, 1928. It was completely independent from KLM, which had not established any air routes *within* the East Indies. In a rare exception, the Dutch government allowed the formation of another airline but limited its area of operations. KLM would retain the sole right to establish a long-distance route from the homeland to Batavia. But KNILM ordered four Fokker F.VIIb/3ms, and two of them began the first regular

Grouping at left *A sampling of several posters of airlines that used Fokker's trimotors: Polish LOT, Belgian Sabena, and Japanese Air Transport Co., Ltd. This demonstrated the worldwide appeal of the Fokker airliners.* [R.E.G. Davies Collection]

Below *Map of the route followed by the* Postduif *from Amsterdam to Batavia, what would become the longest air route in the world during the interwar years*

Natives in the East Indies investigate a Fokker trimotor.

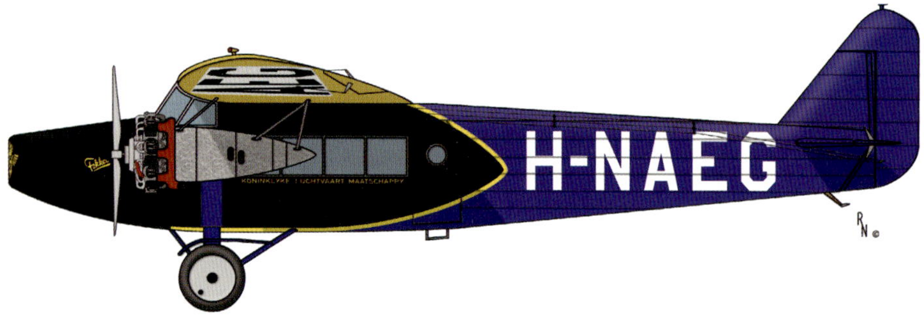

Fokker F.VIII
Length: 55 ft. 1½ in (16.8 m)
wingspan: 75 ft. 5½ in (23 m)
cruising speed: 96 mph (154 km/h)
range: 435 mi (700 km)
power plant: two 480 hp Gnome-Rhône license-built Jupiter radials
passengers: 15

Before Fokker began series production of his F.VII/3m trimotors, KLM requested a new airliner with significantly greater passenger capacity than its F.VIIs and F.VIIas had. The new F.VIII could accommodate fifteen passengers and differed from the new trimotors in that it was wider and had only two engines. Since engines were becoming lighter and more reliable, Platz did not believe that a third engine was necessary. The unique feature of the F.VIII was the loading hatch and cargo compartment in the nose of the aircraft. The F.VIII first flew on March 12, 1927, and KLM purchased seven. [Photo AVIODROME Luchtfotografie, Lelystad, Holland / R. E. G. Davies Collection]

KNILM service within the Dutch East Indies archipelago on November 1, 1928. The first routes were in Java—from Batavia to Bandung and Semarang, then to Sourabaya in 1929; flights to Sumatra began in 1930, with service to Palembang, Medan, and then eventually Singapore. The services provided by KNILM allowed the Dutch in the East Indies to experience regular commercial air service, just as their relatives back in Europe could. More important, it provided an important rapid and efficient transport link within a colony made up of hundreds of islands.[26]

KLM routes in Europe had also expanded considerably. By the end of the decade, KLM was flying to Berlin, Basel, Zürich, Nuremberg, Budapest, Sofia, Athens, and Istanbul, and on to Cairo. Because of increasing passenger demand, Fokker designed and delivered two further airliner types to KLM as the 1920s were drawing to a close. The first, the F.VIII, was a twin-engine high-wing monoplane designed by Platz to fulfill a KLM request for an airliner larger than the F.VIIa. Continuing with standard Fokker construction techniques, he designed a larger welded-steel-tube and canvas-covered fuselage with enough room to accommodate fifteen passengers in five rows (two seats to starboard and one seat to port with an aisle in between).

Although many airlines, KLM included, were pushing for trimotor designs for safety concerns, Platz was confident in the twin-engine arrangement. He selected two new Gnome-Rhône (license-built from Bristol) Jupiter 480-horsepower radial engines that were lighter than the in-line engines used in previous Fokkers and provided enough power so that, if one engine failed, the other was powerful enough to maintain flight. The absence of an engine in the nose allowed for a ten-foot-long cargo compartment in the fuselage; the nose was a hatch on hinges that allowed access. The prototype F.VIII first flew on March 24, 1927, and KLM purchased seven of them. Fokker sold another one to the Hungarian airline Malert, while the Manfred Weiss industrial firm in Budapest also produced three more under license.[27]

The last airliner Fokker produced for KLM in the 1920s was the F.IX, the largest trimotor aircraft to be built by the Fokker Company. Even before air service to the Dutch East Indies began, Albert Plesman believed that the route would become popular and that passenger demand would outstrip the capacity of the F.VIIb/3ms. Already in 1926, Plesman requested a design for a twenty-seat airliner intended for the Indies route. The F.IX, again using the standard Fokker design and construction methods, first flew on August 23, 1929. The first Fokker airliner with a completely enclosed cockpit received praise from pilots who flew it and was considered an aesthetically beautiful aircraft: it won the Grand Prix de Comfort et d'Elegance d'Avions de Transport award at the 1930 Paris Air Show. Although the F.IX showed great potential as a long-distance airliner, the crash of the stock market in October 1929 never allowed it to prove its worth. Fearful of the effects that the crash might have on the airline's business, as well as the potential losses that would be incurred from a large airliner flying long-distance routes with empty seats, Plesman canceled his original request for 10 F.IXs and purchased only two for KLM. The only customer eager for the F.IX was the Czechoslovakian air force, which thought the aircraft could be converted into a large bomber. The Czechoslovak Avia firm license-produced twelve bomber versions of the F.IX, designated the Avia F.39, and built two airliner versions for the national airline Ceskoslovenske Stetne Aerolinie (CSA).[28]

In the late 1920s, with growing passenger demand on the East Indies route, Plesman requested a new airliner capable of carrying up to twenty passengers. Fokker responded with the F.IX, the largest trimotor ever produced by the company. The aircraft made its first flight on August 23, 1929, and its future seemed bright until the stock market crashed only a few weeks later. As a result of fewer passengers because of the Great Depression, Fokker built only two F.IXs, both purchased by KLM. A license to produce the F.IX was purchased by the Czechoslovakian aero firm Avia, which converted the airliner into a bomber, designated the Avia F.39. [Photo AVIODROME Luchtfotografie, Lelystad, Holland]

Avia F.39 (Fokker F.IX)
length: 63 ft 4 in (19.3 m)
wingspan: 89 ft 1 in (27.15 m)
power plant: three 480 hp Gnome-Rhône license-built Jupiter radials
cruising speed: 107 mph (172.2 km/h)
range: 715 miles (1,151 km)
passengers: 20

The Return of Fokker's Fighters

Despite the prohibitions of the Treaty of Versailles, it was not long before Fokker fighters were again being flown by German pilots. In 1921 a group of German technicians under the command of Major Oskar Ritter von Niedermayer, an officer who led a German and Ottoman diplomatic/military mission to Afghanistan during World War I, traveled to the Soviet Union to negotiate the construction of aircraft factories and the use of airfields within Soviet territory. Germany and the Soviet Union were both viewed with disdain by the Allied nations of World War I, and both countries believed they could gain

KLM Routes
By 1923
By 1930
Finland
Norway
Sweden
Latvia
Lithuania
East Prussia
Soviet Union
Ireland
Great Britain
Denmark
Copenhagen
Hamburg
Bremen
Berlin
Amsterdam
The Netherlands
London
Rotterdam
Brussels
Belgium
Paris
Germany
Poland
Nuremberg
Czechoslovakia
Basel
Zürich
France
Switzerland
Austria
Budapest
Hungary
Romania
Yugoslavia
Italy
Bulgaria
Sofia
Istanbul
Albania
Greece
Turkey
Athens
to Cairo
Portugal
French North Africa
ROYAL DUTCH AIR LINES
SEE TWICE AS MUCH OF EUROPE IN HALF THE TIME

something valuable from each other: Germany required a place to test new aircraft and train new pilots, away from the prying eyes of the Inter-Allied Aeronautical Control Commission; the Soviets, for their part, desperately needed advanced German aeronautical technology to build a competitive domestic aviation industry.

Because Germany could not, under the provisions of the Treaty of Versailles, produce military aircraft, the clandestine air arm of the old imperial officers of the Reichswehr looked to their old supplier, Anthony Fokker, to provide them with modern aircraft. In 1923, a former German Eindecker pilot called on Fokker at his home in Amsterdam. Hauptmann Kurt Student, a former commander of Jasta 9 who supervised experimental fighter development later in the war, was accompanied by two representatives of the German industrialist Hugo Stinnes, who was interested in purchasing fighter aircraft from Fokker. The cover story was that Stinnes was going to purchase the aircraft in order to sell them to the Chilean military; but Student and his colleagues were acting officially for the Reichswehr. This secretive leadership of Sondergruppe R[ussia] purchased fifty Fokker D.XIII fighters for the secret German flight-training school located in Lipetsk, Russia. The D.XIII was a refinement of the D.XI fighter, which Fokker had already sold to the Soviets. At the time of its manufacture, the D.XIII was the best fighter in the world, and it broke several speed records. Ironically, the production versions of this aircraft were thus only to be found in a resurrected German air arm.

The crates of D.XIIIs that left Amsterdam supposedly bound for Valparaiso, Chile, never reached their recorded destination. Instead, they ended up deep in Russia, where they were used to train a new generation of German and Soviet pilots. Anthony Fokker had not only provided the Luftstreitkräfte with its first fighter but also equipped the new Luftwaffe (not to mention its future rival, the Red Air Force). Seventeen years later, Kurt Student would return to the Netherlands, this time in command of the German airborne invasion of Holland, spearheaded by the Luftwaffe.[29]

First flown on May 5, 1923, the Fokker D.XI was the first Dutch-produced Fokker fighter to be manufactured in significant numbers. A significant improvement over the D.VII and its later derivatives—though retaining the wooden wing and welded-steel-tube construction—the D.XI failed to find a market in the postwar world, at least in the free world. The Soviet air arm, desperate for modern aircraft, was very interested in purchasing the new fighter. With the tacit support of some government officials, Fokker was able to smuggle 125 of the fighters to the Soviet Union. An additional fifty D.XIs were sold to Romania in 1925 (seen in the color profile). [Photo AVIODROME Luchtfotografie, Lelystad, Holland]

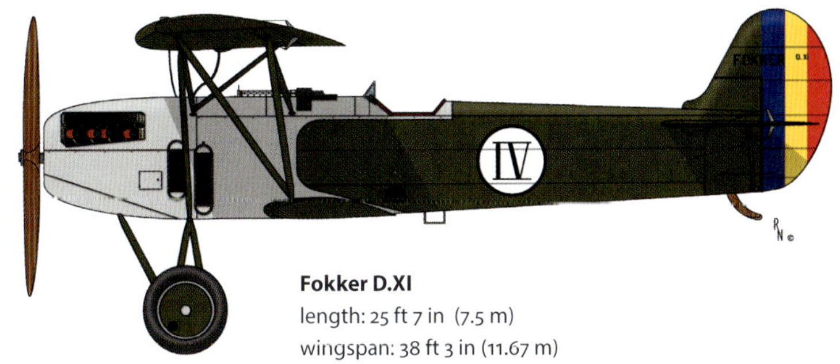

Fokker D.XI
length: 25 ft 7 in (7.5 m)
wingspan: 38 ft 3 in (11.67 m)
power plant: 300 hp Hispano-Suiza 8Fb in-line
maximum speed: 140 mph (225 km/h)
armament: two LMG 08/15 machine guns
crew: 1

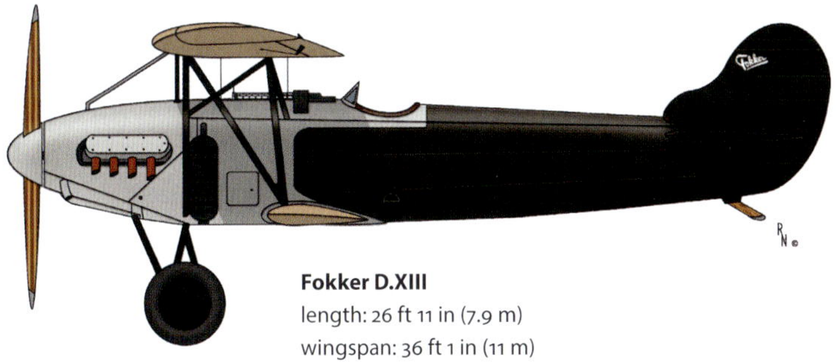

Fokker D.XIII
length: 26 ft 11 in (7.9 m)
wingspan: 36 ft 1 in (11 m)
power plant: 570 hp Napier Lion XI in-line
maximum speed: 168 mph (270 km/h)
armament: two LMG 08/15 machine guns
crew: 1

It seems fitting that the first fighter aircraft of a resurrected German air force was a Fokker. The Fokker D.XIII, developed in 1924, was an improved version of the D.XI tailored to requirements laid out by the German Reichswehr. Fifty-two D.XIIIs, "destined for Chile," arrived in Russia in 1925. A new generation of German fighter pilots was trained on these aircraft at a secret flying school at Lipetsk, in Russia, established in 1925. The Fokker D.XI and D.XIII laid the foundation for the fighter arms of the air forces of what were to become the two most powerful states in Europe: the Soviet Red Air Force and the German Luftwaffe.

Rare photo of a Fokker C.IV in service with the Soviet Red Air Force. [San Diego Air and Space Museum]

Before 1922, all new Fokker designs originated with Reinhold Platz's design team in Schwerin. When Fokker's German factory closed its doors, the first Fokker aircraft to be designed in the Netherlands was the C.IV, a two-seat reconnaissance aircraft, first flown in 1923. The LVA bought thirty, the LA-KNIL ten, and the Soviet Red Air Force fifty. The aero firm of Jorge Loring in Spain purchased a license to build twenty C.IV's for the Spanish Air Force, including this one, preserved at the Museo del Aire in Madrid. [Courtesy of Museo del Aire, Madrid]

Fokker's All-Purpose Combat Aircraft

Fokker's emerging reputation for high-performance and high-quality multipurpose aircraft led him to design what would become the most-produced Dutch military aircraft of all time. Fokker's first aircraft of this type had been the C.IV two-seat reconnaissance aircraft unveiled in 1923. It was used for reconnaissance, training, and early search-and-rescue service and was purchased by the LVA, the U.S. Army Air Service, and the Soviet Red Air Force; in addition, a license for production was purchased by the firm of Spanish aviation engineer Jorge Loring Martínez for an order placed by the Spanish Ejército del Air. The C.IV was important because its demand abroad signified the end of the pariah status—promoted primarily by France—that stigmatized Fokker after World War I because of his association with the German Luftstreitkräfte. One of the frequent notes of praise from military users of Fokker's aircraft was the ability of the Fokker airframes to accommodate a variety of engines. Whether or not this flexibility was purposely intended is unknown, but Fokker made it the primary feature of his next military design. He knew that his tried-and-true combination of a robust wooden cantilever wing and a welded steel-framed fuselage was still

Fokker C.IV
length: 29 ft 4 in (8.85 m)
wingspan: 42 ft 4.3 in (12.91 m)
power plant: 450 hp Napier Lion in-line
maximum speed: 129.9 mph (209 km/h)
armament: one or two .303 machine guns
crew: 2

a design success. Now he sought to create a similar aircraft frame that could, pushing the design and technical limitations of 1924 to the limit, accommodate as many different aero engines as possible.[30]

Fokker retained the basic fuselage design of the C.IV, but he designed several different sets of wings that could be attached to the fuselage, depending on the requirements of whatever engine he used. The result of this careful consideration was the Fokker C.V, an aircraft that could easily be tailor-made to meet not only the performance and service requirements but also the various engine requirements of Fokker's numerous military customers. The C.V was purposely built to accommodate nearly every 350-horsepower to 650-horsepower in-line and radial engine used by all the world's air services. The highlight of this versatility was that skilled mechanics could remove and replace the aircraft's engine and wings within an hour if a rapid change in mission so dictated. The C.V's ability to serve in a reconnaissance, strike, light-bomber, or even fighter role made it the ultimate multirole military aircraft of the decade, and perhaps the first purpose-built multirole military aircraft in history.

Beginning in the summer of 1924, Fokker offered for sale three variants: the C.Va, for tactical observation; the C.Vb, for strategic reconnaissance; and the C.Vc, the light bomber variant, each having a different engine and wingspan to accommodate each one's designated role. All of these early versions of the C.V had rectangular wings with protruding ailerons, descended from the C.I and C.IV designs. Not many of these early C.Vs were sold, but it is interesting that one of Fokker's first customers for the new airplane in January 1925 was the Bolivian Escuela Militar de Aviación, which ordered six Fokker C.Vbs with 520-horsepower Hispano-Suiza in-line engines. General Hans Kundt, a former German general who had become the Bolivian minister of war in 1923, was charged with training and modernizing the Bolivian army along the German model. As part of Kundt's modernization program, he acquired the Fokker C.Vbs as the first modern combat aircraft used by the fledgling Bolivian air arm. A Bolivian C.Vb was the first Fokker C.V of any type to see combat. One of them, in a reprisal raid, bombed a Paraguayan military installation in the Gran Chaco region, a disputed area between Bolivia and Paraguay. The Bolivians used their C.Vbs to train pilots in the late 1920s and early 1930s, and they made several goodwill flights to neighboring

Fokker C.IVa
length: 30 ft 6 in (9.3 m)
wingspan: 44 ft 2.4 in (13.47 m)
power plant: 360 hp Rolls-Royce Eagle VIII V-12 in-line
maximum speed: 130 mph (209.2 km/h)
crew: 2

An interesting example of the versatility of Fokker aircraft is this Fokker C.IVa, preserved at the Owls Head Transportation Museum in Maine and built in 1924 in Amsterdam and exported to the United States. It was converted from a two-seat reconnaissance aircraft into a passenger aircraft with an enclosed cabin by an autobody shop in Seattle. In the late 1920s this aircraft was purchased by pilots Robert Wark and Edward Brown for a nonstop transpacific flight from Tacoma, Washington, to Tokyo, with the passenger seats taken out and additional fuel tanks installed in the cabin. Unfortunately, it crashed shortly after takeoff due to a faulty fuel line. [Courtesy of Owls Head Transportation Museum]

Fokker C.Ve
length: 30 ft 4.2 in (9.25 m)
wingspan: 50 ft 2.4 in (15.3 m)
power plant: 450 hp Napier Lion in-line
maximum speed: 142.9 mph (230 km/h)
armament: two 7.9mm FN machine guns mounted forward, one 7.9mm Lewis gun mounted in the rear cockpit
crew: 2

The C.V was a two-seat biplane that became the world's first purpose-designed multirole combat aircraft. When unveiled to the world in 1924, the C.V was offered in five variants: tactical trainer, strategic trainer, light bomber, fighter/tactical trainer, and bomber/strategic trainer. An innovative feature that was heavily advertised was that the fuselage was designed to accommodate a number of both radial and in-line engines. In a world of slashed military budgets, the idea of a single aircraft that could effectively perform myriad roles was very attractive, and orders began to pour in. Over nine hundred C.V variants were manufactured by Fokker or license-produced abroad. The C.V below is housed in the Aviodrome collection.

countries. Many who flew in the Chaco War of 1932-35 were trained flying the C.Vbs.[31]

Back in the Netherlands, Fokker worked on an improved version of the C.V that had a sesquiplane design and an aerodynamically redefined tapered wing with the ailerons merged into the wing. Initially known as the C.VI, the design became the "d" and "e" variants of the C.V. The Fokker C.Vd fighter/reconnaissance variant and the C.Ve reconnaissance/light bomber variant could fulfill all the roles of the previous C.V variants in two improved production types, and they quickly earned Fokker a number of orders. The air services of the Netherlands were Fokker's best customer, purchasing a total of ninety-five C.V variants.

The C.V was the perfect multirole aircraft for a budget-minded air force of the interwar years, and the LVA kept most of its C.Vs in service throughout the 1920s and 1930s, simply replacing parts or adding more powerful engines as aviation advances dictated. When Germany invaded the Netherlands on May 10, 1940, thirty-four C.Vs were still on active duty, and a number performed reconnaissance, strafing, and bombing missions against the enemy. Other nations that wanted an affordable aircraft that could do just about any aerial combat task, with nearly any kind of power plant, ordered C.Vs from Fokker as well. As the orders began to pour in, Tony Fokker realized the limits of the production capacity of his factory; but he solved the problem with an acumen for business that had been well honed since his early manufacturing days in Schwerin. He sold the rights to license production on a broad scale to a number of nations. The result was that the budget-minded Fokker did not have to invest in the expansion of his facilities but could still receive a substantial profit from licensing fees from C.Vs built in other nations. Foreign sales and license agreements for all variants of the C.V were numerous and profitable. Denmark purchased six and license-built thirty-six, Finland purchased twelve, Hungary purchased fifteen and license-built one hundred fifty, Italy purchased one and license-built four hundred sixty-two (known as the Romeo Ro.1), Norway purchased five and license-built forty-two, Sweden purchased fourteen and license-built thirty-five, and Switzerland purchased six and license-built forty-nine.[32]

Of all the C.Vs purchased or produced by other countries, the Romeo Ro.1s of Italy saw the most combat service in the interwar years with the Regia Aeronautica. Entering service in 1927, a number of Ro.1s were sent to Libya to assist in the Italian army's punitive expeditions against Senussi rebels in the interior of the colony. The Ro.1 was the perfect all-purpose aircraft for policing a remote colony because it could serve as a fighter or bomber, a strike or reconnaissance platform. It was particularly effective in the Senussi uprising as the rebels tried to take advantage of the vast deserts and rugged mountains for defensive purposes: the ability to attack from overhead negated these natural defenses. The Ro.1 was also largely responsible for the Italian victory in the Second Italo-Abyssinian War (October 1935 to May 1936). Representing the most numerous aircraft used by

ABOVE AND RIGHT ***A collection of surviving Fokker C.Vs testifies to the broad international appeal of Fokker's multirole aircraft. Examples are from Switzerland (above)*** [courtesy of Flieger Flab Museum, Dübendorf], ***Norway (upper right)*** [courtesy of Norsk Luftfartsmuseum, Bodø], ***and Sweden (lower right)*** [courtesy of Flygvapenmuseum, Hackås].

BELOW ***A Swedish Fokker C.V, equipped with skis, participated in the rescue of Umberto Nobile, the leader of an Italian polar airship flight, which crashed on May 25, 1928, in the Arctic. A month after the crash, in the middle of an international search for survivors, Lt. Einar Lundborg spotted the survivors' encampment, and he landed. After taking Nobile back with him, Lundborg returned to the encampment to fly the others back, but his C.V crashed and he had to wait with the others until they were rescued by a Russian icebreaker several weeks later. Shown here is Lundborg's crashed C.V..***

Thought to have been purchased from the Polish airline Polskie Linie Lotnicze, or LOT, and powered by a Lorraine-Dietrich in-line, this Fokker F.VIIa was acquired by the tiny Abyssinian air force in 1935 and was frequently used by Emperor Haile Selassie, seen at right boarding the aircraft, as a personal transport. Named **Abba Dagnewt,** ***this aircraft was destroyed on the ground in March 1936 during the Second Italo-Abyssinian War, most likely by IMAM Ro.1 light bombers, the Italian license-produced version of the Fokker C.V.***

General Italo Balbo, head of the Regia Aeronautica, inspects a lineup of Ro.1s. The Ro.1 saw its first major operational service with the Regia Aeronautica in Libya beginning in 1927, and it served in reconnaissance and light-bomber roles as the Italians put down the Senusi revolt led by Omar Mukhtar. By the time of the Second Italo-Abyssinian War, in 1935-36, the Ro.1 was the most numerous aircraft in the Regia Aeronautica. [Photo AVIODROME Luchtfotografie, Lelystad, Holland]

Benito Mussolini peers into the cockpit of an Ro.1. [Photo AVIODROME Luchtfotografie, Lelystad, Holland]

The wrecked fuselage is that of an Ro.1 that crashed at the Oasis of Wau Namus in Libya in 1930 (the crew survived). [Photo AVIODROME Luchtfotografie, Lelystad, Holland/Ro.1 wreck photo courtesy of András Zboray]

the Italians in that war, the ability of the Ro.1s to attack targets independently or in support of ground forces made it the perfect weapon in terrain that was rugged enough to favor the defenders. Italian General Pietro Badoglio summed up the important role intended for the Ro.1 while planning the invasion of Abyssinia:

> We have a weapon that we did not have in 1896: the Air Force. . . . It will allow us to make life almost impossible for the Abyssinians, who total more than three hundred thousand men. This is where our absolute superiority lies: in being able to attack without being attacked. The advance on Adwa must be prepared by a violent bombing action on all the principal Abyssinian cities, including Addis Ababa. Everything must be destroyed with incendiary exploding bombs. Terror must be disseminated throughout the Empire. I expect great results from such a strategy, which is also the only one that the enemy cannot oppose to any appreciable extent, even if he manages to acquire a few planes in the coming months. I repeat: it is through the Air Force that we must crush the Abyssinian resistance.[33]

Individual Ro.1s or swarms of the aircraft were able to break up Abyssinian columns and clear a path for advancing Italian ground forces. When Abyssinian resistance stiffened, Italian aircraft would drop bombs filled with mustard gas in tragically open defiance of the rules established by the Geneva Convention.

The LVA in the 1920s

Most of the Fokker C.Is were retired from frontline service after the arrival of the C.Vs, though the D.VIIs remained the main fighters of the LVA until 1929, ten years after they were acquired. Even after that they stayed in service as trainers until the late 1930s. With little defense funding available, the old Fokkers were simply repaired and given new engines. Already in 1924, the Ministry of Defense had requested a replacement for the D.VII, but budget restraints convinced the ministry that the new C.Vs could fulfill the role of fighter as well as the myriad other tasks it could perform. The D.VII was finally retired as the LVAs main fighter, replaced by the Fokker D.XVI in 1929, when the political leadership could no longer pretend that the C.V could compete with modern fighters being put into production abroad. The prototype of

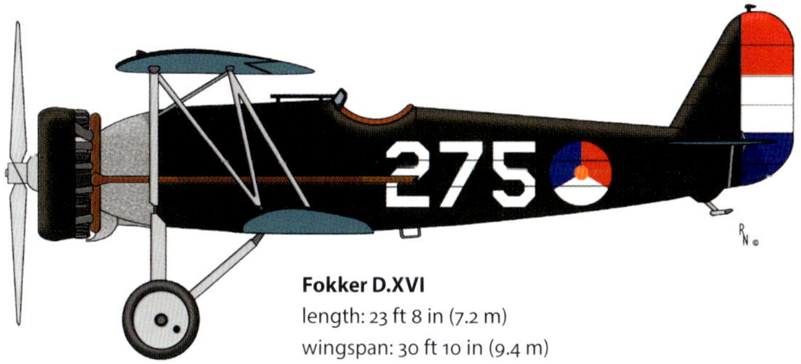

Fokker D.XVI
length: 23 ft 8 in (7.2 m)
wingspan: 30 ft 10 in (9.4 m)
power plant: 450-525 hp Armstrong Siddeley Jaguar VIIA radial
maximum speed: 205 mph (330 km/h)
ceiling: 30,840 ft (9,400 m)
armament: two 7.9mm machine guns
crew: 1

The Fokker D.XVI was one of the best fighters in the world when it debuted in 1930, praised by most of its pilots for its exceptional maneuverability. The short service life of the Armstrong Siddeley Jaguar engines unfortunately restricted frequent use of the aircraft, and the government considered the project a worthless investment. The Great Depression eliminated any chance of large foreign sales for the fighter, and Fokker ended up manufacturing only twenty-four: seventeen went to the LVA; four were ordered by Hungary; and Romania, Italy, and China each purchased one fighter. [Militair Luchtvaart Museum, Soesterberg]

The "Vijf Vingers" performing team of LVA pilots P. J. van der Griend, J. Bakkenes, H. van Weerden Poelman, and J. Jongbloed, led by "Baas" Versteegh (in the lighter-colored Fokker C.I). [Photo AVIODROME Luchtfotografie, Lelystad, Holland]

the D.XVI first flew on July 8, 1929, and it represented a generational leap in performance from the D.VII. Technically, however, it retained many of the D.VIIs characteristic traits: a sesquiplane wing configuration, V-struts, and mixed wood/steel-tube/canvas construction. The large Armstrong Siddeley Jaguar radial engine, coupled with the lightweight fuselage, allowed the aircraft to have good performance. In 1930 the LVA ordered two prototypes and twelve production aircraft, eventually purchasing a total of seventeen. The prospects of D.XVI foreign sales initially looked good when, in the late summer of 1930, one of them won an international fighter competition, sponsored by the Romanian government. Although the Romanians used the competition to select a new fighter for the For ele Aeriene Regale ale României, they did select the D.XVI and no Romanian orders were forthcoming.[34]

By the early 1930s, the effects of the Great Depression were beginning to be felt throughout Europe: the time had to come to tighten rather than expand defense budgets for most countries. At the beginning of 1931, the LVA had 215 aircraft on its roster, but only 137 were combat-ready. As the Depression began to have an impact on the Dutch economy, the government felt that other matters were more pressing than the purchase of new aircraft. It was also difficult for the LVA to retain pilots, who preferred to work for higher salaries offered by KLM or KNILM, or to enjoy the warmer climate of the East Indies by joining the colony's military air service, which was reorganized as the Luchtvaartafdeling-KNIL (LA-KNIL) in 1921. Despite its financial setbacks, the LVA earned an excellent reputation abroad for the quality of its pilots. This was best exemplified by the "Vijf Vingers," an aerobatic team of five D.VIIs led by Willem Versteegh. They first performed before an international audience at the 1923 International Aero Exhibition in Gothenburg, Sweden, where a journalist commented that they flew together so naturally that they looked like the five fingers of a hand. With Versteegh's reputation as the leader of the Vijf Vingers becoming known abroad, a number of countries sent pilots and observers to Soesterberg to study under him. Throughout the 1920s and early 1930s, the quality of the LVA's pilots compensated for the lack of quantity of modern aircraft.[35]

The Defense of the Empire

While the defense of the home country was not a major concern during the 1920s and early 1930s, the defense of the East Indies was of major importance. The British naval blockade during World War I showed how easily the East Indies could be cut off from the motherland and demonstrated that the colony would have to provide its own defense in the event of war with a major naval power. The lack of a substantial aircraft in the colony brought about an eventual expansion of the MLD and LA-KNIL in the 1920s, which were given the task of defending the sea lanes in and around the vast archipelago. In the MLD new pilots were first trained in Spyker V.2s at Soesterberg and De Kooy airfields, and then they were transferred

In 1918 the Rotterdam firm of Van Berkel's Patent, a manufacturer of meat-slicing machines, opened an aviation division that license-manufactured German Hansa Brandenberg W.12 floatplanes. On November 15, 1918, the MLD ordered thirty-five Van Berkel WA floatplanes, the first of which flew on June 6, 1919. The WA was the first Dutch-manufactured floatplane to see service with the MLD, and several saw service until 1933. Pictured here are two WAs stationed at Ambon in the East Indies. The featured profile on page 81 is the Van Berkel WA prototype. [Militair Luchtvaart Museum, Soesterberg]

to the floatplane base at De Mok on the southern tip of Texel for further training, primarily in Friedrichshafen floatplanes that had been interned. The first aircraft purchased by the MLD following the war were copies of the German Hansa Brandenburg W.12 and W.29 floatplanes, which were manufactured by the Rotterdam firm of Van Berkel's Patent, a company that specialized in producing meat slicers and scales, but then expanded to manufacturing munitions during the war. Forty Van Berkel WA (W.12) biplane/floatplanes and six of the Van Berkel WB (W.29) monoplane/floatplanes were built for the MLD. By the end of 1920, twenty WAs and three WBs were sent to the new floatplane base at Tanjong Priok near Batavia. Though MLD pilots liked the Van Berkel floatplanes, the company secured no further aircraft contracts after the WB and closed its aircraft design division in 1921.[36]

By the mid-1920s, the MLD finally ordered a new generation of float- and seaplanes for use in the East Indies. The first new aircraft that the MLD decided on was the Dornier Wal, a German twin-engine high-wing flying boat that had a range of over 500 miles. It could take off and land almost anywhere on the waters around the East Indies and had enough range to serve as a strategic patrol aircraft. The MLD ordered five Wals from Dornier's factory in Pisa, Italy, in 1926 and purchased a license to manufacture the aircraft domestically during the following year. The production license was given to Aviolanda, an aviation firm established in 1926 in Papendrecht, and the company eventually produced forty-one Wals for the

The Dornier Wal was the perfect jack-of-all-trades for the MLD in the Far East. It could serve as a patrol, reconnaissance, bomber, and rescue aircraft. It was particularly remembered as the "local constable" aircraft, which enforced fishing laws, delivered medicines to distant villages in the midst of epidemics, and rescued sailors and travelers marooned at sea. Some Wals would remain on the MLD's roster until World War II. [Militair Luchtvaart Museum, Soesterberg]

Aviolanda-Dornier Wal
length: 57 ft 1 in (17.4 m)
wingspan: 73 ft 11 in (22.53 m)
power plant: two 450 hp Lorraine Dietrich in-lines
maximum speed: 111.9 mph (180 km/h)
armament: two machine guns
crew: 5

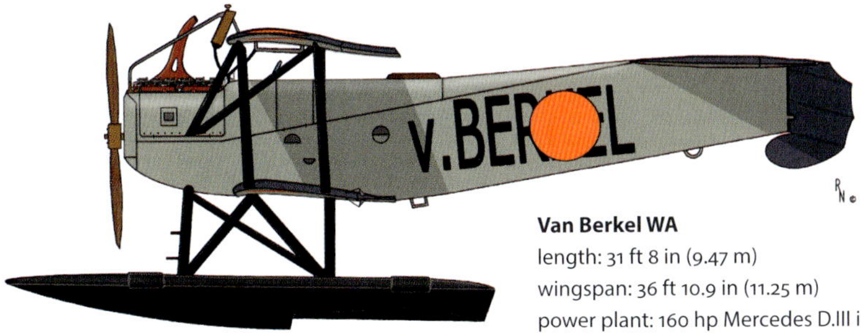

Van Berkel WA
length: 31 ft 8 in (9.47 m)
wingspan: 36 ft 10.9 in (11.25 m)
power plant: 160 hp Mercedes D.III in-line
maximum speed: 93.2 mph (150 km/h)
crew: 2

Fokker T.IVa
length: 37 ft 9½ in (11.52 m)
wingspan: 86 ft 6 in (26.37 m)
power plant: two 750 hp Wright Cyclone radials
maximum speed: 160 mph (257.5 km/h)
armament: three 7.9mm machine guns
crew: 4

MLD. Fokker entered into the production of a series of naval aircraft in 1927: he tried unsuccessfully to sell several flying boats to the MLD in the early 1920s, finally succeeding in selling his T.IV design. The aircraft was a giant twin-engine floatplane that could serve as a torpedo-bomber or a long-range reconnaissance platform. The MLD ordered twelve T.IVs in 1927 for the East Indies and thirty Fokker single-engine C.VIIw floatplanes in 1928, twelve of which were eventually sent to the colony to replace the Van Berkels.[37]

The only other military aircraft in the colony belonged to the LA-KNIL. It began in the 1920s with a substantial force of ex-British RAF aircraft, purchased for a low price from the Aircraft Disposal Company. Thirty-six Avro 504s and thirty-six de Havilland DH.9s were purchased; only six Fokker D.VIIs were acquired from a domestic manufacturer. Training began again at the flight school at Kalidjati, which had closed in September 1918 because of a lack of serviceable aircraft. By 1921 it had grown to a force of 164 men, and two years later a modern new base opened at Andir. The primary responsibility of

The Fokker T.IV was designed in 1926 to an MLD requirement for a long-range scout/bomber. It was a massive twin-engine high-wing floatplane that could accommodate a crew of four, with guns in the nose, dorsal, and ventral positions. The plane could carry a torpedo, and crews trained extensively—but with dummy torpedoes. The navy could not justify the cost of using real ones! [Photo AVIODROME Luchtfotografie, Lelystad, Holland]

the LA-KNIL was reconnaissance and artillery spotting, which required a large number of two-seater aircraft. The rigors of the tropical climate took a heavy toll on the service life of the predominantly wood-and-canvas machines.[38]

When the airport at Sourabaya was finished in November 1929, the LA-KNIL was called upon to provide a fighter squadron to defend the navy's main base in the colony. By that time the KNIL leadership decided to replace the aging D.VII fighters with a modern type: they selected the Curtiss P-6E Hawk. In 1929, Lieutenant Jimmy Doolittle put on an aerobatic demonstration with a P-6E at Andir before the KNIL leadership. Although LA-KNIL purchases had to be approved by the Dutch government, and politicians advocated a "buy-Dutch" policy, the pilots and LA-KNIL leadership were so impressed with the P-6Es performance that they placed an order for eight Hawks. To mollify domestic opposition to this foreign purchase, the LA-KNIL ordered six additional P-6Es from Aviolanda, which had purchased a manufacturing license from Curtiss. This versatile aircraft possessed good performance as a fighter but was also rugged enough to perform prolonged dives, making it very suitable for ground attack missions. The Hawks served as the LA-KNIL's fighter arm until the end of 1930s. By 1932, however, the LA-KNIL was reduced to three operational squadrons, one fighter and two reconnaissance. As was the case with the other armed services, it was difficult to obtain defense funding in a time of peace and a period of economic depression.[39]

Lt. Jimmy Doolittle demonstrates a Curtiss P-6E fighter over the Waalhaven aerodrome.

The purchase of eight Curtiss P-6E fighters from the United States in 1929 signaled the beginning of the LA-KNIL's preference for American aircraft over Dutch aircraft. The LA-KNIL leaders were impressed with the performance of the American fighter, which was readily available, and they did not want to wait for the development of the Fokker D.XVI. As a gesture to domestic industry, the LA-KNIL ordered six additional P-6s from the Aviolanda firm, which had purchased the manufacturing rights from Curtiss, even though Fokker offered his superior D.XVII fighter at a cheaper price.

Aviolanda-Curtiss P-6
length: 22 ft (6.71 m)
wingspan: 31 ft 6 in (9.6 m)
power plant: 631 hp Curtiss V-1570 Conqueror in-line
maximum speed: 187 mph (301 km/h)
maximum ceiling: 22,000 ft (6,705.6 m)
armament: one .303-caliber machine gun, one .50-caliber machine gun
crew: 1

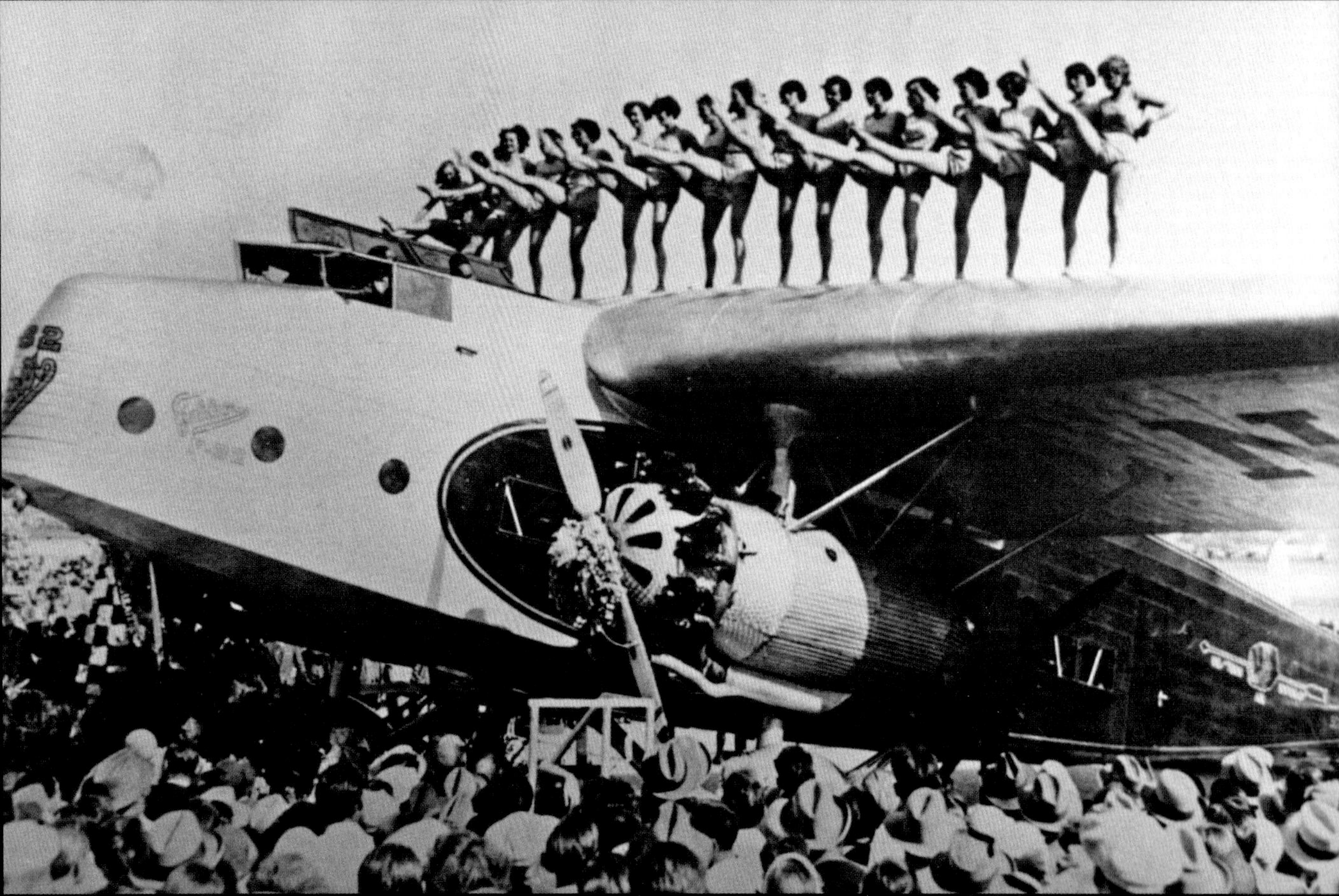

Eighteen showgirls dancing on the wings of the Fokker F.32, demonstrating its strength at its unveiling at Teterboro, New Jersey, in September 1929, the high-water mark of Fokker's domination of commercial aircraft in America.

Chapter Three

THE DUTCH IMMIGRATE TO AMERICA

Strange Bedfellows: Tony Fokker and Billy Mitchell

On August 15, 1918, *The New York Times* featured an article entitled "American Airplanes Scorned by Fokker." Originally published in German in a Berlin newspaper, the article summarized Anthony Fokker's thoughts on American aircraft and the American aviation industry:

> Since its entry into the world war America has failed in many ways, despite its big promises, and so far as aerial warfare is concerned this failure has been complete. There can be no talk about any wholesale delivery of good American airplanes. The first thing we noticed was the appearance of some American fliers, with English and French machines, who were shot down by our veteran air fighters. We have not been able to discover any real American squadrons on the west front as yet....

"But," said the reporter, "America intends to flood the west front with enormous masses of airplanes, and the program approved by the American Government shows that orders have been given to the factories for thousands of machines."

> Such orders are merely fine business for the American concerns," said Fokker. "But the trouble will come with the quality of the airplanes, for the American airplane manufacturer, thousands of miles distant from the front, under no circumstances has the experience possessed by us, who are in constant touch with our air fighters and are able to comply with the wishes of the army administration at once. The more the American airplane industry turns to manufacture by the wholesale the better it is for us, as it is just in aerial warfare where the matter of development has taken such a course that there can be no talk of a really normal, long-continued, uniform process of manufacturing. The United States can do no greater favor to our fliers at the front than to bring the airplanes manufactured some time ago to the west front.
>
> You must not forget that what is new today is distanced already tomorrow, for superiority in air fighting is principally due to the superiority of the airplane. We have new types all the time, and when the manufacture of a series of one of these types is begun there usually is a still newer type at hand that possesses a materially superior quality. It is just this speedy development that first of all benefits our front, and our superiority in the air is often only maintained because a comparatively small number of extremely efficient airplanes turns the balance in our favor. Let the American airplanes manufactured in series come; they are booty for which our air fighters have been

longing for a long time. In air fighting too, it has been shown that quality is superior to quantity.[1]

The capabilities of Fokker's fighter aircraft were well known to the American public, albeit with a degree of notoriety. Many American airmen had been shot down by German pilots flying the superb Fokker D.VII fighter during the last months of World War I, including former president Theodore Roosevelt's son Quentin. Only two years after the armistice, the man who provided the German Luftstreitkräfte with the fighters to achieve air superiority several times over the western front arrived in the United States at the invitation of American military authorities on a surprising mission. He was investigating the possibility of selling combat aircraft to the adversary of his former German clients, the United States, whose aircraft industry he had so descriptively disparaged. *The New York Times* reported Fokker's arrival in New York:

> In an interview with the reporters on the pier Mr. Fokker said:
>
> I am out to get business and naturally have come to the United States. Although I had my business in Germany during the war, I never lost my Dutch nationality. I offered my machines to England and America in 1912, but they did not take me seriously, and as I had to sell my goods somewhere, I found a customer in Germany. I never was in the German army or in the service of the German Government.[2]

Tony Fokker was featured on the cover of* Time *magazine during his third visit to the United States in 1923. The accompanying article said: "Short, stocky, robust, Anthony H.G. Fokker looks like a typical Dutchman, with the rosy complexion of his race, a calm but somewhat stubborn look in his blue eyes. . . ." Eventually, he was being affectionately referred to as "Uncle Tony."

Fokker made sure to point out the American failure to purchase his aircraft before the war. Nevertheless, he was now making a second attempt to sell to the Americans—and this time they would buy. It is surprising that any lingering U.S. resentment toward Fokker's association with the German Luftstreitkräfte quickly dissipated, and, though he maintained his negative attitude toward the American domestic aviation industry, the American armed forces and public were enthusiastic about seeing his superior aircraft coming to the United States. A combination of the high performance of his aircraft and his masterly sales techniques, winning personality, and firsthand aviation knowledge as a pilot would begin not only an American enchantment with Fokker aircraft but also a dominant position for him within the American aviation world that would last for a decade.

It was also poignant that, when Tony Fokker came to New York in November 1920, the best fighter plane that the U.S. Army Air Service (USAAS) had in its arsenal was the Fokker D.VII. The United States had received 142 of the fighters as reparations from the German government in 1919; a number of them, still sporting their German-made lozenge camouflage, were integrated into American squadrons, primarily the USAAS First Pursuit Group. American pilots responded favorably to the performance of the D.VII and were eager for new high-performance aircraft. In the Transcontinental Reliability and Endurance Test of 1919, one of the eight planes to complete the roundtrip transcontinental flight (of the seventy-four that started the test) was a Fokker D.VII flown by Lieutenant Colonel Harold Hartney. The aircraft that Hartney was flying did not go unnoticed, because the majority of the competitors flew American-built Airco DH.4s. Some D.VIIs in American service were refitted with more powerful engines, and a number of fighters were provided to American aircraft manufacturers to study Fokker's construction methods. Boeing's first competitive fighter, the FB-1, was directly designed from the D.VIIs provided to Boeing by the Army Air Service.[3]

One of the American officers who invited Tony Fokker to the United States was Brigadier General William ("Billy") Mitchell, deputy commander of the U.S. Army Air Service, who, two years earlier, had orchestrated a massive aerial offensive against the Fokker fighters of the Luftstreitkräfte at the beginning of the Saint-Mihiel Offensive. Mitchell, forward thinking yet highly outspoken in his native land, recognized Fokker's talents as an innovative designer and had concluded that Fokker's wartime military designs were still more advanced than aircraft under production in the United States. Facing reality and clearly not holding any wartime grudges, Mitchell was willing to discuss with Fokker the purchase

When Tony Fokker first visited the United States in late 1920, he must have felt smug that the best fighter aircraft in the arsenal of the U.S. Army Air Service were ex-German Fokker D.VIIs.

LEFT *A Fokker D.VII confiscated at the end of the war in U.S. Army Air Service markings.*

BELOW *This D.VII was captured by American forces on November 9, 1918, and sent to the United States after the war (currently exhibited in the National Air and Space Museum in Washington, D.C.).*

After testing several requisitioned Fokker D.VIII high-wing monoplane fighters after the war, the U.S. Army Air Service was impressed enough with the plane's performance that it ordered a new high-wing monoplane fighter design from Fokker in 1921. The new Fokker F.VI (designated PW-5 in the United States) had a welded-steel-tube fuselage and a plywood-covered cantilever wing and was powered by a Wright-built 300-horsepower in-line engine. Pleased with its first two examples, the Army Air Service ordered ten more F.VIs in 1922, and they were assigned to the 1st Pursuit Group based at Selfridge Field, Michigan, and served until 1926. [Courtesy of the Museum of the United States Air Force]

Fokker F.VI (PW-5)
length: 26 ft 1 in (7.96 m)
wingspan: 39 ft 5 in (12.00 m)
engine: 300 hp Wright-Hispano 8-cylinder in-line
maximum speed: 144 mph (232 km/h)
armament: two .30 caliber machine guns
crew: 1

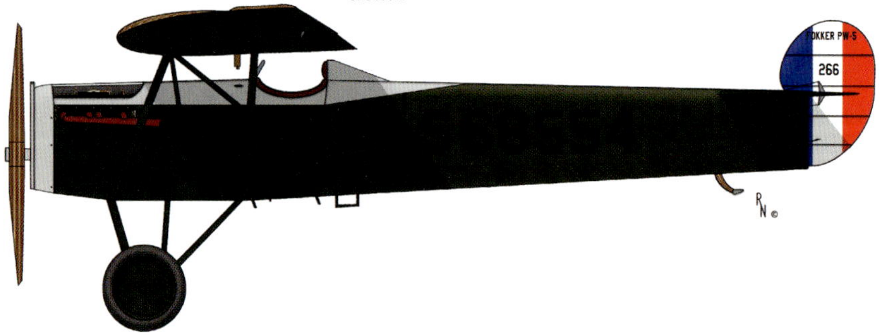

of Dutch-built aircraft for the U.S. Army Air Service. Somewhat unprepared, Fokker hauled out some hastily drawn sketches of potential new designs and presented them to Mitchell. The American general was most interested in a military version of Fokker's F.III transport, which was just beginning to be manufactured.

Mitchell received permission from the army to purchase two militarized Fokker F.IIIs after he had convinced the leadership that the aircraft being manufactured by the Nederlandsche Vliegtuigenfabriek were superior. When Fokker returned to the Netherlands in early 1921, he was ecstatic with the order he had received from Mitchell. Before returning to Europe, Fokker set up a sales office in New York, headed by Robert B. C. Noorduyn, a Dutchman who had previously worked with Frits Koolhoven at Armstrong Whitworth and B.A.T., hoping that more American orders would follow.

While on a tour of aviation facilities throughout Europe from late 1921 to early 1922, Billy Mitchell visited Fokker and his company in Amsterdam. Fokker, munching on *hopjes* (Dutch coffee candies; Fokker was known for always keeping sweets in his pockets), drove Mitchell and his staff around his workshops and showed off the completed F.IV transports that were ready for shipment to the United States. Mitchell was greatly impressed with the variety of designs Fokker had and the quality of his aircraft construction. While in Amsterdam, Mitchell ordered several aircraft from Fokker to be evaluated by the Army Air Service: two F.VI fighter prototypes and one D.IX fighter prototype. The F.VI (designated PW-5 by the Army Air Corps) was a parasol-wing fighter, similar to the D.VIII, powered by a Wright-Hispano 300-horsepower in-line engine and armed with two Browning machine guns. The PW-5 had almost twice the horsepower of the D.VIII, but it had a maximum speed that was only 13 mph faster than that of the wartime fighter. Nevertheless, with the U.S. domestic industry lacking anything better, the Army Air Service was impressed enough to later order an additional ten production models to follow the prototypes. The D.IX (designated PW-6 by the Army Air Corps) was a modernized D.VII equipped with the same 300-horsepower Hispano engine that the PW-5 had.

The performance of the PW-6 was only slightly better than that of the D.VII, and with many D.VIIs in storage, the Army Air Services placed no further orders, keeping the sole example. Fokker also managed to sell Mitchell a C.IV reconnaissance aircraft, as well as a TW.4 two-seat trainer. Meanwhile, Mitchell attempted to persuade Fokker to establish a manufacturing plant in the United States which would more easily facilitate the American military orders that, he hinted, would be forthcoming. Regarding Fokker, Mitchell wrote to his superior, Major General Mason Patrick: "This man has capabilities which are unlimited in the development of aircraft."[4] After his negotiations with Fokker, Mitchell was invited to a dinner in his honor hosted by Queen Wilhelmina. With his factory completing Mitchell's orders and pondering the possibility of further American military orders, Fokker decided to travel again to the United States in May 1922 to look into the possibilities of opening up shop across the Atlantic. The aviation link between the Netherlands and the United States was being forged.[5]

Adversaries-become-friends, Billy Mitchell and Tony Fokker in front of an American DH.4. Although he had faced Fokker's fighters in the skies over the Western Front, Billy Mitchell had no contempt for the Flying Dutchman and hoped to do business with him. Fokker's postwar aircraft were state-of-the-art compared to what the American industry was producing at that time, and Mitchell purchased a number of samples of them so that American pilots could train on up-to-date equipment. Mitchell was also one of the primary motivating forces that compelled Fokker to open a factory in the United States.

Tony Fokker standing next to his D.IX fighter (U.S. designation PW-6), a slightly improved version of the D.VII powered by a 300 hp Hispano in-line. [Courtesy of the Museum of the United States Air Force]

Fokker Goes Transcontinental

The first postwar Fokker aircraft to make a lasting impression on the American population was the F.IV, which Fokker had demonstrated to Mitchell in Amsterdam and which had arrived in the United States two months before. A modified version of the F.III, the F.IV had the cockpit situated to the port side of the engine, and it had a large cantilever wing; but it also had a capacity for eight to twelve passengers in its cabin, as well as a more powerful 400-horsepower Liberty engine. Fokker was extremely pleased with its performance, and after a series of test flights, he had the machine crated and shipped to its new owners across the Atlantic in March 1922. At the moment that Fokker's F.IV arrived in the United States, the Army Air Service was obsessed with the question of transcontinental flight. From a practical standpoint, the leaders

Lieutenant John A. Macready and Lieutenant Oakley G. Kelly standing in front of the Fokker T-2 that they flew nonstop from coast to coast. [Photo AVIODROME Luchtfotografie, Lelystad, Holland]

in the Air Service were interested in charting the best air routes between airfields to reduce the time needed to deploy squadrons from one coast to the other.

From a publicity standpoint, the endurance and speed records achieved by army fliers in the transcontinental test flights captured the attention of the public and demonstrated the transcontinental reach of the nascent air arm of the United States military. Two of those army pilots, Lieutenants Oakley G. Kelly and Muir S. Fairchild, sought to be the first pilots to make a nonstop flight from coast to coast. When the Fokker T-2, the army's new designation for the F.IV, was demonstrated in the spring and summer of 1922, Kelly and Fairchild calculated that the air service finally had a plane large enough to be converted to carry enough fuel for a nonstop flight across the country. They drafted a plan and presented it to the head of the air service, Gen. Patrick, who gave them the go-ahead on August 10, 1922. Since the exposed cockpit was positioned on the port side of the engine, a door had to be made between the cockpit and the cabin, and a set of auxiliary flight controls was installed in the cabin so that the pilot in the exposed cockpit could perform in-flight maintenance on the engine. Furthermore, the pilot's seat was made detachable to make moving from the cockpit to the cabin easier; in addition, a conveyor device was installed between the cockpit and the cabin so that the crew could send messages to each other, because talking above the roar of the engine was nearly impossible. Lieutenant John A. Macready had replaced Lt. Fairchild, who was recovering from injuries he sustained in a previous crash.

Kelly and Macready took off from McCook Field in Los Angeles on November 3, 1922, and headed east. They survived a night of harrowing storms over the Great Plains only to be forced down near Indianapolis due to a cracked cylinder jacket. The winter weather that set in within the next few weeks prevented any further attempts at a transcontinental crossing until the spring. During March and April 1923, Kelly and Macready made several endurance flights in the T-2; in fact, on April 17 they achieved the world's endurance record, staying in the air for 36 hours, 4 minutes, and 34 seconds. To accomplish this feat, the two pilots took six-hour shifts at the controls and, while not flying, ate sandwiches, drank hot broth and coffee from thermoses, and caught what little bit of sleep they could. On May 2, 1923, the two airmen decided to make another attempt at a nonstop transcontinental crossing. This time, however, they took off from Roosevelt Field on Long Island and flew from east to west. The takeoff was the most treacherous part of the flight: with the plane laden with so much fuel, Kelly and Macready barely got airborne and skimmed along at treetop level for much of the first leg of the journey. After a full day and night of taking turns flying and working to keep the engine running, they approached the Rockies at dawn. They crossed the western ranges without incident and appeared over Rockwell Field in San Diego just after noon on May 3. After 26 hours, 50 minutes, and 38 seconds in the air, the T-2 touched down and was greeted by a jubilant crowd.[6]

ABOVE *Lts. Macready and Kelly are standing alongside fuel drums representing the amount of gasoline and oil required for their transcontinental flight.* [Photo AVIODROME Luchtfotografie, Lelystad, Holland]

BELOW *The Fokker F.IV began as a U.S. Army Air Service request for a large transport aircraft and was based on the already successful F.III airliner design. Two F.IVs were built for the U.S. Army Air Service, one being used as an aerial ambulance, and the other used in America's first nonstop transcontinental flight on May 2, 1923, shown below. (The latter aircraft is preserved at the National Air and Space Museum in Washington, D.C.) The second set of controls can be seen through the side windows.*

Fokker F.IV (T-2)
length: 149 ft 3 in (4.97 m)
wingspan: 81 ft 4 in (24.3 m)
engine: 400 hp Liberty 12-cylinder in-line
maximum speed: 77 mph (160 km/h)
range: 2,550 miles (4,103.8 km)
crew: 2

A Brief Military Interlude

The flight of the T-2 garnered a great deal of publicity for the U. S. Army Air Service. According to *Time* magazine:

> Country-wide interest was aroused. The machine was awaited all along its route through Dayton, Indianapolis, St. Louis, Kansas City, Tucumcari, N. M., and Wickenburg, Ariz. A hundred thousand people met them at San Diego, and telegrams of congratulation by the hundred, beginning with one from the President, poured in from every state in the Union.[7]

The flight also brought much positive publicity to Anthony Fokker. He sensed that, in the midst of Kelly and Macready's achievement, the time was right to firmly establish his aerial presence in the United States. Fokker returned to the United States on December 18, 1923, having founded his American company, Atlantic Aviation Corporation (which was renamed the Fokker Aircraft Corporation in September 1925) four days earlier. So as not to

After Tony Fokker established his American factory in Teterboro, New Jersey, he received his first major military order from Billy Mitchell to reconstruct the wooden fuselages of 135 American-built DH.4s with welded-steel-tube fuselages. Not an exciting contract, it was business nonetheless, and it did establish Fokker as an American-based aircraft manufacturer. The featured aircraft is an Atlantic DH-4M-2, rebuilt by Fokker (now housed in the Historic Aircraft Restoration Museum in Maryland Heights, MO). [Photo AVIODROME Luchtfotografie, Lelystad, Holland / color photo courtesy of Don Parsons and Al Stix]

Atlantic DH-4M-2
length: 29 ft 11 in (9.12 m)
wingspan: 42 ft 5 in (12.93 m)
engine: 420 hp Liberty 12A in-line
maximum speed: 123 mph (197.9 km/h)
armament: two .30 caliber machine guns in rear cockpit
crew: 2

arouse any wartime associations, Fokker initially left his name out of the title of the company and allowed others to assume the company's management, while he stayed in the shadows under the title "chief engineer." This was a prudent decision because the American government had encouraged the military to "buy American" after the war.

In May 1924, Fokker purchased the factory buildings of a recently defunct aero manufacturer in Teterboro, New Jersey, just outside New York City. Atlantic Aviation could now officially begin operations. Now that Fokker was established in the United States, Billy Mitchell followed through on the orders he had brought up during his European visit. The company's first order from the Army Air Service was substantial but not particularly glamorous. Mitchell contracted Atlantic Aviation to modernize one hundred thirty-five DH.4s, which involved replacing those aircrafts' wooden fuselages with welded-steel-tube frames, something in which Fokker's factories were the world leaders. This was not the kind of order that Fokker had anticipated, but the U.S. government had decided that it would be cheaper to recondition its war-surplus DH.4s rather than to purchase new aircraft. Fokker's reconditioned DH.4s became known as Atlantic DH-4M-2s. New aircraft were only purchased in small numbers, mainly for evaluation purposes. Mitchell had ordered three D.XI fighters and eight C.IVs in 1923, and Fokker hoped to sell more of this type to the Army Air Service. At the time, the D.XI was the most advanced fighter in the world, and, with an American factory, it seemed logical that further American orders would follow.

Fokker's dreams of equipping the Army Air Service, however, came to an abrupt end in November 1925. Billy Mitchell, his friend and American advocate, was court-martialed for insubordination after he criticized the leadership of the army and navy for the deaths of pilots caused by poor administration and obsolescent equipment (a well-founded charge). Despite the positive testimony of many influential pilots and officers, as well as favorable public opinion, Mitchell chose to resign from the Army Air Service on February 1, 1926. With his primary benefactor gone, Fokker faced the prejudices of the officers who replaced Mitchell and who associated the "foreign" manufacturer with the ousted general. The few contracts that were parceled out by the air service during the 1920s now went primarily to "American" companies.

Tony Fokker speaking with Henry Ford before the beginning of the National Aerial Reliability Tour. Not only did Ford hope to promote the products of his company's own aviation division during the Reliability Tour; he also hoped his engineers would take note of developments made by other aircraft manufacturers, particularly Fokker's new trimotor.

The Trimotor's American Conquest

As military orders dried up after Billy Mitchell's court-martial, Fokker had to look to commercial markets in the United States if his American factory was to survive. Shortly after his resignation from the Army Air Service, Mitchell wrote:

> In America, no system for the development of commercial aviation has ever been developed. As only a few small airplane ventures pay, comparatively little has been done along that line as compared with the airplane lines for passenger and freight plying between London, Paris, Brussels, Berlin, and other parts of Europe.[8]

KLM, with its modern fleet of Fokker F.IIIs and newly arriving F.VIIs, must have certainly been on Mitchell's mind. Fokker also knew all too well the dismal state of commercial aviation in the United States, best represented in his mind by his failure to sell any F.III transports during his 1921 tour in the *Half Moon*. But by the mid-1920s, American political leaders were finally waking up from the national lethargy regarding aerial transport. In an effort to boost the growth of commercial aviation in the United States, President Calvin Coolidge signed into law the Kelly Air Mail Act in February 1925, which allowed the U.S. Postal Service to contract private airlines to carry the mail. Profit could now be readily made by transport aircraft. There was a sudden need for aircraft that could carry large quantities of mail over long distances. Fortunately for Tony Fokker, he was the only aero manufacturer in the country who had extensive experience in building transport aircraft.

Edsel Ford (far right) poses with Tony Fokker (far left) in front of the first F.VIIa/3m. [Photo AVIODROME Luchtfotografie, Lelystad, Holland]

The lineup of aircraft participating in the National Aerial Reliability Tour at Dearborn, Michigan, in late September 1925. Fokker's F.VIIa3/m was clearly the largest participant and was an impressive sight in an age of small single-engine aircraft in the United States. One of the motivating reasons for the Reliability Tour was to encourage the growth of commercial aviation in the country, which was well behind developments in Europe. [Photo AVIODROME Luchtfotografie, Lelystad, Holland]

In early 1925, Henry Ford, his son Edsel, and the Society of Automotive Engineers decided to sponsor the National Aerial Reliability Tour in order to promote and popularize aerial transport in the United States. The tour was not intended to be a race: contestants and their aircraft would depart on September 28, 1925, from Ford's new airport in Dearborn, Michigan, visit twelve cities in the Midwest, and then return to Dearborn six days later. The Fords were not just being generous in their support of the Reliability Tour. Henry Ford had recently purchased the Stout Metal Airplane Company, and he hoped that the tour would highlight Stout's latest design, the all-metal Stout 2-AT monoplane transport, which was influenced by the all-metal designs of Hugo Junkers in Germany. Ford also owned the most extensive airline in the United States at the time, Ford Air Transport Service. Fokker learned about the Reliability Tour in early 1925; at the time, he had one of the most modern transport aircraft in the world at his disposal, the F.VIIa.

Since "reliability" was the most important aspect in Ford's air tour, Bob Noorduyn mentioned to Tony Fokker that the single-engine F.VIIa might not be the ideal aircraft for the competition. The reputation of American aero engine reliability was still somewhat poor, due in large part to the mediocre performance of war-surplus 400-horsepower Liberty engines. After several heated discussions, Noorduyn convinced Fokker that he should enter a three-engine variant of the F.VIIa for added reliability. Fokker sent Platz a telegram instructing him to add an additional engine to each wing of an F.VIIa. He also sent a sketch of the converted transport with the two extra engines embedded into the wings. With only two months to prepare the aircraft before shipment to the United States, Platz ignored Fokker's sketch and suspended the extra engines under the wings. Platz already had a trimotor version of the F.VIIa on paper, so the conversion went smoothly, and the new aircraft, designated F.VIIa/3m, was completed in six weeks. With three engines, the proposed aircraft would easily be able to fly on two should one fail. After several test flights in which he shut down one or two engines at a time and successfully kept the aircraft flying, Fokker had the F.VIIa3/m disassembled and put aboard the ocean liner *Veendam* for shipment to the United States. Upon arrival in New York, the aircraft was reassembled at Teterboro and flown by Fokker to Dearborn. And on September 28, 1925, the contestants in Ford's Reliability Tour began their aerial trek over the Midwest.

Spectators could not have overlooked Fokker's presence in the Ford Reliability Tour, even if they tried to. The F.VIIa/3m was the largest aircraft in the tour, and FOKKER was painted in large letters on the sides of the rear fuselage. Always keen on publicity, Tony Fokker also made sure that he was the first contestant to land at each city along the tour route, a feat he accomplished with one exception. The following is a report from a dinner party in Columbus, Ohio, on the evening of October 3, where one of the tour pilots had this to say about Tony Fokker:

> What a "great thing for aviation" he thought "this Fokker Publicity—No, I mean Ford Reliability Tour" will prove

A cartoon of Tony Fokker from the Ford Reliability Tour. With "FOKKER" clearly painted all over his trimotor and making sure he was the first to land at every stop, Fokker hoped to gain the maximum amount of publicity for his new aircraft. Even he acknowledged that his promotional efforts were a bit over the top; nevertheless, they did bring the attention he desired.

The main competitor for Fokker airliner sales in the United States came from Ford, which had its series of 4-AT and 5-AT trimotors. Ford's engineers closely examined Fokker's F.VIIa/3m one night while it was parked in Ford's Dearborn hangar prior to the Reliability Tour, and used that knowledge in designing the 4-AT. Unlike Fokker, however, Ford opted for an all-metal construction, which resulted in significantly higher production costs. Ford's aircraft division never succeeded in becoming profitable and closed its doors in 1936. This trimotor is the Floyd Bennett, *used by Richard Byrd in his 1929 flight over the South Pole and housed in the Henry Ford Museum in Dearborn, Michigan.*

The Universal was the first Fokker aircraft to be designed and built in the United States, and it first flew in 1926. Designed by Bob Noorduyn, who later founded his own aircraft company and designed the successful Noorduyn Norseman bush plane, the Universal was intended to carry either passengers or cargo, or a combination of both. This multirole design made it one of the first highly successful bush aircraft in North America, and because it could be operated with either wheels, floats, or skis, the majority of Universals were sold to Canadian operators. [Museum of the United States Air Force]

to be. Even Anthony H.G. Fokker, affectionately known to the tourists as "Uncle Anthony," joined in the roar of laughter and his ruddy Dutch countenance glowed more than ever.[9]

When the tour concluded on October 4 (Fokker, of course, being the first to land), Fokker's trimotor was temporarily housed in one of Ford's hangars in Dearborn. During this time several Ford engineers made a profile of the trimotor's wing and took extensive notes about the design. Ford and William Stout had been developing their own trimotor aircraft, the 3-AT, but, with engines buried in the wings and the open cockpit placed above the center engine in the stubby nose, it turned out to be an ugly aerodynamic failure.

In June 1926, when Ford's next trimotor, the 4-AT, was unveiled, it somewhat resembled Fokker's trimotor design, with the exception that the fuselage had been constructed with corrugated aluminum. Upon its unveiling, Fokker was immediately convinced that Ford had copied his trimotor design. When Ford sent some of his new all-metal aircraft to Europe in 1929, Hugo Junkers sued Ford for patent infringement for his use of corrugated aluminum construction; Junkers won the lawsuit. It is unknown to what extent Ford's designers copied or used parts of Fokker's trimotor design as they developed and constructed their trimotors; but Ford's clear interest in the Fokker design demonstrated the respect that he and other aircraft designers had for Fokker's innovation.[10]

The Fokker factory in Glen Dale, West Virginia, which produced a number of Universals, Super Universals, and F.10s, still exists (at the time of this writing) along with the factory's airstrip along the Ohio River, just outside of Wheeling, West Virginia. "Fokker Aircraft" is still barely visible on the front outside wall of the factory.

Universal and Super

The Ford Reliability Tour had done much to put Fokker in the American limelight, but at the time his American factory was still finishing Mitchell's DH-4M-2 modernization order and putting together Fokker aircraft that had been assembled in and shipped from the Netherlands. Bob Noorduyn was about to change that, for when Fokker returned to Teterboro from the Reliability Tour, he was just in time for the unveiling of the first Fokker aircraft to be designed and built in the United States. Noorduyn designed the single-engine Fokker Universal to be the ideal solution to what he perceived were the general American requirements of a transport aircraft at the time. Since the United States did not yet have a well-developed airline network, there was no immediate need for large passenger aircraft. With the recent Kelly Act, the nascent airlines in the United States looked primarily to airmail for profit, and the delivery of mail by air did not require the use of a large aircraft.

Noorduyn's answer to these circumstances was a transport aircraft with windows and room for four seats in a passenger configuration or plenty of room for airmail and freight with the seats removed, hence the model name "Universal." Unlike contemporary Dutch Fokker aircraft, however, the Universal had two peculiar anachronistic features: the cockpit was open, and the wing was not a large cantilever design but rather a thin wing supported by struts attached to the fuselage. These design features were still prevalent among American designers, perhaps justifying Noorduyn's use of them. American airmail pilots, bedecked in their goggles, helmets, and scarves, still expected to be able to gaze out of an open cockpit. A total of forty-five Universals were sold, mostly to Canadian operators, who appreciated the aircraft's interchangeable landing gear, float, or ski configurations for flights throughout the Canadian wilderness.

In 1926 a young airmail pilot named "Slim" Lindbergh approached the Fokker Aircraft Corporation and requested the use of one of its Universals in an attempt to fly nonstop across the Atlantic. Worried about the ramifications that a failed transatlantic flight would have on the company's image, Fokker's sales manager dismissed the proposal. Charles Lindbergh later told the story to Tony Fokker, who told Lindbergh that, had he known of his ambition, he certainly would have offered "Slim" an aircraft to use!

The Universal was quickly superseded by the Super Universal, which made its first flight in March 1928. The Super Universal was derived from the Universal; the main improvements over its predecessor were a larger cabin

Fokker Super Universal
length: 36 ft 7 in (11.15 m)
wingspan: 50 ft 8 in (15.44 m)
engine: 420 hp Pratt & Whitney R 1340 Wasp radial
cruising speed: 118 mph (189.9 km/h)
range: 684 miles (1,101 km)
crew: 2
passengers: 6

Bob Noorduyn gave the Super Universal, an improved version of the Universal, a larger cabin with room for six seats, a more powerful engine, an enclosed cockpit, and landing gear with much simplified struts. The Super Universal was the perfect "jack of all trades" aircraft and was the most numerous American-Fokker design ever produced: over 200 Super Universals were built.

Left *This Super Universal is preserved at the Western Canada Aviation Museum.* [Courtesy of Clarke Seaborn]

Tony Fokker (far left) standing alongside then Secretary of Commerce Herbert Hoover in front of a Fokker F.VIIA/3m operated by Philadelphia Rapid Transit Air Services in 1926. Both Hoover and Fokker believed that there was a lucrative future for commercial aviation in the United States. [Photo AVIODROME Luchtfotografie, Lelystad, Holland]

with room for six passengers, a more powerful engine, a longer wing, and an enclosed cockpit. The Super Universal's versatility and overall good performance made it Fokker's best-selling American aircraft: his plant built eighty Super Universals; fifteen were license-produced in Canada; and more than two hundred were license-produced in Japan, where the aircraft was still in service until after the end of World War II. As increasing American orders grew beyond the manufacturing capacity of his Teterboro factory, Fokker began production in an additional factory in Glendale, West Virginia, on August 9, 1928.

The American Reign of Fokker

The late 1920s finally began to see a rise in passenger travel by air in the United States, and Fokker was ready to market his best-known product to the airlines. By this time he had become known for the Dutch-built F.VIIa/3m and the American-built C-2 trimotors that he sold to Richard Byrd (*Josephine Ford* and *America*), Amy Guest (*Friendship*), and the U.S. Army (*Bird of Paradise*)—and the famous flights they made (all to be told in chapter 4). The Kelly Air Mail Act, passed in 1925, had brought in a large number of orders for the Universal and Super Universal. In 1926, the Kelly Act was followed by the Air Commerce Act, which laid out the guidelines and regulations by which the country's infant airlines could operate. "Passenger air travel" in the United States prior to that time was primarily made up of joy rides in war-surplus aircraft at county fairs. America was far behind Europe in the establishment of passenger airline service.

The Kelly Act and the Air Commerce Act finally prompted the founding of airlines for postal and passenger service. The Universals and Super Universals served well as mail planes: they could accommodate a mix of cargo and a small number of passengers, but as more and more Americans opted to travel by air, the nation's airlines began to look for a commercial aircraft that could accommodate more passengers. Tony Fokker initially offered his Dutch-built F.VIIa/3m and F.VIIb/3m to airlines in the United States; but by the late 1920s he decided to manufacture another version of his hallmark commercial aircraft at his factories in New Jersey and West Virginia. In early 1928, Fokker unveiled the F.10 trimotor to the American civil aircraft market. The fuselage was designed and built in the United States, while the wings on the first seven production aircraft were the same as those of the F.VII series, and they were imported from the Netherlands. Later F.10s would have larger, American-built wings and were redesignated F.10As. The F.10s were powered by three 420-horsepower Pratt and Whitney Wasp radial engines and had a roomy cabin that could comfortably accommodate twelve passengers. The plane was an immediate commercial and public success.

The first major customer for Fokker's American-built F.10 was Western Air Express (WAE), based in Los Angeles. The airline was founded on July 13, 1925, by Harris Hanshue, a former racecar driver, and it began passenger flights on April 17, 1926. WAE had received $180,000 from the Daniel Guggenheim Fund for the Promotion of Aeronautics that January to promote the concept of a "model airway," which would focus on good service for its passengers. With the need for aircraft with higher passenger capacity, WAE used all of the money it received from the Guggenheim fund to purchase the first three F.10s from Fokker, which it received in the spring of 1928. WAE became one of Fokker's best customers, eventually purchasing twenty-five F.10s and F.10As. The F.10 was one of the first commercial aircraft in the United States to offer an enclosed cabin with comfortable seats and in-flight catering; as a result, WAE earned a reputation for excellent service.[11]

One of Fokker's other major customers in America was Pan American Airways, which was founded by Juan Trippe in 1927. Trippe had previously bought Fokker trimotors for Colonial Airways, of which he was the president before he founded Pan Am. While pondering the founding of Pan Am and its first Caribbean route, Trippe chartered a trimotor from Fokker for a proving flight from Miami to Havana and back. Trippe, accompanied by

Western Air Express (WAE) was an early American airline that began passenger operations in 1926 and was one of the first airlines in the United States to purchase Fokker F.10 airliners (above). Beginning as a small mail carrier from Los Angeles to Salt Lake City, WAE soon expanded across the West, eventually becoming Transcontinental & Western Airlines, the forerunner of the American giant TWA. Fokker airliners were heavily promoted as a selling point by WAE, and later by TWA. [Photo courtesy of the Museum of the United States Air Force / brochure courtesy of the R. E. G. Davies collection]

Juan Trippe, best known as the founder of Pan American World Airways, was one of Fokker's first American customers when he purchased two F.VIIs for his first airline company, Colonial Air Transport, in 1926. Believing that the Fokker trimotors were the best airliners available at the time, he bought F.VIIa/3ms and F.10As for Pan Am, which was established the following year. Pan Am's first route was between Key West, Florida, and Havana, Cuba.

LEFT *Charles Lindbergh makes the first Pan Am flight to Havana.*

BELOW *Juan Trippe (far right) speaks with some of his pilots in front of a Pan Am Fokker Universal.* [Photo AVIODROME Luchtfotografie, Lelystad, Holland / brochure courtesy of the R. E. G. Davies Collection]

Fokker, made a successful flight to Havana, where Fokker gave several aerial demonstrations, and Trippe received permission for his new airline to land in Cuba. On the way back to Miami, however, the aircraft experienced trouble in two engines due to low-grade gasoline they had taken on in a refueling stop at Key West (no one at that time had thought to place high-octane aviation fuel along the route). Fokker's pilot, George Pond, made a landing in a shallow stretch of water near Key Largo; but what looked like sand from above turned out to be coral, which shredded the plane's rubber tires upon landing. Pond, Trippe, and Fokker made it ashore and stopped a northbound Florida East Coast Railway train that was headed for Miami. Fokker and his workmen later returned to Key Largo, replaced the trimotor's engines and tires, and flew the plane out using a wooden plank runway.

That little tropical adventure on their first flight to Cuba apparently did not dim Trippe's enthusiasm for the plane. The first aircraft purchased by Pan American were three Dutch-built Fokker F.VIIa/3m trimotors. Charles Lindbergh was the first pilot to make a flight in Pan Am's first Fokker transport, and that gave the airline a great deal of publicity. Trippe was pleased enough by the service of the F.VIIa/3ms that on June 20, 1928, he followed in WAE's footsteps and ordered twelve F.10As from Fokker, planes that were rigorously used on Pan Am's Miami-Cuba-West Indies route. Other American purchasers of Fokker trimotors were Universal Airlines and American Airways (the predecessor of American Airlines). By 1930, there were more Fokker transports flying in the United States than transport aircraft of any American manufacturer. For a brief period, Dutch-inspired aircraft dominated the American skies.[12]

How Long Can You Stay in the Air? A *Question Mark* Answers the Question

Nineteen twenty-nine began with another Fokker aviation triumph. In the summer of 1928, Captain Ira Eaker of the Army Air Corps learned of a plan for in-flight refueling that was being developed by Elwood Quesada, a lieutenant in the Army Air Corps and a Marine Corps aviator. Eaker proposed the plan to Major General James Fechet, the chief of the Army Air Corps. Fechet was enthusiastic and gave his approval, on the condition that Eaker and his fellow airmen could demonstrate the military potential that successful in-flight refueling could offer.[13] Major Carl Spaatz, who was designated the commander of the operation, selected a Fokker C-2 (a military version of the F.10A trimotor) for the endurance record attempt. The other two aircraft involved in the endurance flight were two Army Air Corps Douglas C-1C transport planes that had been converted into aerial tankers. The C-1C had an open cockpit in which the pilot and copilot sat side by side, and two 150-gallon fuel tanks were installed in the fuselage for this endurance flight. The C-1C tankers had a 50-foot fire hose on a reel inside the cargo hold next to a trapdoor, which would be lowered to the Fokker.[14]

On New Year's Day, 1929, at 7:26 a.m., the aircraft, christened the *Question Mark* because no one knew exactly how long it could stay in the air, took off from Los Angeles Metropolitan Airport. Aboard were Major Carl Spaatz, Captain Ira Eaker, Lieutenants Elwood Quesada and Harry Halverson, Staff Sergeant Roy Hooe, and only 100 gallons of fuel as the plane was heavy because of all of the equipment and supplies aboard. Thus the first refueling was scheduled for 8:15 that same morning, only forty-five minutes after takeoff. The second refueling plane, RP#2, piloted by Lieutenant Odas Moon, flew up from Los Angeles Metropolitan Airport and successfully completed the first refueling. The *Question Mark* and the refueling planes had no radios, so contact was made by way of signals, while any messages from the ground to be relayed to the *Question Mark* had to be done by writing them on chalkboards mounted to the sides of air corps pursuit planes. Around noon the crew of the *Question Mark* saw a PW-9D pursuit plane pull up alongside with the following message written on its side: "Don't Forget the Rose Bowl." The Fokker was flying in a continuous circle between Los Angeles and San Diego, where the refueling plane RP#1 was based, but it had been agreed

Construction of Super Universals and an F.10 at Fokker's Teterboro factory. [Photo AVIODROME Luchtfotografie, Lelystad, Holland]

Developed at the same time as the Super Universal, the F.10 became the standard American Fokker airliner in the late 1920s. It was similar to the F.VII/3m but had a larger fuselage and a different cockpit window. The design was ordered by Western Air Express, and it received its first F.10 in May 1928. Because it had a roomy cabin that could seat up to twelve passengers, further orders came from Western, Universal Airlines, Standard Airlines, and Pan Am. Sixty-five F.10s were built and they fared well against their main competitor, the Ford all-metal trimotor.

Fokker F.10A
length: 50 ft 7 in (15.42 m)
wingspan: 79 ft 1 in (24.1 m)
engines: three 420 hp Pratt & Whitney Wasp radials
cruising speed: 121 mph (194.7 km/h)
crew: 2
passengers: 12

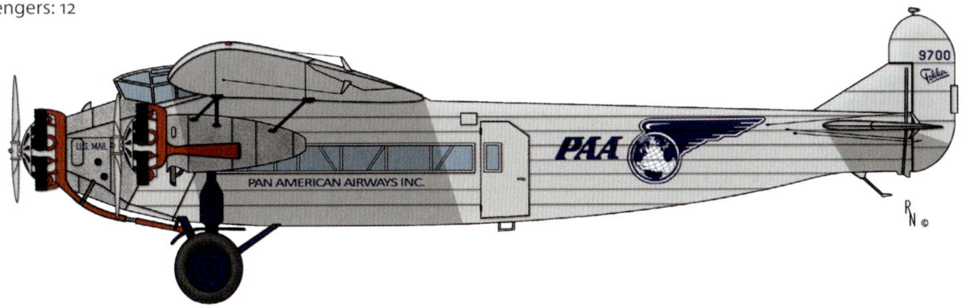

The crew of the record refueling flight of the Question Mark *(from left to right): Major Carl Spaatz, Captain Ira Eaker, Lieutenant Harry Halverson, Lieutenant Elwood Quesada, and Sergeant Roy Hooe. Carl Spaatz served as commander of the U.S. Strategic Air Forces in Europe during World War II, and became the first chief of staff of the United States Air Force in 1947; Ira Eaker commanded at different times the 8th, 12th, and 15th Air Forces in Europe during World War II; and Elwood Quesada commanded the 3rd Air Force during the war.* [Museum of the United States Air Force]

ahead of time that the *Question Mark* would perform a refueling over the Rose Bowl football game going on in Pasadena.

With thousands in the Rose Bowl stadium watching from below, Maj. Spaatz completed the second refueling, giving the football fans a firsthand look at a rare spectacle while at the same time bringing the Army Air Corps a great deal of publicity. Fortunately for the crew of the *Question Mark,* the crowd below could not see what happened at the end of the refueling run (as recalled by Ira Eaker): "We went over the Rose Bowl. It was very bumpy, as you can appreciate, as we should have appreciated, up against those mountains in January, and the refueling plane and the *Question Mark* were torn apart. I was piloting the *Question Mark* and I realized that Major Spaatz had probably been saturated in high octane gasoline."

Because only the refueling plane could control the flow of the fuel, Spaatz was showered with aviation fuel. He was wearing a rubber raincoat, gloves, goggles, and a face mask, so he only suffered burns to his face and was treated with zinc oxide. He ordered the flight to continue and said that, in case he needed medical attention, he would bale out with a parachute so that the endurance attempt would not have to be abandoned. Fortunately for Spaatz, he did not suffer a major injury. In fact, he performed the next refueling wearing only a parachute, not having had time to change into a new set of clothes. Thus Spaatz became the only-known *airborne* streaker at an American championship football game. But as a result of Spaatz's misadventure, the crew learned to cope with the difficulties of the refueling process and the turbulence caused by the winds and the moving aircraft. They were already rewarded for their efforts on the evening of New Year's Day, when a hot turkey dinner prepared by a church ladies' group in Van Nuys was sent down from one of the refueling planes!

Although the cabin was cramped and the noise from the engines almost deafening, the crew of the *Question Mark* were well looked after by their fellow air corps crewmen. Hot meals, water, mail, telegrams, clean towels, and clean underwear were routinely lowered to the Fokker by the refueling planes, and on one occasion a folding bathtub was sent down. The crewmen could take turns sleeping on bunks that were mounted on top of the fuel tanks in the cabin. The monotony of the routine and the constant roar of the engines were the main obstacles faced by the crew. The *Question Mark* was in the air for three days before any serious mechanical problems occurred. On the third day the port engine began to run roughly. Donning a parachute and a safety line, Sgt. Hooe climbed out to the engine and was able to clean out the spark plugs that had become caked with aerial debris.[15] As *Time* magazine reported:

> One motor began spurting oil. Sergeant Roy Hooe pussyfooted along the slim runway leading to the spewing machine, did some windy tinkering. Capt. Ira Eaker, at the joy stick, wore a haggard grin. He headed back toward Los Angeles. The day was sunny, the fog had drifted away. The fourth day, the eighty-seventh hour passed. Had the

five flown directly eastward the same distance from their starting point they would have been winging over Europe.

Finally, on January 7, the port engine cut out altogether. Rather than scrub the mission, Hooe attempted to repair the engine again. This time the engine rockers had failed completely, and Eaker could not keep the heavy Fokker at an adequate altitude without burning out the other two engines. When the *Question Mark* came in for a landing, the aircraft and its crew had been airborne for precisely six days, six hours, and forty minutes; they had taken aboard 5,660 gallons of aviation fuel, 245 gallons of oil, as well as water, food, and the other supplies for the crew. The endurance achieved in this mission could be attributed to the skill of the crew members, but also to the reliability and versatility of the Fokker trimotor design. The crew of the *Question Mark* had successfully proven that sustained in-flight refueling was possible and also suggested that its implementation could allow bombers to carry heavier payloads and fly longer distances with the assistance of refueling aircraft. Although in-flight refueling saw virtually no application during the 1930s or during World War II, it would come to be an integral part of Cold War and post–Cold War aerial strategic planning and operation.[16]

Refueling plane RP#1, an Army Air Corps Douglas C-1C transport loaded with fuel tanks and a fire hose lowered through a door in the cabin floor, pumping fuel down to the **Question Mark** ***over Burbank, California. One of the*** **Question Mark*'s crew can be seen sticking his head out of the upper hatch next to the fuel hose.*** [Museum of the United States Air Force]

The Forsaken Giant

Orders for Fokker aircraft were on the rise in 1928 and 1929, thanks in large part to the continued publicity of the trimotors in airline advertising and the *Question Mark*'s recent feat. Nevertheless, the growing presence of Henry Ford's all-metal 4-AT and 5-AT trimotors was beginning to be felt in the civil aviation market at the end of the decade. Although there were more Fokker aircraft flying in the United States in 1930 than any other civil aircraft, Tony Fokker wanted to nip the growing competition from Ford in the bud. The all-metal construction of Ford's trimotors was particularly appealing to airlines, which had to operate in hot and humid climates. But Fokker was still not convinced that he had to re-equip his factories for all-metal production.

Instead, he decided to counter the rising Ford threat with a transport that would have more than two or three times the passenger capacity of Ford's trimotors. The result was the Fokker F.32, a four-engine, high-cantilevered-wing transport that had a crew of two and a capacity for thirty passengers. Fokker reasoned that what this new aircraft lacked in terms of all-metal construction would certainly be made up for in comfort and capacity. Design on this aircraft had already begun in the Netherlands in 1926, but it was completed in 1929 in the United States by Bob Noorduyn and Albert Gassner, a former wartime designer for the Austrian Albatros works. The wing was a giant solid piece constructed of wood; the fuselage was a

Tony Fokker (center), with America's top-scoring fighter ace Eddie Rickenbacker (left) and renowned Australian polar explorer Sir George Hubert Wilkins (right). Tony Fokker's aviation expertise and jovial nature earned him the respect and friendship of many in the aviation world. Rickenbacker, who incidentally claimed thirteen Fokker D.VIIs in combat during World War I, came to work for Fokker's American company as vice president of sales in the late 1920s. Wilkins used the F.VIIb/3m trimotor* Detroiter *in an expedition flight over the Arctic in 1928. [Photo AVIODROME Luchtfotografie, Lelystad, Holland]

welded-steel-tube frame covered with canvas; and power was provided by four Pratt and Whitney radial engines arranged in tandem pairs under the wing. The passenger cabin was equipped like the interior of a Pullman railroad coach, featuring adjustable arm rests, cushy seats, overhead luggage racks, reading lights, a pantry, and a lavatory. The cabin was divided into "compartments," and sleeping berths could be installed for overnight flights. Fokker was excited about the prospects of the F.32. The number of Americans traveling by air was rapidly growing, and he believed that he was on the threshold of ushering in a new age of mass air transit with large airliners. Unfortunately, this was not to be the case.

Initially, sales looked promising for the new Fokker giant when it was unveiled to the public in September 1929. Both Universal Air Lines and Western Air Express ordered five of the transports. But problems began to arise when the giant took to the air. Test pilots found the aircraft to be underpowered and complained that the controls responded sluggishly. Officials at Universal Air Lines required a series of flights of the prototype carrying a full load before they would purchase the aircraft; but Fokker's test pilot, Marshall Boggs, refused to perform the test flight because he believed that the engines could not keep such a heavy load aloft. Boggs's vote of no confidence cost Fokker the order from Universal Air Lines. Western Air Express kept its order, but the first major publicity that the aircraft received was anything but positive.

On November 28, 1928, Marshall Boggs, who had finally agreed to pilot the giant, was in the F.32 prototype on a test flight out of Teterboro, when two engines quit as he was cruising over a Long Island neighborhood. The aircraft clipped several telephone lines and finally came down into a block of houses. As *The New York Times* reported:

> The pilot and his mechanic could do nothing but wait and brace themselves for the inevitable smash. They saw children below them, and, it seemed, directly in their path. Still settling, the eight-ton air liner stripped the radio wires from the Fagan house and garage, while Mrs. Fagan stood directly underneath on her back stoop, horror stricken. Then the chimney next door and half the roof and chimney of the third house followed as the big plane sank toward the earth. It still held its curving course, and Boggs still fought to control the airplane. It crossed the street at a sharp angle, nosed down and smashed into the Wicks home broadside.

Boggs and Fokker engineer Harry McDonald climbed out of the aircraft with only minor injuries, and fortunately no one was killed on the ground; however, the F.32 burst into flames, and all that was left was a tangle of welded steel tubes. The aircraft was certainly too big for its engines, and more powerful ones were mounted on the next F.32 that was completed.

Despite the crash of the prototype, Western Air Express did not cancel its order; two F.32s were delivered to the airline in March 1930. The more powerful engines in the production series aircraft somewhat improved the aircraft's performance, but the giant was still plagued by two problems. First, the noise from the tandem pairs of engines under the wings made normal conversation in the passenger cabin difficult. Second, there was a tendency for the rear engines to overheat, fouling the spark plugs; that problem was never completely fixed. But the decisive factor that prematurely ended the F.32s career had nothing to do with the aircraft's performance; rather, it was that this high-capacity airliner began service at a time when there were few passengers flying. It was not that travelers did not want to fly; instead, by the time Western Air Express's F.32s entered service, the effects of the Great Depression had made air travel an unnecessary luxury for most people. Western Air Express canceled its remaining order, and buyers were never found for the other four F.32s that Fokker built.[17]

The Plane that Fell from the Sky: The Crash of Fokker's American Fortunes

The failure to find a market for the F.32 was a major setback to Fokker's enterprise in the United States. The F.32 had a retail price of $110,000 (over twice that of the F.10A), and when the company sold only two of the seven it had built, it suffered a financial loss. Yet the setback caused by the F.32 was relatively minor compared to the next incident to befall Fokker's American enterprise. *Time* magazine reported the following:

> A heavy fog hung over Kansas fields near Emporia one morning last week as Edward Baker, farm boy of Bazaar, set forth to feed his cattle. Along about ten o'clock he heard an explosion, then a crash. Soon afterward, in a nearby pasture, Edward Baker came upon the flaming carcass of a ten passenger Fokker of the Transcontinental & Western Air line. Its eight occupants lay dead or dying. . . .[18]

Another witness saw the aircraft drop out of the sky and crash to the ground, and then saw part of a wing come tumbling down a few seconds later. One of the wings of the F.10A had broken off in flight during a thunderstorm, causing the fatal crash. Any crash with fatalities is tragic enough, but one of the passengers who perished on that Fokker plane was Knute Rockne, the popular football coach of the University of Notre Dame, and this brought a blitz of media attention to the incident.

Anthony Fokker immediately went to the scene of the crash to look over the wreck. After examining the twisted wood and steel tubing, Fokker told reporters that "the flight should not have been undertaken in existing weather conditions. I would say the human element entered very strongly into the cause of the crash."[19] The Department of Commerce countered that the "airplane had been operated in accordance with Air Commerce regulations; daily inspections . . . satisfactorily concluded [that it was] . . . thoroughly airworthy.... [N]o blame can be attached to the pilots."[20] Officials of the Department

With increased demand in the late 1920s, Western Air Express requested a new aircraft that would have a significantly higher passenger capacity than the F.10. When it was first flown on September 10, 1929, the four-engine Fokker F.32 was the largest landplane in the world and received a great deal of publicity. Its four engines were housed in pairs in nacelles under the wing in a unique fashion: one tractor propeller pulling from the front and another pushing from the back. [Photo AVIODROME Luchtfotografie, Lelystad, Holland]

Despite its cushy seats, Pullman car–like interior, and high passenger capacity, the days of the F.32 were short-lived. Even with four engines the aircraft was dangerously underpowered and the prototype crashed in November 1929 due to an engine failure. Like the large F.IX trimotor in the Netherlands, the F.32 also became a victim of the Great Depression with dwindling numbers of passengers who could afford to fly. Seven F.32s were built but Fokker only managed to sell two to Western Air Express. [Museum of the United States Air Force]

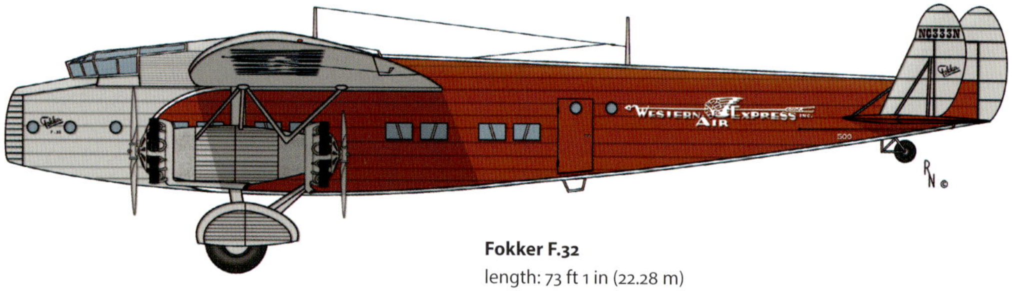

Fokker F.32
length: 73 ft 1 in (22.28 m)
wingspan: 99 ft 1 in (30.2 m)
engines: four 575 hp Pratt & Whitney Hornet B radials
cruising speed: 122 mph (196.3 km/h)
range: 851 miles (1,369.55 km)
crew: 2
passengers: 30

of Commerce began to suspect that the problem lay in the construction of the wooden wings. On May 4, 1931, the aeronautics branch of the Department of Commerce grounded all Fokker F.10s and F.10As that had been assembled at the Glendale factory in 1929 (as the aircraft that crashed on Long Island had been) and ordered that they be returned to the factory for inspection. This was the first time the U.S. government had grounded a specific type of civil transport in the wake of an accident; it was to have a mortal effect on Fokker's American enterprise.

Tony Fokker was furious at the Department of Commerce's action. He was adamantly certain that the cause of the crash had nothing to do with the design of the aircraft or with his wooden construction techniques. Fokker's views on all-wooden construction would later be vindicated, since some successful aircraft were manufactured partially or entirely out of wood throughout the rest of the 1930s and during World War II, the de Havilland Mosquito being the best known. He also wondered why, considering the excellent safety record that his aircraft had earned, the F.10A was being singled out. It was later reported that the crew of a railroad engine in Kansas City saw the TWA F.10A clip its wingtip on a grain elevator shortly after takeoff, and a dent was later found on the grain elevator where the railroad men saw the wingtip strike it. The Department of Commerce paid little attention to this report. Fokker was all the more furious when he was denied access to the meeting between the Department of Commerce and representatives of airlines that used the F.10A:

> Through the corridors of the Department of Commerce building and of Washington's Mayflower Hotel last week stormed an exceedingly irate Dutchman—Anthony Herman Gerhard ("Tony") Fokker. He shouted threats at the Department, at Assistant Secretary Clarence Marshall Young for the "hasty," "hostile" and "prejudiced" action of suspending Fokker planes from U.S. passenger service. . . .[21]

After two weeks of thorough inspections, no major faults were found in the wings of the F.10s and F.10As that were examined. The ban was lifted, and most of the transports went back into service. But a fatal blow had been dealt to the reputation of Fokker aircraft in the United States.

The media circus surrounding the Knute Rockne crash and the grounding of the F.10s was unprecedented and created mass hysteria concerning Fokker's wooden-winged aircraft. Manufacturers of all-metal aircraft took advantage of the situation and touted their designs as standing up to the elements better than those with wooden components. Even though Fokker's design was later vindicated by the Department of Commerce, it had already been sentenced to oblivion in the minds of travelers thanks to a vindictive media. Tony Fokker could not even save himself from the fallout of the F.10 fiasco. By 1931, Fokker no longer had a controlling voice in his American company, since a controlling interest in the Fokker Aircraft Corporation had been purchased by Western Air Express (the holding company for Atlantic Aviation) in October 1928, and then by the General Motors Corporation in May 1929. General Motors engineered the merging of the Fokker Aircraft Corporation and the Dornier Corporation of America into the General Aviation Corporation in May 1930, which took even more influence away from Fokker.

At the end of the decade of the 1920s, Fokker's American design team made an attempt to regain military contracts with prototypes for two modern military aircraft that the company hoped to sell to the Army Air Corps. The first was the YO-27, a twin-engine, cantilever-wing observation aircraft fitted with retractable landing gear, which was designed to replace the older biplane observation aircraft in the Air Corps's inventory. The army ordered two prototypes of the YO-27, the first to be completed as an observation aircraft and the second, designated XB-8, to be completed as a fast medium bomber. The lightweight composite steel-tube/wood/canvas XB-8 was not designed as a bomber and showed only marginally better performance over the types that were about to be replaced. The Air Corps lost interest in that aircraft as a bomber but ordered a dozen of the observation variant.

Fokker manufactured and attempted to market an amphibian, the F.11A, in the United States in the late 1920s and early 1930s. The wings were built in Fokker's American factories, but the all-metal fuselages were built by Werkspoor in the Netherlands and shipped across the Atlantic. Although a unique aircraft, only four were sold to private customers. Tony Fokker is seen here climbing out of the prototype.

Shown here are the forward fuselage and other parts of the only surviving F.11A in storage at the Aviodrome in Lelystad.

A fragment of the wooden wing from the Fokker F.10A of TWA Flight 599, which crashed on March 31, 1931; the wing was examined by the Aeronautics Branch of the U.S. Department of Commerce. Although the cause of the crash was most likely poor maintenance on the part of the operator or the decision of the pilot to fly in poor weather rather than a design or construction flaw, the grounding of this type of airliner on the grounds of safety concerns was unprecedented in American history. [Museum of the United States Air Force]

With a rather limited role, no further YO-27s were built, and the last one was retired from the Army Air Corps service in 1937. Nevertheless, it was one of the first American military aircraft to have retractable landing gear.

The other Fokker aircraft developed for the army was the XA-7 monoplane two-seat attack aircraft. This aircraft had a number of modern refinements: it had a cantilevered low wing, a streamlined fuselage, landing gear covered with spats, and, most important, it was the first Fokker airplane of all-metal construction. The XA-7 was not ordered by the Army Air Corps, and in the end these two attempts by Fokker to reenter the military market came to naught. Commercial sales were down as a result of the Depression before the Knute Rockne crash, and GM realized that Fokker had no replacement designs for the F.10A or Super Universal on the drawing boards. The Rockne crash was used by the GM leadership as a convenient reason to "convince" Fokker to leave the company that he had founded. Fokker and his design team left without a major quarrel, and what was left of the Fokker Aircraft Corporation was eventually absorbed into North American Aviation, Inc. Fokker's factories were closed by October 1931, and the short-lived "Dutch dominance" of the American skies came to an abrupt end.[22]

Fokker's New Deal and Roosevelt's Shenanigans

Although Fokker's manufacturing enterprise in the United States disappeared at the end of 1931, Tony Fokker remained in the shadow of the American aviation scene for the rest of the decade. While in California in 1933, Fokker test-flew Douglas's experimental DC-1. Fokker realized that this was a very advanced aircraft that would have great sales potential, not just in the United States but in Europe as well. In the back of his mind he also realized that his Amsterdam factory would not be able to come up with a similar all-metal design by the time the DC-2 production model would be rolling off the assembly lines. Since Donald Douglas was a personal friend of his, Fokker discussed a radical proposal with the American aircraft manufacturer: Fokker offered to purchase the European sales and manufacturing rights from Douglas, thus becoming the sole distributor of the exceptional new airliner on the Continent.

The offer would give Douglas royalties from the manufacture of Douglas aircraft by the Fokker Company, as well as giving him Tony Fokker's sales expertise and network of European contacts. It was also a very clever and advantageous arrangement for Fokker: rather than compete against the new Douglas airliners in the European market (a battle that he knew he would probably lose), Fokker created a way in which he could profit from an aircraft with which his own contemporary designs could not hope to compete. The deal ensured the security of his company against increasingly excellent airliners coming from American manufacturers. Fokker envisioned his factory assembling the DC-2s destined for European airlines, while his designers could use the time to develop new all-metal airliners that could effectively compete against the new American upstart models.

More important, the deal with Douglas would provide Fokker's Amsterdam factory with a valuable interlude in which to re-equip itself for the production of large all-metal airliners, something the company had not yet taken on. But Fokker never let on that he was a relative latecomer to the production of all-metal aircraft. When Donald Douglas visited the Fokker factory in Amsterdam, Fokker made a point of showing Douglas a new all-metal, low-wing monoplane fighter, which he claimed would be the fastest in the world at 274 mph.[23] The purchase of European rights to the DC-2 was a new deal that helped keep Fokker among the leaders in European civil aviation. (The full story of Fokker and the Douglas airliners will be told in Chapter 5.)

Out of the American spotlight for a few years, Anthony Fokker returned to American headlines in the mid-1930s, but under rather clouded circumstances. His name appeared frequently in the investigations conducted by the Nye Committee, or the Special Committee on Investigations of the Munitions Industry, led by Senator Gerald

Nye of North Dakota. The primary function of the committee was to investigate the role that industrial and banking profiteering had on the decision of the United States to enter World War I; but the committee also assumed a secondary function: investigating "the activities of individuals, firms, associations and of corporations and all other agencies in the United States engaged in the manufacture, sale, distribution, import or export of arms, munitions or other implements of war." The Nye Committee had the support of President Franklin Delano Roosevelt, who pushed for greater government oversight of American munitions sales abroad, stemming from an unrealistic idealism and pacifism that would be discarded as soon as Pearl Harbor happened.

Nye, however, had no idealistic pretentions: he was an advocate of farmers and small businessmen, and he rallied against corporate monopolies. In the middle of this political battle, the Douglas and Lockheed aircraft companies came into Nye's sights. Both companies were eagerly selling their aircraft abroad, and the exclusive foreign export agent for both Douglas and Lockheed happened to be none other than Tony Fokker. Not wishing to invest heavily in research and design to stay competitive with the American aircraft manufacturers, Fokker had made a compromise: not only did he purchase the exclusive rights to sell exports and license-production rights of the DC-2 (as well as the future DC-3) from his friend Donald Douglas in 1934, but he drove directly from Los Angeles to Burbank and also succeeded in purchasing the export rights of the Lockheed Electra from Lockheed president Robert Gross. Fokker's salesmanship worked very well for Douglas, who secured sales throughout Europe, though in some instances it was via bribery. Furthermore, some of the customers were frowned on by the U.S. government. In one of the U.S. Senate's committee hearings, Senator Nye's chief counsel read the following from a letter Fokker wrote to Douglas regarding his attempts to sell the DC-2:

> Selling the license to the Swiss factory of Dornier at Alten Rhein means disclosing all the technical information to

In the late 1920s, the Army Air Corps ordered a reconnaissance aircraft design from Fokker. It was designated the XO-27, and the Fokker company presented a composite-material monoplane with the engines embedded in the wings and retractable landing gear—both used to reduce drag. The second XO-27 was converted into a bomber and given the designation XB-8 (seen in this photo). In 1931, the Air Corps ordered twelve of the reconnaissance version, by that time known as the YO-27. These were the last Fokker aircraft to be purchased by the U.S. Army Air Corps.

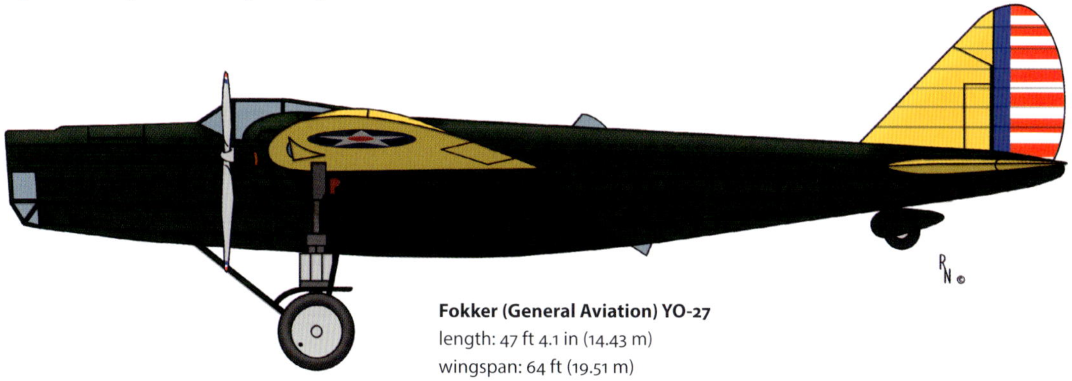

Fokker (General Aviation) YO-27
length: 47 ft 4.1 in (14.43 m)
wingspan: 64 ft (19.51 m)
engines: two 600 hp Curtiss V-1570-23 Conqueror in-lines
maximum speed: 160 mph (257.5 km/h)
crew: 3

the Dornier Company in Germany, and we hope to do a better business with the German Government direct, or with one of the German firms with which we are in negotiation.

Germany probably will not buy officially the license on the Douglas, but unofficially may buy the technical information.

Spain, after my personal visit at Madrid, intends to buy two airplanes for troop transportation.... This business will not be closed for at least half a year, as it takes this time to obtain the necessary funds and pass all the Government departments. Besides that, many people have to be "seen."[24]

The possibility of American aeronautical technology ending up in German hands, as well as the reference to bribery to secure the potential Spanish government order, clearly caught the attention of the Nye Committee members. Another example that called Fokker's business methods into question was the sale of a DC-2 to the Soviet Union for $101,480, when a similar aircraft was sold to the American airline TWA for only $58,000.

Although Fokker's shrewd sales tactics on behalf of Douglas could be considered under the table by some, Fokker had violated no American law when all was said and done. Fokker had no qualms about selling to the Soviets; the Red Air Force had purchased the bulk of his military aircraft production in the years immediately following World War I. Defending itself against the accusations of the Nye Committee, the Douglas company stated that the DC-2 was purely a civil aircraft and that any military application to the airliner was purely the act and responsibility of the purchaser. Furthermore, any export or license arrangements made with governments to which the United States took offense were not the responsibility of the Douglas Aircraft Company but rather of the Fokker Company, a Dutch concern that was not under the jurisdiction of American embargo laws. Fokker succeeded in outmaneuvering the U.S. government on this point.[25]

It was Fokker's relationship with Lockheed and Elliott

Fokker (General Aviation) XA-7
length: 31 ft (9.45 m)
wingspan: 46 ft 9 in (14.25 m)
engine: 600 hp Curtiss V-1570-27 Conqueror in-line
maximum speed: 184 mph (296 km/h)
range: 500 miles (804.67 km)
armament: four .30 caliber machine guns, one .30 caliber machine gun in rear cockpit, up to 488 lbs (221 kg) of bombs
crew: 2

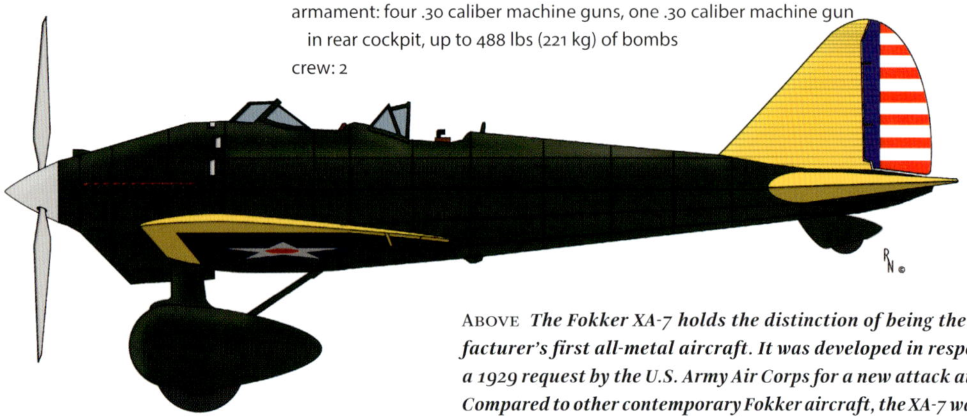

ABOVE *The Fokker XA-7 holds the distinction of being the manufacturer's first all-metal aircraft. It was developed in response to a 1929 request by the U.S. Army Air Corps for a new attack aircraft. Compared to other contemporary Fokker aircraft, the XA-7 was revolutionary not only in its all-metal construction but also in its monoplane low-wing configuration. Only the XA-7 prototype was built.*

RIGHT *Tony Fokker peering out of the first Fokker-Douglas DC-2. His purchase of the European sales and manufacturing licenses to Donald Douglas's new all-metal airliners not only kept him a minor player in American aviation circles, but it also brought much-needed revenue to his Dutch company during the middle years of the Great Depression.* [Photo San Diego Air and Space Museum]

Roosevelt, the son of President Roosevelt, that propelled Fokker temporarily back into the media scrutiny in the midst of the Nye Committee investigations of 1935-36. On September 4, 1935, one of the headlines in *The New York Times* read: "Nye Hunts Fokker in Airplane Deal." Nye issued a subpoena to Fokker to appear before his senate committee regarding Fokker's involvement in foreign aircraft sales, but Fokker was nowhere to be reached. On September 4, Nye requested the assistance of officials in the Justice and State Departments to help locate Fokker. For twenty-four hours there appeared to be a massive manhunt for the elusive Flying Dutchman. As it turned out, Fokker was on a fishing trip on his yacht off Montauk Point, completely oblivious to what was going on ashore. He learned of the manhunt on September 5, after reading the above-mentioned article, and agreed to make a deposition before the Nye Committee on September 18, 1935. What Fokker mentioned at his hearing would become a thorn in the side of Franklin Roosevelt a year later, when the Nye Committee released Fokker's testimony.

An article in *Aero Digest* in October 1936 brought to public light clandestine discussions between Anthony Fokker, Elliott Roosevelt, FDR, and the Soviet Union. In 1934, Franklin Roosevelt had established formal relations with the Soviet Union, which meant normalized trade could begin with the United States. Sensing an opportunity to sell commercial aircraft to the Soviets, Fokker secured the sales and manufacturing rights for Douglas aircraft in Europe (since sales of military equipment were prohibited) and then went over to Lockheed's offices and negotiated a two-year exclusive sales agreement for the Lockheed Electra for Europe, Great Britain, and the Soviet Union. Donald Douglas suggested that Fokker employ the president's son Elliott as a salesman. Through conversations with one of Elliott's associates, Grenville Stratton, Fokker agreed to pay Elliott $25,000 a year for his sales services, but he did not sign a contract. Fokker believed that there was a fortune to be made in aircraft sales, but he was shrewd enough to wait to see if Elliott could actually deliver on his boastful promises. The Soviet sales plan was finalized in a dinner meeting

Despite the closure of his American factories, Fokker was still one of the world's established aircraft manufacturers and was well known and respected on both sides of the Atlantic. During the 1930s he traveled frequently between the Old World and the New and maintained many of his contacts in the aviation world. Here he has a reunion at Tempelhoff Airport in Berlin in December 1931 with two of the foremost Fokker D.VII aces from the First World War, Bruno Loerzer (far left) and Ernst Udet (fifth from left). Both served as Luftwaffe generals in World War II. [Photo AVIODROME Luchtfotografie, Lelystad, Holland]

President Franklin Delano Roosevelt (far left) and his son Elliott (far right). Tony Fokker hired Elliott to sell Lockheed airliners to the Soviet Union in clandestine meetings arranged by Lockheed, Fokker, and the Soviet government—with the approval of President Roosevelt. Elliott, more interested in living the high life than selling aircraft, failed to make a single sale to the Soviets, and Fokker, disgusted, washed his hands of the matter.

on January 25, 1934, at the White House between Donald Douglas, Elliott, and Franklin Roosevelt.[26]

Elliott Roosevelt made a business trip to the Soviet Union and informed Herbert Reed, one of Fokker's sales agents and former secretary-treasurer of the Atlantic Aircraft Corporation, that he was confident that he could sell fifty Electras to the Soviets. Apparently, Franklin Roosevelt approved of the plan, because Elliott phoned Reed and "suggested that his contract be made with Reed rather than directly with Fokker, saying, 'Father objects to my entering the employ of an alien [Fokker], but if the contract is drawn in your [Reed's] name, it will be all right.'" Fokker paid Elliott $5,000 to cement their new business partnership; if the deal were to go through, it would bring Elliott an additional $500,000. A code was established between Elliott Roosevelt, President Roosevelt, and Fokker that would cloud their involvement in the deal.[27]

The fifty Electras, however, were never sold. Not only did Elliott put too high a price on the aircraft, expecting a large profit for himself, but he lacked good sales skills and was more interested in the wining and dining aspects of the sales negotiations. The Russian purchasing delegation returned to Moscow without purchasing a single plane. At the same time—and unfortunately for Gross—Fokker also decided to back out of his deal with Lockheed. Fokker was not particularly impressed with the performance of the Electra: it failed to meet guaranteed speed requirements, and he was only able to sell a handful of the transports throughout Europe. This temporarily left Lockheed in the lurch financially, but it saved the company's reputation two years later. At the same time, Fokker was disgusted with Elliott and his inflated reputation as a master salesman. Although he never chastised Elliott publicly, he wrote a letter to Donald Douglas saying that the president's son and his cronies were "chiselers," and he suggested that Douglas personally oversee sales to Russia and dismiss Elliott Roosevelt.

The story of the younger Roosevelt's involvement in a scheme to sell fifty Lockheed Electras to the Soviets was leaked to the *Chicago Tribune* by a New York publisher who was opposed to Franklin Roosevelt's bid for reelection in 1936—and who also had contact with Herbert Reed. The evidence presented was the initial contract worked out between Fokker, Elliott Roosevelt, and Reed, the code they devised, and the telephone records between the three men.[28] This was followed up by the accusatory article in *Aero Digest*. The Nye Committee also made Fokker's 1935 affidavit public in early October 1936, after charges had been made in the media that, in the case of the Elliot Roosevelt-Fokker deal, the committee was "withholding information from the public."[29]

The Internal Revenue Service became interested in the deal because Fokker's deposition had listed $5,000 paid to Elliott Roosevelt on his 1934 tax statement, but Roosevelt had not declared receiving $5,000 from Fokker. Elliott told reporters that he had never received any money from Fokker, but his business associate Grenville Stratton had. Stratton tried to obtain Elliott's signed receipt for the $5,000 from Fokker, but the Dutchman refused. Stratton then attempted to persuade Herbert Reed to testify that he, not Elliott, had received the payment. Reed refused to falsely testify, and it was clear that Elliott was caught red-handed.[30] Amid attacks from Democratic politicians and lobbyists who claimed that the Nye Committee was using Fokker's affidavit to politically smear the Roosevelt administration, Senator Nye declared the Fokker incident closed the day after the affidavit was made public.

Nye vowed that it was not his intention to use the affidavit for political purposes, and Fokker made a similar statement to the media. The bottom line was that Franklin Roosevelt's naïve son had stumbled into a rather shady military arms deal that was exposed. (This was not the last such incident for Elliott Roosevelt: during World War II, Howard Hughes used lavish Hollywood parties and women to "convince" then-Col. Roosevelt to support a government contract for the Hughes XF-11 reconnaissance plane.)

Fortunately for Roosevelt, no planes were sold to the Soviets, so he was officially cleared of any wrongdoing, though he and Senator Nye bore the damage of the media storm. The one person to come out of this ordeal almost completely unscathed was Tony Fokker. After years of experience with the American media, he knew how to handle them. At the beginning of his depositions to the Nye Committee, Fokker stated that his reputation as an aircraft manufacturer was "sufficient guarantee of his (Elliott's) success in selling those planes he is promoting and that he has, generally speaking, not needed to resort to corruption of government officials."[31] Elliott Roosevelt was out of his league when compared to Tony Fokker's experience in clandestine aircraft sales. The latter was the kind of person who had been able to use the services of egotistical self-promoters such as Hermann Göring and the son of President Roosevelt as salesmen, to dismiss both of them, and to still have made a profit in the end. Although Fokker became an American citizen and spent the rest of his life in the United States, the incident with Roosevelt is a fitting conclusion to the influence that the wily "Flying Dutchman" had in the world of American aviation.

Tony Fokker spent most of his time when he was in the United States in the mid- to late-1930s relaxing on the water or visiting with friends. He had a wide variety of acquaintances and friends, including Howard Hughes (above) and Charlie Chaplain (left). While he did not care to indulge in parties or nightlife, his affable personality drew people to him. [Photo AVIODROME Luchtfotografie, Lelystad, Holland]

A unique photograph of "Uncle Tony" with a number of aviators, all of whom achieved fame via flights in Fokker aircraft. First from the left is Captain James Fitzmaurice, Commandant of the Irish Free State Army Air Corps, who attempted a transatlantic flight from Ireland to Philadelphia in a Fokker F.VIIa named Princess Xenia, *but was forced to turn back by bad weather on September 16, 1927.*

Second from the left is Charles Kingsford-Smith, who made the world's first transpacific flight in the Fokker F.VIIb3/m Southern Cross. *In June 1929, Kingsford-Smith flew from Australia to England, and a year later took the* Southern Cross *across the Atlantic to the United States, completing a circumnavigation of the globe in the aircraft. With him here is his crew from the* Southern Cross's *transatlantic flight: copilot Evert van Dijk (KLM), navigator Jonathan Saul (Irish Free State Army Air Corps), and radio operator John Stannage.*

Fourth from the right is KLM Captain Gerrit Geysendorffer and copilot J. B. Scholte (third from left), who made the world's first long-distance charter flight when they flew American millionaire Van Lear Black from Amsterdam to Batavia and back in a KLM Fokker F.VIIa in 1927.

Finally, second from the right is Bernt Balchen, a Norwegian aviator and Fokker test pilot who was responsible for the success of Richard Byrd's transatlantic flight in the Fokker C-2 America. [Photo AVIODROME Luchtfotografie, Lelystad, Holland

Chapter Four

FOKKER MAKES THE WORLD A LITTLE SMALLER

A Byrd Flies to the North Pole

Fokker's Universals and Super Universals blazed new trails throughout the rural areas and wilderness regions of the United States and Canada, greatly assisting the rapid expansion of the airmail and airfreight services on the continent. Yet it was Tony Fokker's trimotors that he was most recognized for in North America and the rest of the world. Fokker's flying of his first trimotor during the Ford Reliability Tour brought the design even more publicity in its service after the tour than during it. The destiny of Fokker's trimotor was about to become entwined with that of an ambitious young naval officer with a passion for exploration and a love for publicity similar to Fokker's. Lieutenant Commander Richard E. Byrd of the United States Navy had been participating in plans for an American flight to the North Pole as early as 1924. The navy suggested using the rigid airship *Shenandoah* for a flight from Point Barrow, Alaska, to Spitsbergen, an island to the north of Norway, and Byrd was selected to serve as the navigator for the flight. Ultimately, President Calvin Coolidge canceled the flight due to his worry about the feasibility of such a flight in unknown airspace and climate conditions. The following year Byrd took part in an aerial expedition over Greenland that was led by Donald M. MacMillan. The MacMillan-Byrd expedition used three Loening amphibian biplanes loaned from the navy and was sponsored by the National Geographic Society. The expedition put Byrd into the public limelight, but he still desired to be the first person to fly over the North Pole. He eventually found support for his ambition from Henry and Edsel Ford. Edsel Ford personally gave Byrd a check for $20,000 and convinced John D. Rockefeller to give a similar amount. After the Ford Reliability Tour, Byrd purchased the F.VIIa/3m from Tony Fokker for $40,000, not a small price at the time. Fokker

Fokker's first F.VIIa3/m trimotor, veteran of the Ford Reliability Tour and now christened Josephine Ford *after Edsel Ford's daughter, seen after Richard Byrd's purchase of the aircraft with money donated by the Fords and John D. Rockefeller. The aircraft had recently returned from the flight of Tony Fokker and Juan Trippe to Havana and was being disassembled for transport to Spitsbergen.* [Photo AVIODROME Luchtfotografie, Lelystad, Holland]

Byrd checking over the port engine on the Josephine Ford.

was somewhat reluctant to sell the aircraft because it was the only demonstration model of his new trimotor that he possessed; he had thus set a high sale price for the aircraft. In April 1926, Byrd remarked to Edsel Ford: "Fokker has written his name all over the plane, but I could not help that, as he said he would not sell it to me unless I allowed him to do so."[1] Despite Fokker's insistence on turning the aircraft into a flying billboard, Byrd considered it the perfect rugged transport for a flight over the North Pole. Byrd also received donations from a number of media firms, which hoped to capitalize on the story of the flight. With this money, Byrd leased a supply ship, the USS *Chantier,* from the U.S. Navy for six months. Loaded with supplies and the *Josephine Ford* (Byrd named the Fokker trimotor after Edsel Ford's daughter as a show of gratitude, though Tony Fokker insisted that his name still remain predominant on the aircraft), the *Chantier* set sail on April 5, 1926, for the island of Spitsbergen, from which Byrd would begin his polar flight.[2]

The *Chantier* arrived in Spitsbergen on April 29, and Byrd's team began to assemble the *Josephine Ford.* Once the aircraft was ready for test flights, Byrd and his pilot, Floyd Bennett, faced an unexpected problem: they had not anticipated how the aircraft's weight would impact its takeoff on ice. According to Byrd:

> No one knew what a big plane like the *Josephine Ford* would do taking off [on] the snow with skis. We had much to learn. We were truly pioneering. . . .
>
> As there was no level stretch available that was smooth enough to take off from with a heavy load we were forced to try another new stunt—to take off going down hill. To get the snow on our take-off field smooth was the biggest job of all. The boys had to work 18 hours a day but never did I hear a single complaint from any of them.
>
> The plane's first attempt to take off for a trial flight ended in a snow drift and nearly upset—which not only would have hurt us, but would have upset the expedition as well! A ski was broken to bits and the landing gear bent and broken.
>
> Things looked black, but the men refused to lose heart. Then twice again we broke our ski in pretty much the same way. . . .
>
> Profiting by our first experience, we treated the bottom of the skis with a mixture of resin and tar. The runway was fairly smooth for the second attempt and the plane was lightly loaded. We held our breath.
>
> This time our airplane moved forward rapidly, then rose gracefully into the air.[3]

The successful test flight and the new skis were pivotal for Byrd because it turned out that he was now in a race to be the first to fly over the North Pole. Also at Spitsbergen was a Norwegian/Italian team under the command of the renowned polar explorer Roald Amundsen, who was preparing his own flight over the Pole in the *Norge,* an Italian-built airship piloted by its designer, Colonel Umberto Nobile of the Italian Regia Aeronautica. On May 8, Byrd's meteorologist concluded that a patch of good weather was moving in long enough for the projected duration of Byrd's flight. At half past midnight on May 9, 1926, Byrd and Bennett warmed up the *Josephine Ford*'s engines and roared down their makeshift runway, taking off for the North Pole.

The *Josephine Ford* climbed slowly as a result of its 10,000-pound load. The aircraft was filled with 5-gallon gasoline cans, a short-wave radio set, a rubber boat, 10-weeks' worth of supplies, and most important, Byrd's navigational equipment. Flying over an uncharted and barren landscape devoid of any landmarks meant that navigational skills were more valuable on this flight than aeronautical skills, and Byrd was recognized as one of the navy's best navigators. Byrd used a sun compass to determine the northerly direction, a chronometer and a sextant for measuring longitude and latitude, and a drift indicator under the aircraft—which could be accessed via a trapdoor—used in conjunction with smoke bombs to measure to what degree the wind was blowing the aircraft off course. While Bennett manned the controls, Byrd was at work with these instruments. One minor miscalculation and they might not only miss the Pole but lose their way back to Spitsbergen as well. This constant orchestration of collecting calculations was demanding for Byrd, particularly with the instruments outside of the aircraft: "I froze my face and one of my hands in taking sights with the instruments from the trapdoors. But I noticed these frostbites at once and was more careful thereafter in the future."[4]

When Byrd from time to time relieved Bennett, who needed to stretch his legs and also pour gasoline into the tank, he took the controls in one hand and held a sun compass in the other. As hours of white monotony

ABOVE *The* Josephine Ford *being brought ashore at Spitsbergen.*

LEFT *Bennett and Byrd speed down a slope made to assist the heavily laden* Josephine Ford *in its takeoff.*

BELOW *The* Josephine Ford *passing over Byrd's base on Spitsbergen on its way to the North Pole.*

Richard Byrd (second from left) and Floyd Bennett (third from right) being awarded the Medal of Honor (Tiffany Cross) by President Calvin Coolidge. [Library of Congress LC-USZ62-131298]

passed, misfortune struck at about an hour's distance from the Pole. Looking out the window, Byrd noticed an oil leak in the starboard engine. Bennett wanted to land on the ice to repair the leak but Byrd insisted on flying on; he was afraid that the *Josephine Ford* might break one of its skis in a rough landing. Byrd took the controls and hoped that the reputation for reliability earned by Tony Fokker's trimotor would hold true:

> When I took the wheel again I kept my eyes glued on that oil leak and the oil-pressure indicator. Should the pressure drop, we would lose the motor immediately. It fascinated me. There was no doubt in my mind that the oil pressure would drop any moment. But the prize was actually in sight. We could not turn back.
>
> At 9:02 a.m., May 9, 1926, Greenwich civil time, our calculations showed us to be at the Pole! The dream of a lifetime had at last been realized.
>
> We headed to the right to take two confirming sights of the sun, then turned and took two more.
>
> After that we made some moving and still pictures, then went on for several miles in the direction we had come, and made another larger circle to be sure to take in the Pole. We thus made a non-stop flight around the world in a very few minutes. In doing that we lost a whole day in time and of course when we completed the circle we gained that day back again.[5]

Byrd had concluded the first flight over the top of the world, flying from one day to the next and back again. Only thirty years later, that navigational feat would become the daily routine patrol of American and Soviet bombers, lasting throughout the duration of the Cold War. Byrd and Bennett left the Pole at 9:15 a.m. and set a course back to Spitsbergen. After more hours of monotonous but accurate navigating, the *Josephine Ford* touched down at Spitsbergen after being in the air for nearly sixteen hours.

As Byrd disembarked from the trimotor, he was congratulated by Roald Amundsen, who crossed the Pole in the *Norge* less than three days later. When Byrd returned home, he became an instant celebrity. He was promoted to the rank of commander, was awarded the Congressional Medal of Honor by President Calvin Coolidge, and was given a ticker-tape parade in New York. The U.S. Navy and the National Geographic Society both appointed committees of mathematicians and navigators, who, after examining Byrd's charts and records, concluded that the *Josephine Ford* had indeed flown over the North Pole.

However, on May 9, 1996, seventy years after Byrd's flight, the front page of *The New York Times* carried an article entitled "Did Byrd Reach Pole? His Diary Hints 'No.'" The journal Byrd kept during the flight had just been discovered in the archives of Ohio State University. This was not the first instance in which the veracity of Byrd's account had come into question: some had questioned the outcome of the flight beginning already in 1926. It is noteworthy that veteran Norwegian pilot Bernt Balchen, who had helped Byrd build the skis at Spitsbergen that allowed the *Josephine Ford* to take off, later became one of the latter's detractors. Balchen claimed that Bennett, on his deathbed with pneumonia in 1928, told him that he and Byrd took off, circled for several hours, and then returned, claiming that they had reached the Pole. Some researchers, on examining Byrd's journal, came to believe that, at the speed and course the *Josephine Ford* was flying, the North Pole could not have been reached in the time the aircraft was airborne. They believed that the oil leak in the engine that had worried Byrd and Bennett proved to be the decisive factor in the *Josephine Ford* not reaching the North Pole. Byrd had selected the Fokker F.VIIa/3m because, in the event of an engine failure, the aircraft could continue on two engines. With three engines operational, the *Josephine Ford* cruised at 85 mph; but when flying on two engines, the aircraft could only manage 60 mph. Taking into consideration that the aircraft would face headwinds of at least 10 mph on the return journey, reducing the cruising speed to 50 mph or less, the chances of reaching Spitsbergen with enough fuel or without the risk of another engine failure would have been slim. Some aviation historians then concluded that credit for the first flight over the North Pole should go to Roald Amundsen and Umberto Nobile, who were flying the Italian-built airship *Norge* on May 12, 1926.

The question concerning whether or not Byrd and Bennett flew over the North Pole continues, and undoubtedly it will never be definitively answered. But, whatever the true result of Byrd's flight, Tony Fokker basked in the media attention that his aircraft received, albeit in the shadow of Byrd. The *Josephine Ford* was only the first of several Fokker trimotors that would achieve record flights that would be enshrined in the annals of aviation history. Already recognizing the historical significance of the aircraft in 1926, Edsel Ford purchased the *Josephine Ford* to be prominently displayed in the planned Henry Ford Museum, where it remains to this day.[6]

The first of Fokker's iconic trimotors, preserved and on display at the Henry Ford museum in Dearborn, Michigan.

Fokker F.VIIa/3m Josephine Ford
length: 47 ft 11 in (14.61 m)
wingspan: 63 ft 4 in (19.3 m)
power plant: three 200 hp Wright J-4 radials
cruising speed: 93 mph (150 km/h)
range: 620 miles (998 km)

The Misadventures of the *America*

The successful flight of the *Josephine Ford* laid the groundwork for another long-distance collaborative undertaking between Tony Fokker and Richard Byrd: nothing less than the first nonstop crossing of the Atlantic by a heavier-than-air aircraft. On July 9, 1926, Rodman Wannamaker, owner of the Philadelphia-based Wannamaker's department store franchise, who helped to fund Byrd's North Pole expedition, held a luncheon for Byrd and his polar team. There he announced his intention to fund a transatlantic flight, to be undertaken by Byrd, in the interest of the development of commercial aviation. Byrd accepted the opportunity with great enthusiasm and, with Wannamaker's funding, founded the American Trans-Oceanic Company to organize the flight. Having been pleased with the performance of the *Josephine Ford,* Byrd decided to have a new Fokker trimotor purpose-built for the flight.

The choice of a multi-engine aircraft was somewhat unusual for a transatlantic crossing because multi-engine aircraft typically had less range due to the weight

Diagram showing the interior layout of the America.

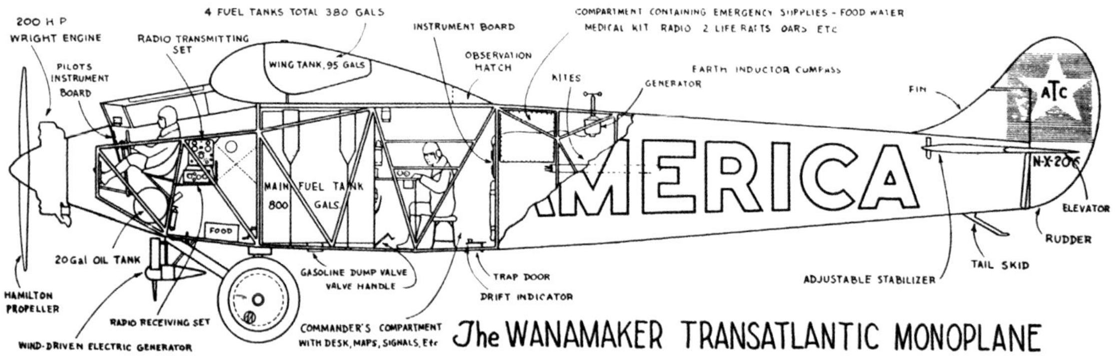

and relatively low horsepower of the contemporary engines. Byrd and Wannamaker, however, wanted to demonstrate that the transatlantic crossing in a multi-engine plane carrying passengers and cargo could be a practical commercial endeavor rather than a one-man stunt in a small single-engine plane. To this purpose, Fokker offered a civil version of his American-built C-2 transport, which he was building for the U.S. Army Air Corps. It had a larger wing than the *Josephine Ford,* which would give Byrd's aircraft a 3,000-pound payload increase. Much of the aircraft's weight would be dedicated to fuel, but Byrd intended to have two pilots, a navigator, a radioman, and 800 pounds of navigational, radio, and survival equipment. One of the more interesting devices Byrd had installed in the aircraft was a large kite that would carry the plane's radio antenna high into the air in the event of an emergency landing. Finally, Byrd intended to carry along a bag of mail, which would go down in history as the first transatlantic airmail.

On April 20, 1927, the new trimotor, christened *America,* was wheeled out of Fokker's factory at Teterboro. Tony Fokker intended to make the *America*'s test flight alone, but Byrd insisted that he, his pilot—who was again Floyd Bennett—and his radioman, George Noville, join him. Fokker was uneasy about bringing passengers up in an untested aircraft, but he consented nevertheless. From this point on, the short life of the *America* turned into a comedy of errors that unleashed a flurry of frustrations and recriminations between Fokker and Byrd that permanently soured relations between the two aviators.

As Fokker took the *America* aloft, the initial stage of the test flight went well. When the aircraft came in for a landing, however, something went wrong: as the *America* touched down, it nosed over and came to a halt on its back. Fokker escaped relatively unharmed from the crash, but Byrd suffered an injury to his left arm, Noville sustained internal injuries, and Bennett had a broken leg and internal injuries. Byrd claimed that when the plane touched the ground "I saw Fokker rise and make frantic efforts to jump out. Bennett was trapped as Fokker occupied the only exit. There was no way Noville and I could even try to get out."[7] Fokker was not amused in the least by Byrd's implication that he was cowardly, and he refuted it in his autobiography: "The weight of the engine then opened up a crack in the cockpit and I fell out on my head. Almost instantly a stream of hot oil covered my face and body as I scrambled to my feet. . . . Bennett was hanging head downward, and with a slight pull he almost dropped down, and I hauled him out."[8]

Observers on the ground confirmed Fokker's testimony of what happened during the crash landing. *The New York Times* reported:

> After the plane struck the ground, it ran along less than fifty yards before the tail suddenly shot up into the air, and the big machine went over on its nose, turning a somersault and landing flat on its back. Fokker was thrown clear of the machine and hurled on his face, but received no injuries except a few scratches and a shaking up. He jumped up in a few minutes and ran to the machine to aid his companions.
>
> Byrd, Bennett, and Noville were pinned underneath the machine, but Byrd was able to crawl out unaided.

He and Fokker hastened to help extricate Bennett and Noville. . . .[9]

Not only did Byrd try to portray Fokker as a coward, but he also neglected to mention how Fokker, after falling out of the aircraft, rushed to Bennett's aid. Precisely why Byrd decided to smear Fokker in that way is unknown, though it seems that he blamed Fokker for the crash and he became vindictive about events to come.

While Byrd, Bennett, and Noville were recovering in the hospital, Fokker immediately went to work repairing the *America*. Bernt Balchen, who was working for Fokker as a test pilot at the time, assisted Fokker with the repairs and had the trimotor already flying again by May 12, 1927 (Byrd erroneously wrote that the aircraft took a month to repair). While repairing the aircraft, Fokker and Balchen discovered that Bennett had not turned the stabilizer trim wheel in the cockpit to the lowest landing position, and that was partly to blame for the *America* flipping upon landing. Fokker also admitted that he had not anticipated what effects the larger wing would have on a slow landing and that he should never have allowed passengers aboard an untested aircraft. The *America* may have been ready for its transatlantic flight, but Byrd and his crew were not. Floyd Bennett's injuries were severe enough to keep him from flying for several months. Fokker immediately suggested Bernt Balchen as the replacement pilot, but Rodman Wannamaker insisted that the primary pilot be an "all-American"—even though the Norwegian Balchen was one of the best pilots in the world. Fokker selected Bert Acosta, a famous pilot who had once held the world speed record, and persuaded Wannamaker to allow Balchen to go along as a copilot since Acosta had no experience flying by instruments alone. This was to be a pivotal decision. Acosta and Balchen were ready to fly, but Byrd continued to delay the departure even though his and Noville's injuries had healed to the point where they could fly. Byrd claimed:

> I felt it important to go through a full series of scientific tests of plane and equipment, fuel and engine, in order

The overturned America *after its crash on April 20, 1927, which left Floyd Bennett injured and unable to participate in the transatlantic flight. The failed trial flight also led to a falling out between Fokker and Byrd, each of whom blamed the other for the accident.*

The crew that flew the America *to France (from left to right): Bert Acosta, Richard Byrd, George Noville, and Bernt Balchen.*

> that we should know exactly what our machine would do. To hasten this laboratory work for the sake of notoriety was to undermine the scientific character of our expedition.[10]

Despite Byrd's "scientific" excuses, Fokker could not figure out why Byrd did not take off. Byrd's seemingly endless tests and experiments irritated Fokker, who disdained scientific experimentation and "experts" throughout his career. Instead, he treated aeronautics in more of a hands-on, aesthetic sense: he admired fliers who gained expertise through experience rather than earthbound calculations.

Fokker found it somewhat fitting that, on the day before Byrd unveiled the *America* to the media and public, Charles Lindbergh took off for Paris in the *Spirit of Saint Louis* on May 20, 1927, from the same field on Long Island where Byrd was making his preparations. Fokker admired Lindbergh's ambition and less than scientific approach to flying. According to Fokker:

> I was the last person to have a long conversation with Lindbergh before he left, while mechanics were filling up the gas tanks. Something was said about Byrd. I told him Byrd, even though burdened with all his scientific equipment, had been ready for some time, yet showed no signs of leaving. I was glad that Lindbergh, playing a lone hand, should get a break.
>
> As soon as he climbed into his cockpit, I jumped into my Lancia and raced to the far end of the runway. My car was full of fire-fighting apparatus. . . .
>
> Fortunately, I had no use for the chemical extinguisher that morning. Lindbergh was off on the wings of destiny.[11]

The following day, as the world was celebrating Lindbergh's successful crossing, Byrd's unveiling of the *America* was simply a media footnote. Watching the celebrations around Roosevelt Field on Long Island, Fokker commented: "Byrd joined in, like a good sport, though it must have irked him to see the unscientific Lindbergh nose him out with as perfect a flight as the world has ever seen." Fokker and his ground crews prepared the *America* for takeoff on three separate occasions, but Byrd canceled each time. Furious, Fokker washed his hands of the enterprise and set sail on his yacht.

Finally, in the early morning hours of June 29, 1927, Byrd ordered the *America* be made ready for flight. The weather forecast was less than ideal, but he insisted that it was now time to go. The trimotor was pulled up to the top of a greased wooden slide, designed by Fokker, which gave the aircraft the equivalent of an additional 500-foot runway. At 5:24 a.m., with the engines running at full throttle, the rope that held the plane in place on top of the slide broke, and the fliers were suddenly on their way across the Atlantic. The heavily laden *America* rolled along the runway for forty-eight seconds before its wheels finally left the ground.

During the first several hours the fliers experienced rain; when they reached Nova Scotia, the skies cleared. But when the *America* reached Newfoundland, the landscape was covered with thick fog, which stretched across the entire ocean, so that the fliers would not be able to see anything below until they reached the French coast. Balchen had been a critical choice as copilot because most of the flight had to be conducted by instruments alone. The *America* flew over the French coast in the early morning hours of June 30, but it again encountered thick fog en route.

Byrd had calculated a course toward Paris, and at his estimated arrival time, Acosta and Balchen spotted a bright revolving light, which Byrd assumed was the tower spotlight at Le Bourget Field. He was wrong: on approach, the fliers discovered that the light belonged

The* America*, engines at full throttle, beginning its takeoff run down the wooden ramp designed by Fokker to help the aircraft build up enough speed to get into the air. [Museum of the United States Air Force]

The America *rests in the surf off of Ver-sur-Mer after the crew had made it safely ashore and before it was torn apart by local souvenir hunters.*

to a lighthouse on the French coast! Byrd's navigation had been way off. Byrd later claimed that their position was due to "some local affection of the compass in the plane, or the pilot's dial had stuck badly."[12] At that point Balchen took the controls and began to navigate toward Paris. But when they arrived over the city, it was storming and Le Bourget could not be located with certainty.

Byrd decided to return to the lighthouse they had spotted earlier and make a landing in the sea because the storm and fog were obscuring the ground below. Though Byrd later wrote how he heroically decided to save his crew at that point, Balchen told Fokker after the flight what the mood in the aircraft was really like:

> Byrd seemed confused and entirely lost; Acosta was a physical wreck; Noville, by damaging his radio, had destroyed his sole usefulness.
>
> Through the black night, whipped by storms, Balchen steered resolutely back to the coast. He communicated with Byrd by notes. One of Byrd's queries read:
>
> "Are we going to crash?"
>
> "Hell, no!" Balchen replied.[13]

Upon reaching the lighthouse, Balchen cruised along the beach until he found a shallow place to land. The crew dropped flares onto the water, creating a navigational aide for Balchen to land. As he slowly brought the plane down, the first impact tore away the landing gear,

In the summer of 1928, Richard Byrd embarked on his first Antarctic expedition in which he would make the first flight over the South Pole in the Ford trimotor Floyd Bennett. *In addition to the Ford, Byrd brought two other aircraft on his expedition: a Fairchild FC-2 monoplane named* Stars and Stripes *and a Fokker Super Universal named* Virginia. *Byrd and veteran pilot Bernt Balchen made several survey flights in the* Virginia *but on March 13, 1929, a storm came in and high winds tore the Fokker from its moorings. The aircraft was thrown airborne and then smashed onto the ice. Here Byrd examines the wreck of the* Virginia.

and on the second impact the plane came to an abrupt halt at 2:30 a.m.[14]

The fliers climbed up onto the wing of the aircraft, and Noville dragged an inflatable rubber boat out of the emergency compartment on top of the fuselage. After pumping up the boat and collecting the mail and other objects for delivery, including pieces of the Betsy Ross original American flag, the exhausted fliers rowed their way toward land. Byrd and his party came ashore at Ver-sur-Mer in Normandy. This was the beach that became known as Omaha Beach, where thousands of American soldiers were to storm ashore just seventeen years later. The crew of the *America* made their way to the lighthouse, and, after convincing the lighthouse keeper and his wife in broken French that they were not a group of transients looking for a place to stay but transatlantic fliers who had just arrived from America, they were finally welcomed in. The fliers were eventually taken from the Ver-sur-Mer lighthouse to Paris and greeted to a hero's welcome similar to the one Lindbergh received, despite being the third aircraft to cross the Atlantic and having made a forced landing in the sea on arrival. While the fliers were in Paris, Norman locals and souvenir hunters pulled the *America* ashore and stripped much of the aircraft. Upon arrival in New York, Byrd became the first person to be honored with a second ticker-tape parade. Byrd was in the limelight again, and a Fokker aircraft gained an added amount of publicity. Nevertheless, Tony Fokker never forgave him for not ensuring that a Fokker trimotor was the first plane to cross the Atlantic. But while Fokker was frustrated with Byrd and the *America* flight, he was able at the same time to rejoice about the triumph in the record flight of another of his aircraft.[15]

Bird of Paradise

Before Richard Byrd and the *America* were halfway across the Atlantic, another Fokker trimotor made a historical long-range flight, which was unfortunately somewhat overshadowed by the worldwide euphoria over "Lucky Lindy" and his transatlantic crossing. Now that the Atlantic had been conquered, aviation promoters were looking for other horizons to pursue. On the other side of the country, the first nonstop flight from the continental United States to Hawaii was being discussed as the route for the world's next major aviation prize. Before any civilian could make the attempt, however, the U.S. Army Air

When Byrd returned to the United States from his Little America base in Antarctic in 1930, he left the wreck of the Fokker Super Universal Virginia *behind. The wreck is still there to this day in the Rockefeller Mountains and has been visited several times in recent years. This photo shows the wreck in December 1998. The frame is clearly visible as well as one of the engine cylinders and a ski.* [Photo courtesy of Max Wenden]

The Bird of Paradise *flies west over San Francisco Bay, headed for Hawaii, on June 28, 1927.* [Museum of the United States Air Force]

Tony Fokker with Army Air Corps fliers Lieutenant Lester J. Maitland and Lieutenant Albert F. Hegenberger. The flight of the Bird of Paradise, *through sheer coincidence, occurred almost simultaneously with Byrd's transatlantic flight in the* America, *and it gave Fokker a tidal wave of publicity for his reliable trimotors.* [Museum of the United States Air Force]

Corps set into motion its plans for such a flight, which it had been considering for years beforehand. Beginning already in 1919, Army Air Service pilots had petitioned their superiors to attempt a flight to Hawaii; on every occasion they had been turned down. But in late 1926 the Air Corps acquired its first Fokker C-2, an aircraft that had the necessary range to make the trip to Hawaii. Furthermore, the Air Corps had developed a system of radio beacons and radio direction-finding equipment that would aid an aircraft to navigate across such a long distance to a point on the map that could easily be flown past by a slight deviation in compass bearing. After successful tests with a Fokker C-2 and the radio equipment, on June 24, 1927, the secretary of war authorized an Air Corps flight to Hawaii.

The two pilots selected for the mission were Lieutenant Lester J. Maitland, who in 1926 convinced his superior, the assistant secretary of war for air, that such a flight was feasible; and Lieutenant Albert F. Hegenberger, who was considered the best navigator in the Army Air Corps. As several civilian pilots were simultaneously preparing their own attempts at the first nonstop flight to Hawaii, the Air Corps decided that the mission could begin on June 28, 1927. At Oakland Municipal Airport, outside of San Francisco, Maitland and Hegenberger boarded their Fokker C-2, now named the *Bird of Paradise.* The aircraft was a flying telecommunications center and navigation room: aboard were radio receivers and transmitters; an earth inductor compass; several magnetic compasses; various navigational tools; and finally, the most important instrument of the ancient mariner, a sextant. The plane was also loaded with emergency rations, five gallons of drinking water, and a rubber raft in the event that the pilots had to ditch in the ocean.

On June 28 at 7:09 a.m., Maitland and Hegenberger boarded the *Bird of Paradise,* revved the engines, took off, and passed over the Golden Gate as they headed out into the vast Pacific. Much of the success of the mission fell on Hegenberger's shoulders; he had to check his bearings constantly and measure for drift, a challenging task when, about two hours into its flight, the *Bird of Paradise* encountered rain and heavy winds. Periodically, Hegenberger checked his bearings via radio contact with ships that were steaming along their route. As the day gave way to night, Maitland took the Fokker above the clouds so that Hegenberger could calculate their course by the stars. Hegenberger concluded that they would arrive over Hawaii before daylight, so Maitland reduced speed in order to avoid having to make a landing in the dark. Even so, they arrived over Kauai before daybreak and circled the island until the sun came up. At 6:29 a.m., the *Bird of Paradise* came in for a landing at Wheeler Field on Oahu after a 25-hour, 50-minute flight. The Army Air Corps had achieved a significant publicity coup, and Maitland and Hegenberger temporarily became the darlings of the media. They even received praise from America's greatest aviation hero, Charles Lindbergh, who called their mission "the most perfectly organized and carefully planned flight ever attempted." Maitland and Hegenberger also received praised from Tony Fokker. Obviously, the flight of the *Bird of Paradise* put the Fokker aircraft in a positive spotlight once again and created a great deal of publicity that boosted sales of Fokker's proven trimotor design.[16]

The interior of the* Bird of Paradise *looking forward toward the cockpit from the navigator's position in the rear of the plane. Note the large fuel tank in the middle of the cabin and the navigator's radio set in the foreground to the left. This photo also gives a good idea of a Fokker trimotor's steel tube-wood-canvas construction. [Museum of the United States Air Force]

The navigator's aperiodic compass in the rear of the aircraft. A compass that did not oscillate when an aircraft changed headings or made abrupt movements due to turbulence was vital for correct navigation. [Museum of the United States Air Force]

The *Southern Cross*

While Richard Byrd had failed to make the Fokker trimotor the first aircraft to cross the Atlantic nonstop, the first aircraft to fly across the Pacific was indeed a Fokker. The origins of this achievement began not along the Pacific rim but rather in the Arctic. In 1926 the Australian-born explorer George Hubert Wilkins began to plan an aerial expedition to the North Pole and, after considering the success Richard Byrd had had the previous year, ordered a Fokker F.VIIa and the first F.VIIb/3m trimotor directly from the Fokker company. The expedition was funded by the *Detroit News* newspaper and was named the *Detroit News* Arctic Expedition. The two aircraft were built in Amsterdam and shipped to Alaska, but a series of misfortunes plagued the expedition. The F.VIIa, named *Alaskan,* broke its wing during a rough landing, and the

Above *Australian pilot Charles Kingsford-Smith and his Fokker F.VIIb3/m* Southern Cross, *affectionately nicknamed the "Old Bus." Kingsford-Smith flew the first transpacific flight in the aircraft and eventually circumnavigated the globe in it.* [Photo AVIODROME Luchtfotografie, Lelystad, Holland]

Below *The* Southern Cross *is preserved at the Kingsford-Smith Memorial at Brisbane Airport in Australia.* [Image provided by Brisbane Airport Corporation. Photographer: Bob Jones]

F.VIIb/3m, named *Detroiter,* broke its undercarriage—also in a bad landing. It would take a long time to make the repairs on the two aircraft in such primitive conditions, so Wilkins decided to cancel the expedition due to the projected delays. He shipped the remains of the *Alaskan* and the *Detroiter* to Seattle, where he hired Boeing to repair the damaged trimotors.

While this was underway, an Australian aviator who was shopping for an airplane that he could fly across the Pacific heard of Wilkins's misfortunes. The aviator's name was Charles Kingsford-Smith, a veteran of the British Royal Flying Corps who had flown SPAD fighters in No. 23 Squadron during World War I. Kingsford-Smith (nicknamed "Smithy") and his copilot, Charles Ulm, had just completed a flight around the entire coastline of Australia, and now they wanted to attempt a flight from the United States to Australia, which would be the world's first transpacific flight. After the around-Australia flight, Kingsford-Smith and Ulm received some funding from the Australian government for their transpacific plan, so the two aviators set sail to the United States. After observing long-range flights that had already been made, the two Australians decided that the most suitable plane for a transpacific flight would be a Fokker trimotor. Richard Byrd had used them on two occasions, and the first nonstop flight from the American west coast to Hawaii had been achieved in a Fokker trimotor. According to Kingsford-Smith:

> It was patent to us or to any one after a study of these important facts that the Fokker undoubtedly was the plane to lift the load, and the Wright Whirlwind motors were undoubtedly the engines to push the Fokker through with sufficient power to meet all requirements.
>
> By one of those strange coincidences, or perhaps it may have been Fate, just as our opinion of the Fokker plane had soared very high indeed, we were brought, so to speak, to close quarters with a Fokker. Quite suddenly and unexpectedly a Fokker was placed within our reach. It was a telegram to us in San Francisco from Sir George Wilkins, who was then in Seattle, that completed this coincidence.

Sir George Wilkins told us in the telegram that he had a Fokker plane that he could sell to us without engines or instruments. We telegraphed back to Seattle, telling Sir George Wilkins that we were decidedly interested in the offer, and asking him to come down to San Francisco to tell us all about the plane. He came down, and in the course of many long chats, we gained a vast fund of valuable information from him. . . .[17]

Kingsford-Smith and Ulm had found their plane; now they had to figure out how to get engines for the plane and, more important, how to pay for it.

The first step for the Australian aviators was to find and purchase three new Wright Whirlwind engines for their Fokker. They contacted the Wright factory only to learn to their dismay that the factory was behind in the production of over eighty engines that had previously been ordered, most of them by the U.S. army and navy. In an effort to expedite the process in obtaining the engines needed for the plane—and through the mediation of the British ambassador to the United States and the Australian commissioner—Kingsford-Smith and Ulm approached the Department of the Navy in San Francisco to see whether they could obtain three of the Whirlwind engines being completed for the navy in return for three engines to be completed later. Admiral Christian J. Peoples, whom the fliers first met with, emphatically declared that he would have nothing to do with a transpacific flight, which he considered a suicidal enterprise. He then called in his adjutant, Lieutenant Ben Wyatt, who was himself a long-distance pilot, and asked Wyatt to further talk the Aussies out of the transpacific flight, as Kingsford-Smith and Ulm related in their book *The Flight of the Southern Cross:*

"If that's what they're going to do," said Wyatt, "I do not want anything to do with them. I don't want to know anything about such an idea. I do not know what equipment you are going to use or anything about it."

This was a little discouraging, as we had expected more sympathy with our plan from Wyatt. But at last, after this devastating barrage of criticism, there came a lull. We could talk. Wyatt was pacing about the room in an impatient way.

"We are going to use a three-motored Fokker," we said.

Wyatt grabbed a chair and sat down.

"Now, that's different," he said.

They were magic words those—"a three-motored Fokker."

"That is different," Wyatt and Admiral Peoples repeated in unison.

They were now both in a much more amiable mood. Their faces were wreathed in smiles. They got down to talking the thing over in a calm and even a sympathetic way. It was an amazing change.[18]

A "three-motored Fokker"—what more could be said for the reputation of Tony Fokker's aircraft! With the help of the navy and other interested military officials, Kingsford-Smith and Ulm were able to obtain three of the U.S. government's Whirlwind engines, and the Fokker trimotor would soon be ready to fly.

However, the political situation back in Australia cast an ominous cloud over the enterprise. A new government

The Southern Cross ***taking off from Oakland on the first leg of its journey across the Pacific.***

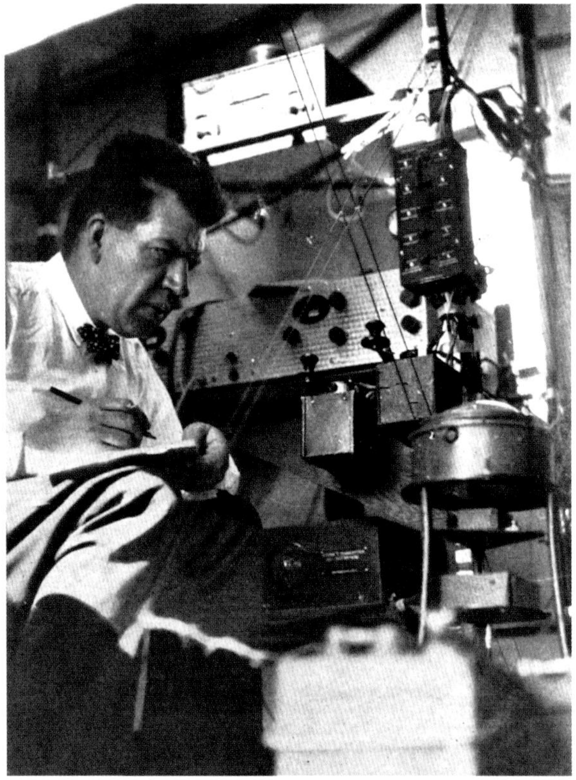

These two images show the interior of the Southern Cross *and some of its navigational equipment: Harry Lyon (right) taking readings from the earth inductor compass, an instrument first used in aircraft in 1924 that was more accurate than a standard magnetic compass. Jim Warner (below) is at the radio set. In the background of this photo one gets a good view of the welded-steel fuselage frame covered with canvas from the outside.*

had been elected, and it decided to withdraw government funding for the transpacific flight of Kingsford-Smith and Ulm, telling the pilots to give up the venture and sell the aircraft. Downcast, the pilots put the plane up for sale. But in March 1928, out of the blue, the pilots were invited to visit Captain G. Allan Hancock, a wealthy California rancher who asked them to join him for a cruise aboard his yacht, where he asked them about their planned flight. The fliers had no idea what Hancock's interest in their venture might be, but at the end of the cruise the latter told them he would purchase the Fokker and give it to them for their attempted flight across the Pacific. The dream of the transpacific flight was about to become a reality.

On the morning of May 31, 1928, Kingsford-Smith and Ulm, along with their navigator, Harry Lyon, and radio operator, Jim Warner, prepared for takeoff:

> [W]hen Kingsford-Smith took his seat at the controls, there was a rush of people anxious for a final handshake. After seeing that everything was O.K. in the after cabin Ulm was the last to enter the plane. The three motors had been warmed up. . . . It was 8:54 AM when we finally took off. The roar of those three great engines quickly assumed for us the pleasing grandeur of a symphony of great music. Their racket normally grated heavily on the eardrums, but so long as they roared in harmony no Wagnerian chorus could have given us greater pleasure.[19]

The Fokker, with the name *Southern Cross* painted across the rear fuselage, cruised away from the gray mists of San Francisco and out into the endless blue. The fact that there were four men aboard the aircraft helped to create a sense of companionship among the fliers, something that helped to ease each man's vigil at his post. Nevertheless, the monotony of hour after hour of staring at the same horizon and control panels took its toll on the mind and body.[20]

Despite the boredom, the *Southern Cross* arrived over the Hawaiian Islands at about 9:00 a.m. on June 1 and landed safely at Wheeler Field in Honolulu at 12:17 p.m.

The first of the flight's three stages had been accomplished. When the *Southern Cross* touched down on Wheeler Field, the fliers were greeted by a large crowd. As is the Hawaiian custom for all those arriving by air, the Hawaiians placed leis around the crew members' necks. This was to be the first of three tumultuous greetings for the crew. After several receptions and some sleep, the fliers took off for Suva in the Fiji Islands at dawn on June 3. Sporadic rain squalls made this leg of the journey more eventful than the first leg to Honolulu, but the *Southern Cross* landed on Suva at 3:50 p.m., June 4, 34 hours and 30 minutes after departing Hawaii. On Suva the fliers were given an ecstatic welcome by a crowd of natives, most of whom had never seen an airplanc before.[21]

After a few days in that tropical paradise, the *Southern Cross* continued with its trek, taking off from Suva at 2:52 p.m. on June 8. The tropical climate of the Fiji Islands gave way to a colder climate, and then worse, to a series of storms that shook the plane and its crew alike. Heavy rains made controlling the aircraft difficult. According to Kingsford-Smith:

> As we flattened out, the assault of the stream of water was too much for the glass windshields. They began to leak near the joint under the wings above us. First came a steady drip of water on to our knees. Then the drip became a shower, and often a cascade, till the pants of our overalls became sodden. The water poured down into our boots, and we faced more miserable hours. Our feet became thoroughly wet, and our legs got numb with the intense cold and dampness. As we tore through the rain and darkness the cold became merciless. The blasts that puffed round the edges of the windshield and slapped our faces, which were already streaming with rain water, seemed as bitter as any whiff from Antarctic floes.[22]

The storms lasted for six hours during the night, but Kingsford-Smith and Ulm braved the elements and stayed on course. After a cold and miserable night, the sun came with the dawn and the Australian coast was in sight at 9:50 a.m. on June 6. An hour later the *Southern Cross* landed at Brisbane, the first aircraft to have crossed the Pacific Ocean. Kingsford-Smith, Ulm, and the rest of the crew were the toast of Australia, as well as the rest of the world. They had been in the air for 83 hours and 11 minutes, almost twice the time it took Richard Byrd to fly across the Atlantic.

The crew of the* Southern Cross *upon arrival in Sydney: Jim Warner, Charles Ulm, Charles Kingsford-Smith, and Harry Lyon.

THE *FRIENDSHIP* OF AMELIA EARHART

In the spring of 1928, a wealthy Englishwoman named Amy Guest, wife of the former British air minister Frederick Guest, decided that she wanted to be the first woman to fly across the Atlantic. She had leased a brand new

The Friendship *was a Fokker F.VIIb3/m originally ordered by Richard Byrd for his 1928 Antarctic expedition and was subsequently sold to Amy Guest, the American-born wife of the British secretary of state for air. Instead, Byrd used a Ford trimotor, the* Floyd Bennett, *on his Antarctic expedition; the* Friendship *went on to carry the first woman across the Atlantic—Amelia Earhart.* [Museum of the United States Air Force]

Fokker F.VIIb/3m, which had been ordered by Richard Byrd for his expedition to the Antarctic. Byrd was forced to find another buyer for his Fokker when the sponsor of his Antarctic expedition, Henry Ford, "reminded" him that Ford also had a trimotor aircraft available for a flight that would garner a great deal of publicity. The particular Fokker trimotor that Byrd had ordered was the fourth production example of the F.VIIb/3m. The Jell-O magnate Donald Woodward purchased it from Byrd on behalf of Amy Guest's transatlantic plan. But Guest's family did not approve of her planned adventure, so she decided instead to *sponsor* the first flight to carry a woman across the Atlantic.

Guest entrusted her lawyer with the task of finding an American woman who was a pilot—and was also attractive, well educated, well mannered, and publicly acceptable to English society. Guest's lawyer turned the search project over to publisher George Putnam, who had just published Richard Byrd's book *Skyward,* and Captain Hilton Railey, an aviation publicist. The men learned about a young social worker in Boston who happened to have a pilot's license and who possessed the qualities sought by Amy Guest. The young woman's name was Amelia Earhart, and Railey interviewed her in his office in April 1928. At that time, Earhart's only claim to fame was that she was the sixteenth woman in the world to have obtained a pilot's license. But she flew only when time and money would permit, and both were limited to her.

Richard Byrd, who had known about the project from the first and who happened to be an associate of Putnam, offered to pick a crew for the flight. Wilmer ("Bill") Stultz, who was a veteran of both the Army and Navy Air Services and who worked for Fokker as a test pilot, was selected as the pilot of the *Friendship.* The copilot/mechanic whom Byrd selected was Louis Edward ("Slim") Gordon, also a veteran of the Army Air Service. Amy Guest had stipulated that Earhart be the commander of the flight, and she was given that title—albeit nominally. At the time Earhart had no experience flying multi-engine aircraft, and the flying would be left to Stultz and Gordon. Furthermore, the new team kept their plans for the flight secret, and

Earhart never even went to the hangar where the Fokker was stored. There were other challengers in the race to become the first woman to cross the Atlantic, and any publicity before the flight would not be welcome. By early May, the *Friendship* had been flight-tested by veteran Fokker pilots Bernt Balchen and Floyd Bennett; now all the crew needed was good weather.[23]

The good weather came on June 3, 1928. At 4:30 a.m., Earhart, Stultz, and Gordon went out into the Boston harbor, where the *Friendship* was moored. The Guest family had decided to replace the Fokker's conventional landing gear with duralumin floats in case an emergency landing would have to be made en route (a number of aviators had already disappeared during transatlantic flight attempts). In addition, the fuselage of the plane was painted a bright red-orange, and the wings gold, to serve as a visual aid for rescuers in case the plane had to land in the ocean. The interior of the plane looked like a flying gasoline station: in addition to the two 95-gallon tanks in the wings, a second set of 95-gallon tanks had been mounted in the wings, and two 245-gallon tanks were loaded into the fuselage (it was thought that 870 gallons of fuel would be enough for the transatlantic flight). Stultz started the three 220-horsepower Wright Whirlwind engines and began to taxi on the water. After shedding some weight by dumping some fuel, he was able to get the *Friendship* airborne and on its way to Trepassey, Nova Scotia, the starting point for the transatlantic flight. For Amelia this was the most dangerous part of the trip, as she recalled:

> I tried to get a picture of the tugboats and harbor as we left, but just before starting the spring lock of the cabin door broke off, and I had to hold the door shut until Slim could get back to repair it. It was at first anchored to a gasoline can, but I saw the can being slowly pulled out, so anchored myself to it instead.
>
> So, a few minutes after the take-off we nearly lost two of our crew. That would have been a jolly beginning! Actually Slim came within inches of falling out when the door suddenly slid open. And when I dived for that gasoline can, edging towards the opening door, I, too, had a nar-

Wilmer Stultz looking back from the cockpit between two large fuel tanks. Fuel consumption was one of the most critical aspects of early transatlantic flights.

Travelers sailing on the liner SS* America *were treated to a rare sight on the morning of June 18: they spotted the* Friendship *approaching and circling overhead. The fliers, who wanted to check their current position, were unable to raise the ship on the radio, so Amelia Earhart attempted to drop two notes to the ship in paper bags weighted with oranges. Unfortunately, both missed.

row escape. However, a string tied through the leather thong in the door itself and fastened to a brace inside the cabin held it shut fairly securely.[24]

With the exception of Amelia's novice attempt at aerial photography, the rest of the flight to Nova Scotia proceeded without further mishap.

The *Friendship* arrived at Trepassey on the afternoon of June 4, but the crew was disappointed to find the weather abysmal: no takeoff attempt could be made in the continuous gales and fog. Boredom set in rapidly among the *Friendship*'s crew at Trepassey, as the tiny fishing community had little to offer in the way of entertainment. Stultz and Gordon continuously looked after the plane, while Earhart visited a small convent school to study maps of the Atlantic in the school's library. The three also passed the time playing cards. When Putnam sent Earhart a telegram saying: "SUGGEST YOU GO INTO RETIREMENT TEMPORARILY WITH NUNS AND HAVE THEM WASH SHIRT ETC." Amelia jokingly replied: "THANKS FATHERLY TELEGRAM NO WASHING NECESSARY SOCKS UNDERWEAR WORN-OUT SHIRT LOST TO SLIM AT RUMMY CHEERIO."

The poor weather continued for days on end, and eventually Stultz and Gordon began to drown their miseries excessively at the local tavern, much to Earhart's chagrin. Finally, on the morning of June 17, the weather at Trepassey was calm with a gentle tailwind. Gordon and Earhart pumped black coffee into Stultz, who was still hung-over from the night before, and the three hurried out to the plane. After two unsuccessful attempts to take off, the crew decided to drain more fuel, until only 700 gallons remained, the minimum amount calculated to get the plane to Ireland. Finally, on the third attempt, after pushing the engines at full throttle for three miles, Stultz managed to get the *Friendship* airborne. There was no turning back. Takeoff occurred in clear weather just before noon, but as the fliers headed out over the Atlantic, the cloud cover became heavy again, and Stultz had to climb to ten thousand feet to avoid turbulence. Due to the thick clouds below, Stultz and Gordon would fly entirely by instruments, occasionally picking up bearings from passing ships below. Amelia sat in the fuselage between the two giant fuel tanks, occasionally sitting in the cockpit when Stultz or Gordon took a break or went to examine the charts on the map table in the rear of the cabin. They kept each other alert during the night, and relief came when daylight gradually appeared over the horizon.

As dawn gave way to morning, however, the fliers began to grow anxious. They were no longer receiving any radio signals, and by 9:00 a.m. (GMT) they had only two hours' worth of fuel left. By Stultz's calculations, they should have passed over Ireland an hour before; but after they dropped to 3,000 feet to get below the cloud cover, all they saw was open ocean. Eventually they spotted an ocean liner in the distance, and that must have been a welcome sight. But they were unable to get the radio to work—so that they could get their bearings. Three thousand feet below, the passengers of the SS *America* were treated to a rare sound and sight: a far-off rumbling they could hear for several minutes before a Fokker airliner appeared cruising overhead. The captain of the *America* realized that the unidentified plane was probably attempting a transatlantic crossing, and he ordered that the ship's current position be boldly painted in white on the deck. But just as the ship's crew began to paint, the plane flew off. After Earhart's attempts to contact the ship by radio proved futile, the crew decided to resume their easterly course, gambling that they would eventually reach land. In her memoir of that flight, Earhart describes their efforts at communicating.

> We circled the America, although having no idea of her identity at the time. With the radio crippled, in an effort to get our position, Bill scribbled a note. The note and an orange to weight it, I tied in a bag with an absurd piece of silver cord. As we circled the America, the bag was dropped through the hatch. But the combination of our speed, the movement of the vessel, the wind and the lightness of the missile was too much for our marksmanship. We tried another shot, using our remaining orange. No luck.

> Should we seek safety and try to come down beside the steamer? Perhaps one reason the attempt was never undertaken was the roughness of the sea, which not only made a landing difficult but a take-off impossible.
>
> Bill leaped to the radio with the hope of at least receiving a message. At some moment in the excitement, before I closed the hatch which opens in the bottom of the fuselage, I lay flat and took a photograph. This, I am told, is the first one made of a vessel at sea from a plane in trans-Atlantic flight.
>
> Then we turned back to the original course, retracing the twelve mile detour made to circle the steamer. In a way we were polling all our chances and placing everything in a final wager on our original judgment.[25]

An anxious half-hour passed before they spotted another vessel, this time a small fishing boat, and then another, and then a fleet of small boats all headed on the same course.

Finally, after another hour, they spotted a coastline, and after searching for a suitable place to land, Stultz brought the *Friendship* down in a sheltered bay. He then taxied up to a buoy, Gordon opened the door, and the fliers had their first glimpse of the Old World. While Gordon moored the plane to the buoy, Earhart looked out onto a small factory town at the end of the bay. They had landed just off the small hamlet of Burry Point in South Wales, and she recorded their first contact with the locals:

> We could see factories in the distance and hear the hum of activity. Houses dotted the green hillside. We were some distance off shore but the beach looked muddy and barren. The only people in sight were three men working on a railroad track at the base of the hill. To them we waved, and Slim yelled lustily for service.
>
> Finally they noticed us, straightened up and even went so far as to walk down to the shore and look us over. Then their animation died out and they went back to their work. The *Friendship* simply wasn't interesting. An itinerant trans-Atlantic plane meant nothing.

Earhart peeks out the door of the Friendship *after landing in Great Britain.*

Anthony Fokker with Amelia Earhart and Wilmer Stultz. [National Air and Space Museum]

In the meantime three or four more people had gathered to look at us. To Slim's call for a boat we had no answer. I waved a towel desperately out the front windows and one friendly soul pulled off his coat and waved back.

It must have been nearly an hour before the first boats came out. Our first visitor was Norman Fisher who arrived in a dory. Bill went ashore with him and telephoned our friends at Southampton while Slim and I remained on the *Friendship*. A vigorous ferry service was soon instituted and many small boats began to swarm about us.[26]

Stultz went ashore aboard one of the boats and contacted Capt. Railey in Southampton, who arrived by seaplane several hours later. Word spread quickly throughout the community, and by the time Earhart was rowed ashore, a huge crowd had gathered by the seaside. This was to be the first of many such receptions for "Lady Lindy," as Earhart was soon dubbed. She would quickly become the toast of both sides of the Atlantic and would go on to have a remarkable aviation career. Stultz, Gordon, and the *Friendship* were virtually ignored by the onslaught of the media, even though they had accomplished the feat. The public was obsessed by the spectacle of the first female to fly the Atlantic. But the groundbreaking flight that launched Amelia Earhart's aviation career in the public eye must be attributed to two skilled pilots and, most important, the rugged design and reliability of Fokker's *Friendship*.

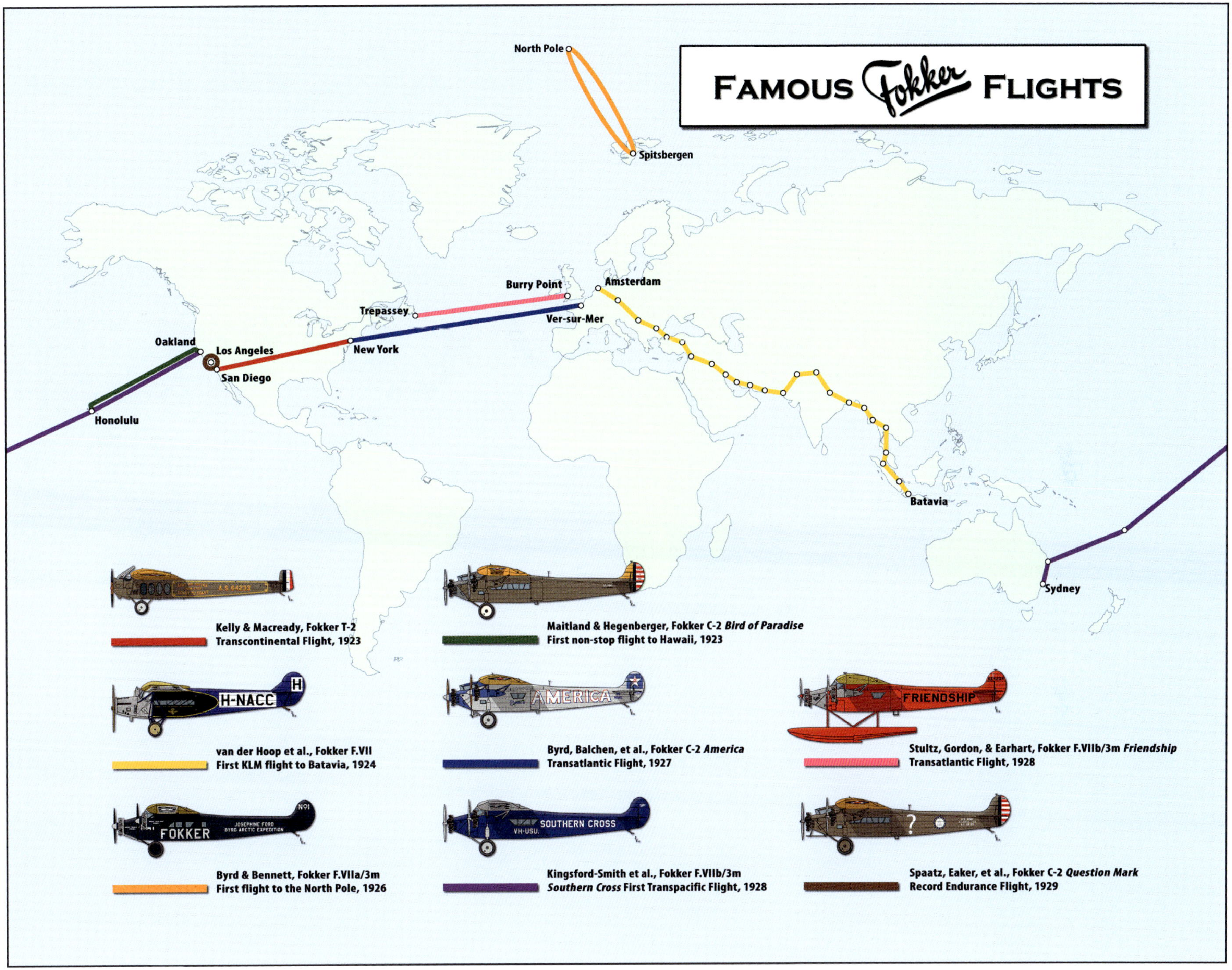
Famous Fokker Flights
North Pole
Spitsbergen
Amsterdam
Burry Point
Trepassey
Ver-sur-Mer
Oakland
Los Angeles
San Diego
New York
Honolulu
Batavia
Sydney
A.S. 64233
Kelly & Macready, Fokker T-2
Transcontinental Flight, 1923
Maitland & Hegenberger, Fokker C-2 *Bird of Paradise*
First non-stop flight to Hawaii, 1923
H
H-NACC
van der Hoop et al., Fokker F.VII
First KLM flight to Batavia, 1924
AMERICA
Byrd, Balchen, et al., Fokker C-2 *America*
Transatlantic Flight, 1927
FRIENDSHIP
Stultz, Gordon, & Earhart, Fokker F.VIIb/3m *Friendship*
Transatlantic Flight, 1928
FOKKER
JOSEPHINE FORD
BYRD ARCTIC EXPEDITION
Byrd & Bennett, Fokker F.VIIa/3m
First flight to the North Pole, 1926
SOUTHERN CROSS
VH-USU.
Kingsford-Smith et al., Fokker F.VIIb/3m
Southern Cross First Transpacific Flight, 1928
?
Spaatz, Eaker, et al., Fokker C-2 *Question Mark*
Record Endurance Flight, 1929

The tarmac at Schiphol Airport in the late 1930s. Gone are the old wood and canvas Fokker trimotors, replaced by modern and streamlined Douglas DC-3 airliners. KLM experienced rapid worldwide expansion and modernization over the course of the decade. [Photo AVIODROME Luchtfotografie, Lelystad, Holland]

Chapter Five

EAST INDIAMEN OF THE AIR

Depressing Peace and Peaceful Depression

As the 1930s began, the effects of the Great Depression, coupled with the effects of a decade of relative peace throughout the world, began to erode the dominating position held by Fokker in both military and civilian aviation circles. Military defense budgets were continually slashed during the 1920s in the wake of the Treaty of Versailles, and governments cut further defense funds as the world's economy continued to spiral downward. On the other hand, civil aviation experienced some growth: new routes were opened, and a consistent number of dedicated passengers still existed. The era of the pioneering and dangerous distance flights was beginning to wane as aviation became less an adventure and more a regular mode of travel. This was due in large part to modern advances in streamlining and the new all-metal construction techniques. Initiated in the United States and Germany, those advances came to be adopted by aircraft manufacturers as the decade moved forward. However, the new technology and construction techniques were expensive for aircraft manufacturers to implement, and since they were receiving only a trickle of both military and civilian orders as the growth in air travel was limited by the effects of the Depression in the first half of the decade, few could afford to convert their factories to accommodate all-metal construction.

Fokker refused to upgrade his factory unless his primary customers, namely, the Dutch Ministry of Defense and KLM, would help subsidize such improvements. After the 1931 Knute Rockne crash and the closure of his American factories, it would not have been fiscally wise for Fokker to independently undertake a modernization program without substantial orders or investment to make up the loss. Furthermore, since all-metal construction was still relatively new at the beginning of the decade, and few airlines could afford these expensive new aircraft, Fokker saw no need to immediately modernize; he figured that his designers could still develop competitive aircraft using his traditional construction methods.

Fokker's first civil transports of the 1930s were simply refinements of his proven F.VIIb/3m design. The F.XII was a trimotor transport ordered by KLM for a new regular service between Amsterdam and Batavia, which would begin in the fall of 1931. It was designed to be larger than the F.VIIb/3m (but smaller than the F.IX) and have better performance. The prototype F.XII first flew on December 5, 1930, powered by three 425-horsepower Pratt & Whitney Wasp radial engines. Compared to the F.VIIb/3m, the F.XII had a longer fuselage, which could accommodate fourteen passengers on European routes and four

Despite the onset of the Depression business along the Amsterdam-Batavia route remained steady at the beginning of the 1930s. KLM's Plesman needed an airliner that was larger than the F.VII/3m but not as large as the F.IX. In late 1930, Fokker presented Plesman with the F.XII design, a trimotor that had better performance than the F.VII/3m and had a passenger capacity of four to six on the Indies route and fourteen to sixteen on European routes. Plesman purchased eight F.XIIs exclusively for Amsterdam-Batavia service. The profile below shows the F.XII **Ibis**. *The wheel covers were later removed because mud from grass runways would tend to clog them.* [Photo AVIODROME Luchtfotografie, Lelystad, Holland]

Two passengers enjoying drinks served by the flight steward on a European-route Fokker F.XII. KLM prided itself on the professional and civilized nature of its service. [Photo AVIODROME Luchtfotografie, Lelystad, Holland]

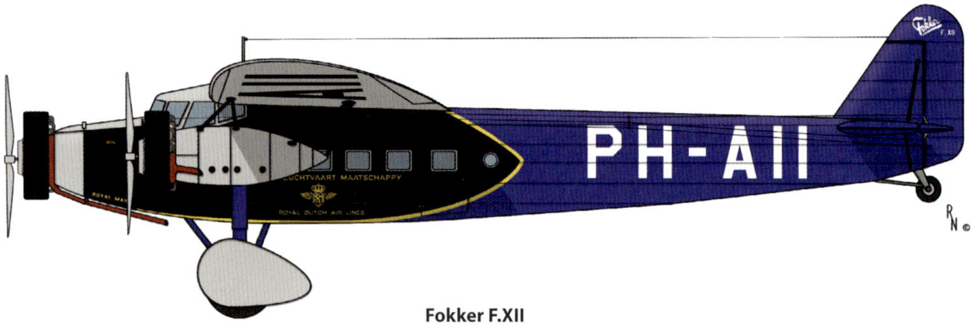

Fokker F.XII
length: 58 ft 5 in (17.8 m)
wingspan: 75 ft. 6 in (23.02 m)
engines: three 425 hp Pratt & Whitney Wasp C radials
cruising speed: 127 mph (205 km/h)
range: 920 miles (1,480 km)
crew: 3-4
passengers: 4-6 (Indies configuration), 14-16 (European routes)

to six passengers on the Amsterdam-Batavia route. KLM ordered eight F.XIIs for the Amsterdam-Batavia route, all of which were equipped with comfortable reclining chairs for the long flight. The first F.XII went into service in March 1931 and reached Batavia in eighty-one hours of flying time. The KNILM bought two F.XIIs, and the Swedish airline Aktie Bolaget Aerotransport (ABA) purchased one; but no other orders were placed for the transport.

Compared to the many F.VII variants sold in the late 1920s, the sale of only eleven F.XIIs did not project an encouraging market forecast, further convincing Fokker that technological investment would probably not bring any dividends at that time. This thinking could be seen in the design of Fokker's next trimotor: when KLM requested a new transport that would be slightly faster than the F.XII, Fokker offered the F.XVIII, a new trimotor that was essentially an F.XII with a longer but narrower fuselage and a handful of other small aerodynamic refinements. The entire research and design costs for the F.XVIII amounted to less than 800 guilders! This epitomized Fokker's posture at that time: do not invest in research at a time when large orders cannot be guaranteed. Despite Fokker's nonchalant attitude toward the aircraft's design, the F.XVII was indeed faster than the F.XII, and it reduced the flying time of the Amsterdam-Batavia route to just seventy-five and a half hours. KLM purchased five of that aircraft, and those were the only F.XVIIIs ever produced.[1]

While KLM's F.XIIs were being built, Plesman requested a new airliner from Fokker that would be faster and have a larger cabin for more passengers. In these respects, the resulting F.XVIII, with a maximum speed that was only 9 mph faster than the F.XII and still with seating for 4-6 passengers, was hardly much of an improvement. Despite this, the F.XVIII proved to be a popular and reliable aircraft. Two F.XVIIIs, the Pelikaan *and* Snip, *also brought a great deal of publicity to KLM with their respective Christmas mail flights to Batavia in 1933 and Curaçao in 1934. The profile featured here is the F.XVIII* Pelikaan. [R. E. G. Davies Collection]

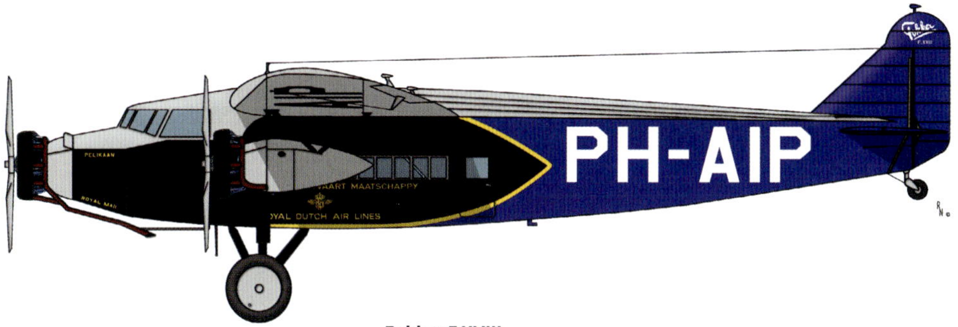

Fokker F.XVIII
length: 60 ft 8 in (18.5 m)
wingspan: 80 ft 5 in (24.5 m)
engines: three 440 hp Pratt & Whitney Wasp C radials
cruising speed: 126 mph (203 km/h)
range: 930 miles (1,500 km)
crew: 3-4
passengers: 4-6 (Indies configuration), 13 (European routes)

Dutch Domination of the Far Eastern Aerial Trade Route

During the 1930s, KLM's most prestigious and highly touted air route was its Amsterdam-Batavia passenger service, which commenced on a weekly basis on October 1, 1931, using Fokker F.XII transports equipped with four sleeper-seats for the ten-day journey. At the time, KLM had a virtual monopoly on the aerial transport of passengers from Europe to the Far East. When KLM inaugurated its regular passenger service to Batavia, British Imperial Airways, KLM's primary competitor along the

The interior of a Fokker F.XII on the Amsterdam-Batavia route. The passenger cabin was appointed with beautiful inlaid wood paneling on the side walls. Fully reclining chairs allowed passengers to sleep if they wished to do so. In the rear of the cabin is a small pantry for light meals and drinks (note the silverware and the thermoses for soup and hot beverages); a restroom is located to the right of the pantry. [Photo AVIODROME Luchtfotografie, Lelystad, Holland]

route, could only take its passengers as far as India. A Handley Page H.P. 42 four-engine biplane flew from London to Paris; then passengers took a journey by rail from Paris to Brindisi, where they boarded a Short S.8 Calcutta biplane/flying boat to Haifa, where they finally boarded a de Havilland DH.66 Hercules biplane trimotor to Karachi. The whole journey took eight days.[2] Through cooperation with Indian Transcontinental Airways, British Imperial passengers were finally able to reach Singapore at the end of 1933, seven months after KLM had established service to Singapore there via Medan. Through cooperation with the Australian airline QANTAS, British Imperial reached Brisbane in December 1934.

British Imperial finally managed to match KLM's route, but Imperial's passengers had to transfer from landplane to flying boat to landplane, and so on, all along the journey, while KLM's passengers were flown in the same aircraft along the entire route. The only other competition KLM faced on its route to the Orient was from the French; but in those early days of long-distance flight, they were a small threat. In January 1931, Air Orient began fortnightly service from Paris to Saigon, partly in conjunction with KLM, which supplied the en route support (it is noteworthy that Air Orient flew Fokker aircraft along parts of the route at the time). On May 5, 1932, a weekly passenger service began. Lioré et Olivier LeO 242 flying boats carried passengers from Marseilles to Beirut, where Breguet 280, Farman F.190, or Potez 32 single-engine airliners flew on to Baghdad. From there Fokker F.VIIb3/m and Farman F.300 trimotors flew the most difficult part of the route to Saigon. Air France continued this service when the airline was formed in 1933, but these aircraft offered little passenger capacity along the route.[3]

By the early 1930s, Albert Plesman could pride himself on KLM's fast and efficient route to the Far East. It was the longest airline route in the world, and it was serviced by reliable Fokker transports. Closely observing the proving flights made to the East Indies during the late 1920s, he soon realized the benefits of a route that used modern landplanes. Speaking before the Royal Aeronautical Society in London on February 2, 1933, he outlined KLM's operating rationale for the East Indies route:

> There were those who pointed out that the route of Amsterdam-Batavia was for a considerable part a sea route, and ought thus, to be run with seaplanes. . . . In the first place there was the problem: land or seaplane. This question was decided in favour of the former, because the view was held that a real seaplane, able to resist a heavy sea, had yet to be constructed, whilst the seaplane as regards acquisition and upkeep is far from economic in operation. Further, the adoption of a sea route would have necessitated either a considerable detour or long flights with seaplanes over the mainland. . . .[4]

As we have seen, Plesman's primary concern regarding operations along the East Indies route was economy. KLM's Far Eastern route had one immediate benefit over British Imperial's: KLM was operating strictly between two points, Amsterdam and Batavia, whereas Imperial had to offer service to many points all along its route. Imperial was limited by the geography of the British Empire, diplomatic squabbles, and the limited range of British-built transport aircraft. Nevertheless, though KLM held a clear advantage in its route to the Far East, Plesman was never content to rest on his laurels. When he addressed the Royal Aeronautical Society, KLM was operating Fokker F.XIIs and the slightly improved F.XVIII trimotor transports along the Amsterdam-Batavia route, both of which could carry four to six passengers with respective cruising speeds of 127 and 126 mph. Plesman wanted better.

Even before the Fokker F.XVIII had made its first flight (in June 1932), Plesman approached Fokker requesting new designs that would replace the F.XII and F.XVIII for the East Indies route. His primary interest was in a large four-engine aircraft with a significantly greater passenger capacity. This was particularly farsighted, but the Fokker company's operational and design mentality was hesitant, even obsolescent in some cases; investment in modernization and research and design for long-term profits was something that Anthony Fokker ignored for many years. Like Plesman, he had a desire for economy, and his desire manifested itself in developing his old designs rather than investing heavily in new ones. He saw no immediate need to modernize his works. Since 1919, KLM had purchased all its aircraft from Fokker; and because the Dutch government was "encouraging" KLM to purchase from a domestic aircraft supplier in the 1920s, Fokker felt he had a guaranteed customer. So he used many of the same design and construction features in the F.XII and F.XVIII aircraft that he had used in his late-model fighter aircraft from World War I and his first transport aircraft in the early 1920s, which included composite welded-steel-tube/plywood/fabric construction, a plywood cantilevered high-wing, and the Fokker hallmark trimotor engine configuration.[5]

A KLM poster showing the interior layout of a Fokker F.XVIII on the Amsterdam-Batavia route. Of interest are the radio operator's station in the passenger cabin directly behind the cockpit and the navigator's table behind the radio. The fuel tank is housed in the thick cantilever wing. Note also the mail compartments in the nose, under the cockpit, and in the rear fuselage—behind the pantry. Postal revenue from long-distance flights was KLM's most important source of profit. [Photo AVIODROME Luchtfotografie, Lelystad, Holland]

Anthony Fokker had had no formal education in aeronautical design; nor had his chief designer, Reinhold Platz, who headed his design team from 1916 to 1931. More than that, both men had a personal disdain for formally trained aeronautical "experts." But as the Great Depression settled in, foreign orders for aircraft began to dry up, and Fokker had demonstrated nothing particularly innovative since his F.VIIb3/m trimotor design of 1925. By 1932, KLM was the sole purchaser of Fokker's new airliners. In addition, the company was in transition during that time: Reinhold Platz departed in 1931, and Fokker brought in new designers in an attempt to design and build modern, commercially competitive airliners that would restore domestic and foreign orders. But economy was an issue that was to plague the relationship between KLM and Fokker for the rest of the decade.

Tony Fokker overlooking the construction of the F.XX. Although a drag-reducing streamlined elliptical fuselage and retractable landing gear were implemented into the F.XX, Fokker and his designers had reached the final limitations of the classic Fokker composite material trimotor design. He could no longer put off the inevitable shift to all-metal research, design, and production taking place in the United States and Germany. The F.XX was stuck between two generations of airliner design. [Photo AVIODROME Luchtfotografie, Lelystad, Holland]

Plesman wanted the best modern airliner at the lowest possible price; Fokker wanted to design and build airliners only at the lowest possible price. Modern research and design required extensive investment, and the fact that neither party wanted to pay for it exclusively created a strained relationship between the two men.

At the time of Plesman's call for a faster, higher-capacity aircraft, Fokker was able to show a design for a new streamlined trimotor, the Fokker F.XX. Plesman wanted an airliner that could fly thirty miles an hour faster than the F.XVIII, and the new F.XX design could easily achieve that. A design preference for the trimotor airliner had developed in the mid-1920s, the basic theory being that, because of the frequent unreliability of early aero engines, three were better than one—or even two. The trimotor layout was a Fokker design hallmark and was present in nearly all of his airliner designs from 1925 to 1933. While a trimotor avoided instability if one engine failed, its layout presented two problems: the engine and propeller in the front of the fuselage obstructed the view of the pilot, and the vibration of the front engine could be felt throughout the fuselage. The F.XX was caught between two generations of airliner design. On the one hand, it still recycled Fokker's high-wing trimotor design formula; on the other hand, it displayed refinements such as a rounded fuselage, engine cowlings, and retractable landing gear. All of these innovations were put in place by Fokker's new chief designer, Engineer Marius Beeling. The F.XX did not have a significantly higher passenger capacity than the F.XVIII did and aero engine reliability had improved to the extent that three engines were no longer necessary for long-distance flights. Nevertheless Plesman showed initial interest in the design.[6]

Fokker and Beeling also presented sketches for a large four-engine airliner, designated the F.XXXVI, which was designed to carry sixteen passengers in great comfort along the East Indies route. In September 1932, Plesman ordered prototypes of the F.XX and F.XXXVI, and Fokker promised that they would be constructed by April 1933. Plesman said that he intended to put the F.XXXVI into East Indies service in August 1933; if it performed well, he said, he would consider purchasing another five. Suddenly the future looked considerably brighter for Fokker's Nederlandsche Vliegtuigenfabriek. But it was not to last. Fokker greatly underestimated the time necessary for his factory to construct such new and innovative designs. The "new" F.XVIII design was simply the F.XII airliner with a narrower fuselage to create less drag, thus giving the plane "improved" performance. Agan, it was a reworking of old methods, which had been the standard Fokker design approach. The new F.XX and F.XXXVI designs, even though they still had the traditional high-cantilever wing and mixed construction, would take considerable development time. The resulting production delays further ruptured the already tenuous relationship between Plesman and Fokker.

Fokker was by far the most significant manufacturer in the Dutch aero industry, but other, smaller firms were showing modernizing initiative that sought to break Fokker's near monopoly on sales in the Netherlands. In 1930, Dirk "Dick" Asjes, a young pilot studying at the Technical University of Delft, developed the concept of a purpose-built mail plane that, with a cruising speed of at least 300 km/h, could fly to the East Indies much faster than the Fokker airliners could. He sketched out a sleek and streamlined trimotor of all-wood construction. The primary motivation for Asjes's design was profit. The rate

The most aesthetically beautiful trimotor built by Fokker was unfortunately the most unsuccessful. When it was unveiled to the world in December 1933 for the Christmas mail flight to Batavia, its American-built engines failed to start, further casting a shadow over the design. Although Plesman had ordered the F.XX design, he had to be persuaded to purchase the sole example since he had become entranced with the all-metal DC-2s being built by Douglas. [R. E. G. Davies Collection]

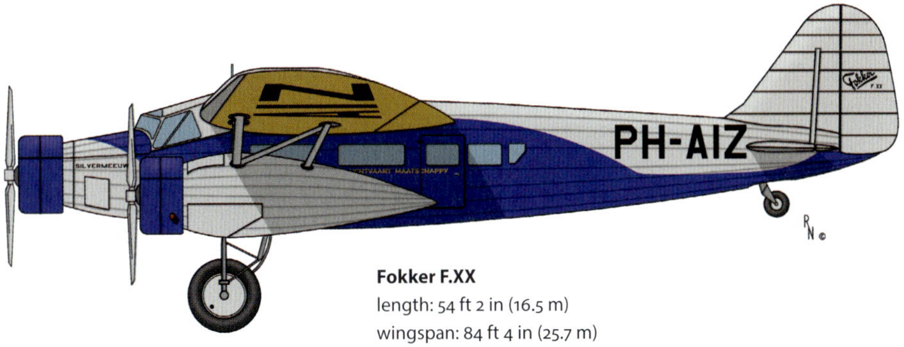

Fokker F.XX
length: 54 ft 2 in (16.5 m)
wingspan: 84 ft 4 in (25.7 m)
engines: three 650 hp Wright Cyclone R-1820-F radials
cruising speed: 155 mph (250 km/h)
range: 1,030 miles (1,660 km)
crew: 2-3
passengers: 12

Developed simultaneously with the F.XX, the giant 4-engine F.XXXVI demonstrated Fokker's growing experimentation with streamlining, coupled with his reliance on the traditional wooden-wing and welded-steel-tube fuselage. Fokker was proud of his giant airliner and its well-appointed and luxurious passenger accommodations. Compared to his older trimotor designs, the F.XXXVI did appear modern and streamlined, as Fokker seems to be showing in this photograph, with his own new streamlined 1934 Chrysler Airflow sedan parked in front of the giant. [Photo AVIODROME Luchtfotografie, Lelystad, Holland]

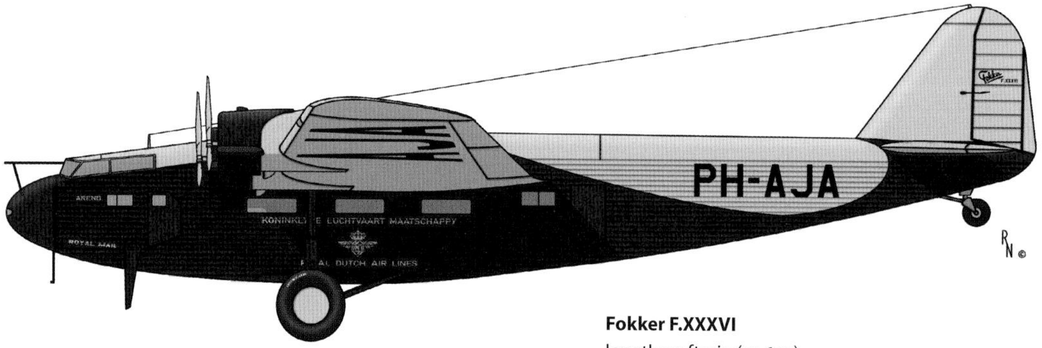

Fokker F.XXXVI
length: 77 ft 5 in (23.6 m)
wingspan: 108 ft 3 in (33 m)
engines: four 750 hp Wright Cyclone F2 radials
cruising speed: 174 mph (280 km/h)
range: 963 miles (1,550 km)
crew: 4
passengers: 16 (Indies configuration), 32 (European routes)

that the government paid at that time was 45 guilders per kilo of mail delivered by air, whereas one kilo of weight devoted to passengers brought only 18 guilders. Asjes approached Tony Fokker with his idea, but Fokker rejected him. The latter was already working on the F.XX at the time. Albert Plesman also rejected the idea of a purpose-built mail plane because KLM was committed to the transport of passengers as well as mail.

Asjes finally found support from two steamship lines, the Stoomvaartmaatschappij Nederland and the Rotterdamsche Lloyd, which hoped to break KLM's monopoly on air transport to the East Indies. Lieutenant Colonel Jacob Jan van Santen, the commandant of the LVA, also offered support to the project, believing that Asjes's design had the potential to be converted into a fast transport or bomber for military use. Asjes then took his concept to the small aviation firm of Pander en Zonen, a furniture maker that had begun small aircraft construction in the 1920s. It was a bold project for a small manufacturer such as Pander to take on, but Theodorus Slot, Pander's designer, created a workable design from Asjes's sketches, and the results were impressive. The Pander S.4 was the first low-wing commercial aircraft with retractable landing gear and streamlined NACA cowlings to be built in the Netherlands. The S.4 prototype, christened the *Postjager,* was unveiled to Prince Hendrik and the public at the Amsterdam Aero Club at Schiphol on September 23, 1933, alongside Fokker's new trimotor, the F.XX named the *Zilvermeeuw*.

The Pander S.4 was even presented to Charles Lindbergh while he was inspecting the Dutch aero industry on a visit to the Netherlands. He praised the streamlined design and fine lines of the aircraft but was critical of the concept of mounting three engines on a relatively small aircraft with a small payload. He commented that similar-sized aircraft in the United States could carry the same load with just one or two engines (he had in mind the new all-metal twin-engine transports being tested by Boeing

Theodorus Slot (left), designer of the Pander S.4, and Henk Pander in a mockup of the cockpit of the Postjager. *Slot went on to work for De Schelde, where he later designed the advanced S.21 fighter project.* [Photo AVIODROME Luchtfotografie, Lelystad, Holland]

Tony Fokker showing Charles Lindbergh, during the latter's 1934 visit to the Netherlands, the unique staggered cockpit layout (the copilot's seat offset behind the pilot's, supposedly giving the pilot a better view) of the then-being-built F.XXXVI. This unusual design feature still shows Fokker's natural inclination to think as a pilot in the design process of his aircraft. [Photo AVIODROME Luchtfotografie, Lelystad, Holland]

Developed by student pilot Dirk Asjes and Theo Slot, of the Pander company, the Pander S.4 Postjager *was funded by several Dutch steamship lines as a purpose-built fast mail plane for service between the Netherlands and the East Indies. Its investors hoped that the* Postjager *would earn a high profit and challenge KLM's monopoly on air mail revenue. It was one of the most aesthetically beautiful trimotor aircraft ever developed. The profile shows the aircraft in its markings for the MacRobertson Air Race in 1934.* [Photo AVIODROME Luchtfotografie, Lelystad, Holland]

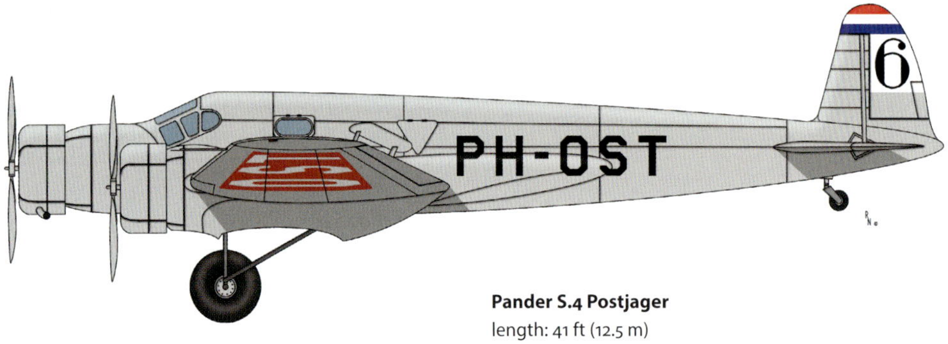

Pander S.4 Postjager
length: 41 ft (12.5 m)
wingspan: 54 ft 5 in (16.6 m)
engines: three 420 hp Wright Whirlwind R-975-E-2 radials
maximum speed: 224 mph (360 km/h)
range: 1,833 miles (2,950 km)
ceiling: 17,717 ft (5,400 m)
crew: 3

and Douglas). These comments did not bother Asjes: he had designed the S.4 as a fast transport, and with a maximum speed of 224 mph, he had achieved his goal.[7]

The 1933 Kerstpostvlucht and the Flight of the *Pelikaan*

During the summer of 1933, the Studiecomité Snelpost Nederland-Indië, made up of members of various shipping companies and colonial business enterprises, decided to sponsor a special Christmas mail flight contest to the East Indies, a competition that would evaluate the effectiveness of a high-speed mail route. The competition was intended to prove that the flight to Batavia could now be made in five days. The competitors in this event were to be KLM's Fokker F.XX and Pander's *Postjager*. These two aircraft brought a great deal of national pride to the Dutch public: they represented great strides in streamlined design, and the public reveled in the fact that their national aero industry was about to do what other international aviation experts from nations with large aero industries said could not be done. Plesman was particularly eager to see what the latest products of the Dutch aero industry could achieve.

Although the *Postjager* was in direct competition with KLM's F.XX, Plesman offered the services of veteran KLM pilot Gerrit Geysendorffer to fly the Pander aircraft, and of KLM radio operator S. van Straten to man the radio equipment. Recognizing the importance of national prestige over corporate aggrandizement, Plesman was certainly making a sporting gesture. Furthermore, Plesman allowed the *Postjager* to take off a week before the F.XX did. It was another kind gesture, but it was also a subtle way of publicly showing his confidence in KLM's new plane and the airline's apparent ability to finish the journey on time. KLM Captain Ivan Smirnoff, who was selected to fly the F.XX, echoed his boss's confidence, but he was somewhat concerned about the F.XX's American-built Wright Cyclone radial engines, which, like many engines of the time, had a reputation for unreliability. He had experienced trouble with them a number of times during test flights, though it now appeared that the problems had been remedied. As the date for the departure of the *Postjager* came, the eyes and ears of the Dutch people and the international aviation world were fixed on Schiphol.[8]

During the early hours of December 9, 1933, the Pander ground crew prepared the *Postjager* for departure. Public enthusiasm for the flight was so great that more than 51,000 letters and postcards had been earmarked for the flight, and a large crowd had gathered at Schiphol to witness the departure. After warming up the engines and giving a final wave to the crowd, Geysendorffer took off for Batavia at 4:15 a.m. The first leg of journey went smoothly as the aircraft cruised over northern and central Europe. But as the *Postjager* approached Rome, it flew into heavy clouds and pouring rain. Geysendorffer landed at Rome at 10:10 a.m.; despite the downpour, the *Postjager* was refueled and airborne again an hour and a half later. As it continued to fly to the southeast, the weather became worse, and they encountered storms over the Gulf of Taranto. Suddenly, Geysendorffer noticed a loss of oil pressure in the right engine, and then it sputtered to a stop.

Not wanting to fly through storms over the Mediterranean on only two engines, Geysendorffer reversed course, intending to land at Brindisi to inspect the engine and wait out the storm. The tower at Brindisi radioed the *Postjager* to say that the airfield was saturated by the rain, making it unsuitable for landing, and it directed the aircraft to land at the military airfield at Grottaglie. After landing, the crew discovered that an oil leak, caused by a loose nut from the starter, had caused the American-built Wright Whirlwind engine to overheat, wrecking it. A new engine was needed, and it would have to come from the Wright factory in the United States. Henk Pander purchased a new engine and had it loaded aboard the Italian liner SS *Conte di Savoia,* one of the fastest liners on the Atlantic run. It still took that ship seven days to reach Naples, arriving on December 22. It would take further time to send the engine to Grottaglie and to install it. And thus, because of the failure of one of the plane's American-built engines, Asjes and Geysendorffer spent a depressing Christmas stranded at an Italian air base.[9]

The reports of the *Postjager*'s condition were received somberly by the Dutch public. So much had been expected of the new aircraft. This put extra pressure on Smirnoff to make sure that the F.XX *Zilvermeeuw* would arrive in Batavia before Christmas or Dutch aviation would be humiliated before the world. At 3:00 a.m. on December 18, Smirnoff and his crew boarded the Fokker F.XX. Only a partial mail load was put aboard because the F.XX was instructed to stop at Brindisi and pick up the mail stranded aboard the *Postjager*. A large crowd had gathered once again, this time to watch the departure of KLM's *Zilvermeeuw*, despite the chilling cold of the early morning hours. Smirnoff began to turn the engines over, but suddenly one of them started sputtering and came to a stop—followed shortly by a second one. Smirnoff shut down the other engine and made his way out of the cockpit. Before he had exited the aircraft, Plesman and a team of mechanics were already at work examining the engines. The inspection showed that cogwheels in each engine were defective and had broken apart. The chief mechanic calculated that it would take twenty-four hours to fully repair the engines.

The Pander Postjager *preparing for takeoff at Schiphol on its Christmas mail flight to Batavia in the early morning hours of December 9, 1933.* [Photo AVIODROME Luchtfotografie, Lelystad, Holland]

After the engines of the F.XX Zilvermeeuw *failed, Plesman ordered the F.XVIII* Pelikaan *made ready for the Christmas mail flight to the East Indies. Capt. Smirnoff and his crew would have quite a task making it to Batavia before Christmas: the* Pelikaan *was 40 mph slower than the* Zilvermeeuw*! In this photograph, crowds are gathered in the snow at Schiphol on December 18, 1933, to watch the* Pelikaan *take off.* [Photo AVIODROME Luchtfotografie, Lelystad, Holland]

Smirnoff was furious. The American-built Cyclones, which had already given him trouble, failed him at the most critical moment. However, Plesman was not to be defeated: the mail had to go through. He asked whether there was any aircraft available for immediate takeoff and was told that the F.XVIII *Pelikaan* could be made ready within an hour. Plesman ordered that aircraft to be made ready and had the mail transferred from the F.XX to the *Pelikaan*. He then told Smirnoff that he would be flying the *Pelikaan* and asked the pilot whether he could arrive on Christmas Day. Smirnoff told Plesman he would reach Batavia before Christmas! This seemed like an outlandish boast, since the *Pelikaan* flew 40 mph slower than did the *Zilvermeeuw*. Nevertheless, Smirnoff and his crew boarded the aircraft and took off only an hour and sixteen minutes after the scheduled departure of the *Zilvermeeuw*.

Smirnoff and his crew, like the *Pelikaan*, were veterans of the Amsterdam-Batavia route, but they had a unique challenge ahead of them. They had to shorten the time flying the longest air route in the world without the advantage of a faster aircraft if they were to live up to Smirnoff's boast that the *Pelikaan* would arrive in Batavia before Christmas. This could only be accomplished by round-the-clock flying and short stopovers for refueling; but all of it would be complicated by the poor December weather, which increased the probability of an increase in unscheduled stopovers or delays. Though the odds were stacked against a timely arrival, Smirnoff was determined to make it.

As the *Pelikaan* approached the Mediterranean, it encountered a number of cloudbursts and rainstorms as evening settled in, and Smirnoff decided to land in Rome for a few hours, not wanting to fly over the mountains of Italy and Greece in the dark and in poor weather. When Smirnoff radioed KLM headquarters about his unscheduled stop in Rome, Plesman shot back a message saying that he was very disappointed and expected Smirnoff to get moving as soon as possible. This infuriated Smirnoff. Plesman sat at a desk and had no firsthand experience of piloting a large aircraft through treacherous weather halfway around the world. Perhaps due to his boss's impertinence, Smirnoff radioed Plesman after arriving in Athens that, despite the delay in Rome, he intended to arrive in Batavia on December 23. This meant that he expected the *Pelikaan* to make the flight in half the travel time of KLM's regularly scheduled flights between Amsterdam and Batavia.

Plesman sent no reply; he must have thought Smirnoff was out of his mind. As if Smirnoff did not have enough on his mind, there was also the mail from the stranded *Postjager* to pick up. Geysendorffer and Asjes had made an arrangement with British Imperial Airways to load the mail from the stranded *Postjager* aboard an Imperial Airways transport in Brindisi, which would then fly on to Cairo to rendezvous with a KLM transport. At Cairo the mail was loaded aboard the Fokker F.XII transport *IJsvogel,* which then took off for the Far East. Plesman radioed Smirnoff that the *Pelikaan* had to meet the *IJsvogel* somewhere along the Far East route and pick up the *Postjager*'s mail. Not only did Smirnoff have to reach Batavia on schedule, but now he had to locate and catch up with the *IJsvogel*.

Fortunately for the crew of the *Pelikaan,* the weather improved when they were halfway across the Mediterranean, and it stayed clear as they flew from Cairo to Baghdad to Bushire to Djask to Karachi. Smirnoff had requested that the *IJsvogel* rendezvous with the *Pelikaan* in Karachi, but when he arrived there he learned that the *IJsvogel* had already left. As soon as the *Pelikaan* was refueled, Smirnoff took off impatiently, hoping to catch the *IJsvogel* at the next refueling point. Several hours later, the *Pelikaan* landed at Jodhpur in British India. Smirnoff found the *IJsvogel* there waiting for him, along with a large crowd, including passengers from another KLM transport who wanted to wish the *Pelikaan* fliers good luck. Word had spread around the world about the *Pelikaan*'s flight and its intended arrival time in Batavia, and the KLM agent at Jodhpur had arranged a publicity reception. Smirnoff and his crew smiled for the cameras, but all of this publicity meant that there was all the more pressure on them to reach Batavia on schedule.

So, after overseeing the transfer of the *Postjager*'s mail to the *Pelikaan,* Smirnoff quickly took off again. For the rest of the journey, weather was not the greatest impediment to reaching Batavia on time; rather, it was the dignitaries and crowds at every refueling stop along the rest of the route who implored the Dutchmen to make speeches and attend lavish civic receptions. The largest reception was at Palembang, the first stop in the Dutch

Special postcards like the one shown here were sold for the Postjager*'s Eerste Snelpostvlucht (first fast mail flight). They would be carried aboard the* Postjager *to and from the Indies and be returned to the purchaser as a unique souvenir of the flight. The December 9, 1933, postmark for the* Postjager*'s outbound flight (in red, bottom right) and the December 26, 1933, return flight aboard the* Pelikaan *(in black, middle left) are visible on the back of the card.*

***Special envelopes and stamps were issued for the Versnelde KLM Kerstvlucht Naar Indie (KLM Fast Christmas Flight to the Indies) aboard the Fokker F.XX* Zilvermeeuw*. The irony of this item was that it was only aboard the* Zilvermeeuw *on the runway at Schiphol for a very short time; along with all the other mail, it was transferred to the* Pelikaan *that same morning*.**

East Indies, where a feast with gallons of champagne had been prepared by the civil authorities. After a brief speech and a cup of black coffee, Smirnoff and his crew were back in the air within a half hour. With only 300 miles to go to Batavia, the crew spent most of the last leg of the flight shaving and making sure their uniforms were spotless. Finally, on December 22, a full day ahead of schedule, Smirnoff radioed Plesman that the *Pelikaan* had touched down in Batavia. The crew members were carried out of the aircraft on the shoulders of a jubilant crowd. The *Pelikaan* had reached Batavia in a hundred hours and forty minutes: incredibly, Smirnoff had beaten the schedule planned for the *Zilvermeeuw* by fifty minutes! Smirnoff and his crew were the toast of the colony and allowed themselves some well-deserved time to celebrate and rest. But their ordeal was not over: they still had to deliver the New Year's mail to Amsterdam on or before New Year's Day.

Smirnoff and his colleagues spent Christmas day in Batavia preparing the *Pelikaan* for the return flight to Schiphol, which was scheduled to begin in the early morning hours of the next day. Smirnoff radioed Plesman that he planned to arrive in Amsterdam on December 30, and so at 2:00 a.m. on December 26, the *Pelikaan* took off on its westward journey. The runway at Batavia had been lined with searchlights, and the fliers were cheered on by a massive crowd. The crew was eager to return home on schedule, but Smirnoff was in a particular hurry. On Christmas day he had learned via a radio call from his neighbor that his wife had been taken to the hospital for surgery several hours after he had left Schiphol. His neighbor assured him that she was okay, but did not tell him what kind of surgery she had had. As if the responsibilities of the flight did not cause him enough stress, Smirnoff had his wife to worry about on the long journey home.

The westbound flight was much more difficult than the eastbound one had been. Not only did Smirnoff have headwinds to contend with, but the closer the *Pelikaan* got to Europe, the worse the weather became. When the *Pelikaan* crossed over the Greek Peloponnesus from the Mediterranean, the cloud cover was so thick that the *Pelikaan* could not fly above it; as Smirnoff dropped to below a thousand feet, a mist set in and he could not see the ocean. While he was trying to determine his exact location along the coast, radio operator Cor van Beukering received a message from the Greek air command saying that the *Pelikaan* had strayed into a restricted zone, and that if it did not land immediately, Greek antiaircraft batteries would open fire. Having no intention of being delayed by Greek military authorities, Smirnoff had Van Beukering stall by sending apologies to the Greek air command and requests for directional bearings, a strategy that proved successful when Smirnoff calculated that they were back over the Mediterranean. The *Pelikaan* then made its way toward Italy—even as the Greeks continued to demand that Smirnoff land.

The threat of being blown out of the sky by the Greek air command did cause Smirnoff some concern, but the most dangerous part of the journey home was the last leg, from Marseilles to Amsterdam. Sixty-mile-per-hour winds were blowing at Marseilles when the *Pelikaan* touched down there, and Schiphol reported that it was experiencing heavy, blinding snow. Smirnoff asked his crew if they wanted to continue the flight under such conditions, and they unanimously responded, "You're the boss!"

As the *Pelikaan* took to the air and struggled through winter storms across France, Belgium, and the Netherlands, thousands had gathered at Schiphol to welcome the fliers home. The airport authorities continuously used loudspeakers to ask the crowd to be quiet so that the approach of the *Pelikaan* could be heard. After several hours, the still of the peaceful snowfall was ruptured by the approaching drone of aircraft engines. As the spotlights were switched on, Smirnoff spotted the runway at Schiphol and made one of the most dangerous landings in his career: it was dangerous not because of the weather but because of the congestion of well-wishers surrounding the runway. After Smirnoff and his colleagues made a perfect landing, they emerged from the aircraft to a public gone mad with delight and pride. They were congratulated by Plesman, Gen. Snijders, and the minister of transport, who awarded the fliers the titles of Knights of the Orde van Oranje-Nassau on behalf of Queen Wilhelmina. Smirnoff had made the return flight to Amsterdam in 100 hours and 32 minutes, beating his eastbound time by eight minutes! It was an astonishing feat for the fliers and for the sturdy trimotor.[10]

The crew of the Pelikaan *on the Christmas mail flight, from left to right: commander Ivan Smirnoff, copilot Piet Soer, flight engineer Sjef Grosfeld, and radio operator Cor van Beukering.*

The All-Metal Airliner

The flight of the *Pelikaan* was widely celebrated in the Netherlands and the East Indies, but it gave Albert Plesman a stark realization. He became convinced that the day of the mixed-construction trimotor was over, and that all-metal construction was superior to composite construction and would become the industry standard in the future. The failure of the *Zilvermeeuw* in the Kerstpostvlucht competition to the East Indies further convinced him of this. The success of the *Pelikaan*'s flight was due primarily to the professionalism and almost superhuman efforts of Smirnoff and his crew rather than the performance of the aircraft. Plesman realized that the flight could easily have ended in failure. As KLM's profits increased into the 1930s, requiring less in governmental subsidies to balance its books, Plesman had more leeway in his choice of aircraft. He turned his attention to the emerging generation of streamlined all-metal airliners that were being designed across the ocean in the United States. In a somewhat bitter irony (at least for the Dutch aero firms), the director of KLM began to look to the American aero industry for new airliners shortly after defective American-built engines had crippled both of the Dutch aero industry's latest airliners in one of the highest-profile aviation events of the decade.

Across the Atlantic, TWA was eager to clear its reputation after the Knute Rockne crash in one of that airline's Fokker F.10As. In August 1932, TWA issued a specification to several manufacturers for an all-metal monoplane with a cruising speed of 150 mph and a passenger capacity of twelve. Two weeks after the Douglas Aircraft Company of Santa Monica, California, had received TWA's specifications, its representatives offered a design for a streamlined all-metal, low-wing, two-engine monoplane—designated the DC-1. After being extensively tested to ensure that it met the specifications laid out by the airline, the aircraft surpassed TWA's expectations. It offered a smooth ride; it could fly on one engine if the other one failed; and it could fly at 190 mph. It was the largest airplane with retractable landing gear at that time. The airliner drew a great deal of attention for TWA and Douglas when it achieved a transcontinental speed record of 13 hours and 4 minutes on February 19, 1934.[11] Douglas had spent $182,000 on the development of this airliner, but the company quickly recouped its losses. Orders poured in to Douglas from TWA and other American airlines for the twelve-seat DC-2 (the production version of the ten-seat DC-1).

Anthony Fokker and KLM Captain Koene Dirk Parmentier with the first Fokker-Douglas DC-2 demonstration model, showing the aircraft to a potential client in England. With its all-metal construction and streamlined fuselage, the DC-2 can be considered the world's first modern airliner. The profile shows the first DC-2 acquired by KLM, the* Uiver*, in its markings for the 1934 MacRobertson Air Race. [Photo San Diego Air and Space Museum]

American airlines were not the only parties interested in the DC-2. Albert Plesman learned about the airliner's development and quickly recognized its modern potential on the East Indies run. The DC-2 held a clear advantage over the Fokker aircraft used by KLM on its East Indies route. The Fokker F.XII, put into service in 1931, had a cruising speed of 127 mph (205 km/h), a disposable weight of 6,390 pounds, and a four- to six-passenger capacity for the East Indies route. The Fokker F.XVIII, in service by 1932, had a cruising speed of 122 mph (203 km/h), a disposable weight of 7,058 pounds, and a four- to six-passenger capacity. By contrast, the DC-2, which entered commercial service in 1934, had a cruising speed of 190 mph (338 km/h), a disposable weight of 6,105 pounds, and a five-passenger capacity (configured for the Far East route). Although the DC-2 had slightly less disposable weight than did the F.XII or the F.XVIII, its cruising speed showed a 35 percent improvement. The cost of maintenance per flying hour for the DC-2 was 5 percent cheaper than the F.XII and 30 percent cheaper than the F.XVIII. Overall, the total maintenance costs for the DC-2 were 60 percent less than those of the F.XII and F.XVIII. The DC-2 achieved this superiority over the previous Fokker types on the basis of its streamlined all-metal construction and the use of two Wright Cyclone 730-horsepower engines.

In October 1933, Plesman sent KLM pilot Koene Dirk Parmentier to the United States to examine American airliner development. While in California, he had the opportunity to test-fly the Douglas DC-1 and was astonished by its performance, which he reported to Plesman, who was very enthusiastic about the aircraft. He immediately saw that here was an airliner whose performance far surpassed anything that was being developed in the Netherlands—or even in the rest of Europe—and he longed for such an aircraft. When Parmentier further informed him that the DC-1 was going into series production as the DC-2, Plesman decided to act. But what he needed was someone familiar with the American aero industry to make the detailed arrangements to obtain the new Douglas airliners.[12]

On November 23, 1933, Plesman and other KLM representatives invited Anthony Fokker to a dinner and asked if he would be interested in traveling to the United States in order to obtain an agreement to produce the DC-2 under license in his Amsterdam factory. Several days later Fokker was on an ocean liner for New York. Once in the United States—and after visiting other major American aero manufacturers—Fokker traveled to Santa Monica and test-flew the DC-1. He quickly realized that the DC-1 was clearly superior to any design currently on the drawing boards at his company. He had to face reality, but he also wished to remain a significant player in the world of commercial aviation. So he cleverly negotiated—for $100,000—the production and sales rights for the DC-2 (and subsequent Douglas aircraft) for the whole of Europe. According to an agreement signed on January 15, 1934, Fokker would receive 25 percent of each sale. On September 13, 1934, the first KLM DC-2 airliner arrived in Rotterdam aboard the SS *Statendam*. And even before that first DC-2, christened the *Uiver* ("stork"), made its first flight in the Netherlands, Plesman and KLM's board of directors had decided to replace all of its Fokker airliners on the East Indies route with the new DC-2s.

Plesman may have been ecstatic about the possibilities offered by the new planes, but Fokker had mixed emotions on the subject. On the one hand, the DC-2 clearly demonstrated how far Fokker's own designs lagged behind; on the other, he had just secured the European sales and production rights for this modern marvel—the world's first "modern" airliner to deserve that description. If Plesman wanted the plane, he would have to buy it from Fokker, whose only trump card to remain competitive in the civilian market at that moment was his contract with Douglas for the DC-2.[13]

Plesman was clearly tantalized by the streamlined, fast, all-metal airliners that were coming out of Santa Monica, but Fokker still wanted to market the products of his factory. On June 22, 1934, more than a year after its promised finish date (but before the first DC-2 arrived), the Fokker F.XXXVI was wheeled out of its hangar and made its first flight. To observers on the ground, it was a mighty sight to behold: it was one of the largest land

RIGHT *A publicity photo of the sleeping berth arrangement in the Fokker F.XXXVI. Fokker knew the F.XXXVI lacked the all-metal refinements and superior speed of Douglas's airliners, but he hoped to compensate for that by providing an unparalleled spacious and comfortable passenger cabin.*

BELOW *This poster shows the interior layout of the aircraft. The F.XXXVI had a kitchenette, refrigerator, and two lavatories—thus coming to be known as the "Flying Hotel." The aircraft would have offered passengers a high degree of comfort on the long route to the East Indies, but the F.XXXVI never flew to Batavia. Instead, it was used only in its higher-capacity daytime layout on European routes.* [Photo AVIODROME Luchtfotografie, Lelystad, Holland]

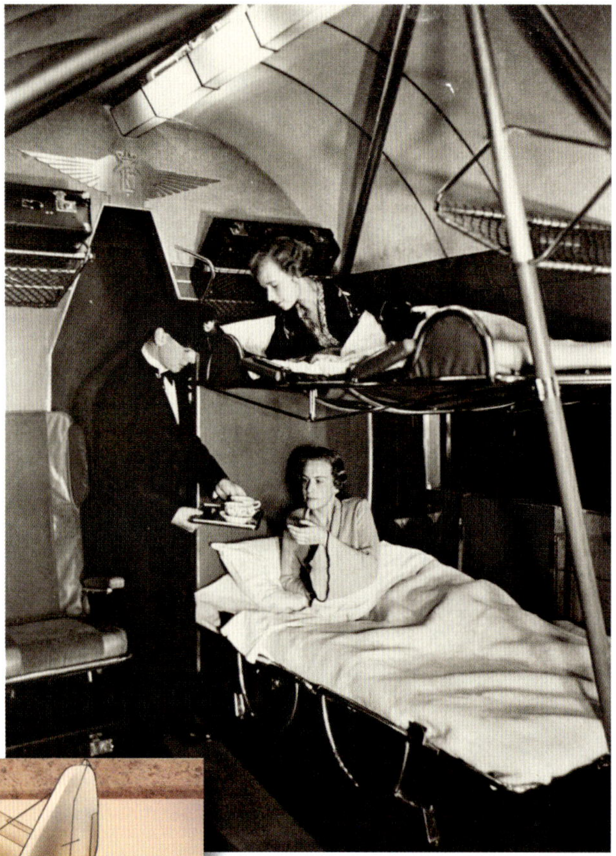

planes in existence, the largest Fokker aircraft built up to that time. Its spacious interior had sleeping berths for sixteen passengers, two washrooms, a wardrobe, and a kitchenette equipped to prepare hot meals. The cushy seats were upholstered with red leather, the walls were covered with blue leather, and behind the walls was a layer of sound-absorbing material that lowered the noise level of the four radial engines.

Fokker was particularly proud of the high degree of comfort that the airliner would allow its passengers on the long East Indies flight. Its rounded fuselage, similar to that of the F.XX, gave the F.XXXVI an impressive exterior appearance along with its comfortable passenger amenities. But in Plesman's eyes, this giant was not a modern airliner. Fokker had still relied on his previous design and construction techniques: a high-wing, steel-tube and fabric-covered fuselage, and fixed landing gear. Fokker countered that the greater comfort and better amenities of the "Flying Hotel" would appeal to travelers more than speed would.[14]

Indeed, the public was enthusiastic about the giant airliner, and it received a good deal of publicity when it was shown at the fifteenth anniversary celebration of the International Air Transport Association in The Hague. Had Fokker completed the F.XXXVI as scheduled in the spring of 1933, Plesman might have purchased six of that type; a year later, he could scarcely be convinced to purchase the prototype. Early in 1934 he abandoned the idea of putting six F.XXXVIs into service and instead decided to purchase a new fleet of DC-2s. Although the DC-2 could only carry five passengers to the F.XXXVI's sixteen (as configured for the East Indies route), Plesman found that he could still meet commercial demand by offering two flights per week to Batavia.

Fokker had invested heavily in the F.XXXVI, so, without forthcoming orders, his company was on the verge of bankruptcy. Despite his sense of having been betrayed by Plesman, however, he was compelled to concentrate on his exclusive European sales rights for the DC-2 for his ultimate financial salvation. Fokker did not have to wait long to profit from his contract with Douglas, as one of the last great air races was about to bring the world's attention to the DC-2.

The MacRobertson Race and the Flight of the *Uiver*

In April 1933, the city of Melbourne, Australia, was planning its centenary celebration for the following year, and the lord mayor of the city, Sir Harold Gengoult-Smith, thought that one way to stimulate interest in the 100th anniversary of the city's founding during the midst of the economic gloom of the Great Depression would be to hold an air race from London to Melbourne. To sponsor the race, Sir Gengoult-Smith approached a wealthy Melbourne confectioner and philanthropist, Sir Macpherson Robertson, who agreed to give $75,000 to the prize fund of the race. MacRobertson, as Robertson liked to call himself, made it clear to the air race committee that by funding such a race, he hoped to promote the development of fast and safe commercial aviation to Australia:

> You have been convened to make arrangements for an International Air Race from London to Melbourne in connection with the Centenary Celebrations. Make it the greatest race yet conducted in the world, make as few conditions as possible consistent with reducing risks to the minimum. Give attention to Australia's geographical isolation, and in this connection direct your thoughts towards the possibility of reducing this handicap consistent with safety.[15]

When the race committee sought the endorsement of the Royal Aero Club of Great Britain for the race, it mentioned that MacRobertson insisted on two requirements for his financial support: first, the race would have to be open to contestants and aircraft from around the world; second, safety was to be promoted first and foremost. The Royal Aero Club granted its endorsement and selected October 20, 1934, as the start date for the race. But the British may have endorsed the race a bit hastily because,

KLM luggage label with a silhouette of the F.XXXVI.

in late 1933, no British airliner in production could fly as fast as KLM's Fokker F.XII and F.XVIII trimotors, which were operating along the Amsterdam-Batavia route. The de Havilland DH.86 Express, a four-engine biplane airliner of composite construction, which first flew in January 1934, was Britain's latest civilian transport, but it had already been made obsolescent by airliner developments in the Netherlands, Germany, and the United States. The international character of the race would unveil before the world the weaknesses of the British aero industry unless the Brits could develop a new aircraft that might win the race.

While British aero manufacturers reflected on the predicament they were in, the mood across the English Channel in the Netherlands was significantly more optimistic. On May 24, 1934, Albert Plesman decided to enter two of KLM's new airliners, the Fokker F.XXXVI and its first Douglas DC-2, into the race. But in Plesman's mind, winning the race was not necessarily the most important part of the event. He calculated that his new generation of airliners could adhere to the normal Amsterdam-Batavia

ABOVE *KLM's DC-2* Uiver, *parked behind the all-metal Boeing 247D, which Plesman believed would be the* Uiver's *primary competitor in the MacRobertson race. The Boeing 247 was the first all-metal airliner to go into production, but the DC-2 was more aerodynamically refined, faster, and had greater range; it also had a higher passenger capacity.*

BELOW *The Boeing 247D* Warner Bros. Comet, *flown in the MacRobertson race by Roscoe Turner and Clyde Pangborn, is on display in the Smithsonian National Air and Space Museum in Washington, DC.*

route, while carrying passengers and cargo, and still be among the first contenders to finish in Australia. Plesman would use the race as a worldwide publicity event to demonstrate the speed, efficiency, comfort, and safety of KLM's service to the Far East. He knew he had the right aircraft and crews to succeed in that.

As the date of the race drew closer, Plesman saw the need for speed as becoming more and more important if the KLM entries were to perform well in the race. To avoid international embarrassment due to the slow pace of modernization in the British aeronautic industry, Sir Geoffrey de Havilland had developed a streamlined, twin-engine monoplane that was purpose-designed to win the MacRobertson Race. Three de Havilland DH.88 Comets were ordered by race contestants, and de Havilland paid for the development cost of the aircraft out of his own pocket, a generous bit of British patriotism. Powered by two 285-horsepower de Havilland Gypsy 6R in-line engines and able to achieve a top speed of 255 mph, the Comet "mail plane" was in fact a race plane. When word of the Comet's development leaked out, a number of contestants backed out of the race, unwilling to compete against a purpose-built race plane. For his part, Plesman realized that the Fokker F.XXXVI, with its maximum speed of 174 mph, had no chance of competing against the Comets in terms of speed. And there was other serious competition besides the de Havilland Comets. Americans Roscoe Turner and Clyde Pangborn entered the race with a Boeing 247D monoplane airliner: it was named the *Warner Bros. Comet,* and its maximum speed was only 10 mph less than that of the DC-2.

Compared to the DH.88, DC-2, 247D, and the *Panderjager,* the Fokker F.XXXVI, with its fixed-landing gear, looked like an aircraft from a previous generation. Plesman withdrew the giant airliner, which had not made its first flight until June 22, 1934, from the race in September. He was in the middle of a protracted fight with Fokker over the purchase of the F.XXXVI and the pricing of the DC-2s, and he had no intention of displaying what he considered to be an obsolescent design on the world stage in such a high-publicity event. Fokker was furious:

> The race will be of no benefit to commercial aviation whatever, and the only man who will profit is the chocolate manufacturer who is giving the prizes. Stunt and record flights may help to make the public air-conscious, but their advertising value is out of all proportion to the expense and the risks involved. Not a single plane has been built by a commercial aviation company because of the reputation gained in some single sensational record.[16]

Due to the bad blood between them at that point, Plesman could care less what Fokker thought. He was determined to present to the world a modernizing and efficient image of KLM, which he saw as embodied in the DC-2.[17]

To pilot KLM's new DC-2, Plesman designated Koene Dirk Parmentier, the KLM captain who had selected the DC-2 for purchase by KLM in 1933, and a man who had extensive experience in night-flying. Parmentier was joined by Jan Johannes Moll, himself a KLM veteran captain of the Amsterdam-Batavia route, as copilot; Bouwe Prins as flight engineer; and Cornelis van Brugge as radioman. Once the crew was selected, Plesman had Parmentier and his colleagues fly its DC-2, the *Uiver,* on the Amsterdam-Berlin route for a week, giving the aircraft a shakedown run before flying on to Great Britain. The *Uiver* and its excellent flight crew gave KLM good prospects for the race.

The KLM DC-2 was not the only Dutch aircraft to register for the MacRobertson Air Race. Pander's *Postjager,* the streamlined trimotor now rechristened the *Panderjager,* was entered by Dirk Asjes. The Nederlandsch Syndicaat Londen Melbourne Race, headed by the chairman of the N.V. Bataafsche Petroleum Maatschappij and represented primarily by the firms that originally supported Pander's trimotor project, subsidized the *Panderjager*'s entry into the race and hoped that a good showing by the aircraft before the world media might still result in the creation of a separate mail airline to the East Indies. Gerrit Geysendorffer would again serve as pilot for the *Panderjager.*

In mid-October 1934 the contestants in the MacRobertson Air Race assembled at the starting point at RAF Mildenhall Airfield. The twenty-one contestants were divided into two categories according to the cruising speeds of their aircraft. The aircraft in the upper speed category with KLM's *Uiver* were three de Havilland Comets, one Boeing 247D, the *Panderjager,* an Airspeed Viceroy, a Granville Gee Bee, and a Lambert Monocoupe. Of these aircraft, six were purpose-built race planes. Despite the fast competition, Plesman insisted that Parmentier and his crew follow KLM's Amsterdam-Batavia air route and perform the flight as if it were a routinely scheduled commercial one. To further emphasize its service efficiency over raw speed, the *Uiver* was to carry cargo, mail, and three passengers, one of whom was Thea Rasche, Germany's first female pilot. The day before the race began, King George V, Queen Mary, and the Prince of Wales paid a visit to Mildenhall to inspect the aircraft and meet the pilots. Parmentier and his crew stood at attention in spotless uniforms when introduced to the royal party, an

The crew of the Panderjager, *from left: radioman Pieter Pronk, Captain Gerrit Geysendorfer, and copilot Dirk Asjes.*

The outright winner of the MacRobertson Air Race was the de Havilland DH.88 Comet Grosvenor House, *flown by Charles W. A. Scott and Tom Campbell Black. The DH.88 was a purpose-built race plane designed by Sir Geoffrey de Havilland to win the race. It had a top speed of 255 mph (415 km/h), 45 mph faster than KLM's* Uiver. *But the purpose design and high speed of the DH.88 made the* Uiver's *performance in the race all the more impressive. The DH.88* Grosvenor House *is preserved in the Shuttleworth Collection in Bedfordshire, England.* [Courtesy of the Shuttleworth Collection]

The Uiver *being refueled in the middle of the night in Baghdad.*

image of professionalism that was to catch the attention of the public throughout the race. Anthony Fokker also showed up at Mildenhall on October 19. Despite his outrage over Plesman's withdrawal of his F.XXXVI, he still had a vested interest in the performance of the DC-2, and he watched over the aircraft's maintenance in its hangar. In the early hours of October 20, Parmentier, Moll, and all of the other pilots made their way to their aircraft, which were lined up for takeoff, scheduled at 6:30 a.m. A crowd of 13,000 had gathered to watch the contestants take off at 45-second intervals. Much of the crowd's attention was drawn to the sleek Dutch aircraft, which represented a new era in aviation. Both the *Panderjager* and the *Uiver* impressed the bystanders as they taxied into takeoff position:

> In the hangar itself the Douglas DC-2 was slowly being moved, and the *Panderjager* was already on the tarmac.
>
> Presently, against a background of a dawn fit for the occasion—layer upon layer of jagged orange clouds climbing into starlit purple—the Douglas and the Pander were being taxied along the front of the aerodrome enclosure. A flutter of handkerchiefs from the cabin windows and an answering wave from the crowd.
>
> Probably more effective than anything for the average sightseer was the realization that the Royal Dutch Air Lines were taking fare-paying passengers and mails in their new 200-m.p.h. Douglas. This was business, not racing, and they were seeing the last word in high-speed transport machines—the result of many years of steady research and development.[18]

As the passengers boarded the *Uiver,* Parmentier took satisfaction in the fact that they were elegantly dressed compared to the other fliers, who were bundled up in their flight suits, scarves, and caps. The passengers would be served breakfast after takeoff, and the KLM crew would treat the experience as a regular commercial long-distance flight. Finally, at 6:30 a.m., the mayor of London waved off the first contestant. The *Panderjager,* piloted by Asjes and Geysendorffer, was the fourth plane to take off, and the *Uiver* was the seventh. The race was on.

A look at the map of the race made matters look as though the *Uiver* would not stand a chance of beating the Comets to Melbourne. The race committee stipulated that there would only be five mandatory stops: Baghdad, Allahabad in British India, Singapore, and then Darwin and Charleville, both in Australia. The maximum range of the de Havilland DH.88 was nearly 3,000 miles, so the racers flying the Comets would have no difficulty making only those five required stops. The maximum range of the DC-2 was only slightly over 1,000 miles, and Plesman dictated that the *Uiver* would make all of KLM's routine stops along the route to Batavia. Between Mildenhall and Batavia, KLM aircraft stopped at twelve airfields; so Parmentier and Moll had to land at all of those, plus six additional stops to Melbourne, making a total of eighteen stops for the *Uiver* (plus an unexpected stop at Albury, Australia), compared to five for the Comets. The de Havillands also had a maximum speed advantage over the DC-2: 255 mph to 210 mph, respectively.

On paper, therefore, things did not look particularly optimistic for the *Uiver*; but calculations were to prove quite different from actual performance. One factor that gave the *Uiver* an advantage over its competition was reliability. DC-2s had been in operation in the United States for months before the race, and Plesman had given the *Uiver* an adequate shakedown period. The Comets, on the other hand, were tested only six weeks before the start of the race. So Plesman was confident that the demonstrated reliability of the DC-2 might give the *Uiver* a chance at first place. The race started off smoothly for her and her crew.

The *Panderjager* had a good start to the race as well. When Geysendorffer and Asjes reached Baghdad, they found out that they were in third place, with the Comet *Grosvenor House,* flown by Charles William Anderson Scott and Tom Campbell Black, and the *Uiver* ahead of them. En route to Allahabad via Karachi, the *Panderjager* maintained its place, and it looked as though the Dutch might dominate the race. Unfortunately for Asjes and Geysendorffer, misfortune struck on their arrival at Allahabad. The *Panderjager* arrived over Bamrauli Airfield during the night, and as Geysendorffer brought the plane down for a landing, the darkness prevented him from noticing that the starboard landing gear was not down. The aircraft hit hard, spun around, bending the port landing gear, and finally careened to a halt. Geysendorffer burst out of the aircraft weaving a tapestry of profanity. This was the second time the Pander had failed him, and he had completely lost faith in the design. After he had cooled down, he and Asjes examined the aircraft and discovered a ruptured fuel tank and a bent propeller. The aircraft could be repaired, but not with the limited facilities at Allahabad.

The repairs, undertaken in Calcutta, took three days, ending any chance that Geysendorffer and Asjes might have had to win the race. The Dutchmen decided that they should finish the race nonetheless, and once the repairs were completed, Geysendorffer decided to make a test flight on the evening of October 26. As he taxied the *Panderjager* into takeoff position, his view was obstructed by the bright beam of a landing light at the end of the runway, which was mounted on a trailer and pulled by an ambulance. Geysendorffer asked the tower to turn off the light, and his request was granted. He revved the Pander's engines and was rolling down the runway when suddenly an object appeared in the aircraft's headlights. The airfield ground crew had parked the ambulance and trailer, with the light now turned off, right in the path of the oncoming plane! The stunned ground crew in the ambulance switched the landing light on, but it was too late. Geysendorffer tried to veer to the left, but the right wingtip smashed into the landing light and ignited the starboard wing tank. The right side of the plane burst into flames before it came to a halt. Since the left side of the aircraft was undamaged, Geysendorffer and Asjes were able to escape. Within minutes, though, only a burning frame remained of the beautiful *Panderjager.*

That was to be the end of the Pander trimotor project. No commercial orders were forthcoming, and the LVA, which initially showed interest in a military version of the trimotor, withdrew any lingering support of the project. The crash of the *Panderjager* also spelled the end of Pander's aviation division, which was sold to the De Schelde firm. The *Panderjager* was a very promising and advanced

The flaming wreck of the* Panderjager *at Allahabad, India. It was a sad end for this beautiful aircraft. [Photo AVIODROME Luchtfotografie, Lelystad, Holland]

design for its time, but it never fully matured due to a series of random misfortunes.[19]

Back aboard the *Uiver,* things could not have been going better for Parmentier and Moll. Their flight had been relatively uneventful. The only mishap on the way to Batavia was that one of the passengers had been left behind at Allahabad, and the *Uiver* had to return to pick him up; but that delay was hardly noticed in the overall schedule. Parmentier and Moll were rigorously adhering to Plesman's proposed airline schedule, spending between twenty minutes and an hour at each one of their airfield stops. When the *Uiver* reached Batavia, Parmentier and Moll were still in second place, preceded only by Scott and Campbell Black in the *Grosvenor House.* While flying over the East Indies and the Timor Sea, Parmentier gained 500 miles on the *Grosvenor House.* During the refueling at Rambang, the *Uiver* crew learned that the Comet was experiencing engine trouble. Parmentier and Moll's efficient flying was paying off, and it looked as though they might have a chance to win the race.

Then came the final leg of the race—from Charleville to Melbourne in Australia. The *Uiver* took off in the early evening of October 23, but soon began to receive radio warnings of storms along the route to Melbourne. Parmentier tried to climb above them; but he was unable to, so he turned east in order to navigate along the Australian coast. On the way to the coast, Parmentier began to notice that the ground beneath him was beginning to rise up: the *Uiver* was heading into a chain of mountains that run along the coast. In order to safely pass over them, the *Uiver* would have to climb to above 7,000 feet. But the aircraft could not gain altitude: ice from the storm was coating the wings, making it impossible for the plane to climb. Parmentier had no choice but to turn around and head west in the hope of flying out of the storm. It did not take long for the pilots to realize that now they had no idea of their exact position. Hoping to get a contact for directional bearings, van Brugge, the radio operator, sent out SOS signals; but the thunder and noise of the rain pounding against the fuselage made it impossible to hear any incoming messages. After some time, van Brugge made contact with a radio station in the village of Albury, which was only 188 miles from Melbourne. By the time van Brugge received this message, the crew had no idea what the weather conditions were along the remaining route to Melbourne, had little idea of their exact location, and had only two hours of fuel remaining. In light of all that, Parmentier made the decision to head for Albury in order to refuel.

On the ground at Albury, the mayor ordered that the town's street lights be turned on and off in a sequence that would spell the town's name in Morse code. In the air it presented a curious sight to the pilots when they approached the town. According to Parmentier:

> While I kept track on the map, Moll guided our plane through the mountains until I [could] see the light of a city in the distance. That must be Albury. While I was busy with the compass, setting a course for Cootamundra, I discovered something strange. Albury suddenly disappeared, only one row of lights remained visible. It looked like an airfield. A few seconds later all the lights in the city were blazing again. It seemed they wanted to draw our attention there. Or did someone think that war had broken out and the city was threatened by an enemy bomber? In any case, it seemed worthwhile to follow the lights, as they suggested the presence of an airfield.
>
> As we circled over this area, we saw on both sides a large number of cars with their headlights illuminating the field, apparently with the intention to help us to land. But at the same time we saw that it was no airfield; the dimensions were too small for such. While van Brugge [hauled] in the trailing radio aerial, I turned on both our floodlights and flew low over the field several times to see if it was big enough to touch down without damaging our *Uiver.* . . .[20]

After dropping two flares over the field to make sure it was level and long enough for a landing, Parmentier took the aircraft down. Since Albury had no airfield, the cars had positioned their headlights along a racetrack outside the town. Despite the poor weather and poor visibility, Parmentier came in and made a perfect landing.

Although they arrived in the middle of the night, the crew and passengers on the *Uiver* were given a hearty welcome by the local population. As the storm was still raging overhead and having no desire to fly blind over unfamiliar terrain in these conditions, Parmentier and Moll decided to wait until morning to take off again, and so headed into town for a few hours of sleep. When the crew came back to the racetrack in the morning they were frustrated to see that the *Uiver* had sunk into the rain-soaked ground. But before they could contemplate what to do, Mayor Alf Waugh arrived on the scene with over 300 men from the town, all equipped with shovels and ropes, and all determined to dig the *Uiver* out of the mire. Parmentier recalled:

> We sought the help of the bystanders to push the *Uiver,* but the machine was stuck. Only a few people stood around the landing gear: I asked for shovels and ropes, which were soon brought. Then the ground behind the wheels was dug out: a few planks were laid in the trench, then long ropes were fastened to the landing gear and the whole of Albury pulled on the ropes to back our aircraft out of the soft earth. People were excited and happy that they could help us. It was a pleasure to see how cheerfully everyone dredged through the mud up to the ankles, getting their feet wet without concern. Then suddenly one of the ropes broke with a loud snap, sending thirty Alburians down onto the wet grass, laughter rose up, and among great amusement they scrambled to their feet and reattached the rope. Finally it succeeded and the *Uiver* was brought to a place where the soil was slightly firmer.[21]

The problem still remained that the plane would have to attempt a takeoff from a muddy field. Parmentier realized that there was no chance of the *Uiver* doing so with the passenger and cargo load it was carrying. Nevertheless, he was determined to finish the race, so he decided to try to take off without the cargo, the passengers, and

Citizens of Albury, Australia, working together to pull the Uiver *out of the mud.*

The crew of the Uiver, *from left: radio operator Cornelis van Brugge, Captain Koene Dirk Parmentier, copilot Jan Moll, and flight engineer Bouwe Prins.*

van Brugge and Prins—leaving them behind on the ground. After Parmentier revved its engines, the *Uiver* strained down the muddy runway but managed to lift off the ground just at the end of the racetrack. Due in large part to the efforts of the mayor and citizenry of Albury, the *Uiver* was back on course for Melbourne and the finish.

After only fifty-seven minutes of flying time, the *Uiver* crossed the finish line at the Flemington Racecourse outside of Melbourne at 2:52 p.m. on October 24. Although Scott and Campbell Black had won the speed race, arriving in the *Grosvenor House* nineteen hours and nineteen minutes before the *Uiver* landed, Parmentier and Moll won the handicap event while coming in second in the speed event. A crowd of 20,000 had gathered to welcome the Dutchmen around midnight the evening before; but they dispersed after hearing about the *Uiver*'s emergency landing at Albury. The next morning, after hearing that the *Uiver* was airborne again, the crowd again converged on the Flemington Racecourse. The fact that Parmentier and Moll were not Australian or British made no difference to the enthusiastic crowd. The Dutch achievement demonstrated that Australia was now capable of being reached by airliner.

After first being greeted by officers of the Royal Australian Air Force, Parmentier and Moll were welcomed by the Dutch consul, Colonel H. Wright, who proceeded to make Parmentier and all the members of his crew knights of the Orde van Oranje-Nassau by a decree from Queen Wilhelmina. During the rest of their time in Australia, Parmentier and his colleagues were announced as Chevalier Parmentier, Chevalier Moll, and so on. Parmentier joked that this should stop, or the city of Melbourne would assume that they were brothers of Maurice Chevalier! After this presentation, the Dutch fliers were presented to Sir Macpherson Robertson, who praised them with these words: "This was just the result I wanted—to show that a transport plane could reach Australia in four days."

Back in the Netherlands, the public had gone mad with *Uiver* fever. To the Dutch population, their plane had accomplished a great achievement with the whole world watching. Many businesses closed so that people could listen to the details of the *Uiver*'s flight over the radio. Prime Minister Colijn radioed the *Uiver*'s crew to give his personal congratulations. The mood of the Netherlands was well summed up in a story that Colijn told Parmentier:

> I would like to say a few words to you, not on my own behalf but on behalf of the government and entire people of the Netherlands. There's been tremendous excitement: from old to young and from rich to poor, the whole nation waited in suspense, especially in the last twenty-four hours, to see what would happen. There's been a shockwave of enthusiasm throughout the country, when we heard that the *Uiver* arrived well. I'll tell you an amusing anecdote that I heard by chance yesterday. On Monday there was a pastor who was having catechism. And he had wanted the children to report what things they had learned about [John] Calvin and then at that moment he asked, when Calvin was born. But the children paid absolutely no attention. And then he asked: Where is the *Uiver* at this moment? Then they all jumped up, and knew the precise location position of the *Uiver*.[22]

Although the *Uiver* was an American-designed and -built aircraft, it was a triumph for the Netherlands, KLM, and its pilots.

Albert Plesman and Prime Minister Hendrikus Colijn congratulating the crew of the* Uiver *on their success over the radio.

An "*Uiver *craze" broke out in the Netherlands after the MacRobertson race in the form of songs, books, and commemorative souvenirs. This delft plate, made by De Koninklijke Porceleyne Fles, is one such example.

Fokker-Douglas

As the *Uiver* and KLM basked in the spotlight of public attention, Plesman realized that the need for DC-2s on the East Indies route was immediate—in order for the airline to retain the modern image it had created for itself. Plesman had already anticipated good performance from the DC-2 and he ordered fourteen of the airliners from Fokker. Fokker responded with a price of 160,000 guilders per aircraft, much higher than Plesman had anticipated. Plesman was furious and demanded a lower price; but Fokker would not budge. The sales rights to the DC-2 were the only way he would be able to make a profit

The original DC-2, the Uiver, *crashed en route to Batavia at Rutbah Wells in Iraq on December 20, 1934. The Aviodrome museum in Lelystad, the Netherlands, possesses a flying example of a DC-2 painted in the original* Uiver's *color scheme. Shown here are the cockpit and passenger cabin of the "new"* Uiver.

on commercial aircraft before his factory could develop modern competitive designs. With so much publicity surrounding the *Uiver,* KLM needed more DC-2s immediately. Plesman knew this, and he knew that it would require an agreement with Fokker, who was now all too aware of the advantage he had in the sales negotiations. Not wishing to waste any more time, KLM's board of directors eagerly decided that they were willing to pay up to 176,000 guilders per aircraft. But the negotiations between Plesman and Fokker continued; the latter, who was in no hurry, was intent on holding out for the best price possible. Finally, on August 15, 1935, KLM and Fokker reached an agreement by which the airline would pay 166,000 guilders per aircraft. Fokker thus managed to save his company; but on the other side of the scale, Plesman saw the whole affair as extortion.[23]

On March 30, 1935, KLM received the first of seventeen DC-2s manufactured by Douglas and sold by Fokker (the *Uiver* had crashed near Rutbah Wells en route to Batavia on December 20, 1934). Fokker may have purchased the license to manufacture the DC-2 in the Netherlands, but both he and Donald Douglas agreed that the airliners would all be built in Douglas's factory in California since it would take too long to retool Fokker's factory for all-metal

Douglas DC-2
length: 61 ft 11¾ in (18.89 m)
wingspan: 85 ft (25.91 m)
engines: two 730 hp Wright GR-1820-F53 Cyclone radials
maximum speed: 210 mph (338 km/h)
ceiling: 22,450 ft (6,845 m)
range: 1,000 miles (1,609 km)
crew: 3-4
passengers: 14 (European flights), 5-8 (Indies flights)

construction. Nevertheless, all of the DC-2s shipped to Europe had "Fokker-Douglas" painted on them, in turn giving Fokker an association with the most modern airliner of the day even though he had no hand in its design or production. On June 12, 1935, KLM began a twice-weekly service from Amsterdam to Batavia with its new DC-2s. The airliner's high cruising speed brought the time in the air to just fifty-seven hours (six days total travel time), reducing the travel time on that route by a third, since the F.XVIII's regular flight time had been seventy-four hours (nine days total travel time). KLM's last DC-2 was delivered on April 16, 1936, by which time nearly all of its Fokker trimotor transports had been sold.

KLM was developing a reputation as the most modern airline in Europe. The soundproofed and ventilated cabin of the DC-2 certainly gave passengers a much more comfortable flight, and in 1935 passenger service was upgraded by the inclusion of a stewardess with the crew of most airliners; her sole purpose was to ensure the comfort of passengers. Between 1935 and 1940 new routes were opened on the Continent between Amsterdam and Prague, Frankfurt, Milan, Vienna, Stockholm, Manchester, Kristiansand, Oslo, and Lisbon. KLM also became the first European airline to operate the DC-2's more famous successor, the DC-3, a widened and lengthened DC-2 with greater capacity, range, and speed. It was a relatively easy project for Douglas, and over time this airliner came to epitomize the new generation of all-metal airliners. When configured for the East Indies route, it carried eleven passengers, double the number of the DC-2.

KLM received the first of twenty-two DC-3s on March 23, 1937, and in October of that year the airline began three weekly flights along the Amsterdam-Batavia route. The slightly faster DC-3 reduced the time in the air along the route to fifty-five hours (six days total travel time). KLM thus maintained its title as the fastest and most frequent airline to the Far East. The fast and streamlined image of the DC-3 was widely marketed by KLM, and that garnered a great deal of publicity. This airliner was also good for Fokker, who sold sixty-three of that type before World War II began. KLM's DC-2/DC-3 service also forced

Plesman, Lindbergh, and Fokker at the Fokker factory. This was at the time of the falling out between Plesman and Fokker over KLM's reluctance to purchase the F.XX and F.XXXVI prototypes and Fokker's acquisition of the European sales rights for the Douglas DC-2. Plesman's contempt for Fokker almost seems visible in this photograph. [Photo AVIODROME Luchtfotografie, Lelystad, Holland]

A jovial Tony Fokker with representatives of Swissair after the airline's purchase of five new Fokker-Douglas DC-2s. While still coming to grips with modern design manufacturing methods in the late 1930s, Fokker was still the master salesman he had always been. He was able to sell a total of 39 DC-2s and 63 DC-3s throughout Europe. [Photo AVIODROME Luchtfotografie, Lelystad, Holland]

KLM advertisement with two little Dutch boys. This was an era when an airline captain had almost the same prestige as racing drivers, explorers, or athletes. KLM also took particular care to make sure that its flight officers were always impeccably dressed regardless of the length or duration of the flights they made. [R. E. G. Davies Collection]

its competitors to reevaluate and modernize their own Far Eastern services.[24]

To the Ends of the Empire

The Dutch public did not have to wait long to celebrate another KLM aviation triumph after the exploits of the *Uiver.* While KLM's participation in the MacRobertson Race was still being discussed in 1934, Albert Plesman had another groundbreaking KLM flight in mind. Plesman planned for a KLM aircraft to make the airline's first *transatlantic* crossing with one of its airliners. This was not to be an attempt to make a nonstop Amsterdam-to-New York flight (though Plesman hoped that such a flight would be possible in the not-too-distant future). Rather, a KLM airliner would fly across the Atlantic in stages, and its destination would be Willemstad on the island of Curacao, the capital of the Dutch West Indies. There were two motivations for the flight: first, to commemorate three hundred years of Dutch rule in Curacao (since 1634); second, to deliver an aircraft to the island in order to inaugurate regular KLM air services within the Dutch West Indies.

The establishment of KLM air service in the Western Hemisphere was the true impetus of the flight. Inter-island services could be created among the Dutch Antilles and other islands in the Caribbean, as well as to Dutch Guyana. Service among the Dutch Caribbean territories, however, would be just the first step; Plesman's ultimate goal was to create a KLM trans-Caribbean air network stretching from cities in Venezuela and Colombia north to Miami. But time was already running out, since Pan American Airways already had a strong presence in the region, and the French Compagnie Générale Aéropostale (CGA) and German-owned Sociedad Colombo Alemana de Transporte Aéreo (SCADTA) were looking to expand into the Caribbean. Although the establishment of a KLM network in the Caribbean offered profit potential, especially with the development of large oil facilities on Curacao, on Aruba, and in Venezuela, the trans-

Poster showing the interior arrangement of the passenger cabin of one of KLM's Douglas DC-2s. [Photo AVIODROME Luchtfotografie, Lelystad, Holland]

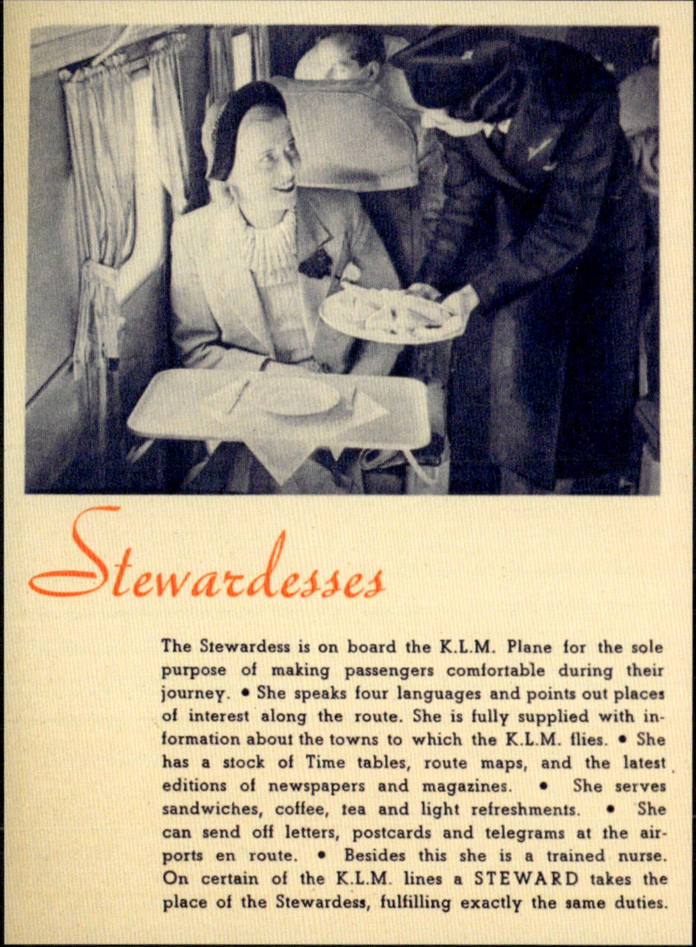

Stewardesses

The Stewardess is on board the K.L.M. Plane for the sole purpose of making passengers comfortable during their journey. • She speaks four languages and points out places of interest along the route. She is fully supplied with information about the towns to which the K.L.M. flies. • She has a stock of Time tables, route maps, and the latest editions of newspapers and magazines. • She serves sandwiches, coffee, tea and light refreshments. • She can send off letters, postcards and telegrams at the airports en route. • Besides this she is a trained nurse. On certain of the K.L.M. lines a STEWARD takes the place of the Stewardess, fulfilling exactly the same duties.

KLM introduced stewardess service to their airliners beginning in 1935 as the new DC-2s came into service. [R. E. G. Davies Collection]

RIGHT *The Douglas DC-3 was essentially a lengthened, wide-bodied development of the DC-2 airliner that offered more seating for daytime flights and sleeping berths for long-distance night flights. With its roomier cabin and higher passenger capacity, this became an ideal aircraft for KLM's Amsterdam-to-Batavia route, and KLM became the aircraft's first non-American purchaser. As with the DC-2, Fokker held the European production and sales rights to the DC-3.*

BELOW *A DC-3 of the Aviodrome's collection painted in 1939–40 neutrality markings.* [Photo AVIODROME Luchtfotografie, Lelystad, Holland]

Douglas DC-3
length: 64 ft 8 in (19.7 m)
wingspan: 95 ft 2 in (29.0 m)
engines: two 1,100 hp Wright R-1820 Cyclone radials
maximum speed: 230 mph (370 km/h)
ceiling: 23,200 ft (7,100 m)
crew: 3-4
passengers: 14-28

atlantic flight was an expensive endeavor. Furthermore, landing rights had to be obtained in foreign territories.

Given the limited range of KLM's aircraft, the airline mapped out a flight route from Amsterdam that would proceed to Casablanca in French Morocco, to Porto Praia in the Cape Verde Islands, across the Atlantic to Paramaribo in Dutch Guyana, and finally to Willemstad on Curacao. In addition to organizing the fueling and maintenance arrangements along the route, KLM had to set up and maintain radio and meteorological stations, and it would have to modify an aircraft to accommodate extra fuel tanks to give it enough range to make it across the Atlantic. The economy-minded Plesman had no intention of having KLM subsidize the entire cost of the flight, and thus he decided to borrow an idea from the previous year: the flight would be scheduled for December, and it would be designated a Kerstpostvlucht, like the flight made by the *Pelikaan* to Batavia, which would bring in revenue from the sale of special covers, stamps, and seals. In November 1934, Plesman announced to the public the Kerstpostvlucht to the West Indies and that the aircraft making the flight would be the Fokker F.XVIII *Snip*. With the Dutch public still riding a wave of aeronautical enthusiasm brought on by the recent successful return of the *Uiver* to the Netherlands, KLM had no problem marketing the upcoming flight of the *Snip*.

The pilot selected to fly the *Snip* was KLM Captain Jacobus Johannes Hondong, a veteran pilot of the Amsterdam-Batavia route. The rest of his crew were copilot and navigator Jan J. van Balkom, radio operator Simon van der Molen, and flight mechanic Leonardus D. Stolk. Before the flight commenced, Hondong and KLM had to make preparations for a flight over a route they had never traveled before. Deutsche Lufthansa was now regularly operating flying boats across the South Atlantic, from Bathhurst in Gambia to Recife in Brazil, but the route from Porto Praia to Paramaribo was new and longer, and the Germans had the luxury of catapult depot ships stationed along their route. For proper navigation, the *Snip* was equipped with brand-new Philips high- and low-frequency radios. KLM requested the assistance of the Koninklijke Nederlandse Stoomvaart Maatschappij (Royal Netherlands Steamship Company), which arranged for one of its ships, the SS *Stuyvesant,* to arrive at a location halfway between Porto Praia and Paramaribo around the time the *Snip* would be on that route in order to serve as a navigational beacon and also to relay navigational and meteorological information to the flight crew. Special radio assistance was provided by the Dutch submarine *K.XVIII,* which was in the Central Atlantic in the middle of a scientific and goodwill voyage around the world. Further navigational and meteorological assistance would be given by the French and the Portuguese

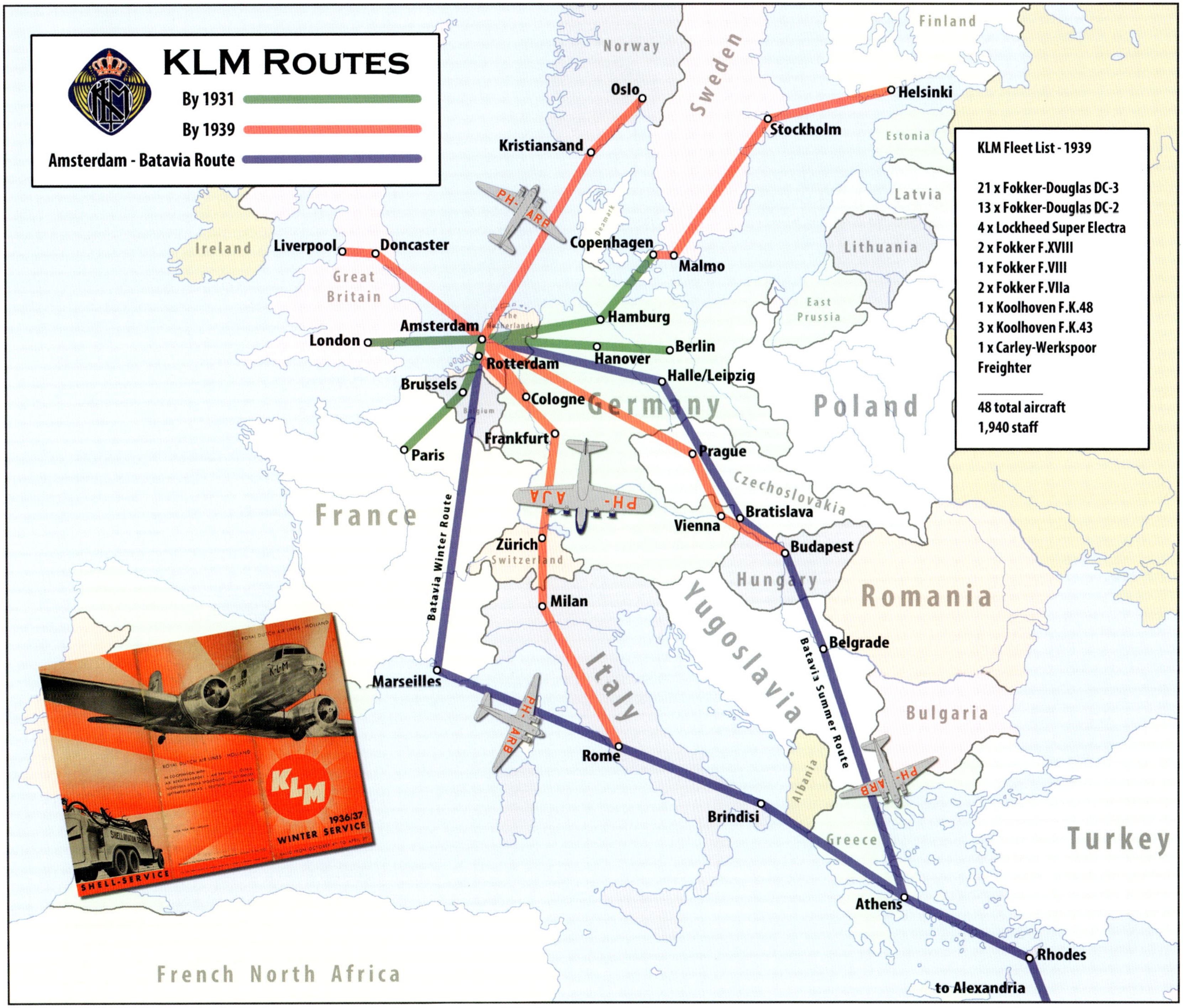
KLM Routes
By 1931
By 1939
Amsterdam - Batavia Route
KLM Fleet List - 1939
21 x Fokker-Douglas DC-3
13 x Fokker-Douglas DC-2
4 x Lockheed Super Electra
2 x Fokker F.XVIII
1 x Fokker F.VIII
2 x Fokker F.VIIa
1 x Koolhoven F.K.48
3 x Koolhoven F.K.43
1 x Carley-Werkspoor Freighter
48 total aircraft
1,940 staff
Norway
Sweden
Finland
Estonia
Latvia
Lithuania
East Prussia
Poland
Ireland
Great Britain
The Netherlands
Belgium
France
Germany
Czechoslovakia
Switzerland
Hungary
Romania
Yugoslavia
Italy
Bulgaria
Albania
Greece
Turkey
French North Africa
Oslo
Kristiansand
Stockholm
Helsinki
Copenhagen
Malmo
Liverpool
Doncaster
Amsterdam
London
Hamburg
Berlin
Hanover
Rotterdam
Halle/Leipzig
Brussels
Cologne
Paris
Frankfurt
Prague
Bratislava
Vienna
Budapest
Zürich
Milan
Belgrade
Marseilles
Rome
Brindisi
Athens
Rhodes
to Alexandria
Batavia Winter Route
Batavia Summer Route
PH-ARE
PH-AJA
PH-ARB
KLM
1936/37
WINTER SERVICE
SHELL-SERVICE

Sacks of mail for the 1934 Kerstpostvlucht to the West Indies being loaded into the forward cargo compartment of the Snip. [Photo AVIODROME Luchtfotografie, Lelystad, Holland]

1934 Kerstpostvlucht envelope carried aboard the Snip *on its transatlantic flight.*

over their territories during the first legs of the journey. Finally, the cabin of the *Snip* was stripped bare to allow for the installation of four additional fuel tanks, and the aircraft was re-equipped with three new 525-horsepower Pratt & Whitney Wasp radial engines, increasing its horsepower and speed. Plesman's idea of promoting the flight as a Kerstpostvlucht was an outstanding success, and public support was immense: 26,521 letters and packages were loaded aboard the aircraft, perhaps the most interesting being a bottle of beer that a Rotterdam brewery was sending to its agent in Curacao! At midnight on December 15, 1934, the engines of the *Snip* were turned over before a crowd of well-wishers at Schiphol. The weather was miserable: heavy wet snow was falling, and visibility was poor. Nevertheless, Capt. Hondong decided to take off on schedule.

After the engines were warmed up and the crew was aboard, the *Snip* took off at ten minutes after midnight on December 15 and headed in the direction of the Mediterranean. They encountered heavy snow and strong headwinds over northern Europe and France, and ice was collecting on the wings, making it impossible for the *Snip* to rise above the inclement weather. Radio operator van der Molen had received reports that the weather around Casablanca was equally bad, so Hondong decided against trying to fly there and instead landed at Marseille to wait for better conditions. After refueling in Marseille, Hondong took off again and landed at Alicante in Spain, again deciding to postpone the leg to Casablanca until the poor weather had passed. Unlike the *Uiver* in its flight to Australia, the *Snip* was not in a race, and there was no reason to risk damage to the aircraft. On the 16th, after the weather had improved, the *Snip* flew to Casablanca and on the following day on to Porto Praia. On the 18th, the crew rested while KLM and Royal Dutch Shell mechanics made a thorough check of the aircraft's engines and fuel tanks.

On the afternoon of December 19, the *Snip* taxied into the wind and took off for the Western Hemisphere. Radio contact was established almost immediately with the *Stuyvesant,* the *K-XVIII,* and Paramaribo, and it appeared that the journey would proceed smoothly. Halfway across the Atlantic, however, the *Snip*'s high-frequency radio malfunctioned: it could only receive, not send, messages. For several hours radio listeners throughout the Dutch Empire held their breath, wondering what had happened to the aircraft. Finally, van der Molen fixed the set and reestablished contact with Paramaribo, where an anxious crowd breathed a sigh of relief. In the early morning hours of the 20th, land was spotted over the horizon. Despite the inability of the crew to send messages for several hours, navigator van Balkom, via a combination of navigating by the stars and information passed along by the *Stuyvesant* and *K-XVIII*, had charted a course that took the *Snip* over the South American mainland less than four miles from the point planned out prior to departure, which was yet another excellent example of KLM operational efficiency. Shortly after 8:00 a.m. on December 20, the *Snip* came to a landing at Zandery Airfield near Paramaribo.

For two days Hondong and his crew were treated to a number of official receptions, and it appeared as though most of the population of the city had come out to welcome them. On December 22, the *Snip* took off for a diplomatic visit to La Guaira in Venezuela and received a warm welcome there. This visit had been planned ahead by Plesman in order to make a good impression on the Venezuelans in hopes of obtaining KLM landing rights throughout the country. After several official presentations, Hondong and his crew boarded the *Snip* and took off for Willemstad, their final destination. When the *Snip* touched down at Hato Airfield near Willemstad, a crowd of thousands was on hand to greet the fliers. The crew was then rushed to a nearby platform, where the governor of the colony made all the crew members knights of the Orde van Oranje-Nassau. It was a proud moment for KLM and the Dutch population: as of that moment, all corners of the empire had been reached from the fatherland by air.[25]

On January 19, 1935, KLM officially opened its West Indies division, with the *Snip* making regularly scheduled flights between Curacao and Aruba. The *Snip* was joined by the F.XVIII *Oehoe*, which was shipped by boat from Amsterdam in July 1935. Only a few weeks after it arrived, however, a novice pilot damaged its nose in a landing on Aruba, and it was out of service until November. KLM was eager to begin services to South America, but the Venezualan government took its time arranging the necessary landing permits. As it was, two aircraft could not provide a broad-ranging service alone, but they did manage to carry over 2,600 passengers between Curacao and Aruba during KLM's first year of service in the West

Crowds and cameramen gathering at Schiphol while the ground crew prepares the Snip *for its flight to the West Indies late in the evening of December 15, 1934.* [Photo AVIODROME Luchtfotografie, Lelystad, Holland]

Bystanders gather at Hato Airfield on Curacao to welcome the Snip.

The crew of the Snip *from left to right: Captain Jacobus Hondong, copilot Jan van Balkom, radio operator Simon van der Molen, and flight engineer Leonardus Stolk.*

Indies. KLM finally opened its first international route in the Caribbean on July 1, 1936, with service to Maracaibo—after the Venezuelan government finally granted the airline landing rights.

As the prospects for further route expansion grew in 1937, KLM decided to send some of its newly ordered Lockheed Model 14 Super Electras to the West Indies. Four of the all-metal modern airliners arrived in 1938, the first one flown from Lockheed's plant in California to Curacao by Capt. Geysendorffer, who was assigned to instruct the West Indies pilots on how to fly a faster and more modern aircraft. By the end of 1939, war was raging in Europe, but KLM's West Indies Division was rapidly expanding, with routes to as far away as Barranquilla, Colombia, and Maracaibo (with a connection via Pan Am flying boat service to Miami) to the west, and Trinidad, Barbados, and Paramaribo to the east.[26]

In early 1940, KLM began to examine the possibility of scheduling regular transatlantic flights following the route pioneered by Capt. Hondong in 1934. Of its roster of aircraft at the time, DC-3s could be equipped with extra fuel tanks and turned into long-range mail planes. The airline planned to have a long-range airliner in service by the following year. KLM's ultimate goal was entry into the United States via Miami from Curacao. Since 1937, the United States government and the Civil Aeronautics Board (lobbied heavily by Pan Am) had refused to grant landing rights in Miami to KLM, hoping to maintain an American monopoly on flights into and out of the country. The excuse frequently cited for not giving foreign airlines landing rights in the the United States was national defense. In August 1938, Deutsche Lufthansa flew one of its Focke-Wulf Fw 200 Condor airliners nonstop from Berlin to New York. Though the cabin of that airliner was packed with extra fuel tanks, the leadership of the U.S. Army Air Corps feared that the east coast of the United States would soon be within range of bombers from Europe. What was perceived to be even more threatening was the purchase of two Fw 200s by the Brazilian-based Sydicato Conder airline, a subsidiary of Deutsche Lufthansa, in 1939.

When World War II began, Deutsche Lufthansa and its Latin American subsidiaries, as well as the Italian airline Linee Aeree Transcontinentali Italiane (LATI), operated over 20,000 miles of routes in South America. Long-range German and Italian airliners, if converted to bombers and if operating from their airline bases, had the necessary range to attack the Panama Canal. This argument came to American national attention in 1941 and was promoted by Pan Am, which operated over 15,000 miles of routes in South America and took over a number of the German routes in 1942, with the rest being taken over by the respective South American governments. The Army Air Corps's fears of aerial bombardment from South America by the Axis powers proved, in reality, to be ungrounded (the German Luftwaffe never seriously entertained the idea because it would have been impossible logistically); but Pan Am nonetheless exploited those fears to their fullest. And though KLM only operated over 1,850 miles in the Caribbean and posed no threat to the defense of the United States or its Caribbean outposts, Pan Am and its political backers continued to promote national defense against foreign aircraft incursions in

As with the Uiver, *there was a "*Snip *craze" in the Netherlands that produced a number of souvenir items. The* Snip *was marketed on a rusk tin while this children's puzzle shows the crew of the* Snip *and the aircraft flying over the Atlantic, aided by the submarine* K-XVIII. [Photo AVIODROME Luchtfotografie, Lelystad, Holland]

Fokker F.XVIIIs Snip *and* Oehoe *parked in front of KLM's hangars at Hato Airfield (left). These trimotors served on KLM's West Indies routes until the end of the World War II. As a memorial to its transatlantic flight, the cockpit of the* Snip *(below) was preserved and is housed in the Curacaosch Museum in Willemstad.* [Courtesy Het Curacaosch Museum]

order to curtail any possible transatlantic competition from the Dutch—even after the German occupation of the Netherlands in May 1940. KLM did not receive landing rights in Miami until August 1943, a year and a half after the U.S. and Dutch governments had allied against Germany and Japan.[27]

KLM's Lockheed Super Electra Troepiaal *cruises over Willemstad on Curacao in the Dutch West Indies. Designed as Lockheed's response to the Douglas DC-2, the Model 14 Super Electra was faster than the DC-2 but was overshadowed by the larger capacity DC-3. Nevertheless it was a modern all-metal aircraft that attracted a number of European customers, including KLM. Four were purchased for the West Indies division in 1938.*

The Violent End of Fokker's Trimotors

As deliveries of new Douglas DC-2s and DC-3s arrived in Amsterdam, KLM began to sell off its fleet of Fokker trimotors. Although they were obsolete in Plesman's mind, the Fokker trimotors were still in good shape, and a number of European airlines were looking for aircraft that were cheaper than the new generation of expensive all-metal airliners. Perhaps the two most interesting customers for KLM's Fokker trimotors were the Republican and Nationalist movements that were locked in combat in Spain and were willing to pay nearly any price for any aircraft at the time. After the outbreak of the Spanish Civil War in July 1936, the Spanish air attaché in Paris, who had joined the Nationalist cause, covertly purchased two Fokker F.VIIb/3ms from KLM via Crilly Airways in Great Britain. The Nationalists hired the famous British pilot Captain T. Neville Stack, an experienced race pilot who had flown the Airspeed Viceroy in the MacRobert-

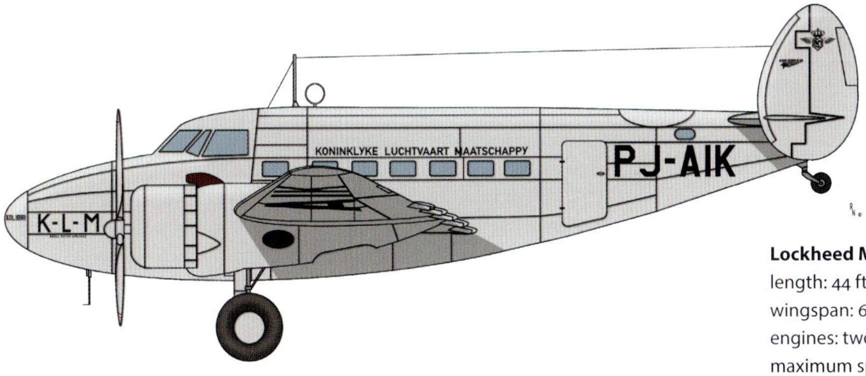

Lockheed Model 14 Super Electra
length: 44 ft 4 in (13.51 m)
wingspan: 65 ft 6 in (19.96 m)
engines: two 760 hp Wright SGR-1820-F62 radials
maximum speed: 250 mph (402 km/h)
ceiling: 24,500 ft (7,470 m)
range: 2,125 miles (3,420 km)
crew: 2
passengers: 12

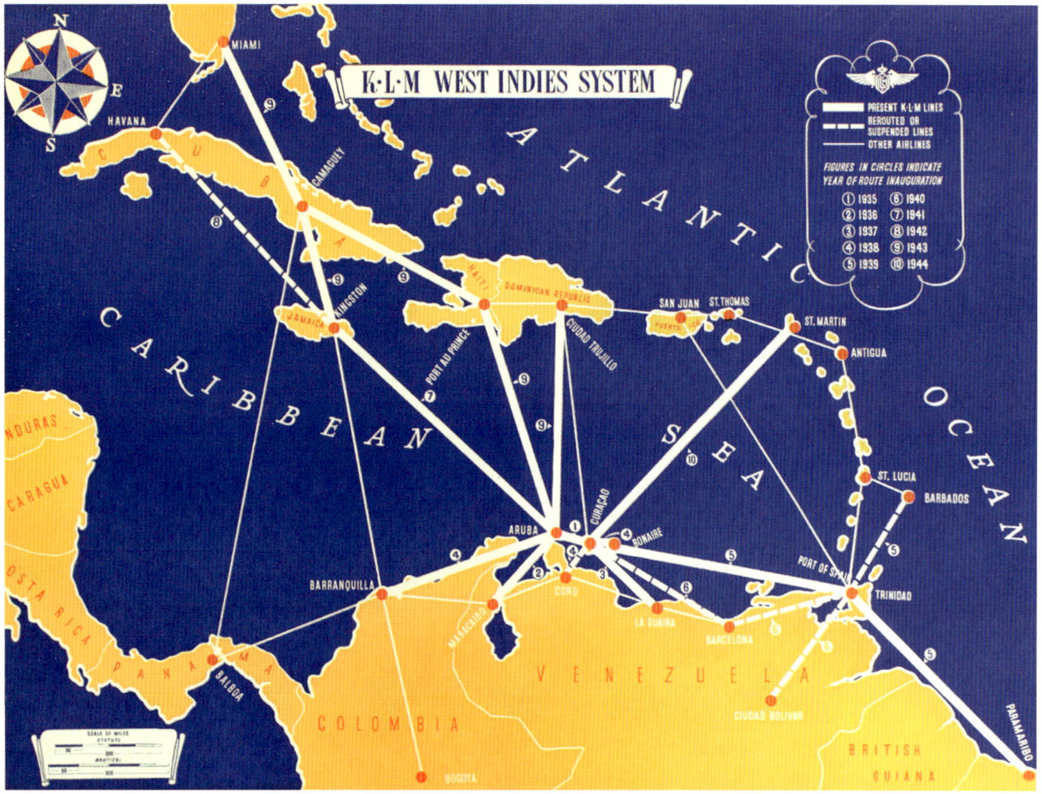

Map of KLM's West Indies Division.

son Race, and fellow pilot Donald Salisbury Green to fly the trimotors to Spain. Equipped with extra fuel, which was pumped into the tanks from containers inside their fuselages, both aircraft were safely flown nonstop from Great Britain to Nationalist-held Burgos.

These were not the first Fokker trimotors to be used by the Nationalists: three F.VIIb/3ms were taken over from the Spanish national airline Líneas Aéreas Postales Españolas (LAPE) and were instrumental in beginning the airlift of troops from General Francisco Franco's Army of Africa to the mainland, where they were desperately needed to secure territory held by the Nationalists. These three Fokkers had transported nearly 2,000 men across the Straits of Gibraltar before Adolf Hitler sent a fleet of Luftwaffe and Deutsche Lufthansa Junkers Ju 52/3ms to assist in the transit of the rest of Franco's forces. The Nationalists also covertly acquired four former KLM Fokker F.XIIs from British airlines through the assistance of a Polish arms dealer. Unfortunately, the Polish pilots hired by the arms dealer were fighter pilots who were unaccustomed to flying multi-engine aircraft. Two of the F.XIIs crashed at the hands of these inexperienced pilots on their delivery flights, but the other two were eventually delivered safely. The F.VIIb/3ms and F.XIIs were formed into the "Esquadrilla Fokker," which carried out transport and bombing missions (rudimentary bomb racks had been installed on the aircraft) until the unit was disbanded in December 1936. Afterward, the surviving Na-

In late 1937, KLM transferred the Fokker F.VIII Duif *to the West Indies for cartography service. In March 1939 the aircraft was sold to the Venezuelan government but it crashed near an airfield in the jungle of the Gran Sabana region in April of that year. In 1999 the wreck was rediscovered and was retrieved by staff of the Aviodome Museum in 2001. Bits and pieces of the aircraft were located in native villages around the airfield. The wreck was briefly put on display in a diorama (shown here) at the Aviodome near Schiphol until 2003 when the Aviodome was reorganized as the Aviodrome and relocated to Lelystad. The wreckage of the* Duif *is currently in storage at the Aviodrome.* [Photo courtesy of Henk van den Os]

tionalist Fokkers were used only in noncombat transport and training roles.[28]

Likewise, the Republicans made use of several ex-LAPE F.VIIb/3ms for bombing and transport missions early in the war. Also like the Nationalists, the Republicans had purchasing agents abroad, and La Société Française des Transports Aériens, a French dummy corporation set up to purchase aircraft for the Spanish Republican government, managed to buy four Fokker trimotors from KLM in September 1936. These included the F.IX *Adelaar,* the F.XII *IJsvogel,* and two particularly famous KLM transports, the F.XVIII *Pelikaan* and the F.XX *Zilvermeeuw.* It was reported to the media that these aircraft were to be the backbone of a new French West African airline Air Tropique, which was another front organization, and the four trimotors made their way to Spain from Le Bourget with the tacit support of the ruling French socialist government. The *Zilvermeeuw* was put into service with LAPE as a high-speed transport and flew a number of flights to Paris carrying gold bullion for Republican weapons purchases—before it crashed in February 1938. The other three trimotors were equipped with bomb racks and served as bombers until they were replaced by purpose-built aircraft. The *Pelikaan* was destroyed on the ground shortly before the end of the Spanish civil war during a bombing raid conducted by the German Legion Condor in February 1939.

Of all the Fokker trimotors brought into the Spanish civil war, only a single F.VIIb/3m, an F.IX, and an F.XII survived the conflict. However, the air battles taking place in the skies of Spain during the late 1930s did have an indirect impact on the Dutch military aviation industry. Germany, Italy, and the Soviet Union all used the Spanish civil war as a sort of live-fire exercise to test the latest generation of their combat aircraft. Foreign military observers examined the performance of these foreign machines, and their reports to their respective governments helped inaugurate a new period of intense technological development in Europe's military aviation industries. The German, British, Soviet, Italian, and French air forces all began a series of modernization pro-

Fokker F.VIIb/3m Veterano *was one of three built for the Aeronáutica Militar Española under license by the Loring company. It was requisitioned by the Nationalists in Spanish West Africa at the beginning of the Spanish Civil War and initially used to ferry troops across the Straits of Gibraltar. This airlift of troops into southern Spain played a pivotal role in the survival of Franco's Nationalist movement.* Veterano *was later employed as a bomber and made several raids on Spanish Republican ships.*

The Fokker F.XX with a camouflage paint scheme seen at Le Bourget outside Paris in 1937. It was purchased by the Spanish Republican government and used as a high-speed transport by the Spanish airline LAPE. It made several flights carrying gold to France to pay for weapons purchases before it crashed in February 1938. [Photo AVIODROME Luchtfotografie, Lelystad, Holland]

Top *After the Nationale Vliegtuig Industrie was dissolved, Frits Koolhoven took over its remaining assets and founded his own company, N.V. Koolhoven Vliegtuigen. He would never go on to produce airliners in quantity as Fokker did, but Koolhoven had success in the late 1920s and 1930s with small private aircraft. The first aircraft of the new company to be produced in quantity was the F.K.41, a high-wing 3-passenger sport/business plane that was first flown in July 1928. Koolhoven's company only built seven F.K.41s, but a license to produce the design in Great Britain was purchased by Marcel Desoutter, a famous prewar aviator who founded his own aviation company, Desoutter Aircraft Company, Ltd., in 1928. Desoutter manufactured twenty-eight Desoutter Mk.Is (powered by the 130 hp de Havilland Gipsy Major I) and thirteen Desoutter Mk.IIs (powered by the 120 hp de Havilland Gipsy III). This Desoutter Mk.II resides in the Shuttleworth Collection in Bedfordshire, England.* [Courtesy of the Shuttleworth Collection]

Bottom *Frits Koolhoven (center) relaxing with friends.* [Photo AVIODROME Luchtfotografie, Lelystad, Holland]

Koolhoven F.K.41
length: 25 ft 7 in (7.8 m)
wingspan: 34 ft 5½ in (10.5 m)
engine: 130 hp de Havilland Gipsy Major I in-line
maximum speed: 121 mph (195 km/h)
crew: 1

grams, and the smaller nations of Europe, including the Netherlands, had to follow suit or be technologically left behind.[29]

Forsaking the Flying Boat

What made KLM different from its foreign rivals was its refusal to invest in or commit to a flying-boat system on its Far Eastern route—or on any of its routes. In the mid-1930s, when Imperial Airways of Britain, Air France, and Pan American Airways were purchasing giant flying boats and investing in infrastructure to support them on their Far Eastern routes, Plesman had already concluded that the days of the flying boat were numbered. The reasoning for operating flying boats on long-distance routes was that they had a greater long-distance payload than the land-based aircraft of the time. Greater payload meant more passengers, more cargo, and more mail. However, the greater size of the flying boat, which allowed for the greater payload, also meant greater takeoff weight, resulting in a higher weight-to-horsepower ratio. Because more horsepower was required to lift the flying boat out of the water and keep it aloft, it had a slower airspeed and a higher consumption of fuel. In the end, the revenue gained from the increased payload did not make up for the increased fuel costs. For example, the cost per seat-mile of a Short Empire–class flying boat, despite its greater passenger capacity, was almost twice that of a DC-3.

That was Plesman's view of flying boats; but British Imperial saw things in a different light. Since Imperial had more destinations to service along its Far Eastern route than did KLM, it would require massive investment to construct the necessary ground infrastructure and concrete runways to support the new generation of all-metal four-engine airliners that were in development. At this technological juncture, Imperial decided to chart a course that would give it modern, fast, and luxurious airliners and also avoid the costs of infrastructure redevelopment. In 1934, Imperial began the Empire Flying Boat program: based on the development of large flying boats, Imperial ordered thirty-one of the Short S.23 C Empire–class flying boats, each of which had seventeen seats and an attractive upper-deck lounge. The first one entered service in 1936, but regular service to as far away as Singapore did not begin until February 23, 1938. Another reason for the use of flying boats—aside from infrastructure savings—was that, in the event of an engine failure, landing on water provided a higher safety factor (which was the main reason for Pan American's faith in flying boats). The final advantage offered by the flying boat was prestige: the larger interior allowed for more spacious and comfortable accommodations for its passengers. To the economically minded Plesman, this was a frivolous waste that would create a longer schedule. KLM's Douglas fleet offered the fastest service to the Far East, and Plesman prided himself especially on his airline's speed and efficiency. Furthermore, he preferred to wait until the new generation of American-built four-engine airliners went into service. Meanwhile, he allowed his new fleet of Douglas DC-2s and DC-3s to maintain their service to the East Indies.[30]

Dutch aircraft designer and manufacturer Frits Koolhoven, of N.V. Koolhoven Vliegtuigen, pushed KLM to reevaluate the flying boat for its long-distance routes, using the argument of Pan Am and Imperial that flying boats required no runways, only access to the water. He said that, despite the higher operating costs of the flying boats, it would be more economical for the Netherlands to invest in flying boats than to commit massive sums to a complete redevelopment of the airfields used by KLM. In 1937, Koolhoven wrote:

> The greatest advantage of a seaplane is its independence from airfields, as there is much more water in the world than land.
>
> All of the great commercial cities [lie] on water, wherever there is a Dutch port facility the opportunity to land costs nothing, except the expenses of a motorboat and a buoy.
>
> Had less money been spent on land airfields and landplanes, we could have perhaps developed 50-ton flying boats with the same money. . . .
>
> Our colonies are thousands of miles removed from the Motherland, both of which are rich with islands; they are surrounded by the same water here and there from which we could take-off and land without cost.[31]

Inspired by the Clipper flying boats that Pan Am was operating on its transpacific route, Koolhoven began to design a massive 100-ton flying boat in 1938. With a wingspan of 230 feet and a length of 200 feet, the Koolhoven Oceaanvliegboot would have been roughly twice the size of the Boeing 314, the largest flying boat to see commercial service before the outbreak of World War II. It was to be powered by a set of two in-line engines, mounted in tandem, to drive a single propeller from each wing. It was to have a capacity for sixty or seventy passengers, twelve crew members, and forty-two tons of cargo.

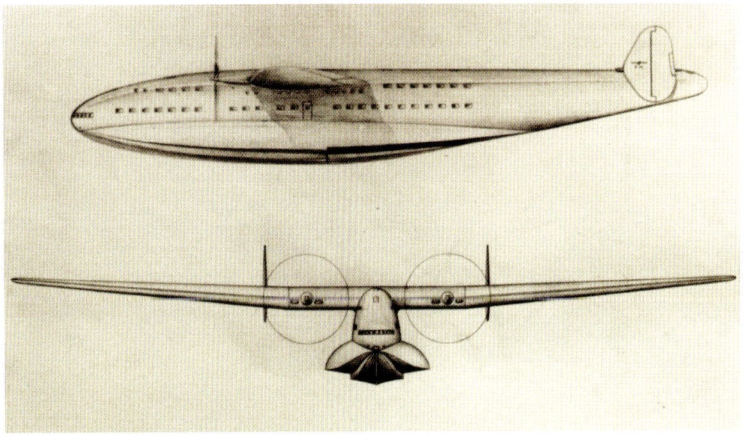

A sketch of Koolhoven's 100-ton Oceaanvliegboot proposal. Research into such a design began in 1936, but the project was dropped in 1938. It was yet another prime example of Koolhoven's creative yet eccentric approach to aircraft design. [Photo AVIODROME Luchtfotografie, Lelystad, Holland]

When Koolhoven showed his Oceaanvliegboot project to Albert Plesman, the latter was not interested. Plesman was fully confident in the progress being made in increasing the range of large, land-based aircraft, and he believed that they represented the future of long-distance air travel. His view was vindicated after the war, when similar massive flying boats, such as the British Saunders-Roe Princess (which never went into service) and the French Latécoère 631 failed to be commercially successful. The reason was that World War II had rapidly accelerated the development of long-range land-based aircraft, plus the concrete runways and ground infrastructure necessary to accommodate them. In the end, it became clear that Plesman had made a wise decision not to pursue a flying-boat program for KLM.[32]

The Pursuit of the Intercontinental Airliner

With KLM's route to the Far East upgraded with its newly purchased Douglas airliners, there was only one geographical challenge left before the airline could fully embrace the entire globe: developing the capability of

KLM's primary maintenance hangar at Schiphol in the late 1930s, filled with DC-2 and DC-3 airliners. By the beginning of World War II, KLM boasted one of the world's most modern aircraft fleets. [Photo AVIODROME Luchtfotografie, Lelystad, Holland]

opening a regular transatlantic air route. While KLM was taking delivery of its new DC-2s and DC-3s, Albert Plesman was already researching how to create such a route and seeking to determine the type of aircraft required for the job. In the fall of 1935, Donald Douglas was already considering a four-engine, all-metal airliner that would have twice the capacity of the DC-3, a range of 2,200 miles, and a pressurized cabin. Such a revolutionary design required extensive research, and several major airlines, including KLM, encouraged Douglas to develop a prototype. At the time, KLM's fleet was increasingly relying almost exclusively on Douglas airliners. The fact that Plesman, who had adamantly refused to give Anthony Fokker funding to help with research and design costs, offered investment in an unproven and radical design demonstrated his firm conviction that the future of long-distance air travel lay in such a design and that the Douglas Company had the necessary industrial infrastructure to create and build a new long-distance airliner in a timely manner. Not only could Douglas's new design be used on a transatlantic route, but it could also be put into service on the Amsterdam-Batavia route, eliminating several stops and reducing the flying time.

The resulting DC-4, which took two years to design and build, made its first flight in May 1938. The prototype was not pressurized, but the cabin was air-conditioned, and the airliner cruised at 200 mph. The prototype did not fully meet expectations because of its underpowered performance, and the complex new electrical systems required substantial maintenance. As a result, the model, by that time designated DC-4E, did not go into production.[33] Instead, the single prototype was exported to Japan, where it was used as the basis for an unsuccessful long-range bomber design. A simplified but more efficient DC-4 design was developed and would later go into series production. Unfortunately for KLM, the first DC-4 was not completed until February 1942, when the Netherlands had already been occupied by Germany for nearly two years.

Plesman's interest in the DC-4E project came as no surprise to Anthony Fokker, even when, in November

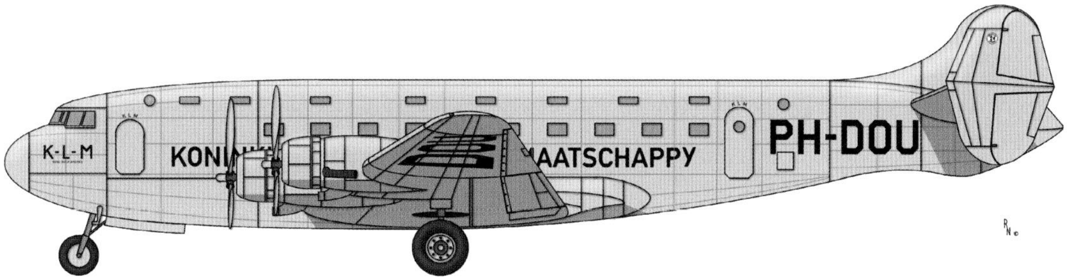

Douglas DC-4E
length: 97 ft 7 in (29.74 m)
wingspan: 138 ft 3 in (42.14 m)
engines: four 1,450 hp Pratt & Whitney R-2180-S1A1-G Twin Hornet radials
maximum speed: 245 mph (394 km/h)
ceiling: 22,900 ft (6,980 m)
range: 2,200 miles (3,540 km)
crew: 4
passengers: 30-42

1936, the KLM director wrote to Fokker that, if KLM was going to purchase any further aircraft from Fokker, they would have to be similar in design to the DC-4E. As Douglas's business partner, Fokker was well aware of the new project being discussed in Santa Monica. As a surprise to Plesman, Fokker sent him a new design, Ontwerp 132, only a few days later. Ontwerp 132 was a streamlined, low-wing, four-engine airliner with fully retractable landing gear; it was perhaps the most aesthetically pleasing airliner design to emerge from Fokker's drawing boards. In a first for Fokker, the front and rear of the fuselage was made of duralumin, but the wings and center fuselage were still made of wood. In its East Indies configuration, Ontwerp 132 would have seats for twenty passengers and would cruise at 200 mph, with a range of 1,500 miles. Ontwerp 132 was not to be pressurized, and Fokker argued that it would take years for American manufacturers to perfect a fully pressurized airliner (he was correct: the supposedly first fully pressurized airliner, the four-engine Boeing 307 Stratoliner which entered service in 1940, was only partially pressurized). He also said that the wooden wings, though heavier, were less complex to maintain and that their increased weight would be offset by the lower weight of the partial-metal fuselage. Fokker sent KLM a memorandum in which he compared the projected performance of the DC-4E and Ontwerp 132: he concluded by saying that the 132 would be slightly faster, could be put into service sooner, and would be 10 percent more economical to operate than would the DC-4E. Had Ontwerp 132 gone into production, KLM could

Already in 1935, before the first DC-3 had made its first flight, Douglas began design work on a four-engine airliner that would have a range of 2,200 miles and carry twice the number of passengers as the DC-3. Designated the DC-4E, the aircraft showed great potential in its early developmental stages; but it had a number of complex innovations that were yet to be technically perfected, and it appeared that it would be an overly expensive aircraft to operate. KLM invested in the airliner's initial development but withdrew its financial support—as did other interested airlines—when the DC-4E's numerous problems became apparent.

TOP *This profile shows the DC-4E in a hypothetical KLM livery.*

BOTTOM *The DC-4E cruises over New York City.*

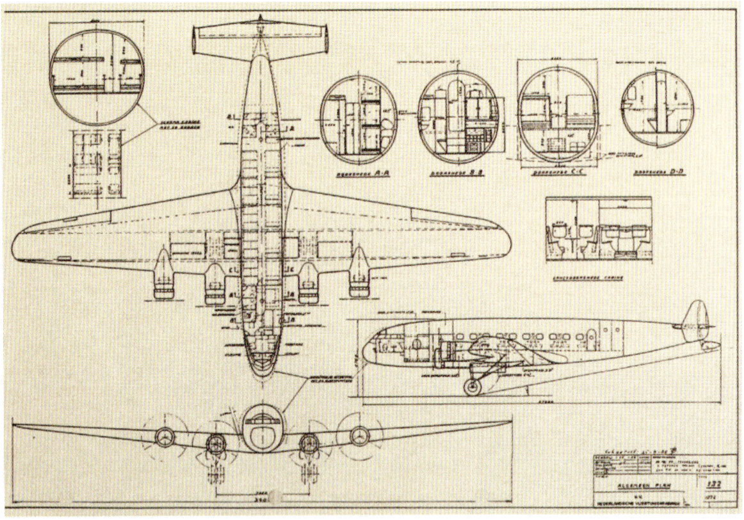

Left *Blueprints for Fokker Ontwerp 132. The project was an attempt by Fokker and his engineers to create an airliner of the company's own manufacture that could directly compete with the Douglas DC-4E. Although it was not of all-metal construction, it nevertheless showed that Fokker was moving toward modern aircraft construction methods. Having already invested in the DC-4E project, Plesman refused to consider this aesthetically beautiful Fokker design.* [Photo AVIODROME Luchtfotografie, Lelystad, Holland]

Below *The Focke-Wulf Fw 200 Condor airliner proved Albert Plesman's belief that land-based aircraft would be able to fly nonstop across the Atlantic when one flew nonstop from Berlin to New York City on August 10-11, 1938. At the time, the Condor trumped all other airliners in the world in terms of range, something not lost on American manufacturers, who went to work on a new generation of long-range designs. For a time, Plesman considered purchasing several Condors for KLM while waiting for Douglas to finish the DC-4E project; however, always forward thinking, he decided to wait for a fully pressurized airliner to be developed. The beginning of World War II also curtailed the possibility of aircraft purchases from Germany. This profile features a Condor in hypothetical KLM livery.*

Focke-Wulf Fw 200B Condor
length: 78 ft 3 in (23.85 m)
wingspan: 108 ft 3¼ in (33 m)
engines: four 830 hp BMW 132H radials
cruising speed: 226.7 mph (365 km/h)
ceiling: 23,622 ft (7,200 m)
range: 932 miles (1,500 km)
crew: 4
passengers: 26

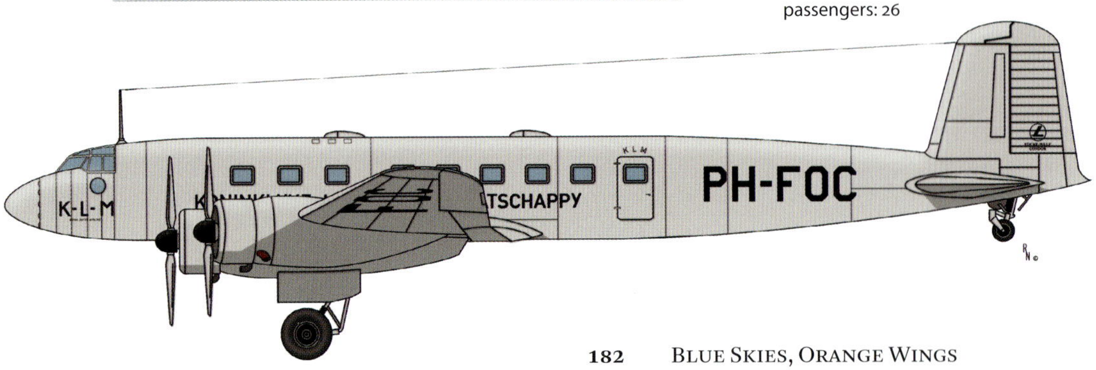

have purchased a Dutch-built airliner that was similar in performance to Germany's Focke-Wulf Fw 200, the first of the new generation of long-range four-engine airliners. Plesman was somewhat impressed with the leaps in modernization that Fokker's company was making—at least on the drawing board. But he was still determined to purchase only all-metal airliners, and he was still dubious about any completion date that Fokker might give.[34]

The board of directors of KLM was hesitant to have the airline's Far Eastern four-engine aircraft program reliant on a single prototype, and that was a wise decision. By the summer of 1938, KLM's board was beginning to learn about the teething troubles of the DC-4E. Furthermore, the airliner was not meeting the required cruising speed, and KLM did not want to commit to an aircraft whose performance might rapidly be superseded by another. For a time KLM considered the Focke-Wulf Fw 200 for the Far Eastern route, as it was already in series production; but as more modern pressurized airliners were just over the horizon, the airline decided to wait. This time the American aero industry let KLM down. First, Donald Douglas decided not to pursue the DC-4E project and focused his efforts on the definitive DC-4, which did not fly until February 14, 1942. Second, the prototype of the Boeing 307 Stratoliner, which KLM wanted to purchase for its European routes, crashed on March 18, 1939, during a demonstration flight for KLM officials in Seattle. Pieter Guilonard, the vice director of KLM, was killed in that crash. Subsequently, KLM turned to new long-range designs being developed by Lockheed. The wind suddenly appeared to be shifting in Fokker's favor.[35]

The fortunes of the Nederlandsche Vliegtuigenfabriek suddenly changed in 1936, thanks in large part to the European rearmament race instigated by Adolf Hitler. Fokker began to receive orders for a variety of military aircraft, not just from the LVA and MLD but from the air arms of other nations as well. His company had invested the earnings from the DC-2 and DC-3 sales into new military designs, such as the revolutionary G.I and D.XXIII fighters. With the fortunes of his company restored, as well as his reputation as a modern military manufacturer,

Fokker sought to reenter the now highly competitive airliner market and win back contracts from KLM. He had submitted numerous modern designs for new airliners to KLM in the late 1930s, but the airline paid little attention to them. Finally, in 1939, Fokker approached KLM with a new long-range four-engine airliner for the East Indies route, and this time he had the backing of the Dutch government. Fokker had been petitioning the government to intervene on his behalf by encouraging KLM to "buy Dutch." The laissez-faire economic nature of previous governments only took these appeals under consideration, but in 1939 the government recognized the strategic importance of having a modern domestic aircraft manufacturer. In the event of war, the Netherlands needed to be self-sufficient for its military and civil aviation needs.

On September 26, 1939, the ministry of waterworks instructed KLM to purchase an example of Fokker Ontwerp 180, a radical all-metal four-engine pressurized giant with the passenger cabin located in the giant wing. The government would help to subsidize the construction of Ontwerp 180 and in return KLM would be granted permission to order six long-range airliners from the United States. Fokker had finally forced his way back into the commercial aviation market. Unfortunately, he was not able to cherish this success: Anthony Fokker died of complications after sinus surgery on December 23, 1939. Nor was Plesman able to inaugurate his four-engine airliner plan for the Amsterdam-Batavia route as he had scheduled, because World War II intervened. KLM did not receive its first modern four-engine airliner until 1945.[36]

The Boeing 307 Stratoliner, a civil transport derived from the B-17C bomber, was seen as a potential replacement for the failed DC-4E, since it had both long-range and partial pressurization. KLM's interest in the aircraft waned after the prototype broke up in the air and crashed outside of Seattle, Washington, on March 18, 1939, killing all on board. Inspecting the aircraft for potential purchase at the time was Pieter Guilonard, KLM's assistant general manager, and Albert von Baumhauer, chief engineer of the Dutch government's airworthiness board. The Smithsonian National Air and Space Museum's Steven F. Udvar-Hazy Center houses the sole surviving Boeing 307. The profile shows another KLM "what could have been."

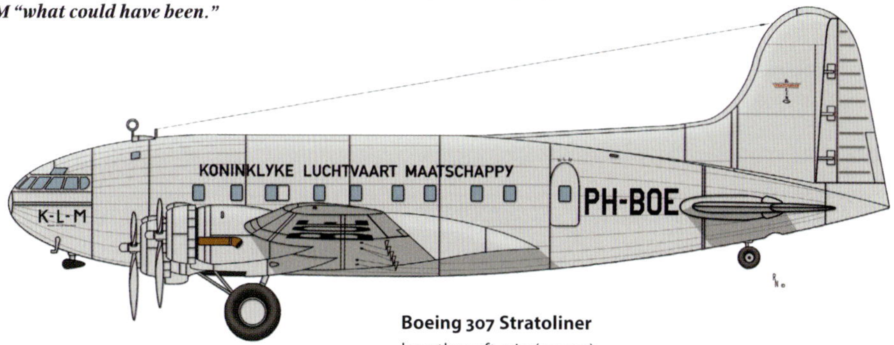

Boeing 307 Stratoliner
length: 74 ft 4 in (22.7 m)
wingspan: 107 ft 3 in (32.7 m)
engines: four 900 hp Wright GR-1820 Cyclone radials
maximum speed: 246 mph (396 km/h)
ceiling: 26,200 ft (7,986 m)
range: 2,390 miles (3,846 km)
crew: 5
passengers: 33

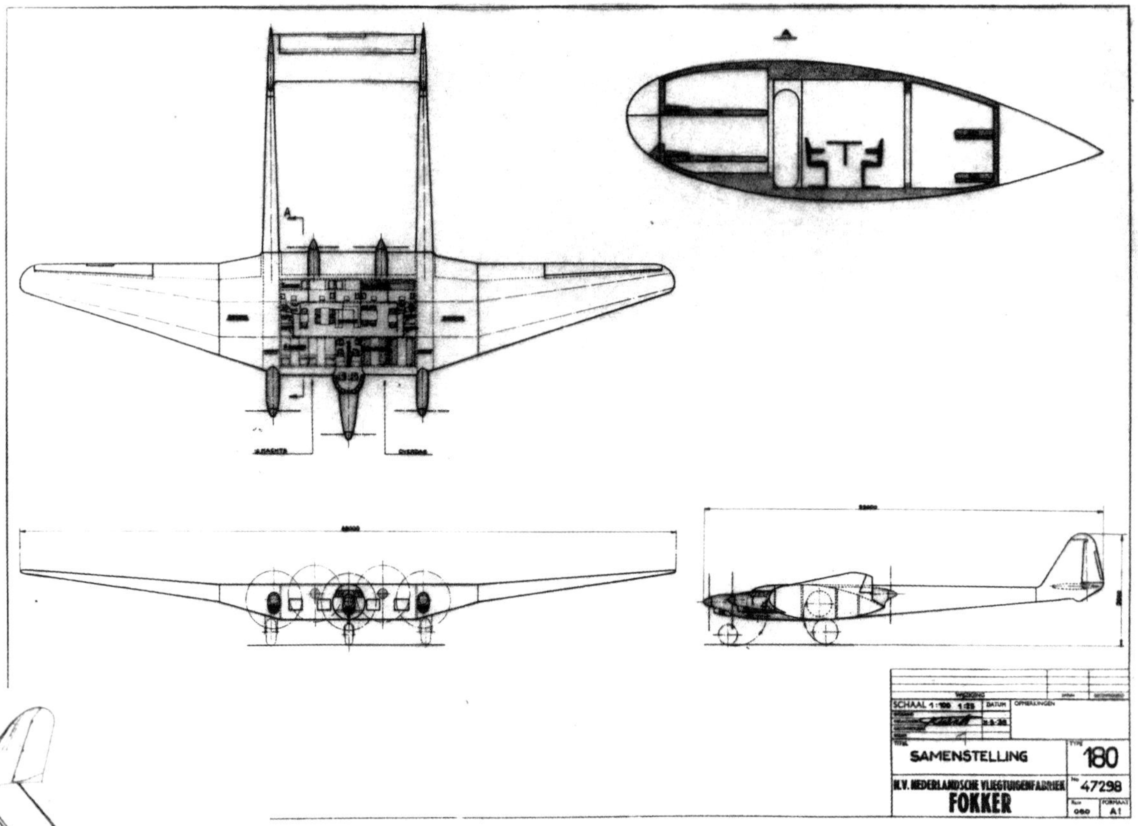

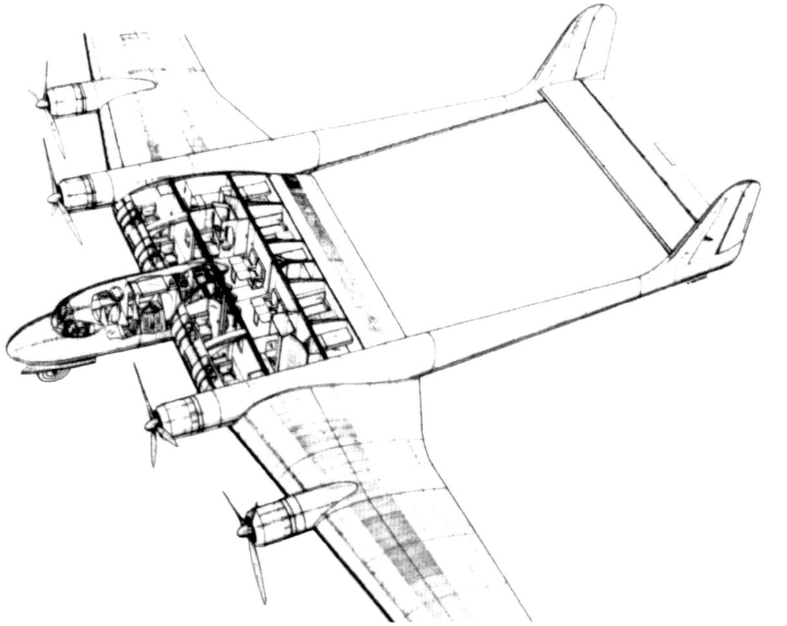

A preliminary sketch and later blueprint for Fokker Ontwerp 180. The transatlantic project was inspired by the flying-wing designs of American aircraft designer Vincent Burnelli. The passenger cabin was situated in the middle of the wing with luxurious accommodations for twenty-six. Ontwerp 180 was an all-metal design that had four engines in its early sketches but ultimately would have five as the project took shape. The massive flying-wing airliner seemed to be a quantum leap from Fokker's designs of only a few years earlier. Unfortunately, World War II brought an abrupt halt to the project. [Photo AVIODROME Luchtfotografie, Lelystad, Holland]

The evolution of KLM posters over a decade shows not only an advancement in technology but also a refinement in advertising style; the first is from the early 1920s, the second from toward the end of the decade.

The "Flying Dutchman" motif was the primary theme in KLM advertising and is evidenced in these posters from 1933 and 1939.

Photo of the Fokker factory in the late 1930s with D.XXI single-engine and G.1 twin-engine fighters under construction. Rearmament across Europe in the late 1930s gave Fokker a much-needed boost in sales as the LVA and other air forces needed new fighters and bombers. In May 1940 these aircraft would be defending Dutch skies against a sudden Nazi onslaught. [Photo AVIODROME Luchtfotografie, Lelystad, Holland]

Chapter Six

TRYING TO FLY ABOVE THE STORM

Defending Neutrality Once More

When World War II began on September 1, 1939, the Netherlands hoped to maintain neutrality similar to what it had during World War I. But world politics and balances of power had changed rather significantly since the Treaty of Versailles. Prior to the outbreak of war, the Dutch desired a *strict neutrality,* which they defined as making no alliances or nonaggression pacts with any of the European powers. Indeed, the Dutch had turned down a nonaggression pact offered by Adolf Hitler in 1936, fearing that it might compromise the Dutch notion of strict neutrality. Hitler would continue to make nonaggression pact overtures to the Dutch well into 1939, but if the Dutch government had accepted one of these offers, the British and French would have interpreted it as a sign that the Netherlands had become a quiet ally of Der Führer. Part of the rationale for a policy of strict neutrality came from the seeming lack of interest and the powerlessness of the League of Nations in dealing with acts of aggression against weaker nations, for example, the Japanese occupation of Manchuria in 1931 and the Italian invasion of Abyssinia in 1936. The Dutch realized early on that, if the Netherlands were to be invaded by a foreign power, it could not count on the League to come to its aid. Therefore, defiant, self-sufficient neutrality seemed to be the practical course.

As the decade came to a close, however, strict neutrality would prove almost impossible to keep in place. The Dutch were not particularly worried about their sovereignty when the Germans annexed the Sudetenland in the latter part of 1938 and Bohemia and Moravia in early 1939, or even when the Germans invaded Poland on September 1, 1939. The Dutch population had no reason at this point to be anti-German. A large proportion of the Dutch continental trade took place with Germany, and there was a cultural affinity between the two peoples. Furthermore, business would greatly suffer if there was to be any disruption of trade with Germany. In addition, most Dutch businessmen and industrialists could relate to the Nazi government's disapproval of socialists and communists. There was little love for communism in the Netherlands. On the other hand, Dutch business concerns did not want any disruption in trade with Great Britain either. In this regard, therefore, strict neutrality again seemed like a reasonable approach to the deteriorating situation on the Continent.

The leadership of the Netherlands was divided as to

Colonel Hans Oster was deputy chief of the German Abwehr intelligence service under Admiral Wilhelm Carnaris, who began to plot against the Nazis with other conspirators already in 1938. Oster passed a wealth of top secret information on to Maj. Sas prior to the invasion of the Netherlands. Oster was arrested after the failed July 20, 1944, bomb plot against Adolf Hitler and was executed the following year. [Wikimedia Commons]

Major Gijsbertus J. Sas was the military attaché at the Dutch embassy in Berlin from March 1939 to May 10, 1940. He learned in advance through his friend, Colonel Hans Oster of the German Abwehr, about the German invasions of Poland, Scandinavia, and the West and passed this information on to General Izaäk Reijnders and later General Henri Winkelman. Reijnders refused to believe that the Germans would violate Dutch neutrality; but after the war began, Sas's information was taken more seriously by Winkelman, Defense Minister Dijxhoorn, Prince Bernhard, and Queen Wilhelmina. [Wikimedia Commons]

Queen Wilhelmina speaking with King Leopold of Belgium in front of the Dutch royal train in Brussels. Fearing that Hitler could not be trusted, the Queen wanted the Dutch armed forces to begin joint defensive planning with the Belgians. Prime Minister Dirk Jan de Geer and Opperbevelhebber Reijnders, however, pushed for a strict interpretation of neutrality and refused to initiate defense planning with the Belgians and the Allies.

how strictly the country's neutrality should be defined and carried out. After war broke out in September 1939, Eelco Nicolaus van Kleffens, the Dutch foreign minister, Adriaan Quirinus Hendrik Dijxhoorn, the defense minister, and Queen Wilhelmina desired a less strict version of neutrality that would allow further communications with the British, French, and Belgians in the event of a German invasion of the Netherlands. The reason for these negotiations came from intelligence sources, principally Major Gijsbertus Sas, the Dutch military attaché in Berlin. Sas had a well-placed friend within the upper ranks of the Third Reich, a person who happened to be opposed to Hitler's expansionist policies: Colonel Hans Oster, deputy to the commander of the Abwehr, the German Military Intelligence Service. Oster, a German monarchist opposed to the National Socialist government of Hitler, had a special affinity for the Netherlands because of Queen Wilhelmina's generous protection of Kaiser Wilhelm II after World War I; he had developed a further appreciation for the Dutch through his friendship with Sas. Oster belonged to a group of traditional Prussian officers, including his superior, Admiral Wilhelm Canaris of the Abwehr, who hoped to remove Hitler and his Nazis from power in Germany.

In October 1939, Oster began conveying information to Sas about German plans to cross through the southern Netherlands near Maastricht in order to conquer Belgium and split the British and northern French armies off from Paris, thus circumventing the Maginot Line. In October 1939, Sas learned from Oster of an upcoming German invasion of western Europe, scheduled for November 12, that would send the German army through the southern Netherlands. Sas passed this information on to his superiors, and Queen Wilhelmina made a surprising move to offset this pending invasion. Along with King Leopold of Belgium and Grand Duchess Charlotte of Luxembourg, the Queen issued an offer of peace mediation between both sides of the conflict. Both the Germans and the Allies dismissed this proposal, but November 12 passed and no invasion came. This did not make the Queen any more relaxed as she gazed on the German army stationed all along the eastern border of the Netherlands. During World War I, she had felt that she could trust the word of her cousin, Kaiser Wilhelm II. But she did not feel that she could trust the word of an egocentric Austrian corporal who surrounded himself with opportunists prone to violent actions and vitriolic speech.[1]

In January 1940, another invasion warning came from the Belgian intelligence service through an unlikely source. On the morning of January 10, 1940, two Luftwaffe officers made a forced landing due to the failure of the engine of their Messerschmitt Bf 108 liaison aircraft while they were on their way from Loddenheide to Cologne. Because of the heavy fog, they were unsure about their exact location and ended up landing just inside the Belgian border near the town of Michelen. The passenger in the plane, Major Helmuth Reinberger, happened to have detailed plans regarding a German paradrop in

Belgium for the planned German invasion of the West on January 17 in his briefcase. Before Reinberger was able to destroy the documents after the emergency landing, two Belgian gendarmes arrived on bicycles and saved the papers from being burned. They sent the documents on to Belgian intelligence, and they misled Reinberger into believing that the documents had in fact been damaged beyond any use. This was done so that he would convey this information to the German military attaché in Brussels, thus allowing the Germans to believe that their plans had not been compromised. Second, the Belgians passed this information on to the British, French, and Dutch. On January 13, Belgian intelligence received a message from Maj. Sas, who had also contacted his own military, that he had learned through his source (Oster) that the Germans planned to move up their attack from the 17th to the 14th, because they now believed that their invasion plans had been compromised. But both January 14 and 17 passed without any German invasion.[2]

While the Queen, van Kleffens, and Dijxhoorn were seeking a somewhat more progressive approach to defensive planning, the prime minister, Dirk Jan de Geer, and General Izaäk Reijnders, the Opperbevelhebber van Land-en Zeemacht, were strongly opposed to anything that might violate strict Dutch neutrality. De Geer took a primarily economic view of the matter: in following strict neutrality, the Dutch could trade with both sides of the conflict and also maintain their empire abroad. However, one of de Geer's weaknesses in this decision-making process was that he had only come to power as the head of a new coalition government on August 10, 1939. His predecessor as prime minister, Hendrikus Colijn, who was a strong conservative and had been in power since 1933, was well respected and was considered by many to be more qualified to make the important decisions facing the nation in 1939–40. By contrast, de Geer was cautious and passive. (He was eventually removed from power by Queen Wilhelmina, while the government was in exile, for his lack of resolve against the German invaders; after the war he was tried for publishing a leaflet instructing the Dutch on how to cooperate with the occupying Germans.)

Jonkheer Dirk J. de Geer became prime minister of the Netherlands on August 10, 1939, after the fall of the fifth Colijn government. A lifelong pacifist, de Geer was hardly the dynamic leader the Netherlands needed when World War II began. He was reluctant to do anything that might violate the rules of strict neutrality; he also believed that Dutch resistance to an invading power would be futile. Although he escaped to Great Britain after the German occupation in May 1940, he later returned to the occupied Netherlands and advocated for peace and passive collaboration with the Germans. Here de Geer (third from left) stands with his cabinet, including Defense Minister Dijxhoorn (fourth from left) and Foreign Minister van Kleffens (second from right). [Wikimedia Commons]

Gen. Reijnders did not believe Sas's reports from Berlin. Twice the chicken had cried "wolf," and twice no wolf had appeared. On one occasion Reijnders intercepted Sas, who was on his way to give an intelligence report to the Queen, and refused to allow him entry into the royal palace. Another reason Reijnders doubted a potential German invasion was that the Dutch military was in the middle of a series of important arms purchases and negotiations with Germany. The air force was ordering a number of bombers from Germany, while the Koninklijke Marine was working with German shipyards on a design for a series of new Dutch battle cruisers. Why would the Germans invade the Netherlands if they were making important weapons deals with the Dutch armed forces?

On August 28, 1939, the de Geer government declared a general mobilization of the armed forces, anticipating the outbreak of hostilities on the Continent. Maj. Sas learned of Germany's plans to invade Poland from Col. Oster in advance, and, despite the skepticism of Gen. Reijnders, Queen Wilhelmina insisted on immediate mobilization, making the Netherlands the first neutral nation to do so. Here the royal family is given an antitank gun demonstration after the mobilization. [Militair Luchtvaart Museum, Soesterberg]

Finally, Reijnders did not wish to provoke the Germans into attacking because he knew full well the state of the army. Much of the Dutch army's equipment was considered to be of vintage status, particularly its artillery. Many of the artillery guns dated back to the turn of the century, and some had to be moved out of coastal forts and placed on improvised carriages. A few were even removed from museums for combat! The army had no tanks, five tankettes, twenty-six imported and domestically produced armored cars, and a variety of trucks for transport purposes. Typically, the most common form of transportation offered to Dutch troops was the bicycle. However, the average soldier's equipment was a little better: Dutch troops were issued modern steel helmets, somewhat similar to the German design, grayish-green uniforms, 6.5mm model 95 Mannlicher-Steyr rifles and carbines, pistols, and grenades. The primary heavy machine gun in the Dutch arsenal was the water-cooled Schwarzlose 08 machine gun; but units were also equipped with the very portable Madsen 6.5mm M1929 light machine gun.

However, with only 200,000 regular troops and 50,000 reservists, the Dutch army would not be expected to last long against the impressive might of the German Wehrmacht.[3] In the midst of all of this pessimism regarding the capability of the Dutch army, another branch of the Dutch military was better prepared and approached contemporary standards: that branch was the Luchtvaartafdeeling (LVA). The LVA was considerably weaker when the 1930s began, but general European rearmament in the mid- to late 1930s led to a reinvigorated domestic aircraft industry and a strengthened Dutch air force.

The LVA in the 1930s

When the 1930s began, the LVA purchased only a trickle of new aircraft from Fokker. During 1932, Fokker developed a beautifully streamlined version of the D.XVI fighter, powered by a Curtiss Conqueror in-line engine, that he designated the D.XVII. The LVA became interested in the project and decided that the fighter had great potential. Although it had no immediate need for additional fighters at the time, the LVA ordered ten D.XVIIs from Fokker in December 1932. The primary motivation for this order was to give Fokker's company a desperately needed cash infusion, since it was in the defense ministry's best interests to ensure that the nation's primary military aircraft manufacturer remain in business. Beyond the ten ordered by the LVA and the prototype, Fokker was not able to secure any other orders, despite the fact that the D.XVII had the best overall performance of any fighter in the world at its unveiling. They were loved by LVA pilots and served as advanced fighter trainers as late as 1940.[4]

The only other Fokker combat aircraft designed in

the first half of the 1930s that was to be manufactured in any numbers was the C.X observation/light bomber aircraft. The C.X was a streamlined, aesthetically beautiful biplane designed as a replacement for the C.V. Like the D.XVII, the C.X had several aerodynamic refinements over the C.V, while maintaining its predecessor's ability to take on a number of different combat roles. The C.X prototype made its first flight on October 9, 1934. The LVA ordered twenty C.Xs, which were delivered in 1935 and 1936. Like the C.V before it, the C.X was loved by pilots for its maneuverability, while the LVA leadership praised its versatility. Fokker had success marketing the C.X beyond the LVA: the LA-KNIL ordered thirteen, Finland purchased four and license-manufactured thirty-five, and Switzerland purchased a manufacturing license and produced eighty-eight examples of a modified version, which was designated the EKW C-35. Despite the growing obsolescence of the biplane concept when it entered service, the C.X represented the pinnacle of biplane technology.[5]

The small number of military aircraft sales in the first half of the 1930s was not due to a lack of effort on the part of Fokker or his designers. A wide variety of designs, ranging from low-wing monoplane fighters to large four-engine bombers and transports, were drafted between 1930 and 1935. With the world at peace at that time, the LVA felt it had absolutely no need for expensive offensive aircraft such as long-range bombers or transports. Even new fighters were deemed unnecessary. When Adolf Hitler unveiled his new Luftwaffe to the world in 1935, the idea of peaceful European skies came to an abrupt halt, and a new period of rapid rearmament was suddenly triggered. The potential threat of German, French, and British bombers blackening the skies over the Continent forced small neutral air forces to modernize and expand. Fortunately for the LVA, Fokker's designers were already working on three new designs that would serve as the Netherlands' primary frontline aircraft during the German invasion in 1940.

The first of these designs, the D.XXI, made its debut flight on March 27, 1936. The D.XXI was a monoplane fighter-interceptor of mixed metal-wood-fabric construc-

The Fokker D.XVII was an aesthetically beautiful and high-performance biplane fighter that saw limited construction due to defense cutbacks in the midst of the Depression. The D.XVII was originally designed for the LA-KNIL as a replacement for its long-serving D.VII fighters. The LA-KNIL decided not to purchase the D.XVII, opting for the American Curtiss P-6 fighter instead. The LVA had been observing the fighter's development and in December 1932 ordered ten of the fighters—and later purchased the prototype tested by the LA-KNIL. In the late 1930s, as the LVA reequipped its fighter squadrons with Fokker D.XXIs, the D.XVIIs were reassigned as advanced trainers. A few D.XVIIs flew again as fighters during the **Meidagen.** [Photo AVIODROME Luchtfotografie, Lelystad, Holland]

Fokker D.XVII
length: 23 ft 7½ in (7.2 m)
wingspan: 31 ft 6 in (9.6 m)
powerplant: one 580 hp Roll Royce Kestrel HS in-line
maximum speed: 190 mph (305 km/h)
ceiling: 25,263 ft (7,700 m)
range: 214 miles (345 km)
armament: two 7.9mm machine guns

In 1933 the LA-KNIL approached Fokker with requirements for a new light bomber/scout aircraft. Fokker presented the C.X, a streamlined two-seat biplane powered by a 650 hp Rolls Royce Kestrel in-line engine. Compared to the C.V, the C.X was nearly as fast and maneuverable as a fighter when it was designed and was very popular among its pilots. The C.X could also take on the myriad roles performed by the C.V. The LA-KNIL ordered thirteen C.Xs and the LVA ordered twenty, the last sixteen of which were delivered with an enclosed cockpit for the pilot. Purchased and license-manufactured by the Finns, the C.X served well against more modern Soviet aircraft in the Winter War of 1939–40 and World War II. [Photo AVIODROME Luchtfotografie, Lelystad, Holland]

Fokker C.X
length: 28 ft 10½ in (8.8 m)
wingspan: 39 ft 4½ in (12 m)
powerplant: one 640 hp Rolls Royce Kestrel V in-line
maximum speed: 221 mph (355 km/h)
ceiling: 28,871 ft (8,800 m)
range: 578 miles (930 km)
armament: three 7.9mm machine guns, 882 lbs (400 kg) of bombs

tion, armed with four FN Browning M-36 machine guns, and powered initially by a 645-hp Bristol Mercury VI-S radial engine. This new fighter, developed by Fokker's new designer, Doctor of Engineering Erich Schatzki, was certainly no record-breaking design, especially compared with the Messerschmitt Bf 109 and the Supermarine Spitfire, both under development at the same time. The D.XXI had fixed landing gear, and its mixed construction demonstrated Fokker's refusal to re-equip his factory for all-metal aircraft construction. The commander of the LVA, Colonel Petrus Wilhelmus Best, at first showed no interest in acquiring the fighter because of its initial low speed (255 mph, only a 25 mph improvement over the D.XVII biplane fighter that it was intended to replace). Best was concerned about countering the perceived threat of fast medium bombers under development in other countries, particularly the new *Schnellbombers* in Germany.

However, the D.XXI did have some advantages: its light weight gave it exceptional maneuverability. It also had a significantly lower price tag than all-metal monoplane fighters and the adaptability to accept several different power plants and armament suites. The lower cost and the engine and armament flexibility were particularly appealing to smaller air forces, which were eager to modernize but had to work with very limited funds. Export orders and license-manufacture orders came from Finland, Republican Spain, and Denmark. After observing a series of flight tests of a Finnish D.XXI that was equipped with a more powerful Bristol radial, the LVA finally became interested in the fighter and placed an order for thirty-six D.XXIs, which were powered by 830-hp Bristol Mercury VIII radials, on December 31, 1937.[6]

When Col. Best initially rejected the D.XXI in 1936, his interest was focused on a completely different Fokker design. Best was fascinated with the concept of the *luchtkruiser* ("air cruiser"), a medium bomber that could serve in an offensive role but also a defensive role as a heavily armed battle plane that could wade into and attack enemy bomber formations. Fokker began experimenting with the *luchtkruiser* concept in 1933, and in 1935 the

No Fokker-built C.X survives but the Flieger Flab Museum in Dübendorf, Switzerland, possesses a Swiss-built version. The EKW C-35 (Eidgenössische Konstruktions Werkstätte) was a modified version of the Fokker C.X, the main difference being a 20mm cannon installed in the propeller hub of the Swiss aircraft. EKW built 88 C-35s between 1936 and 1942. [Photo courtesy of Peter de Jong]

first serious design drafted on the drawing board became the T.V, a mid-wing medium bomber. But Fokker had problems melding the LVA's bomber and battle plane requirements into a single aircraft; the larger the armament, the smaller the bomb payload, and vice versa. Although initially advertised as a bomber, battle plane, and sixteen-man transport, the ever-evolving design of the T.V began to look more and more like a medium bomber. The Ministry of Defense was pleased enough with this resulting design that it ordered sixteen T.Vs off the drawing board—that is, without a prototype—on December 7, 1936. With the tempo of rearmament across Europe accelerating, and the realization growing among air force officers of the futility of a high-performance heavy battle

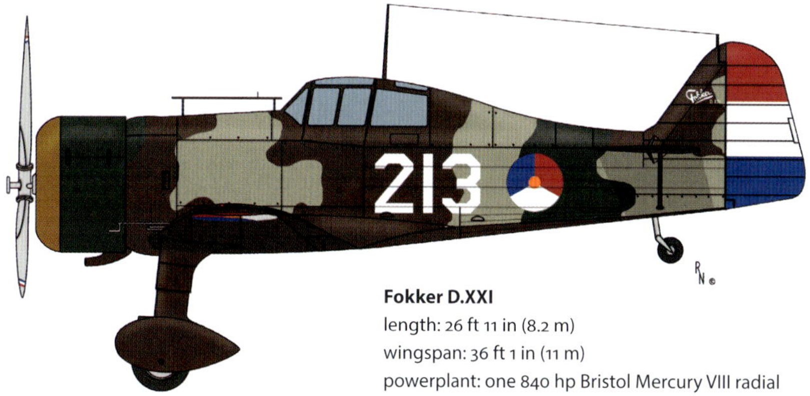

Fokker D.XXI
length: 26 ft 11 in (8.2 m)
wingspan: 36 ft 1 in (11 m)
powerplant: one 840 hp Bristol Mercury VIII radial
maximum speed: 286 mph (460 km/h)
ceiling: 33,137 ft (10,100 m)
range: 578 miles (930 km)
armament: four FN/Browning M-36 machine guns

Originally designed for—but ultimately rejected by—the LA-KNIL, the Fokker D.XXI fighter was evaluated and purchased in numbers by the LVA to replace its aging biplane fighters. The D.XXI bridged two eras of fighter aircraft design: its mixed steel-wood-fabric construction and fixed landing gear harked back to designs of the early 1930s, while its low-wing monoplane layout and enclosed cockpit reflected developments being made abroad in the mid-1930s. Nevertheless, it did bring the LVA's fighter arm out of the biplane era and gave its pilots a more competitive aircraft. [Photo AVIODROME Luchtfotografie, Lelystad, Holland]

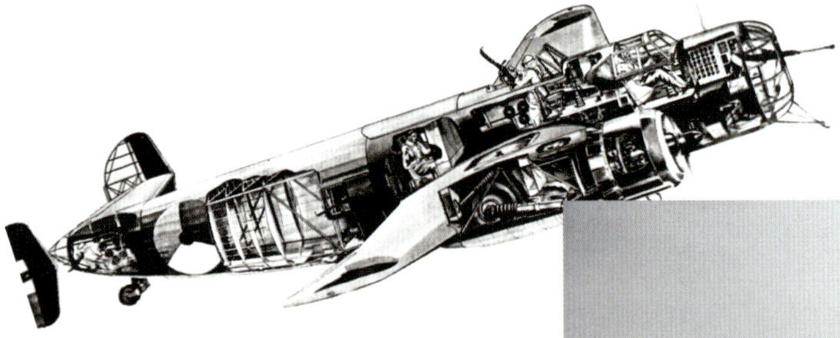

The Fokker T.V was designed according to the concept of a luchtkruiser *(aerial cruiser), a heavily armed battle plane that was intended to intercept and attack formations of enemy bombers. For this purpose, the manufacturer installed a pivoting 20mm cannon in the nose where the gunner would serve as aircraft commander. With sleek and fast monoplane fighters going into production in the mid- to late 1930s, the battle plane/bomber-destroyer concept was dismissed, and the T.V was redesignated as a medium bomber, a role in which it performed adequately.* [Photo AVIODROME Luchtfotografie, Lelystad, Holland]

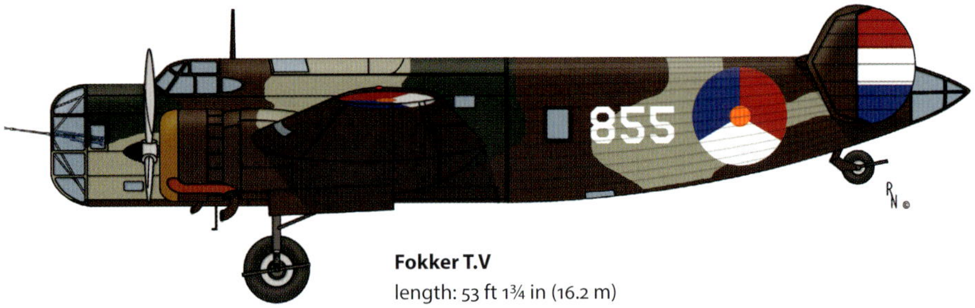

Fokker T.V
length: 53 ft 1¾ in (16.2 m)
wingspan: 68 ft 10¾ in (21 m)
powerplant: two 925 hp Bristol Pegasus XXVI radials
maximum speed: 264 mph (425 km/h)
ceiling: 26,247 ft (8,000 m)
range: 963 miles (1,550 km)
armament: one 20mm Solothurn cannon, four 7.9mm machine guns, 2,205 lbs (1,000 kg) of bombs
crew: 5

plane, the LVA was satisfied to receive the T.V as a medium bomber. Construction began on the first aircraft in February 1937, and it made its first flight on October 16. The T.V was of mixed steel-wood-fabric construction, powered by two 925-hp Bristol Pegasus XXVI radials, had a payload of 2,205 pounds, and was armed with one 20mm Solothurn cannon in the nose and four 7.9mm FN Browning machine guns.[7]

While the D.XXI and the T.V were rather pedestrian in their intended roles compared to some foreign designs, Fokker's *jachtkruiser* design concept was revolutionary and was a domestic and international sensation. The *jachtkruiser* ("fighter cruiser") was a heavy fighter that could also perform the roles of fighter-bomber and reconnaissance platform. The *jachtkruiser* project, known as the G.1, was a private venture by Fokker, and Erich Schatzki began design work on it in 1934. The project was kept secret by Tony Fokker until he unveiled it to the world at the Salon de l' Aéronautique in Paris in November 1936. The G.1 had a large wing with a small fuselage in the center, had twin tail booms, and was powered by two Hispano-Suiza radials (Dutch production models would be powered by Bristol Mercury VIII radials, the same used in the D.XXI, as the LVA hoped to simplify power-plant logistics through the use of a single engine). The heavy fighter's armament was perhaps its most impressive feature: eight 7.9mm FN Browning machine guns in the nose and a single one in the rear nose.

The formidable firepower of the G.1 earned it the nickname of "le Faucheur" ("the reaper") at the Salon. German Luftwaffe planners in particular were surprised by the G.1, since they were developing in secret a similar *Zerstörer* ("destroyer") aircraft—the Messerschmitt Bf 110. The G.1 was more heavily armed and performed better than the initial versions of the Bf 110. The LVA showed immediate interest in the G.1 as Fokker's *jachtkruiser* better fulfilled the role of a bomber-killer than the T.V *luchtkruiser*. After a number of tests with the prototype, the LVA ordered 36 G.1A's (Bristol Mercury powered) from Fokker on October 21, 1937. Export orders and manufacturing licenses rapidly followed from

If the D.XXI fighter seemed conventional at the time of its unveiling, the twin-engine, twin-tail Fokker G.1 was anything but. Designed in secret as an internal project within the Fokker company, the G.1 came as an impressive surprise when first shown to the world at the 1937 Paris Salon International de l'Aéronautique. Despite its size, it was quite maneuverable and it packed a powerful punch: eight machine guns in the nose. It was eagerly acquired by the LVA, which referred to the aircraft as a jachtkruiser *("fighter" cruiser), a heavy fighter that could not only engage enemy fighters but also attack bombers and serve effectively in the ground attack role.* [Photo AVIODROME Luchtfotografie, Lelystad, Holland]

Republican Spain, Sweden, Denmark, and Hungary. The construction of the D.XXI, T.V, and G.1 not only gave the LVA a respectable force of modern aircraft on the eve of World War II; their orders also provided Fokker with a sorely needed income after only a trickle of civilian and military orders in the early and mid-1930s.[8]

In 1937, Col. Best, who would command the air defenses of the country during the German invasion, recognized the great need for an effective air force and air-defense infrastructure in the event of an invasion of the Netherlands. According to Best:

> Another possibility for a strategic surprise-attack is one where the attacking force directs the first phase of the combined air-ground operation against the Netherlands to obtain a jumping-off place against a more important enemy and by this to prevent our nation to take an important and active part in further air and ground operations.

Best had anticipated what Hitler's intention and method of invading the Netherlands would be two years before the Führer had even contemplated violating Dutch neutrality (though British or French violation of Dutch

Fokker G.1A
length: 35 ft 9 in (10.9 m)
wingspan: 56 ft 5 in (17.2 m)
powerplant: two 800 hp Bristol Mercury VIII radials
maximum speed: 295 mph (475 km/h)
ceiling: 30,840 ft (9,400 m)
range: 932 miles (1,500 km)
armament: nine 7.9mm FN machine guns
crew: 2

While the Netherlands had many inept politicians and commanders in leadership positions on the eve of World War II, one exception was Major General Petrus W. Best, commander of the Militair Luchtvaart (ML). Already in March 1937 he gave a lecture in which he predicted that any future invasion of the Netherlands would involve the airborne capture or suppression of Dutch airfields, combined with a rapid thrust made by motorized and mechanized units on the ground. A leading member of the IML, Best pushed for the acquisition of the best combat aircraft for the ML but was thwarted by Defense Minister Jannes van Dijk. One area where he had success was his procurement of modern antiaircraft weapons in quantity, the effective organization of these weapons, and a modern communications network for the defense of Dutch airfields. The foresight of this preparation would have grave effects on the German airborne invaders in May 1940. Here Best speaks with Prime Minister Hendrikus Colijn. [D. Dildy Collection]

neutrality in a new European war was not entirely ruled out at the time either). In order to effectively coordinate the aerial defense of the country in the event of an attack, officials undertook a restructuring of the LVA on November 1, 1938. Now renamed the Wapen der Militair Luchtvaart (more commonly referred to as the Militair Luchtvaart, or ML), the LVA was given equal status with other branches of the army. The new ML consisted of three organizations: the Luchtvaartbrigade, which was organized into three air regiments, made up of most of the army's aircraft and placed under the command of veteran air officer Lieutenant Colonel Floris van Heyst; the Commando Luchtverdediging (Air Defense Command, or LVD), headquartered in The Hague, which included ML fighter aircraft, antiaircraft batteries, and searchlight units; and finally, the Vrijwillige Landstormkorps Luchtwachtdienst (Voluntary Observer Corps), which maintained observation posts all over the country.

The Search for Modern Aircraft: Too Little, Too Late

At the time of Dutch mobilization in 1939, the ML had twenty-three Fokker G.1 *jachtkruisers,* twenty-eight Fokker D.XXI fighters, eleven Douglas 8A-3N light-bombers (a designation of the plane made only by the Dutch, since the Americans considered it strictly a ground-attack aircraft), and nine Fokker T.V bombers—all relatively modern aircraft. In reserve, the ML also had thirteen Fokker D.XVII fighters, twenty-four Fokker C.V attack/reconnaissance aircraft, eleven Fokker C.X attack/reconnaissance aircraft, and sixteen Koolhoven F.K. 51 trainers—all of which were biplanes. Although there had been little spending on the part of the army during the 1930s, the LVA received better funding and was even able to expand in the latter part of the decade. While the new generation of monoplanes, such as the Fokker G.1, D.XXI, and T.V, were being constructed in the late 1930s, the ML formed a commission called the Inspectie der Militair Luchtvaart (IML), made up of Gen. Marius Raaijmakers, who became its director; Jannes van Dijk, the defense minister at that time; and Gen. Reijnders. The IML commission decided to embark on a four-year program, beginning in 1938, to further the ML's modernization efforts.

Although the ML was re-equipping with its new D.XXI, G.1, and T.V aircraft, the technical developments in aviation in Great Britain and Germany were moving at such a rapid pace that modern replacements for these new aircraft would be required soon. Though the Netherlands did not have manufacturing concerns for the construction of tanks and artillery, the nation did possess a modern and competitive aviation industry, particularly in the companies of Fokker, Koolhoven, and De Schelde. The

A Quartet of Foreign Aircraft Considered for ML Service in Hypothetical Dutch Colors and Markings

1 Heinkel He 112E

On July 12, 1938, Heinkel flew one of its He 112B fighters to Soesterberg for several days of demonstration flights. Having lost the Luftwaffe's competition for a new fighter to the Messerschmitt Bf 109, Heinkel was eager to find export customers for its He 112. It was a well-armed and maneuverable aircraft, and it was highly praised by the Dutch pilots who flew it. Heinkel offered the Dutch the He 112E variant, which was powered by a 1,100 hp Daimler-Benz engine and would have been faster and more maneuverable than the Bf 109. But the He 112 had a high price tag, and despite the positive review by the Dutch pilots, the Defense Ministry refused to purchase the fighter.

length: 30 ft 6 in (9.3 m)
wingspan: 29 ft 10¼ in (9.1 m)
power plant: 1,100 hp Daimler-Benz DB 601Aa in-line
maximum speed: 354 mph (570 km/h)
ceiling: 27,890 ft (8,500 m)
range: 715 miles (1,150 km)
armament: two 7.9mm MG 17 machine guns, two 20mm MG FF cannons

2 Hawker Hurricane Mk.I

The Hawker Hurricane was Great Britain's first low-wing monoplane fighter with retractable landing gear; it was the mainstay fighter of the RAF by 1940. It became a popular fighter for export production, and a large number were sold to Belgium, Finland, Romania, Turkey, and Yugoslavia before the war began. In 1938, Gen. Best requested the immediate purchase of eighteen Hurricanes for the ML, because the British could accommodate the order and because it would give ML pilots modern fighters to train on while the Fokker D.XXIII and De Schelde S.21 projects were being completed. Defense Minister van Dijk ignored this request, and by the time Dijxhoorn assumed office the British were at war and were focused on their own production needs and those of their allies.

length: 31 ft 5 in (9.6 m)
wingspan: 40 ft (12.2 m)
power plant: 1,030 hp Rolls-Royce Merlin II in-line
maximum speed: 316 mph (509 km/h)
ceiling: 33,200 ft (10,119 m)
range: 460 miles (740 km)
armament: eight 0.303 cal. machine guns

3 Supermarine Spitfire Mk.Ia

Like the Heinkel He 112E, the Supermarine Spitfire could have given the Dutch a fighter that would have been an equal match for the Luftwaffe's Messerschmitt Bf 109s, which sped into Dutch air space on May 10, 1940. Before the war began, it may have been possible to arrange an order for the Spitfire with the British; but just as with the He 112E, such an order fell victim to van Dijk's frugality.

length: 29 ft 11 in (9.1 m)
wingspan: 36 ft 10 in (11.2 m)
power plant: 1,030 hp Rolls-Royce Merlin II in-line
maximum speed: 355 mph (571 km/h)
ceiling: 34,000 ft (10,363 m)
range: 500 miles (805 km)
armament: eight 0.303 cal. machine guns

4 Dornier Do 215B-1

The Dornier Do 215 was initially developed as an export version of the Do 17Z medium bomber but equipped with Daimler-Benz in-line engines for better performance. The Dutch, Swedish, and Yugoslav air forces all showed interest in the Do 215. Defense Minister Dijxhorn placed an order with Dornier for eighteen Do 215B-1s, an agreement that Dornier nominally agreed to honor despite the outbreak of war. Ironically, Dornier refused a similar order from the Swedish air force, which in turn ordered eighteen G.1Bs from Fokker.

length: 51 ft 10 in (15.8 m)
wingspan: 59 ft 1 in (18 m)
power plant: two 1,150 hp Daimler-Benz DB 601 Ba in-lines
maximum speed: 292 mph (470 km/h)
ceiling: 29,500 ft (9,000 m)
range: 1,522 miles (2,450 km)
armament: four 7.92 MG 15 machine guns, 2,205 lbs (1,000 kg) of bombs
crew: 4

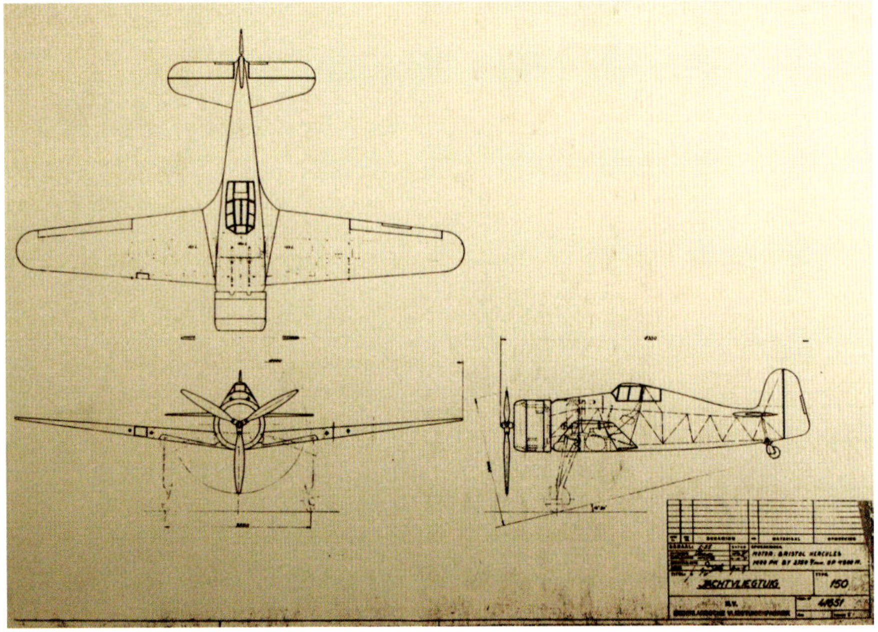

Fokker Ontwerpen 150 and 151 were new single-seat fighter designs, developed in part from the D.XXI, which were presented to the IML for its new fighter requirement. Both designs had a composite construction similar to the D.XXI but had the added refinement of retractable landing gear. Ontwerp 150 was to be powered by a Bristol Hercules radial engine, while Ontwerp 151 was the same airframe but was to be powered by either a Daimler-Benz DB 600H or a Rolls Royce Merlin in-line. The ML showed interest in these designs but the IML did not, instead preferring Ontwerp 155 (later the D.XXIII), which was also being developed at the time. Fokker continued design work on the Ontwerpen 150 and 151, but the projects were dropped in late 1939, when the Ministry of Defense was no longer able to purchase aero engines from Germany or Great Britain. [Photo AVIODROME Luchtfotografie, Lelystad, Holland]

ML's four-year-plan called for the acquisition of thirty-six single-seat air defense fighters, eighteen *jachtkruisers*/light bombers, eighteen two-seat ground attack aircraft, and twenty trainers.

While Fokker was continuing to finish the construction of the G.1s, D.XXIs, and T.Vs, the ML leadership first looked abroad for aircraft to meet the requirements of their four-year plan. The first fighter they examined was the Heinkel He 112B from Germany. One of Heinkel's test pilots demonstrated the plane to Dutch observers at Soesterberg and De Kooy. The elliptical wing of the plane gave it exceptional maneuverability, but the demonstration model had a Junkers Jumo 210Ea engine, with only 650 horsepower, and the Dutch were not particularly impressed with the resulting low speed. Heinkel was aware of this and offered the Dutch exclusive rights to purchase the He 112B with the new state-of-the-art Daimler Benz DB.601a 1,100-hp engine. This He 112E with the new engine would be faster than the Messerschmitt Bf 109E and would have outperformed both the 109s and British Spitfires that dueled over the skies of southern England in the summer of 1940!

The next foreign fighter that the ML examined was the British Hawker Hurricane. The Hurricane was a modern monoplane fighter with retractable landing gear, but it did not show as good a performance as did the projected DB.601a-powered He 112E. Nevertheless, the Hurricanes were available for purchase, they were cheaper than the He 112Es, and there was a discussion of having the aircraft built under license by the N.V. Nederlandsche Vliegtuigfabriek. For the *jachtkruiser*/light bomber role, the ML was quite impressed with the German Dornier Do 215, an export version of the Dornier Do 17Z. Gen. Best and Gen. Reijnders turned to the United States for a modern ground-attack aircraft, and they selected the Douglas 8A-3N, which was armed with four machine guns and could carry 600 kg of bombs. The easy availability of the plane and its rugged construction helped them make the decision to acquire this aircraft.

Finally, for a multi-engined trainer for bomber and *jachtkruiser* pilots, the ML examined several different aircraft from Focke-Wulf, Avro, Airspeed, Caproni, and Lockheed, as well as the domestic manufacturers. The trainer they selected was the Focke-Wulf Fw 58 Weihe, partly because of the good rapport that Focke-Wulf had with ML officials. The ML's purchase of foreign-built aircraft did not sit well with Fokker, Koolhoven, or De Schelde. What it did demonstrate was that they would have to take more modern and creative approaches to their designs in order to secure ML contracts.[9]

The Dutch aviation companies realized in the mid- to late 1930s that they were losing ground in technical innovation to German and British companies, as well as to the upstart American air industry. The first attempts by

Left and Below *The F.K.51 became the first Koolhoven-designed aircraft to see large-scale production since his F.K.8, designed for and built by Armstrong Whitworth during World War I. The F.K.51 was selected as a new trainer for the LVA in the autumn of 1935, primarily because of its cheap price tag. As the F.K.51 went into production, it demonstrated good service in the LVA, the MLD, and the LA-KNIL; even the Spanish Republican air force was attracted to this modern and inexpensive trainer. A large number of orders came pouring in, and for the first time Koolhoven's factory had to try to cope with mass production. Here Prince Bernhard (fourth from left) meets with new LVA pilots in front of their F.K.51 trainer as Frits Koolhoven (third from left) looks on. The F.K.51 replica shown below is housed in the Nationaal Militair Museum in Soest.* [Militair Luchtvaart Museum, Soesterberg]

Koolhoven F.K.51
length: 25 ft 11 in (7.9 m)
wingspan: 29 ft 6¼ in (9 m)
powerplant: one 365 hp Armstrong Siddeley Cheetah IX radial
maximum speed: 146 mph (235 km/h)
ceiling: 18,373 ft (5,600 m)
range: 454 miles (730 km)
armament: one 7.7mm Lewis machine gun
crew: 2

Fokker and Koolhoven to remedy this consisted of offering high-performance aircraft using their construction methods they had been using for years. Fokker initially proposed two variants of his D.XXI, using the same airframe but with retractable landing gear: the Ontwerp 150, powered by a Bristol Hercules radial engine, and the Ontwerp 151, powered by either a Daimler Benz DB.600H in-line engine or a British Rolls Royce Merlin II in-line engine. Neither variant had spectacular performance compared to new foreign developments, so they never went beyond the drawing board.

Meanwhile, Koolhoven had hired Fokker's principal designer, Erich Schatzki, the designer of the D.XXI, after he left Fokker's company due to arguments with the company's leadership. Schatzki went on to design Koolhoven's first successful fighter, the F.K.58. Outwardly, the F.K.58 rather closely resembled the D.XXI, except that it had retractable landing gear and a different engine. Originally, the F.K.58 was developed for export to the French, whose aviation industry was in a relatively poor state in the mid- to late 1930s—because of the socialist government's amalgamation of all the major aircraft companies. The bureaucratic red tape caused by this government interference meant that design and production were hampered in the mid-1930s. In the late 1930s, as war threatened, the French aircraft industry was desperately trying to catch up—in numbers and quality—

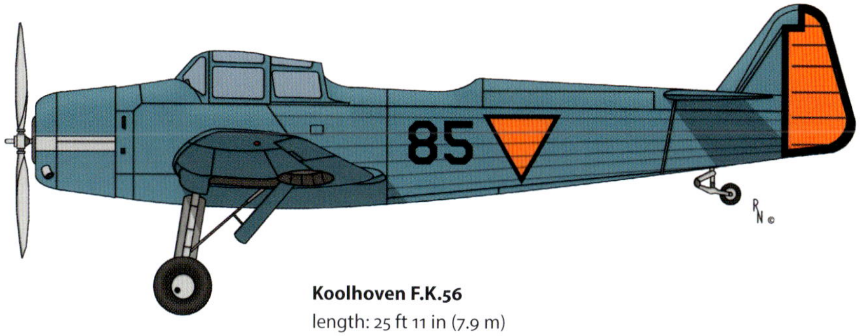

Koolhoven F.K.56
length: 25 ft 11 in (7.9 m)
wingspan: 37 ft 8¾ in (11.5 m)
powerplant: one 420 hp Wright Whirlwind R-975-E3 radial
maximum speed: 186 mph (300 km/h)
ceiling: 23,950 ft (7,300 m)
range: 746 miles (1,200 km)
crew: 2

Left *While the orders were good for Koolhoven, and the F.K.51 served well as a trainer, the large orders placed by the Dutch air services gave the false sense that Koolhoven was a major manufacturer. Koolhoven nevertheless followed the F.K.51 in 1938 with the F.K.56, a monoplane fighter trainer with retractable landing gear that was ordered by the LVA and the Belgian Aéronautique Militaire. Koolhoven was not able to complete either F.K.56 order before May 1940 and this should have been a warning to the Dutch Defense Ministry that Koolhoven's factory was not capable of rapid production in time of war, let alone peacetime.*

Described at the 1938 Salon International de l'Aeronautique as "l'avion le plus rapide du monde" (the fastest aircraft in the world), this supposedly promising fighter turned out to be anything but. The F.K.58 was designed for and first ordered by the French Armée de l'Air, which was desperately seeking foreign fighters to remedy slow domestic output and which was looking for a cheaper alternative to American-built fighters. Also desiring a cheap fighter, Dutch Defense Minister van Dijk ordered the F.K.58 for the ML. However, his successor, Adriaan Dijxhoorn, and the ML leadership were not enthusiastic about the F.K.58's performance and hoped to buy better fighters abroad. But as World War II began, Great Britain and Germany were no longer willing to sell any modern fighters to the Dutch, and Dijxhoorn was forced to keep the Koolhoven contract. But no F.K.58s ever reached the pilots of the ML. The Bristol Taurus engines Koolhoven had ordered from Great Britain were confiscated by the RAF, leaving only the less powerful Bristol Mercury VIIIs available from ML stocks. The Germans invaded the Netherlands before those engines could be mounted to any airframes. [Militair Luchtvaart Museum, Soesterberg]

Koolhoven F.K.58
length: 28 ft 6½ in (8.7 m)
wingspan: 36 ft 1 in (11 m)
powerplant: one 1,030 hp Gnome Rhône 14N39 radial
maximum speed: 295 mph (475 km/h)
ceiling: 32,808 ft (10,000 m)
range: 466 miles (750 km)
armament: four 7.9mm FN-Browning machine guns

with its German and Italian rivals, and with its British ally. Since these nations were solely committed to their own national production, the only other major aircraft manufacturing state left in Europe was the Netherlands.

In the early months of 1938, when the French aviation authorities approached Frits Koolhoven, he told them that he could provide them with a fighter better than the American-built Curtiss Hawk 75A, an aircraft the French were considering for purchase. A few months later, in July 1938, Koolhoven unveiled his new fighter: it had a Hispano-Suiza 14AA radial engine, giving the plane a top speed of 300 mph (500 km/h), and it mounted four machine guns. Since the performance of the F.K.58 was slightly better than that of the French mainstay fighter, the Morane-Saulnier M.S.406, the French aviation authorities decided to order fifty F.K.58s in January 1939. In the Netherlands, the IML likewise showed some interest in the F.K.58; however, they were concerned about its lower performance compared to the Ontwerp 150 and 151 designs offered by Fokker. To address this, Koolhoven looked to upgrade the F.K.58 with a Daimler Benz DB.600 in-line engine, or with a more powerful radial.[10]

Fokker's Ontwerpen 150 and 151 and Koolhoven's F.K.58 may not have been able to compete on a par with the Supermarine Spitfire or the Heinkel He 112E (with its DB.601 engine), but Tony Fokker had several other designs up his sleeve that he thought would bring his company back to the forefront of European aviation. One specific area within the IML's four-year plan, which Fokker was especially able to address, was that of the *jachtkruiser*. Fokker responded to the IML's new *jachtkruiser* requirement with Ontwerp 154, whose design in its later variants (Ontwerpen 195, 198, and 199) would eventually come to be known as the Fokker CG.2. The new *jachtkruiser* looked quite different from the G.1: the nose would be a glazed-gun/observation position; there would be glazed-gun positions in the back of the cabin, one behind the pilot and one at the bottom rear of the fuselage; and the fuselage would extend back to the tail, unlike the twin booms of the G.1, where there would be twin rudders. Armament arrangements could be altered based

Beginning in October 1938, Fokker began work on Ontwerp 154, a jachtkruiser *replacement for the G.1, which was still in production. With all-metal construction and armed with two 20mm cannon and six 7.9mm machine guns, Ontwerp 154, later designated the CG.2, would have been a formidable attack aircraft. The project was rejected by Defense Minister van Dijk in the summer of 1939, but put back into motion by Defense Minister Dijxhoorn in September 1939. Dijxhoorn ordered twenty CG.2s from Fokker on November 21, 1939, to replace the Fokker C.X biplanes of the 2e Ver.V.A. Fokker prepared a mockup of the CG.2 (shown here under construction) in the winter of 1940, but a prototype was not finished before the German invasion.* [Photo AVIODROME Luchtfotografie, Lelystad, Holland]

on the type of mission being flown, but the *jachtkruiser* variant's armament consisted of a 20mm Solothurn cannon in the glazed nose, four 7.9mm machine guns under the nose, one 7.9mm machine gun in the aft upper and lower positions, and another 20mm Solothurn cannon in the aft lower position, which was unseen from above and thus designed to shoot down bombers appearing from below, a variant of the Schräge Musik ("jazz music") cannon arrangement later developed by the Germans and used with great success against RAF bombers. Fokker proposed all-metal construction and either DB.600H engines, which would give the *jachtkruiser* a top speed of 316 mph (527 km/h), or Merlin II engines.

Fokker also sought to capitalize on the ML's *luchtkruiser* concept and submitted a design for what he considered to be the ultimate *luchtkruiser,* the Cruiser Study Project 1939. Little is known about this design, especially since it was not even issued an Ontwerp number; but it was revolutionary. Two engines, most likely Merlins, DB.601s, or Junkers Jumo in-lines, were placed in a tandem push-pull arrangement in the center of the wing between two full-length fuselages. The fuselages were similar to those of the all-metal T.IX bomber being developed for the ML-KNIL. The technical drawings of the 1939 *luchtkruiser* show the plane to be very well armed (since it would have had double the armament of a T.IX) and would have had a considerable bomb load capacity.[11] De Schelde also submitted *jachtkruiser* and *luchtkruiser* designs to the IML, though little information remains about these proposals. The De Schelde *jachtkruiser* had two inline engines in the wings, retractable landing gear, a gun position in the nose, and two retractable gun turrets aft—one on top of the fuselage and one on the bottom. The *luchtkruiser* design was a sleek, streamlined trimotor, powered by three radials, with retractable landing gear, somewhat reminiscent of the Pander *Postjager.* (Pander had turned its aircraft division over to De Schelde in 1935 after the destruction of the *Panderjager.*) De Schelde made a mockup of the bomber, but that was as far as the design progressed. War intervened before serious developmental work on the *jachtkruiser* and *luchtkruiser* designs of Fokker and De Schelde could begin.[12]

Fokker and De Schelde also intended to create new, if somewhat unorthodox, fighter designs that would put their companies back on par with Europe's other premier aviation firms. Fokker's Ontwerp 155 was nothing short

The Fokker T.IX began as a medium bomber project for the LA-KNIL in 1938, which was already seeking a modern replacement for its Glenn Martin 139 bombers. The T.IX was the first all-metal aircraft built by Fokker in the Netherlands; the prototype made its first flight on September 11, 1939. Its performance was similar to that of other modern medium bombers being used in Europe and the United States, but again, further development ended with the German invasion. Here construction proceeds on the T.IX prototype in Fokker's factory. Note the noses for G.1 fighters hanging on the wall. [Photo AVIODROME Luchtfotografie, Lelystad, Holland]

Fokker T.IX
length: 54 ft 2 in (16.5 m)
wingspan: 81 ft (24.7 m)
power plant: two 1,375 hp Bristol Hercules radials
maximum speed: 273 mph (440 km/h)
ceiling: 26,247 ft (8,000 m)
range: 1,690 miles (2,720 km)
armament: one 20mm cannon, four 12.7mm machine guns, 4,409 lbs (2,000 kg) of bombs
crew: 5

of a revolutionary design that had shed any of the traditional and orthodox design and construction methods for which the company was previously known. In 1938, Fokker presented Ontwerp 155 to the IML, which certainly found the design to be a revolutionary experiment; but it committed no tangible support for the design until its capabilities had been proven in flight. Ontwerp 155 was a single-seater fighter with two in-line engines placed in the fuselage in a tandem push-pull arrangement, with twin tail booms, and with an armament of six 7.9mm Browning machine guns. This fighter would be of all-metal construction and powered by two Sagitta 528-hp air-cooled in-line engines from the Czechoslovakian engine firm of Josef Walter in Prague.

Fokker went to work on the prototype, at that point referred to as the D.XXIII, and it took its first flight on May 30, 1939. With the Walter Sagitta engines, the fighter reached a top speed of 326 mph (525 km/h), but the test pilot, Gerben Sonderman, found that the rear engine tended to overheat and that the engines in general were not very reliable. But Fokker could not consult with the Walter Company about these problems because Bohemia and Moravia had been annexed by Germany earlier in the year. So Fokker then decided to turn to other engines, such as the Junkers Jumo 210Ga (745 hp) and the Rolls Royce Kestrel IV (755 hp) to increase the fighter's performance. The Jumo engine would have given the plane a top speed of 345 mph (555 km/h), and the Kestrel 351 mph (565 km/h), both of them close to the speeds of the Spitfire and the Bf 109E. The IML proved to be interested in the prototype and encouraged Fokker to proceed with further tests.

De Schelde also created a revolutionary design to meet the single-seater fighter requirements of the IML's four-year-plan. In 1938, De Schelde's designer, Theo Slot, began work on the S.20, a four-person cabin plane with the 160-hp Hirth HM 506A air-cooled engine located behind the cockpit in a pusher arrangement with twin tail booms. It was a rather unusual engine configuration, but Slot believed that it held promise for a high-performance fighter.

That same year, Slot began designing the De Schelde

In early 1938, Fokker's chief designer, Marius Beeling, drafted a radical new fighter design of all-metal construction with two engines on the fuselage centerline, fore and aft, and twin tail booms. Anthony Fokker was interested and pushed for its immediate development. A mockup of the new Fokker D.XXIII was presented at the 1938 Paris Salon de l'Aéronautique and drew international acclaim. The prototype of the Fokker D.XXIII made its first flight on May 30, 1939, and it attracted immediate LVA interest. The prototype was damaged at Schiphol during the German invasion, but was it later examined by Luftwaffe engineers. [Photo AVIODROME Luchtfotografie, Lelystad, Holland]

S.21 single-seat fighter, which had an extensively glazed nose, twin tail booms, wings constructed in an inverted gull shape, and an in-line engine located behind the cockpit and firewall. Armament consisted of a Madsen 23mm cannon in the nose and four Browning 7.9mm machine guns, two located on each side of the cockpit alongside the pilot's seat. The fully glazed nose would give the pilot exceptional visibility, and the aircraft's small size allowed for less weight and an overall excellent performance. The S.21 would be powered by a 1,050-hp Daimler-Benz DB.601Ga, which would produce a projected top speed of 367 mph (590 km/h). By the summer of 1939, the S.21 prototype was beginning to take shape, and the IML was willing to consider the aircraft pending the performance of the prototype. Fokker and De Schelde were certainly beginning to prove their ability to design modern high-performance aircraft, but the outbreak of war in Europe on September 1, 1939, would greatly hinder those developments.[13]

On October 22, 1938, after examining numerous foreign and domestic designs, the IML submitted its suggestion for the purchase of aircraft to meet the requirement for the thirty-six single-seat fighters of the four-year plan to the defense minister, van Dijk, who had the final say on the allocation of government defense funds. The IML's proposal was this:

Fokker D.XXIII
length: 33 ft 5½ in (10.2 m)
wingspan: 37 ft 8¾ in (11.5 m)
power plant: two 528 hp Walter Sagitta I-SR in-lines
maximum speed: 326 mph (525 km/h)
ceiling: 29,530 ft (9,400 m)
range: 522 miles (840 km)
armament: two 7.9mm FN-Browning machine guns, two 13.2mm FN-Browning machine guns

Developed at the same time as the Fokker D.XXIII, the De Schelde S.21 was a small all-metal fighter with twin tail booms and the engine mounted in a pusher arrangement in the rear of the fuselage. It was intended to be a fast, maneuverable, and heavily armed fighter that could be used in both air superiority and ground attack roles. The LVA was interested in the S.21, but the prototype was only nearing completion at the time of the German invasion. [Photo AVIODROME Luchtfotografie, Lelystad, Holland]

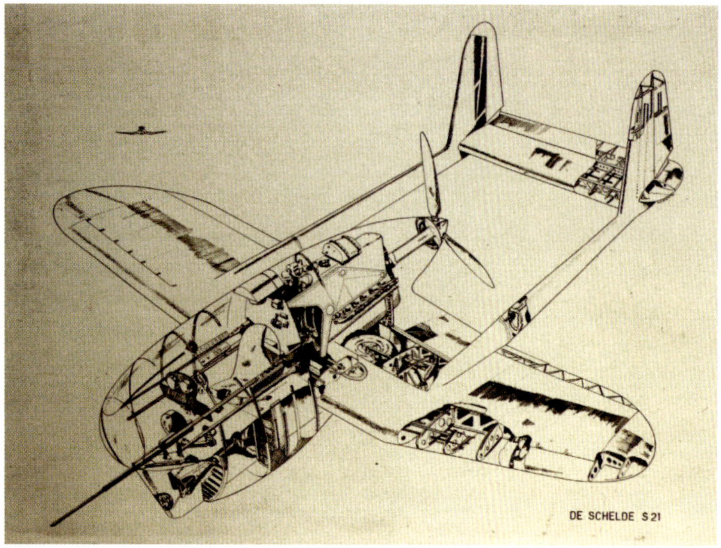

De Schelde S.21
length: 24 ft 4¾ in (7.4 m)
wingspan: 29 ft 6 in (9 m)
power plant: one 1,050 hp Daimler Benz DB 600Ga in-line
maximum speed: 367 mph (590 km/h)
ceiling: 32,810 ft (10,000 m)
armament: one 23mm Madsen cannon, four 7.9mm FN-Browning machine guns

Jannes J. C. van Dijk was the minister of defense under the first and second de Beerenbrouck governments (1921-25) and during the fourth and fifth Colijn governments (1937-39). Beginning in 1937 he served on the Inspectie der Militair Luchtvaart (IML), which was given the task of developing a four-year plan for the acquisition of modern aircraft for the Militair Luchtvaart. A number of high-performance aircraft were available for purchase on the foreign market, such as the Supermarine Spitfire, Hawker Hurricane, and Heinkel He 112E, and domestic developments such as the Fokker D.XXIII, CG.2, and De Schelde S.21—all of which the IML recommended for immediate purchase or construction. Van Dijk, however, ignored the IML's proposal and opted for the cheapest aircraft available: the Koolhoven F.K.58 for the fighter role and the Douglas 8A-3N for the attack role. This poor decision had grave consequences for the aircraft the ML had at its disposal when the Germans invaded on May 10, 1940. Here van Dijk (far left) sits with other cabinet members of the Colijn (far right) government. [Wikimedia Commons]

> Purchase as quickly as possible 18 Hurricanes: wait for the development of the prototypes of the Fokker [O]ntwerp 155 (D.XXIII) and the De Schelde S.21, and from these two, one must be chosen for the 2e *afdeling*; should neither of these two types by 1939 turn out to be satisfactory, then a choice should be made between the Spitfire and the He 112 with the Daimler Benz engine.[14]

Although the He 112E had significantly better performance than did the Hurricane, and even slightly better performance than the Spitfire, Gen. Best recommended the immediate purchase of eighteen Hurricanes because there were finished examples in England ready to be bought right away, whereas Heinkel would have to install DB.601 engines into existing He 112B airframes, which would take some time, and the British would probably not be particularly willing to sell any examples of their premier fighter, the Spitfire. The IML also recommended the purchase of eighteen Dornier Do 215A (export version of the Do 17Z) bombers and to pursue the construction of Fokker Ontwerp 154 (Fokker CG.2) to fulfill the four-year plan's *jachtkruiser* requirement.

Despite all of the high-performance aircraft placed before him, plus a very large defense budget to spend, van Dijk made a very curious decision: he picked the single-seat fighter with the lowest performance from among the options available to him, the Koolhoven F.K.58. Part of van Dijk's rationale for his decision was that, despite the fact that he had funds available for better aircraft, the F.K.58 had the cheapest price tag of all of the contenders. (I shall refrain here from making any comments about the Dutch penchant for always seeking the best deal.) On July 22, 1939, van Dijk placed an order with Koolhoven for the purchase of thirty-six F.K.58s, to be powered by 1,050-hp Bristol Taurus radials that would give the F.K.58 a top speed of 298 mph (497 km/h), thus denying Gen. Best's request for Hurricanes or better. To make matters worse, van Dijk did not heed the IML's *jachtkruiser* suggestions and instead ordered no Do 17s and canceled further development and construction of Fokker's Ontwerp 154. Finally, for the IML's attack plane requests, van Dijk ordered eighteen Douglas 8A-3Ns, refusing to consider Fokker and De Schelde *luchtkruiser* designs for similar (and probably more suitable) aircraft. Unfortunately, van Dijk's decisions would have a grave impact on the quantity and quality of modern aircraft available to the ML when war came to the Netherlands.[15]

When Adriaan Dijxhoorn replaced van Dijk as defense minister in the new cabinet formed by de Geer after his electoral win on August 10, 1939, the preparations for the defense of the nation in the event of war were not in good shape. Dijxhoorn learned of van Dijk's aircraft acquisitions for the ML's four-year-plan and he immediately went to work to replace van Dijk's orders with those for aircraft of higher quality and better performance. He tried to drop the order for the Koolhoven F.K.58s in order to obtain better aircraft from abroad, but events on the Continent interfered. Germany's invasion of Poland on September 1—and the declaration of war on Germany by Great Britain and France two days later—made the proactive Dijxhoorn's attempts to remedy the aircraft order situation much more difficult; he had been appointed to his office just a little too late. Great Britain and Germany both refused to export combat aircraft to neutral nations due to their own immediate wartime demand, so the Spitfire, Hurricane, and He 112E were no longer available. However, Germany did pledge to honor the Dutch contract for the Dornier bombers; not surprisingly, however, no Do 215As ever reached the Netherlands.

Dijxhoorn and the ML then turned to Fokker to provide an improved fighter. Fokker could have put Ontwerpen 150 and 151 into production fairly quickly, but no mention can be found of the ML pursuing either of these designs after the war broke out. Perhaps it was because they required foreign-built engines, which were no longer available. But Dijxhoorn did encourage Fokker to continue work on the D.XXXIII, and he quietly arranged for several Daimler Benz in-line engines to be purchased from questionable sources in neutral Switzerland so that Fokker and De Schelde could continue prototype construction on their single-seat fighter designs.

On March 2, 1940, Bristol informed Koolhoven that it

Adriaan H. Q. Dijxhoorn, minister of defense in the de Geer government (which assumed power on August 10, 1939), had the unenviable task of trying to rapidly modernize and improve the equipment of the Dutch armed forces after the miserly tenure of Jannes van Dijk. Dijxhoorn took intelligence reports of a German invasion seriously, and he replaced Gen. Reijnders with General Henri Winkelman, who likewise believed the reports of imminent invasion. One of Dijxhoorn's most challenging tasks was to equip the Militair Luchtvaart with modern aircraft as quickly as possible. Aircraft from Great Britain or Germany were no longer available for purchase, since they were already at war; this left the United States as the only other primary manufacturer to turn to. But the designs the Americans were exporting were little better than the Fokker aircraft the ML already possessed. Had van Dijk been willing to spend more on aircraft procurement, the fighters over Dutch skies could have been Spitfires, Hurricanes, or Heinkel 112Es. [Wikimedia Commons]

would not be able to provide the Taurus III engines that were designated for the F.K.58s originally ordered by van Dijk. The only British engines available were thirty-six Bristol Mercury VIII radials, which the ML already had in its possession for forthcoming Fokker D.XXIs and G.1s. With only 760 horsepower, the Mercury VIIIs would have made the already mediocre performance of the F.K.58 considerably worse. Dijxhoorn found the underpowered F.K.58s to be an unacceptable option; even the initially planned Bristol Taurus-powered F.K.58s would be barely faster than the Do 215s that he had ordered! Therefore, the defense minister turned to the last major source of modern aircraft open to the Netherlands: the neutral United States. One fighter that the United States offered for export in February 1940 was the Vultee Vanguard V-48, an all-metal fighter armed with four 30-caliber (7.62mm) and two 50-caliber (12.7mm) machine guns and powered by a Pratt & Whitney 1,200-hp radial with a top speed of 340 mph (544 km/h). As the fighter had not yet entered series production, it was immediately available for purchase.

The American fighter that really captured Dijxhoorn's attention, however, was the Curtiss CW-21B, a lightweight, all-metal plane that had an incredible rate of climb and was advertised by the company as the "Mile a Minute Intercepter." Dijxhoorn was particularly impressed that the CW-21B was able to climb to 6,000 meters in five minutes, whereas a Spitfire, in 1938, was only able to climb to 4,000 meters in five minutes. The CW-21 was powered by a Wright Cyclone R-1820-G5 radial, had a top speed of 322 mph (536 km/h), and would be armed with four Belgian FN 7.9mm machine guns. On April 17, 1940, Dijxhoorn ordered twenty-four CW-21Bs, as he was eager to equip the ML with as many modern fighters as he could obtain. The feeling of desperation to prepare for the ML's defense of Dutch skies in the event of war was not exclusive to the ML; indeed, the military in general was beginning to feel uneasy as winter gave way to spring in 1940.[16]

The purchase of new aircraft was only one part of creating an efficient air-defense system. Modern antiaircraft guns were also desperately needed. During the late 1930s, the Dutch government purchased a variety of antiaircraft guns abroad for the Commando Luchtverdediging, including one hundred fifty-five Oerlikon and Scotti Isotta Fraschini 2cm guns, forty-six Bofors 4cm guns, and seventy-two Vickers 7.5cm guns and fire-directional computers to aim them. The Dutch purchased a license to produce the Vickers gun and planned to supplement them with a superior Hazemeyer fire-directional computer, which was domestically designed. Although the government was investing heavily in rearmament, the budget-minded politicians encouraged private industrial concerns to purchase antiaircraft guns to protect their own facilities. These were manned by members of the air defense corps volunteers. The vast majority of the Dutch antiaircraft capability fell within three air defense zones: Amsterdam, Rotterdam/The Hague, and Utrecht/Soesterberg. The Dutch also had mobile air defense units that were attached to the field army, as well as mobile units that were stationed in other parts of the country outside the three main air-defense zones. These mobile units were also connected to the air-defense radio network, and thus Air Defense Command could coordinate their actions as well. On the eve of the German invasion, the army was even experimenting with a prototype of a radar system that could detect aircraft up to fifteen kilometers away.

Throughout the country, members of the Vrijwillige Landstormkorps Luchtwachtdienst were positioned in watchtowers, tall buildings, and church towers equipped with radios to first detect and report incoming aircraft. These watchtowers were connected to an extensive radio network, which was in turn supervised by the Commando Luchtverdediging and could immediately relay information to airfields and antiaircraft batteries. This system was much more advanced than what France and Belgium could boast. Despite France's significantly larger air force and large number of antiaircraft batteries, the French air-defense system relied on visual observation posts whose only contact with the Armée de l'Air command was made through the nearest local public telephone—hardly an efficient means of command control. Although still in the process of modernizing in the spring of 1940, the Dutch armed forces maintained the most sophisticated and effective air-defense network in Western Europe.[17]

A Change in Leadership

For van Kleffens, Dijxhoorn, and others who wished to take a more proactive approach to Dutch defensive measures (albeit still maintaining neutrality), the year 1940 began with a glimmer of hope when Gen. Reijnders was relieved of his post as supreme commander. In the end, Gen. Reijnders was dismissed because of his stubborn unwillingness to change the military's defensive planning despite the ominous information forwarded to him by

Dutch troops training with modern Oerlikon 2cm antiaircraft guns. [Militair Luchtvaart Museum, Soesterberg]

In October 1939, all Dutch aircraft had their red-white-blue with orange center roundels changed to an orange triangle with a black border. These "neutrality markings" were introduced in order to avoid confusion with British and French red-white-blue roundels. This was the second time Dutch aircraft markings had been changed since the foundation of the Dutch air services. The first Dutch identification marking, a plain orange circle, was changed to the red-white-blue with orange center roundel in 1921 after officials in the East Indies complained that the orange circle too closely resembled the Japanese red "meatball" roundel.

Dutch Military Aircraft Markings

1914-1920

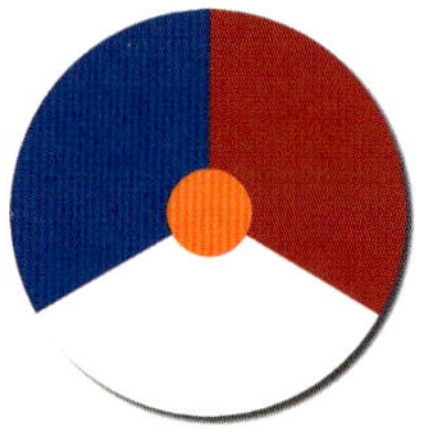

1921-1939

1939-1940

Sas and the GS-III, the intelligence division of the Dutch army, and because of his relentless arguments with civilian officials and his own superior, defense minister Dijxhoorn. (At one point, due to the bad blood between them, Reijnders referred to Dijxhoorn as a jealous mother-in-law hovering over him!) Furthermore, Reijnders dismissed any intelligence reports regarding Germany's plans of aggression. Indeed, he once replied to one of Sas's warnings thus: "Ze komen toch lekker niet" ("They aren't coming, so thanks for nothing!"). Reijnders still believed that the noble Prussian leadership of the German army would not violate the neutrality of the Netherlands, and he also believed that any German officer, Hans Oster in particular, who divulged secret information to a foreign power should be considered a traitor.

The bottom line was that Reijnders was trapped in a World War I mentality of honor among noble officers. What he failed to realize was that the rational and honorable Prussian officer corps no longer had the final say in German military matters. That prerogative had been seized by the irrational, politically driven, and amoral Hitler, who had as much contempt for the German officer corps as he had for his political rivals. In one regard, the Netherlands was fortunate, because Reijnders's replacement, General Henri Gerard Winkelman, was more open to the intelligence warnings coming from abroad.

A major problem, however, was that Gen. Reijnders had left the overall defense plans in an absolute state of disorganization, and there was no communication between the service branches, the Defense Ministry, and the cabinet. Reijnders had originally intended to place the bulk of the Dutch army along the Peel-Raam Line in the southern Netherlands, a series of casemates along canals and marshes that followed the German border up to the Belgian border. The reason for this troop deployment was that, in the event of a forceful German invasion of the Netherlands, the Dutch army could link up with the Belgian army and fall back in a line until French reinforcements would arrive in force. The problem with this strategy was that Reijnders, due to the perceived risk of violating strict neutrality, had allowed for no official military coordination between the Dutch, Belgian, French, and British forces. Hence his belief in Dutch-Belgian-French cooperation was merely a wishful assumption rather than a grounded reality. Furthermore, the Belgian high command refused to commit to any agreement to send Belgian troops to the Dutch border, which was further north of the Belgian defense line along the Albert Canal. It should be said in Reijnders's defense, however, that he had wanted to declare martial law after the outbreak of the war to better mobilize the country and to crack down on foreign espionage activities within Dutch borders. But the Dutch government had denied his request.[18]

Winkelman, the new Opperbevelhebber van Land- en Zeemacht, went straight to work revising the military's defense plans in the event of a German invasion of the Netherlands. Rather than defend the Peel-Raam Line in the south, which would have left the heart of the country open to attack, Winkelman decided to place the bulk of Dutch forces along the north-south Grebbelinie and then along the Waal-Linge Line, which ran almost 90 degrees west to connect with the Southfront Line of the Vesting Holland defenses. The Grebbelinie was perhaps the most modern and developed fortification line east of the Vesting Holland. It followed roughly the eastern border of the province of Utrecht (which also happened to parallel the only significant ridge in the Netherlands), running into Gelderland and ending at the Waal River. And it was equipped with pillboxes for machine and antitank guns. Nevertheless, it was not considered modern by the standards of other foreign militaries, and it could not compare with the more highly developed Belgian defenses and the French Maginot Line.

Turning directly north along the Waal, Winkelman stationed units along the hastily improvised Waal-Linge Line that connected the Grebbelinie with the Waterlinie of the Vesting Holland, which then ran to the sea. This limited the amount of terrain for the Dutch military to defend; at the same time it protected the vital urban areas in North and South Holland, as well as in Utrecht. All major Dutch airfields were also located within the Vesting Holland, so an aerial defense could be concentrated within Winkelman's defensive boundaries as well. While the abandonment of the Peel-Raam Line allowed an opening between the Dutch and Belgian lines, which the Germans could quickly drive through, the vital central portion of the Netherlands was closed off, and the only entrance into the area was via the Moerdijk bridges over the Maas River south of Dordrecht.

Winkelman also allowed unofficial secret conversations between Dutch military attachés and the French regarding a combined Allied effort in the event of a German invasion of the Low Countries. At the outbreak of war, the French Seventh Army would move up along the Belgian left flank and hold the area between the Albert Canal defenses in Belgium and the Dutch Waterlinie just to the east of the Moerdijk bridges. This had already been part of French General Maurice Gamelin's Dyle-Breda Plan, but the exact details of it were not known to the Dutch because the government was still officially maintaining a stance of strict neutrality.

Another benefit of Winkelman's appointment to the position of supreme commander of land and sea forces was that he took Maj. Sas's warnings from Berlin much more seriously. Winkelman paid attention to Sas when the attaché learned, via Oster, of the plans for the German invasion of Denmark and Norway, especially when Sas's information was confirmed by the Dutch intelligence agency, the GS-III. Indeed, the German invasion of Scandinavia happened just as Sas warned it would. But some in the Dutch high command were still critical of Sas's continuous warnings. Perhaps the worst irony of the entire situation was that Sas had conveyed revised plans for the German invasion of the Netherlands, involving airborne troops (something that had never been mentioned before) to Reijnders just before the latter was dismissed—but Reijnders had locked them away in a safe. He had never even informed his successor of their existence! With so much information coming in about potential German invasions from many different sources—and with the tension in the West growing—it was difficult for Winkelman to choose a clear course of action.[19]

General Izaäk H. Reijnders was made chief of the general staff of the Dutch army in 1934 and was appointed as Opperbevelhebber van Land- en Zeemacht when Dutch mobilization began on August 28, 1939. Reijnders was an advocate of strict neutrality and refused to believe the reports from Maj. Sas and his German informant, Col. Oster, regarding the imminent German invasion. He was an argumentative individual who frequently challenged his new superior in 1939, Defense Minister Adriaan Dijxhoorn, and adamantly refused to make better preparations for a potential German invasion based on intelligence reports. He was relieved of his command in February 1940 due to his uncooperative behavior with Dijxhoorn. [Wikimedia Commons]

Just as Minister of Defense Dijxhoorn inherited a mess from his predecessor, so did General Henri Winkelman (far left), who became Opperbevelhebber van Land- en Zeemacht after Gen. Reijnders was relieved of the post on February 5, 1940. When he took command, Winkelman found Dutch defensive planning in total disarray and fervently went to work on an effective defensive plan that would take advantage of Dutch military strengths and territorial advantages rather than trying to defend too much territory. Winkelman based his planning on intelligence reports from Maj. Sas and the GS-III, which Reijnders had refused to consider and had locked up in a safe. It was fortuitous that Winkelman found them, because Reijnders had neglected to tell him of their existence! Here Gen. Winkelman inspects a troop of grenadiers. [Netherlands Institute for Military History]

Case Yellow

What, then, were the exact plans being developed by the Germans during this period? The Germans had indeed considered invading the Netherlands in their original October 1939 plans for a greater Western offensive against the Belgians, French, and British—called *Fall Gelb* (Case Yellow)—initially scheduled for mid-November. General Franz Halder, chief of staff to the Oberkommando des Heeres (OKH), the German army's high command, presented the first plan for the invasion of Western Europe in October 1939. It involved a large force going directly through the Netherlands and attacking Belgium and northern France with the goal of occupying the Low Countries and destroying a significant portion of the British and French armies so that the Kriegsmarine and the Luftwaffe could focus their attention on attacking Great Britain. This plan differed from the Schlieffen plan in that it was not a strategy for all-out victory in the West; rather, it was one that would shift the balance in Germany's favor, and it did involve an attack on the Netherlands.

The impetus for attacking the Dutch came from Reichsmarschall Hermann Göring and his Luftwaffe, who wanted to gain control of Dutch air bases within the Vesting Holland in order to prevent aircraft of the British RAF from operating from those bases. Göring's plan came under criticism almost immediately from Hitler and the general staff of the army. They favored not violating Dutch neutrality, or only moving through the southern Maastricht corridor (hoping that the Dutch could be convinced not to declare war in return for a promise of full sovereignty), so that a stronger and more aggressive attack could be made through Belgium, aiming at a deeper push into France. The revised version of Halder's plan was scheduled to begin on November 12, but it was postponed by Hitler several times because of poor weather; it was finally canceled, partly due to the rather mediocre results it envisioned.

In the meantime, a more ambitious strategy was developed by General Erich von Manstein, along with his superior, General Gerd von Rundstedt, which called for total victory in the West—as opposed to securing a better strategic position on the front. Manstein, who had begun talks with General Heinz Guderian (recognized as one of the fathers of modern mobile and armored warfare), developed a plan focused on the deployment of three army groups: Army Group B was to attack the Netherlands and Belgium and secure the German right flank; Army Group A, containing the bulk of Germany's panzer forces, was to attack through the Ardennes Forest in Belgium and to inflict a defeat against the French at Sedan and then push to the coast, cutting off the British expeditionary force and the northern French armies and annihilating them; Army Group C, the weakest of the three, was to make a diversionary attack against the Maginot Line on the German left flank in order to keep French reserves pinned to the line so that they could not reinforce Allied forces in the north.

Committing most of the panzers to one area was a very risky gamble (not to mention a new and unorthodox strategy); but if everything went according to plan, after defeating the British expeditionary force and the northern French armies, the German army could then swing south toward Paris, thus having completely circumvented the Maginot Line. Rundstedt submitted Manstein's operational concept to the officers of the general staff beginning on October 31, 1939; the general staff dismissed the plan as far too radical and difficult to implement. But the "Manstein Variant" of *Fall Gelb* suddenly resurfaced in January 1940. The "Michelen Incident" triggered the need for a new Western strategy, since the *Fall Gelb* plans had most likely been passed on to the Allies. Rundstedt contacted Generalfeldmarschall Walther von Brauchitsch, Oberbefehlshaber des Heeres, and encouraged him to reconsider the "Manstein Variant." Halder and von Brauchitsch began to work details of the "Manstein Variant" into their new plans for *Fall Gelb* after a series of war games. Hitler first learned of Manstein's concept at an officers' dinner on February 17, 1940, and he was impressed. The following day Halder took his finalized new plan to Hitler, who approved it, and on February 24 the OKH began to prepare for the implementation of the finalized plan.

After Hitler launched Operation Weserübung, the invasions of Denmark and Norway on April 9, 1940, he and the high command finally settled on May 10, 1940, as the date on which *Fall Gelb* would commence (the operation had been canceled twenty-nine times during the preceding several months!). Hitler's order that the occupation of the Netherlands would now become part of the German plan was a result of Göring's stubborn insistence on the occupation of Dutch air bases. The German assault against the Grebbelinie called for mostly second-rate infantry divisions supplemented by the Der Führer, Deutschland, and Germania groups of the SS Verfügungstruppe (SS-VT), as well as the Leibstandarte Adolf Hitler (Hitler's personal bodyguard force). Only one armored division, the 9th Panzer Division, was allocated to the invasion of the Netherlands, and its task was to push west, parallel to the Waal defenses, and then turn north to break into the Vesting Holland.

The swift occupation of the territory within the Waterlinie, however, hinged on a revolutionary and untried strategy: the largest airborne assault ever attempted. The idea of a large-scale airborne assault tantalized Hitler, because it would represent the modern innovations of the German military and demonstrate the strength of Nazi-developed airpower. To its planners and leaders, it represented an innovative gamble to storm the Vesting Holland without a frontal attack. Just as warriors in the

The 1939–40 Winter War between Finland and the Soviet Union inadvertently gave Dutch pilots an opportunity to see how their Fokker aircraft performed in a combat environment. A large number of the Finnish air force was made up of Fokker D.XXI fighters and C.X (one is shown here taking off on the snow) and C.V light bombers/observation aircraft. Although outnumbered by over thirty to one in the air, Finnish pilots shot down 207 Soviet aircraft, while the total number of Finnish aircraft lost in the war was 48, giving the Finns a kill ratio of at least 4 to 1. Combat experience showed the D.XXI to be a particularly maneuverable and agile fighter, something Dutch pilots would take advantage of when they later found themselves in combat. Here is a surviving Finnish Fokker D.XXI on metal skis at the Keski-Suomen Ilmailumuseo. [Photo AVIODROME Luchtfotografie, Lelystad, Holland / Keski-Suomen Ilmailumuseo]

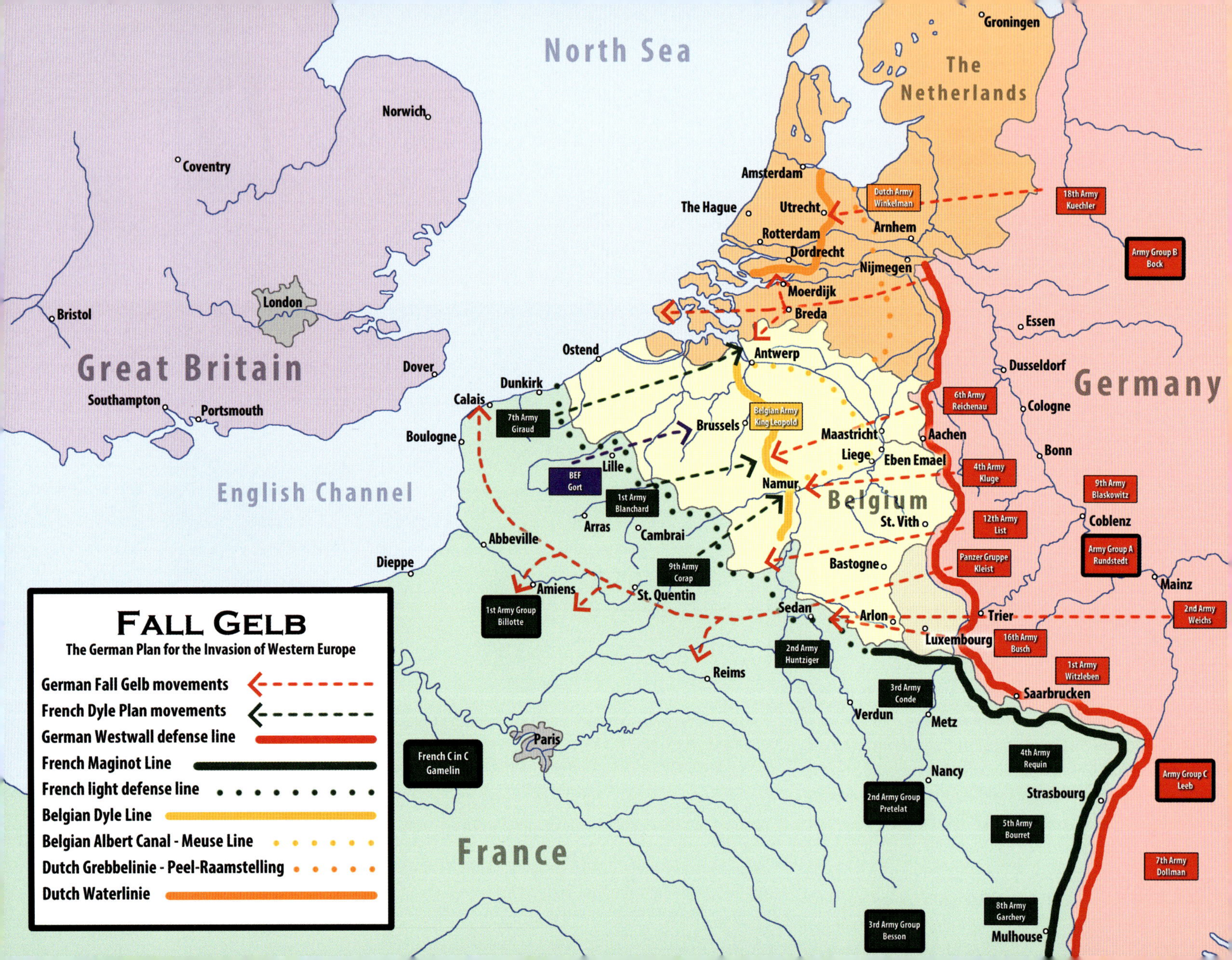
North Sea
The Netherlands
Groningen
Amsterdam
The Hague
Utrecht
Rotterdam
Dordrecht
Arnhem
Nijmegen
Moerdijk
Breda
Dutch Army Winkelman
18th Army Kuechler
Army Group B Bock
Essen
Dusseldorf
Germany
Cologne
Bonn
Aachen
Coblenz
Mainz
Trier
Saarbrucken
Norwich
Coventry
Bristol
London
Great Britain
Dover
Southampton
Portsmouth
English Channel
Ostend
Antwerp
Dunkirk
Calais
Boulogne
Brussels
Belgian Army King Leopold
Maastricht
Liege
Eben Emael
Namur
Belgium
St. Vith
Bastogne
Arlon
Luxembourg
Lille
Arras
Cambrai
Abbeville
Dieppe
Amiens
St. Quentin
Sedan
Reims
Verdun
Metz
Nancy
Strasbourg
Mulhouse
Paris
France
7th Army Giraud
BEF Gort
1st Army Blanchard
9th Army Corap
1st Army Group Billotte
2nd Army Huntziger
3rd Army Conde
French C in C Gamelin
4th Army Requin
2nd Army Group Pretelat
5th Army Bourret
8th Army Garchery
3rd Army Group Besson
6th Army Reichenau
4th Army Kluge
9th Army Blaskowitz
12th Army List
Army Group A Rundstedt
Panzer Gruppe Kleist
2nd Army Weichs
16th Army Busch
1st Army Witzleben
Army Group C Leeb
7th Army Dollman
FALL GELB
The German Plan for the Invasion of Western Europe
German Fall Gelb movements
French Dyle Plan movements
German Westwall defense line
French Maginot Line
French light defense line
Belgian Dyle Line
Belgian Albert Canal - Meuse Line
Dutch Grebbelinie - Peel-Raamstelling
Dutch Waterlinie

OPPOSITE PAGE *Map showing the German* Fall Gelb *plan for the invasion of France and the Low Countries and the Allied Dyle Plan designed to counter a German invasion of the West.*

Middle Ages scaled the ramparts of a castle to open the gates to an army waiting outside, so would Germany's airborne warriors fly over the defenses and open the gates of Fortress Holland. This task was assigned to the German Luftlande Korps, commanded by Lieutenant General Kurt Student and made up of the 4,000-man 7. Flieger-Division (7th Airborne Division), entirely made up of *Fallschirmjäger* (paratroopers), and the 13,500-man 22. Luftlande-Division (22nd Air-Landing Division), which was a lightly equipped infantry division carried into battle by transport aircraft.

Student, who served as a fighter pilot in the First World War, drafted an attack plan consisting of three parts. The first phase was to drop the paratroopers of the 7th Airborne Division around the Waalhaven airfield near Rotterdam as well as the Moerdijk bridges over the Waal River and the bridges over the Maas River at Dordrecht, the southern entrance of Fortress Holland. The first phase would be completed when the paratroopers attacked and secured the airfield and bridges. The second phase of the plan was to land transport planes carrying the 22nd Air-Landing Division on the airfields around The Hague, which would be heavily bombed before the landings, and these troops would then secure the airfields and attempt to capture the Dutch royal family and the government and military leaders in The Hague. The third and final phase of the plan was for the airborne divisions inside Fortress Holland to hold their positions until the arrival of the 9th Panzer Division, which would then create a breach through which infantry could proceed to occupy the remainder of the region. The German airborne arm had been in development since 1935, but its activities were a top secret prior to the beginning of World War II and during its first few months. Much of the success of Student's strategy lay in the element of surprise that the air landings in Fortress Holland would have. It was certainly a bold and innovative plan. But the Dutch were not going to be taken completely by surprise.

German Fallschirmjäger *(paratroopers) jumping from Ju 52 transports during a Luftwaffe paradrop exercise. The swift capture of the Netherlands according to the* Fall Gelb *plan required the rapid capture of airfields and vital bridges by paratroopers and* Luftlande *(air-landing) troops.* [Militair Luchtvaart Museum, Soesterberg]

SUSPICIONS GROW

The Germans began conducting photographic reconnaissance flights over the Netherlands even before the war began. The unit primarily responsible for this was the Kommando Rowehl, a special reconnaissance wing organized by the Abwehr. Before the war, Kommando Rowehl installed hidden cameras in three Heinkel He 111 and three Focke-Wulf Fw 200 airliners of Deutsche Lufthansa. Dutch air defense commanders along the Raam-Peel Line noticed that Deutsche Lufthansa airliners, while coming into and going out of Schiphol, frequently dropped to 200

Deutsche Lufthansa's Focke-Wulf Fw 200 **Westfalen** ***at Schiphol on June 25, 1938. The Westfalen was one of the civilian airliners equipped with secret cameras and used by Kommando Rowehl for photographic reconnaissance flights over Dutch airfields and defensive positions.*** [Photo AVIODROME Luchtfotografie, Lelystad, Holland]

or 300 meters, then proceeded to climb away. They also noticed that Deutsche Lufthansa airliners occasionally deviated from their normal commercial air routes and sometimes were spotted flying over the air base at Soesterberg. During the summer they began to notice high-altitude flights over Schiphol, Rotterdam, Waalhaven, and the area surrounding The Hague. In an attempt to curtail this activity, the Dutch government, at the beginning of the war, instructed the airlines of the belligerent powers that their aircraft could fly only along designated corridors at a height of 300 meters.

Deutsche Lufthansa flights into the Netherlands were suspended for a time after the war commenced—to the relief of Dutch air-defense commanders. However, German photographic reconnaissance flights became more obvious; in addition, occasional high-altitude flights were made by military aircraft of Luftwaffe Aufklärungsgruppen reconnaissance units. On October 26, 1939, a Dornier Do 17P reconnaissance aircraft made a crash landing near the village of Usquert in Groningen, the aircraft and crew were interned, and the plane and its equipment thoroughly examined by the GS-III. Yet, despite the Dutch capture of this Do 17P, German high-altitude photo reconnaissance flights continued. The Dutch government protested to the German government, but those protests were rebuffed: the typical German response was that these overflights were either German aircraft that had lost their way or were British reconnaissance aircraft (indeed, the British *were* making reconnaissance flights over the Netherlands). In any event, by the time of the German invasion, Kommando Rowehl and the Luftwaffe had thoroughly photographed the key defensive positions and air defenses inside the Netherlands.

The initial reason that the Germans made such a large number of these reconnaissance missions was to thoroughly document the capabilities of Dutch airfields in case the British and French would make use of them—either by invitation or by force. The second reason for the frequent German reconnaissance flights was to prepare for airborne operations. When Deutsche Lufthansa flights were resumed into Schiphol on March 15, 1940, Kommando Rowehl resumed the reconnaissance missions in the airline's civilian aircraft. But the Germans were not the only ones using civilian airline flights as cover for reconnaissance flights. KLM pilot Karel Steensma, who was also a member of GS-III, made a point to observe new airfields under construction in western Germany while on flights to Berlin. The KLM office at Tempelhof Airport in Berlin attempted to gain information about these airfields by requesting information about them and permission for KLM airliners to use them in case of an emergency.[20]

As I mentioned previously, the Dutch learned from intelligence reports that paratroopers would play a part in a German invasion of the Netherlands. They also knew firsthand about the nature of German paradrop operations that were conducted during the invasion of Denmark and Norway on April 9, 1940. KLM pilot Evert van Dijk was at Fornebu Airport in Oslo when German paratroopers captured Norway's airfields, and he was able to report what he saw to the Dutch military. Hitler's carefully guarded secret was out, and the Dutch did not sit on their hands and do nothing. The ML repositioned the bulk of its antiaircraft arsenal to the major airports and airfields in Fortress Holland, and machine gun pits were dug around the fields in case of an airborne attack. These measures, combined with the alert status of the ML, gave the Dutch an effective air-defense system. Armored-car units were also stationed near the most important airfields: their 37mm cannons would prove a devastatingly effective weapon against the lightly armed paratroopers. Their mobility and speed also allowed them to move to various hot points as needed. Further, the Dutch blocked the highways around The Hague and Dordrecht with parked cars positioned several yards apart so that German transport aircraft could not utilize the roads as improvised runways.

When one takes all of this into account—and considering the nation's well-defined defensive lines—one can argue that the Netherlands was the nation best prepared for the coming German onslaught, even though its military may have been the most underequipped and inexperienced. And the onslaught *was* coming, as indicated by further intelligence that came to the Dutch high command. Reports from the GS-III told of German troop buildups along the border. These reports continued to

Luftwaffe Dornier Do 17P reconnaissance aircraft shot down near Usquert in Groningen on October 26, 1939. These flights convinced many Dutch officers that the Germans were extensively photographing Dutch military installations. [Netherlands Institute of Military History]

On April 8, 1940, KLM Captain Evert van Dijk flew the DC-3 Kemphaan *into Fornebu Airport at Oslo, Norway, on a routine passenger flight. The following day the Germans launched the invasion of Denmark and Norway. On that morning van Dijk witnessed firsthand the rapid and successful capture of Fornebu Airport by German* Fallschirmjäger *and* Luftlande *units. The Germans could not detain van Dijk and the* Kemphaan *because they belonged to a neutral nation; thus he flew the DC-3 back to Schiphol on April 14. Upon his return he reported what he saw to the Dutch military. This bit of unintended intelligence convinced the Dutch army and the ML to reinforce the defenses around airfields behind the Waterlinie and to prepare carefully for similar airborne attacks.* [Fornebu photo—Deutsches Bundesarchiv via Wikimedia Commons]

come in until May 10, 1940. On the night before, Sas phoned from Berlin warning the Dutch high command that the German invasion would indeed begin in the early hours of the 10th. Sas's last warning was finally heeded that evening, at least to some degree, because something out of the ordinary certainly seemed to be stirring across the border in Germany. Dutch guards posted along the German frontier were phoning The Hague with reports of the noise of large numbers of motors turning over and orders being shouted from the German side. In response, Gen. Winkelman sent a preliminary invasion alert to troops stationed at the border crossings and went home to retire for the evening. He would not sleep long that night.[21]

A troop-laden Ju 52 transport comes in for a landing at Fornebu over a crashed Messerschmitt Bf 110 fighter during the invasion of Norway.

A flight of German Junkers Ju 52 transports disgorging their cargo: Fallschirmjäger, *highly trained paratroopers. The German invasion of the Netherlands on May 10, 1940, was the world's first major airborne military operation.*

Chapter Seven

LIGHTNING STRIKE IN MAY

THE FIRST DAY OF THE *MEIDAGEN:* THE BATTLE FOR THE AIRFIELDS (MAY 10, 1940)

In the darkness at 3:30 a.m. (Amsterdam time)[1] on May 10, 1940, the early-morning calm gave way to the sound of aircraft engines turning over and warming up at the airfields. Dutch pilots were roused from their bunks and told to be ready to scramble at a moment's notice. The airfield commanders had received phone calls reporting that border guards stationed along the German border had reported groups of Germans in Dutch uniforms crossing the border, and that the border bridges over the Maas were being blown up as a precautionary measure. No word had come from the Dutch high command about an all-out German invasion, but the airbase commanders felt that something was amiss. At about the same time that the Dutch ground crews were starting up and arming their fighters, a low rumbling could be heard in the distance; large formations of twin-engine aircraft were approaching at high altitude. But then the droning became quieter as the planes headed off toward the west.

At the Ypenburg airfield, the ML base near The Hague (the home of the Veldleger's *jachtgroep* and a unit of C.V observation planes), the base commander gave the command to switch off the aircraft engines. He had concluded that the aircraft in the distance heading out to the

Luftwaffe bomber crews suiting up prior to a mission.

Militaire Luchtvaart Order of Battle May 10, 1940

1e Luchtvaartregiment

Strategische Verkenners Afdeling

10 Fokker C.Xs operational / 3 in reserve at Bergen

Bombardeervliegtuig Afdeling

9 Fokker T.Vs operational / 3 in reserve at Schiphol

1e Jachtvliegtuig Afdeling

11 Fokker D.XXIs operational / 1 in reserve at De Kooy

2e Jachtvliegtuig Afdeling

9 Fokker D.XXIs operational / 3 in reserve at Schiphol

3e Jachtvliegtuig Afdeling

11 Fokker G.1s operational / 1 in reserve at Waalhaven

4e Jachtvliegtuig Afdeling

12 Fokker G.1s operational / 2 in reserve at Bergen

2e Luchtvaartregiment

1e Jachtvliegtuigenafdeling

8 Fokker D.XXIs operational / 1 in reserve at Ypenburg

3e Jachtvliegtuigenafdeling

11 Douglas 8A-3Ns operational / 1 in reserve at Ypenburg

Ie Verkenningsgroep, attached to IV Legerkorps (army corps)
- 8 C.Vs, 4 F.K.51s, and 1 C.X at Hilversum

IIe Verkenningsgroep, attached to II Legerkorps
- 9 C.Vs and 6 F.K.51s at Ypenburg

IIIe Verkenningsgroep, attached to 1 and 2 Brigaden
- 9 C.Vs and 3 F.K.51s at Ruigenhoek

IVe Verkenningsgroep, attached to III Legerkorps
- 8 C.Vs and 5 F.K.51s at Gilze-Rijen

3e Luchtvaartregiment

71 aircraft (mostly training types) at the Elementaire Vliegschool at Souberg, the Voortgezette Vliegschool at Haamstede, and the Jachtvliegschool at De Vlijt.

North Sea were German aircraft en route to attack Great Britain. The commander at Waalhaven ordered two G.1s of the 3e Jacht Vliegtuig Afdeeling (3e Ja.V.A.) to take off for a patrol over the airport at 3:50. At that moment the early morning calm was broken again: in the distance the drone of a large number of aircraft could be heard again, as well as the rumble of antiaircraft guns in The Hague. Captain O. K. Bartels, commander of the Ypenburg ground defenses, and his driver were in his staff car touring the base perimeter when suddenly a Heinkel He 111 bomber swooped down and strafed the road ahead of them. Bartels turned around and headed for the airfield just as a group of He 111s arrived overhead. The planes that had been thought to be headed for England were actually on a mission to attack the Dutch airfields.

The German bombers had headed northwest over the North Sea to a point fifteen or twenty miles off the coast and then curved to the southwest as part of a ruse to confuse the Dutch. Fortunately, pilots and antiaircraft crews had stayed on alert, and thus the Dutch were not caught completely by surprise. As soon as the base commander at Ypenburg heard the incoming aircraft and the ground fire, he scrambled all of the aircraft that could get airborne. Just as the base's eight Fokker D.XXIs of the 1e Ja.V.A. Jachtgroep Veldleger were taking off, Capt. Bartels arrived at the edge of the airfield and saw bombs begin to drop from the He 111s overhead. Shortly after that, eleven 8A-3Ns of the 3e Ja.V.A. Jachtgroep Veldleger took off amid the falling bombs; one had its left wing damaged from a blast as it was getting airborne. Along with the D.XXIs, they found themselves in the middle of a massive swarm of German bombers escorted by Bf 110C fighters. The D.XXIs immediately took aim at the German aggressors: Second Lieutenant A. M. van de Vaart shot down a Do 215 reconnaissance plane; Second Lieutenant F. G. B. Droste bagged a Junkers Ju 88 bomber; and Sergeant P. J. Aarts claimed a Bf 110C.

In the air battle for Ypenburg, however, Germany's overwhelming numbers eventually claimed almost all of the Dutch defenders: three D.XXIs were shot down in air-to-air combat, while the other five had to make forced

Douglas 8A-3N
length: 31 ft 8⅝ in (9.7 m)
wingspan: 47 ft 8½ in (14.5 m)
power plant: 1,065 hp Pratt & Whitney R-1830-SC3G Twin Wasp radial engine
maximum speed: 258 mph (416 km/h)
range: 650 miles (1,046 km)
ceiling: 25,263 ft (7,700 m)
armament: five 7.9mm M36 machine guns
payload: 1,200 lbs (544 kg) of bombs
crew: 2

A new light bomber/scout aircraft was one of the requirements of the IML's four-year modernization plan, and the Douglas 8A-3N was one of the few aircraft within this category that was available for purchase when the IML's plan was tardily put into motion in the summer of 1939. Defense Minister van Dijk ordered 18 8A-3Ns in July 1939, to arrive in the Netherlands during September and October of that year, for the 2nd Air Regiment of the of the Field Army Air Group. The Ministry of Defense also tried to order a large number of American bombs for the 8A-3Ns, but they were not delivered before the German invasion. Since the 8A-3Ns could not fulfill their light bomber role without an adequate supply of bombs, the ML leadership made the inexplicable decision to assign the planes the role of auxiliary fighter. These planes had a top speed of only 206 mph and poor maneuverability, and that decision was to have tragic consequences during the German invasion. This photo shows the eighteen 8A-3Ns at Soesterberg before they were sent to the air base at Ypenburg. The Northrup A-17A (early production version of the Douglas 8A-3N) at the top of the page is housed at the Museum of the United States Air Force [Militair Luchtvaart Museum, Soesterberg]

Crashed Douglas 8A-3N #390 of Sergeant J. J. de Bruin, shot down near Delft. Pressed into the battle as fighters, the unwieldy Douglas bombers stood no chance against the Messerschmitt Bf 110 fighters escorting the German bombers over Ypenburg. [Photo AVIODROME Luchtfotografie, Lelystad, Holland]

landings due to damage or were running out of ammunition or fuel (one of the D.XXIs was able to land at the Ruigenhoek airfield, which German reconnaissance had not detected). The 8A-3Ns fared even worse: six were shot down almost immediately after takeoff by the roving Bf 110Cs, while the other four had to make forced landings, in which two were destroyed. On the ground, the aerial bombardment of Ypenburg continued until 4:45 a.m., and just as the bombers were returning home, a large group of Ju 52s began to fly over. While Capt. Bartels was watching the end of the bombardment from the edge of the airfield, his driver shouted at him and pointed to the sky: small puffs of white were appearing to come out of the transport aircraft. Dozens of paratroopers were coming down all around the area.[2]

High above the Ypenburg area, as the bombers were attacking the airfield, a Ju 52 transport group dropped two companies of paratroopers northeast of the airfield; they landed along the highway between Delft and Ypenburg. Their mission was to secure the airfield for a large group of transports carrying air-landing troops scheduled to land soon. The air-landing troops were to then disembark and race to The Hague in order to capture the royal family, the government, and the military high command. These troops carried road maps of The Hague showing the locations of their objectives, as well as the location of automobile dealerships (information obtained by Germans living in The Hague), where they could commandeer improvised ground transport. Once the paratroopers landed and made their way to the airfield, they could see antiaircraft guns firing at a group of incoming Ju 52s. To their horror, they saw several of the transports being shot out of the sky, victims of Dutch antiaircraft fire, and falling to earth engulfed in flames (the fuel tanks of the Ju 52s did not have armor protection and were not self-sealing). The paratroopers came to a stark realization: the defenses at Ypenburg had not been taken out by the bombing raid that had preceded them.

The surviving and damaged transports aborted from the skies over their planned drop zones and dropped their paratroopers off target. The effectiveness of the Dutch defense was further reinforced when the German paratroopers on the ground ran into the machine-gun positions and two platoons of Landsverk armored cars that made up Capt. Bartels's defensive screen. Since the paratroopers were not dropped on their designated drop zones, their situation was confused when they hit the ground, and they were in no position to fulfill their mission to secure the airfield for the incoming air-landing units. At 6:15, the Dutch antiaircraft gunners spotted the first wave of air-landing troop transports coming in to land on the airfield, their pilots not knowing what the circumstances on the ground were. As the thirteen unsuspecting Ju 52s approached to land, the Dutch antiaircraft batteries opened fire and shot down the first eight before they even touched the ground; the remaining five were either destroyed on landing or shot up by machine guns stationed around the airfield perimeter. Three additional waves of Ju 52s carrying air-landing units made the same approach on Ypenburg, and many German paratroopers shared the same fate as those who preceded them.

The Dutch defense and antiaircraft units certainly earned their keep that morning. The antiaircraft batteries, machine guns, and the squadron of armored cars kept up a murderous fire on the incoming German

Ju 52/3m transports coming in from over the sea at dawn.

planes. They shot some down on approach, and those that landed crashed into the burning wreckage of other Ju 52s on the airfield. The lucky ones managed to rev their engines and bank away from the airfield, most making forced landings on the highway to Delft or on the beach; only seven of the twenty-eight planes that landed near

LEFT ***Dutch troops rushing to man a Vickers 7.5cm antiaircraft gun.*** [Militair Luchtvaart Museum, Soesterberg]

BELOW ***The Dutch army did not build up a tank force before World War II, believing that the many rivers, canals, and waterlines would deny an attacker the use of armored units in the field en masse. Instead, the army purchased twenty-six Landsverk M.36 and M.38 armored cars from Sweden between 1936 and 1938. Eight armored car platoons (3 cars each) were formed as rapid-response units that, as part of the cavalry, could be quickly sent along Holland's excellent road network to support embattled infantry units (one armored car shown here training with a cavalry unit during mobilization*** [Militair Luchtvaart Museum, Soesterberg]. ***Armed with a Bofors 37mm semi-automatic cannon, which could fire high-explosive or armor-piercing shells, and three 7.9mm Lewis guns, the Dutch Landsverk was the best armored car deployed by any nation in the West in the spring of 1940, and it was used extensively during the battles for the airfields and the defense of Rotterdam. A Landsverk M.38 survives in the Cavaleriemuseum in the Bernhardkazerne in Amersfoort.***

One of the Ju 52s that aborted from Ypenburg and made a crash landing on Highway 13, between Delft and Rotterdam. [Netherlands Institute of Military History]

Delft were able to take off again. Back at the airfield, the Dutch were pouring machine-gun rounds into the crashed Ju 52s, cutting down the Germans who were trying to fight their way out. When the Dutch ceased fire, only three Germans were found alive out of all the troops flown into Ypenburg, and they were promptly taken prisoner. At that point on May 10, round one of the battle for the Netherlands had gone decisively to the Dutch.[3]

The German paratroopers who landed in the vicinity of Delft came down in a disorganized fashion on all sides of the city. While they were trying to re-form their units, they heard the roar of antiaircraft fire coming from the city. The Dutch were firing at the transports that had aborted from Ypenburg and were now making for their secondary landing area, the highway between Delft and Rotterdam. The paratroopers watched helplessly as a number of the transports were shot out of the air by the accurate fire of the Dutch gunners in Delft. Inside the planes that survived the antiaircraft barrage, the pilots began to panic when they made their landing approach along the highway: the lanes were purposely blocked with cars and trucks. Without any other place to land and the sky filled with Dutch flak, the Ju 52 pilots put their planes down as best they could on the embankments along the highway. One German soldier remarked:

> In front of us small white puffs of smoke appeared and glided past the cockpit windows. Anti-aircraft fire! So, the Dutchman was resisting. He was even shooting. This appeared to us to be foolhardy and unwise of our small neighbour. In any case we instinctively went and sat on our helmets to thus protect another precious part of our body from below. . . . Suddenly a heavy blow hit the plane. We fell pell-mell. I landed in front of the horse that had also fallen, but luckily the suspension straps prevented it from falling on me. The pilot regained control of the plane. What happened? A hit by the anti-aircraft took away one of the wheels of the landing gear. The plane captain didn't tell us in order to save us from worry. . . . We stared along the road in front of us. Would the plane come to halt before the car that the Dutch parked across the road to prevent a landing? It was a useless thought, for the plane had already tilted over to one side, brushed along a hedge in its path, and turned around. Plane parts were being strewn in all directions and the plane was thrown onto a field.[4]

Nearly all of the transports that landed were damaged, some losing their landing gear or wings, and only a handful were able to take off again back to Germany. The air-landing troops that managed to make their way out of the wrecked planes along the highway then attempted to link up with the paratroopers around Delft. If they could take the city and the highway to Rotterdam, they would be able to set up a link between troops attempting to take Ypenburg and the paratroopers and air-landing troops who were simultaneously making an attack on Rotterdam.

Although the Dutch garrison in Delft was outnumbered by the survivors of the German attack groups in the vicinity, they apparently were in no mood to casually leave their city to the invaders. Some paratroopers had occupied the Porcelyne Fles Delftware Works in the city after landing. Upon hearing this, the Dutch garrison and a number of students from the Technical University of Delft began a spirited attack that drove the Germans not only out of the factory but out of the town completely. The fighting in and around Delft was very disorganized, mainly scattered planeloads of Germans dueling with small numbers of Dutch garrison troops, policemen, and armed students. In almost every instance, the Dutch were able to attack and overwhelm the small groups of invaders and force them to capitulate.

In some instances, small groups of Dutch held out against determined German attacks. The best example was that of Warrant Officer J. C. P. Walraven, who, along with seven soldiers and three policemen, successfully defended the Kruithuis of Delft (an old gunpowder house containing a large stock of artillery and antiaircraft shells) against a group of paratroopers armed with submachine guns and grenades. The Dutch managed to repulse all of the German attacks on Delft, and, as an added bonus, they collected a large number of rifles, submachine guns, ammunition, and several motorcycles from their prisoners. This stiff resistance by a greatly outnumbered foe was becoming more and more of a demoralizing shock to the Germans.[5]

As if matters were not going badly enough for the Germans around Ypenburg and Delft, they were about to experience another series of nasty surprises outside of The Hague. One of the German objectives in their assault on The Hague was the auxiliary airfield near the village of Valkenburg, outside the city. The airfield had no aircraft based there and was only defended by two infantry companies and a heavy machine-gun platoon. At the time that the other attacks were beginning around The Hague, at 3:45 a.m., troop-laden transports began their landing approach. Although the few defenders at the airfield were on their own against the incoming horde, Mother Nature came to their assistance. There was a good reason why there were no Dutch planes based at Valkenburg: unbeknownst to the Germans, the airfield had not yet been completed, and the soil on the field was still far too soft to support the landing of heavy aircraft. As fifty Ju 52s touched down onto the airfield, they shuddered to an abrupt stop as their landing gear sank into the soft, muddy soil. The stranded planes and their passengers became perfect targets for the defenders ringing the airfield. The Dutch poured rifle, machine gun, and howitzer fire into the transports and the disembarking troops for over two hours before the numerically superior Germans on the airfield, supported by paratroopers who had landed behind the defenders' position, were able to drive the Dutch from their positions. Although the Germans had secured the airfield, their victory was hollow at best. Because of the condition of the soil, the airfield could not be reused, and not one of the fifty transports that had landed there could take off again; they had all either been damaged or had sunk to their bellies in the soft mud. Witnessing the carnage on the ground from a distance, and realizing that there would be no safe place to land, a second group of twenty Ju 52s bound for Valkenburg turned around and returned to Germany with their troops still aboard.[6]

Disaster likewise struck the air-landing troops making their assault at the auxiliary airfield at Ockenburg,

Two Ju 52s stuck in the mud on the airfield at Valkenburg. The weight of the aircraft had sunk them down to their bellies, and not a single transport was able to take off again. [Militair Luchtvaart Museum, Soesterberg]

A reconnaissance photo showing the German aerial assault on the airfield at Valkenburg. The white specks in the circles numbered "1" are parachutes from the Fallschirmjäger *that landed around the airfield. A number of Ju 52s stuck in the mud on the airfield are in the circle numbered "2." On the left side of the photo in the circles numbered "3," three Ju 52s are approaching the airfield for a landing (note the low altitude of the aircraft from their shadows).*

another town outside the The Hague. The story there was the same as it was at Ypenburg and Valkenburg: the paratroopers who were supposed to secure the airfield for the incoming transport planes had failed in their objective, and the transports were met with unexpected defensive fire as soon as they touched down. The defenders at Ockenburg numbered only ninety-six men—with three light machine guns and no antiaircraft guns—but they had been on alert since the evening before. Throughout the night the pickets patrolling the airfield perimeter had noticed flashing red-and-white signal lights coming from the nearby sand dunes. Although the sentries did not find anyone on the dunes, the airfield commander kept his troops on alert, correctly assuming that something dangerous was coming. After the Ockenburg defenders had been watching the air battle over Ypenburg for some time, a group of German fighters swooped in and began strafing the field. Afterward came the transports, but they were met with ground fire. The Dutch managed to destroy several planes and inflict heavy casualties on the Germans. But as at Valkenburg, they were badly outnumbered and eventually outflanked by the paratroopers who had finally made their way to the scene. But the defenders' resistance was so fierce that the air-landing troops were forced to take the machine guns off the transports and turn them on the Dutch. Although the Dutch were driven from the airfield shortly before 8:00 a.m., they had managed to inflict enough damage on the enemy that only thirteen of the forty-seven Ju 52s that landed at Ockenburg were able to take off again.[7]

The ML units based at Schiphol and De Kooy airfields fared much better than did their compatriots to the south. The situation at Schiphol Airport was tense, and the pilots were in their aircraft already by 3:00 a.m. However, the alarm of invasion had not been confirmed by the fighter command in The Hague, and the commander of the 2e Jacht Vliegtuig Afdeeling (2e Ja.V.A.), Captain P. J. E. Janssens, gave the order for the pilots to leave their aircraft at 3:15. The aircrews had hardly settled back down in the hangar when, at 3:58, they spotted three German bombers speeding in from the northwest at an

Left *A Heinkel He 111 bomber seen from the cockpit of another.* [Museum of the United States Air Force]

Above ***Fokker T.V #854 survived the Luftwaffe's early morning attack on Schiphol and was able to land and re-arm at another airfield. It later took off successfully and attacked the German-held airfield at Waalhaven but was shot down shortly after noon by a group of six Bf 109 fighters. Only one of the crew of five was able to bail out.*** [Photo AVIODROME Luchtfotografie, Lelystad, Holland]

altitude of only 25-30 meters. When the incoming aircraft were reported to Janssens, he sounded the general alarm, ordering all available fighters to scramble. The Fokker T.V bombers of Bombardeer Vliegtuig Afdeeling (Bom.V.A.) were also ordered to take off immediately after the D.XXIs. Eight of the Dutch bombers were able to get airborne; one was damaged by bomb fragments on takeoff and had to abort. Meanwhile, the D.XXIs, which were already airborne, swept in on the invaders. A number of He 111s were shot up, and First Lieutenant N. W. Sluijter managed to shoot down a Junkers Ju 88 bomber. The T.Vs quickly went to work in their originally intended role as *luchtkruiser,* or bomber-destroyer aircraft, as they wove into the formations of German planes overhead, claiming damage to a number of Ju 52s. Surprisingly, eight of the D.XXIs and all of the T.Vs that made it into the air during the first raid on Schiphol were able to land at the battered airport or at other airfields. Some made it back into the air for further combat during the day, while one T.V was damaged during landing, one had irreparable engine damage, and another was damaged by indiscriminate Dutch antiaircraft fire.

As the German bombers flew away, the ground crew at Schiphol began to survey the damage. The ML barracks, KLM canteen, and a number of private homes bordering the airport were completely destroyed, and Fokker T.V #860, which was parked on the tarmac in front of the terminal, was a completely burnt-out loss. The airport terminal building itself did not suffer much damage, mainly windows blown out, with shards of glass everywhere. The conditions of the airport's hangars varied: Hangar A was only slightly damaged; Hangar B received several direct hits, damaging or destroying the KLM aircraft parked inside; inside Hangar C, bomb hits started fires that engulfed Fokker T.V #851, which burned along with the training aircraft of the Nationale Luchtvaartschool (National Aviation School). T.V #863 was damaged, along with the engines destined for T.V #857, which was parked, engineless, inside Military Hangar I. Hangar D received the most damage: three KLM DC-3s and a Focke Wulf Fw 58 were destroyed by fires caused by the bomb blasts, and a number of other DC-3s were heavily damaged. Military Hangar I, along with T.V #857 inside, was heavily damaged, but the ground crews managed to quickly extinguish the fires. It is amazing that Military Hangar II, which housed the base's ammunition and the

Damage at Schiphol following the Luftwaffe attack. One of KLM's DC-2s sits damaged on the tarmac. Most of the ML's aircraft at Schiphol were able to scramble and survive, but KLM lost fourteen of its aircraft. [Netherlands Institute of Military History]

Three of the Fokker D.XXIs of the 1e Jacht Vliegtuig Afdeeling based at De Kooy. The 1e Ja.V.A.'s fighters had already been warmed up at 3:00 a.m. as base personnel detected German aircraft to the north, and all of the aircraft were in the air when the first German attack came. The pilots and fighters of 1e Ja.V.A. were in the air most of the morning, at one point eight of their number dueling against nine Bf 109s over De Kooy shortly before 5:00 a.m. [Militair Luchtvaart Museum, Soesterberg]

bombs for the T.Vs, came through the attack virtually unscathed, which was very important because it allowed the T.Vs to begin counterattacks as soon as they returned to base.

The damage to the airport had indeed been heavy, but the hard-working ground crews were able to get many of the facilities operational within a relatively short period of time. Bomb craters on the airfield and tarmac were filled and debris was removed while the wreckage of burnt-out machinery and aircraft was bulldozed out of the hangars. Fortunately, the antiaircraft defenses were undamaged, and Schiphol was back in the fight within a matter of hours. It was the fleet of commercial KLM aircraft that suffered the highest degree of damage at Schiphol on the morning of May 10. A total of four DC-3s, five DC-2s, the Werkspoor Jumbo cargo freighter, three Koolhoven F.K.43s, and an F.K.48 were written off in the aftermath of the attack.[8]

To the north of Schiphol, the D.XXI pilots of 1e Jacht Vliegtuig Afdeeling (1e Ja.V.A.), based at the De Kooy airfield, gave a much more impressive accounting of themselves. All eleven of the squadron's fighters were scrambled just before 4:00 a.m., after reports came in of Luftwaffe attacks on other Dutch airfields. Patrolling in the dawn skies, the squadron came across no large groups of German aircraft, but suddenly they received a radio message from the squadron commander back at De Kooy: the base was under attack by Bf 109 fighters. Since not every D.XXI was equipped with a radio (a prewar cost-saving measure that would have tragic consequences), only nine of the fighters received the message, some by hand signals. When the nine D.XXIs returned to De Kooy, there was not a single enemy aircraft overhead, so six of the D.XXI's went down to refuel while the remaining three stayed airborne, providing cover for those on the ground. When the six refueled fighters took off again, the remaining three came in to refuel. Just as they were landing, a group of eight Bf 109s sped in and commenced a strafing run that left one of the landing Fokkers in flames. Second Lieutenant Henk van Overvest, who had just touched down, gunned his engine and took off after the intruders. Overvest quickly came up behind one of the Bf 109s and poured a stream of bullets into it, knocking out its engine. The German fighter went down and made a belly landing, skidding across the airfield. After the plane had come to a stop, the pilot, Lieutenant Dieter Robitzsch, who happened to be the squadron commander, climbed out and in all seriousness demanded of the Dutch: "Why do you resist?" Later he remarked: "I did not want this!"

Back in the air, the maneuverability of the Fokkers gave them the upper hand in the ensuing air battle. Despite their obsolescent appearance, with their fixed landing gear and wood-and-canvas construction, the D.XXIs could easily outturn the faster Bf 109s: it took only three complete turns for a D.XXI to go from being prey in front of a Messerschmitt to being the predator behind it. Lieutenant Francois Focquin de Grave damaged one of the attackers, which made an emergency landing on the island of Borkum, and Lieutenant Herman Doppenberg sent another German fighter down. Within ten minutes, the Germans were high-tailing it back to base minus one-third of their force, while all eight D.XXIs that participated in the air battle came down safely—albeit all damaged.[9]

On the ground at Waalhaven Aerodrome near Rotterdam at 3:50, First Lieutenant Piet Noomen, a veteran KLM pilot, was standing in front of the airbase's command post when he noticed three aircraft speeding in from the southwest at a low level. The three were Heinkel He 111s, and they dropped their bombs and strafed with their machine guns as they sped over the airfield. Fully aware that the war was now on for the Netherlands, Noomen raised the alarm and ran off toward Fokker G.1 #312, which was sitting on the tarmac in front of the base's hangars. Noomen and his rear gunner, Cpl. De Vries, jumped into the plane and gave the signal for the ground crew to start the engines. The left engine started quickly but the right one would not turn over. The mechanics feverishly worked on the engine, even as bombs were striking the hangars behind them, hurling large pieces of debris everywhere. Calmly working through all that, they finally got the motor to start.

At that point Noomen scrambled and took off after the same Heinkels, which had just completed a second pass on the airfield. At first Noomen flew close to the deck, figuring that the Germans would not be able to spot his earthen-camouflaged fighter against the ground in the early morning darkness. Flying at full throttle, Noomen crept up on the three Heinkels and then climbed to get into an attack position. Then from a distance of sixty meters, Noomen opened fire on the lead plane, flying in the middle of the formation. Smoke began to erupt from the bomber and it went down, making a belly landing in a field. Unbeknownst to Noomen at the time, he had just shot down the plane carrying the commander of Kampfgeschwader 4, Oberst Martin Fiebig. Of the two remain-

The crashed Bf 109 of Lieutenant Dieter Robitzsch, commander of a squadron of nine Messerschmitts that raided De Kooy at 4:50 a.m. Robitzsch was shot down over the airfield by Second Lieutenant Henk van Overvest. When the German climbed out of his cockpit, he impudently asked, "Why do you resist?" [Militair Luchtvaart Museum, Soesterberg]

Pilots of 1e Ja.V.A. at De Kooy: Second Lieutenants Jan Bosch, Herman Doppenberg, and Henk van Overvest. Doppenberg and van Overvest each claimed a Bf 109 from Robitzsch's squadron on the morning of the 10th. [Douglas Dildy Collection]

Three Heinkel He 111s on a low-altitude attack approach. [Museum of the United States Air Force]

Rear gunner climbing into a Fokker G.1. [Douglas Dildy Collection]

ing Heinkels, the one on the right veered off to make a run for it after taking a number of bullets while the one on the left stayed on course while the gunner in the dorsal machine-gun post opened fire. The German bomber soon felt the wrath of the Fokker's eight machine guns: Noomen took out its dorsal gun and then knocked out its left engine, sending it toward the ground.

Noomen had shot down two of the invaders in fifteen minutes, but any victory celebration would have to wait. De Vries signaled to Noomen that the right fuel tank had been hit, and the latter switched off the right engine to prevent a potential fire. The airmen headed for home, landing in the swampy ground at the northwest corner of the airfield. With only one engine, it was impossible to taxi the plane toward the repair shops, so Noomen and De Vries left the fighter where it was. Running across the airfield to the headquarters, they dove into the wet ground several times to avoid being strafed by the German fighters circling overhead. When Noomen and De Vries finally reached the base's command post, they were disappointed to learn that there were no other fighters available to take off in. In fact, Noomen was not able to get into the air again during the Dutch campaign due to a lack of operable aircraft. But at least he could take satisfaction in the fact that within the fifteen minutes of combat that he saw (out of a flying career that spanned over 16,000 flight hours with KLM), he had managed to achieve two kills.[10]

Noomen's wingman, Second Lieutenant Gerben Sonderman, followed him into the air but set his course to intercept an incoming group of Ju 52s escorted by Bf 109s. Sonderman shot down one of the transports, a Do 17Z reconnaissance aircraft loitering in the area, and a Bf 109D. Back on the ground at Waalhaven, the remaining G.1s of 3e Jacht Vliegtuig Afdeeling (3e Ja.V.A.) were ordered to scramble. First Lieutenant K. W. Woudenberg, Sergeant H. F. Souffrée, and First Lieutenant J. P. Kuipers were able to get their G.1s into the air before a second wave of Heinkels struck the airfield. They were joined overhead by Sonderman, who waded into the bomber formation. Souffrée and Kuipers attacked a second wave of incoming bombers, and the two pilots claimed one and two kills respectively. Woudenberg attacked the incoming wave of Ju 52s carrying the paratroopers destined for the drop on Waalhaven, which was first engaged by Sonderman. Woudenberg claimed one transport. Kuipers ran into friendly antiaircraft fire and returned to Waalhaven to land, but his fighter, along with Noomen's, was destroyed in the ensuing airborne attack. Sonderman was still in the air when the German paratroopers began their attack on the airfield, and he decided to land on a beach south of The Hague. He was spotted there by Souffrée and Woudenberg, who had also landed on the beach out of both ammunition and fuel.

In the middle of the second bombing raid on the airfield, two more G.1s, piloted by Second Lieutenant J. van der Jagt and Sergeant Major Jan Buwalda, were able to get airborne, but they did not last long in the melee overhead, now saturated with Bf 109 fighters. Van der Jagt went down in flames into the Maas River, but Buwalda was able to shoot down a He 111 and a Do 215 reconnaissance aircraft before he, too, was downed by a swarm of Messerschmitts; fortunately, he and his gunner survived. Although the pilots of 3e. Ja.V.A. put up a fierce resistance over Waalhaven, the damage to the airfield and its adjacent facilities was severe: many of the hangars were destroyed; the Koolhoven factory and its production lines were obliterated; and a number of aircraft were destroyed

The burden of air-to-air combat for the ML fell upon the Fokker D.XXI and G.1 fighters. They were opposed by the Luftwaffe's Messerschmitt Bf 109 and Bf 110 fighters. The Messerschmitts were faster and were better armed than their respective Dutch counterparts, having two 20mm cannons. However, the Fokkers were more maneuverable than the German fighters and proved to be nimble dogfighters. The Fokker D.XXI (below) and G.1 (top right) replicas shown here are housed in the Nationaal Militair Museum in Soest. The Bf 109 (right) and Bf 110 (bottom right) are preserved in the Royal Air Force Museum in Hendon and the Deutsches Technikmuseum in Berlin respectively.

on the ground.[11] Only one G.1 of the 3e Ja.V.A. escaped to Bergen to fight again. When it arrived, it found yet another scene of destruction. At 3:59 a.m., a force of He 111s and Ju 88s had struck the Bergen airfield, destroying or damaging eleven of the twelve Fokker G.1s of the 4e Jacht Vliegtuig Afdeeling (4e Ja.V.A.). The fighters had been parked wingtip to wingtip on the concrete tarmac in front of the hangars because the ground of the rest of the airfield was too soft to support the weight of the twin-engine fighters.

Gerben Sonderman scrambling into the cockpit of his Fokker G.1 (above). Before the war Sonderman worked as a test pilot for Fokker, flying the prototypes of the D.XXIII fighter (shown right in a prewar photo behind a D.XXIII with the aircraft's designer Marius Beeling). Sonderman shot down three German aircraft during the Meidagen *and later joined the* Ordedienst *(OD), the largest secret intelligence gathering and resistance group in the Netherlands. Sonderman assisted with communications between the OD and the London-based* Bureau Inlichtingen *(BI), the Dutch equivalent of the British SIS, for the remainder of the war. Sonderman returned to work as a test pilot for Fokker after the war but tragically was killed when a Fokker S.14 jet trainer he was demonstrating in the United States crashed in October 1955.* [Douglas Dildy Collection / Photo AVIODROME Luchtfotografie, Lelystad, Holland]

The Urban Assault on Rotterdam

Hauptmann Karl Lothar Schulz was lucky: the Ju 52 carrying him and his men had not been attacked by the Fokker G.1s swarming around Rotterdam. But his mission was pivotal to the success of the campaign: he and his 600-man battalion had the task of capturing the Waalhaven Aerodrome and securing it in time for the arrival of airlanding troops. Once the airfield was secure, Schulz and his men would have to make their way through Rotterdam and capture the two main bridges across the Maas River. As Schulz's plane neared the drop zone, the cabin began to shake as the wings began to absorb antiaircraft fire. As soon as the green light in the cabin came on, Schulz and his men hastily made their way out of the aircraft, hoping to elude the antiaircraft fire targeting their plane. As soon as Schulz hit the ground on the perimeter of the airfield, he found he was under fire from Dutch defensive positions on the ground; the earlier bombings of the airfield had not neutralized the defenses. As the paratroopers were regrouping after landing, Schulz spotted three trucks carrying Dutch infantry coming toward them. Schulz ordered a machine gun to fire, and the trucks stopped; their passengers jumped out and took cover. A group of Germans surged forward, captured the trucks, and drove off toward the headquarters building of the airfield. The Dutch defenders were not blind to this, and they turned one of their 20mm Oerlikon guns on the trucks speeding across the airfield. Now it was the

Personnel of 3e Jacht Vliegtuig Afdeeling based at Waalhaven in front of a Fokker G.1 (from left to right): H. de Vries, H. F. Souffrée, O. W. P. Kappelmeier, J. J. Buwalda, and J. A. Pouw. Both Souffrée and Buwalda were able to achieve kills over Waalhaven. [Photo AVIODROME Luchtfotografie, Lelystad, Holland]

Ground crew at Bergen running away from a Fokker G.1 they had just camouflaged with tree branches as a siren warns of another German air raid. Most of the G.1s based at Bergen were destroyed or damaged because they were all parked on the tarmac during the first German raid, since the field itself had been too wet to support the weight of the heavy fighters. [Photo AVIODROME Luchtfotografie, Lelystad, Holland]

Germans who were bailing out and taking cover. Peering through the tall grass on the field, Schulz saw that the fire was coming from a canon in a concrete pillbox. Crawling on their bellies, Schulz and another paratrooper approached the pillbox without being seen, and when they came within about fifty yards of it, they sprang to their feet, ran forward, and tossed a smoke and a stick grenade in through the window slit. There was an explosion, and the defenders staggered out, wounded and with their hands in the air. Shortly after that, the rest of the firing on the airfield ceased, and Schulz saw his men running toward him. The German paratroopers had captured or driven off the remaining Dutch defenders in the vicinity.

After the firing had ceased on his end of the airfield, Hauptmann Schulz gathered up his men, boarded their captured trucks, and drove across the field to the aerodrome buildings. Once they pulled up to the building and faced fire coming from within them, the Germans dashed toward the aerodrome's control tower. Schulz kicked in the door and inside he found a number of Dutch officers, who dropped their weapons and surrendered. Major J. C. M. Simon Thomas, the commandant of the air base, indignantly declared that the attack was an illegal act against a neutral country. Schulz asked whether any mines had been laid on the field, and the commandant replied that none had been. Knowing that the security of the field was necessary for the safe landing of the incoming transports carrying air-landing troops, Schulz ordered the commandant to go with him. They sped off in an Opel sedan that belonged to one of the G.1 pilots and drove around the field looking for mines. When Schulz was satisfied that there were no mines and that the field was secure, he ordered that a message be radioed to Luftwaffe command stating that the airfield was in German hands and ready for the landing of incoming transport aircraft.

The first Ju 52 made a smooth landing on the airfield; Schulz headed over to the plane in the commandant's staff car and was happy to see Oberstleutnant Dietrich von Choltitz, commander of the first battalion of Luftlande troops to touch down at Waalhaven, jump out. But before Schulz could brief von Choltitz on the current situation, an antiaircraft battery on an unoccupied portion of the airfield's perimeter began to fire at the next incoming transport. The plane was hit and crashed in flames on the field, and the next two incoming aircraft shared the same fate. The Dutch then began to drop mortar rounds and send machine-gun fire into the mass of burning wreckage and the groups of Germans on the airfield. Schulz left von Choltitz on the field and took his paratroopers in the direction of the Dutch fire. Along the way he was joined by Maj. Thomas, the airfield commandant, who suggested that he might be able to convince the Dutch troops to surrender. Schulz and his men took cover before they reached the Dutch defensive position; but the Dutch commandant went out into the open, waving his hands in the air in an attempt to get his countrymen to cease their fire. Lieutenant J. H. Hasewinkel, who was in charge of the position, refused to surrender. Tragically, Thomas was struck by a bullet in the ensuing fight. He

A 20mm Oerlikon antiaircraft cannon like the ones used at Waalhaven and other Dutch airfields in the collection of the Militair Luchtvaart Museum. One hundred twenty of these guns were delivered from Switzerland prior to the German invasion. With a rate of fire of 180 rounds per minute, they were devastatingly effective against both aircraft and ground targets.

was pulled into the Dutch position by Hasewinkel's men, but he died soon thereafter.[12] Shortly after that, Schulz and his men stormed the Dutch position and took it after a brief firefight. The full perimeter of the airfield was now in German hands, and the rest of von Choltitz's men could now be safely flown in. At about the same time General Student landed on the airfield and took personal command of all forces at and coming into Waalhaven. The time was about 6:30 a.m.[13]

Apart from the paradrop at the Waalhaven Aerodrome, the Germans made other attacks of a smaller scale within Rotterdam. To the northeast of Waalhaven, a group of fifty paratroopers under the command of Oberstleutnant Horst Kerfin dropped over Feijenoord "De Kuip" Football Stadium, a perfect drop zone from the air. Kerfin's men landed unopposed. Once they had organized themselves, they ran out into the street and stopped a tram filled with civilians on their way to work, who were apparently unaware that there was a war on. Kerfin ordered the people off and, followed by a small number of commandeered Dutch civilian automobiles, he and some of his men took off in the tram. This odd procession made its way toward the Willemsbrug, the tram bells ringing all the way and Dutch civilians staring after them, wondering what on earth they were witnessing. Kerfin was equally surprised that his group passed by a number of armed traffic policemen and soldiers who were too shocked or confused at what they saw to fire a shot.

While Kerfin's paratroopers were dropping over Feijenoord Stadium, twelve old and unarmed Heinkel He 59C-2 floatplanes came in for a landing on the Nieuwe Maas and taxied up to the northern side of the river near the Willemsbrug. Aboard the floatplanes were 120 troops and combat engineers under the command of Oberleutnant Herman-Albert Schrader. The troops climbed out of the aircraft into inflatable rubber boats and rowed to the bridge, some being helped up onto the pier by Dutchmen on their way to work, people who obviously thought that this operation was a Dutch military exercise. Schrader's men quickly ran past the shocked civilians to the Willemsbrug, and his engineers began dis-

Hauptmann Karl Lothar Schulz, commander of the Fallschirmjäger tasked with capturing the airfield at Waalhaven. Schulz would go on to be part of the German invasion of Crete in 1941 and would later be promoted to the rank of major general, serving as the last commander of the 1. Fallschirmjägerdivision during the final stages of the Italian Campaign. [Deutsches Bundesarchiv via Wikimedia Commons]

Aerial photo of the airfield at Waalhaven after Schulz's men had secured it. Notice the wrecked Ju 52 and the smoldering remains of Dutch aircraft. With the airfield taken by 6:30 a.m., Ju 52s carrying Luftlande troops could safely fly in. [Deutsches Bundesarchiv via Wikimedia Commons]

connecting the demolition charges on the bridge. Shortly thereafter, Schrader heard a great commotion of bells and horns coming from the southern end of the bridge, and his men took up defensive positions. Just then, to Schrader's relief, Obstlt. Kerfin's tram and improvised motorcade pulled up to the bridge, and the paratroopers disembarked. After this rendezvous, the Germans secured the southern ends of the Willemsbrug on Noordereiland, and the adjacent railway bridge, as well as the northern ends of both bridges.

While a small number of troops stayed with the bridges to await the arrival of reinforcements from von Choltitz's forces coming into Waalhaven, the rest surged forward from the northern bridgehead into the city. The few Dutch troops stationed around the bridge did not perform very impressively: most retreated on the Germans' arrival at the bridge. Some policemen took shots at the invaders, and three were killed by the Germans. The paratroopers captured a small number of policemen and soldiers north of the bridge and confined them at the Maashotel. The Germans then moved into the Beursstation, a suburban railway station north of the Willemsbrug; again, the few Dutch troops that were there took off without a fight. So far, in this part of the Netherlands it appeared that the invasion plan was going like clockwork: these special assault groups had secured both the main bridges over the Maas intact with no loss, and they had secured a small perimeter around the northern bridgeheads. All they had to do was wait for reinforcements to arrive from the Waalhaven Aerodrome.[14]

But this is where the rapid success of the Germans in Rotterdam came to a halt. Although completely surprised in the wee hours of the morning, the Rotterdam populace was quick to respond to the German invaders. Fortunately for the defenders, some of the best troops in the country—the marines, professional soldiers known as the "Black Devils" because of their black uniforms—were stationed in the city. From their barracks in the Oostplein, they were ordered by Gen. Winkelman to force the Germans from their positions around the bridges. The marines made their way toward the Beursstation and the bridges via nar-

Fallschirmjäger *next to a Dutch car. Oberstleutnant Kerfin's* Fallschirmjäger *unit that landed near the Feijenoord "De Kuip" Stadium commandeered a tram and a number of cars to take them speedily to the Willemsbrug. Prior to the invasion,* Fallschirmjäger *commanders were given maps of Rotterdam and The Hague with the locations of car dealerships highlighted as places where they and their men could acquire impromptu transport.* [Netherlands Institute of Military History]

The objective of the Kerfin's Fallschirmjäger *unit: the Willemsbrug traffic bridge and the adjacent railway bridge over the Maas in the center of Rotterdam. This image of Rotterdam looking toward the northeast shows Noordereiland in the middle of the Maas, with the Willemsbrug to the north of the island in the foreground and the railway bridge running parallel behind it. The capture of these bridges intact was vital if the German armored and mechanized units, coming up from the south, were to eventually make their way toward The Hague and Amsterdam.* [Netherlands Institute of Military History]

row streets so as not to be seen by the enemy. Eventually they reached Boompjes Street, which ran along the Maas on the north side of the river. Captain Willem Schuiling, the commander of the marines who were approaching the bridges, managed to position his men on both sides of the German position at the northern end of the Willemsbrug, from which they attacked. This initial attack was rebuffed by three German machine-gun nests on the bridge. Marine Sergeant T. C. Karstanje and his men probed the area but were fired on again by the German machine gunners. Karstanje did not want to send his men on a suicidal charge and decided to sneak up on the German machine-gun positions by climbing along the roofs of the buildings along the Boompjes. They finally made it to the roof of the Maashotel after an hour of climbing, maneuvering, and even coming under fire from Dutch troops positioned in the upper floors of the Witte Huis office building. Karstanje was able to see the German positions from the roof: the machine-gun nests were beneath him on Boompjes Street, and the Germans were using a tram and a truck as cover. Karstanje believed that the nests could be taken out with well-placed grenades, and he sent two marines to the roof's edge to attempt it. Marine Boers's grenade took out one of the nests, but Marine Verhoeven's missed—though it still caused damage to the German position below.

From their location atop the Maashotel, the Dutch were not in a good position to fire at the machine-gun nests, and they had very few grenades to spare. Karstenje then sent five marines into the hotel to try to find a better firing position from the windows. Inside the hotel, the marines were surprised to find a number of policemen and civilians who had been taken prisoner and locked up by the Germans. Making their way to the second floor, the marines found a number of large windows facing the street that offered an excellent position from which to fire on the German machine guns. The marines divided into two units, one on the right side of the floor and the other on the left. The recently freed policemen and civilians threw rocks through the center window, hoping to draw the attention and fire of the machine guns. The ruse worked: the marines opened fire and caught the machine

Heinkel He 59C-2 floatplane taxiing on the Maas. Twelve He 59s of the Staffel Schwilden, an air unit organized for this special mission, landed 120 assault troops and combat engineers in rubber boats on the northern side of the Maas. Their mission was to disable the demolition charges on the Willemsbrug. Amazingly these German troops met little resistance, in part because most Dutch people were completely taken aback by the brazen act of German aircraft calmly landing on the Maas River just as people were beginning to go to work that morning. [Netherlands Institute of Military History]

A tram, similar to the one used by Kerfin's men to travel to the Willemsbrug, passing the Marinierkazerne (marine barracks) on the Oostplein. The marines stationed at these barracks were sent out to attack Kerfin's Fallschirmjäger *and the combat engineers who had secured the northern end of the Maas bridges.* [Netherlands Institute of Military History]

gunners by surprise. After a brief firefight, the remaining Germans abandoned their position and ran.

But the marines had little time to celebrate; shortly thereafter, from their position near the Maashotel, the Germans began bombarding the hotel with mortar fire. Initially, the thick walls of the building withstood the mortar fire; but then the Germans began dropping rounds on the roof, and those began to penetrate the building. The marines made their way to the back of the hotel, but there they came under fire from a German plane making a strafing run. Not accustomed to such a sudden attack from all sides, the marines scattered in all directions. They made their way into the nearby streets, reorganized themselves, and then made their way back to the Maashotel to remove their wounded comrades.

Karstanje's storming of the Maashotel was a pivotal turning point in the battle on the north side of the Maas River. Throughout the rest of the day, the Germans on the northern end of the Willemsbrug were pushed out of their forward positions around the Beursstation. By the end of the day, the invaders had been confined to the Nationale Levensverzekering-Bank building just across the Boompjes from the Willemsbrug. The Germans held the bridges, but they could go no further.[15]

While the battle for the northern end of the Willemsbrug was raging, the Koninklijke Marine, with a long and proud fighting tradition, refused to sit silently by. The old gunboat *Z 5*, with two 75mm guns and four light machine guns, was patrolling off the coast when it received orders to proceed to the Nieuwe Waterweg in Rotterdam and to come to the aid of the Dutch ground troops in the early hours of May 10. The *Z 5* was joined by the new motor torpedo boat *TM 51*, which had been patrolling along the Nieuwe Maas. The commanders of the two ships decided to team up and attack the German positions around the Willemsbrug. At about 8:00 a.m., the guns of the *Z 5* and *TM 51* opened fire on German positions on Noordereiland. The heavy guns aboard the *Z 5* and the two 20mm canons on the *TM 51* were an unwelcome surprise to the Germans and wreaked havoc among their positions. The Germans opened fire with their machine guns and eventually brought up several light antitank guns. The *TM 51*, filled with machine-gun holes and with its engines overheating from the sharp maneuvering in the river, turned back, and the *Z 5* eventually withdrew as well, but only after its 75mm ammunition had been totally spent.

Buoyed by the successful attack made by the *Z 5* and *TM 51*, the Koninklijke Marine decided to send the Admiralen-class destroyer *Van Galen*, armed with four 120mm guns, two 75mm, and four 40mm antiaircraft guns, up the Nieuwe Maas to make a similar attack. The *Van Galen* entered the Nieuwe Waterweg during the afternoon, but as it approached Rotterdam, it was pounced on by thirty Stukas. Amazingly, the dive bombers achieved no direct

***A contingent of the Dutch marines, who were known as the "Black Devils" because of their black uniforms and their elite combat skills. They would tenaciously engage the Germans on the northern side of the Maas throughout the rest of the* Meidagen.** [Netherlands Institute of Military History]

hits on the ship, but the many near misses caused enough damage for the captain to decide to abort the mission. With steam pipes ruptured, rivets popping, and the ship taking on a dangerous roll, the captain ordered the damaged destroyer to pull up along the quay at the Merwehaven, where she later sank at her moorings. Though the brief naval campaign on the Nieuwe Maas had been inconclusive, the tenacity of the Dutch in repelling the German invaders from the Maas bridges by any means necessary came as a rude shock to the Germans.[16]

Compared to the aircraft of the Militair Luchtvaart, those of the Marine Luchtvaart Dienst (MLD) did not have much of an opportunity to respond to the German onslaught: since there was no major naval activity on the part of the Germans against the Netherlands, there was little that the MLD's floatplanes could do. In fact, the majority of the MLD's planes were lost on the ground or at their moorings on May 10. Although the Fokker D.XXIs of 1. Ja.V.A. put up an outstanding fight over De Kooy early on the morning of May 10, once they had landed there was little protection for the airfield. The ground crews at De Kooy moved the base's eighteen obsolete Fokker S.III trainers out onto the field when they learned of the invasion, intent on using them as decoys while they tried their best to disperse the rest of the base's fifteen Koolhoven F.K.51 and the fifteen Fokker S.IX trainers. Unfortunately, it mattered little: in three subsequent raids following the dogfight over De Kooy, strafing Bf 109s managed to

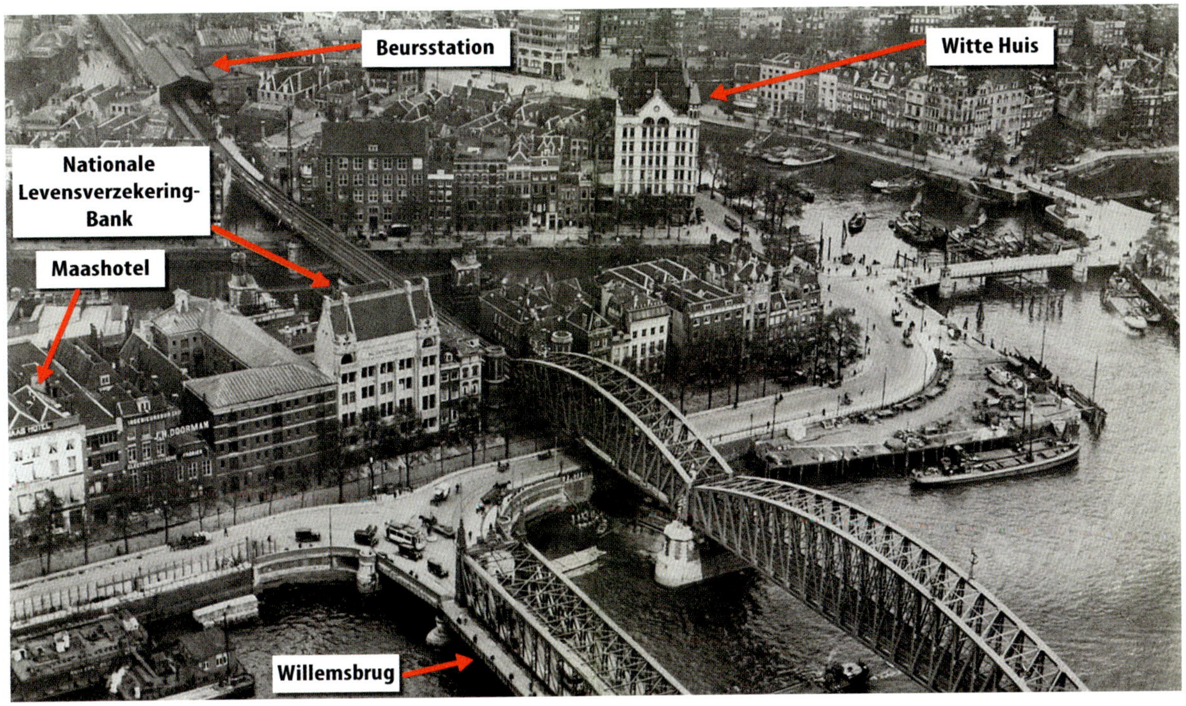

The area along the Boompjes at the northern end of the Maas bridges, which saw the heaviest fighting between the marines and the Germans. On the extreme left is the Maashotel, which Sgt. Karstanje and his marines stormed from the roof. Five buildings to the right of the hotel is the Nationale Levensverzekering-Bank building (the white building with the steeply sloped roof) in which the Germans took refuge after the marines had pushed them out of their initial defensive positions, including the Beuersstation (at top left along the railway).

Dutch torpedo boat TM 51, *which, along with gunboat* Z 5, *attacked German positions on Noordereiland until they were driven off by German light anti-tank guns.* [Netherlands Institute of Military History]

destroy or damage all forty-eight of the base's training aircraft. Many of the MLD's floatplanes based near De Mok did not fare well either. Ten Fokker C.VIIws were destroyed or damaged by strafing attacks on the 10th, and most of the base's remaining floatplanes would be destroyed in further attacks over the next two days.

However, the MLD did accomplish one very important mission on May 10. Beginning at 8:00 a.m., four Fokker T.VIIIws and a Fokker C.VIIIw were ordered to take off and fly to Scheveningen. Their mission was for one of the floatplanes to pick up Foreign Minister van Kleffens and his wife and fly them to England in an effort to encourage British support for the defense of the Netherlands. With so many German aircraft roving Dutch airspace, the MLD sent five floatplanes, hoping that at least one would arrive at Scheveningen to pick up van Kleffens. When the foreign minister reached Scheveningen, only two T.VIIIws, R-1 and R-3, had arrived. Both had been attacked by German fighters en route, but van Kleffens was hurried aboard the R-3, whose pilot had determined that he could make it to England despite the damage to his aircraft. Just as the R-3 was taking off, a German fighter dove from overhead and made a strafing run on the Dutch plane. Fortunately, R-3 was not hit, and as the German pilot flew past, he turned his sights on R-1, which was still sitting on water. Van Kleffens escaped, and the R-3 landed in Brighton Harbor just after 11:00 a.m. R-1 managed to escape as well, but the other two T.VIIIws and the C.VIIIw were not so lucky: all were destroyed by patrolling German fighters.

The Admiralen-class destroyer Van Galen *also sailed into the Maas to attack German positions in the city. After sustaining damage from an attack by thirty Stuka divebombers, the* Van Galen *was pulled along a quay, where she later sank. This image shows the* Van Galen *being raised later in the war.* [Netherlands Institute of Military History]

The rest of the MLD's operational Fokker T.VIIIws, after flying several reconnaissance missions, survived the day and landed at Kudelstaart, where they were moored under the branches of large overhanging trees. They were never spotted by the Germans under this natural camouflage. Nevertheless, with no fighter cover of its own, and in the face of an almost constant German aerial presence, there was little that the pilots and aircraft of the MLD could do in this campaign.[17]

The Wrath of Orange

Despite the ferocity of the German attack, the Dutch did not sit idly by and concede the initiative without a fight. While the bases of the Militair Luchtvaart had been pounded hard and the situation in the air may have been chaotic at best, the Dutch did not wait long to mount a limited aerial counteroffensive against the enemy. After scrambling and achieving two air-to-air kills, T.V #855, commanded by Lieutenant Bernardus Swagerman, landed back at Schiphol in the early daylight hours. After refueling, Swagerman and his crew took off at 6:45 and headed for Ockenburg. While the fighting over the airfield was still underway at about 7:00, the Germans looked up and spotted a lone T.V as it approached and dropped six bombs on the Ju 52s parked on the grass. Swagerman's attack destroyed one Ju 52 and damaged several others. While returning to base, however, Swagerman's T.V was pounced on by a group of patrolling German fighters and shot down over the sea. Three of the crew bailed out, but Swagerman was the only one to survive by swimming ashore. But this was not the end of the war for Lt. Swagerman.

Shortly thereafter, German Major General Hans Graf von Sponeck, commander of all the Luftlande troops coming into the Netherlands, finally arrived on the scene. The general was supposed to have landed at Ypenburg, but the pilot of his transport found that airfield a mess

As part of the general modernization of the Dutch armed forces in the Netherlands in the late 1930s, the navy ordered a new twin-engine floatplane from Fokker in September 1938 for the MLD, which was in desperate need of modern aircraft in the home country. The T.VIII was intended to serve as a reconnaissance platform as well as a torpedo bomber; it was the last series-production military aircraft built by Fokker before the beginning of World War II. Designed by Marius Beeling, the first production T.VIIIs (T.VIIIw/G) were of composite construction, though Fokker intended to later produce an all-metal series (T.VIIIw/M) of the aircraft. The MLD initially ordered five T.VIIIw/Gs, but then followed up with an order for an additional nineteen T.VIIIw/Gs and twelve T.VIIIw/Ms. Belgium, Denmark, Finland, Norway, Portugal, and Sweden were interested in the aircraft, but only eleven T.VIIIw/Gs were completed for the MLD before the Netherlands was drawn into World War II. On the morning of May 10, T.VIIIs R-1, R-2, R-3, and R-4 were sent to Scheveningen to pick up Dutch politicians and fly them to England. R-3 managed to fly Foreign Minister van Kleffens and his family to Britain. R-2 (shown here at its base on the Braassemermeer) was shot down by German fighters and burned by its crew. [Photo AVIODROME Luchtfotografie, Lelystad, Holland]

Fokker T.VIIIw
length: 42 ft 8 in (13 m)
wingspan: 59 ft 1 in (18 m)
power plant: two 451 hp Wright R-975-E3 Whirlwind radial engines
maximum speed: 177 mph (285 km/h)
range: 1,709 miles (2,750 km)
ceiling: 22,310 ft (6,800 m)
armament: two 7.92mm machine guns
payload: 1,323 lbs (600 kg) of bombs, or one aerial torpedo
crew: 3

Undoubtedly one of the most courageous airmen to fly during the Meidagen, *Lieutenant Bernardus Swagerman, as commander/observer (the commander in a T.V was not the pilot but rather the observer who also acted as the bombardier), led his Fokker T.V #855 in the air during the first raid on Schiphol, and he and his crew managed to shoot down at least two enemy aircraft, ironically using their T.V in the* luchtkruiser *role for which it had been intended. After a brief return to Schiphol to rearm and refuel, T.V #855 made a bombing raid against Ju 52s parked on the Ockenburg airfield, destroying four of them. On the return flight to Schiphol, #855 was pounced on by German fighters, and Swagerman was the crew's only survivor when they bailed out and landed in the sea. Despite this ordeal, Swagerman reported for duty back at Schiphol later that evening! He would fly two more missions in T.Vs during the* Meidagen. [Militair Luchtvaart Museum, Soesterberg]

of smoldering German aircraft. When Gen. von Sponeck's plane arrived over Ockenburg, it took fire from the ground; the pilot made a rough landing in a field surrounded by woods, since the Ockenburg airfield was also clogged with aircraft. While the general was trying to grasp how the ground campaign was shaping up, a group of three other T.Vs that had landed at Ruigenhoek took off to attack Ockenburg, following Lt. Swagerman's lead. This group arrived over the Ockenburg airfield just before 8:00 a.m. and dropped their bombs from medium altitude. Three more Ju 52s were destroyed in that run, and more were damaged. Gen. von Sponeck and the German paratroopers were beginning to realize that the striking power of the Militair Luchtvaart had not yet been eliminated. Another ominous sign for them regarding the course of the battle was that only thirteen of the forty-seven Ju 52s that had landed in the vicinity of Ockenburg were able to take off for Germany. The rest were damaged in landing or destroyed by Dutch bomber attacks or were damaged by the Dutch artillery fire that was beginning to come down on the field. It appeared that Gen. von Sponeck's scheduled "date" with the royal family was going to be delayed.[18]

In another area of the combat zone, the ML had a C.V reconnaissance plane of the 3e Verkennings Vlieg Groep, which was based at the secret airfield at Ruigenhoek, reconnoitering the German air landings at Valkenburg already by 6:30 that morning. The Dutch high command promptly ordered bombing raids against the airfield at Valkenburg as well as the airfield at Waalhaven. Around 11:00, the base commandant at the Bergen airfield stepped forward to address the crews of the Strategische Verkennings Vliegtuig Afdeeling (Strat.Ver.V.A.). He told them that they were going to attack the German-held airfields at Valkenburg and Waalhaven. The pilots were ready for a fight, wanting to avenge the destruction of the G.1s of the 4e Ja.V.A. earlier that morning. The Fokker C.X bombers of the Strat. Ver.V.A. had escaped the devastating early-morning German raids because they were camouflaged and parked away from the airfield. The base commander had the G.1s prepped for action, giving the older C.Xs secondary consideration. Now, in a twist of fate, the biplane bombers were called upon to attack a numerically and technologically superior enemy. The role to be played by pilots and aircraft of the Strat.Ver.V.A. would best exemplify the ML's dogged determination to resist the onslaught of the Luftwaffe.[19]

As the C.X crews disembarked from the bus that drove them to their awaiting aircraft, the captain of the squadron said nothing but shook each man's hand, as Second Lieutenant S. J. Postma recalled: "In that firm handshake were expressed these thoughts: have courage, men, do your duty, farewell." It was a reverent departure for air crews courageously going into such a fierce battle—and with such obsolescent aircraft.

A group of three C.Xs took off to strike Valkenburg, which had already been attacked by a group of five C.V reconnaissance bombers from Ruigenhoek at about 8:30 a.m. The three C.Xs made a successful attack, bombed the airfield, strafed several Ju 52s on the beaches near Katwijk, and returned to base. Another group of five C.Xs, including Postma's, took off twenty minutes after the first group; their target was Waalhaven. The C.Xs flew over the Dutch coastline at an altitude of about 5,000 feet and then turned west over the Nieuwe Maas, and followed it toward Rotterdam. As the planes approached Waalhaven and prepared to attack, Postma noted the following:

> The fist of the observer of the command aircraft went into the air; he gestured as if he wanted to say: men, we are here, now the turn is ours; soon he dropped his fist, the signal at which the bombs had to be released. 2,000 kilograms of explosives will speed to the ground, destroying everything at the first impact.... The bombs accurately fell into the middle of a grey mass of aircraft, finding their mark.[20]

As the smoke rose from Waalhaven airfield, the C.Xs circled overhead, surveying the damage they had caused. But Postma and the other Dutch pilots could not really determine the amount of damage they had inflicted, and they could not dive down for a closer look, because they had to return immediately to Bergen in case they were needed for another mission. While the C.Xs banked over Rotterdam and dove to a lower altitude in the direction of Bergen, Postma spotted something:

> Then I suddenly saw a squadron of Messerschmitts high above us. Some broke away from the group and dove

BELOW LEFT *Major General Hans Graf von Sponeck, the unlucky commander of the 22. Luftlande-Division. The initial German plan called for Sponeck's troops to land on the captured Dutch airfields and proceed immediately to The Hague to capture Queen Wilhelmina, the Dutch high command, and the Dutch government. Since Waalhaven was the only airfield held by the Germans at the end of May 10, Sponeck's troops were scattered across the countryside wherever their transports were able to land. Sponeck himself was separated from most of his division throughout the* Meidagen, *and the 22. Luftlande-Division ended up playing little part in the Battle of Holland. Here Sponeck digs his own foxhole in the woods outside of The Hague.*

BELOW RIGHT *Fokker C.Xs of the Strategische Verkennings Vliegtuig Afdeeling (Strat.Ver.V.A.) at Bergen, armed with bombs. The C.Xs were camouflaged away from the airstrip when the Luftwaffe attack destroyed and damaged most of Bergen's G.1 fighters.* [Douglas Dildy Collection]

down as swift as an arrow, we had been discovered! I put my aircraft more and more on its nose, gave it more and more gas, and we also dove at a furious speed; beginning a dogfight with our trainers against six fighters was, however, too optimistic. Too late! We were already caught up with. Suddenly a fiery stream shot from the nose of a Messerschmitt, which struck the aircraft of the escadrille-commandant; immediately a gray-black trail streamed from the tail of his aircraft, he was hit, lost. As I pushed against my rudder controls, debris flew to the left of me. Immediately my pursuer shot past me, accelerated, and disappeared. . . . An enormous shower of petrol and oil; my tanks were hit. . . . I hauled my stick back, pieces of plywood flew off the wing, the nose of my aircraft righted itself up. The old Fokker held together well. . . . finally the wheels touched the ground, slowed down, the aircraft came to a stop. . . . In less than a second my observer and I stood beside the aircraft. . . . My comrade did an Indian dance around me, shook my hand: "Charley, we're alive, beautifully done!"[21]

Looking around the area where they landed, Postma and his observer saw several abandoned Ju 52s and parachutes blowing on the ground. They then examined their aircraft. A temporary repair was out of the question; the damage was simply too extensive.

Postma and his observer began making their way across a field toward the nearest houses they could see—until they came across a group of Dutch soldiers lying flat along a dike. One of the soldiers made a motion for them to lie down, because in a nearby Ju 52 there were still paratroopers armed with machine guns. Suddenly, a DKW motorcycle approached, driven by a paratrooper with another in the sidecar. As the motorcycle came within range, the Dutch soldiers rose up and leveled a volley into the oncoming Germans. After surviving this engagement, Postma and his comrade continued their journey on foot until they came upon a fast Oldsmobile, which they promptly commandeered. Arriving in a nearby town, Postma went to the town hall and received necessary papers of transit as well as information on the military activities in the local surroundings from an army officer. He was also given important route advice from an armored car officer, who told Postma to head to the west to avoid German paratroopers around The Hague and also the battle raging at Ypenburg. Finally, at dusk, the two fliers drove into the air base at Bergen and to their surprise discovered that all of the pilots and observers of Strat.Ver.V.A. had returned alive! After swapping tales of their individual exploits, all were in high spirits, and Postma remarked: "Had the cook not come, I would have completely forgotten about my stomach that day!"

ABOVE ***Fokker C.Xs of Strat. Ver.V.A. in flight*** [Photo AVIODROME Luchtfotografie, Lelystad, Holland]

LEFT ***Second Lieutenant S. J. Postma's Fokker C.X #708 after its forced landing.*** [Photo AVIODROME Luchtfotografie, Lelystad, Holland]

OPPOSITE PAGE ***Map of German air attacks and paradrops***

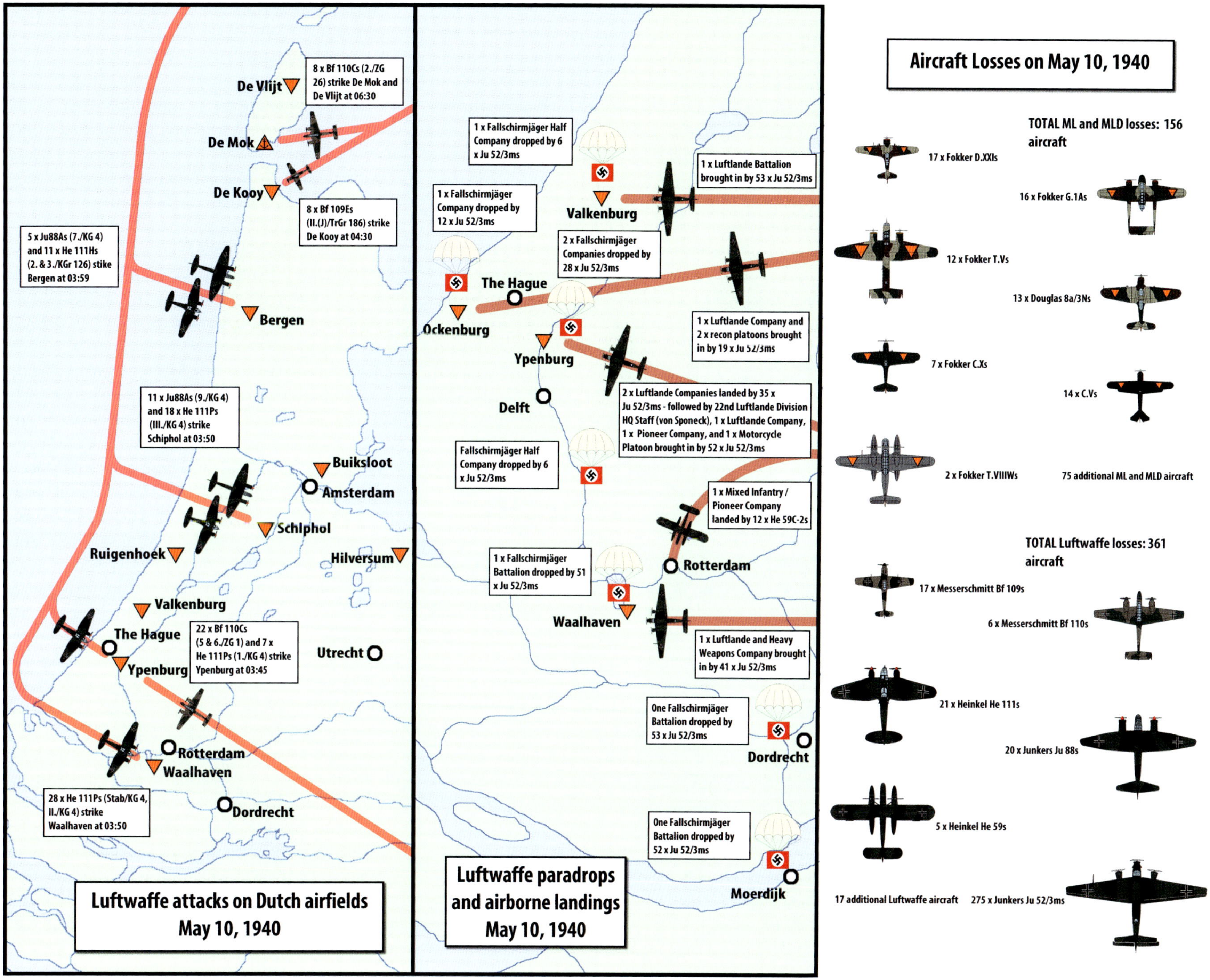

De Vlijt
8 x Bf 110Cs (2./ZG 26) strike De Mok and De Vlijt at 06:30
De Mok
De Kooy
8 x Bf 109Es (II.(J)/TrGr 186) strike De Kooy at 04:30
5 x Ju88As (7./KG 4) and 11 x He 111Hs (2. & 3./KGr 126) strike Bergen at 03:59
Bergen
11 x Ju88As (9./KG 4) and 18 x He 111Ps (III./KG 4) strike Schiphol at 03:50
Buiksloot
Amsterdam
Schiphol
Ruigenhoek
Hilversum
Valkenburg
The Hague
22 x Bf 110Cs (5 & 6./ZG 1) and 7 x He 111Ps (1./KG 4) strike Ypenburg at 03:45
Ypenburg
Utrecht
Rotterdam
Waalhaven
28 x He 111Ps (Stab/KG 4, II./KG 4) strike Waalhaven at 03:50
Dordrecht
Luftwaffe attacks on Dutch airfields May 10, 1940
1 x Fallschirmjäger Half Company dropped by 6 x Ju 52/3ms
1 x Luftlande Battalion brought in by 53 x Ju 52/3ms
1 x Fallschirmjäger Company dropped by 12 x Ju 52/3ms
Valkenburg
2 x Fallschirmjäger Companies dropped by 28 x Ju 52/3ms
The Hague
Ockenburg
1 x Luftlande Company and 2 x recon platoons brought in by 19 x Ju 52/3ms
Ypenburg
Delft
2 x Luftlande Companies landed by 35 x Ju 52/3ms - followed by 22nd Luftlande Division HQ Staff (von Sponeck), 1 x Luftlande Company, 1 x Pioneer Company, and 1 x Motorcycle Platoon brought in by 52 x Ju 52/3ms
Fallschirmjäger Half Company dropped by 6 x Ju 52/3ms
1 x Mixed Infantry / Pioneer Company landed by 12 x He 59C-2s
1 x Fallschirmjäger Battalion dropped by 51 x Ju 52/3ms
Rotterdam
Waalhaven
1 x Luftlande and Heavy Weapons Company brought in by 41 x Ju 52/3ms
One Fallschirmjäger Battalion dropped by 53 x Ju 52/3ms
Dordrecht
One Fallschirmjäger Battalion dropped by 52 x Ju 52/3ms
Moerdijk
Luftwaffe paradrops and airborne landings May 10, 1940
Aircraft Losses on May 10, 1940
TOTAL ML and MLD losses: 156 aircraft
17 x Fokker D.XXIs
16 x Fokker G.1As
12 x Fokker T.Vs
13 x Douglas 8a/3Ns
7 x Fokker C.Xs
14 x C.Vs
2 x Fokker T.VIIIWs
75 additional ML and MLD aircraft
TOTAL Luftwaffe losses: 361 aircraft
17 x Messerschmitt Bf 109s
6 x Messerschmitt Bf 110s
21 x Heinkel He 111s
20 x Junkers Ju 88s
5 x Heinkel He 59s
17 additional Luftwaffe aircraft
275 x Junkers Ju 52/3ms

The first day of the German invasion had been long and costly, but it was meritorious for Dutch pilots. And, though a significant portion of the Militair Luchtvaart had been destroyed, the remaining pilots and aircraft were ready to continue the battle. Throughout the late morning and afternoon, the Germans continued their attacks on Dutch airfields and managed to destroy more aircraft. Some Dutch aircraft that had landed after combat on May 10 were unable to take off again for various reasons and took no further part in the campaign. A total of one hundred forty (seventy-six combat aircraft) Dutch ML and MLD aircraft were written off on the first day of the German invasion, twenty-two of them shot down in air-to-air combat. Other Dutch aircraft were damaged, but the ML and MLD ground crews began a furious effort to repair and to get the damaged planes rearmed, refueled, and airborne around the clock for the next five straight days. ML ground crews also managed to arm and make ready fourteen additional aircraft for combat duties, including one Fokker G.1A, three Fokker G.1Bs, six Fokker D.XVIIs, and four Fokker C.Vs.

From the perspective of the German high command's ambitious plans, the strategic results of the first day of the Battle of Holland were little short of a failure. Granted, they had destroyed much of the Dutch air force, and the bridges at Moerdijk and Dordrecht were in German hands; but the outlook for the success of the rest of the campaign was ominous. The attack on The Hague had failed completely. Units of the Dutch army in the Vesting Holland had initially been surprised and thrown into disarray (as the Germans had anticipated), but they reorganized themselves, quickly got a grasp of the situation, and began a series of well-executed counterattacks against the Germans. The airfield at Ypenburg, from which the Dutch defenders had never been completely forced, was back in Dutch hands before 3:00 p.m. on May 10. Dutch troops recaptured the airfield at Ockenburg early in the afternoon as well, and the airfield at Valkenburg was retaken by 5:30 p.m. At each location the Dutch captured large amounts of German weapons and ammunition, much of which was still aboard the wrecked transport planes. The Germans who were not killed or captured on the airfields retreated into the surrounding villages and countryside.

Of the 9,300 troops scheduled to land at the airfields around The Hague on May 10, only 3,800 made it to the ground alive, and of that total, over 1,500 were taken prisoner by the Dutch. General Graf von Sponeck's remaining scattered troops could only be resupplied by airborne drops and were ordered by the Luftwaffe command to move south toward the northern end of Rotterdam. The remnants of the 22nd Air-Landing Division played no further major role in the Battle of Holland. The only airfield that the Germans still held at the end of the day was Waalhaven. The situation at Rotterdam was at a stalemate. The Germans had secured the airfield and the southern end of city, as well as the bridges over the Maas, but the Dutch still securely held the northern side of the Maas and were receiving reinforcements. Student could only receive reinforcements from air landings at Waalhaven, which he did; a total of 3,700 troops were landed there on the 10th. The problem facing Student was that these troops could not be solely committed to the battle in Rotterdam; he also had to use them to reinforce the German positions between Rotterdam and Moerdijk. Student could count on no help from Gen. von Sponeck, and his supply base at Waalhaven was not completely safe. On the night of May 10, the British Royal Air Force sent thirty-six Wellington bombers to attack the airfield, adding to the damage caused by the air attacks earlier that day. The airfield was also subjected to sporadic artillery bombardment throughout the campaign.

Luftwaffe losses over the Netherlands were very heavy on that first day of the invasion: seven fighters, twenty bombers, almost two hundred transports, and five other combat aircraft. A total of 231 Luftwaffe aircraft were written off, fourteen of which were shot down in air-to-air combat. Dutch anti-aircraft batteries were proving to be extraordinarily lethal, and the morale and tenacity of the Dutch ground forces was much stronger than the Germans had anticipated.[22]

The Second Day (May 11, 1940)

While May 10 had ended on a positive note for the Dutch ground forces within the Vesting Holland, the 11th heralded a major setback that compromised any foreseeable chance for a protracted defense of their country. In the early hours of May 10, as the invasion commenced, the Germans were thwarted in all their attempts to capture a bridge crossing the Maas River intact except at one vital location due to a daring ruse. At Gennep, three Brandenburger commandos, dressed as Dutch MPs, escorted a group of German "prisoners" toward the garrison that defended the railway bridge over the river. The "prisoners" suddenly hauled out machine pistols from under their overcoats and took the bridge intact. German trains began rolling over the bridge shortly thereafter, and German troops disembarked with equipment for an assault on the Peel-Raam Line. The Dutch stubbornly held the line for most of the day, despite heavy air and artillery bombardments and the fact that they were increasingly becoming outnumbered. Finally, in the late hours of the 10th, the Germans breached the line, and the Dutch decided to withdraw toward the Vesting Holland early on the 11th.

In addition to the loss of the Peel-Raam Line, the Dutch were to lose any possibility of Allied ground support on May 11. On May 10 French General Henri Giraud sent the motorized units of the 1st Division Légère Méchanique of the French Seventh Army into Belgium on their way to the Netherlands in order to move into position between the Dutch and Belgian defensive positions,

Fallschirmjäger descend near the bridges at Moerdijk (above)—then rush to secure those bridges (left). The successful capture of the bridges across the wide Hollands Diep gave Wehrmacht units approaching from the south entry into the Vesting Holland through the back door. This, along with the capture of the airfield at Waalhaven and the bridges over the Maas in Rotterdam, were the critical successes achieved by the Germans on the first day of the invasion. Had these objectives not been achieved, German momentum in the Netherlands would have come to a complete halt. [Photo AVIODROME Luchtfotografie, Lelystad, Holland / Militair Luchtvaart Museum, Soesterberg]

The Dutch received little aerial assistance from the British and the French on the first day of the German invasion, but during the night of May 10-11, the RAF sent thirty-six Wellington bombers on a raid against Waalhaven (right), damaging German aircraft on the airfield and disrupting operations. An RAF reconnaissance photo (below) taken after the raid shows that the airport, hangars, and the adjacent Koolhoven factory were obliterated by the morning of May 11. One interesting feature of this photo is the relatively intact Fokker G.1 sitting on the tarmac.

according to Gen. Gamelin's prewar strategy. At first, the anticipated arrival of this force bolstered the morale of the Dutch troops; but what followed turned into a melodramatic failure due to French truculence regarding cooperative action. The Dutch commanders, eager to counterattack, were disgusted to learn that the French refused to take the offensive even while, at the same time, being unwilling to cooperate with the improvised defensive plans prepared by the Dutch. The only units of the French Seventh Army to arrive on May 10 were a handful of Panhard 178 armored cars, hardly the kind of weapon needed to stop an oncoming panzer division. As May 11 wore on, the Dutch wondered where Giraud's promised tanks were. As it turned out, the French tank commander decided to hold back his forces in case the Belgians could not hold the German advance against them.

When the Dutch forces around Moerdijk finally convinced some forward elements of the French Seventh Army to assist them in their attempt to recapture the bridges there, many wasted hours passed while the French commander was dawdling over how to attack. As the combined Dutch-French attack on the Moerdijk bridges was about to begin, an entire group of Stukas flew over and attacked. The French armored cars were hit hard and retreated; the Dutch stayed in their positions, waiting for the order to attack. As the 9th Panzer Division approached Moerdijk on May 11 and 12, Giraud was ordered to withdraw the French Seventh Army from the Netherlands, having hardly put up a fight. The failure of the French to counterattack in concert with the Dutch and the French abandonment of their positions left a wide avenue open for the Germans to secure Moerdijk and push on toward Rotterdam, an opening that had a decisive consequence on the ground and air war in the Netherlands.[23]

Early on the morning of May 11, the fighting resumed in Rotterdam. The German paratroopers under Obstlt. Kerfin still held the northern end of the Maas bridges, but they were effectively surrounded on all sides by the Dutch. No one ventured onto the Maas bridges themselves because both sides could bring heavy fire to bear on anyone or anything that attempted to cross them. With the Germans securely holding the southern bank of the Maas, Colonel Pieter Wilhelmus Scharroo, commander of the Dutch ground forces in Rotterdam, decided to attempt to blow up the bridges, thus cutting off Kerfin's men on the northern bank and preventing a possible German mechanized or armored advance from the south. But the Dutch could not bring any artillery to bear on the bridges from the northern side without being exposed to heavy German fire from Noordereiland.

Scharroo then phoned the ML for an airstrike against

the bridges. Two Fokker T.Vs were deployed for that mission. At 10:30 a.m. on May 11, they arrived over the city and made an unopposed attack. Six of the eight 50-kg bombs dropped by the lead plane hit the southern entrance of the Willemsbrug and several adjacent houses. The bridge was not damaged, but fires broke out in the surrounding houses on Noordereiland, forcing the Germans from them. Both bombers returned without damage, and the ML decided to make another try at destroying the bridges.

The T.Vs returned from Schiphol at 1:30 p.m., accompanied by an escort of three D.XXI fighters. This time the bombers flew at a low altitude of 200 feet to avoid detection, climbing on the approach to the targets, and making diving attacks on the bridges. The attack was again executed without any aerial opposition, but this time all sixteen bombs missed their targets, falling into the river. On the return route, the Dutch attack force was intercepted by eight Bf 110s. The D.XXI escorts peeled off to attack the Germans while the bombers attempted to flee. Lt. Focquin de Grave engaged four of the Messerschmitts and claimed one shot down before he made a crash landing in his damaged fighter. While Focquin de Grave was

ABOVE *On May 11, the Dutch prepared to attack the* Fallschirmjäger *positions at Moerdijk and retake the bridges over the Hollands Diep. The day before, the French had promised to send armored units from the Seventh Army under the command of General Henri Giraud to assist with this operation and to help the Dutch defend against German panzers that had breached the Peel-Raam Line; but no French tanks arrived. Only a small force of French Panhard armored cars came up from the south, and their commander was reluctant to support the Dutch counterattack at Moerdijk. When the Dutch finally convinced the French armored cars to support their attack, it was too late. A group of Stukas arrived overhead and began their attack dives.*

LEFT *Here the* Fallschirmjäger *defenders at Moerdijk looked up with a sigh of relief as the Stukas went about their deadly work.* [Stukas: Deutsches Bundesarchiv via Wikimedia Commons]

Wrecks of French Panhard 178 armored cars, destroyed by the Stuka attack at Moerdijk on May 11. [Douglas Dildy Collection]

in the middle of a dogfight, T.V #856, commanded by Lt. Swagerman, managed to escape into the clouds. T.V #850 was not so lucky: it was shot down by the other four Messerschmitts, but not before its tail gunner had shot down one of the attackers. Another D.XXI, #229, was shot down by this group of Bf 110s, while the other escaped back to Buikksluit. The rest of the aerial activity of the ML on May 11 consisted of strafing attacks mounted by two Fokker G.1s against Ju 52s landing on the highway between Delft and Rotterdam.[24]

May 11 happened to be a bad day for the Holland-Amerika Line as well. Several large ocean liners were moored along the Wilhelminakade on the south side of the Maas, including the *Statendam*, one of the largest ships of the Holland-Amerika Line. The Germans had boarded the ship on May 10 and had taken the crew prisoner, forcing them below decks. On the aft deck, the Germans had positioned a machine-gun post on the 11th and had opened fire on the Dutch in the Boompjes across the river. On the other side of the Maas, the Dutch quickly turned their artillery on this new threat and began firing shells into the stately ship. Fortunately, the crew managed to escape from below decks, but the shelling started the ship on fire. By the time the Germans abandoned the *Statendam*, she was an inferno that burned for several days—because she had 4,000 barrels of oil in her fuel stores. A fireboat pulled alongside and attempted to put out the fire, but it was forced to withdraw after its captain was shot in the crossfire. The large vessels *Bosdijk, Dinteldijk*, and *Veendam* shared the same fate as the *Statendam*. Nothing was safe along the riverfront since neither side could dislodge the other, and, at the same time, neither would give up. The dark, thick smoke billowing out from the fuel stores of these vessels clouded the riverfront of the city for the next several days, and it would hamper any aerial operations overhead. This would eventually prove lethal to city on May 14.[25]

The Third Day (May 12, 1940)

On May 12, the ML decided to use as many of its available aircraft to support Dutch defenders along the Grebbeberg as possible, even pulling a number of its obsolete C.V observation biplanes and D.XVII biplane fighters out of their virtual retirement. Every possible aircraft was needed. Three Fokker G.1s, four C.Vs, one C.X, and three D.XVIIs strafed and bombed the German lines at the Grebbeberg for about a half hour before dusk, which certainly let the Germans know that the ML was still in the fight, though the Dutch did lose one C.V to enemy flak and another C.V and two D.XVIIs to landing accidents

The only surviving remnant of the Fokker fighters that defended Dutch skies during the Meidagen *is the engine and cockpit of Fokker D.XXI #229. This aircraft, piloted by Sergeant Jacobus Koos Roos, was shot down by a Bf 110 while escorting two Fokker T.Vs in an attack on the Maas bridges in Rotterdam in the afternoon of May 11. Koos Roos survived by bailing out. The wreck of his aircraft was not discovered until 1993, and it has since been put on display at the Stichting Crash 40-45 Museum in Aalsmeerderbrug, near Schiphol.*

On May 10, German troops boarded and set up machine-gun positions aboard the **Statendam,** ***which was moored along the Wilhelminakade on the southern side of the Maas River. From across the river, Dutch artillery targeted these gun positions on the 11th, but the shelling started fires aboard the liner. The stately ship burned for several days and was a complete loss.*** [Netherlands Institute of Military History]

at Schiphol. Irritated by these continuous pinprick raids by the ML, the Luftwaffe resumed its attacks on Dutch airfields; its pilots shot at any aircraft with orange triangles they could find. At the same time, the Luftwaffe conducted a series of raids on strategic Dutch positions in northern Rotterdam. It targeted the Delftsche Poort railway station and the Beursstation and the Maasstation.

The German bombers were also detailed to hit one of the prime military targets on the north side of the city: the Marinierskazerne, from which the marines had been assembling and launching their attacks against the paratroopers. The marines were by now desperately clinging to their bridgehead on the north side of the river. Just before noon, a group of Ju 87 Stukas approached Rotterdam and spotted the self-identifying red flares fired by the Germans on Noordereiland. As they cruised over the river, the Stukas began going into their dives, their target being the Marinierskazerne. As luck would have it, however, the precision weapons of the Luftwaffe were completely off their mark on that particular mission: their bombs struck all around the building, but they did not achieve a single direct hit. This was fortunate for the Dutch, because at that moment a large group of marines were in the barracks getting a much-deserved rest. A small hospital nearby suffered a direct hit; but by an amazing stroke of luck, all of the staff and patients were in the cellar, whose thick ceiling withstood the blast.

Not so lucky was the old zoo on the Kruiskade. Eighteen of the bombs aimed for the Delftsche Poort railway station slammed into the zoo grounds, killing and injuring a large number of animals. In light of the ongoing battle and out of fear that another air attack might cause further damage to the zoo, allowing the animals to escape, the Dutch military decided that it was necessary to shoot the remaining large predators in the zoo. Sadly, they shot seven lions, nine tigers, four panthers, three jaguars, and two bears. Despite the Luftwaffe's attempts at precision bombing, no one could fully predict where the bombs would fall, and this made the civilians on the ground all the more nervous.[26]

The Fourth Day (May 13, 1940)

The early morning hours of Monday, May 13, found the remaining C.X pilots of Stat.Ver.V.A. at Bergen waking up eagerly. Though they were tired and had already seen three exhausting days of combat operations, the start of the day's first mission came as a relief from the nervous tension and waiting from the night before. In the late hours of the 12th, the pilots had been told that their first mission of the next day was going to be a ground strike against the German forces attacking the Grebbeberg, which would coincide with a scheduled Dutch counterattack. Taking off in the gray dawn, the C.Xs repeated their well-honed phrase HUBOBE (short for *Huisjes, Boompjes, Beestjes,* or "houses, trees, and animals"). This referred to Dutch pilots flying at the deck to avoid detection from German fighter patrols, skimming over fields and buildings. They were joined by an escort of D.XXIs flying from Buiksloot. Along the way, Lt. Postma noticed groups of Messerschmitts flying high overhead, but they did not intercept. The HUBOBE tactics kept the Dutch out of sight, and they reached their target without being discovered. According to Postma:

Suddenly, before the spectators on the ground, we appeared behind the Grebbeberg and began to climb to approximately three hundred meters, which is the necessary altitude, if we want our bombs to explode. Yet a few moments passed, then we were over the target of our flight, the woods in the area of Wageningen, where the hostile artillery batteries had positioned themselves, which continually harassed the fortifications on the Grebbeberg. . . . For their part our fighters sent many fiery rounds into the woods under us, almost simultaneously with the bombs, which the observers now dropped. . . . With the greatest possible speed we flew back; the enemy fighters could have been alerted and then easily caught up with us, we had to avoid combat as much as possible with the few aircraft we still had. . . . We returned to Bergen, where we [were] received with joy. . . . [A] few hours later a phone call came, with the request, once again, to fly a mission to the area near the Grebbeberg. This time it would not be any less dangerous; it was later in the day and the battle was in full swing. The reports indicated that the enemy air force was very active there; volunteers were asked for. However, our captain did not need to wait long for names; all gave themselves without hesitating. . . . [27]

The C.Xs were rearmed, refueled, and back in the air before noon for another strike on the Grebbeberg. Again, amazingly, the HUBOBE tactics prevailed: the planes made their attack and were not intercepted on the way to or from the target. HUBOBE allowed the Dutch to effectively utilize aircraft that would have otherwise been considered obsolete for battle. Although these bold attacks did not cause significant damage or alter the situation on the ground, they briefly raised the morale of the Dutch troops on the Grebbeberg; those troops had seen nothing but German aircraft since the first day of the war.

The attacks made by those old biplanes made the Luftwaffe realize that the striking power of the Militair Luchtvaart and the morale of its pilots was not yet completely destroyed. In the afternoon hours of May 13 the

On May 12 the ML, desperate for operational aircraft, pressed its surviving Fokker D.XVII biplanes into service as escort fighters. Three D.XVIIs, along with three G.1s, escorted a group of C.V and C.X light bombers on a strike against the German lines opposite the Grebbeberg. Although the strike caused little damage, it raised the morale of the Dutch defenders and made it clear to the Germans that the ML was not yet out of the fight. Here a D.XVII prepares for takeoff. [Photo AVIODROME Luchtfotografie, Lelystad, Holland]

Dutch troops kneeling in makeshift rifle positions behind parked cars and trucks along the Boompjes. On May 12, the Luftwaffe launched a Stuka attack against the Marinierkazerne and surrounding buildings, hoping to relieve pressure on the beleaguered German defenders trapped on the northern end of the Maas bridges. The attack was poorly executed, most bombs missing their targets, and the Dutch marines and other ground troops continued to attack and besiege the German positions on the north side of the Maas until the Dutch surrender. [Netherlands Institute of Military History]

Fokker C.X #714, one of the aircraft of Strat.Ver.V.A. that carried out two HUBOBE strikes against the Germans attacking the Grebbeberg on May 13. [Photo AVIODROME Luchtfotografie, Lelystad, Holland]

***Here the observer from Fokker C.V #648 climbs out from his rear position with the aircraft's camera after a reconnaissance mission. Note the bullet holes in the orange triangle. Most C.Vs were deployed during the* Meidagen *as observation aircraft for Dutch army units on the ground. Some C.Vs were also sent on HUBOBE strike missions during the latter days of the* Meidagen.** [Photo AVIODROME Luchtfotografie, Lelystad, Holland]

Germans conducted a bombing raid on Bergen; again, however, the camouflaged C.Xs were not detected from the air and received no damage. After the raid, the base mechanics once again went to work patching up the planes in anticipation of further missions on the following day. The base commander received a phone call from Buiksloot saying that the D.XXI fighters were being repaired and would again be available for escort duties the next day. The commander also learned that Buiksloot was going to be abandoned that night due to the fear by the high command of a possible German landing on the western side of the Ijsselmeer. It was then decided that the airfield at Bergen be evacuated as well. In light of the earlier German bombing, it probably would not be long before the Germans figured out where the Dutch attacks were coming from; then the Germans would most certainly step up their own attacks.

The preparations to abandon the base began that night. Important documents and photos were burned while the ground crew loaded trucks with ammunition, bombs, and spare parts—yet another night without rest for the airmen. Early on the morning of the May 14, a truck convoy set out from Bergen to Schiphol, the new base of operations for the C.X squadron. The remaining aircraft took off among the empty remains of Bergen at 10:00 a.m., after the morning mist had dissipated. Fifteen minutes later, the pilots put their aircraft down on the runway at Schiphol. As they taxied around the airfield of the country's largest airport, Postma felt they had entered a wasteland:

> Mounds of earth, broken concrete, bent pieces of iron, the sun shining between layers of hundreds of shards of glass, buildings, more like ruins than hangars, and fuselage ruins lying about; the picture of this was what we saw of such a proud airport for a few days.
>
> No living being could be found. This all together did not particularly work to calm us. We imagined ourselves in a kind of haunted land, where witches and ghosts would manifest themselves at any moment, possessed with the most terrifying plans.

Furthermore our position was not particularly safe, as we stood totally defenseless in an open area.

At last, after ten minutes, which seemed like hours, came one of the observers, who had searched around, with a gratifying report, which someone had found for him, that we had to start and land at Noordwijkerhout.[28]

The C.Xs took off from Schiphol and made their way without incident to the Ruigenhoek airfield near Noordwijkerhout, on the dunes along the North Sea, using their HUBOBE tactics to avoid detection. After landing on the dunes, the pilots camouflaged their aircraft as best they could and waited for the arrival of the truck convoy from Bergen. As the pilots tried to relax, almost any sound they heard made them drop to the ground, thinking that an attack was incoming. After four continuous days of battle their nerves were frayed.

May 13 saw the last mission carried out by Bom.V.A. Beginning at midnight, the high command was trying to decide how best to use its last remaining bomber. At 3:40 a.m., the commander of Bom.V.A. received a phone call from the high command ordering T.V #856 to be armed with two 300-kg bombs and to phone back as soon as the bomber was ready for takeoff. Since eight 50-kg bombs were already loaded in the bomb bay, it took the ground crew some time to rearm the bomber. Finally, at 5:05, the call came through to army headquarters: T.V #856 was ready for takeoff. Then the Bom.V.A. commander received his orders: with the greatest possible precision, bombard the vehicle bridge at Moerdijk with the 300-kg bombs. Two Fokker G.1s would be provided as escort. After the bombardment, the three aircraft had to report whether there were any large armored columns approaching or on the bridges.

After being given their orders, Lts. Swagerman (T.V #856), Bodo Sandberg (G.1 #308), and Paul Schoute (G.1 #315) plotted their attack. Using the well-honed HUBOBE tactics, they would fly as low as possible in the direction of Dordrecht and on reaching the city, quickly climb to 1,000 meters and attack the bridge from the north. The G.1s would provide a tight escort, flying only 300 meters above the T.V. After that preparatory plan, the bomber crew and fighter pilots boarded their aircraft and took off from Schiphol at 5:19 a.m. They approached Dordrecht unopposed, just skimming over the trees and polders. When Dordrecht was in sight, the T.V climbed to 1,000 meters and made its bombing run on the bridge. One bomb was dropped, landing 50 meters from the bridge and exploding in the water. The bomber then swung around and approached the bridge from the south; Swagerman was determined to fulfill his mission. On the second approach the T.V made a perfect drop, and the bomb was seen to hit the ground beside the bridge.

However, it did not explode! There must have been a deep sense of frustration among the airmen in the bomber, but there was little time to reflect on it. They spotted an incoming group of Bf 109s overhead, which dove in to attack. The German fighters divided into three groups, each attacking one of the Dutch planes. Swagerman and his crew bravely tried to put up a fight, but the Germans had the advantage. Riddled with 20mm canon shells, T.V #856 plummeted into the ground near Ridderkerk, with no survivors among the crew. Only Lt. Sandberg made it back to Schiphol in his G.1, and to him fell the unenviable task of reporting that Bom.V.A. no longer existed.[29]

After the French Seventh Army's withdrawal on May 12, there was no hope of any Allied armored intervention against the rapidly advancing 9th Panzer Division. Although the overall situation for the Dutch armed forces in the Netherlands was becoming more and more dire, the possibility of stalling or even halting the German advance into the Vesting Holland from the south was not entirely lost. In the early hours of May 13, tanks of the 9th Panzer Division began to move over the Moerdijk bridges onto the Island of Dordrecht. The Dutch garrison on the island, not having been told of the French Seventh's retreat, heard the creaking treads approaching and thought that the long-expected French tanks were arriving. It was quite a shock when they saw the black crosses on the tanks, which quickly began firing. The Dutch fell back into the city of Dordrecht, but along the way and within the city, they put their antitank guns to good use. In the

The commander/observer of a Fokker T.V getting up from his stool in the nose of the aircraft and heading aft through the cockpit. This and the subsequent photo give a good idea of the position that Bernardus Swagerman manned in his T.V, and also of the view he had in the nose on his last mission on May 13. [Photo AVIODROME Luchtfotografie, Lelystad, Holland]

fighting on the island and in the city, the Dutch antitank crews, primarily using the very effective Böhler 47mm antitank gun, managed to knock out fifteen German tanks, after which the Germans withdrew from the city.

The forward units of the 9th Panzer Division then decided to bypass Dordrecht and proceed to the Island of Ysselmonde and drive from there to Rotterdam. Again, the German tanks were ambushed by the well-positioned Dutch antitank guns, which took out another three tanks. Despite that, the Germans succeeded in holding the vital bridges along the southern approach to Rotterdam. In the city, the Germans on the north side of the Maas had been isolated into four groups, the largest of which contained twenty paratroopers with Obstlt. Kerfin in the National Life Insurance Building on the Boompjes; there were ten paratroopers in a house between the Willemsbrug and the railway bridge; a machine-gun nest on the railway bridge itself; and eight paratroopers at the base of the Willemsbrug. On the night before, Col. Scharroo received orders from Gen. Winkelman to push the Germans out of their last strongholds on the north side of the river and to destroy the bridges before the tanks of the 9th Panzer Division arrived in southern Rotterdam. The marines were again sent into action, along with naval auxiliary troops, supported by two DAF armored cars and artillery fire.

The attack was well planned but poorly executed: the company of marines was not told that the Germans still held the National Life Insurance Building; the artillery fire was not coordinated with the infantry assault; and when it did fire, its shots fell short and long. Nevertheless, the marines pressed the attack so fiercely that Obstlt. Kerfin was contemplating the surrender of his isolated position. Then, suddenly, the Dutch fell back. Dutch officers were growing concerned about the increasing enfilading fire coming from the opposite side of the river, and they did not believe they could complete the attack from such a dangerous position. Most of the marines withdrew to their lines, while a handful sought cover under the Willemsbrug, where they stayed for the rest of the campaign, serving as snipers against any German who came within their sights.

The Final Day (May 14, 1940)

In the early morning hours of May 14, units of the 9th Panzer Division and the SS Leibstandarte Adolf Hitler began arriving on the south side of Rotterdam. For Gen. Student, at last the cavalry had arrived. Although the Germans were arriving in overwhelming force, the immediate situation on the Maas front looked no better for the Germans. Paratroopers still held the northern end of the Maas bridges, but the Dutch could still lay down an effective defensive fire against anyone or anything that attempted to cross the bridges. An attack with panzers across the narrow bridges was deemed to be too risky, because the Dutch had antitank guns, and there would be little room to maneuver. Bearing all this in mind, the newly arrived tanks did practically nothing to alter the strategic situation.

Frustrated by these immediate circumstances, the German commanders met to come up with a plan of action. First, they decided that all of the German units present, including the 9th Panzer Division, the SS Leibstandarte Adolf Hitler, the 7th Airborne Division, and the remnants of the 22nd Air-Landing Division, would be merged under the aegis of the newly activated 39th Armee Korps, which would act as a single, organized assault force under the command of Colonel General Rudolf F. K. Schmidt. Next, due to an order from the German high command that the city of Rotterdam be taken as soon as possible, even if it would be destroyed in the process, Schmidt decided to call on the Luftwaffe to attack the Dutch defensive positions on the north side of the river—prior to an all-out assault. Gen. Student had already called on Luftwaffe support on May 13, but he insisted that an aerial attack be *kurz und wuchtig* ("short and heavy"). Schmidt had something heavier in mind: he intended to have the He 111 bombers of Kampfgruppe 54 pound the northern side of the riverfront. Finally, at 2:00 a.m. on the 14th, Schmidt unveiled his plan: at 1:00 p.m., a general artillery bombardment would commence, and then at 1:05 the bombardment would focus on select targets. At 1:20, KG 54 would bomb the Dutch defenses, and at 1:50 the German infantry would launch an all-out assault over the bridges.

Before 9:00 on the morning of the 14th, Gen. Schmidt sent three officers, bearing a white flag, across the Willemsbrug to attempt to negotiate the surrender of the

Above *Swagerman and his crew were not the only Dutch losses in the attack on the Moerdijk vehicle bridge. This photo, supposedly taken from a German aircraft, is believed to be the Fokker G.1 #315 of Lt. Schoute going down in flames. Schoute's G.1 was flying escort for Swagerman's T.V when a group of Bf 109s attacked and shot down both aircraft. Later it was discovered that this photo was a doctored fabrication of the German Propaganda Ministry.* [Photo AVIODROME Luchtfotografie, Lelystad, Holland]

Left and Bottom Right *Dutch troops wheel a Böhler 47mm antitank gun into action. The Dutch army had ordered a number of the Böhler guns from Austria before the war, and those guns were put to good use attacking German panzers attempting to advance through Dordrecht on their way to relieve the* Fallschirmjäger *and* Luftlande *troops held down in Rotterdam. The Dutch antitank gun crews knocked out eighteen panzers on May 13. Here is a Böhler 47mm antitank gun preserved in the Cavalerie Museum in Amersfoort.* [Militair Luchtvaart Museum, Soesterberg]

Dutch marines behind a barricade on the north bank of the Maas (above), shooting at German positions on Noordereiland on May 14. The "De Hef" vertical lift railway bridge, in the background, is one of the few landmarks in this area of Rotterdam that survived the Luftwaffe's bombardment of the city center on May 14, as seen in this view of modern Rotterdam (right) taken from near the same position. [Stadsarchief Rotterdam 1990-1030-1 / photo courtesy of Mr. Jeroen Noppen]

Dutch. The officers, led by Hauptmann Raymund Hoerst, carried with them an ultimatum addressed to the military commander and mayor of Rotterdam that demanded the surrender of the city by 12:30 p.m., or they would face an incoming attack. Hoerst and the other two officers, Hauptmann Pesendorfer and Oberleutnant Friedrich Plutzar, approached the Dutch near the Beursstation and were then driven by car to Col. Scharroo's headquarters on the Staatenweg, in the northern part of the city. They finally arrived there at 10:30, and were told to wait until the city commander was ready to receive them. Hoerst was very annoyed that the Dutch seemed to be in no hurry to get on with the negotiations. Ten minutes later they were brought before Col. Scharroo.

After reading the ultimatum, Scharroo said that he would have to consult with Opperbevelhebber Winkelman, and he sent the Germans back to Noordereiland with a message saying that he would send a negotiator to them by 12:30. Hoerst and his comrades made their way back to the German lines, reporting to Student on Noordereiland—and finally to Schmidt. By that time, it was about noon. Back at Scharroo's headquarters, the mayor of Rotterdam, Burgemeester Pieter Oud, had arrived at the same time that the colonel was speaking with the Germans. After they had gone, Scharroo met with Oud and handed him the copy of the ultimatum, which the Germans had also addressed to the mayor. Oud had decided earlier to leave the fate of the city in the hands of the military; nevertheless, the two men discussed the matter. Oud was concerned by the phrase "sternest measures of destruction" in the ultimatum: he assumed that the Germans would unleash their bombers on the city as they had on Warsaw a year before.

Scharroo, on the other hand, was bothered that the ultimatum was generically from "De Kommandant van de Duitse troepen," not signed by a specific officer. This was an unusual error in basic military protocol. Lieutenant Colonel Johannes J. C. P. Wilson, Winkelman's representative at Scharroo's headquarters, thought that the unsigned message was worthless. Scharroo concurred, especially since he had just reinforced the northern side of the Maas with antitank guns and antiaircraft guns in preparation for a German attack, and to be used, ultimately, to destroy the bridges. Scharroo then phoned Winkelman in The Hague, requesting further instructions. Winkelman took some time considering the matter and later returned Scharroo's call, instructing him that he could not act on an ultimatum that had not been properly signed. In doing so, Winkelman hoped to buy time to prepare defenses between Rotterdam and The Hague in the event of the capitulation of Rotterdam. After Winkelman's call, Scharroo sent Captain Jan Dam Backer with a message requesting a formal ultimatum with the signature of the German commander. The time was now noon.

While these negotiations were taking place between Hptmn. Hoerst and Col. Scharroo, there was a flurry of activity at the airfields of Quakenbruck, Vechta, and Varrelbusch in western Germany. The ground crews of these airfields were preparing the 90 He 111 bombers of KG 54 for their mission over Rotterdam. 50-kg and 250-kg bombs were loaded into the bomb bays of the aircraft, while the aircrews were briefed on their mission. It was decided that the Geschwader would be divided into two forces: the formation of fifty-four bombers under the KG 54 commander, Oberst Walter Lackner, would approach from the east, while Oberstleutnant Otto Höhne's formation of thirty-six bombers would fly in from the southwest. The two attack angles would form a triangle with the Maas River as the base, with the building where Obstlt. Kerfin's men were holding out as the base center. The apex of the triangle, where the bombing runs would intersect, would be the Delftse Poort railway station in the center of the city. The bombardment plan was to isolate the battlefield by creating a swath of destruction that would prevent the defenders from being easily reinforced, while at the same time obstructing their line of withdrawal.

At 11:50 a.m., the bombers took off from their airfields so that they would promptly arrive over the target at 1:20. It is interesting to note that Gen. Student had already requested an aerial bombardment on the 13th against the Dutch defensive positions; but Student had said that the bombardment should be "kurz und wuchtig." For this he had in mind using the dive bombers of Stuka Gr. IV (L1) to make precision strikes against the Dutch defenses along the river. During the conference of the German commanders on Noordereiland on the night of the May 13-14, Schmidt concurred with Student's request for a precision strike, but he believed that the bombers of KG 54 should be added for extra weight. This is what Schmidt and Student assumed would be incoming on the 14th (though, unbeknownst to Schmidt, the Stuka group earmarked for the attack on Rotterdam had actually been diverted to another pressing situation in France).

In Hitler's headquarters, the tenor was not as calm. Early on the morning of May 14, Hitler, furious with the slow progress of the German forces in the Netherlands and the stubborn resilience of the Dutch armed forces, issued the Führer-Weisung nr. 11, which declared:

> On the northern flank the strength of the Dutch Army has proven to be stronger than expected. Political, like military reasons require (us) to break this resistance in a short period of time. The mission of the Army is to quickly bring about the collapse of Fortress Holland with

Forward units of the 9th Panzer Division arrive at the southern end of the Willemsbrug on May 14. The panzers could not drive across the bridge to the aid of the few remaining* Fallschirmjäger *positioned at the northern end of the bridge because the Dutch had antitank guns and artillery covering the bridge and the northern approach to it. With the German panzers unable to proceed across the Maas, the situation in Rotterdam continued to be a stalemate. [Deutsches Bundesarchiv via Wikimedia Commons]

Colonel General Rudolf Schmidt, who was made commander of all German units in and around Rotterdam on May 14. Schmidt requested an air precision strike against Dutch defenses on the afternoon of the 14th in preparation for a German assault across the Willemsbrug. [Deutsches Bundesarchiv via Wikipedia Commons]

sufficient forces from the south in conjunction with the attack against the east front.[30]

There was an implicit disgust within Hitler's message about the lack of progress in the Vesting Holland, one that certainly could not have escaped Hermann Göring. The Luftwaffe's airborne assault had failed, and the army had to come to its rescue. Eager to be back in good favor with his Führer—and desperate to demonstrate that the Luftwaffe could decide a campaign independently, as he had initially promised—Göring decided to use the brute strength of his bombers and hoped that what in effect was a terror bombing by KG 54 would force the Dutch as a nation to capitulate, especially if other Dutch cities were threatened with similar aerial bombardment. General Wilhelm Speidel, chief of staff of the Second Air Fleet during the Dutch campaign, took particular notice of Göring's interference in the Luftwaffe's operations over Rotterdam on May 14:

> Renunciation of the command of a strategic air war—and with it renunciation of all centralized command—had the inevitable result that the Commander in Chief, Luftwaffe, now began to interfere in the minor details of command in the field, and this to an ever increasing degree. There was a repetition of the same sort of thing which had been noted during the campaign in Poland. We lack the documentary evidence to substantiate these statements with facts. Nevertheless, the "interminable excited discussions" between Göring and the Commander in Chief of the Second Air Fleet regarding the attack on Rotterdam are an indication that the Reichmarschall's tendency to interfere in trivial matters was early given its head. Although in this particular instance there may have been political factors and aspects of international law which really justified the concern of the Commander in Chief of the Luftwaffe, the author is able to confirm from personal experience that there were many occasions on which the Luftwaffe Operations Staff, acting on Göring's orders, displayed uncommon interest in the commitment of individual air units, down to squadron level. It is clear that this sort of thing is more likely to disrupt and confuse the orderly course of command than to promote it.[31]

"Aspects of international law" certainly did not play a part in Göring's interference in KG 54's planned bom-

Colonel Pieter Wilhelmus Scharroo, commander of the Dutch units in Rotterdam, in his Ford V-8 coupe. Scharroo did not respond to Schmidt's first ultimatum demanding surrender because it was improperly signed. Scharroo, who sent the negotiators back with a request for a proper ultimatum, and Gen. Winkelman used this as an excuse to gain more time to prepare for the impending German assault. [Netherlands Institute of Military History]

bardment of Rotterdam. Speidel was rather too generous there, but "political factors," such as the Luftwaffe's reputation—and the Reichmarschall's own in Hitler's eyes—certainly motivated Göring's interference in this "trivial matter." Therefore, Göring altered Student and Schmidt's request for a precision attack to a heavy bombardment of the city. If Rotterdam—and possibly the Netherlands as a whole—were to capitulate, his credibility with Hitler would be improved, and the reputation of the Luftwaffe as a force that could decisively determine a military campaign would be restored. However, he did not inform Student and Schmidt of this change in tactic.

Back on the ground at around noon, Hptm. Hoerst reported to Gen. Schmidt that the Dutch were in the process of discussing the ultimatum, and he gave the impression that the Dutch would surrender the city. Since the Dutch were going to send a negotiator at 12:30, Schmidt, in his optimism, radioed the commander of Fliegerkorps z.b.V., General Richard Putzier, that the attack was to be postponed due to ongoing negotiations; if necessary, a new attack time would be scheduled later. Putzier responded that the bombers were already airborne and on their way to the target but that the abort message would be sent. At the same time, Capt. Backer arrived on Noordereiland with Scharoo's message and was escorted to an ice-cream parlor where he was told that the commanding German general would meet with him. When Schmidt learned that the city had not yet capitulated, he was furious, at the same time realizing that his initial optimism was perhaps too hasty. All of this back and forth was taking too much time.

Schmidt barked at his chauffeur to drive him to where the Dutch negotiator was waiting. At nearly the same moment, the sound of an approaching aircraft was heard. The Germans thought nothing of it, but a number of Dutch prisoners of war who were being guarded near Schmidt's headquarters suddenly became excited. Lt. Noomen, who four days earlier had shot down two He 111s, but who had been captured in the interim, watched in awe as a Fokker C.X (#706 from Ruigenhoek) roared in from a low altitude, photographing the buildup of German forces

German pilots, aircrew, and ground crew rushing to man their Heinkel He 111 bombers warming up on an airfield. Developed in the guise of a high-speed civilian airliner when the Luftwaffe was still being built in secret in 1934, the Heinkel He 111 became the most numerous Schnellbomber *in the German service when the war began in 1939. When operating in air-superiority conditions or with fighter escort, however, the He 111 served as an effective medium bomber. It was the most numerous German bomber to see action over the Netherlands during the* Meidagen *and was also responsible for the Rotterdam Blitz on May 14, 1940. Armed with 50- and 250 kg bombs, the He 111s of KG 54 were intended to create a swath of destruction in central Rotterdam rather than the precision Stuka strike against specific Dutch defenses requested by Schmidt. Shown here is a profile of one of the He 111's belonging to KG 54.* [Photo via the Museum of the United States Air Force]

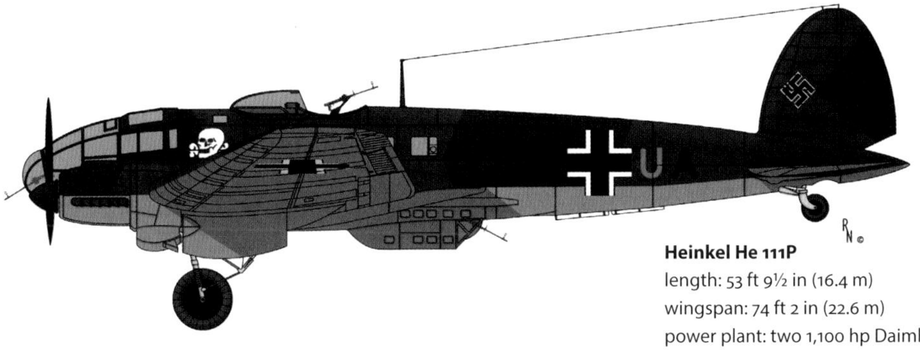

Heinkel He 111P
length: 53 ft 9½ in (16.4 m)
wingspan: 74 ft 2 in (22.6 m)
power plant: two 1,100 hp Daimler Benz DB601A-1 in-line engines
maximum speed: 242 mph (390 km/h)
range: 745 miles (1,200 km)
ceiling: 25,590 ft (7,800 m)
armament: three 7.92mm MG 15 machine guns
payload: 4,409 lbs (2,000 kg) of bombs
crew: 5

Eager to get back into Hitler's good graces after it became clear that the airborne aspects of the invasion of the Netherlands had more or less failed—for which the Luftwaffe was responsible—Hermann Göring ordered that KG 54's bombardment be altered to a terror-bombing rather than a precision strike at selected targets. Göring believed that the terror-bombing of Dutch cities would force the nation to capitulate and end a campaign that was supposed to have taken only one day, according to the German strategists' original timetables. [Deutsches Bundesarchiv via Wikipedia Commons]

for the scheduled ground attack. The sudden appearance of a Dutch plane so shocked the Germans that many of their antiaircraft gunners stood dumbfounded without firing a shot. This flyover must have added to Schmidt's frustration at the Dutch forces' stubborn refusal to immediately capitulate. Schmidt arrived at the ice-cream parlor, where Capt. Backer was waiting at 12:35. On the back of Scharroo's message Schmidt wrote out a new ultimatum demanding a response by 4:20 p.m., and signed it. Backer left the ice-cream parlor at 1:20 p.m., and was escorted toward the Willemsbrug by Lt. Col. von Choltitz and his adjutant, bearing a white flag. Before they reached the bridge, the three officers paused; they could hear the low roar of large formations of planes coming in from the south and the east.

The incoming planes were Höhne's and Lackner's formations of Heinkel He 111s. Unbeknownst to Schmidt, Gen. Putzier had been unable to reach KG 54 by radio and, by the time Schmidt's postponement order was sent out, the bombers had drawn in their long-range radio aerials as they were approaching the target. On the ground there was only a minute or so to react. Von Choltitz ordered his men to fire red warning flares into the sky, the prearranged signal for the bombers to abort the mission. But the aircraft kept coming. Von Choltitz suggested that Capt. Backer stay on Noordereiland, since he felt that the danger of bombardment was quickly becoming more and more real. Backer then asked if he could have an extension to the ultimatum, because of the air raid; when he learned that that was impossible, Backer insisted on returning to the Dutch lines as quickly as possible. While he, von Choltitz, and a German officer bearing a white flag set out for the Willemsbrug, Backer noticed air raid sirens beginning to howl and civilians scrambling into shelters and cellars. Halfway across the bridge, von Choltitz quickly said farewell and took off running with his adjutant to the southern end of the bridge. In the distance Backer saw Schmidt and Student immediately running toward their staff cars, which were waiting at the south end of the bridge at the Koningshaven. Something was terribly wrong.

Just as Backer reached the northern end of the Willemsbrug, the explosions began. Rotterdam was being bombed! Lackner's formation of fifty-four bombers, coming in from the southeast, was releasing its deadly payload over their prearranged targets in the center of the city. For Lackner and his pilots, it was a perfectly executed bombing run; and there was no antiaircraft fire because Winkelman had ordered that all of Rotterdam's antiaircraft guns be sent to The Hague during the capitulation negotiations. As Höhne's formation approached the beginning of its bombing run, Höhne himself was very tense. The release of his formation's bombs had to be absolutely precise since the bombs would be falling within the vicinity of the remnant of German troops trapped on the northern end of the Maas bridges. Suddenly he noticed two red flares bursting in the air to the starboard side of the aircraft flares, coming up from Noordereiland. He knew that this was the prearranged signal to abort the mission, and he immediately called over his radio, "Abdrehen (Abort)!" All of the bombers veered off except for the lead formation of three planes; those had released their bombs just as they received Höhne's command. This maneuver perhaps saved Rotterdam from further destruction, but what was caused by Lackner's bombers was devastating enough. The bombs were accurately dropped into the center of the city.[32]

In the middle of the bombardment, Capt. Backer made his way across the Willemsbrug and, partially through bombed-out rubble, to the Beursstation, where his car was still waiting for him. Although there was pandemonium going on all around him, Backer realized that he must get back to Scharroo's headquarters; there was still Gen. Schmidt's ultimatum to be answered. After a lengthy journey—as a result of the damaged buildings and streets—Backer finally arrived at Scharroo's headquarters and handed the colonel the German ultimatum. Burgomeister Oud, who had arrived just before Backer, pleaded with Scharroo to surrender since, in his opinion, the city had already suffered enough at the hands of the Germans. For a time Scharroo did not know what to do, and he could not consult Gen. Winkelman because the telephone network in the city had been knocked out by the bombing. Finally, after a period of silence, Lt. Col. Wilson stepped forward and said that, since he was the representative of Gen. Winkelman present at this meeting, and since communications with the Dutch high command had been severed, he would accept Col. Scharroo's decision on behalf of the commanding general. After another period of silence, Scharroo said that he would capitulate. Wilson approved of Scharroo's decision and left for The Hague to inform Gen. Winkelman.

At 3:00 p.m., Scharroo ordered his men to cease their fire and to await further orders. Immediately afterward, he and Backer got in a car and began to drive toward the German headquarters on the other side of the Maas. The ultimatum was due to expire at 4:20, and negotiating the drive through the center of the devastated city would take some time. Finally, at 3:50, Scharroo arrived at German headquarters at the Maaspoort, where he was received by Gens. Schmidt and Student. Scharroo made no attempt to hide his disgust over the bombardment and what he saw as a deliberate breach of negotiations. Schmidt responded by saying: "I understand that you are bitter, Herr Oberst." He went on to say that he himself had not approved of the bombing, nor had he requested such a bombardment, and that he had done everything in his power to call it off. Scharroo was not moved by the general's comments and curtly signed the unconditional surrender of Rotterdam at 4:20 p.m., the exact time of the expiration of the German ultimatum. Scharroo simply wrote *angenommen* ("accepted"), signed his name and rank, and left to return to his headquarters.

As Scharoo left, Schmidt felt that he could not blame the colonel for his disdainful attitude. But other events shifted his attention. At 4:43 he radioed his superior, General Georg von Küchler, that the city had been handed over and that the German push north of the Maas had begun. Around fifteen minutes later, Schmidt received a disturbing message from Gen. Student: a bomber formation was underway for a second aerial bombardment of Rotterdam, and it was scheduled to arrive over the city between 5:20 and 6:20 p.m. Schmidt was furious. What was the Luftwaffe doing? It had already ignored his request for a precision tactical bombardment; it had seemingly ignored his message to abort while surrender

Oberstleutnant Otto Höhne and Oberst Walter Lackner, the commanders of the two formations of KG 54 ordered to bomb Rotterdam. Lackner's group of 54 He 111s released their bombs according to plan, but Höhne noticed red flares being shot up from Noordereiland (a prearranged signal to abort the attack) and was able to stop all but three of his thirty-six bombers from releasing their bombs. Nevertheless, the damage had been done: Lackner's planes had bombed Rotterdam in the middle of the surrender negotiations.

Fokker C.X #706 (second from the front) in a lineup of other aircraft of Strat.Ver.V.A. at Schiphol before the war. #706 was still operationally active on May 14 and made a low-altitude reconnaissance pass over Gen. Schmidt's headquarters around noon to photograph the German buildup prior to their scheduled ground attack. The Germans ground forces were bothered that the Luftwaffe was still unable to deal a deathblow to the Dutch ML. [Photo AVIODROME Luchtfotografie, Lelystad, Holland]

Col. Scharroo and Captain Jan Backer coming down the southern approach of the Willemsbrug behind a flag of truce after the bombardment. Scharroo was clearly enraged by the bombardment and simply signed the surrender ultimatum and marched off. Gen. Schmidt had been embarrassed by the attack and was irritated by the Luftwaffe's clumsy and severe handling of the matter. [Netherlands Institute of Military History]

General Henri Winkelman arriving in Rijsoord on the morning of May 15 to sign the formal surrender of the Dutch armed forces.

negotiations were underway; now it appeared as though it had not received the message that Rotterdam had surrendered. The first bombardment was bad enough, but a second one would further blacken an already dark reputation the Germans had with the Dutch in the city.

Gen. Student learned that the second bombardment had come as a direct order from Göring. The reason for the attack was to open up a path for Schmidt's panzers to race through in order to relieve Gen. von Sponeck's air-landing troops, who were still besieged in Overschie. Bombers of KG 54 had already taken off between 4:00 and 4:20 p.m.—at the same time that the Dutch had surrendered the city. At 5:15, Schmidt hurriedly radioed the Luftwaffe: "The northern part of Rotterdam is occupied. Do not drop bombs!" Schmidt was lying: the Germans had not yet moved over to the north side of the Maas River. But he was not about to let a second terror-bombing take place. Almost a half hour later the roar of incoming aircraft was heard approaching the city; but at 5:43 the planes veered off. At that moment, the bomber crews picked up a recall order over the radio and aborted the mission. Rotterdam was spared a second bombing.[33]

One bombardment was horrible enough. The entire center of the city had been demolished, and what was still standing was ablaze. Burgomeister Oud and the city aldermen had decided earlier in the day not to inform the population about the threat of aerial bombardment in order to avoid panic. Thus, when the bombardment began, it took the civilians in the city completely by surprise. Fortunately, a large number of the population had already left the city during the previous four days of fighting, so casualties were not as high as they could have been. Nevertheless, at least 800 civilians were killed—some quickly from the bombardment itself, some slowly from burns or suffocation, some from being trapped under rubble in cellars and basements. With water and gas lines ruptured and the electrical grid knocked out, the city's fire departments could do little to contain the blaze. At first the fires moved eastward, but during the evening the winds began to blow from the east, sending the fires into previously undamaged neighborhoods. Over one square mile of the city burned to the ground, leaving more than 85,000 civilians homeless. Many people fled to safety in the Kralingerhout woods just outside the city, where they spent a restless night as the city burned before their eyes. Firemen and emergency workers poured in from other cities and villages, but the major fires were not extinguished for two days. As Rotterdam burned, the fate of the whole country lay in the balance.[34]

At 3:30 on the afternoon of May 14, Lt. Col. Wilson reported the situation in Rotterdam to Gen. Winkelman in The Hague. Rotterdam was an inferno, and Scharoo and the garrison had surrendered. Shortly thereafter, a message came from the Germans demanding the immediate surrender of Utrecht, under pain of an aerial bombardment similar to what had befallen Rotterdam. Winkelman called a conference with the commander of the field army, Maj. Gen. Baron Van Voorst tot Voorst, and the two quickly came to the conclusion that the Germans were turning to carpet- and terror-bombing to force the Netherlands into a decision. With the ML shattered and the antiaircraft units scattered, Winkelman concluded that there could be no effective defense against aerial bombardment without Allied aid. He contacted the Germans with his intent to surrender, and he sent a capitulation message to all Dutch forces in the country; but he also instructed them to destroy as many weapons and military matériel as possible, using the appropriate password for the day: "wrath."

At 7:00 p.m., Winkelman went on the radio and announced to the Dutch population the surrender of the armed forces that remained in the Netherlands. This news reached Queen Wilhelmina just as she was about to dine with King George VI in Buckingham Palace. The Queen later recalled a feeling of helplessness and despair at that moment: "My army had surrendered, and I was to dine." The following morning at 8:00, Winkelmann met with Gen. von Küchler in the Rijsoord Christian Elementary School to sign the formal terms of surrender. Since von Küchler demanded the surrender of all vessels of the Dutch navy and merchant marine, the

Opperbevelhebber took smug contentment in the fact that nearly all of the navy's ships and 90 percent of the merchant marine had already escaped to England, along with 1,350 valuable German airborne prisoners and most of the gold reserves of the Netherlands. At 10:00 a.m., Winkelman signed the articles of surrender, and the German occupation of the Netherlands began. At one point during the surrender negotiations, von Küchler made the demand that Dutch pilots who had escaped abroad could no longer fight in the war. Winkelman rejected this out of hand: the battle for the Netherlands may have concluded, but the war was far from over. A number of the pilots of Orange would continue the fight against Germany from England and later against the Japanese from the East Indies, Australia, and the United States.[35]

As German forces pushed forward into Belgium and France after the Dutch surrender, Hermann Göring briefly toured parts of Rotterdam to see his crude handiwork. The once-proficient fighter ace—but now a fat martinet whose responsibilities were greatly beyond the reach of his capabilities—boasted that his Luftwaffe had decisively ended the campaign in the Netherlands. He showed no remorse for the terror-bombing of a civilian center; it was merely a means to an end in placating his Führer. While on the witness stand during the Nuremburg Tribunal on March 15, 1946, Göring declared his reasons for and selections of targets for the bombardment of Rotterdam, while at the same time claiming that the damage caused by the bombing was tactical in nature and not as destructive as claimed by the Dutch:

> The great amount of destruction was not caused by bombs but, as has been said, by fire. That can best be seen from the fact that all the buildings which were built of stone and concrete are still standing in the ruined part, while the older houses were destroyed. The spread of this fire was caused by the combustion of large quantities of fats and oils. Secondly—I want to emphasize this particularly—the spread of this fire could surely have been prevented by energetic action on the part of the Rotterdam fire department, in spite of the storm coming up.[36]

As mentioned above, the Dutch defensive positions north of the Maas were not along the attack path targeted by KG 54, showing that Göring's testimony regarding this incident had no credibility, and blaming the Rotterdam fire departments for the extent of the damage showed a complete absence of tact. In the ensuing trials, Göring was not prosecuted for his decisions regarding Rotterdam. Given the number of other atrocities he had to account for, they were overlooked. Ultimately, Göring's belief that the Luftwaffe had secured a major victory in the Netherlands was shortsighted at best. A look at the tangible results of the air assault on the Netherlands reveal a tactical success, achieved at a high cost, that led to strategic failure.

During the five *Meidagen* ("May Days"), 528 aircraft of the Luftwaffe were either written-off or temporarily

The center of Rotterdam ablaze following KG 54's terror bombardment. With most of the city's waterlines ruptured, there was little that firemen could do to stop or contain the fires. It took two days for the fires to be extinguished, after which one square mile of the city had burned to the ground. [Militair Luchtvaart Museum, Soesterberg]

knocked out of action. This number accounted for over half of the Luftwaffe strength deployed over the Netherlands between May 10 and 14. The 328 aircraft completely destroyed in the Netherlands included 37 fighters, 52 bombers, 220 transports, and 19 other combat aircraft. The fighters and bombers could easily be replaced, but the destruction of so many transport aircraft constituted a strategic loss. Kampfgeschwader z.b. V.1 lost 61 of 215 transports, and Kampfgeschwader z.b. V.2 lost 140 of 215, 73 percent of the unit's strength. A significant number of pilots were lost along with the Ju 52s, many of whom were veteran airline pilots and flight instructors, as well as aircrew. Many of the Ju 52s that force-landed in the Netherlands or returned to Germany were shot up and required repairs that lasted anywhere from weeks to months. Until the end of 1940, the Fokker works in Amsterdam alone repaired a minimum of fifty Ju 52s. The loss of so many transport aircraft in the Netherlands echoed throughout the rest of the war. There certainly would not be enough Ju 52 transports available for airborne operations for Hitler's planned invasion of Great Britain in the fall of 1940. The success of that invasion (Unternehmen Seelöwe) depended largely on the capture of a British airfields by airborne troops, and the lack of Ju 52s was an important factor in Hitler's decision to cancel it. The Luftwaffe's transport units still had not fully recovered from their operations in the Netherlands when Hitler launched the airborne invasion of Crete in May 1941. A similar number of Ju 52s were lost during the Crete invasion, leaving the Luftwaffe's transport units decimated for the rest of the war. The lack of sufficient transport aircraft to supply the German Sixth Army under General Friedrich Paulus became a pivotal factor in the German defeat during the siege of Stalingrad in early 1943.

The absence of transport aircraft was not the only loss felt by the Luftwaffe as it planned for the invasion of Great Britain. Although the exact number of German *Fallschirmjäger* and airborne troops lost in the Battle for the Netherlands is not known, the best estimates place German casualties in the Netherlands at about 4,000 men. It is known that the 22. Luftlande-Division had at least 42 percent of its officers and 20 percent of its enlisted men killed. There would not be enough of these elite troops to meet the original airborne requirements of Unternehmen Seelöwe. During the rest of 1940 and early 1941, the Luftwaffe undertook an extensive training program of new *Fallschirmjäger* to replace those lost in the Netherlands offensive. And finally, the remnants of the 7. Flieger-Division were left without a leader for the remainder of 1940. Gen. Student was accidentally shot in the head by troops of the Leibstandarte Adolf Hitler who were returning fire at supposed Dutch sniper fire from Col. Scharoo's headquarters on May 14. As Student was being put into an ambulance, he prevented the trigger-happy SS troops from massacring a group of Dutch soldiers and civilians in revenge for their own impulsiveness.

The Battle for the Netherlands thus handicapped Germany's airborne element at a time when it was most critically needed if victory in the West was to be achieved. This fact has been and continues to be overlooked in histories of World War II. Through a narrow view, taken by many surveys of World War II, the Netherlands was conquered by a numerically superior German force after five days of combat. By taking a broader look at the Battle for the

The center of Rotterdam before the bombing was a vibrant section of a modern city. Almost miraculous was the survival of the Witte Huis, to this day a famous Rotterdam landmark, the tallest building in the city at the time, it is seen here through an arch of a destroyed building. [Militair Luchtvaart Museum, Soesterberg]

Netherlands and its impact on the entire Western Theater, however, one can see that the rugged and effective resistance put up by the Dutch armed forces inflicted severe enough losses on the Germans to prevent them from conducting a blitzkrieg invasion of Great Britain. Learning from the heavy losses sustained in the Dutch campaign, German commanders calculated that air superiority over southern England would have to be achieved before any airborne or amphibious landings could take place, limiting the freedom of operations for an invasion and lessening its odds for success. This realization forced the Germans into the Battle of Britain, a battle that the Luftwaffe, with its fixation on ground-support tactical doctrines, was ill prepared to fight. The losses attributed to antiaircraft fire over Holland demonstrated the deadly capability of an efficiently organized and operated air-defense network. Furthermore, the urban fighting that took place in Dordrecht and Rotterdam demonstrated that armored units were vulnerable to a determined defender and that the pace of the blitzkrieg could not be maintained in such environments.

Finally, the bombardment of Rotterdam and the ensuing Dutch capitulation gave Luftwaffe commanders the false notion that similar aerial attacks against cities could be used to compel enemies to surrender. This was achieved in the Netherlands because Rotterdam was defenseless against aerial attack on May 14; the ML had largely been swept from the sky; and the British and the French had abandoned any notions of sending aid to the Dutch. When the Luftwaffe made similar attacks on London, Moscow, and Stalingrad, its commanders realized that it was up against nations that could draw upon greater resources, were committed to fighting a protracted war, and had access to matérial support from the United States. Bearing in mind the German losses in the Netherlands, we can fairly argue that the Dutch helped to preclude the invasion of Britain and put the first nail into the coffin of the Luftwaffe.

However, the Dutch paid heavily for their brief but significant contribution to the Allied cause: during the five *Meidagen,* the Dutch armed forces as a whole suffered

The most iconic German aircraft of the* Meidagen *was the Junkers Ju 52/3m transport, a 1932-vintage airliner, covered with corrugated metal and lacking any streamlined refinements. Flying over the skies of the Netherlands early in the morning of May 10, 1940, the Ju 52 represented the bold initiative of the world's first major airborne operation; however, the burnt-out shells of hundreds of Ju 52s across the Dutch landscape on May 14 testified to Dutch tenacity in the defense of their homeland. A Ju 52 could carry eighteen fully armed* Fallschirmjäger *or* Luftlande *troops into battle. Although larger and faster transport aircraft had been developed in the late 1930s, the Ju 52 remained the primary German aerial transport until the end of the war and was used by the air forces of other nations into the 1970s. Here a Ju 52 makes a low approach before landing to let out a contingent of* Luftlande *troops. [Militair Luchtvaart Museum, Soesterberg]

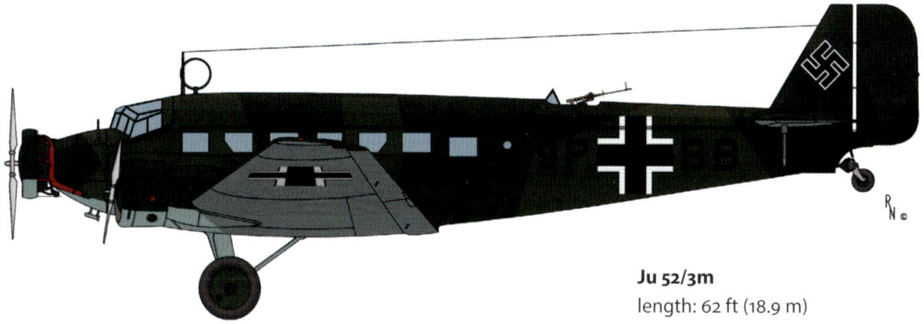

Ju 52/3m
length: 62 ft (18.9 m)
wingspan: 95 ft 11½ in (29.25 m)
power plant: three 715 hp BMW 132T radial engines
maximum speed: 168 mph (270 km/h)
maximum range: 795 miles (1,280 km)
armament: one to three 7.92 MG 15 machine guns

The losses suffered by the Luftwaffe of Ju 52s during the invasion of the Netherlands was staggering. Some that were fortunate enough to make a forced landing, such as this Ju 52 (right), which crashed into a greenhouse near Ypenburg, could later be repaired. Others, such as this burnt-out wreck of a Ju 52 (above), were complete write-offs, in many cases losing some or all of their crews and passengers. [Photo AVIODROME Luchtfotografie, Lelystad, Holland]

2,336 servicemen killed. The Dutch ML went to war with 221 aircraft, 139 of which could serve in a combat role; 94 combat aircraft were lost to German aerial bombardment or in combat operations. Yet, though the five days during which the Dutch fought the German invaders to a standstill may have been costly and resulted in the destruction of Rotterdam, they demonstrated a strong Dutch resolve against a foreign invader and dealt the mighty German Luftwaffe and its vaunted airborne forces a critical blow.

The Netherlands may have been occupied, but many Dutchman were determined to oppose the invaders until the latter were expelled from Dutch soil. In the weeks following the Dutch surrender, Frederick Seekatz, the Fokker Company's German sales manager, decided to build a modified D.VII sportsplane as a gift for Hermann Göring. Working from the original D.VII blueprints, Fokker workers went to work on a nearly perfect replica of the plane in which Göring had earned the Pour le Merite. Before the new D.VII was completed, however, the project suddenly came to a halt. As Seekatz looked over the aircraft and its specifications, a rather weighty matter dawned on him: since the D.VII could only accommodate the combined weight of a pilot and parachute at 194 lbs, there was no possible way the corpulent Reichsmarschall could fly the plane. Even if the plane were made to support Göring's weight, the cockpit would have to be substantially widened for him to fit inside. Not even the most creative use of physics could fit someone of Göring's girth into a D.VII, and Seekatz had to cancel the project rather than risk embarrassing the Reichsmarschall. The fact that not one of Fokker's designers or workers mentioned this small oversight is silent testimony to the creative willingness to defy the German occupiers of their homeland. The air war would go on for the Dutch.

Dicke Hermann ("fat Hermann," as many of his troops pejoratively called him) toured the wreckage of the Fokker factory near Schiphol Airport after the Dutch surrender. Göring also toured Rotterdam to observe the swath of destruction caused by his Luftwaffe bombers. [Militair Luchtvaart Museum]

General Kurt Student, commander of the 7. Flieger-Division, and his Fallschrimjäger *troops around Rotterdam, Waalhaven, and Moerdijk played instrumental roles in preventing the airborne part of the German invasion of the Netherlands from becoming a total disaster. Following the Dutch surrender during the afternoon of May 14, he was accidentally shot and wounded by troops of the SS Leibstandarte Adolf Hitler unit who believed that there was Dutch sniper activity in the area. Before he was taken away in an ambulance, he prevented an SS attempted massacre of Dutch troops and civilians, telling the SS men that they were the fools who shot him.* [Deutsches Bundesarchiv via Wikimedia Commons]

An MLD Dornier Do 24 flying boat resting at anchor in the Dutch East Indies. Before the war, one of the perks for ML
KNIL and MLD aircrews was the tropical surroundings in which they served. [Militair Luchtvaart Museum, Soesterberg]

Chapter Eight

A RISING SUN IN ORANGE SKIES

A Good Defense Is a Good Bomber Offense

As war clouds began to gather over Europe in the mid-1930s, they were simultaneously gathering over the Pacific Ocean and Southeast Asia. In 1931 the Japanese invaded and occupied the northern Chinese province of Manchuria, an act that brought widespread international condemnation. In March 1933, Japan withdrew from the League of Nations after the League's refusal to recognize the puppet state of Manchukuo, which was set up by the Japanese in Manchuria. On January 15, 1935, Japan withdrew from the London Naval Conference, which had been established to regulate the size of the world's great navies in an effort to prevent another naval arms race like the one that preceded World War I. Militarists from the army and the navy began to swell the ranks of the Japanese government in the mid-1930s, and the Japanese navy began a new military building program.

A growing Japanese navy meant an increased Japanese need for oil, and that, in turn, began to concern the colonial government of the Dutch East Indies, which was the crown jewel of European colonies in Southeast Asia because it had been the only colony to consistently generate revenue for the home country. In the twentieth century much of that revenue came from the vast oil fields throughout the archipelago. This made the colony a prime target of Japan's industrial and military leaders, especially because Japan had to rely completely on foreign imports of oil. Renewed Japanese aggression against China in 1937 prompted the Dutch to look to increasing its defenses of the East Indies, since it did not take a military expert to realize that it would only be a matter of time before Japanese military aggression would target the resource-rich European colonies in Southeast Asia.

When World War II broke out in Europe on September 1, 1939, the Militair Luchtvaart van het Koninklijk Nederlands-Indisch Leger (Royal Netherlands Indies Army Air Force), or ML-KNIL, did not possess a single modern fighter aircraft. This is somewhat surprising because, as late as 1937, the ML-KNIL was the United States' primary aircraft export customer, though almost all of the American aircraft that the ML-KNIL purchased were all-metal Glenn Martin monoplane bombers. In making those purchases, the leadership of the ML-KNIL was displaying its belief in a concept that was promoted at that same time by the German Luftwaffe: the fast bomber will always get through. The performance of fighter aircraft in service in the mid- to late 1930s gave a degree of credibility to this concept. The German monoplane bombers called *Schnellbombers,* many derived from the designs of cotemporary fast airliners, were just as fast, if not faster, than the fighters of the day. But the Glenn Martin com-

Prewar photo of the oil wells and refinery complexes at Balikpapan on Borneo.

Martin 139 WH-3A
length: 44 ft 9 in (13.6 m)
wingspan: 70 ft 10½ in (21.6 m)
power plant: two 1,200 hp Wright GR-1820-G-102 Cyclone radial engines
maximum speed: 241 mph (388 km/h)
range: 1,250 miles (2,010 km)
ceiling: 28,215 ft (8,600 m)
armament: three 7.62mm machine guns
payload: 4,409 lbs (2,000 kg) of bombs
crew: 3

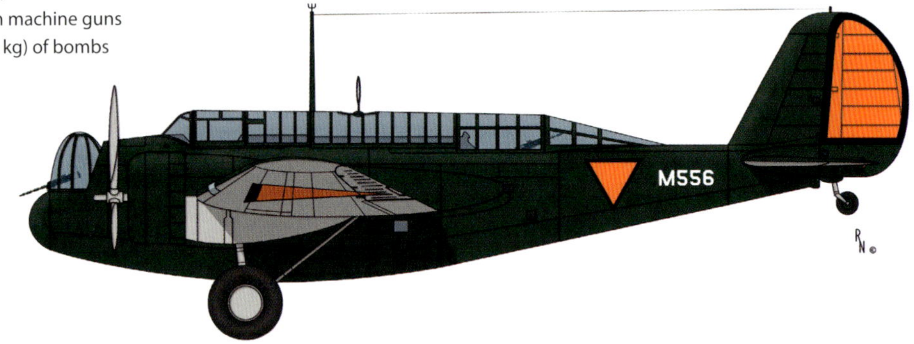

In the mid-1930s, the LA-KNIL embarked upon a purchasing policy of acquiring a large fleet of bombers for the defense of the East Indies at the expense of a balanced air force of fighters and bombers. The logic was that bombers could strike an enemy invasion fleet far off the coast and at the time this decision was made new all-metal twin-engine bombers were almost, if not just, as fast as fighters then in operation. The aircraft chosen for this role was the Martin 139, an export version of the Martin B-10, which was the first all-metal monoplane bomber that was mass-produced for the United States Army Air Corps. By March 1940, the LA-KNIL had acquired one hundred twenty Martin 139s. These bombers served bravely during the East Indies Campaign, but they stood no chance when intercepted by Japanese Zero and Oscar fighters, aircraft that LA-KNIL planners had not anticipated in their prewar planning. The world's only surviving complete B-10 (above) is preserved in the Museum of the United States Air Force in Dayton, Ohio. [Museum of the United States Air Force]

pany in the United States had taken on this modernizing imperative in 1932, even before the Germans did. That year saw the flight of the first prototype of the Martin B-10 all-metal, twin-engine monoplane bomber. The B-10 was the first all-metal bomber acquired in numbers by the United States Army Air Corps, and it had modern features such as enclosed cockpits, rotating gun turrets, retractable landing gear, and an internal bomb bay.

At that time the B-10 was perhaps the most modern military aircraft in the world, with a top speed faster than nearly all contemporary fighters. These qualities did not escape the attention of the leaders of the ML-KNIL. A fast modern bomber with long range would allow Dutch pilots to take the fight to the enemy far out to sea away from the beaches, and the speed of the bomber would allow it to fly unescorted, since it was unlikely that any enemy fighters would be able to catch up with it. Furthermore, this idea was economically appealing to both the ML-KNIL leadership and the Dutch government: with the world in the midst of the Great Depression, fighter aircraft would not have to be purchased, thus keeping defense expenditures down. Although there was an obligation on the part of the ML-KNIL to give Dutch aircraft manufacturers priority in terms of procurement and production, the East Indies air service made an effective argument against doing so in this case. Fokker was in the middle of designing the T.V bomber, and he offered it to the ML-KNIL; but the East Indies leadership rejected the plane because of its partial wood and canvas construction, arguing that the tropical climate of Southeast Asia would cause serious maintenance problems for the T.V. The ML-KNIL insisted on an all-metal bomber suitable for Southeast Asian weather conditions; it also argued that it could not wait for the Fokker factory to re-equip itself for the production of all-metal aircraft. The Dutch government concurred with the ML-KNIL's case and allowed the air arm to place an order with the Glenn Martin company for the B-10.

On February 27, 1936, the ML-KNIL placed an order for seven Martin 139 WH-1s (the export designation of the B-10), and it followed with an order for six more on May 11 of that year—in order to create a full *afdeling*, or squadron. These bombers most likely had two Wright Cyclone G-102 radial engines with 775 horsepower each, giving the bomber a top speed of 217 mph. On March 11, 1937, the Dutch government placed a third order, this one for twenty-six Martin 139 WH-2s, which was a result of the KNIL's worry about increasing international tensions in Asia. The WH-2 variant had two Wright Cyclone G-3 engines with 875 horsepower, bringing the top speed of the plane up to 242 mph, just as fast as most of the Japanese fighters of the time. Though the Dutch were interested in a new Martin design, the 146 (which proved to be a little-altered improvement on the original B-10 design, and since its performance was little better than the B-10s, no contracts were sought and development was canceled), they ordered thirty-nine Martin 139 WH-3s on December 27, 1937, and forty WH-3As on November 17, 1938. The WH-3A, which was the final bomber series purchased by the Dutch from Martin, had two GR1820-G102 radial engines with 1,200 horsepower, which resulted in a top speed of 241 mph and a maximum range, with the addition of an internal bomb-bay tank, of 1,884 miles. The range of this plane was good, but its maximum speed would show its age three years later in combat. All variants included, the ML-KNIL ordered a total of one hundred twenty Martin 139s from the United States, all of which were ready for action in the East Indies by April 1940.[1]

Prewar planning and exercises justified the ML-KNIL's focus on the purchase of bomber aircraft. The ML-KNIL was meant to work in concert with the aircraft and ships of the MLD and Koninklijke Marine. Since the 1920s, the MLD had equipped its reconnaissance flying boats and floatplanes with radios so that information could be immediately passed along to ships, submarines, and air bases. With that intent, the MLD invested heavily in long-range flying boats during the 1930s; they would serve as the eyes of the fleet. Once they spotted an enemy at sea, ships, submarines, and land-based aircraft would then be vectored to the target. The idea was that incoming invasion forces would be struck and turned back before they reached the shores of the archipelago. It was a brilliant strategy, foreshadowing the one that German admirals would later use to great success during the Battle of the Atlantic, when the Luftwaffe's Condor reconnaissance aircraft located British shipping and directed German U-boat wolf packs to their prey. (Unfortunately for the Germans, squabbling between the commanders of the Luftwaffe and the Kriegsmarine kept this sound strategy from being fully implemented.) The Dutch maintained a sizable submarine force in the East Indies early on for that very purpose. Also stationed in the colony was the navy's surface force of light cruisers and destroyers.[2]

Fighters, Fighters, Fighters!

As the war in Europe progressed, the idea that "the bomber will always get through" was shot down, particularly in the skies over southern England during the Battle of Britain in the summer of 1940. Germany's *Schnellbombers* (most of which had been designed shortly after the ML-KNIL's Martin 139s had been) were being driven out of the skies in droves, especially when there was no adequate accompanying fighter cover. This led the leadership of the ML-KNIL to reevaluate its aerial strategy for the defense of the East Indies. The only fighters in

In 1936 the MLD looked for a replacement for the Dornier Wals in the East Indies and settled on a new long-range flying boat design being developed by Dornier. The Dutch government demanded that the MLD's new aircraft be built in the Netherlands, and the MLD arranged a license production contract with Dornier. The Do 24 would be built by Aviolanda and De Schelde, the only aircraft builders in the Netherlands at the time with experience in all-metal construction. While these companies prepared for production, which began in the Netherlands in March 1938, the first thirty Do 24s were built in Germany. Only seven Aviolanda-built Do 24s were completed before May 10, 1940. This photo (below left) shows a Do 24 taxiing off the coast of Scheveningen on September 3, 1938, during a naval review celebrating the fortieth anniversary of the coronation of Queen Wilhelmina. This surviving Do 24 in MLD colors (below right) is preserved at the Nationaal Militair Museum in Soest. [Militair Luchtvaart Museum, Soesterberg]

Dornier Do 24K
length: 72 ft 2 in (22 m)
wingspan: 88 ft 6 in (27 m)
power plant: three Wright R-1820-F52 Cyclone radial engines
maximum speed: 190 mph (306 km/h)
range: 2,048 miles (3,300 km)
ceiling: 17,390 ft (5,300 m)
armament: two 7.92mm machine guns, one 20mm cannon
payload: 1,320 lbs (600 kg) of bombs
crew: 3-4

Curtiss-Wright CW-21B
length: 26 ft 4 in (8 m)
wingspan: 35 ft (10.7 m)
power plant: 1,000 hp Wright R-1820-G5 Cyclone radial engine
maximum speed: 333 mph (536 km/h)
range: 630 miles (1,014 km)
ceiling: 34,300 ft (10,455 m)
armament: four 7.7mm machine guns
crew: 1

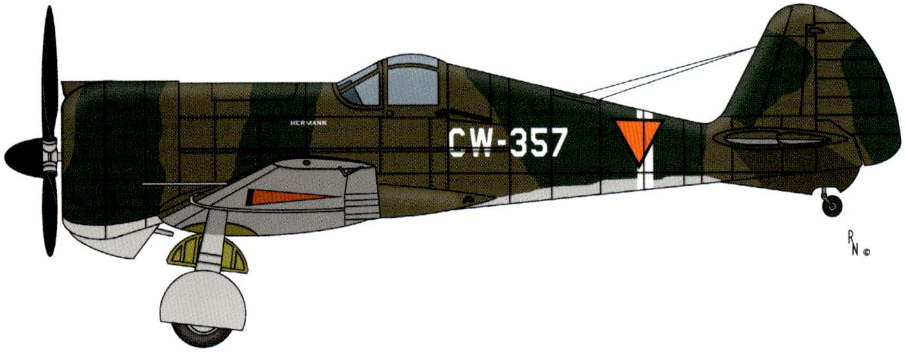

The Curtiss-Wright CW-21B Demon, *developed as a private venture of the Curtiss-Wright company for export, was a lightweight fighter that had a very rapid rate of climb. It was not intended as a dogfighter but rather as a bomber interceptor that could quickly reach formations and make quick diving attacks, hence the aircraft's title, the "Mile-a-Minute Interceptor." The CW-21B was much lighter and did not have the armored protection of a conventional dogfighter, but neither would the Japanese fighters it would face in combat in late 1941 and early 1942. Nevertheless, in tests the CW-21B turned out to be a superb dogfighter due to its light weight. The 24 CW-21Bs that saw service in the East Indies were originally intended for the ML in the Netherlands, but they would not have arrived there before the* Meidagen, *so they were shipped from the United States to the colony.*

service in the East Indies at the time of the purchase of the Martins were the eight Curtiss P-6s that were put into service in 1930, and those obsolete machines were scrapped in 1938 due to a shortage of pilots; by that time, pilots were needed to fly the newly acquired bombers. In the mid- to late 1930s the ML-KNIL leadership had been somewhat justified in its strategy of a defense based on land-based fast bombers. The emergence of the German *Schnellbombers,* such as the Heinkel He 111 and the Dornier Do 17, had demonstrated during combat in the Spanish Civil War that these aircraft could accurately attack their targets and then speed away from any pursuing fighters. The fighters that took part in the Spanish Civil War were predominantly biplanes such as the Heinkel He 51, Fiat CR.32, and Polikarpov I-15, whose top speeds were less than or equal to the German *Schnellbombers.* Only the Messerschmitt Bf 109D could top 300 mph. Most of the Japanese aircraft of the mid- to late 1930s fell into the same category as the biplanes flying over Spain, while the few monoplanes that were introduced at the end of the decade did not match the performance of their European contemporaries.

But while the Spanish Civil War raged, a new generation of high-speed, low-wing monoplane fighters were finishing their prototype phases and coming into production—just as World War II was about to begin. Fighters such as the Supermarine Spitfire, the Messerschmitt Bf 109E, and the Dewoitine D.520 all represented a dramatic leap forward in the performance and effectiveness of the fighter, a leap that was not anticipated by the strategists who had become reliant on the *Schnellbomber* strategy during the interwar period. Fortunately for the ML-KNIL, after the occupation of the Netherlands the East Indies government inherited the contracts made by the Dutch home government. On June 3, 1940, the East Indies government took over the ML's contract for the twenty-four Curtiss-Wright CW-21B Demons, which had been ordered just before the *Meidagen.* They were shipped to the East Indies in late 1940 and assembled at Andir airbase in February 1941. There they formed the 2e Afdeling (2VLG-IV) of IVe Vliegtuiggroep on March 1, 1941. Although the planes had an adequate top speed and the armament of four 7.7mm Colt machine guns, and an excellent rate of climb, the other features of the aircraft were the bare minimum: extra fuel tanks were decided against; there was no bullet-proof glass and no self-sealing fuel tanks; and the radio transmitter was extremely basic. Nonetheless, with every other Allied power trying to purchase American aircraft for their own air forces, the Dutch could not be overly picky as to what was offered to them.[3]

The ML-KNIL actually had another Curtiss-Wright fighter at its disposal prior to the arrival of the CW-21Bs. In 1939, the Koninklijke Marine was growing concerned about the lack of fighters in the archipelago. Several cases in the Spanish Civil War had shown that antiaircraft fire could not, by itself, deter incoming bombers from attacking ships and naval facilities. To appease the navy, the East Indies government ordered twenty Curtiss H75A-7 Hawk fighters in September 1939, which were to be used primarily for the defense of Soerabaya, the main Dutch naval base in the colony. The ML-KNIL leadership was not particularly ecstatic about the purchase. The Hawk was the best American aircraft available for purchase at that time, and it was of all-metal construction; but it was anything but revolutionary when compared to the fighters under development and production in Germany and Great Britain. The Hawk was powered by a 1,200-horsepower Cyclone engine, giving the plane a top speed of 322 mph, and it was armed with four 7.7mm machine guns. Dutch pilots were not enthusiastic about the aircraft's performance because the engine tended to stall during inverted aerobatic maneuvers. Lieutenant General Ludolph van Oyen, commander of the ML-KNIL, had wanted a twin-engine, heavily armed, long-range *jachtkruiser* similar to the Fokker G.1 that had been acquired by the LVA. A twin-engine heavy fighter would have had the range to escort bombers out to sea and could have acted offensively in their own right. But the fall of the Netherlands meant that no such aircraft would be coming from the mother country, and there were no similar types available on the foreign market; so the ML-KNIL had to content itself with its Curtiss Hawks.[4]

The final fighter that the ML-KNIL acquired in some quantity before the beginning of the war in the Pacific was the Brewster B-339 Buffalo. It was similar to the other American fighters in the ML-KNIL inventory at that time: a mediocre and outclassed performer that was available for export sales. Although it was hardly a desirable purchase, the Dutch needed fighters, and even securing an order for this obsolete aircraft was a significant and difficult task. The purchasing commission of the ML-KNIL in the United States was up against stiff competition from the British, who also were trying to purchase any available aircraft for use throughout its empire. The Buffalo turned out to be a difficult plane to purchase for the ML-KNIL. The Netherlands Purchasing Commission in the United States knew that, prior to the German invasion, Belgium had ordered thirty-nine B-339s from Brewster, and since the Belgians had capitulated, the Dutch believed

The Curtiss Hawk 75 was the first all-metal monoplane fighter acquired by the LA-KNIL and the first new fighter in the East Indies since the Curtiss P-6 biplanes of 1932. The LA-KNIL ordered twenty of the fighters in October 1939 after belatedly realizing that its all-bomber policy of a few years earlier was about to be negated by a recent surge in fighter development in Europe and the United States. The Hawk 75 was obsolete by European standards in 1939, but it was available for purchase, and the LA-KNIL leadership assumed (incorrectly) that it would be more than a match for Japanese fighters. Heavy use of the Hawk 75s in training missions in 1940 and 1941 took a toll on their engines, and by the time the war in the Pacific began, only sixteen were operational. This surviving Curtiss Hawk (below left) is housed in the Museum of the United States Air Force.

Curtiss Hawk 75A-7
length: 28 ft 6 in (8.7 m)
wingspan: 37 ft 4 in (11.4 m)
power plant: 1,200 hp Wright R-1820-G205A Cyclone radial engine
maximum speed: 322 mph (519 km/h)
range: 650 miles (1,046 km)
ceiling: 32,350 ft (9,860 m)
armament: four 7.7mm machine guns
crew: 1

that they could assume the Belgian order, in addition to thirty-three airframes for which they already had engines. This request was denied by the Allied Joint Aircraft Committee, which determined the priority of aircraft orders for the various Allied parties (six B-339s were granted to the French, and thirty-three to the British), and several further requests for seventy-two B-339s were also denied.

Finally, a Dutch request, made on October 28, 1940, for seventy-two B-339 airframes without engines was approved, and the Dutch had engines from the thirty-one 1,100-horsepower Cyclone engines that the MLD already possessed and fifty-four 1,200-horsepower Cyclones from Brewster, which they had obtained secondhand from Trans World Airlines. The B-339s were delivered in the spring of 1941 to Java, where they were assembled at Andir. The Dutch ground crews at Andir addressed several of the shortcomings of the Buffalo. They installed armor plating around the fuel tanks and the pilot's seat, while they remedied the lack of self-sealing fuel tanks by encasing the tanks in latex rubber. Fuel and ammunition were reduced to offset the increase in weight caused by these defensive measures, but with two 30-caliber and two 50-caliber machine guns and a reasonable top speed of 321 mph, the Dutch Buffalos were made into respectable fighters.[5]

The ungainly looking Brewster F2A Buffalo became the United States Navy's first monoplane carrier-based fighter, originally beating out the early prototypes of Grumman's F4F Wildcat in a competition in late 1937. By 1940 the Buffalo was clearly obsolescent compared to later prototypes of the Wildcat, and Brewster's fighter became a second-tier product that could be sold only to foreign purchasers. Initially unable to obtain anything better during its tardy fighter buildup, the ML-KNIL purchased and received seventy-one Brewster B-339s (the Buffalo's export designation) before the war in the Pacific began, making it the most numerous Dutch fighter in the Indies. While the Buffalo could hold its own against the Japanese Ki-27 and Ki-43 army fighters, it was ill-equipped to deal with the Japanese navy's Zero fighters and its elite pilots.

The Blinding Glare of the Rising Sun

The Japanese had looked to the Dutch East Indies as early as the beginning of the twentieth century as a source of natural resources to feed Japan's rapid and insatiable industrialization process. Like the great industrial powers of Europe, Japan sought to create a colonial empire that would provide the raw materials necessary for expanding domestic industry. With most of Asia already divided among European powers, the Japanese could look only to China as a potential target for imperial reach—or they would have to confront the Europeans. Since the East Indies was one of the wealthiest colonies in Southeast Asia, and possessed many of the natural resources that the Japanese home islands lacked, conflict with the Dutch became inevitable in the minds of Japan's strategic military planners. The Dutch surmised that Japanese espionage had begun in the East Indies already before the beginning of World War I, when Japanese workers, particularly photographers and fishermen, began to migrate to economically unprofitable yet militarily strategic regions of the archipelago. The KNIL became aware of Japanese espionage activities in the Indies as early as 1907, and in response to these growing encroachments, the colonial administration founded the Politieke Inlichtigendienst (Political Intelligence Service) in 1916. In the years following World War I, several other Dutch counterintelligence organizations were established in the Indies, including Section I of the Koninklijke Marine, Section VII of the KNIL, and the Kantoor voor Oost-Aziatische Zaken (Bureau of East Asian Affairs). Prior to the outbreak of World War II in the Pacific, these organizations had succeeded in breaking several Japanese diplomatic codes.[6]

During the 1930s, several hundred Japanese fishing boats, some acting as surveillance and reconnaissance vessels for the Imperial Japanese Navy, operated throughout the archipelago, making depth soundings and charting waterways, beaches, and naval facilities. Numerous Japanese boats were intercepted by MLD flying boats and patrol boats. The MLD occasionally found suspicious material aboard the boats, and in some instances the Japanese crews attempted to escape from or fire on their pursuers. The Japanese also used commercial fronts to cover up their espionage activities. The Nanyo Kohatsu Kabushiki Kaisha (South Seas Development Company) was a trading company established throughout the East Indies during the 1930s that received direct patronage and agents from the Japanese navy. In mid-1941, the government-owned airline Dai Nippon Kōkū Kabushiki Kaisha (Greater Japan Airways) opened a route from Palau to Portuguese Timor, and its aircraft coincidentally flew over a good portion of the East Indies. Not surpris-

This replica of Lieutenant Gerardus Bruggink's B-339C is housed in the Nationaal Militair Museum in Soest.

Brewster B-339D
length: 26 ft 4 in (8 m)
wingspan: 35 ft (10.7 m)
power plant: 1,200 hp Wright R-1820-40 Cyclone radial engine
maximum speed: 321 mph (517 km/h)
range: 965 miles (1,554 km)
ceiling: 33,200 ft (10,600 m)
armament: two 12.7mm and two 7.7mm machine guns
crew: 1

A Kawanishi H6K2 Mavis flying boat of the Japanese government-owned Dai Nippon Kōkū Kabushiki Kaisha airline off Portuguese Timor in early 1941. Navy photo reconnaissance equipment was fitted into these airliners and they extensively photographed areas of the Dutch East Indies while on their "civil" flights between Palau and Timor. On one occasion Portuguese customs officers discovered reconnaissance cameras in one of these aircraft. Well before the war in the Pacific began, the Dutch knew the Japanese were photographing their military bases. [Museum of the United States Air Force]

Admiral Osami Nagano, commander of the Japanese Naval General Staff, who calculated that the capture of the oilfields in the Dutch East Indies was necessary not only for Japanese military expansionism but for the survival of its military and domestic industry as well in the light of American, British, and Dutch oil embargoes against Japan beginning in mid-1941. The Dutch oil embargo was particularly harsh for the Japanese army and navy air forces as 86 percent of Dutch-produced aviation fuel was purchased by Japan.

ingly, Portuguese customs agents found military reconnaissance equipment aboard the Japanese flying boats; but the aircrews claimed that the "cargo" had been mixed up on departure. Japanese army and navy agents were also sent to the East Indies under cover as employees of legitimate businesses such as the Mitsui Industrial Concern and Kubota and Company. By the opening of World War II in the Pacific, the Dutch East Indies was thoroughly infested with Japanese spies.[7] Japan began to make demands for further oil concessions from the Dutch during the summer of 1940, after the Netherlands had surrendered to Germany. This reinforced the idea among the leadership of the air, land, and naval forces in the East Indies that increased defensive measures had to be pursued, especially since no further assistance could now be offered from the homeland.

The planning for a Japanese invasion of the Dutch East Indies began in April 1941, when Admiral Osami Nagano took command of the Japanese Naval General Staff. Nagano was a supporter of Japanese expansion into Southeast Asia, particularly the Dutch East Indies. Nagano did not want the navy to have to depend on a foreign power for oil. He did not wish to attack the United States, but was eventually convinced to do so by Admiral Isoroku Yamamoto. The catalyst that set in motion the Japanese planning for an invasion of the Dutch East Indies came at the end of July 1941. Since the summer of 1940, Japan had forced the Vichy French to allow the Japanese to make use of airfields in northern French Indochina, which could be used to support the Japanese southern front in China. In the summer of 1941, Japan insisted on sending troops through Indochina. Since this was a blatant act of aggression against a Western power, and it posed a threat to the operation of the Burma Road, the United States declared an oil embargo against Japan, and the British and the Dutch followed suit. This was a crippling blow to a nation engaged in a large war in China, one whose navy (the third largest in the world) and large air forces were absolutely dependent on foreign oil imports. Nagano realized that, if the situation was not remedied, Japan's oil reserve could fuel their armed forces under wartime requirements for only a further eighteen months. That realization caused the Japanese high command to put its war plans into immediate motion.

Nagano's plan for the conquest of Southeast Asia through joint army and navy operations would take place in three stages: the first stage would be attacks on the Philippines, Malaya, Borneo, Celebes, and Sumatra; the second stage would be the encirclement and conquest of Java; and the third stage was the conquest of Burma.[8] The Japanese Imperial Army's contribution to the invasion of the Dutch East Indies was primarily the Sixteenth Army, under General Hitoshi Imamura, and the Special Naval Landing Force of the Southern Expeditionary Army, under General Count Hisaichi Terauchi. The primary targets of the Japanese invasion were the major oil fields on Borneo and Sumatra. Perhaps the most important objective was the refineries of the Bataafsche Petroleum Maatschappij and the Nederlandsch Koloniale Petroleum Maatschappij at Pladjoe (near Palembang) in Sumatra, which were the largest source of aviation fuel produced in the Far East. Although Dutch aviation fuel was sold throughout Southeast Asia, the Japanese were responsible for the purchase of nearly 86 percent of the fuel produced in the Dutch refineries in 1939 alone. This percentage increased up until the embargo, and it represented Japan's dependency on not only the crude oil in the Dutch East Indies but on its manufacturing and refining infrastructure as well.[9]

Preparations for the Coming Storm

Although the Dutch maintained a polite façade toward their trade agreements with the Japanese up until the oil embargo, there was now little doubt as to what Japan's ultimate intentions for the islands were, should the opportunity arise.[10] Since there was very little intelligence sharing among the Americans, British, French, and Australians in the Pacific, the Dutch had to interpret Japanese intentions by themselves up until a few weeks before the attack on Pearl Harbor. When a Dutch intelligence officer visited Singapore in January 1941, the British officers present were very impressed with the extent of Dutch decryption of Japanese codes. But the British high command refused to work together with the Dutch; instead, they allowed only selected information to be passed on to the Dutch. Within the Indies, however, Governor-General Jonkheer Alidius W. L. Tjarda van Starkenborgh Stachouwer did not allow Dutch intelligence services to send spies to Japan or to work freely with other foreign intelligence services because of the state of neutrality that officially existed between the Netherlands and Japan (and also because the Dutch were decrypting Allied and other neutral nations' codes as well as those of the Japanese).[11]

Excessive espionage activity in the East Indies was not the only indicator to the Dutch that the Japanese were planning eventual military action in the Pacific. The KNIL had its own organization of cryptanalysts, known as Kamer 14, at the army's headquarters under the command of Lieutenant Colonel J. A. Verkuyl. During the late 1930s, Kamer 14 was able to break the Japanese Red diplomatic code, the J-19 consular code, and the JN-25 naval code. Kamer 14 also intercepted and decoded a Japanese diplomatic message, the infamous *Higashi No Kaze Ame* (or East Winds Rain message) in early December 1941, declaring the execution of hostilities in the Pacific, though the exact locations were not mentioned. The message was passed on to the Americans, who did not take it seriously.

The Americans may have failed to act on the secret message passed along to them by the Dutch, but the ML-KNIL likewise failed to respond to a vital piece of information it received from the Americans. During the summer of 1941, while on a visit to China, General Henry B. Clagett, the commander of the American Army Air Force in the Philippines, was shown technical data about the new Japanese Zero fighter, which had been analyzed by the Chinese after they had shot down two of the fighters. Clagett then went to Java in August 1941 and met with the commander of the ML-KNIL, Maj. Gen. van Oyen. It is thought that Clagett shared the information on the revolutionary new fighter with van Oyen; even so, for some reason Dutch pilots knew nothing about the aircraft's existence until they met it in combat in the skies over the East Indies. By that time the capabilities of the Zero came as a nasty shock to Dutch airmen.[12]

Although the Dutch did not want to unnecessarily antagonize the Japanese, they began a series of defense talks with the British in Singapore to discuss mutual assistance in the event of military aggression. The United States and Australia were eventually also drawn into these talks, which laid the groundwork for potential Allied cooperation, should war in the Pacific break out. Unfortunately for the Dutch, when the war in the Pacific did begin, their integrated defensive plans were cast aside by the creation of the American-British-Dutch-Australian Command (ABDACOM). The Americans and the British insisted on a unified Allied command organization in an attempt to stem the Japanese advance into the South Pacific. Although it sounded like a reasonable plan in theory, what it did in reality was place all Allied units under de facto American and British command. Not a single Dutch officer was placed in a position to influence naval or aerial policy. ABDACOM naval forces were placed under the command of American Admiral Thomas Hart; air forces were put under British Air Marshal Sir Richard Peirse; and the role of supreme commander of ABDACOM was given to British General Sir Archibald Wavell, with American Lieutenant General George Brett as deputy commander. The only Dutchman to receive any command position of note in the beginning was Lieutenant General Hein ter Poorten, commander of the KNIL, who was given command of the ABDA ground forces.

This lack of adequate representation within the ABDACOM did not sit well with Dutch military and colonial officials. The Dutch maintained the largest air, sea, and land forces in the theater, and much of the future fighting was going to take place within their territory. Admiral Conrad Helfrich of the navy and Maj. Gen. van Oyen of the ML-KNIL were particularly frustrated with the situation. Not only did they not have direct command over their respective forces, but different languages used within the ABDACOM caused delays in sending and re-

Small Japanese fishing boats off the coast near Batavia, photographed by the Dutch destroyer Kortenaer, *whose sailors are preparing to inspect the smaller vessels. Operating from larger mother ships, Japanese "fishing" craft charted and photographed the numerous beaches and inlets of the main islands in the Dutch archipelago for potential beachheads for amphibious landings.* [Netherlands Institute of Military History]

ceiving critical messages. The British were quick to dictate their policies to the Dutch air forces, ignoring the comprehensive defense planning made by the Dutch before the war. As a result of the directives of ABDACOM, Dutch ships and submarines frequently found themselves "blind"—without their accompanying aerial reconnaissance. Although individual national forces were given a degree of latitude within which they could interpret orders and operate, the bulky command structure did much to hamper an effective Allied defense of the East Indies.[13]

Two major breaches in British security further undermined the aerial defense of Singapore and the Malay Peninsula, to which the ML-KNIL had committed itself as part of the ABDACOM agreements. On November 11, 1940, the converted German merchant raider *Atlantis* attacked and sank the British merchant ship *Automedon* in the Indian Ocean. Before the *Automedon* sank, a boarding party from the *Atlantis* found a British War Cabinet report that the British crew had been unable to throw over the side of the ship. The report outlined the defensive weaknesses of the air and ground forces in Singapore and Malaya, and it also said that necessary reinforcements could not be forthcoming due to the need for equipment in Europe and the Middle East. On December 5, the *Atlantis* sailed into Tokyo and relayed the British report to Berlin. On Hitler's orders, the German naval attaché in Tokyo passed this information on to the Japanese. This gave Japanese war planners a full year to take into account the British weaknesses in Southeast Asia as they calculated their strategies for the conquest of Southeast Asia.

Of greater danger to the aerial defense of the Malay Peninsula was the presence of a Japanese agent serving in

The supreme commander of the tardily organized and largely ineffective ABDACOM (American-British-Dutch-Australian Command), General Sir Archibald Wavell (fourth from the left), arriving at Kemajoran Airport near Batavia at the beginning of 1942. Wavell was an able commander; unfortunately, he had to cope with commands that encompassed vast areas with few troops and little equipment. As British commander in the Middle East in late 1940 and early 1941, he led British forces to victory over the Italians in Libya and Ethiopia but was defeated by Rommel when he was forced to deplete his command to bolster the attempted British defense of Greece and Crete. Here in East Asia he was again given the task of defending a large theater with few resources at hand. [Netherlands Institute of Military History]

Lieutenant General Hein ter Poorten, commander of the KNIL and also commander of all ABDA ground forces. With only 75,000 troops in the KNIL, the effective defense of the entire archipelago would be hopeless without substantial reinforcements from the other Allied powers.

one of the British Royal Air Force's intelligence sections in Malaya. Captain Patrick Heenan was a mixed-race New Zealander who was a strong believer in the Irish Republican cause and thus an enemy of Great Britain. He was recruited by the Japanese between 1938 and 1939 and was responsible for passing along sensitive information about the RAF to his handlers. From the time of his recruitment until a few weeks before the beginning of the war in the Pacific, Heenan relayed information about the numbers and dispersal of RAF aircraft via a hidden radio transmitter. From these details, the Japanese were able to determine that they outnumbered the British at least two to one and that all of the British aircraft in the theater were largely obsolete.[14] This information only encouraged the Japanese to further accelerate their timetable for the invasion of Southeast Asia.

The MLD Draws First Blood

When the Japanese attacked Pearl Harbor on December 7, 1941, most of the Japanese Imperial Navy's major warships either were involved in the attack on Hawaii or were covering the Japanese army invasion of Malaya because of the presence of a powerful British surface force based in Singapore. Initially, the first Japanese ships to operate in the waters of the Indies were cruisers and destroyers, as anticipated by Dutch prewar military planners. These Japanese surface groups were deprived of carrier-based air cover; but they were accompanied by a number of seaplane tenders, which carried floatplane fighters and reconnaissance aircraft. The Mitsubishi F1M "Pete" floatplane fighter, based aboard the Japanese seaplane tenders, was a surprisingly maneuverable plane that be-

Major General Ludolph van Oyen, commander of the ML-KNIL. Van Oyen had the unenviable task of defending the skies over the Indies archipelago with a force of obsolete bombers, three different types of second-line American fighters, and many raw pilot recruits who were forced to undergo accelerated training.

Vice-Admiral Conrad E. L. Helfrich (center) shown here with his Allied counterparts, British Vice-Admiral Sir Geoffrey Layton (left) and American Admiral Thomas Hart (right). ABDACOM's multinational naval force of cruisers, destroyers, and submarines was outmatched compared to the number of ships the Japanese would eventually muster for the invasion of the Dutch East Indies. Furthermore the Japanese could use uniform and well-honed tactics, whereas the separate Allied nationalities all had their own unique methods of operations. Helfrich resented British and American meddling in Dutch naval operations as it interfered with prewar sea and air coordination strategies between the Koninklijke Marine and the MLD.

Opposite Page *Indies Airfields Map*

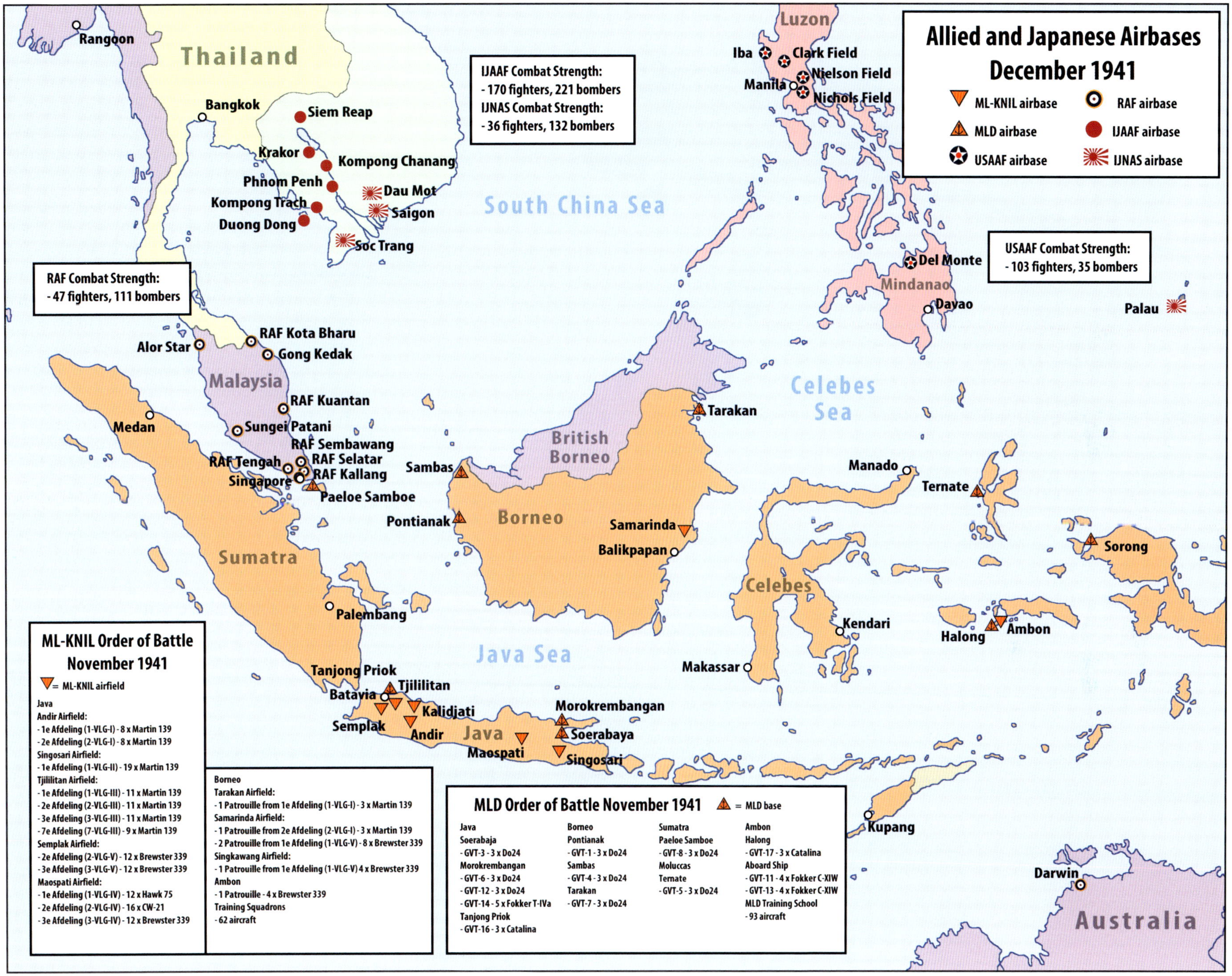

Allied and Japanese Airbases December 1941
ML-KNIL airbase
RAF airbase
MLD airbase
IJAAF airbase
USAAF airbase
IJNAS airbase
IJAAF Combat Strength:
- 170 fighters, 221 bombers
IJNAS Combat Strength:
- 36 fighters, 132 bombers
RAF Combat Strength:
- 47 fighters, 111 bombers
USAAF Combat Strength:
- 103 fighters, 35 bombers
Rangoon
Thailand
Bangkok
Siem Reap
Krakor
Kompong Chanang
Phnom Penh
Dau Mot
Kompong Trach
Saigon
Duong Dong
Soc Trang
Luzon
Iba
Clark Field
Nielson Field
Manila
Nichols Field
South China Sea
Del Monte
Mindanao
Davao
Palau
Alor Star
RAF Kota Bharu
Gong Kedak
Malaysia
RAF Kuantan
Sungei Patani
RAF Sembawang
RAF Tengah
RAF Selatar
Singapore
RAF Kallang
Paeloe Samboe
Medan
Sambas
Pontianak
British Borneo
Borneo
Tarakan
Celebes Sea
Samarinda
Balikpapan
Manado
Ternate
Sorong
Sumatra
Celebes
Palembang
Kendari
Halong
Ambon
Java Sea
Makassar
Tanjong Priok
Tjililitan
Batavia
Kalidjati
Semplak
Andir
Java
Morokrembangan
Soerabaya
Maospati
Singosari
Kupang
Darwin
Australia
ML-KNIL Order of Battle November 1941
= ML-KNIL airfield
Java
Andir Airfield:
- 1e Afdeling (1-VLG-I) - 8 x Martin 139
- 2e Afdeling (2-VLG-I) - 8 x Martin 139
Singosari Airfield:
- 1e Afdeling (1-VLG-II) - 19 x Martin 139
Tjililitan Airfield:
- 1e Afdeling (1-VLG-III) - 11 x Martin 139
- 2e Afdeling (2-VLG-III) - 11 x Martin 139
- 3e Afdeling (3-VLG-III) - 11 x Martin 139
- 7e Afdeling (7-VLG-III) - 9 x Martin 139
Semplak Airfield:
- 2e Afdeling (2-VLG-V) - 12 x Brewster 339
- 3e Afdeling (3-VLG-V) - 12 x Brewster 339
Maospati Airfield:
- 1e Afdeling (1-VLG-IV) - 12 x Hawk 75
- 2e Afdeling (2-VLG-IV) - 16 x CW-21
- 3e Afdeling (3-VLG-IV) - 12 x Brewster 339
Borneo
Tarakan Airfield:
- 1 Patrouille from 1e Afdeling (1-VLG-I) - 3 x Martin 139
Samarinda Airfield:
- 1 Patrouille from 2e Afdeling (2-VLG-I) - 3 x Martin 139
- 2 Patrouille from 1e Afdeling (1-VLG-V) - 8 x Brewster 339
Singkawang Airfield:
- 1 Patrouille from 1e Afdeling (1-VLG-V) 4 x Brewster 339
Ambon
- 1 Patrouille - 4 x Brewster 339
Training Squadrons
- 62 aircraft
MLD Order of Battle November 1941
= MLD base
Java
Soerabaja
- GVT-3 - 3 x Do24
Morokrembangan
- GVT-6 - 3 x Do24
- GVT-12 - 3 x Do24
- GVT-14 - 5 x Fokker T-IVa
Tanjong Priok
- GVT-16 - 3 x Catalina
Borneo
Pontianak
- GVT-1 - 3 x Do24
Sambas
- GVT-4 - 3 x Do24
Tarakan
- GVT-7 - 3 x Do24
Sumatra
Paeloe Samboe
- GVT-8 - 3 x Do24
Moluccas
Ternate
- GVT-5 - 3 x Do24
Ambon
Halong
- GVT-17 - 3 x Catalina
Aboard Ship
- GVT-11 - 4 x Fokker C-XIW
- GVT-13 - 4 x Fokker C-XIW
MLD Training School
- 93 aircraft

The most feared opponent of Dutch fighter pilots was the Mitsubishi A6M2 "Zero" fighter. While it was a very maneuverable fighter with a powerful armament of two machine guns and two 20mm cannon, the most lethal feature of the Zeros was its pilots; Japanese naval aviators were among the most highly trained and experienced combat pilots in the world at the time, and they were well-versed in exploiting the Zero's strengths against their opponents. This Zero is preserved in the Museum of the United States Air Force. [Museum of the United States Air Force]

came a dangerous opponent for the Dutch Martin bombers. On the other hand, their performance could not match that of the Dutch land-based fighters. What the Dutch did not anticipate in the ensuing Japanese attack on the East Indies was a new generation of land-based fighters and bombers with exceptionally long range. The Japanese committed the 11th Air Fleet to the East Indies campaign; it was made up of 430 modern aircraft based in Indochina, Formosa, and Palau.

The eventual appearance of these aircraft over the Indies in large numbers was an unexpected and demoralizing shock to the Dutch. The Imperial Japanese Navy's Mitsubishi A6M "Zero," with its armament of two 7.7mm machine guns and two 20mm cannons, had a top speed of 331 mph, and its maximum range of 1,930 miles made it the deadliest fighter in the Pacific at the time. The plane also had a level of maneuverability which was virtually unknown to European aircraft designers. But it came at a price: the Zero's maneuverability and long range was a result of very lightweight construction, virtually no armor protection, and no self-sealing fuel tanks. In the early days of the war, however, the extensive training of the Zero pilots and the combat experience they gained over China negated the aircraft's deficiencies.

For bombers, the Japanese navy deployed its Mitsubishi G3M "Nell" and G4M "Betty" long-range bombers. The Nell had a maximum speed of 232 mph, a bomb load of 1,764 pounds, and a maximum range of 2,722 miles. The performance of the Nell, which was designed in 1933, only exceeded that of the Dutch Martin in range; but range was an extremely crucial factor in the upcoming campaign. The more modern Betty, designed in 1937, had a maximum speed of 266 mph, a bomb load of 1,764 lbs, and a maximum range of 3,749 miles. Both bombers achieved their incredible range the same way the Zero did: little armor protection and no self-sealing fuel tanks, in addition to a rather light bomb load compared to other bombers of similar size. For reconnaissance, the Japanese navy depended on the Kawanishi H6K "Mavis," a large four-engine flying boat with a range of 3,779 miles. At the beginning of hostilities, the Imperial Japanese Army committed its 3rd Air Division, made up of 465 aircraft, in Malaya. Although the Japanese army's aircraft did not have the same long-range capabilities of the navy's planes, these aircraft would be within range of the East Indies as air bases were eventually acquired in Malaya. At the beginning of the war in the Pacific, the Dutch were initially pitted against nearly 1,000 Japanese aircraft, thus being outnumbered roughly five to one.[15]

The first blood the Dutch drew in the war in the Pacific was accomplished by a Do 24 X-25 of the MLD. On December 9, 1941, the X-25 was called in over the Bourgainville Strait off New Guinea, and it dropped four 100-pound bombs, sinking the schooner *Koukoku Maru,* which was towing a small convoy of sailboats. Another MLD Do 24, the X-22, apparently claimed the first Dutch aerial kill of the war when the plane's 20mm turret gunner shot down a Nell over Sumatra. Things continued to go well for the MLD when the Do 24s of GVT.7, operating out of Tarakan on December 17, intercepted Japanese ships off the coast of British Borneo. The X-32 spotted what appeared to be a cruiser and attacked with its six 500-pound bombs from 15,000 feet. Five of the bombs were released with two hitting the warship and two just missing. At some point afterward, a huge explosion erupted from the stern of the ship and she sank in five minutes. It is thought that the lone Dutch flying boat had sunk the Fubuki-class destroyer *Shinonome* from high altitude, an exceptional feat.[16]

The MLD did not stay solely on the defensive for long, but rather plotted an offensive strike against the Japanese. Adm. Helfrich decided to launch an air strike against the port of Davao in the southern Philippines, which was occupied by the Japanese on December 20. The Japanese presence there posed a threat to the eastern islands of the Indies. In preparation for the strike, the three Do 24s of GVT.2, under the command of First Lieutenant W. J. Reijnierse, were ordered to proceed to the small seaplane base of Kalkas on Lake Tondano, on the far northeastern tip of Celebes; meanwhile, the Do 24s of GVT.5, under First Lieutenant Hugo V. B. Burgerhout, were sent to the island of Talisei, directly north of Lake Tondano. During the night of December 22-23, the flying boats were fueled and armed. GVT.2 took off at 3:00 a.m., and GVT.5 was ordered to take off a half hour later so that both groups would arrive over Davao within five minutes of each other and attack in two separate waves. En route to the target the aircraft of GVT.5 experienced heavy clouds, which broke up the formation, and the pilots were forced to find their way by instruments alone.

At about 6:00 a.m., just outside Davao, X-27 and X-30 located each other, but X-26 was nowhere to be found. Burgerhout decided to press on with the attack anyway, and as they approached the harbor, the Dutch crews spotted a large number of ships and flying boats. X-27 made its attack run against nine Mavis flying boats moored near the shore and damaged a number of them. X-30 bombed a warehouse complex and left the target and its surrounding docks exploding in flames. A Pete floatplane, which was part of a group flying cover over the harbor, attacked the X-27, filling its hull and fuel tanks with bullet holes; the X-27, in return fire, damaged the Pete's center float, and the floatplane capsized on landing. As X-27 and X-30 were making their departure under fire, X-26, the lost sheep of GVT.5, flew past and made an unsuccessful bombing run on a light cruiser before retiring.

A Mitsubishi G3M "Nell" bomber of the Imperial Japanese Navy preparing for takeoff on a bombing mission. The Nell's range of over 2,700 miles gave the Japanese the ability to strike at Dutch targets from far-off bases early in the East Indies Campaign before the Japanese were able to capture airfields in the Indies. However, that range was achieved due to minimal protection for the crew and a lower payload. [Museum of the United States Air Force]

The 2,050-ton Fubuki-class destroyer Shinonome, ***supposedly sunk after taking two bomb hits from Do 24 X-32 on December 17, 1941. The precise circumstances surrounding the destruction of the*** Shinonome ***are not exactly known (she was also attacked by Dutch Martin bombers) but she was hit by bombs from the Dutch flying boat and sank as the result of a massive explosion. Whatever the ultimate cause, the sinking was a morale boost for the Dutch army and navy pilots.*** [Kure Maritime Museum via Wikimedia Commons]

Two Do 24s flying in formation. On the morning of December 23, six Do 24s made a successful attack against Japanese flying boats and ships stationed at Davao in the Philippines. The Japanese were taken aback by this small but bold attack because it demonstrated that the Dutch were not afraid to take the initiative despite being heavily outnumbered in the air. [Militair Luchtvaart Museum, Soesterberg]

Five minutes after X-26 made its attack, the three Do 24s of GVT.2 arrived over Davao and commenced their attack. The target they focused on was the 19,209-ton oil tanker *Tonan Maru No. 2,* which appeared to be in the middle of refueling a cruiser. One of GVT.2's bombs landed on the bow of the tanker and two narrowly missed the ship; the Dutch aircrew reported that they left both ships on fire, but only the *Tonan Maru No. 2* was damaged. GVT.2 made it safely back to Lake Tondano without incident, but X-27 of GVT.5 was struggling to stay aloft. Leaking fuel after its dogfight with the Pete, X-27 just made it out to sea before it made an emergency landing on the water. X-30 came back and picked up the crew of X-27 and eventually the remainder of GVT.5 flew on to Lake Tondano. Although they did not sink any ships at Davao, for the loss of one flying boat the Dutch inflicted several hundred casualties on the Japanese and caused considerable damage to the shore facilities. Furthermore, it demonstrated the tenacity of the Dutch airmen.[17]

A Do 24 flying boat taking off from a lake on a mission. Most of the MLD's flying boats were based in small groups on remote lakes or inlets throughout the Indies archipelago. [Militair Luchtvaart Museum, Soesterberg]

The Japanese did not take the December 23 attack on Davao lightly; they set out on a mission of vengeance shortly thereafter. They correctly suspected that the attack could have come from Lake Tondano, because that was one of the known Dutch flying-boat staging areas within range of Davao. Earlier Japanese reconnaissance flights had located the flying-boat base at Kalkas. The Dutch had observed these enemy reconnaissance planes, but since no earlier had attacks followed, they believed that Kalkas was safe for the time being. Dutch reconnaissance reports also noted that there were no Japanese aircraft carriers in the area, further relaxing Dutch fears about the vulnerability of their flying-boat base. On the morning of December 26, X-30 took off on a reconnaissance flight over Davao, while the remainder of the Do 24s of GVT.2 and GVT.5 prepared for a raid on a Japanese invasion convoy forming up near the island of Jolo in the southern Philippines.

While the Do 24s were warming up their engines on Lake Tondano, the base at Kalkas received a phone call from the northern tip of the island that six Zeros had just been spotted flying in the direction of the lake. Three minutes later, three Zeros descended on Lake Tondano and strafed the flying boats. Three more Zeros hovered above and then took their turn shooting up the nearly helpless Dutch aircraft while a Japanese reconnaissance plane circled above, assessing the results. As the attackers headed back out to sea, they left all of the remaining Do 24s of GVT.2 and GVT.5 on fire, as well as a KNILM Sikorsky S-42B flying boat. As a result, the Dutch abandoned the base and pulled the surviving air crews out of Kalkas and sent them to Java to form a new MLD unit made up of Consolidated PBY Catalina flying boats, ordered for the MLD from the United States before the war. What the Dutch learned from this attack was the remarkable range the Zeros had when they were equipped with external fuel tanks. Japanese fighters could now attack from land bases hundreds of miles away. After this setback, the MLD was primarily restricted to reactionary defensive operations against an aggressive enemy.[18]

The Defense of Borneo and Celebes

The fighters of the ML-KNIL drew first blood on December 19, 1941, when three Buffalos from 1-VIG-V took off after a raid by Nells on Pontianak in western Borneo. One of the Nells was damaged and had to ditch. On the next day, a Buffalo escorting a flight of Martins claimed an aircraft from the floatplane tender *Kamikawa Maru*. But two days later, on December 22, the ML-KNIL experienced its first major setback of the campaign when twenty-four Nells attacked the Singkawang II airfield, where the Martins of 2-VIG-I were based. Two of the bombers were destroyed, and the runway was damaged, temporarily putting the airfield out of action. Singkawang II airfield was bombed again on December 24; fortunately, nearly all of the 2-VIG-I Martins were off on a bombing raid, and only one Martin was destroyed. This raid convinced the Dutch that Singkawang II had to be abandoned, and they sent the Martins to Palembang in Sumatra. Martins based at Samarinda in eastern Borneo took over from the Singkawang group after its withdrawal and commenced attacks on Japanese shipping off Kuching on December 26. The Dutch scored well on that day: they managed to sink the Japanese minesweeper *W-6* and the ammunition-laden transport *Unyo Maru No. 2*, which erupted in a huge explosion after being hit. The Martin bombers made many attacks against the Japanese invasion forces in the areas around Miri and Kuching, but ultimately they were unable to severely hamper Japanese plans. At the end of December the focus of the air units of the ML-KNIL shifted to eastern Borneo.[19]

The next Japanese objective in Borneo was the island of Tarakan, just off the eastern coast of the larger island, where there were numerous oil fields, refineries, and an airfield. The Japanese bombed the airfield on December 26, damaging the takeoff field to the extent that loaded bombers could not take off. A flight of Zeros again attacked the airfield on December 28, and four Buffalos took off in pursuit. In what was the first fighter-on-fighter engagement between the Dutch and the Japanese during the war, the Dutch managed to shoot down two Zeros, but the Japanese claimed three of the Buffalos; the fourth crashed on returning to base. In one mission Tarakan lost its fighter cover. The remaining Martins based at Tarakan were relocated to Samarinda II.

This was a less than auspicious beginning for the fighter pilots of the ML-KNIL, because they certainly could not afford to trade loss for loss with the Japanese, let alone take more losses than they inflicted.[20] These initial losses reflected some of the problems facing the ML-KNIL from the beginning of the conflict. Most ML-KNIL pilots were recent recruits who had limited training and no combat experience. Their Japanese adversaries, on the other hand, were extensively trained, and many had flown combat missions in China in the years leading up to Japan's entry into World War II. Another problem was that, throughout the entire East Indies campaign, Dutch fighter units would always be outnumbered by their Japanese adversaries in the air. The Dutch realized this numerical disadvantage early on, and East Indies

One of the Do 24s based on Lake Tondano on Celebes early in the war. On December 26, 1941, a flight of six Zeros attacked the Do 24s on the lake and destroyed them all. Since no Japanese aircraft carrier was known to be in the vicinity, the Dutch assumed that this forward base was safe from enemy fighters. It was this attack that rudely awakened the Dutch to the extremely long range of the Zero. [Militair Luchtvaart Museum, Soesterberg]

A group of Mitsubishi G3M Nells on a bombing mission. [Museum of the United States Air Force]

A ML-KNIL Martin 139 being loaded with bombs. [Militair Luchtvaart Museum, Soesterberg]`

officials contacted representatives of the Dutch government in the United States to appeal for more aircraft, particularly fighters, for the East Indies theater.

There was a respite for the Dutch during the first week of January 1942, and the ground crews took advantage of the quiet to perform maintenance on the Samarinda II-based aircraft. MLD flying boats continued to operate out of Tarakan, primarily conducting reconnaissance missions. The calm before the storm ended on January 10, however, when a Do 24 spotted a Japanese invasion convoy headed for Tarakan. The Dutch high command ordered two flights of Martins from 1-VLG II based at Palembang to fly to Samarinda II in order to reinforce the bomber units already stationed there, as well as the 7e Afdeling of Martin bombers that had been formed at the beginning of the war from training aircraft and flight-school personnel. Anticipating that it could not push back the impending invasion, the KNIL garrison on the island began demolishing the oil fields and refineries on Tarakan on January 10. The next day, amid the smoke from the burning oil facilities, a Dutch Catalina headed out to sea and noticed that the invasion convoy spotted the day before had broken up into two groups. One group was sitting off Tarakan, while another was heading for Menado on northern Celebes. The Japanese invaders outnumbered the Tarakan defenders by five to one, and the island garrison held out for only about twenty-four hours. The Dutch attempted a raid on the invasion fleet on January 11, but rain squalls prevented a successful attack.

On January 13, the Dutch planned to implement a prewar strategy for the defense of the Tarakan area: five flights in succession of three Martins each were to attack targets at intervals of one and a half hours. The mission turned out to be a disaster for the Dutch. The first flight aborted before it reached Tarakan because there was no cloud cover over the area to hide the attackers from Japanese fighters flying cover overhead; the second flight was pounced on by defending Zeros, and there were no survivors; the third flight made its attack but suffered two bombers shot down and the third crashed on landing back at Samarinda II. The surviving pilot of the third flight sent a radio message warning about the fighters; the fifth flight aborted after that warning, but the fourth flight was close to Tarakan and hidden by the cloud cover that had just built up over the area. The Martins made an attack on the Tarakan airfield, where several Zeros were parked. They damaged the airfield, but none of the Zeros. After losing six bombers in one day, the ML-KNIL gave up its attack on the enemy forces at Tarakan and was forced to disband the 7e Afdeling. The increasingly frequent sight of Zeros providing cover for Japanese operations was beginning to have a demoralizing effect on Dutch bomber crews; but the fight was far from over.[21]

To the east of Tarakan, shortly before 10:00 a.m. on January 11, 1942, Dutch ground forces at Langoan Airfield at Manado, on the northeastern tip of Celebes, spotted a large formation of Japanese aircraft flying overhead. Suddenly little black specks began to drop from the transports followed by puffs of white appearing above each speck. What these Dutchmen were witnessing was the first Japanese airborne operation of the war. Descending onto the Langoan airfield was the bulk of the Yokosuka

ABOVE *Martin 139s flying a bombing mission. The bomber Afdelings of the ML-KNIL fought hard and suffered heavy losses during the air battles over Borneo.* [Militair Luchtvaart Museum, Soesterberg]

LEFT *Three ML-KNIL Buffalos flying in formation. In the first fighter-on-fighter engagement between the Dutch and the Japanese, which took place over Tarakan on December 28, the Dutch lost three Buffalos while downing two Zeros. This fight showed that the inexperienced but enthusiastic Dutch pilots could draw blood, but the ML-KNIL could certainly not afford to lose aircraft on an equal basis with the Japanese.* [Militair Luchtvaart Museum, Soesterberg]

1st Special Naval Landing Force, led by Commander Toyoaki Horiuchi. The Japanese army and navy had only begun experimenting with paratroopers beginning in late 1940, having observed the supposed successful use of the German *Fallschirmjäger* units in Europe earlier in the year. Horiuchi's drop was part of a larger amphibious invasion of the Manado area in which the Yokosuka 1st SNLF would secure the airfield while the Sasebo Combined Landing Force of 2,500 marines and a light tank company would storm ashore and capture the town of Manado.

The troops of the Sasebo Combined Landing Force landed in the early morning hours of January 11; the Dutch garrison at Langoan airfield knew an attack on the area was underway only when they spotted the paratroopers overhead. The descending Axis troops were an eerie reminder of the German invasion of the Netherlands nearly two years earlier. The Dutch ground commander at the airfield, Lieutenant J. G. Wielinga, ordered his troops to open fire, and a number of Japanese paratroops were shot dead before they hit the ground. But as the Japanese landed in force, they methodically knocked out the pillboxes defending the airfield. Wielinga had an armored car at his disposal, but it was eventually captured by the Japanese. Outnumbered nearly six to one, the Dutch gave up the airfield and retreated into the interior. Their situation was further complicated when two Japanese Mavis flying boats loaded with twenty-two troops and an antitank gun landed on nearby Lake Tondano. After the Japanese had secured the airfield, they executed a number of KNIL prisoners in retaliation for the heavy losses they sustained in the operation. This barbarous act was a foretaste of the treatment that many Dutch prisoners could come to expect from the enemy.[22]

Japanese transport planes drop paratroopers of the Yokosuka 1st Special Naval Landing Force, commanded by Commander Toyoaki Horiuchi (above), over the Langoan airfield near Manado on Celebes. The paratroopers secured the airfield but executed a number of Dutch prisoners out of anger over their losses sustained during the battle. Horiuchi was executed as a war criminal after the war for the barbarous actions of his men at the Langoan airfield. [Netherlands Institute of Military History via Wikimedia Commons]

At this point it was becoming increasingly clear to the Dutch that the initiative for the campaign lay solely with the Japanese. On January 21 the Japanese invasion fleet at Tarakan reembarked most of its troops and set sail for the next major objective in eastern Borneo—the oil facilities at Balikpapan. The Dutch spotted the fleet at sea on January 23 and prepared to attack the invaders again. This time, however, the ML-KNIL made a significant attack: a force of two Martins and twenty Buffalos armed with two 50-kg bombs took off to intercept the enemy ships in the Makassar Strait. Although the invasion fleet was covered by Pete floatplanes from the *Sanuki Maru* and the *Sanyo Maru,* the Dutch attackers scored a number of hits on four ships. For the loss of one Buffalo, the Dutch sank the 6,794-ton transport *Nana Maru.*

When the attack was over, the Dutch planes flew on to the airfield at Makassar on Celebes, as they had been instructed to do, hoping that Japanese aircraft in the area would not follow them back to the still unknown airfield at Samarinda II. Unfortunately, a group of Zeros flying over the Balikpapan area on January 24 spotted a KNILM DC-3 and followed it to its destination, the Samarinda II airfield, unbeknownst to the forces there. The Zeros bounced the DC-3 and strafed the field, but one was brought down by antiaircraft fire. The Martins based there were away on a bombing mission over Balikpapan, where the Japanese had landed amid air attacks in the early morning hours of the 24th. But now that they knew where they were being attacked from, the Japanese set out to destroy the airfield with another attack force of six Zeros in the early afternoon. The Buffalos at the airfield took to the air and claimed two of the attackers, but the Dutch also lost two fighters. As the attack was underway, three Martin bombers coming in from Java were attempt-

Left *A Buffalo armed with two 50-kg bombs prior to takeoff. On January 23, 1942, twenty Buffalos attacked a Japanese invasion fleet in the Makassar Strait headed for Balikpapan, damaging three ships and sinking a transport.* [Militair Luchtvaart Museum, Soesterberg]

Above *Aerial reconnaissance photo of oil wells and storage facilities set ablaze by the Dutch before withdrawing from Balikpapan. KNIL engineers and civilian oil workers worked hard to destroy as much of the colony's oil infrastructure before the Japanese could capture these prized objectives.*

ing to make a landing, but all three were shot down on their landing approaches.

On January 25, 1942, the Dutch decided to abandon Samarinda II (Balikpapan was taken by the Japanese the same day), and they sent out the ten remaining Martins for one final raid on the Balikpapan area; from there they were to make their way to Java for maintenance and reorganization. Over the target the pilots noticed that there was very little flak; the reason was that a group of Zeros were patrolling overhead, ready to pounce. One Martin was shot down, three were damaged, and the rest aborted their mission. As if to add insult to injury, on January 27 a group of six Zeros took off from Tarakan and strafed a number of bombers on the ground at the airfield near Bandjermasin in southern Borneo. Seven Martins were destroyed (six belonging to 3-VIG-III, which had just arrived from Java to relieve those of the 1-VIG-II that had returned to Java for repairs), and two were damaged. The air battle for Borneo was over.[23]

On January 24, the Japanese Sasebo Combined Special Naval Landing Force had sailed south from Menado and captured the airfield at Kendari in southeastern Celebes. On January 25, aircraft from the carriers *Hiryu* and *Soryu* had attacked the defenses on Ambon. Japanese troops landed on the island on January 30, and the Allied garrison surrendered on February 3. The loss of Ambon meant that the Japanese controlled the skies over the eastern end of the archipelago, putting them within range of all of the airfields on Java and allowing them to intercept any incoming aerial reinforcements from Australia.

Dutch Assistance in Malaya and Singapore

At the western end of the archipelago, in accordance with prewar planning, the Dutch sent one squadron of Buffalos, the 2-VIG-V, under the command of Captain Jacob Pieter van Helsdingen, to Singapore to assist the British in the defense of Malaya. They arrived on December 12, 1941. Although the Dutch Buffalos were not equipped with bulletproof glass, their ground crews raided the damaged or wrecked British Buffalos for replacements. The British were excited about the arrival of the Dutch. They recognized that these Dutch pilots were experienced ca-

Nakajima B5N "Kate" bombers fly over the Java Sea. Aircraft from the carriers* Hiryu *and* Soryu *attacked the island of Ambon prior to the Japanese amphibious assault. The capture of Ambon gave Japanese land-based aircraft airfields from which they could launch attacks on Java. [Wikimedia Commons]

reer pilots and that their Buffalos, with their more powerful engines, were faster and also that they were equipped with self-sealing fuel tanks. But the Dutch debut in aerial operations over Malaya on December 21, 1941, was not a remarkable success. Two flights of Hawk 75 fighters from 1-VIG-IV had been rebased to Medan in northeastern Sumatra to aid in the ABDACOM defense of the Malayan peninsula. A flight of four of these aircraft, under the command of Lieutenant Max van der Poel, was ordered to bomb the railway station at Singora, in Japanese-occupied northern Malaysia. Each of the aircraft was fully fueled and loaded with four 100-kg bombs per plane.

Just as the fighters were getting airborne at takeoff, the planes of Ensign J. F. Sanders and Sergeant P. C. van Breen collided, and the two unfortunate pilots crashed into the jungle below. After observing the fiery end of their comrades, van der Poel and his wingman, Sergeant H. J. Mulder, continued on their mission. As they approached Singora, the cloud cover was very heavy, and Mulder lost his way. Only van der Poel arrived on schedule over the target, but the thick cloud cover made a precision attack nearly impossible. Nevertheless, van der Poel attacked, dropping his bombs on a signal box and then flew back to Medan where he made a safe landing. Mulder eventually found his way to the railway line about sixty miles south of Singora and bombed it since he was running low on fuel. Without enough fuel to make it back to Medan, Mulder made for the Allied airfield at Ipoh in Malaysia. On his approach to the airfield, the British defenders mistook his plane for a Japanese aircraft and opened fire. As Mulder banked away from the British flak, his fuel ran out and he crashed in the nearby jungle. He awoke three days later while being rescued by British ground troops who found him unconscious in the wreck of his plane. The Dutch lost three of four aircraft in that unfortunate operation, not an auspicious beginning in Malaya.[24]

A Curtiss Hawk 75 preparing for takeoff. [Militair Luchtvaart Museum, Soesterberg]`

The Dutch Buffalo pilots fared a little better. At 2:00 p.m. on January 12, a force of seventy Nakajima Ki-27 "Nate" fighters appeared over the city, and the British, along with three Dutch Buffalos, rose to intercept. In the ensuing melee, Lieutenant August Deibel claimed two fighters that he shot down, though he himself was attacked and forced to bail out, and Capt. van Helsdingen and Sergeant Gerardus Bruggink each claimed a fighter. However, the pilots of 2-VIG-V were not to see extensive combat in the Malayan theater. On January 17, Capt. van Helsdingen removed the survivors of 2-VIG-V to Palembang and then flew on to Java the following day.[25]

The Airborne Assault on Sumatra

February 14, 1942, proved to be another pivotal day in the aerial campaign over the Netherlands East Indies. Again, the Dutch had to deal with an airborne attack on a strategic target. This time the Japanese objective was the Pladjoe oil refineries of the Nederlandsche Koloniale Petroleum Maatschappij and the Bataafsche Petroleum Maatschappij, which were located just to the east of Palembang at the southern tip of Sumatra. These refineries were extremely important to the future of the Japanese war effort, and their capture by airborne assault had been planned as early as September 1940. The unit selected for this mission was the 2nd Raiding Regiment of the Teishin Shudan, an airborne unit of the Imperial Japanese Army Air Force. Although the capture of the Pladjoe refineries was of the utmost concern, the primary objective of the Palembang airborne operation, code-named "L Operation," was the capture of the Pangkalanbenteng Airfield, known to the Allies as P1, north of Palembang. By this time the P1 airfield was no longer being stationed by ML-KNIL units but rather by several squadrons of RAF and RAAF Hurricane fighters and Lockheed Hudson and Bristol Blenheim bombers. In the morning hours of February 14, a force of fifteen Hurricanes, fifteen Blenheims, and fifteen Hudsons took off from airfields P1 and P2 to attack a Japanese convoy entering the Banka Strait. A number of Hudsons were shot down, but the attack group managed to sink a Japanese transport.

As the British and Australians returned to the base, they were shocked at what they saw on their approach. A group of Blenheims, which had taken off late for the attack on the convoy in the Banka Strait, was heading toward the coast when it passed through a large group of what looked like Hudsons flying toward P1. The passing aircraft did not proceed to land at P1 but rather began releasing paratroopers from 2,000 feet. On closer inspection, the Brits and Aussies could see that the incoming "Hudsons" were actually Kawasaki Ki-56 "Thalia" transports that were license-produced versions of the Lockheed Model 14 Super Electra, of which the Hudson was a militarized version. Unbeknownst to the Allies, at 8:30 a.m. on February 14, there had been a takeoff of a large Japanese aerial force, made up of thirty-three Kawasaki Ki-56 and Mitsubishi Ki-57 "Topsy" transports carrying 180 paratroopers, twenty-seven Mitsubishi Ki-21 "Sally" bombers carrying canisters of weapons and supplies, nine Kawasaki Ki-48 "Lily" light bombers for ground support, and eighty Nakajima Ki-43 Hayabusa "Oscar" fighters as escorts. This attack was to be Japan's largest airborne operation during all of World War II. The attack force approached P1 undetected for much of its route because of the large clouds of smoke from the fires in Singapore. At a hundred miles out of Palembang, however, the Japanese air group was spotted by an observer, who contacted the 226 Fighter Group headquarters of the incoming attack. Air Commodore S. F. Vincent warned the ground crew at P1 to be prepared for a potential airborne assault; but as chance would have it, they were unarmed. The only defense of the airfield was a few Bofors antiaircraft guns and some Dutch native infantry in the area. The ground crew improvised a defense as best they could by removing machine guns from inoperable aircraft and mounting them on mounds of dirt and training the Bofors guns to fire horizontally. They were to offer a spirited defense against the Japanese.

Meanwhile, in the skies above the Palembang area, the Japanese transport planes began to drop their para-

Sergeant H. J. Mulder of 1-VIG-IV, who attacked the railway line near Singoara in Malaya on December 21, 1941, crashed in the jungle near the British-held airfield at Ipoh in southern Malaya, and lay unconscious in the cockpit of his Hawk 75 for three days until he was finally located by British troops. [Netherlands Institute of Military History]

Nighttime photo of one of the oil refinery complexes at Pladjoe near Palembang in southern Sumatra. The Japanese had planned for the capture of these refineries by airborne assault since the autumn of 1940.

troopers at 11:26 a.m., and most landed two miles to the southeast of P1. The group of Sallys followed and dropped the paratroopers' equipment canisters, while the Lilys and the Oscars bombed and strafed the airfield. Much to the chagrin of the Japanese, however, there were few aircraft on the field to attack, because most of them were out on the mission over the Banka Strait. The drop of one group of paratroopers was delayed due to a jammed door on one of the transport aircraft, and this group landed along the road between Palembang and P1. As the Japanese proceeded with the drop, the Hurricanes and Blenheims were returning from the Banka Strait and began to fly through swarms of descending paratroopers. Most of the Allied pilots picked up a radio message about the raid and were advised to proceed to P2 to land, refuel, and rearm. Some of the pilots were unable to receive the message and proceeded to attack the bombers and paratroopers over P1 before running out of ammunition and fuel. One hundred eighty paratroopers were dropped two miles southeast of the P1 airfield and were able to block the road from the airfield to Palembang, thus preventing any Allied ground reinforcements from reaching their target.

During the day, the Allied aircrews and ground crews at P1 were able to keep the paratroopers from taking the airfield, long enough to destroy the unserviceable aircraft and fuel stores there. In the early evening, the Allies abandoned the burning airfield, which was occupied by the Japanese paratroops shortly thereafter. To the south of P1, the Japanese dropped an additional sixty paratroopers near the BPM refinery at Pladjoe. The paratroopers advanced into the refinery and managed to secure it relatively intact, despite fierce Allied counterattacks. The paratroopers also managed to capture the NKPM refinery; but at 6:00 a.m. on the following day, hidden Dutch demolition charges exploded, destroying over 80 percent of the refinery and its storage tanks. Despite that setback, the Japanese capture of the BPM refinery intact was a major victory for them. Although the Japanese had not discovered the P2 airfield, and the RAF and RAAF units stationed there were making successful attacks on Japanese amphibious forces proceeding up the Musi River toward Palembang, the Allies decided to remove all of their aircraft stationed in Sumatra to Java on February 17, 1942.[26]

Pushed back to Java

By mid-February, all of the ML-KNIL units that were operational in the East Indies had fallen back to bases on Java. The fierce actions over Borneo and Malaya had left the ML-KNIL with sixty-five fighters and forty-five Martin bombers. One positive aspect of the withdrawal of all

Mitsubishi Ki-57 "Topsy" transports, loaded with paratroopers, preparing to take off. [Museum of the United States Air Force]

ML-KNIL aircraft to Java was that the Dutch would have all of their air assets closer together rather than spread through the entire archipelago, and they could potentially counter an incoming raid with greater force. On the other hand, Java was the last line of defense for the Dutch, and their backs were now up against the wall. The Japanese realized that, and they would not let up on the pressure. As the Dutch withdrew from Borneo and Celebes, the Japanese moved more and more aircraft onto the abandoned airfields, all of which were within striking range of Java. On February 1, two reconnaissance aircraft made a flight over Sourabaya, providing vital intelligence on the new disposition of the ML-KNIL units in the area. The next day a group of Zeros operating from Balikpapan made a raid on the airfield at Maospati, followed on the 3rd by perhaps the most disastrous raid encountered by the ML-KNIL in the East Indies campaign.[27]

On February 3, the Japanese began their all-out effort to eliminate Dutch aerial opposition over Java. From newly acquired and repaired airfields in Borneo and Celebes, the Japanese launched a raid of twenty-six Nells against Sourabaya and twenty-seven Nells against Madioen, both bomber groups covered by a force of twenty-seven Zeros and a reconnaisance plane. Another raiding group of seventeen Zeros and two reconnaissance planes were sent against Malang, bringing the total number of Japanese aircraft approaching the Sourabaya area to one hundred. As the Japanese were seen approaching the coast, the Dutch scrambled every available fighter they could get airborne: seven Curtiss Hawks and twelve CW-21s. As the Curtiss Hawks were ascending, they noticed an unescorted group of Nells heading toward Sourabaya. But what appeared to be an opportune target turned out to be a deathtrap. As the Hawks commenced their attack, they were pounced on by Zeros that had just arrived on the scene. Five of the Curtiss Hawks were shot down in the ensuing dogfight; the Japanese lost just one Nell.

The CW-21s flying out of Perak divided into flights of four and were similarly hard-pressed by the numerically superior Zero formations. As First Lieutenant Ricardo A. D. Anemaet, the commander of 2-VIG-IV, was climbing

Japanese paratroopers of the 2nd Raiding Regiment of the Teishin Shudan of the Japanese Army Air Force coming down near the P1 airfield at Palembang in the late morning of February 14, 1942. This rather crude photo was taken by one of the paratroopers on the ground. Note the parachutes on the ground and the light from the flames burning the aviation fuel and ammunition stores at P1 in the background.

Mitsubishi Ki-21 "Sally" bombers then flew overhead and dropped canisters filled with weapons and supplies. The Japanese paratroops captured about half of the Pladjoe refineries intact. Only on a handful of occasions during the war did the Japanese use paratroops in airborne operations, and the two largest happened to be against the Dutch at Manado and Palembang. [Museum of the United States Air Force]

Aerial bombardment of the port of Tandjong Perak near Sourabaya. On February 3, 1942, the Japanese navy launched bombing raids against the port facilities of Sourabaya, hoping to lure Dutch fighters into the skies and eliminate the Dutch aerial presence in eastern Java. [Netherlands Institute of Military History]

to intercept, he heard an eerie voice over the Dutch air defense frequency, speaking in Dutch, but with a Japanese accent: "Ha ha ha, we are already over the city." Japanese informers had passed on vital air defense information to the enemy. Nevertheless, the Dutch pressed on with their attack. The CW-21 flight under First Lieutenant J. Kingma was hit from behind by a group of sixteen Zeros. Two planes of the CW-21 flight were almost immediately shot down, but Kingma managed to shoot down two Zeros. Following this, Kingma was attacked by a separate incoming group of twelve Zeros, and, though he made one attack pass, his fighter was hit and he bailed out. Kingma's wingman, Sergeant H. M. Haye, managed to shoot down one of the incoming Zeros before he, too, was hit and was forced to make a landing. The two other flights of CW-21s did not make any confirmed kills: of the flight under First Lieutenant W. A. Bedet, three of the fighters were damaged and had to make forced landings; of the flight under 1st Lt. Anemaet, one CW-21 was shot down, two returned safely to Perak, and Anemaet destroyed his plane when he accidentally rolled into a bomb crater after landing at Perak.

Of the twelve CW-21s that took off against the raiders, only three returned in serviceable condition. Although the number of confirmed Japanese losses would appear to be low, apparently the Dutch aerial defense of Sourabaya left a deep impression on the attackers. While undergoing interrogation in a POW camp after the East Indies campaign, a Japanese officer told 1st Lt. Anemaet that they had lost eighty aircraft in the raid! After dispatching the CW-21s, the Zeros turned their attention to the MLD's Morokrembangen flying-boat base at Sourabaya. Unfortunately, the Dutch flying boats moored in the harbor were sitting ducks. The Japanese destroyed three Do 24s, one Dornier Wal, three Fokker C.XI floatplanes, and two large Fokker T.IV floatplanes. The Zeros claimed two more Dornier Wals and a Ryan STM floatplane in the air, all of which were on training flights, as well as a Catalina. American Curtiss P-40 fighters, which had recently arrived at a secret airstrip at Ngoro, took off in pursuit of the attackers and managed to shoot down a Zero and a Nell for the loss of one P-40.

Although the Dutch pilots showed great courage in this air battle, the damage suffered was severe: fourteen fighters, seven flying boats, and six floatplanes were destroyed, and the airfields at Perak, Singosari, and Madioen sustained heavy damage, in addition to what was sustained by the main Dutch naval base at Sourabaya. On February 5, the Japanese again struck Sourabaya with a raid of twenty-seven Zeros. This time there were only four CW-21s and two Curtiss Hawks available to engage the enemy. It was a brave show of force, but the results were predictable: both of the Hawks and a CW-21 were shot down, and two more CW-21s were damaged. The only Dutchman to get away was Lt. Anemaet, who rolled into the formation of the Zeros, shot one down, and made a break for home.[28] The Japanese target was again the Morokrembangen flying-boat base, and again the Zero pilots racked up an impressive score: three Do 24s and two Catalinas destroyed on the water, and a Catalina and a Ryan STM shot down in the air. This raid effectively neutralized the remaining Dutch air strength on eastern Java.

The skies over western Java remained clear of Japanese attackers during the first week of February, when the Japanese were concentrating their aerial efforts against the air defenses and facilities of Sourabaya on the eastern side of the island. On February 3 a group of transports arrived in Batavia carrying RAF pilots; but, more important, the British aircraft transport *Athene* docked and offloaded thirty-nine crated Hurricane fighters. The Hurricane fuselages were towed from the docks through the streets of Batavia to Kemajoran Airport, where ground crews assembled their wings and remaining components. There were great hopes for the combat potential of these Hurricanes: finally, a battle-tested European fighter to counter the Japanese Zero. Twelve of the Hurricanes were handed over to the ML-KNIL and were sent to Andir, where they were taken over by Lt. Anemaet and other 2-VIG-IV pilots who had lost their CW-21s in the intense dogfights over Sourabaya several days earlier.

While the remaining Dutch aircraft and pilots from eastern Java were being reassembled at Andir, the Japanese mounted their first major strike against western

Eight Hawk 75s intercepted what seemed to be an unescorted flight of Nell bombers over Sourabaya on February 3, but they were themselves ambushed by a group of Zeros that had been lingering behind. Five of the Hawks were lost in the engagement. With bases on Celebes and Borneo, Japanese naval aircraft could strike at will over eastern Java and always with superior numbers. [Militair Luchtvaart Museum, Soesterberg]

The ML-KNIL's CW-21s made a spirited defense over Sourabaya on February 3, 1942, but were ultimately no match for the numerically superior force of Zeros over the port. Nine of the twelve CW-21s that scrambled were shot down or damaged. [Militair Luchtvaart Museum, Soesterberg]

In order to train the large number of pilots needed for the new Curtiss and Buffalo fighters coming from the United States, the ML-KNIL ordered 84 Ryan STM-2 trainers in 1940. The MLD also ordered 24 Ryan STM-S2s, some of which were equipped with pontoons as floatplane trainers. The majority of Dutch pilots who served in the East Indies Campaign were trained in these little airplanes, and some of them were even used for reconnaissance missions during the campaign. A number of Ryan STMs, including the one shown here in ML-KNIL markings, still fly in the present day. [Militair Luchtvaart Museum, Soesterberg]

Ryan STM
length: 21 ft 5 in (6.5 m)
wingspan: 30 ft (9.2 m)
power plant: one 125 hp Menasco C4 in-line engine
maximum speed: 126 mph (203 km/h)
range: 366 miles (589 km)
ceiling: 17,200 ft (5,243 m)
crew: 2

Java on February 9. The targets of the incoming twenty-seven bombers and thirteen escorting Zeros were Tjililitan military airfield, where many of the ML-KNIL's operational Buffalos had rebased, and Kemajoran Airport, outside Batavia. The air-raid warning was sounded late, and only four Buffalos were able to scramble against the attackers; three of the four Buffalos were shot down, and the other returned undamaged—with no confirmed kills against the Japanese. At Tjililitan, two Martins coming in for a landing were shot down, and two F.K.51 trainers and four Buffalos were destroyed on the ground. At Kemajoran, two KNILM airliners were destroyed, as well as four Australian Buffalos, which had recently arrived from Singapore. Poor weather spared western Java from further attacks for a few days after that, and this allowed Lt. Anemaet to re-form 2-VIG-IV with the newly arrived Hurricanes. The respite also gave the pilots some vital time to adjust to the new fighters. The remaining CW-21s from eastern Java were also relocated to Andir, and the defense of the Sourabaya area was left to recently arrived American P-40 groups. The six CW-21s were placed under the command of First Lieutenant Wim Boxman, and they were based along a stretch of highway outside Andir that was hidden from the prying eyes of Japanese reconnais-

A Dutch pilot preparing to scramble in his CW-21 (right). The Japanese struck Sourabaya again on February 5 with a strike of twenty-seven Zeros. The ML-KNIL could only scramble four CW-21s, of which one was lost and two were damaged. One CW-21, flown by Lieutenant Ricardo A. D. Anemaet (shown here on left), managed to shoot down a Zero and escape without damage. Anemaet would command 2-VIG-IV throughout the rest of the campaign after it was replenished with Hawker Hurricanes after the loss of nearly all of its CW-21s. [Militair Luchtvaart Museum, Soesterberg / Netherlands Institute of Military History]

sance planes. Every Dutch plane would be needed as the Japanese readied themselves for a massive assault on the last major outpost of Dutch strength in the East Indies.[29]

February 19 brought with it a new threat to western Java: units of the Imperial Japanese Army Air Force had occupied the P1 and P2 airfields at Palembang several days before and were now within easy reach of Java. That morning a group of nineteen Oscars and five Lily light bombers attacked the military airfield of Semplak, outside Batavia, and Kemajoran Airport. Eight Buffalos from 1-VIG-V and 2-VIG-5 intercepted and managed to claim two of the fighters; in return, the Japanese downed four Buffalos. At Semplak, four RAAF Hudsons were destroyed, as were three KNILM flying boats, one airliner, and a Ryan trainer at Kemajoran. This attack convinced the KNILM to remove the rest of its fleet from Kemajoran, but its airliners would be used throughout the rest of the campaign to carry evacuees to Australia and to bring in supplies for Java's beleaguered defenders. In the late afternoon of February 19, the IJAAF mounted a raid made up of twenty-eight Oscars and nine Lilys against Andir. Meeting them in the air were twelve Buffalos of 3-VIG-V, under the command of Lieutenant Pieter Tideman, with some of the fighters being flown by volunteer KNILM pilots. Again, more Buffalos than Oscars were shot down, but one of the Dutch pilots, Sergeant J. P. Adam, was determined not to go down empty-handed. He rammed his Buffalo into an oncoming Oscar, bringing the enemy fighter down and bailing out of his own damaged plane! As in almost all of the dogfights over the East Indies, Japanese numerical superiority always shifted the odds in their favor, as described by Lt. Tideman:

> As for myself, I can only say that I had several severe dogfights. Although I must have hit quite a few Navy 0s,* I did not see one of them go down to the deck because the Japs operated in groups of three: one taking up the fight, the second staying close behind him, and the third taking a position higher on his tail. So, as soon as I got No 1 in my gunsight and opened up with my machine-guns, after a burst or two, I saw No 2 or No 3 coming in on me. So as

In August 1941 the Dutch government in exile arranged to purchase one hundred Hawker Hurricane Mk.IIs for the ML-KNIL from the Canadian Car and Foundry Co. Ltd. This order was later canceled due to the rapid tempo of the Japanese advance in Southeast Asia, but a number of Hurricanes did serve under the ML-KNIL colors during the battle for Java. Twenty-nine RAF Hurricane Mk.IIs were rerouted from Singapore to Batavia, arriving on February 4, 1942, to help reinforce the increasingly depleted ML-KNIL fighter arm. The Hurricanes were used by 2 VLG-IV to replace earlier losses of CW-21s. Because it took time for the Dutch pilots to adjust to the new fighters, the Hurricanes were active only during the last three weeks of the East Indies Campaign, most seeing combat in the skies over east Java. Shown here are two Hurricane fuselages on the road to Kemajoran Airport where they were assembled by RAF ground crews. [Netherlands Institute of Military History]

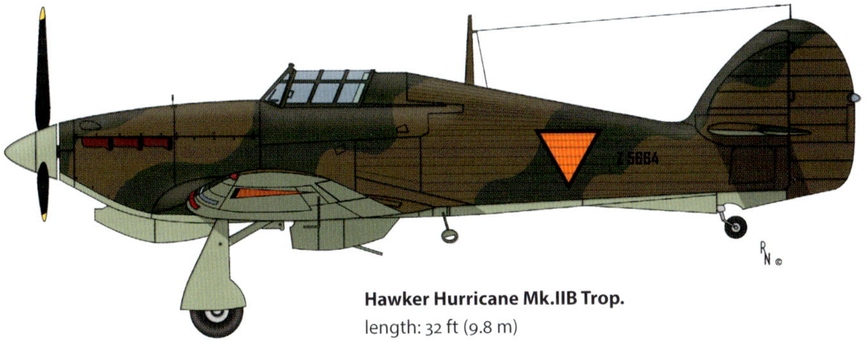

Hawker Hurricane Mk.IIB Trop.
length: 32 ft (9.8 m)
wingspan: 40 ft (12.2 m)
power plant: 1,280 hp Rolls-Royce Merlin XX in-line engine
maximum speed: 339 mph (546 km/h)
ceiling: 35,600 ft (10,851 m)
range: 460 miles (740 km)
armament: twelve 0.303 cal. machine guns
crew: 1

The pilots of the ML-KNIL met aircraft of the Imperial Japanese Army Air Force (IJAAF) over western Java after the Japanese began operating aircraft out of the airfields around Palembang on Sumatra. The Nakajima Ki-43 "Oscar" fighter (right) was more maneuverable than the Dutch fighters, but it lacked the 20mm cannons of the Zero. Dutch fighters were more heavily armed and just as fast (if not faster) than the Oscars, but the Japanese army pilots had extensive combat experience. Dutch pilots may have scored better against the fighters of the IJAAF if they had not been constantly outnumbered. The Kawasaki Ki-48 "Lily" (below right) light bombers were rather unexceptional aircraft but served as an effective strike aircraft when provided with fighter escort. [Museum of the United States Air Force]

not to get shot down myself, I had to turn my attention to the one behind.[30]

[*The Dutch mistook the Oscars for Zeros in this engagement.]

The raid on Andir took a heavy toll: a number of training aircraft, three Curtiss Hawks, two CW-21s, and a Buffalo. Nor did the Japanese let up the pressure of their aerial offensive. On February 21 a group of Oscars and Lilys attacked Kalidjati, destroying five Martins and a ML-KNIL Lockheed Lodestar transport. The Dutch intercepted with nine Buffalos of 3-VIG-V under Lt. Tideman, shooting down one Oscar for the loss of one Buffalo. Semplak was hit by twenty Zeros on February 22, with the Australians losing six Hudson bombers and the Dutch one Lodestar. The IJAAF returned in force on the 24th, as twenty-seven Oscars and thirty-three Sallys attacked Kalidjati and Andir. More Hudsons, Blenheims, and Martins were destroyed on the ground, while the Dutch lost two Hurricanes and three CW-21s. Tjililitan and Batavia were also attacked that day.

The continued Japanese attacks and increasing numerical superiority were quickly eroding the remaining Dutch air defenses on Java. Virtually nowhere on the island was safe from air attack. The Dutch were running out of fighters and the situation was about to be made even worse by events at sea over the next several days.[31]

The Battle of the Java Sea and the Loss of the *Langley*

Perhaps the campaign in which the Dutch most desperately needed aerial reconnaissance and cover was the Japanese naval invasion of Java. By mid-February 1942, the MLD had lost nearly half of its long-range reconnaissance flying boats, while the ML-KNIL was hard-pressed to provide air cover for Allied warships at sea. Meanwhile, following their conquests of Celebes and Borneo, the Japanese were preparing for a two-pronged invasion of Java. The Western Expeditionary Force, under the command of Rear-Admiral Takeo Kurita, was to land at Bantam Bay, northwest of Batavia, while the Eastern Expeditionary Force, under the command of Rear-Admirals Shoji Nishimura and Takeo Takagi, was to land near Kragan, northwest of Sourabaya. It was thus fortunate for the Allies that the Dutch Do 24 X-28 was able to find the Eastern Force on February 26 in the Makassar Strait, shadow the force for a few hours, even attempt to bomb a destroyer, and make it back to base alive. On receiving this report, Rear-Admiral Karel Doorman, in command of ABDA's combined naval strike force, set sail from Sourabaya with the bulk of the remaining Allied warships in the region.

As Adm. Doorman steamed along the northern coast of Java, searching in vain for the Japanese invasion force on the night of the 26th and into the morning and midday of the 27th, he was at a distinct disadvantage when it came to naval aerial reconnaissance. Several ships in his striking force had the capacity to carry reconnaissance aircraft; but for a number of reasons they were not available for use. The only Dutch ship with a catapult under Doorman's command was the light cruiser *De Ruyter*. She had a Heinkel catapult amidships and typically carried two Fokker C.XIs; but as fate would have it, the planes were not aboard when Doorman sailed to intercept the Japanese. In an interesting historical footnote, one of the *De Ruyter*'s C.XIs, W-12, happened to be flying over Sourabaya harbor on February 16, when an escorted group of Japanese bombers attacked the naval base and airfield. A pilot of one of the Zero escorts noted: "En route to Malang we encountered a Dutch floatplane and I broke formation long enough to send him crashing into the ocean." The *De Ruyter*'s W-12 became one of the early victims of Japan's second-highest scoring ace of World War II, Saburo Sakai.[32]

Doorman hoped for land-based air support against the incoming Japanese invasion fleet. Sadly, it was not to come. In fact, the Americans at Sourabaya refused to give Adm. Helfrich any reconnaissance aircraft that he had requested for Doorman's sake; the Americans argued that the temporary loss of any of their reconnaissance aircraft would hamper their own aerial operations. So much

Just as the fighters of the Imperial Japanese Navy were sent in force to neutralize the ML-KNIL over eastern Java in early February, those of the IJAAF were tasked with the same mission over western Java in late February. The Dutch rallied their remaining fighters to defend the area around Batavia to the last. The Buffalo units were particularly heavily engaged. [Militair Luchtvaart Museum, Soesterberg]

Admiral Karel Doorman entered the Battle of the Java Sea blind, with no land-based aerial reconnaissance and no aircraft aboard his ships. His flagship, De Ruyter, *usually carried two catapult-launched Fokker C.XI floatplanes for reconnaissance and gunnery spotting (left). One had been left behind in Sourabaya while the other had been shot down over the harbor on February 16 by a Zero piloted by Saburo Sakai (above), who would go on to become Japan's second-highest-scoring fighter ace.* [Photo AVIODROME Luchtfotografie, Lelystad, Holland]

for ABDA cooperation. Fortunately for Doorman, a Dutch Catalina spotted the Japanese invasion fleet at 1:50 p.m. on February 27. Doorman then set an intercept course. At 3:30 p.m., his ships were unsuccessfully attacked by Japanese aircraft. Doorman requested fighter cover for his own ships and for Allied bombers to attack the Japanese ships. Again, the Americans denied his request; they had launched a small raid of their own against the Japanese ships and had neglected to inform Doorman of this. Finally, the ML-KNIL sent a flight of five Buffalos to cover Doorman's ships; but there were no further attacks by air, and the fighters returned to base.

Meanwhile, the Japanese cruiser *Nachi* launched one of its scout planes, which kept an eye on the movement of Doorman's ships. Adm. Takagi proceeded toward Doorman's position at top speed in order to be in a good position to intercept the Allied advance on the invasion convoy. The Battle of the Java Sea began shortly after 4:00 p.m., when the Japanese were sighted. In the first stage of the battle the Allied ships scored some hits on the Japanese, but in turn lost the Dutch destroyer *Kortenaer* and the British destroyer *Electra*. The Japanese gunnery and torpedo aiming were undoubtedly helped by their scout planes directing fire from above. Doorman had no aircraft to assist in this. While Doorman was hunting in vain for the invasion convoy, Takagi's scout planes were keeping the latter informed of Doorman's movements so that Takagi could eventually plan an effect attack. At 11:00 p.m., Takagi attacked Doorman's remaining ships with the *Nachi* and *Haguro*. Torpedoes launched from the Japanese cruisers hit Doorman's flagship, the cruiser *De Ruyter,* and the Dutch cruiser *Java*; both were sunk, and Doorman went down with his ship. The two remaining Allied cruisers, the USS *Houston* and HMAS *Perth,* made a retreat for Tandjong Priok. A lack of adequate aerial reconnaissance had kept Adm. Doorman "blind" during the Battle of the Java Sea and ultimately led to his fleet's—and his own—tragic end.[33]

Prior to the Battle of the Java Sea, Adm. Doorman expected to have significant air cover over his fleet for the first time in the campaign. En route to Tjilatjap in southern Java was the American seaplane tender USS *Langley*, with thirty-two Curtiss P-40 fighters on her deck. Accompanying the *Langley* was the cargo ship *Seawitch*, which had an additional twenty-seven disassembled P-40s in her hold. American pilots accompanied the P-40s, but Gen. Brett and Field Marshal Wavell wanted to send the planes and pilots on to India, believing that Java could not hold out after the fall of Singapore. The Dutch, however, intended to defend Java to the last man. Adm. Helfrich, who had taken over command of ABDA naval operations on February 14, could not stop the full removal of American and British resources to India; but he demanded that at least the P-40s be sent to Java so that ML-KNIL airmen could continue the fight against the Japanese. Gen. Brett relented and allowed the *Langley*, with thirty-two planes and thirty-two green pilots aboard, and the *Seawitch*, with her cargo of crated fighters, to proceed to Java; but the remainder of his more veteran aircrews were to proceed to India. Thus the *Langley* and the *Seawitch* departed Fremantle, Australia, on February 22 and planned to reach Tjilatjap, a port that had not been attacked by Japanese bombers up to that point, in the early morning hours of February 28, with the darkness of the night of the 27th covering their approach to the port.[34]

Unfortunately for the Dutch, a Japanese reconnaissance plane spotted the ships at 9:00 a.m. on February 27. Shortly before noon, a force of sixteen Bettys and fifteen Zeros began to approach the *Langley* at a height of 15,000 feet. In the ensuing attack, the Bettys scored five direct hits on the *Langley*. Four of the bombs hit near or on the flight deck, destroying several of the P-40s parked on top. Two near misses from the first bombing attack resulted in leaks below and knocked out the engines. About an hour after the attack, the *Langley* was ordered abandoned and after all of her survivors were taken off, she was torpedoed by her own escorting destroyers. The *Seawitch* reached Tjilatjap on schedule under the cover of morning darkness on February 28, but her twenty-seven P-40 s never made it out of their crates—or even ashore, for that matter. On March 2 the crated aircraft were sitting on lighters in the harbor when they

Admiral Takeo Takagi (top), commander of the eastern Java invasion force, not only had the advantage of catapult-launched aircraft aboard his ships, but he also had more ships, more heavy guns, and crews that had been extensively trained in night-fighting tactics. His heavy cruisers, the* Haguro *and* Nachi *(above), each mounted ten 8-inch guns; these ships, along with Takagi's other light cruisers and destroyers, carried the effective "Long Lance" torpedoes.
[Wikimedia Commons]

were pushed into the bay to prevent their capture by the Japanese.[35]

The Abandonment of Eastern Java

With the loss of the Battle of the Java Sea and the lack of any significant number of fighter reinforcements, the Dutch prepared to make their last stand on Java in the face of the incoming Japanese invasions. Already on February 26, the Dutch moved six Hurricanes and six Buffalos from Andir to Ngoro, outside of Sourabaya, in preparation for the expected invasion in the east. Although Japanese raids continued on the western and eastern ends of the island, a more threatening impending storm was about to hit Java. The Dutch knew from their flying-boat reconnaissance that Japanese invasion fleets were making their way to both ends of the island. On February 28, the Dutch began the demolition of the naval base at Tanjong Priok near Batavia and dispersed the remaining flying boats there. In the early morning hours of the next day, the Japanese began their landings on the northwestern tip of Java. The remaining Dutch and Allied air units

In the Battle of the Java Sea, Karel Doorman showed great courage in commanding his motley task force of heavy cruisers, light cruisers, and destroyers, but they were no match for the numerically superior and better-prepared Japanese. Doorman went down with his flagship, De Ruyter, *shown here with the Dutch light cruiser* Java, *which was also lost in the battle.* [Netherlands Institute of Military History]

in the west planned to make an all-out counterattack at dawn. Two flights of four Buffalos and three Martins, one led by Capt. van Helsdingen and the other led by Captain Andrias A. M. van Rest, took off at dawn to attack the invasion fleet and the landing beaches. Unfortunately for the Dutch and their Allies, the Japanese were making their way inland much more rapidly than anticipated. In the late morning, while the RAF crews were waiting by their bombers for orders at the airfield at Kalidjati, a Japanese tank rolled onto the airfield followed by rifle and mortar fire from Japanese troops who were hidden in the jungle nearby. A few British bombers were able to take off and escape but most were unable to get away. Meanwhile the remaining air and ground crews tried to destroy the planes that could not escape while under fire and made a retreat as best they could.[36]

In eastern Java the remaining Dutch fighters and bombers, along with American units stationed there, took off and strafed and bombed the transports and landing craft along the invasion beaches. Most of the attacking aircraft returned to refuel and rearm at Ngoro, but the secret airfield was finally discovered by a flight of four Zeros patrolling the area. Two of the Zeros swooped down and strafed the refueling aircraft, destroying ten American P-40s, five Dutch Hurricanes, and five Martin bombers. The Japanese also attacked other airfields around Sourabaya, destroying more P-40s and Buffalos that were under repair on the ground. In the face of these attacks—as well as their inability to drive the Japanese from their invasion beaches—the Dutch decided to abandon the airfields in the Sourabaya area and to destroy all of the remaining aircraft that could not be flown out. The following day, realizing that the naval campaign for the East Indies had been decided, Adm. Helfrich requested to be relieved of his command, quietly boarded a Dutch Catalina, and flew to Ceylon to coordinate further Dutch naval operations from there. The air war in eastern Java was over.

The Raid on Broome and Smirnoff's Finest Hour

As the month of March opened with the Japanese landings on the western and eastern ends of Java, another aerial setback was unfolding for the Dutch and their Allies in northwest Australia. By this time, all available Allied transport planes on the island of Java were committed to the removal of refugees from the island, since it was becoming clear that the island's defenders could not hold out much longer. On March 2, a Japanese Mavis reconnaissance flying boat was spotted circling over the small Australian port of Broome. The harbor and airstrip of this small hamlet had become a major thoroughfare for flying boats and transports evacuating Allied personnel and their families out of Java in the last weeks of February. This large concentration of Allied aircraft was a tempting target for the Japanese, especially since the Mavis spotted no fighters in the region. The Mavis's droning over the area did not go unnoticed by the Allied pilots in the harbor and on the ground. Some nervously saw an attack as imminent, but the crews of the aircraft were exhausted from their previous trips, and many of the aircraft were not fueled. Thus, on the morning of March 3, the aircraft that the Mavis had spotted the day before were still there, much to the delight of Lieutenant Zenziro Miyano, who arrived with a flight of nine Zeros and one Mitsubishi C5M "Babs" reconnaissance aircraft over Broome at 9:30 a.m., having flown from Koepang on the intelligence gathered by the reconnaissance flight of the previous day. An additional surprise for Miyano was that there were a number of flying boats in Roebuck Bay, off Broome, that had not been reported the day before. Unfortunately for those aboard them, they had arrived during the night of March 2 and the early morning hours of March 3, and there had not been enough time to refuel them.

Three Zeros dove on the bombers and transports on the Broome airfield; three descended toward Roebuck Bay to attack the flying boats anchored there; and another three initially flew top cover in case Allied fighters were to intercept. (Since none were there to intercept, they later joined the attack.) On the airfield, the Japanese strafed and destroyed two American B-17s, an Australian Hudson, and a Dutch Lodestar. Fortunately, no one was killed on the airfield. The pilot of the Dutch Lodestar, Lieutenant Gus Winckel, grabbed a machine gun from his aircraft at the beginning of the attack and actually managed to shoot down one of the Zeros as he fired the machine gun from his hip! An American B-24 attempted to take off from the airfield during the raid but

The Dutch suffered another major setback on February 27 in the wake of the loss in the Java Sea, when the American seaplane tender Langley *was sunk by Japanese navy bombers off the eastern coast of Java. The* Langley *was carrying thirty-two Curtiss P-40 fighters destined for the defense of Java. This photo shows a near miss alongside the* Langley*; the P-40 fighters are visible on the* Langley*'s deck.* [United States Navy via Wikimedia Commons]

TOP *Japanese Special Naval Landing troops coming ashore in the Dutch East Indies. The amphibious assault on Java began on March 1.*

BOTTOM *By late morning, Japanese tanks had already reached the airfield at Kalidjati, which was filled with British and Dutch aircraft whose crews were still waiting for orders.*

was quickly shot down by the attackers; thirty-one of the thirty-three airmen aboard the plane perished.

Perhaps more tragic was the fate of the Allied flying boats in Roebuck Bay. Most of the Dutch aircraft were still loaded with women and children refugees since it had not been possible to take them ashore the previous night due to strong tides in the bay and the lack of facilities on shore to house them. The flying boats were perfect, motionless targets for the attackers. As the Zeros made their strafing runs, the Dutch aircrews and their passengers attempted to escape from the aircraft into the water. Some servicemen and refugees who were shot or trapped within the sinking flying boats died, and several who managed to escape were fatally attacked by sharks in the bay. At least forty of the Dutch perished; the rest were hauled into rescue boats and taken ashore. The loss of life was tragic, and so was the loss of aircraft: nine Dutch, two American, two British, and two Australian flying boats were lost in the attack, a major setback to the Allied airlift effort in the middle of the evacuation of Java.[37]

Fifty miles north of Broome, the KNILM DC-3 airliner *Pelikaan,* carrying eight refugees, including a woman and a baby, and four flight crew from Bandoeng in Java to Broome, was making its way toward the Australian coast when its pilot noticed something peculiar. The pilot, Captain Ivan Smirnoff, one of KLM's best pilots and veteran of the 1933 Kerstpostvlucht to Batavia, noticed smoke rising above his intended destination, and his radio operator was not able to raise the Broome tower. Smirnoff worried that something was amiss and shortly thereafter saw three small aircraft approaching him. A moment later, bullets began to tear into the fuselage and wings of the *Pelikaan* as three Zeros roared past the plane. Smirnoff was hit by two bullets in the left arm, one in the right, and one in his left hip. Screaming was coming from wounded passengers behind him, and suddenly the left engine erupted in flames. However, Smirnoff kept his cool and realized that he had to land the plane before the engine exploded or the Zeros made another pass. He spotted a stretch of beach below him and put the plane in a dive toward it. He carefully belly-landed the plane

A group of Dutch airmen pose in front of a P-40 fighter belonging to the No. 120 Squadron (NEI) of the Royal Australian Air Force. The phrase written on the bomb translates as: "The Netherlands will rise again." A number of Dutch pilots and aircrews who escaped from the Netherlands and the East Indies, as well as other young Dutchmen who trained in Allied flight schools, went on to serve in Dutch units in the British Royal Air Force in Europe and the Royal Australian Air Force in the Pacific. They contributed to the greater Allied effort to defeat the Axis for the remainder of the war. [Militair Luchtvaart Museum, Soesterberg]

Even though the Japanese enjoyed air superiority over Java, the remaining aircraft of the ML-KNIL continued to attack the Japanese where they could. On March 2 a flight of Dutch Martins bombed and sank two Japanese transport ships off the northwest coast of the island. [Militair Luchtvaart Museum, Soesterberg]

Before the war in the Pacific, the ML-KNIL purchased sixteen Lockheed 212s to use as trainers for bomber pilots flying the Martin 139s. The 212s were equipped with bomb racks on the wings and a rotating gun turret on the top of the rear fuselage. It was in Lockheed 212 L-201 that Ensign Frederik Pelder, along with two Australian, one Canadian, and one New Zealand fighter pilots, made a daring escape flight from Java to Ceylon on March 9-11, 1942.

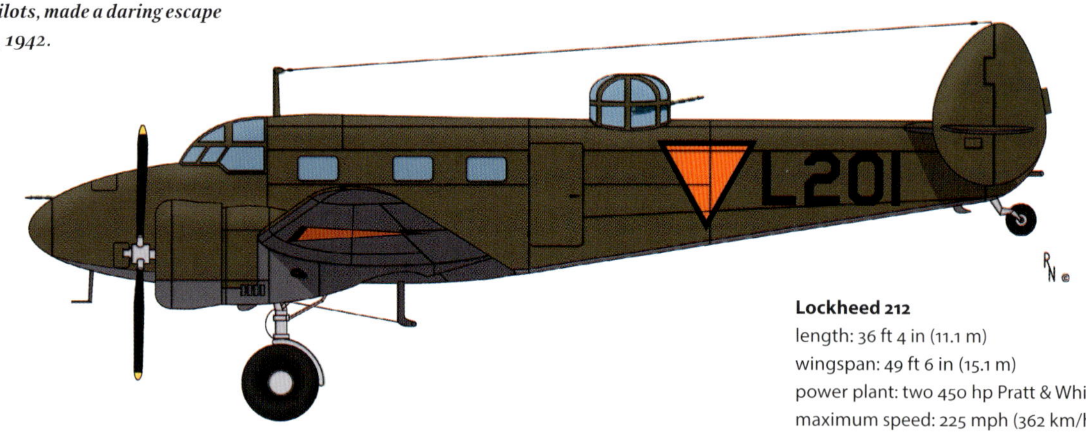

Lockheed 212
length: 36 ft 4 in (11.1 m)
wingspan: 49 ft 6 in (15.1 m)
power plant: two 450 hp Pratt & Whitney R-985 Wasp Junior SB radial engines
maximum speed: 225 mph (362 km/h)
range: 800 miles (1,300 km)
ceiling: 22,900 ft (6,980 m)
crew: 2

Captain J. P. van Helsdingen, who shot down three Japanese aircraft throughout the East Indies Campaign, led the last ML-KNIL fighter mission on March 7. He was shot down and killed in an ensuing dogfight. [Netherlands Institute of Military History]

way—beginning already several days before. On March 7, Capt. van Helsdingen led the last four operational Buffalos based at Andir on a final raid against Kalidjati. Before reaching their target, they were intercepted by Japanese fighters. In the ensuing fight, van Helsdingen was shot down and killed, while the other three pilots returned to base. On the following day, the governor general of the East Indies announced the surrender of the colony to the Japanese.

A number of Dutch and Allied pilots escaped from Java when the Indies capitulated, most of them heading for Australia. But one of the most adventurous of these escapes involved Buffalo fighter pilot Ensign Frederik Pelder and four other Commonwealth pilots. At Pameungpeuk Airfield in southern Java, Pelder and his comrades located three Lockheed 212s (a military version of the Lockheed Model 12 Electra Junior, sixteen of which had been purchased as bomber trainers by the ML-KNIL). All three of the Lockheeds had been damaged by their ground crews to some degree in order to prevent their use by the Japanese. Using the Lockheed that still had its landing gear intact, the pilots stripped the other two aircraft of parts needed to replace those that had been damaged on the former. Through a bit of jerry-rigging involving rope and bamboo, the group put together an airworthy aircraft, Lockheed L-201. They then siphoned petrol out of the other two wrecks to top off the tanks of L-201, and they removed fuel tanks from the damaged fighters and placed them inside the cabin, where the fuel in them could be fed into the L-201s tanks via a hand pump. After a day of getting the L-201 prepared for flight, Pelder and his colleagues took off on the morning of March 9. They decided that Ceylon would be their ultimate destination despite the great distance involved. First they flew to Medan in northern Sumatra, which was still under Dutch control. After refueling there, they proceeded to a small airfield on the northern tip of Sumatra, dodging Japanese reconnaissance planes along the way, for a final fill-up before the leg to Ceylon. Pelder's efforts paid off when L-201 touched down in Ceylon on the afternoon of March 11. This adventurous episode represents the resolve of Dutch and Allied airmen, despite the demoralizing defeat in the East Indies, to continue the fight against the Japanese. Although Holland and the East Indies had been occupied by the Axis powers, the Dutch Empire would strike back.

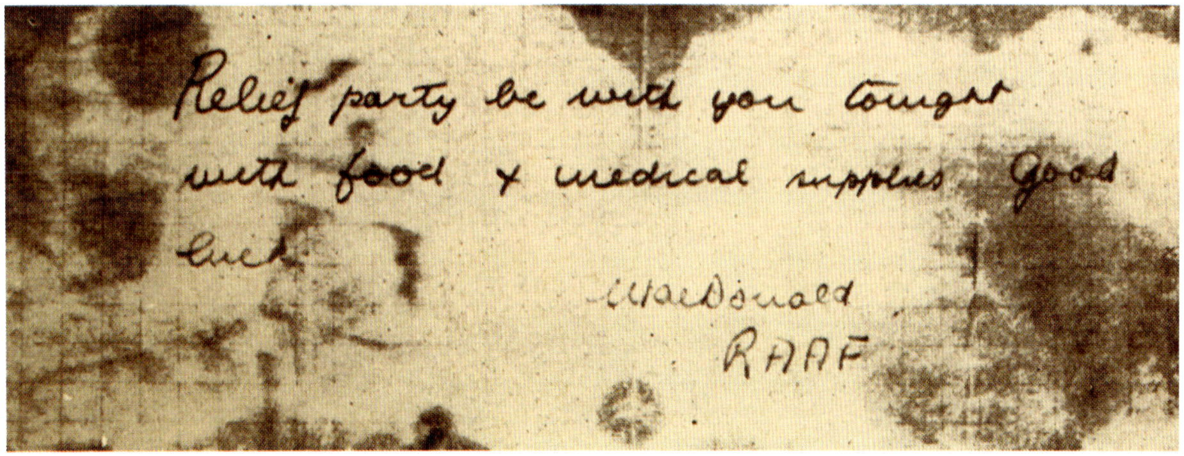

Relief party be with you tonight
with food & medical supplies Good
luck

MacDonald
RAAF

Photo of the note dropped with emergency supplies from an Australian aircraft for Smirnoff and the other survivors of the **Pelikaan.**

medical supplies, food, milk, and cigarettes. Inside one of the containers were notes saying that a relief party was on its way from a mission and that it would arrive by dusk. As it turned out, an aborigine had spotted the wreck of the *Pelikaan* a few days after it had crashed and walked to the Beagle Bay Mission to report what he had found to the Catholic brothers there. In a touch of irony, the mission was operated by German monks who were allowed to remain at their post provided they did not leave the area or attempt to aid the enemy in any way. Bishop Raibel of the mission traveled to Broome to relay the information about the downed aircraft, and this resulted in the Australian aircraft's dropping the emergency rations and medicines.

One of the German brothers, an Australian soldier stationed to the mission, and an aborigine set out from the mission with a mule train loaded with supplies. On their way to the crash site they came upon the four Dutchmen whom Smirnoff had dispatched earlier to try to search for help. Finally, on the afternoon after Smirnoff had received the emergency supplies from the Australian planes, the rescuers from the Beagle Bay Mission arrived. Sadly, the van Tuyn baby had died in Smirnoff's arms the night before; but the rest of the survivors were saved. Smirnoff and the other Dutch survivors were slowly taken back by mule train to the Beagle Bay Mission and nursed back to health by the German brothers there. Smirnoff himself found it somewhat ironic that he had been saved by men who were from the country that he had fought against in two world wars. Nevertheless, he survived to continue to serve his adopted homeland.[40]

The End on Java

After the disasters at Kalidjati and Sourabaya on March 1, the Dutch sent most of their remaining aircraft in western Java to Andir. On March 2, the ML-KNIL enjoyed some success when Dutch Martins bombed and sank two Japanese troop transports, the *Sakura Maru* and the *Horai Maru,* of the Japanese Western Expeditionary Force. But air superiority over Java still rested clearly with the Japanese; both their army and navy pilots continued in their mission to eradicate the remaining Allied air power on the island. The invaders raided Andir heavily on March 2 and 3, but the remaining Dutch fighters still flew up against them. Dutch fighters and bombers also continued to raid and strafe the Japanese on the ground near Kalidjati over the next few days. But March 7 was to be the last battle fought by the ML-KNIL during the East Indies campaign. The fate of the islands had already been mainly decided, since any aircraft with the range to reach Australia was loaded with refugees and sent on its

Below Left ***KNILM's DC-3* Pelikaan, *sitting on the beach in northern Australia, where Ivan Smirnoff made a forced landing after being attacked by three Zeros that had just finished their strike on Broome.***

Below Right ***The interior of the* Pelikaan, *riddled with bullet holes. The seats and other furnishings in the passenger cabin had been removed in order to install an extra fuel tank and to provide additional room for more evacuees.***

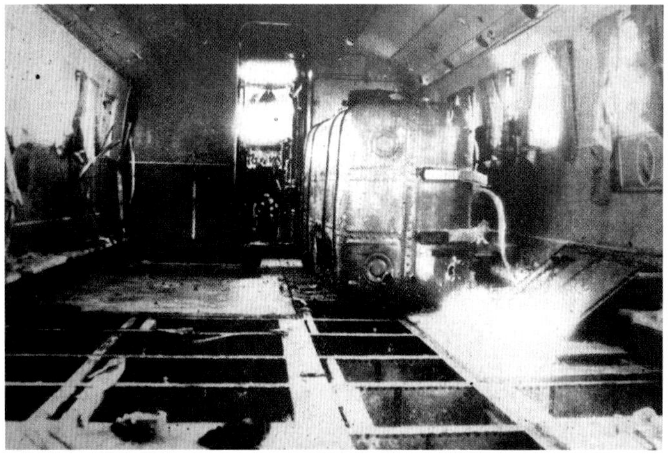

in the sea just off the beach, and the pounding surf put out the fire in the left engine. But Smirnoff and his passengers were not safe yet: the Zeros began to make strafing runs on the downed *Pelikaan.* He ordered those who were able to dive into the water under the plane in order to take cover in between the Zeros' strafing passes. Most of the men aboard made it safely into the water, but the plane's mechanic, N. J. Blaauw, mistimed his escape and was shot through the legs by an oncoming Zero. Shortly thereafter, the Zeros flew away from the crash site, low on fuel, and Smirnoff was eager to assess the condition of his passengers and the equipment and emergency supplies aboard the aircraft. He paid little attention to his injuries, simply washing his wounds in the salt water of the surf. As he climbed back into the aircraft, he noticed that a Dutch lieutenant and the young woman were lying wounded and unconscious on the floor, while the baby was screaming, having been shot through the arm. It was a grim beginning of the war for these poor people, who now began a struggle for survival.[38]

The situation for Smirnoff and his refugees looked grim indeed. Almost everyone in the group had been wounded, and the area where they landed was desolate, with no signs of food or potable water. From the plane the survivors recovered the radio, emergency rations of food and water, and the parachutes, which they used to make a tent to create some shade for the wounded. Muller, the radioman, managed to send out an SOS, but received no response. During the first night on the beach, the first two casualties among the group occurred: Mrs. van Tuyn and Lt. Hendriksz both died of their wounds and were buried, with Smirnoff reciting Russian Orthodox prayers for the departed. He also attempted to feed and keep alive Mrs. van Tuyn's wounded baby. The next day, the survivors grew excited as they heard the sound of aircraft engines approaching in the distance. Expecting to see an Allied rescue aircraft, the party was shocked to see a four-engine Japanese Mavis reconnaissance plane fly over; they were even more shocked when, on the return pass, the plane dropped five bombs on the wreck of the DC-3. As the Japanese flew off, the survivors realized that the wrong party had received their radio SOS.

After this bit of excitement, Smirnoff sent two men inland to try to locate some water. At night they came back empty-handed, but the survivors received the respite of a brief tropical storm, which gave them at least a small amount of drinkable water. On the fourth day, Smirnoff decided to send off all of those who were able to walk in search of help. Before they left, the group, in an effort to remove the salt from the seawater, assembled a makeshift distillation device from pipes and other equipment they scavenged from the plane. Smirnoff stayed behind with the remaining wounded; on the fifth night, the mechanic Blaauw died. All that the remaining members of the party could do was siphon what little water they could from the distillation device and pray for rescue.[39]

The afternoon of the sixth day brought the roar of aircraft engines, and Smirnoff ordered the remaining members to lie down and play possum, fearing that another Japanese bombing attack was imminent. As the two aircraft approached, however, Smirnoff glanced upward and did not see the Japanese "meatball" markings on the planes; rather, they had the roundels of the Royal Australian Air Force. Smirnoff sprang to his feet and began waving at the aircraft, which spotted him and made a low pass to drop, by parachute, several containers of

The elimination of serious Dutch aerial opposition on Java allowed the Japanese to operate freely over not only the skies of the island but also against targets in northern Australia. On March 3 a force of nine Zeros, flying from Koepang on Timor, went south to attack Dutch and other Allied flying boats and transports located at the small port of Broome in northwest Australia. [Museum of the United States Air Force]

Surviving wreck of one of the MLD Dornier Do 24 flying boats that was destroyed in the air raid on Broome. One of the engines and part of the wing is in the background. In front of it is the rear half of the fuselage; the circular opening for the 20mm cannon turret is visible just to the right of the center of the photo while the port side of the tail is partially out of the water to the right. Several flying boat wrecks are visible at low tide at Broome, a unique reminder of those

STUBBORN DUTCHMEN

Prince Bernhard with a "wingman" in the cockpit of a Spitfire. The Prince learned to fly a Spitfire and became a keen pilot. He pushed for the creation of an all-Dutch fighter squadron within the RAF—which later became No. 322 Squadron.

Orange in the RAF

The loss of the homeland and the East Indies to the forces of the Axis did not spell the end of the war for many Dutch airmen. Many would continue to fight against the aggressors in Europe and the Pacific until the end of the war. Only weeks after the fall of the Netherlands on May 14, 1940, Dutch pilots were back in the air. Although most of the ML's aircraft were shot down or damaged during the *Meidagen,* or destroyed by their crews prior to surrender, a number of MLD aircraft escaped to France and then on to England. The most useful of these were eight Fokker T.VIIIw floatplanes that, after a brief interlude at Calais, were ordered by the Dutch government-in-exile to fly to England, where they were eventually assigned to Pembroke Dock in southwestern Wales. On June 1, 1940, the T.VIIIws and their crews were formed into No. 320 Squadron RAF, part of RAF Coastal Command. This unit had the distinction of being the first non-British squadron of the RAF to be equipped exclusively with non-British aircraft. The squadron's first missions were as antisubmarine patrols over the Irish Sea, and to escort convoys entering the South-West approaches. During the summer and early fall the T.VIIIws attacked several German reconnaissance aircraft and made attacks on several U-boat sightings. Unfortunately, by October, after several months of service in the harsh elements of the seas around the British Isles, the T.VIIIws were in need of maintenance, but there was a lack of spare parts. The Fokkers made their last operational flights in November 1940, and their crews began to transition to American-built Lockheed Hudson bombers. No. 320 Squadron and its Dutch pilots and airmen went on to serve for the duration of the war, flying Hudsons and B-25 Mitchells for RAF Bomber Command and the RAF Second Tactical Air Force.[1]

Unlike the MLD, the ML was unable to relocate its surviving aircraft to England. A number of trained pilots and

Members of the Dutch government in exile in a cabinet meeting. From left to right: Minister of Colonies Charles J. M. Welter, Foreign Minister Eelco N. van Kleffens, Minister of Defense Colonel Adriaan Dijxhoorn, Navy Minister Admiral Johannes T. Furstner, and Prime Minister Pieter S. Gerbrandy. Queen Wilhelmina appointed Gerbrandy prime minister after Dirk Jan de Geer advocated a separate peace with the Germans. Gerbrandy would lead the Dutch government in exile throughout the war, and he actively supported the formation of Dutch military units to serve alongside those of the United States and British Commonwealth.

Former MLD Fokker T.VIIIw floatplanes in RAF camouflage and markings at Pembroke Dock being inspected by British Secretary of State for Air Sir Archibald Sinclair. Merged into No. 320 Squadron RAF Coastal Command on June 1, 1940, these aircraft and their pilots served as the first Dutch military unit in exile to fight with the Allies. No. 320 Squadron flew the Fokker T.VIIIws until lack of spare parts forced them to switch to British and American aircraft several months later.

many students from the military flying schools were able to escape. No. 320 Squadron drew a significant number of these airmen, while several others made their way to the East Indies to join ML-KNIL or MLD units. Beginning in the Battle of Britain, a handful of fighter squadrons made up of foreign pilots had been formed and activated within the RAF. In March 1942, Prince Bernhard, who earned his pilot's wings from an RAF flight school in the spring of 1941, began to lobby for the creation of an all-Dutch fighter squadron in the RAF. Initially there were not enough Dutch pilots and ground crew to form a completely Dutch squadron, since most of them had gone to serve with the fighter units of the ML-KNIL. The Prince managed to find a few, and they were sent to serve with No. 167 Squadron until more Dutchmen could be trained as pilots. Finally, on June 12, 1943, after enough pilots had been assembled and a number of mechanics had been recruited from the Dutch Princess Irene Brigade in the British Army, No. 167 Squadron was redesignated No. 322 "Dutch" Squadron. It was equipped with Spitfire Mk.Vbs with orange triangles painted on the fuselages, and its pilots adopted a squadron badge with a parrot in the center, since the squadron's mascot was an African gray parrot that one of the pilots had purchased at the London Zoo. The squadron spent the rest of 1943 practicing dogfighting and ground attacks.

No. 322 Squadron saw its first serious action on January 4, 1944, when it carried out the first of several escort missions, protecting B-25s from No. 320 Squadron on bombing raids over France. In April, No. 322 Squadron was moved to Hartford Bridge Aerodrome in Hampshire, near the southern coast of England. Prior to D-Day, most of the squadron's missions were scrambles against German reconnaissance aircraft attempting to photograph

Dutch pilots of No. 322 Squadron and one of their Spitfire fighters. The first aircraft used by the pilots of No. 322 Squadron was the Spitfire Mk.VB. This improved version of the Mk I had a more powerful engine and clipped wingtips that allowed for better performance at lower altitudes. The Mk.VB had already been outclassed in late 1941 by the new Focke-Wulf Fw 190 fighter but was still in use with second-line units in June 1943 when No. 322 Squadron was formed. In March 1944 the squadron was reequipped with the Spitfire Mk.XIV and would later use Mk.IXb and Mk.XVIe versions. The higher performance of these later version Spitfires gave the aircraft of No. 322 Squadron the speed required to intercept V-1 "buzz bombs," something that the squadron excelled at in the summer and autumn of 1944. [Wikimedia Commons]

Supermarine Spitfire Mk.Vb
length: 29 ft 11 in (9.1 m)
wingspan: 36 ft 10 in (11.2 m)
power plant: 1,440 hp Rolls-Royce Merlin 45 in-line engine
maximum speed: 374 mph (602 km/h)
ceiling: 37,000 ft (11,278 m)
range: 470 miles (756 km)
armament: two 20mm cannon, four 0.303 cal. machine guns

the preinvasion buildup in the Channel ports. After the Allied invasion of Normandy, the Dutchmen were tasked with an important defensive duty: interception missions against the V-1 cruise missiles launched in London's direction. The pilots became experts at taking down the "Buzz Bombs": the squadron chalked up a total of 110 official V-1 kills up to the middle of August. From then on, No. 322 Squadron was assigned to do fighter sweeps and tactical support missions over northern France and the Netherlands during Operation Market Garden. Many of the pilots were eager to be flying over their homeland once again and proud of their role in the gradual Allied push into the Netherlands. Early into 1945, the squadron was moved to a series of bases in the Allied-liberated areas of the Netherlands. The rest of the war they spent primarily flying close air-support missions. When Germany surrendered in May, No. 322 Squadron had flown 4,896 sorties since its formation in 1943. During the last two months of the war—and until it was disbanded on October 7, 1945—No. 322 Squadron was led by perhaps its most colorful commander, Squadron Leader Bram van der Stok, a veteran of the prewar ML and a Fokker D.XXI pilot during the *Meidagen*. Van der Stok is perhaps best remembered for his role in the "Great Escape" from the

Pilots of No. 322 Squadron RAF in front of a Spitfire Mk.XVIe. Sitting in the middle directly under the propeller is squadron leader Bram van der Stok. [Netherlands Institute of Military History]

KLM's DC-3 Zilverreiger *in BOAC wartime livery, but still flying KLM's flag, at Whitechurch.*

Luftwaffe's Stalag Luft III prisoner-of-war camp. Bram was one of three pilots who made good their escape from the camp out of a total of seventy-six who made the attempt (fifty of the remaining seventy-three were shot on Hitler's orders). In the award-winning Hollywood film *The Great Escape,* Bram van der Stok was inexplicably portrayed as an Australian named Sedgwick, played by James Coburn.[2]

KLM Flies On

KLM was particularly hard hit after the Dutch surrender to the Germans on May 14, 1940. The surviving airliners that had not been destroyed or damaged beyond repair in the aerial bombardments of Schiphol were requisitioned by the Luftwaffe. The German authorities considered KLM a state-operated company, and thus they considered the airliners legal war booty. Albert Plesman brazenly challenged the confiscation of the airliners, providing evidence that KLM was a private firm. Although the airliners were not returned, the German authorities—amazingly—granted the airline over 2.8 million florins in compensation for the aircraft. Although he no longer had any airliners, the indomitable Plesman planned for the resurgence of KLM once the war was over, and he started and improvised a radio and navigation school in Amsterdam. In May 1941, after Dutch airmen escaped to Great Britain in a Fokker G.I and a T.VIII, the Germans became wary of any kind of Dutch aviation-related activity, and

Lisbon's Portela Airport was one of the few places in Europe where Axis, Allied, and neutral aircraft could be parked only a few yards away from each other.

Right Top *From left to right, an Aero Portuguesa Lockheed Lodestar, a Fokker-built Deutsche Lufthansa DC-3 (requisitioned from the Czech airline CLS [Ceskoslovenska Letecka Spolecnost]), and a Fokker-built DC-2 of Iberia Líneas Aéreas de España.*

Right Bottom *A group of British Overseas Airways Corporation (BOAC) DC-3s and demilitarized B-24s on the same tarmac. Naturally, Portela became a hotbed of spies from all sides of the conflict, as they routinely watched and reported on the arrivals and departures of airliners and passengers. KLM's surviving airliners, flying for BOAC, were regular visitors to Portela throughout the war.*

they arrested Plesman. He was imprisoned for eleven months and released in May 1942 on the condition that he stay out of the western part of the country. He moved to Twenthe and continued to plan for a resurgent KLM, but any tangible plans would have to wait until the liberation of the Netherlands.[3]

The KLM airliners and pilots that managed to escape to Great Britain, however, did not sit dormant. One DC-2 and five DC-3s made good their escape, and the Dutch government-in-exile, along with KLM representatives in London, offered to fly charter flights for the British Overseas Airways Corporation (BOAC). On July 26, 1940, KLM Captain Quirinus Tepas, BOAC copilot Jimmy Weir, and KLM radio operator Cornelis van Brugge, aboard the DC-3 *Ibis,* made the first KLM wartime flight, traveling from London to Lisbon. The KLM airliners were moved from London to Whitchurch when the blitz of London began, but not even Whitchurch was immune to attack. A Luftwaffe bombardment on November 24, 1940, destroyed the DC-3 *Wulp*. For two years, however, the KLM flights to Lisbon continued uninterrupted, and the airliners were not attacked by German aircraft patrolling off the coast of France. German pilots had orders not to attack KLM aircraft because the Germans frequently used the Lisbon to London flights to send messages via neutral diplomatic mail to agents operating in England. The offices of Deutsche Lufthansa at Lisbon's airport were next to those of BOAC, and British and German agents routinely kept tabs on each other's flights and passenger lists in and out of Lisbon.

The détente between the Luftwaffe and KLM abruptly ended, however, on April 19, 1943. En route to Lisbon, the DC-3 *Ibis,* piloted by none other than KLM's top captain, Koene Dirk Parmentier, was attacked by six Me 110s. Parmentier dove the airliner to 50 ft. above the ocean and after a series of erratic maneuvers on the deck steeply climbed into the clouds and lost his pursuers. After landing in Lisbon, Parmentier found bullet and cannon holes all throughout the port wing and engine of the airliner. Despite this attack, the Whitchurch-to-Lisbon flights continued; but a far graver incident occurred only five weeks later, on June 1 Capt. Tepas, piloting the *Ibis* to England, noticed he was being shadowed by several aircraft while flying over the Bay of Biscay. His last radio message to Whitchurch was the following: "I am being followed by strange aircraft. Putting on best speed. . . . We are being attacked. Cannon shells and tracers are going through the fuselage. Wave-hopping and doing my best."[4] A group of eight Ju 88s that belonged to KG40, based at Bordeaux-Merignac and on patrol over the Bay of Biscay, spotted a lone enemy aircraft. According to a postwar interview with Oberleutnant Herbert Hinze, commander of the Staffel, two of the Ju 88s closed in, one attacking from above and the other from below. When Hinze realized that the "enemy" was a civilian airliner, he called off the attack, but by then it was too late. The *Ibis* and all seventeen people aboard crashed into the sea.

There has been a continuing controversy since the war as to whether or not KG40 intentionally shot down the *Ibis.* One theory is that the *Ibis* was targeted because it was carrying renowned actor Leslie Howard, best remembered today for his role as Ashley Wilkes in the 1939 epic film *Gone with the Wind.* Howard made a number of propaganda films for the British during the war and supposedly collected intelligence for the British military while on his visits to neutral countries. Some have sug-

KLM's DC-3 Ibis *appears below in RAF camouflage, which was standard livery for BOAC aircraft during the war (though they were given civil registration numbers). It was in this aircraft, during Flight 777 between Whitechurch and Lisbon, that* Gone With the Wind *actor Leslie Howard (left), Jewish activist Wilfrid B. Israel, and fifteen other passengers and crew lost their lives when the airliner was shot down over the Bay of Biscay by German fighters on June 1, 1943. One of the crew members on this flight was radio operator Cornelis van Brugge, who had served aboard KLM's DC-2* Uiver *during the MacRobertson Air Race in 1934.* [Wikimedia Commons]

Douglas DC-3
length: 64 ft 8 in (19.7 m)
wingspan: 95 ft 2 in (29 m)
power plant: two 1,200 hp Pratt & Whitney R-1830-S1C3G Twin Wasp radial engines
maximum speed: 224 mph (360 km/h)
range: 1,600 miles (2,575 km)
ceiling: 26,400 ft (8,045 m)
crew: 4
passengers: 21-32

Ju 88C-6 long-range fighters, similar to those that equipped Staffel 14 of Kampfgeschwader 40 based at Bordeaux-Merignac. Eight of these fighters attacked and downed the Ibis. *It is not exactly clear why the Ju 88 pilots downed the civilian airliner. The most likely explanation, supported by interviews with some of the Ju 88 pilots after the war, is that the Germans mistook the airliner for a British military aircraft due to its camouflage. Nevertheless, a number of conspiracy theories exist, ranging from a deliberate attempt to kill Leslie Howard (who was heavily involved in British propaganda films) to the mistaken belief that Winston Churchill was aboard the aircraft during the flight. Ultimately, the route flown was a dangerous one because of its proximity to Luftwaffe patrol areas, and a number of other Allied airliners were attacked on the route at various times during the war.* [Deutsches Bundesarchiv via Wikimedia Commons]

gested that, due to Howard's extensive propaganda activities, Josef Goebbels had a personal vendetta against the actor and ordered the plane to be shot down. Another conspiracy theory is that German military intelligence had learned that Winston Churchill would be flying from North Africa to Britain in early June. Leslie Howard's friend Alfred Chenhalls, who accompanied him on the flight, seemed to resemble Churchill from a distance, and German agents tracking BOAC departures from Lisbon could have sent mistaken information to Berlin, which was all too eager to find a way to assassinate Churchill. Nevertheless, the only documented information about the shoot down that is not hearsay or theory is the transcript of Tepas's last radio message and the accounts given by the Staffel commander and pilots of KG40 involved in the incident.

After the loss of the *Ibis,* KLM switched to flying the Lisbon route only at night; fortunately, there were no further encounters with the enemy for the rest of the war. Once the Germans were pushed out of the coastal regions of France in the summer of 1944, KLM resumed daytime flights to Lisbon. After Operation Market Garden in the fall of 1944, KLM began service to newly liberated Eindhoven. Parmentier and his fellow pilots were finally able to fly back to Dutch soil.[5]

The stubborn Dutch resolve to fight the Axis throughout the world was perhaps best exemplified in the Caribbean, of all places. Lacking purpose-built naval patrol aircraft, the colonial government in the Dutch West Indies chartered the Fokker F.XVIII *Oriol* from the KLM West Indies Division for conversion into a bomber shortly after the German invasion of the Netherlands. The passenger seats were removed and an opening was cut into the fuselage floor through which bombs or depth charges could be dropped. The first "bombs" had been made from artillery shells and they were aimed with a rudimentary targeting device. The effectiveness of the *Oriol* as a combat aircraft was limited not only by its original passenger design role but by a lack of financial resources in the West Indies; early in the war the colonial government only had enough money to fund twelve hours of flight operations per month for the old Fokker trimotor. Despite these early difficulties, the *Oriol* did make a contribution to the war effort against Germany in the Caribbean. Its first combat flights were patrols against German merchantmen attempting to escape to Germany from neutral Caribbean ports. In November 1940, the *Oriol* spotted the German ship *Idarwald* off the western coast of Cuba and radioed its position to a British cruiser, which later intercepted the fugitive vessel. The following year the *Oriol* strafed the bow of a suspicious sailing ship en route to Venezuela, and stopped it. As it turned out, the crew and passengers of the vessel were Germans and National Socialists attempting to escape an internment camp on Bonaire. The *Oriol* flew anti-U-boat patrols until the spring of 1942, when

From the summer of 1940 to the spring of 1942, KLM's old Fokker F.XVIII airliner Oriol *(above) was painted in military camouflage and used as a makeshift maritime patrol aircraft in the West Indies. An opening was made in the fuselage floor to roll depth charges out of, and another opening was made in the fuselage roof for a machine gun mount (below).* [Photo AVIODROME Luchtfotografie, Lelystad, Holland]

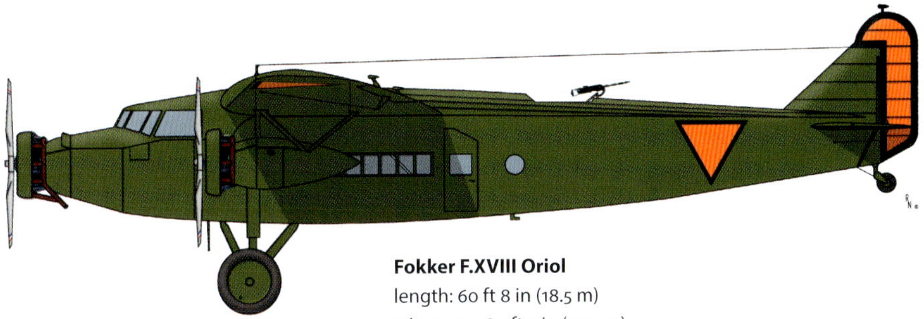

Fokker F.XVIII Oriol
length: 60 ft 8 in (18.5 m)
wingspan: 80 ft 5 in (24.5 m)
power plant: three 440 hp Pratt & Whitney Wasp C radials
cruising speed: 126 mph (203 km/h)
range: 930 miles (1,500 km)
armament: one 7.7mm Lewis light machine gun
crew: 3-4

A group of young pilots and aircrew from the East Indies at the Royal Netherlands Military Flying School at Jackson Army Airfield in Jackson, Mississippi. A number of Dutch pilots, pilot trainees, and aircrews escaped to Australia during the occupation of the East Indies and traveled to the United States for training. These airmen would form the nucleus of the No. 18 (bomber) and No. 120 (fighter) squadrons (NEI) of the Royal Australian Air Force, and they would continue the fight against the Japanese until the end of the war. [Conrad Kiewiet De Jonge Collection]

American military aircraft arrived on Curacao to take over those duties.

In the Far East, KLM continued its service to Batavia, with its western terminus being Tel Aviv. As the airline's prewar leadership was stuck in the occupied homeland, control of its remaining assets was turned over to KNILM, headed by Willem Versteegh. Seven DC-3s were along that route when the Netherlands fell, thus avoiding the fate that had befallen the airline's other aircraft at Schiphol. With seven aircraft where only four were needed, KLM easily maintained a weekly service to Batavia, even adding a second weekly flight in July 1941, because BOAC was not able to keep up with the increases of wartime demand on the Far Eastern route. The airliners of KNILM assisted KLM with the Far Eastern route until several weeks after December 7, 1941, when marauding Japanese aircraft began to appear along the route. KNILM airliners continued to operate within the East Indies, evacuating soldiers and civilians from the ever-changing front lines, despite the almost constant presence of Japanese fighters in the vicinity. Finally, on February 19, 1942, with the remaining KNIL and ML-KNIL forces falling back to Java, Willem Versteegh, director of KNILM since his retirement from the LVA in 1935, ordered the KNILM fleet to rebase to Australia and assist with evacuation flights from there (the most famous of those evacuation flights being the one piloted by Ivan Smirnoff, as told in chapter 8). When the East Indies surrendered on March 8, 1942, KNILM managed to transfer two DC-2s, two DC-3s, three DC-5s, and four Lockheed Super Electras to Australia.

Down But Not Out in the Far East

Despite the chaos of the final days of the campaign against the Japanese in the East Indies, a large number of ML-KNIL, MLD, and KNILM personnel managed to escape from the archipelago to Australia. The students and instructors of the ML-KNIL and MLD flying schools were evacuated in February, while a number of veteran military pilots were able to escape by ship or via the Herculean ferry flights made by the remaining KNILM transports. The new problem facing the ML-KNIL was that it was now an air force without any aircraft. Only a handful of Dutch military aircraft were able to fly to Australia, including eleven Lockheed Lodestar transports and a lone Martin 139 bomber. The MLD, likewise, was able to relocate only a few flying boats and thirty-four Ryan STM trainers. To compound matters, all surviving ML-KNIL and MLD aircraft were quickly requisitioned by the USAAF, RAF, and RAAF, including new aircraft purchased in the United States that had been diverted to Australia. Even KNILM was forced to sell its remaining airliners to the USAAF after the American authorities requisitioned spare parts previously allocated for the Dutch airline. It became clear that the Dutch were now at the bottom end of the totem pole in terms of Allied consideration and priority in the Pacific theater, despite having fought hard and contributed substantial resources in the first months of the war in the Pacific. Nevertheless, the surviving Dutch pilots and ground crews were eager to get back into the fight.

Less than a month after the Dutch surrender to the Japanese on Java, the No. 18 (Netherlands East Indies or NEI) Squadron was formed in Canberra under the command of Lieutenant Colonel B. Fiedeldij as part of the RAAF on April 4, 1942. There had been a contingent of Dutch airmen waiting in Canberra for the delivery of the first of one hundred sixty-two North American B-25 Mitchell bombers that the East Indies government had purchased well before the colony surrendered. As with other Dutch aircraft orders in the United States, these bombers were requisitioned by the USAAF; but the Americans did promise to provide eighteen Mitchells to eventually equip No. 18 Squadron. To begin operations as soon as possible, No. 18 Squadron brought in KNILM pilots and ground crew, as well as RAAF ground and logistics crew, to bring its ranks to full strength. In late April the first five Mitchells arrived and were immediately put to use training the pilots on the new aircraft. The Mitchell was quite an adjustment and upgrade for those who had previously flown Martin 139s, DC-2s, or Lockheed

Lodestars. The Americans sent fourteen Douglas A-20A Boston bombers to round out the squadron, but Lt. Col. Fiedeldij militantly insisted that his men have the originally agreed on—and better—eighteen Mitchells. His demand was granted, and the Bostons were rotated out for the last of the eighteeen Mitchells throughout the late summer of 1942.

Halfway around the world, fresh Dutch pilots were being trained for eventual service in the Pacific Theater. Students and instructors from the ML-KNIL and MLD flying schools were shipped to the United States in April 1942, and a new Royal Netherlands Military Flying School was established at the Jackson Army Airfield (Hawkins Field) in Jackson, Mississippi. The pilots trained at Jackson were not just previous ML pilots and pilot-trainees. Dutchmen who had escaped from the occupied Netherlands as well as Dutch expats from the United States, Canada, and all over the world came, eager to liberate the home country and empire. American Lend-Lease provided 165 single- and twin-engine trainers for the flying school. During its operation, the school graduated about two hundred forty pilots, ninety-nine of whom were trained as fighter pilots destined for a new Dutch fighter squadron under RAAF command. Advanced training took place on Mitchells and Curtiss P-40 Kittyhawks. The school was initially headed by the commander of the ML-KNIL, Major General Ludolph van Oyen, until October 1943, when he was appointed acting commander of the KNIL.[6]

Back in Australia, 18 Squadron had enough training, aircraft, and personnel to begin combat operations in late 1942. The training center was moved from Canberra to MacDonald Airfield just south of Darwin in the Northern Territory. Since this was a very remote region, the squadron had to be completely self-sufficient and had a total force of 558 men (250 Dutch and 308 Australians, the latter primarily making up the ground and logistics crews). Finally, on January 18, 1943, the Mitchells of No. 18 Squadron flew their first operational mission, searching for Japanese shipping. From then on the Dutch Mitchells and their crews began flying regular reconnaissance and supply drop missions to Dutch guerillas in the East Indies as well. The No. 18 Squadron's specialty, however, was antishipping attacks throughout the waters of the East Indies archipelago. The Dutch pilots specialized in making risky mast-high attacks on Japanese ships and some of their Mitchells were fitted with eight machine guns for this very purpose. These attacks were dangerous, and losses eventually came from Japanese antiaircraft fire, fighters, and even damage to the bombers from their

No. 18 Squadron (NEI) RAAF pilots and crews in front of a B-25. The primary aircraft of No. 18 Squadron was the North American B-25C Mitchell medium bomber. The B-25 was a versatile aircraft that possessed good range and, when equipped with multiple forward-firing machine guns, could perform devastatingly effective strafing and antishipping missions. The squadron received its first eighteen B-25s by the end of September 1942, and the unit became operational in mid-January of the following year. Operating out of northern Australia, Dutch B-25s flew reconnaissance missions and ground and antishipping strikes throughout the East Indies. Dutch pilots and aircrews received 150 B-25s by the end of the war, including the later B-25J model, which could be equipped with up to eighteen .50 cal. machine guns. [Conrad Kiewiet De Jonge Collection]

North American B-25C Mitchell
length: 52 ft 11 in (16.1 m)
wingspan: 67 ft 7 in (20.6 m)
power plant: two 1,700 hp Wright R-2600-13 radial engines
maximum speed: 284 mph (457 km/h)
range: 1,500 miles (2,414 km)
ceiling: 21,200 ft (6,462 m)
armament: six .50-cal. machine guns
payload: 5,200 lbs (2,359 kg) of bombs
crew: 5

Dutch pilot trainee and instructor taxiing in a Vultee BT-13 Valiant trainer at Jackson Army Airfield in Mississippi. Operating for almost three years, the Royal Netherlands Military Flying School trained nearly 900 pilots and aircrew. Fighter pilots were trained on either Vultee BT-13 Valiants or North American AT-6 Texans, while bomber pilots were trained on Beech AT-11 Kansans or Lockheed 12 twin-engine trainers. P-40 fighters and B-25 bombers ordered for the Dutch squadrons in the Pacific were delivered to Jackson not only for advanced training purposes but also so that their new pilots could then fly them to the Pacific theater themselves.

Maj. Gen. van Oyen of the ML-KNIL inspects a group of students at the Royal Netherlands Military Flying School at Jackson, Mississippi.

A B-25 of No. 18 Squadron in flight. The Dutch national flag insignia replaced the orange "neutrality" triangle marking early in 1942, and it was used on all subsequent ML-KNIL aircraft until the end of the war. [Conrad Kiewiet De Jonge Collection]

own bombs dropped on ships at such precise but low levels. Nevertheless, morale was high and the pilots and aircrews were eager to take the fight to the enemy over Dutch territory. In May 1943 the squadron moved to Batchelor, which was closer to Darwin, as well as its area of operations. Throughout the rest of 1943 and into early 1944, the Mitchells honed their antishipping tactics, making many treetop raids (similar to the HUBOBE tactics of the *Meidagen*) on Japanese-held ports; they now had fighter cover provided by long-range Bristol Beaufighters of the RAAF. In six weeks alone, between mid-November 1943 and early January 1944, No. 18 Squadron sank over 22,000 tons of Japanese shipping.

While No. 18 Squadron continued to harass the enemy from Batchelor, a new Dutch squadron began to make its presence known in the East Indies in the spring of 1944. On December 10, 1943, the Dutch fighter pilots who had been eagerly training in Mississippi were finally formed into the No. 120 (NEI) Squadron. This unit numbered twenty-four Curtiss P-40 Kittyhawk fighters, twenty-eight pilots, and two hundred sixty ground crew (two hundred fifteen of whom were Australian). Upon arrival in Australia in early 1944, the Dutch pilots underwent several weeks of training to acclimate themselves to RAAF tactics, which differed some from what they were taught in the United States. Finally, in April, the No. 120 Squadron was deemed ready for combat and sent to Merauke in southern Dutch New Guinea in April. The squadron's move was simultaneous with the beginning of an Allied assault on the region with amphibious landings at Hollandia and Aitape on April 22, 1944. The aircraft and pilots of the No. 120 Squadron would support the Allied effort to wrest control of Dutch New Guinea from the Japanese.

The Dutch Kittyhawks primarily flew ground support missions, assisting the Allied advance on the ground; but like their fellow countrymen in No. 18 Squadron, they also undertook antishipping missions. Fortunately, there was little opposition from the enemy in the skies as the Allies made a concentrated effort to destroy Japanese aircraft and neutralize their airfields throughout the region.

The No. 18 and 120 Squadrons were now also supported by two Dutch transport units. The first, NEI Transport Section Brisbane (or NEI-TSB) was formed in January 1943 to supply No. 18 Squadron. The second, NEI Transport Section Melbourne, or NEI-TSM, was a completely independent Dutch unit formed in February 1944. Both units flew Mitchells, Lodestars, C-47s, and Lockheed 12As, and a number of the sections' pilots were KLM or KNILM veterans. In November 1944, both sections were merged into the No. 1 NEI Transport Squadron, which was for a time under the command of the old man of the LVA, Colonel "Baas" Versteegh.

Throughout the summer and fall of 1944, the No. 18 Squadron continued its operations throughout the Timor Sea. On July 1, 1944, it received a new commanding officer who had quite an aviation pedigree, Lieutenant Colonel Dirk L. Asjes. After his misadventures with the *Pander Postjager,* Asjes worked for Koolhoven for some time but eventually went to the East Indies to work for Royal Dutch Shell. There he joined the ML-KNIL and piloted a Martin 139 against the Japanese invasion of the colony. After training to fly the Mitchell in Jackson, Mississippi, he returned to the Far East to become an integral member of the No. 18 Squadron. The Dutch pilots also became more daring as the war pushed on. On September 24, 1944, the squadron flew two missions over Java, where it dropped propaganda leaflets over internment camps in Batavia and Bandung to raise the morale of the Dutch civilians imprisoned there. To strike a blow against Japanese morale, several Mitchells strafed the governor-general's residence at Buitenzorg, which had become a Japanese military headquarters. Throughout the fall, the Mitchells continued their relentless attacks on Japanese shipping, sinking or damaging eighty-three vessels between October 1944 and January 1945.

As the war moved into 1945, the No. 18 and No. 120 Squadrons did not see as much action as they had previously. The Australians wanted to move the Dutch squadrons to the New Britain theater, but the Dutch colonial government insisted that they support operations in the East Indies. The squadrons were inactive for much of the

A group of Dutch P-40s in flight. No. 120 (Netherlands East Indies) Squadron RAAF received twenty-four new Curtiss P-40N fighters from the United States in January 1944, a little over a month after the squadron had been formed. At the end of the war, the reorganized ML-KNIL had sixty-seven P-40Ns at its disposal. The P-40N was the best and final version of the Curtiss fighter and was received in large numbers by the Royal Australian Air Force. While originally intended by Curtiss as a high-altitude interceptor, the P-40Ns of No. 120 Squadron were primarily used for strafing and ground attack missions. [Militair Luchtvaart Museum, Soesterberg]

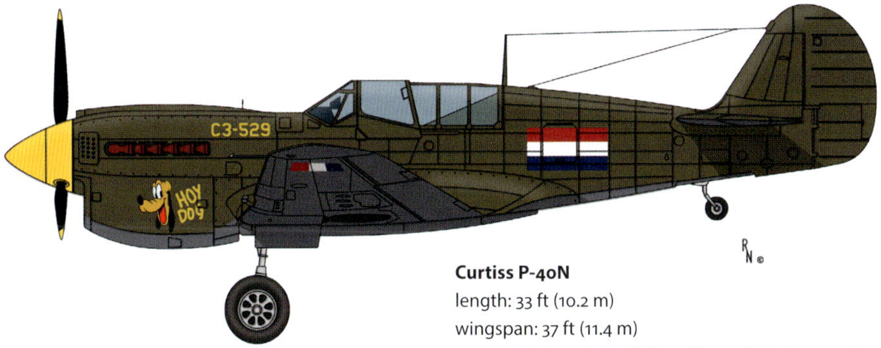

Curtiss P-40N
length: 33 ft (10.2 m)
wingspan: 37 ft (11.4 m)
power plant: 1,360 hp Allison V-1710-81 in-line engine
maximum speed: 378 mph (608.2 km/h)
range: 750 miles (1,207 km)
ceiling: 38,000 ft (11,582 m)
armament: four .50 in (12.7mm) machine guns
crew: 1

Lieutenant Colonel Dick Asjes (second from the right), veteran crew member of the Pander Postjager *in the 1933 Kerstpostvlucht and the MacRobertson Air Race, pictured as the commander of No. 18 Squadron RAAF in July 1944. After moving to the East Indies in 1939, Asjes joined the ML-KNIL and became a bomber pilot just in time to see action in a Martin 139 during the battle for the Indies in early 1942. He trained with other Dutch pilots at Jackson, Mississippi, and became commander of No. 18 Squadron on July 1, 1944. He commanded the squadron until October 7, 1944, and he personally led many missions, often serving as the pathfinder.*

The air war over the Dutch East Indies was truly an international effort involving Dutch, American, and British Commonwealth pilots and ground crews. Included in that group were expatriate and second-generation foreign-born Dutchmen as well. Here Oris Op't Holt (born in Cicero, Illinois, of Dutch parents) of the American Army Air Force poses on the left with two Sikh soldiers in Dutch New Guinea in 1944. [Photo courtesy of Dr. Timothy Op't Holt]

first part of the year as their new destination was being debated, but eventually the Dutch squadrons got their way. A joint Allied invasion of Borneo began on May 1, 1945, and it was decided that No. 18 Squadron would support operations there. The squadron began to relocate to Balikpapan in July, but the war ended before it could become fully operational. However, along with the NEI Transport Squadron, it flew numerous important transport missions bringing food and medical supplies to recently liberated POW camps and returning to Australia carrying liberated POWs and civilian internees. No. 120 Squadron, also earmarked for tactical support for ground operations on Borneo, was moved to Biak and became operational there on June 12, 1945. The Dutch Kittyhawks flew ground support missions until the war in the Pacific ended on September 2, 1945.[7]

The End of the Golden Era and a New World Order

As the war came to a close in the fall of 1945, the role to be played by Dutch aviation in the postwar world was unclear at best. Peace may have descended on the homeland, but the arduous task of reconstruction loomed ahead. The vibrant Dutch aviation industry of the interwar years lay in ruins. Smaller aviation firms like Koolhoven and De Schelde never again opened their doors. In the last years of the war, the Fokker factory had been ransacked by the Germans and then nearly obliterated by Allied bombing raids. The company began to rebuild after the war, but building and selling new aircraft in a postwar world that was glutted with thousands of surplus aircraft of all varieties proved to be initially difficult. Nevertheless, Fokker launched its first new postwar aircraft, a small trainer designated the S-11, in 1947 and designed and manufactured the world's first purpose-built jet trainer, the S-14 Machtrainer, beginning in 1951. The company began designing and selling small- to mid-size airliners starting with the F-27 Friendship in the mid-1950s. KLM likewise required major rebuilding and re-equipping when the war ended. It began operations with surplus C-47 Dakotas, but finally began to receive the DC-4s it had long sought in 1946. KLM also received the distinction of being the first Continental airline to begin regular transatlantic service, beginning with a DC-4 flight from Amsterdam to New York on May 21, 1946. Although KLM purchased a number of the smaller airliners manufactured by Fokker for Continental routes, the airline began to rely exclusively on American-built airliners for all of its long-distance routes in the postwar world.

A sense of normality may have begun to return to airports and the Fokker company in the Netherlands, but there was no immediate peace for the pilots and aircrews who had fought throughout the war. In the Far East, Indonesian rebels declared independence and began an insurrection against Dutch rule. The defeated Japanese handed over large numbers of weapons and supplies to the rebels, who had, in turn, collaborated with the Japanese during the war. After taking time to rebuild and re-equip an army, the Netherlands dispatched troops to the East Indies in early 1946, along with the pilots and aircraft of No. 18 and No. 120 Squadrons, which formed the core of a re-created ML-KNIL. New ML-KNIL squadrons were formed with American-built P-40s, P-51s, B-25s, and C-47s; further,

No. 322 Squadron, reactivated in the Netherlands by the resurgent ML, was sent with its Spitfires to the East Indies in 1947. Dutch pilots and airmen fought the rebels in the skies over the archipelago until 1949, when the Netherlands was compelled by the United States to recognize an independent Indonesian state or lose its Marshall Plan funding that was vital to the reconstruction of the devastated homeland. In 1950, as the result of virtual extortion by the United States, the ML-KNIL and the Dutch aerial presence in the East Indies ceased to exist. The devastation caused by World War II and the onset of the Cold War brought an end to the influential role played by the Dutch in the field of aviation in the interwar years. Tony Fokker passed away in the opening months of World War II, many veteran Dutch pilots and airmen died during the war, and several of the surviving influential flying Dutchmen were also lost in the early years of the Cold War: Frits Koolhoven (who died in 1946 after a stroke); Gerrit Geysendorffer (who perished in 1947 when the C-47 he was piloting crashed on takeoff in Copenhagen); Koene Dirk Parmentier (who perished in 1948, when he crashed in a Lockheed Constellation at Prestwick, Scotland, due to bad weather); and, finally, Albert Plesman (1953). The empire—to the ends of which pioneering long-distance flights brought great publicity, acclaim, and achievement—was gone. The Koninklijke Luchtmacht, founded as an independent force in 1953, came to be viewed in the world as yet another force within NATO's air armada during the Cold War and beyond. The Fokker company declared bankruptcy in 1996, and even the great KLM fell victim to globalization, becoming part of the KLM-Air France SkyTeam conglomerate in 2004. Who knows what the future holds for the Dutch and aviation, but the critical role played by this nation, its people, and its aircraft during the Golden Age of Flight deserves an important place in the annals of the history of manned flight.

On September 13, 1945, eleven days after the formal Japanese surrender in Tokyo Bay, Lieutenant General Hatazo Adachi surrendered all Japanese forces in Dutch New Guinea and Papua New Guinea. Here are two Mitsubishi Ki-21 Sally bombers, whitewashed and with green crosses painted on their sides as neutrality/surrender markings, which flew Adachi and his staff to the surrender ceremony at Cape Wom airfield in Papua New Guinea. The last Japanese troops left the Dutch East Indies in October 1945. [Photo courtesy of Dr. Timothy Op't Holt]

Shortly after the end of the war the pilots and B-25s of No. 18 Squadron had a new yet important mission to fulfill: dropping supplies to and transporting recently released Dutch prisoners of war throughout the East Indies. Weapons and equipment were stripped out of the B-25s for maximum transport capacity. On some flights, up to eighteen passengers were carried in a single bomber. These flights provided a happy ending to soldiers and civilians who spent over three years suffering at the hands of brutal Japanese prison guards. Here a group of civilian ex-POWs prepares to board a Dutch B-25. [Conrad Kiewiet De Jonge Collection]

NOTES

Notes to Chapter One

1. Hubert P. van Tuyll van Serooskerken, *The Netherlands and World War I: Espionage, Diplomacy, and Survival* (Leiden: Brill, 2001), 118-19. For further information on Snijders's interest in aviation, see R. de Winter, *Luchtmachtstructuren in Beweging: 80 Jaar Luchtmachtorganisatie* (Den Haag: Sectie Luchtmachthistorie van de Luchtmachtstaf, 1994), 13-15; see also R. de Winter, *Hendrik Walaardt Sacré, 1873-1949: Leven voor de Luchtvaart* (Den Haag: Sectie Luchtmachthistorie van de Luchtmachtstaf, 1992), 33; Willem Helfferich, *Squadrons van de Koninklijke Luchtmacht* (Rotterdam: Drukkerij Wyt & Zn., 1994), 11; Wim Schoenmaker and Thijs Postma, *Aviateurs van het Eerste Uur* (Weesp: Romen Luchtvaart, 1984), 119-20.

2. Enzo Angelucci, *The Rand McNally Encyclopedia of Military Aircraft* (New York: The Military Press, 1983), 21; see also Helfferich, *Squadrons,* 12.

3. Amry Vandenbosch, *The Neutrality of the Netherlands During the World War* (Grand Rapids: Eerdmans, 1927).

4. Angelucci, *Encyclopedia of Military Aircraft,* 29.

5. Serooskerken, *The Netherlands and World War I,* 200, 143. Chapters 3 and 4 of Serooskerken's book discuss the strategic problems facing the Dutch in their military planning in detail. The Waterlinie was a planned inundation line running south from the Zuyder Zee and then west to the North Sea. It consisted of sixty-five fortified positions, and the line called for roughly 200,000 troops for its defense. Originally, it was thought that this line would allow Amsterdam to hold out for months, but later in the war Gen. Snijders became skeptical of this because of the increases in German long-range artillery (pp. 104-5, 232).

6. *Ibid.,* 128-29; see also H. R. H. Wilhelmina, *Lonely But Not Alone* (New York: McGraw-Hill, 1960), 89-113.

7. For a full list of the aircraft interned by the Netherlands during World War I, see Johan G. H. Visser, "Dutch Military Aircraft: 1910-1920," *Over the Front* 14, no. 4 (Winter 1999): 348-55.

8. De Winter, *Sacré,* 70-71. See also Angelucci, *Encyclopedia of Military Aircraft,* 26; see also Giorgio Apostolo, *Color Profiles of World War I Combat Planes* (New York: Crescent Books, 1974), 41-48; Willem Helfferich, *Nederlandse Koninklijke Luchtmacht: Van Vliegclub tot Strijdmacht* (Rotterdam: Wyt Uitgevers, 1981), 11.

9. Captain A. Poillon, *Aeroplanes and Aeroplane Motors in Holland* (Spijker File 1, National Air and Space Museum, Washington, DC, Feb. 2, 1917).

10. Theo Wesselink and Thijs Postma, *De Nederlandse vliegtuigen* (Haarlem: Romen, 1982), 13-14; see also Visser, "Dutch Military Aircraft: 1910-1920," 320.

11. Wesselink and Postma, *Nederlande vliegtuigen*, 14.

12. Poillon, *Aeroplanes and Aeroplane Motors,* 4.

13. Hugo Hooftman, *Van Farman tot Neptune: Vijftig Jaar Nederlandse Marinevliegtuigen* (Zwolle: La Rivière & Voorhoeve, 1964), 62-65; see also Henri Hegener, *Fokker: The Man and The Aircraft* (Fallbrook: Aero Publishers, Inc., 1961), 35; Goran Lundin, "Thulin," *WWI Aero: The Journal of the Early Aeroplane* 153 (August 1996): 20.

14. Harry van Dorssen and Frits Gerdessen, "Interned! A List of Aeroplanes of All Nationalities That Were Interned by the Dutch Authorities After Landing in Holland During 1914-1918," *Cross & Cockade Great Britain Journal* 16, no. 1 (1985): 21; see also Serooskerken, *The Netherlands and World War I,* 205-6.

15. Paul Leaman, *Fokker Aircraft of World War One* (Ramsbury: The Crowood Press, 2001), 69-73; see also Alex Imrie, *Fokker Fighters of World War One* (London: Arms & Armor Press, 1986), 25; C. Smit, *Bescheiden Betreffende de Buitenlandse Politiek van Nederland 1848-1919: Derde Periode 1899-1919, Vijfde Deel 1917-1919, Eerste Stuk* (Den Haag: Martinus Nijhoff, 1964), 402; Hegener, *Fokker,* 35.

16. H. Walaardt Sacré, W. P. van den Abeelen, and F. Spittel, *Vijf-en-Twintig Jaar Luchtvaart in Nederland* (Amsterdam: A. J. G. Strengholt, 1932), 112-13, 150-56; see also B. van der Klaauw, Armand van Ishoven, and Peter van der Gaag, *De Geschiedenis van de Nederlandse en Belgische Luchtvaart* (Rotterdam: Lekturama B.V., 1982), 18-19.

17. C. Smit, *Bescheiden Betreffende de Buitenlandse Politiek van Nederland 1848-1919: Derde Periode 1899-1919, Achtste Deel Buitenlandse Bronnen 1917-1919, Eerste Stuk* (Den Haag: Martinus Nijhoff, 1973), 183, 189, 611; see also Serooskerken, *The Netherlands and World War I,* 189-93.

18. Hegner, *Fokker,* 35-36; see also C. G. Grey, ed., *All the World's Aircraft* (London: Sampson Low, Marston & Co., 1920), 236a; Dorssen, "Interned!" 20.

19. Oliver Tapper, *Armstrong Whitworth Aircraft Since 1913* (London: Putnam, 1973), 52-69; see also Theo Wesselink and Thijs Postma, *Koolhoven: Nederlands vliegtuigbouwer in de schaduw van Fokker* (Haarlem: Romen, 1981), 15-24.

20. Wesselink and Postma, *Koolhoven,* 21, 25-26.

21. Serooskerken, *The Netherlands and World War I,* 245-54, 268-77.

22. Anthony H. G. Fokker and Bruce Gould, *Flying Dutchman: The Life of Anthony Fokker* (New York: Henry Holt, 1931), 15, 20.

23. *Ibid.,* 116.

24. Hilary St. George Saunders, *Per Ardua: The Rise of British Air Power, 1911-1939* (New York: Arno Press, 1972), 84.

25. The true inventor of the machine-gun interrupter gear is a matter of debate among historians. During the war, Fokker claimed to be the inventor of the device, but already in his autobiography (published in 1931) he admits that the German August Euler had already patented the idea of a fixed forward-firing machine gun in 1910. Swiss aircraft designer Franz Schneider also had a patent on a synchronization device prior to the war. Schneider later sued Fokker for patent infringement. The German courts ruled against Fokker, but the war ended as his lawyers were appealing the verdict, and Fokker got off the hook. For further details, see Robert Hucker, "The Fokker Scourge: Fact or Fiction?" *Air Classics* 15, no. 8 (June 1979): 15-18, 96-97; see also Marc Dierikx, *Fokker: A Transatlantic Biography* (Washington, DC: Smithsonian Institution Press, 1997), 29-35.

26. A. R. Weyl, *Fokker: The Creative Years* (London: Putnam, 1965), 192-244.

27. Michael O'Leary, "Fokker's Last Scourge: The Deadly D VII," *Air Combat* 2, no. 1 (1974): 20; see also Richard K. Schrader, "The Army's Forgotten Fokkers," *Air Classics* 24, no. 5 (May 1988): 65-66.

Notes to Chapter Two

1. C. Smit, *Bescheiden Betreffende de Buitenlandse Politiek van Nederland 1848-1919: Derde Periode 1899-1919, Vierde Deel 1914-1917* (Den Haag: Martinus Nijhoff, 1962), 22.

2. Fokker and Gould, *Flying Dutchman,* 217-18.

3. *Ibid.,* 218-19.

4. *Ibid.,* 224-25.

5. *Ibid.,* 225-26.

6. *Ibid.,* 240.

7. *Ibid.,* 241-42; see also Peter Westburg, "Deadly D-VIII: A Detailed Look at Tony Fokker's Ultimate Fighter. . . .WWI's Best," *Wings* 9, no. 2 (Apr. 1979): 53.

8. Colin Owers, "Especially . . . the D.VII . . . ," *Air Enthusiast* 61 (Jan./Feb. 1996): 57-58.

9. Radko Vašíek, "Fokker D.VII's and the Founding of the Czechoslovak Air Force," *Cross and Cockade Journal* 21, no. 3 (1980): 265.

10. Owers, "Especially . . . the D.VII," 53, 70.

11. René de Leeuw, *Albert Plesman: Luchtvaartpionier en Visionair* (Den Haag: Uitgeverij van de Vereniging van Nederlandse Gemeenten, 1989), 13-19; see also Rob J. M. Mulder, *E.L.T.A.: The First Aviation Exhibition Amsterdam* (Spikkestad: European Airlines Rob Mulder, 2009), 22-30.

12. Mulder, *E.L.T.A.,* 146-82.

13. Wesselink and Postma, *Koolhoven,* 39-40.

14. Walaardt Sacré et al., *Vijf-en-Twintig Jaar Luchtvaart in Nederland,* 228-40; see also Mulder, *E.L.T.A.,* 33-35.

15. Leeuw, *Plesman,* 22-23; Mulder, *E.L.T.A.,* 128-41.

16. Roy Allen, *Pictorial History of KLM Royal Dutch Airlines* (London: Ian Allen Ltd., 1978), 9-13; see also Mulder, *E.L.T.A.,* 140-42.

17. Weyl, *Fokker,* 366-72.

18. Thijs Postma, *Fokker: Aircraft Builders of the World* (London: Jane's, 1979), 49; see also Dierikx, *Fokker,* 88-89.

19. René de Leeuw, ed., *Fokker Commercial Aircraft* (Amsterdam: N. V. Koninklijke Nederlandse Vliegtuigenfabriek Fokker, 1994), 22-27; see also Dierikx, *Fokker,* 90-91.

20. Fokker and Gould, *Flying Dutchman,* 246-47.
21. "Fast Fokker Plane Makes Debut Here," *The New York Times,* July 22, 1921, p. 16.
22. A. N. J. Thomassen À Thuessink van der Hoop, *Door de Lucht naar Indië* (Amsterdam: Scheltens and Giltay, 1926), 97-99.
23. Van der Hoop, *Door de Lucht naar Indië,* 104.
24. Wesselink and Postma, *Koolhoven,* 55-56.
25. H. A. Taylor and Peter Alting, "Fokker's 'Lucky Seven,'" *Air Enthusiast* 12 (April/July 1980): 35.
26. Klaauw et al., *Nederlandse en Belgische Luchtvaart,* 33-34.
27. R. E. G. Davies, *A History of the World's Airlines* (London: Oxford University Press, 1964), 35, 63-64; see also John Stroud, "Wings of Peace: Fokker VIII," *Aeroplane Monthly* (May 1988): 297-300.
28. Leeuw, *Fokker Commercial Aircraft,* 68-70.
29. Edward L. Homze, *Arming the Luftwaffe: The Reich Air Ministry and the German Aircraft Industry 1919-1939* (Lincoln: University of Nebraska Press, 1976), 8-9; see also Weyl, *Fokker,* 388-91.
30. Wim Schoenmaker and Thijs Postma, *KLu Vliegtuigen* (Alkmaar: Uitgeverij De Alk, 1987), 36-37.
31. Schoenmaker and Postma, *KLu Vliegtuigen,* 40-43; see also Dan Hagedorn and Antonio L. Sapienza, *Aircraft of the Chaco War* (Atglen, PA: Schiffer Military/Aviation History, 1997), 58-59.
32. Colin Owers, "Fokker's Fifth: The C.V Multi-role Biplane," *Air Enthusiast* 53 (Spring 1994): 60-68.
33. Quoted in Giorgio Rochat, "The Italian Air Force in the Ethiopian War (1935-1936)," in Ruth Ben-Ghiat and Mia Fuller, eds., *Italian Colonialism* (New York: Palgrave, 2005), 38.
34. Schoenmaker and Postma, *KLu Vliegtuigen,* 45-46.
35. Klaauw, *Nederlandse en Belgische Luchtvaart,* 38-39.
36. *Ibid.,* 40-41; see also Thijs Postma, *Vermetele Vliegende Hollanders* (Bussum: Unieboek, 1975), 37-39.
37. Sacré et al., *Vijf-en-Twintig Jaar Luchtvaart*, 107-49.
38. *Ibid.,* 150-68.
39. Gerard J. Casius, "The Curtiss P-6 in the Netherlands East Indies," *Air Combat* (March 1976): 66-69.

Notes to Chapter Three

1. "American Airplanes Scorned by Fokker," *The New York Times*, August 15, 1918, p. 6.
2. "Fokker Sees 1-Day Flights to Europe," *The New York Times*, November 11, 1920, p. 8.
3. Colin A. Owers, "The Fokker D.VII in US Service," *Skyways* no. 86 (2008): 18-25. See also Owers, "Especially... the D.VII..." 58.
4. Quoted in Burke Davis, *The Billy Mitchell Affair* (New York: Random House, 1967), 140.
5. Spencer Lane, *First World Flight: The Odyssey of Billy Mitchell* (Daytona Beach, FL: U.S. Press, 2002), 133-37.
6. Maurer Maurer, *Aviation in the U.S. Army, 1919-1939* (Washington, DC: Office of Air Force History, United States Air Force, 1987), 177-82.
7. "Coast to Coast," *Time*, May 12, 1923.
8. William Mitchell, *Winged Defense: The Development and Possibilities of Modern Air Power—Economic and Military* (New York: G. P. Putnam's Sons, 1925), 88-89.
9. C. B. Allen, "The Ford Tour," *Aero Digest* (Nov. 1925): 606, 634.
10. Timothy J. O'Callaghan, *The Aviation Legacy of Henry and Edsel Ford* (Ann Arbor, MI: Proctor Publications, LLC, 2000), 67-68.
11. R. E. G. Davies, *TWA: An Airline and Its Aircraft* (McLean, VA: Paldwr Press, 2000), 8, 14-15, 22.
12. R. E. G. Davies, *Pan Am: An Airline and Its Aircraft* (New York: Orion Books, 1987), 6-7, 27; see also Dierikx, *Fokker,* 119-21.
13. Collin Bakse, ed., *Airlift Tanker: History of U.S. Airlift and Tanker Forces* (Paducah, KY: Turner Publishing Co., 1995), 52-53.
14. Richard K. Smith, *Seventy-Five Years of Inflight Refueling: Highlights, 1923-1998* (Washington, DC: Air Force History and Museums Program, 1998), 3-7.
15. David R. Mets, *Master of Airpower: General Carl A. Spaatz* (Novato, CA: Presidio Press, 1988), 69-73.
16. Maurer, *Aviation in the U.S. Army,* 260-65; see also Bakse, ed., *Airlift Tanker,* 52-53.
17. R. H. Scheppler, "Fokker's Four-Engined Failure," *Air Classics* 11, no. 6 (June 1975): 54-64; see also Chan King, "Four-Engined First: Fokker's F.32," *Wings* 32, no. 6 (Dec. 2002): 14-23.
18. "Death of Rockne," *Time,* April 6, 1931.
19. "A Piece of Ice?" *Time,* April 13, 1931.
20. *Ibid.*
21. "Fokker Fuss," *Time,* May 18, 1931.
22. Alain J. Pelletier, "Fokker Twighlight," *Air Enthusiast* 117 (May/June 2005): 62-66; see also Dierikx, *Fokker,* 138-45.
23. Wilbur H. Morrison, *Donald W. Douglas: A Heart With Wings* (Ames, IA: Iowa State University Press, 1991), 84.
24. Wayne Biddle, *Barons of the Sky* (New York: Simon and Schuster, 1991), 203.
25. *Ibid.,* 202-6.
26. Frank A. Tichenor, "Roosevelt and Farley Charged with 'Fraud and Collusion'!!" *Aero Digest* (October 1936): 18-19.
27. Biddle, *Barons of the Sky,* 222-23.
28. Richard Norton Smith, *The Colonel: The Life and Legend of Robert R. McCormick, 1880-1955* (Boston: Houghton Mifflin Company, 1997), 347-48.
29. "Elliott Roosevelt Linked to Air Deal," *The New York Times,* Oct. 7, 1936.
30. Tichenor, "Roosevelt and Farley," 24.
31. "Fokker Affidavit Tells Roosevelt's Son Deal," *The Los Angeles Times,* Oct. 7, 1936.

Notes to Chapter Four

1. Quoted in O'Callaghan, *The Aviation Legacy,* 100.
2. Raimund E. Goerler, *To the Pole: The Diary and Notebook of Richard E. Byrd, 1925-1927* (Columbus: Ohio State University Press, 1998), 41-48.
3. Richard Evelyn Byrd, *Skyward* (New York: G. P. Putnam's Sons, 1928), 178-80.
4. *Ibid.,* 192.
5. *Ibid.,* 197.
6. Dennis Rawlins, "Byrd's Heroic 1926 Flight and Its Faked Last Leg," *Dio: The International Journal of Scientific History* 10 (Jan. 2000): 9-22; see also "Did Byrd Reach Pole? His Diary Hints 'No,'" *The New York Times*, May 9, 1996, 1; and Goerler, *To the Pole,* 52-59.
7. Byrd, *Skyward,* 235-36.
8. Fokker and Gould, *Flying Dutchman,* 257-58.
9. "Byrd Plane Crashes in its First Trial," *The New York Times*, Apr. 17, 1927, 1, 22.
10. Byrd, *Skyward,* 240.
11. Fokker and Gould, *Flying Dutchman,* 261.
12. Byrd, *Skyward,* 267.
13. Fokker and Gould, *Flying Dutchman,* 263.
14. Commander Richard E. Byrd, "Our Transatlantic Flight," *Aero Digest* (July 1927): 10.
15. "Uncle Tony," *Time*, May 4, 1931.
16. Maurer, *Aviation in the U.S. Army, 1919-1939* (Washington, DC: Office of Air Force History United States Air Force, 1987), 256-60.
17. C. E. Kingsford-Smith and C. T. P. Ulm, *The Flight of the Southern Cross* (New York: Robert M. McBride & Company, 1929), 23-24.
18. *Ibid.,* 35-36.
19. *Ibid.,* 81
20. *Ibid.,* 111-12.
21. *Ibid.,* 226-27.
22. *Ibid.,* 252-53.
23. Doris L. Rich, *Amelia Earhart: A Biography* (Washington, DC: Smithsonian Institution, 1989), 63-65.
24. Amelia Earhart, *20 Hrs. 40 Min.: Our Flight in the Friendship* (New York: G. P. Putnam's Sons, 1928), 119-20.
25. *Ibid.,* 191-95.
26. *Ibid.,* 199-200.

Notes to Chapter Five

1. Leeuw, *Fokker Commercial Aircraft,* 76-79; see also John Stroud, "Wings of Peace," *Aeroplane Monthly* (November 1985): 602-5.
2. The Short S.8 Calcutta had a cruising speed of 97 mph, the de Havilland D.H.66 Hercules had a cruising speed of 110 mph, and the Fokker F.XII of KLM had a cruising speed of 127 mph. Figures taken from Enzo Angelucci, *The Illustrated Encyclopedia of Civil Aircraft* (Edison: Chartwell Books, 2001), 106, 200; see also Leeuw, *Fokker Commercial Aircraft,* 77.
3. Davies, *A History of the World's Airlines,* 173-74; see also R. E. G. Davies, *British Airways: An Airline and Its Aircraft Volume 1: 1919-1939* (McLean, VA: Paldwr Press, 2005), 35.
4. Albert Plesman, "The Amsterdam-Batavia Weekly Service," *Flight* 25 (February 9, 1933): 128-31.
5. Peter W. Brooks, *The Modern Airliner: Its Origins and Development* (London: Putnam, 1961), 57-59.
6. Leeuw, *Fokker Commercial Aircraft,* 93-94; see also "Fokker F.XX Commercial Airplane (Dutch)," *National Advisory Committee for Aeronautics Aircraft Circular No. 187* (February 1934), National Air and Space Museum Technical File #AF-700490-01.
7. Harm J. Hazewinkel, *Pander: Een Haagse vliegtuigbouwer* (Hilversum: All Media Productions, 2006), 98-104.
8. Anne Robertson Coupar, *The Smirnoff Story* (London: Jarrolds Publishers Ltd., 1960), 94-98.
9. Hazewinkel, *Pander,* 106-7.

10. Coupar, *Smirnoff,* 100-127; see also René de Leeuw, *KLM: De Geschiedenis van de KLM vanaf 1919* (Weesp: Unieboek, 1984), 43-47.

11. René J. Francillon, *McDonnell Douglas Aircraft Since 1920: Volume I* (Annapolis: Naval Institute Press, 1979), 150-54.

12. N. Geldhof and P. C. Kok, *Douglas DC-2: De eerste blikken vogel van de KLM en de KNILM* (Bergen: Bonneville, 1997), 41-46.

13. Geldhof and Kok, *Douglas DC-2,* 56-58; see also Johan P. Nater, *De Uiver: Glorie en tragiek in de Melbourne race* (Rotterdam: Ad. Donker, 1983), 56-60.

14. Leeuw, *Fokker Commercial Aircraft,* 100-103; see also "The Fokker Fours," *Air Enthusiast* 1, no. 6 (November 1971): 293; see also C. M. Poulsen, "Speed and Comfort: Some Impressions of an Afternoon Spent in Flying Around Holland in an F.36 and a Douglas D.2," *Flight* (Sept. 27, 1934): 994-96.

15. Quoted in Arthur Swinson, *The Great Air Race: England-Australia 1934* (London: Cassell, 1968), 14.

16. *Ibid.,* 78.

17. *Ibid.,* 94-96.

18. "The Story of the Australia Race," *Flight* 26, no. 1348 (Oct. 25, 1934): 1110-11.

19. Hazewinkel, *Pander,* 111-15.

20. K. D. Parmentier, *In Drie Dagen naar Australië* (Amsterdam: Scheltens & Giltay, 1935), 152-53.

21. *Ibid.,* 164.

22. *Ibid.,* 183.

23. Dierikx, *Fokker,* 161-62.

24. Francillon, *McDonnell Douglas Aircraft Since 1920,* 218-23.

25. Wibo Burgers, *De Geschiedenis van de Luchtvaart in Nederland* (Rijswijk: Uitgeverij Elmar, 1988), 58-65.

26. *KLM's Caribbean Decade, 1934-1944* (Curacao: Koninklijke Luchtvaart Maatschappij voor Nederland en Kolonien, n.v., 1944); see also R. E. G. Davies, *Airlines of Latin America Since 1919* (McLean, VA: Paldwr Press, 1997), 148-50.

27. Melvin Hall and Walter Peck, "Wings for the Trojan Horse," *Foreign Affairs* 19, no. 2 (January 1941): 347-69.

28. Instituto de Historia y Cultura Aérea, *Historia de la Aviacion Española* (Madrid: Instituto de Historia y Cultura Aérea, 1988), 195-202; see also Gerald Howson, "Fokker's Trimotors Go To War," *Air Enthusiast* 13 (August/November 1980): 43-47.

29. Howson, "Fokker's Trimotors," 47-49.

30. Brooks, The *Modern Airliner,* 91.

31. F. Koolhoven, "Vliegboot of Landvliegtuig," *Het Vliegveld* (September 1937): 280-82.

32. Harry Van der Meer, "Koolhovens Oceaanvliegboot," *Verenigde Vleugels* (November 2007): 16-17.

33. Francillon, *McDonnell Douglas Aircraft Since 1920,* 265-68.

34. "Beschrijving Fokker Ontwerp 132" (N.V. Nederlandsche Vliegtuigenfabriek Fokker), 1-5; "Opmerkingen Vergelyking Douglas DC-4 en Fokker 132" (N.V. Nederlandsche Vliegtuigenfabriek Fokker), 3; Fokker Ontwerp 132 file, Fokker Heritage Trust, Aviodrome, Lelystad.

35. Notulen van de 193ste Vergadering van den Raad van Bestuur, gehouden op Dinsdag 8 November 1938, KLM Historical Archives; see also "Huge Stratoliner Wreck in Test; 10 on Board Killed," *The New York Times,* March 19, 1939, p. 1.

36. See Bericht op brief van 15 September. 1939 Betreffende aanschaffing nieuw materieel. La.A.A.Luchtvaartdienst van het Ministerie van Waterstaat aan de Voorzitter van de Raad van Bestuur van de K.L.M. 26 September 1939, and Brief van den Waarnemend Algemeen Secretaris aan den Leden van de Raad van Bestuur, 6 November 1939, KLM Historical Archives. See also "Concept Ontwerp 180" (25 October 1939), Fokker Ontwerp 180 file, Fokker Heritage Trust, Aviodrome, Lelystad.

Notes to Chapter Six

1. Peter Hoffmann, "Peace Through Coup d'Etat: The Foreign Contacts of the German Resistance 1933-1944," *Central European History* 19, no. 1 (March 1986): 21.

2. Raoul François Casimir van Overstraeten, *Albert I-Leopold III, vingt ans de politique militaire belge 1920-1940* (Bruges: Desclee de Brouwer, 1946), 458; see also Jean Vanwelkenhuyzen, *Le 10 janvier 1940 a Mechelen-sur-Meuse: le plan de Hitler aux mains des Belges* (Bruxelles: Goemaere, 1955).

3. Walter B. Maass, *The Netherlands at War: 1940-1945* (London: Abelard-Schuman, 1970), 18.

4. Schoenmaker and Postma, *KLu Vliegtuigen,* 48-49; see also Peter Westburg, "Fokker's Last Biplane Fight," *Air Classics* 1, no. 7 (July 1975): 60-73.

5. Schoenmaker and Postma, *KLu Vliegtuigen,* 51-53.

6. *Ibid.*, 54-57; see also Frits Gerdessen and Luuk Boerman, *Fokker D.XXI: historie, camouflage en kentekens* (Zwammerdam: Dutch Profile, 2007), 41-43.

7. Schoenmaker and Postma, *KLu Vliegtuigen,* 62-64; see also Bart van der Klaauw, "Frustrated Fokker," *Air International* (November 1986): 241-49.

8. Schoenmaker and Postma, *KLu Vliegtuigen,* 58-61.

9. W. Schoenmaker and F. Postma, *Mei 1940: De verdediging van het Nederlandse luchtruim* (Amsterdam/Dieren: Bataafsche Leeuw, 1985). See also Rob de Bruin et al., *Illusies en Incidenten: De Militair Luchtvaart en de neutraliteitshandhaving tot 10 mei 1940* ('s-Gravenhage: Koninklijke Luchtmacht / Bureau Drukwerk en Formulierenbeheer DMKLu, 1988), 35-51.

10. Fokker Ontwerp 150 and 151 files, Fokker Heritage Trust, Aviodrome, Lelystad. See also Bruin et al., *Illusies en Incidenten,* 38, and T. J. M. Wesselink, "The Fighter That Missed the War . . . The Last of the Koolhovens," *Air International* (April 1976): 185-89.

11. L. Th. van't Hof, "Dit had onze jachtkruiser voor 1941 moeten worden: De Fokker G-2, opvolger van een geweldenaar," *Vliegende Hollander* (December 1962): 408-11; see also Frits Gerdessen, "Fokker's 'Paper' Fighters: Interwar Projects," *Air Enthusiast* 95 (September/October 2001): 38-42; Bruin et al., *Illusies en Incidenten,* 46-47; and Luchtkruiser Studie-Ontwerp Fokker tek. 47992, 1939, Fokker Heritage Trust, Aviodrome, Lelystad.

12. Gerdessen, "Fokker's 'Paper' Fighters,'" 38-42.

13. Willem Vredeling, *Fokker D.23* (Maarssen: Geromy, 2007); see also Ontwerp 155 file, Fokker Heritage Trust, Aviodrome, Lelystad.

14. Bruin et al., *Illusies en Incidenten,* 38.

15. *Ibid.*, 56-57; see also Wesselink, "The Fighter That Missed the War . . . ," 188.

16. *Ibid.*, 42, 56-57; see also *Ibid.*, 198.

17. F. J. Molenaar, *De luchtverdediging in de meidagen 1940, twee banden* (Den Haag: Staatsuitgeverij, 1970); see also Brian Cull, Bruce Lander, and Heinrich Weiss, *Twelve Days in May* (London: Grub Street, 1995), 7-8.

18. Henry L. Mason, "War Comes to The Netherlands: September 1939–May 1940," *Political Science Quarterly* 78, no. 4 (December 1963): 558.

19. Jeffery A. Gunsburg, *Divided and Conquered: The French High Command and the Defeat of the West, 1940* (London: Greenwood Press, 1979), 150-52; see also Andre Ausems, "The Netherlands Military Intelligence Summaries 1939-1940 and the Defeat in the Blitzkrieg of May 1940," *Military Affairs* 50, no. 4 (October 1986): 190-99; see also Ernest R. May, *Strange Victory: Hitler's Conquest of France* (New York: Hill and Wang, 2000), 312-13.

20. Geoffrey J. Thomas and Barry Kelly, *KG 200: The Luftwaffe's Most Secret Unit* (Crowborough: Hikoki Publications, 2003), 15-19; see also Bruin et al., *Illusies en Incidenten*, 150-63.

21. John Mosier, *The Blitzkrieg Myth: How Hitler and the Allies Misread the Strategic Realities of World War II* (New York: HarperCollins, 2003), 121-22; see also Mason, "War Comes to The Netherlands," 563-66.

Notes to Chapter Seven

1. All times given in the rest of the chapter are Amsterdam time.

2. Gerdessen, *Fokker D.XXI*, 37-38.

3. Lieutenant Colonel E. H. Brongers, *The Battle for The Hague* (Soesterberg: Uitgeverij Aspekt, 2004), 42-62.

4. *Ibid.*, 63-65.

5. *Ibid.*, 67-76.

6. *Ibid.*, 90-101.

7. *Ibid.*, 76-90.

8. Molenaar, *De luchtverdediging in de meidagen 1940*, 119-57.

9. Douglas Dildy, "Meidagen 1940: The Dutch Air Arms Defense Against the German Invasion, May, 1940; Part 2a, Chapter 3," *Small Air Forces Observer* 28, no. 2 (October 2004): 44-45; see also Peter D. Cornwell, *The Battle of France: Then and Now* (Old Harlow: Battle of Britain International Ltd., 2007), 205.

10. K. Mallan, *Als de Dag van Gisteren . . . De Duitse Overrompeling en Vernietiging van Nederlands Eerste Havenstad* (Weesp: De Gooise Uitgeverij, 1985), 94-98.

11. *Ibid.*, 98-122.

12. Several Dutch accounts maintain that Schulz forced the airfield commandant, Major Simon Thomas, to act as a human shield riding on the sideboard of his own car, to go forward and order the Dutch soldiers still firing on the airfield to surrender. A Dutch sergeant major in command of the position refused to surrender and opened fire on the car. Two Germans were killed, but the commandant was hit as well. The Dutch then surged forward and picked up their commander, who died shortly thereafter. The exact details of this encounter are still unknown.

13. Mallan, *Als de Dag van Gisteren,* 126-30, 137-42.

14. *Ibid.*, 131-36; see also E. H. Brongers, *Opmars naar Rotterdam, Deel I* (Soesterberg: Uitgeverij Aspekt, 2004), 146-49.

15. Mallan, *Als de Dag van Gisteren,* 143-48; see also Wim Horn-

man, *De helden van de Willemsbrug: Rotterdam, mei 1940* (Amsterdam: Omega Boek, 1984).

16. Mallan, *Als de Dag van Gisteren*, 153-56.

17. Theo Wesselink, "The Saga of the T VIIIw," *Air Enthusiast* 20 (December 1982): 66-68; see also Cornwell, *Battle of France*, 194.

18. Molenaar, *De luchtverdediging in de meidagen 1940*, 144-50.

19. *Ibid.*, 239-65, 283-93.

20. S. J. Postma, *HU-BO-BE: De strategische VerVa in de oorlogsdagen van 1940* (Assen: Born's Uitgeversbedrijf N.V., 1945), 25-26.

21. *Ibid.*, 26-29.

22. Brongers, *The Battle for The Hague*, 128-63; see also Cornwell, *The Battle of France*, 206-29.

23. Alistair Horne, *To Lose a Battle: France 1940* (Boston: Little, Brown, 1969), 242.

24. Molenaar, *De luchtverdediging in de meidagen 1940*, 150-51.

25. Mallen, *Als de Dag van Gisteren*, 159; see also Wilhelmina Steenbeek, *Rotterdam. Invasion of Holland* (New York: Ballantine, 1973), 81.

26. Mallen, *Al de Dag van Gisteren*, 158-62.

27. Postma, *HU-BO-BE*, 41-43.

28. *Ibid.*, 51-52.

29. Molenaar, *De luchtverdediging in de meidagen 1940*, 152-55.

30. *Führer-Weisung nr. 11*, http://der-fuehrer.org/reden/deutsch/Weisungen/1940-05-14.htm; see also Martin Moll, *"Führer-Erlasse" 1939-1945: Edition sämtlicher* überlieferter, *nicht im Reichsgesetzblatt abgedruckter, von Hitler während des Zweiten Weltkrieges schriftlich erteilter Direktiven aus den Bereichen Staat, Partei, Wirtschaft, Besatzungspolitik und Militärverwaltung* (Stuttgart: F. Steiner, 1997).

31. Wilhelm Speidel, *The German Air Force in France and the Low Countries 1939-1940*, Volume 3 (Karlsruhe: Studiegruppe Geschichte des Luftkrieges, 1958), 480-81. See also declassified document, USAF Historical Study 152, Microfilm Reel IRIS Number (E) K1026U 468153pt6, Air Force Historical Research Agency, Maxwell AFB.

32. Mallan, *Als de Dag van Gisteren*, 196-213.

33. J. L. van der Pauw, *Rotterdam in de Tweede Wereldoorlog* (Rotterdam: Uitgeverij Boom, 2006), 84-100; see also Brongers, *Opmars, Deel III*, 222-42.

34. Mallan, *Als de Dag van Gisteren*, 218-21; see also Steenbeek, *Rotterdam*, 127-29.

35. C. W. Star Busmann, *De Tweede Wereldoorlog: De bange Meidagen van '40* (Rotterdam: Lekturama, 1978), 65-67.

36. Transcripts from International Military Tribunal, *The Trial of German Major War Criminals: Proceedings of the International Military Tribunal Sitting at Nuremberg, Germany*, 23 volumes (London: Published Under the Authority of H.M. Attorney-General by H.M. Stationery Office, 1946).

Notes to Chapter Eight

1. Gerard Casius, "Batavia's Big Sticks," *Air Enthusiast* 22 (Aug.-Nov. 1983): 1-4.

2. William H. Garzke, Jr. and Robert O. Dulin, Jr., *Battleships: Allied Battleships in World War II* (Annapolis, MD: Naval Institute Press, 1980), 153-56.

3. Gerard Casius, "The St. Louis Lightweight," *Air Enthusiast* 16 (1983): 37-39.

4. Gerry Beauchamp, "The 90-Day War," *Air Combat* 4, no. 1 (Jan. 1976): 72-74.

5. Gerard Casius, *Brewster B-339C/D/-23: historie, camouflage en kentekens* (Zwammerdam: Dutch Profile, 2008), 21-25, 30-34.

6. Bob de Graaff, "Hot Intelligence in the Tropics: Dutch Intelligence Operations in the Netherlands East Indies during the Second World War," *Journal of Contemporary History* 22, no. 4, *Intelligence Services during the Second World War: Part 2* (Oct. 1987): 563-64.

7. *Ten Years of Japanese Burrowing in the Netherlands East Indies* (New York: The Netherlands Information Bureau, 1942); see also Davies, *A History of the World's Airlines*, 192.

8. John B. Lundstrom, *The First South Pacific Campaign: Pacific Fleet Strategy December 1941–June 1942* (Annapolis: Naval Institute Press, 1976), 8; see also John Toland, *The Rising Sun: The Decline and Fall of the Japanese Empire 1936-1945* (New York: Random House, 1970), 86.

9. Ellen van Zyll de Jong, "Netherlands Indies to Produce Aviation Fuel for Far East," *Far Eastern Survey* 9, no. 10 (May 8, 1940): 116-17.

10. Louis Allen, "Japanese Intelligence Systems," *Journal of Contemporary History* 22, no. 4, *Intelligence Services during the Second World War: Part 2* (Oct. 1987): 551-52. See also Rupert Emerson, "The Dutch East Indies Adrift," *Foreign Affairs* 18, no. 4 (July 1940): 739.

11. Richard J. Aldrich, *Intelligence and the War Against Japan* (Cambridge, UK: Cambridge University Press, 2000), 81-82.

12. Rear Admiral Edwin T. Layton, U.S.N., *"And I Was There": Pearl Harbor and Midway—Breaking the Secrets* (New York: William Morrow, 1985), 206-7, 521-22; see also Casius, *Brewster B-339C/D/-23*, 40.

13. Layton, *"And I Was There,"* 53-55; see also John Costello, *The Pacific War* (New York: Rawson, Wade, 1981), 188-89.

14. Aldrich, *Intelligence*, 45-46.

15. René J. Francillon, *Japanese Aircraft of the Pacific War* (Annapolis, MD: Naval Institute Press, 1988), 350-87. See also Tom Womack, *The Dutch Naval Air Force Against Japan: The Defense of the Netherlands East Indies, 1941-1942* (Jefferson, NC: McFarland, 2006), 45-48.

16. Womack, *The Dutch Naval Air Force*, 52-56. The exact fate of the *Shinonome* is a mystery. One source notes that the destroyer was sunk by Martin bombers of 2-VLG 1 on December 17 (Casius, "Batavia's Big Sticks," 9); P. C. De Boer, in *De Luchtstrijd rond Borneo* (Houten: Van Holkema & Warendorf, 1987), claims that Martins sank the destroyer on December 18. To this day, the wreck of the ship has not been found.

17. Womack, *The Dutch Naval Air Force*, 64-69.

18. *Ibid.*, 69-70.

19. Christopher Shores and Brian Cull, with Yasuho Izawa, *Bloody Shambles: Volume 1* (London: Grub Street, 1992), 204-5; see also Casius, "Batavia's Big Sticks," 10.

20. Shores et al., *Bloody Shambles: Volume 1*, 202, 208-9; Brian Cull, with Paul Sorthaug and Mark Haselden, *Buffalos Over Singapore* (London: Grub Street, 2003), 205.

21. Casius, "Batavia's Big Sticks," 12-14; see also Shores et al., *Bloody Shambles: Volume 1*, 208, 212-16.

22. Gordon L. Rottman and A. Takizawa, *Japanese Paratroop Forces in World War II* (Oxford: Osprey Publishing, 2005), 20-24.

23. Casius, "Batavia's Big Sticks," 14-15; see also Shores et al., *Bloody Shambles: Volume 1*, 223-28.

24. Beauchamp, "The 90-Day War," 74-75; see also Shores et al., *Bloody Shambles: Volume 1*, 142-43.

25. Cull, *Buffalos Over Singapore*, 91-92, 120.

26. Rottman and Takizawa, *Japanese Paratroop Forces*, 31-43.

27. Shores et al., *Bloody Shambles: Volume 2*, 146-50.

28. Casius, "The St. Louis Lightweight," 42-43; see also Shores et al., *Bloody Shambles: Volume 2*, 150-55.

29. Shores et al., *Bloody Shambles: Volume 2*, 168-69.

30. *Ibid.*, 208.

31. C. C. Küpfer, *Onze Vliegers in Indië* (Haarlem, Netherlands: Uitgave Boom-Ruigrok N.V., 1947), 290-97; see also Shores et al., *Bloody Shambles: Volume 2*, 202-16.

32. Shores et al., *Bloody Shambles: Volume 2*, 201.

33. F. C. van Oosten, *The Battle of the Java Sea* (Annapolis: Naval Institute Press, 1976), 46-55.

34. Dwight R. Messimer, *Pawns of War: The Loss of the USS* Langley *and the USS* Pecos (Annapolis, MD: Naval Institute Press, 1983), 21-50.

35. Messimer, *Pawns of War*, 51-117; 199.

36. Shores et al., *Bloody Shambles: Volume 2*, 292-302.

37. Mervyn W. Prime, *WA's Pearl Harbour: The Japanese Raid on Broome* (Bullcreek, UK: Royal Australian Air Force Association, 1985), 4-9.

38. William H. Tyler, *Flight of Diamonds: The Story of Broome's War and the Carnot Bay Diamonds* (Victoria Park: Hesperian Press, 1987), 11-13.

39. *Ibid.*, 13-15.

40. *Ibid.*, 16-20.

Notes to the Conclusion

1. Wesselink, "Saga of the T.VIIIw," 68-71.

2. Tieme Festner, "No. 322 Squadron, Royal Netherlands Air Force," *Wings of Fame* 15 (1999): 22-26; see also Kolonel A. P. de Jong, *Vlucht door de tijd: 75 jaar Nederlandse luchtmacht* (Houten: Unieboek, 1988), 104-6.

3. Leeuw, *KLM: De Geschiedenis van de KLM vanaf 1919*, 61-64.

4. "Foreign News: The Luftwaffe Intercepts," *Time*, June 14, 1943, 30.

5. Leeuw, *KLM: De Geschiedenis van de KLM vanaf 1919*, 64-67.

6. Gerard Casius and Peter Boer, "NEIAF: The Story of an Unusual Air Force, Part II," *Air Combat* 3 (1975): 65-71.

7. See RAAF Historical Section, *Units of the Royal Australian Air Force: A Concise History*, Volumes 2 and 3 (Canberra: Australian Government Publishing Service, 1995); Doug Hurst, *De vierde bondgenoot: de Nederlandse strijdkrachten in Australië tijdens de Tweede Wereldoorlog* (Zwolle: Waanders Uitgevers, 2006); and René Wittert, *Het Vergeten Squadron* (Franeker: Uitgeverij T. Wever B.V., 1983).

BIBLIOGRAPHY

Archives and Collections

Boeing Corporate Archives, Bellevue, WA
Cavaleriemuseum, Bernhardkazerne, Amersfoort
Deutsches Technikmuseum, Berlin
Douglas Commercial Aircraft Archive, Cypress, CA
Fokker Heritage Trust, Aviodrome, Lelystad
KLM Historical Archives, Amstelveen
Koninklijke Bibliotheek, Den Haag
Henry Ford Museum, Dearborn, MI
Het Legermuseum, Delft*
Maria-Austria Instituut, Amsterdam
Militair Luchtvaart Museum, Soesterberg*
Museum of the United States Air Force, Dayton, OH
National Air and Space Museum, Washington, DC
Stichting Koolhoven Vliegtuigen, Aviodrome, Lelystad

**At the time of publication, the former Legermuseum in Delft and the Militair Luchtvaart Museum in Soesterberg are being combined into a new Nationaal Militair Museum in Soesterberg.*

Published Sources

Aarssen, Kees. *Van Berkel's Patent, de luchtvaartafdeling: van weegschaal tot vliegtuig.* Maarssen: Geromy, 2010.

Aldrich, Richard J. *Intelligence and the War against Japan.* Cambridge: Cambridge University Press, 2000.

Allen, C. B. "The Ford Tour." *Aero Digest* (Nov. 1925): 606, 634-36.

Allen, Louis. "Japanese Intelligence Systems." *Journal of Contemporary History* 22, no. 4, *Intelligence Services during the Second World War: Part 2* (Oct. 1987): 547-62.

Allen, Roy. *Pictorial History of KLM Royal Dutch Airlines.* London: Ian Allen, 1978.

Angelucci, Enzo. *The Illustrated Encyclopedia of Civil Aircraft.* Edison, NJ: Chartwell Books, 2001.

——. *The Rand McNally Encyclopedia of Military Aircraft.* New York: Military Press, 1983.

Apostolo, Giorgio. *Color Profiles of World War I Combat Planes.* New York: Crescent Books, 1974.

Ausems, Andre. "The Netherlands Military Intelligence Summaries 1939-1940 and the Defeat in the Blitzkrieg of May 1940." *Military Affairs* 50, no. 4 (1986): 190-99.

Avery, Norm, ed. "Fokker Views." *Skyways: The Journal of the Airplane, 1920-1940* 31 (1994): 18-31.

Bakse, Collin, ed. *Airlift Tanker: History of U.S. Airlift and Tanker Forces.* Paducah, KY: Turner Publishing, 1995.

Beauchamp, Gerry. "The 90-Day War." *Air Combat* 4, no. 1 (1976): 72-78.

Beeling, Marius. "Dutch Digression." *Air Enthusiast International* (Feb. 1974): 69-75.

Belcarz, Bartołomiej, and Robert Pęczkowski. *White Eagles: The Aircraft, Men, and Operations of the Polish Air Force, 1918-1939.* Ottringham: Hikoki Publications, 2001.

Ben-Ghiat, Ruth, and Mia Fuller, eds. *Italian Colonialism.* New York: Palgrave Macmillan, 2005.

Bennett-Bremner. E. *Front-Line Airline: Air Transport during the South-West Pacific War, 1939-44.* London: Paul Elek, 1945.

Biddle, Wayne. *Barons of the Sky.* New York: Simon and Schuster, 1991.

Boer, P. C. *De luchtstrijd rond Borneo: operaties van de Militair Luchtvaart KNIL in de periode december 1941 tot februari 1942.* Houten: Van Holkema & Warendorf, 1987.

Bowers, Peter M. "Famous Ocean-Spanning Fokkers: Part 1." *Air Progress* (Dec. 1967): 52-58, 82.

——. "Famous Ocean-Spanning Fokkers: Part 2." *Air Progress* (Jan. 1968): 49-51, 62-64.

Boyd, Alexander. *The Soviet Air Force Since 1918.* New York: Stein and Day, 1977.

Brongers, Lt. Col. E. H. *The Battle for The Hague.* Soesterberg: Uitgeverij Aspekt, 2004.

——. *Opmars naar Rotterdam, Deel I.* Soesterberg: Uitgeverij Aspekt, 2004.

Brooks, Peter W. *The Modern Airliner: Its Origins and Development.* London: Putnam, 1961.

Bruin, Rob de, et al. *Illusies en Incidenten: De Militair Luchtvaart en de neutraliteitshandhaving tot 10 mei 1940.* The Hague: Koninklijke Luchtmacht/Bureau Drukwerk en Formulierenbeheer DMKLu, 1988.

Burgers, Wibo. *De Geschiedenis van de Luchtvaart in Nederland.* Rijswijk: Uitgeverij Elmar, 1988.

Busmann, C. W. Star. *De Tweede Wereldoorlog: De bange Meidagen van '40.* Rotterdam: Lekturama, 1978.

Byers, Richard. "An Unhappy Marriage: The Junkers-Fokker Merger." *Journal of Historical Biography* 3 (2008): 1-30.

Byrd, Richard Evelyn. "Our Transatlantic Flight." *Aero Digest* (July 1927): 8-14.

——. *Skyward.* New York: Putnam, 1928.

Casius, Gerard J. "American-Built Civilian Airplanes in the Netherlands East Indies, 1935-1942." *American Aviation Historical Society Journal* 28, no. 2 (1983): 144-48.

——. "Batavia's Big Sticks." *Air Enthusiast* 22 (1983): 1-20.

——. *Brewster B-339C/D/-23: historie, camouflage en kentekens.* Zwammerdam: Dutch Profile, 2008.

——. "The Curtiss P-6 in the Netherlands East Indies." *Air Combat* (Mar. 1976): 66-69.

——. "Glenn Martin's Biplanes in Dutch Service." *Air Combat* (Mar. 1976): 18-21, 74-78.

——. "The St. Louis Lightweight." *Air Enthusiast* 16 (1983): 33-44, 65.

Casius, Gerard, and Peter Boer. "NEIAF: The Story of an Unusual Air Force, Part I." *Air Combat* 3, no. 2 (1975): 62-69, 78.

——. "NEIAF: The Story of an Unusual Air Force, Part II." *Air Combat* 3, no. 3 (1975): 65-71.

——. "NEIAF: The Story of an Unusual Air Force, Part III." *Air Combat* 3, no. 4 (1975): 22-25, 68-74.

Copp, DeWitt S. *A Few Great Captains: The Men and Events That Shaped the Development of U.S. Air Power.* New York: Doubleday, 1980.

Cornwell, Peter D. *The Battle of France: Then and Now.* Old Harlow: Battle of Britain International, 2007.

Costello, John. *The Pacific War.* New York: Rawson, Wade, 1981.

Coupar, Anne Robertson. *The Smirnoff Story.* London: Jarrolds Publishers, 1960.

Cull, Brian, Bruce Lander, and Heinrich Weiss. *Twelve Days in May.* London: Grub Street, 1995.

Cull, Brian, with Paul Sortehaug. *Hurricanes Over Singapore.* London: Grub Street, 2004.

Cull, Brian, with Paul Sortehaug and Mark Haselden. *Buffalos Over Singapore.* London: Grub Street, 2003.

Cynk, Jerzy B. *History of the Polish Air Force, 1918-1968.* Reading: Osprey Publishing, 1972.

——. *The Polish Air Force at War: The Official History, Vol. 1, 1939-1943.* Atglen, PA: Schiffer Military History, 2004.

Davies, R. E. G. *Airlines of Latin America Since 1919.* McLean, VA: Paldwr Press, 1997.

——. *British Airways: An Airline and Its Aircraft Volume 1: 1919-1939.* McLean, VA: Paldwr Press, 2005.

——. *A History of the World's Airlines.* London: Oxford University Press, 1964.

——. *Pan Am: An Airline and Its Aircraft.* New York: Orion Books, 1987.

——. *TWA: An Airline and Its Aircraft.* McLean, VA: Paldwr Press, 2000.

Davis, Burke. *The Billy Mitchell Affair.* New York: Random House, 1967.

Dierikx, Marc. *Bevlogen jaren: Nederlandse burgerluchtvaart tussen de wereldoorlogen.* Houten: Romen, 1986.

——. *Blauw in de lucht: Koninklijke Luchtvaart Maatschappij 1919-1999.* The Hague: Sdu Publishers, 1999.

——. *Clipping the Clouds: How Air Travel Changed the World.* London: Praeger, 2008.

———. *Fokker: A Transatlantic Biography.* Washington, DC: Smithsonian Institution Press, 1997.
———. "Struggle for Prominence: Clashing Dutch and British Interests on the Colonial Air Routes, 1918-42." *Journal of Contemporary History* 26, no. 2 (1991): 333-51.
Dierikx, Marc, and Bram Bouwens. *Building Castles of the Air: Schiphol Amsterdam and the Development of Airport Infrastructure in Europe, 1916-1996.* The Hague: Sdu Publishers, 1997.
Dildy, Douglas C. "Meidagen 1940: The Dutch Air Arms Defense against the German Invasion, May, 1940; Part 1." *Small Air Forces Observer* 28, no. 1 (2004): 17-36.
———. "Meidagen 1940: The Dutch Air Arms Defense against the German Invasion, May, 1940; Part 2a." *Small Air Forces Observer* 28, no. 2 (2004): 43-54.
———. "Meidagen 1940: The Dutch Air Arms Defense against the German Invasion, May, 1940; Part 2b." *Small Air Forces Observer* 28, no. 3 (2005): 79-84.
———. "Meidagen 1940: The Dutch Air Arms Defense against the German Invasion, May, 1940; Part 3." *Small Air Forces Observer* 28, no. 4 (2005): 129-35.
Dorssen, Harry van, and Frits Gerdessen, "Interned! A List of Aeroplanes of All Nationalities That Were Interned by the Dutch Authorities after Landing in Holland during 1914-1918." *Cross and Cockade Great Britain Journal* 16, no. 1 (1985): 18-31.
Dull, Paul S. *A Battle History of the Imperial Japanese Navy (1941-1945).* Annapolis, MD: United States Naval Institute, 1978.
Earhart, Amelia. *20 Hrs. 40 Min.: Our Flight in the Friendship.* New York: Putnam, 1928.
Festner, Tieme. "No. 322 Squadron, Royal Netherlands Air Force." *Wings of Fame* 15 (1999): 22-35.
Flanagan, Brian P. "The U.S. Air Service's Fokker D.VIII Monoplanes." *Cross and Cockade Journal* 16, no. 1 (1975): 83-92.
Fokker, Anthony H. G. "Air Transportation." *Annals of the American Academy of Political and Social Science* 131 (1927): 182-87.
Fokker, Anthony H. G., and Bruce Gould. *Flying Dutchman: The Life of Anthony Fokker.* New York: Henry Holt, 1931.
Fokker Aircraft Corporation of America. *Some Practical Considerations concerning Fokker Aircraft.* New York: Fokker Aircraft Corporation of America, 1928.
"The Fokker Fours." *Air Enthusiast* 1, no. 6 (1971): 292-96.
Forden, Lesley. *The Ford Air Tours: 1925-1931.* New Brighton, MN: Aviation Foundation of America, 2003.
Francillon, René J. *Japanese Aircraft of the Pacific War.* Annapolis, MD: Naval Institute Press, 1988.
———. *Lockheed Aircraft Since 1913.* Annapolis, MD: Naval Institutes Press, 1982.
———. *McDonnell Douglas Aircraft Since 1920: Volume I.* Annapolis, MD: Naval Institute Press, 1979.
Froesch, Charles. "The Fokker Aircraft Corporation of America." *American Aviation Historical Society Journal* 47, no. 3 (2002): 216-25.
Garrison, Peter. "The Perfect Wing." *Aviation History* 24, no. 3 (2014): 44-49.
Garzke, William H., Jr., and Robert O. Dulin, Jr. *Battleships: Allied Battleships in World War II.* Annapolis, MD: Naval Institute Press, 1980.
Geldhof, Nico. *De Fokker D.VII: in dienst van de Nederlandse Militair Luchtvaart.* Maarssen: Geromy, 2008.
Geldhof, N., and P. C. Kok. *Douglas DC-2: De eerste blikken vogel van de KLM en de KNILM.* Bergen: Bonneville, 1997.
Geldhof, N., et al., eds. *70 Jaar Marineluchtvaartdienst.* Leeuwarden: Uitgeverij Eisma B.V., 1987.
Gerdessen, Frits. "The Douglas DB-8A/3N." *American Aviation Historical Society Journal* 44, no. 4 (1999): 298-307.
———. "Fokker's 'Paper' Fighters: Interwar Projects." *Air Enthusiast* 95 (2001): 32-44.
———. "Netherlands' Fokker D.VII's." *Cross and Cockade Journal* 22, no. 4 (1981): 349-54.
Gerdessen, Frits, and Luuk Boerman. *Fokker D.XXI: historie, camouflage en kentekens.* Zwammerdam: Dutch Profile, 2007.
Glines, Carroll V., and Wendell F. Moseley. *The Story of a Fabulous Airplane: The DC-3.* Philadelphia: J.B. Lippincott, 1966.
Goerler, Raimund E. *To the Pole: The Diary and Notebook of Richard E. Byrd, 1925-1927.* Columbus: Ohio State University Press, 1998.
Goss, Chris. *Bloody Biscay: The Story of the Luftwaffe's Only Long Range Maritime Fighter Unit, V* Gruppe/Kampfgeschwader *40, and Its Adversaries. 1942-1944.* Manchester: Crécy Publishing, 1997.
Graaff, Bob de. "Hot Intelligence in the Tropics: Dutch Intelligence Operations in the Netherlands East Indies during the Second World War." *Journal of Contemporary History* 22, no. 4, *Intelligence Services during the Second World War: Part 2* (Oct. 1987): 563-84.
Green, William, and Gordon Swanborough. "The Ubiquitous Hawk: Part I." *Air Enthusiast* 1, no. 6 (1971): 307-14.
———. "The Ubiquitous Hawk: Part II." *Air Enthusiast* 1, no. 7 (1971): 374-78.
———. "The Ubiquitous Hawk: Part III." *Air Enthusiast* 2, no. 1 (1972): 47-52.
Grosz, Peter M. "Fokker's D VIII . . . the Reluctant Razor." *Air Enthusiast* 17 (1981): 61-73.
———. "Reinhold Platz and the Fokker Company." *Over the Front* 5, no. 3 (1990): 213-22.
Gunsburg, Jeffery A. *Divided and Conquered: The French High Command and the Defeat of the West, 1940.* London: Greenwood Press, 1979.
Hagedorn, Dan, and Antonio L. Sapienza. *Aircraft of the Chaco War.* Atglen, PA: Schiffer Military/Aviation History, 1997.
Hagens, G. J., C. Roelofs, and J. van Driel. *This Is Your Flight Engineer Speaking . . .* Amsterdam: Vereniging van KLM-Boordwerktuigkundigen, 1988.
Hall, Melvin, and Walter Peck. "Wings for the Trojan Horse." *Foreign Affairs* 19, no. 2 (1941): 347-69.
Hazewinkel, Harm J. *Pander: Een Haagse vliegtuigbouwer.* Hilversum: All Media Productions, 2006.
Hegener, Henri. *Fokker: The Man and the Aircraft.* Fallbrook, CA: Aero Publishers, 1961.
Helfferich, Willem. *Squadrons van de Koninklijke Luchtmacht.* Rotterdam: Drukkerij Wyt & Zn., 1994.
Hof, L. Th. van't. "Dit had onze jachtkruiser voor 1941 moeten worden: De Fokker G-2, opvolger van een geweldenaar." *Vliegende Hollander* (Dec. 1962): 408-11.
Hoffman, Peter. "Peace through Coup d'Etat: The Foreign Contacts of the German Resistance 1933-1944." *Central European History* 19, no. 1 (1986): 3-44.
Homze, Edward L. *Arming the Luftwaffe: The Reich Air Ministry and the German Aircraft Industry, 1919-1939.* Lincoln: University of Nebraska Press, 1976.
Hooftman, Hugo. *Van Farman tot Neptune: Vijftig Jaar Nederlandse Marinevliegtuigen.* Zwolle: La Rivière & Voorhoeve, 1964.
Horne, Alistair. *To Lose a Battle: France, 1940.* Boston: Little, Brown, 1969.
Howard, Ronald. *In Search of My Father: A Portrait of Leslie Howard.* New York: St. Martin's Press, 1981.
Howson, Gerald. "Fokker's Trimotors Go to War." *Air Enthusiast* 13 (1980): 43-49.
Hucker, Robert. "D-VIII . . . Was It the Best Fokker?" *Air Classics* 14, no. 2 (1978): 70-79.
———. "The Fokker Scourge: Fact or Fiction?" *Air Classics* 15, no. 8 (1979): 14-18, 96-98.
Hurst, Doug. *De vierde bondgenoot: de Nederlandse strijdkrachten in Australië tijdens de Tweede Wereldoorlog.* Zwolle: Waanders Uitgevers, 2006.
Imrie, Alex. *Fokker Fighters of World War One.* London: Arms & Armor Press, 1986.
Ingells, Douglas J. *The Plane That Changed the World: A Biography of the DC-3.* Fallbrook, CA: Aero Publishers, 1966.
Instituto de Historia y Cultura Aérea. *Historia de la Aviacion Española.* Madrid: Instituto de Historia y Cultura Aérea, 1988.
International Military Tribunal. *The Trial of German Major War Criminals: Proceedings of the International Military Tribunal Sitting at Nuremberg, Germany.* 23 vols. London: Published under the Authority of H.M. Attorney-General by H.M. Stationery Office, 1946.
Isaacs, Keith, Gerard J. Casius, and A. P. De Jong. "Brewster's Benighted Buffalo." *Air Enthusiast Quarterly* 1 (1974): 66-83.
Jackson, A. J. "Bats and Bantams." *Aeroplane Monthly* 11, no. 3 (1983): 150-55.
———. "Bats and Bantams." *Aeroplane Monthly* 11, no. 4 (1983): 205-8.
———. "Bats and Bantams." *Aeroplane Monthly* 11, no. 5 (1983): 274-77.
———. "Bats and Bantams." *Aeroplane Monthly* 11, no. 6 (1983): 339-42.
Jackson, Robert. *The Red Falcons: The Soviet Air Force in Action, 1919-1969.* London: Clifton Books, 1970.
Jong, Ellen van Zyll de. "Netherlands Indies to Produce Aviation Fuel for Far East." *Far Eastern Survey* 9, no. 10 (1940): 116-17.
Jong, Kolonel A. P. de. *Vlucht door de tijd: 75 jaar Nederlandse luchtmacht.* Houten: Unieboek, 1988.
Jong, L. de. *Het Koninkrijk der Nederlanden in de Tweede Wereldoorlog.* Deel I-III. The Hague: Staatsuitgeverij, 1969.
Kavelaars, H. C. "The DC-2, the Dutch, and the 1934 Melbourne Race." *American Aviation Historical Society Journal* 29, no. 4 (1984): 256-74.
King, Chan. "Four-Engined First: Fokker's F.32." *Wings* 32, no. 6 (2002): 14-23.

Kingsford-Smith, C. E., and C. T. P. Ulm. *The Flight of the Southern Cross.* New York: Robert M. McBride & Co., 1929.
Klaauw, Bart van der. "East Indies Pioneers: The KNILM Story—1928-1947." *Air Enthusiast* 113 (2004): 52-57.
——. "Fokker's American Heydays: 'Flying Dutchmen' Built in the US." *Air Enthusiast* 68 (1997): 2-11.
——. "Frustrated Fokker." *Air International* (Nov. 1986): 241-49.
Klaauw, B. van der, Armand van Ishoven, and Peter van der Gaag. *De Geschiedenis van de Nederlandse en Belgische Luchtvaart.* Rotterdam: Lekturama B.V., 1982.
Koninklijke Luchtvaart Maatschappij voor Nederland en Kolonien. *KLM's Caribbean Decade, 1934-1944.* Curacao: Koninklijke Luchtvaart Maatschappij voor Nederland en Kolonien, N.V., 1944.
Koolhoven, F. "Vliegboot of Landvliegtuig." *Het Vliegveld* (Sept. 1937): 280-82.
Kroon, Kapitein-luitenant ter Zee b.d. L.D. de, and Haye Thomas. *Van Linieschip tot Vliegkampschip: De Koninklijke Marine sinds het ontstaan van het Koninkrijk der Nederlanden.* Amsterdam: Elsevier, 1964.
Kuhn, Volkmar. *German Paratroopers in World War II.* London: Ian Allan, 1978.
Küpfer, C. C. *Onze Vliegers in Indië.* Haarlem: Uitgave Boom-Ruigrok N.V., 1947.
Lamberton, W. M. *Fighter Aircraft of the 1914-1918 War.* Los Angeles: Aero Publishers, 1964.
Lane, Spencer. *First World Flight: The Odyssey of Billy Mitchell.* Daytona Beach, FL: U.S. Press, 2002.
Layton, Rear Admiral Edwin T., U.S.N. *"And I Was There": Pearl Harbor and Midway—Breaking the Secrets.* New York: William Morrow, 1985.
Leaman, Paul. *Fokker Aircraft of World War One.* Ramsbury: Crowood Press, 2001.
Leeuw, René de. *Albert Plesman: Luchtvaartpionier en Visionair.* The Hague: Uitgeverij van de Vereniging van Nederlandse Gemeenten, 1989.
——, ed. *Fokker Commercial Aircraft.* Amsterdam: N.V. Koninklijke Nederlandse Vliegtuigenfabriek Fokker, 1994.
——. *KLM: De Geschiedenis van de KLM vanaf 1919.* Weesp: Unieboek, 1984.
Loveday, E. Colin. "Southern Cross Enigma: Piecing Together an Icon's Past." *Air Enthusiast* 88 (2000): 58-65.
Lundin, Goran. "Thulin." *WWI Aero: The Journal of the Early Aeroplane* 153 (1996): 18-37.
Lundstrom, John B. *The First South Pacific Campaign: Pacific Fleet Strategy, December 1941–June 1942.* Annapolis, MD: Naval Institute Press, 1976.
Maass, Walter B. *The Netherlands at War: 1940-1945.* London: Abelard-Schuman, 1970.
Mallan, K. *Als de Dag van Gisteren . . . De Duitse Overrompeling en Vernietiging van Nederlands Eerste Havenstad.* Weesp: De Gooise Uitgeverij, 1985.
Mason, Henry L. "War Comes to The Netherlands: September 1939–May 1940." *Political Science Quarterly* 78, no. 4 (1963): 548-80.
Maurer, Maurer. *Aviation in the U.S. Army, 1919-1939.* Washington, DC: Office of Air Force History, United States Air Force, 1987.
May, Ernest R. *Strange Victory: Hitler's Conquest of France.* New York: Hill and Wang, 2000.
Messimer, Dwight R. *Pawns of War: The Loss of the USS* Langley *and the USS* Pecos. Annapolis, MD: Naval Institute Press, 1983.
Mets, David R. *Master of Airpower: General Carl A. Spaatz.* Novato, CA: Presidio Press, 1988.
Mitchell, William. *Winged Defense: The Development and Possibilities of Modern Air Power—Economic and Military.* New York: Putnam, 1925.
Molenaar, F. J. *De luchtverdediging in de meidagen 1940.* 2 vols. The Hague: Staatsuitgeverij, 1970.
Moll, Martin. *"Führer-Erlasse" 1939-1945: Edition sämtlicher überlieferter, nicht im Reichsgesetzblatt abgedruckter, von Hitler während des Zweiten Weltkrieges schriftlich erteilter Direktiven aus den Bereichen Staat, Partei, Wirtschaft, Besatzungspolitik und Militärverwaltung.* Stuttgart: F. Steiner, 1997.
Morrison, Wilbur H. *Donald W. Douglas: A Heart with Wings.* Ames: Iowa State University Press, 1991.
Mosier, John. *The Blitzkrieg Myth: How Hitler and the Allies Misread the Strategic Realities of World War II.* New York: HarperCollins, 2003.
Mulder, Rob J. M. *E.L.T.A.: The First Aviation Exhibition Amsterdam.* Spikkestad: European Airlines Rob Mulder, 2009.
Nater, Johan P. *De Uiver: Glorie en tragiek in de Melbourne race.* Rotterdam: Ad. Donker, 1983.
O'Callaghan, Timothy J. *The Aviation Legacy of Henry and Edsel Ford.* Ann Arbor, MI: Proctor Publications, 2000.
Odgers, George. *Air War against Japan, 1943-1945.* Canberra: Australian War Memorial, 1957.
O'Leary, Michael. "Fokker's Last Scourge: The Deadly D VII." *Air Combat* 2, no. 1 (1974): 18-26.
Oosten, F. C. van. *The Battle of the Java Sea.* Annapolis, MD: Naval Institute Press, 1976.
Overstraeten, Raoul François Casimir van. *Albert I–Leopold III, vingt ans de politique militaire belge 1920-1940.* Bruges: Desclee de Brouwer, 1946.
Overvest, H. J. van. "Airborne in the D VII." *Air Enthusiast* 38 (1989): 48-54.
Owers, Colin. "Especially . . . the D.VII . . . Part One." *Air Enthusiast* 60 (1995): 63-70.
——. "Especially . . . the D.VII . . . Part Two." *Air Enthusiast* 61 (1996): 52-63.
——. "The Fokker D.VII in US Service." *Skyways* 86 (2008).
——. "Fokker's Fifth: The C.V Multi-role Biplane." *Air Enthusiast* 53 (1994): 60-68.
——. "USAAS Fokker D.VII Fighters." *Windsock International* 9, no. 3 (1993): 16-19.
Parmentier, K. D. *In Drie Dagen naar Australië.* Amsterdam: Scheltens & Giltay, 1935.
Parton, James. *"Air Force Spoken Here": General Ira Eaker and the Command of the Air.* Bethesda, MD: Adler & Adler, 1986.
Pauw, J. L. van der. *Rotterdam in de Tweede Wereldoorlog.* Rotterdam: Uitgeverij Boom, 2006.
Pearson, Frederic S. *The Weak State in International Crisis: The Case of the Netherlands in the German Invasion Crisis of 1939-40.* Washington, DC: University Press of America, 1981.
Pelletier, Alain J. "Fokker Twilight." *Air Enthusiast* 117 (2005): 62-66.
Penrose, Harald. *British Aviation: The Great War and Armistice: 1915-1919.* New York: Funk & Wagnalls, 1969.
Plesman, Albert. "The Amsterdam-Batavia Weekly Service." *Flight* 25 (Feb. 9, 1933): 128-33.
Postma, S. J. *HU-BO-BE: De strategische VerVa in de oorlogsdagen van 1940.* Assen: Born's Uitgeversbedrijf N.V., 1945.
Postma, Thijs. *Fokker: Aircraft Builders of the World.* London: Jane's, 1979.
——. *Vermetele Vliegende Hollanders.* Bussum: Unieboek, 1975.
Postma, Thijs, and Nico Geldhof. *Nederlandse Marine Vliegtuigen.* The Hague: Omniboek, 1978.
Poulsen, C. M. "Speed and Comfort: Some Impressions of an Afternoon Spent in Flying around Holland in an F.36 and a Douglas D.2." *Flight* (Sept. 27, 1934): 994-96.
Prime, Mervyn W. *WA's Pearl Harbour: The Japanese Raid on Broome.* Bullcreek, UK: Royal Australian Air Force Association, 1985.
RAAF Historical Section. *Units of the Royal Australian Air Force: A Concise History*. Vols. 2 and 3. Canberra: Australian Government Publishing Service, 1995.
Rawlins, Dennis. "Byrd's Heroic 1926 Flight and Its Faked Last Leg." *Dio: The International Journal of Scientific History* 10 (2000): 9-106.
Rich, Doris L. *Amelia Earhart: A Biography.* Washington, DC: Smithsonian Institution, 1989.
Rottman, Gordon L., and A. Takizawa. *Japanese Paratroop Forces in World War II.* Oxford: Osprey Publishing, 2005.
Rusman, E. *Wings across Continents: The KLM Amsterdam-Batavia Line*. Amsterdam: Andries Blitz, 1935.
Saunders, Hilary St. George. *Per Ardua: The Rise of British Air Power, 1911-1939.* New York: Arno Press, 1972.
Scheppler, R. H. "Fokker's Four-Engined Failure." *Air Classics* 11, no. 6 (1975): 54-64.
Schoenmaker, Wim, and Thijs Postma. *Aviateurs van het Eerste Uur.* Weesp: Romen Luchtvaart, 1984.
——. *KLu Vliegtuigen.* Alkmaar: Uitgeverij De Alk, 1987.
——. *Mei 1940: De verdediging van het Nederlandse luchtruim.* Amsterdam/Dieren: Bataafsche Leeuw, 1985.
Schrader, Richard K. "The Army's Forgotten Fokkers." *Air Classics* 24, no. 5 (1988): 64-67.
Seaborn, Clark G. "The Rebirth of CF-AAM: The History and Restoration of a Fokker Super Universal." *C.A.H.S.: The Journal of the Canadian Aviation Historical Society* 35, no. 1 (1997): 18-29.
Shores, Christopher, and Brian Cull, with Yasuho Izawa. *Bloody Shambles.* 3 vols. London: Grub Street, 1992.
Sloan, John. "Fokker in the United States: Part 1." *Skyways* 43 (1997): 34-45.
——. "Fokker in the United States: Part 2." *Skyways* 45 (1998): 35-50.
Smit, C. *Bescheiden Betreffende de Buitenlandse Politiek van Neder-*

land 1848-1919: Derde Periode 1899-1919, Vierde Deel 1914-1917. The Hague: Martinus Nijhoff, 1962.
——. *Bescheiden Betreffende de Buitenlandse Politiek van Nederland 1848-1919: Derde Periode 1899-1919, Vijfde Deel 1917-1919, Eerste Stuk.* The Hague: Martinus Nijhoff, 1964.
——. *Bescheiden Betreffende de Buitenlandse Politiek van Nederland 1848-1919: Derde Periode 1899-1919, Achtste Deel Buitenlandse Bronnen 1917-1919, Eerste Stuk.* The Hague: Martinus Nijhoff, 1973.
Smith, Richard K. *Seventy-Five Years of Inflight Refueling: Highlights, 1923-1998.* Washington, DC: Air Force History and Museums Program, 1998.
Smith, Richard Norton. *The Colonel: The Life and Legend of Robert R. McCormick, 1880-1955.* Boston: Houghton Mifflin, 1997.
Speidel, Wilhelm. *The German Air Force in France and the Low Countries, 1939-1940, Volume 3.* Karlsruhe: Studiegruppe Geschichte des Luftkrieges, 1958.
Steenbeek, Wilhelmina. *Rotterdam: Invasion of Holland.* New York: Ballantine Books, 1973.
Stroud, John. *European Transport Aircraft Since 1910.* London: Putnam, 1966.
——. "Wings of Peace." *Aeroplane Monthly* (Sept. 1985): 489-501.
——. "Wings of Peace: Fokker VIII." *Aeroplane Monthly* (May 1988): 297-300.
Swanborough, Gordon, and Peter M. Bowers. *United States Military Aircraft Since 1909.* Washington, DC: Smithsonian Institution Press, 1989.
Swinson, Arthur. *The Great Air Race: England-Australia 1934.* London: Cassell, 1968.
Tapper, Oliver. *Armstrong Whitworth Aircraft Since 1913.* London: Putnam, 1973.
Taylor, H. A., and Peter Alting. "Fokker's 'Lucky Seven.'" *Air Enthusiast* 12 (1980): 24-38.
Ten Years of Japanese Burrowing in the Netherlands East Indies. New York: The Netherlands Information Bureau, 1942.
Thetford, O. G., and E. J. Riding. *Aircraft of the 1914-1918 War.* Harleyford: Harborough, 1954.
Thomas, Geoffrey J., and Barry Kelly. *KG 200: The Luftwaffe's Most Secret Unit.* Crowborough: Hikoki Publications, 2003.
Thomassen À Thuessink van der Hoop, A. N. J. *Door de Lucht naar Indië.* Amsterdam: Scheltens and Giltay, 1926.
Tichenor, Frank A. "Roosevelt and Farley Charged with 'Fraud and Collusion'!!" *Aero Digest* (Oct. 1936).
Toland, John. *The Rising Sun: The Decline and Fall of the Japanese Empire, 1936-1945.* New York: Random House, 1970.
Tuyll, Hubert P. van. "The Dutch Mobilization of 1914: Reading the 'Enemy's' Intentions." *Journal of Military History* 64, no. 3 (2000): 711-37.
Tuyll van Serooskerken, Hubert P. van. *The Netherlands and World War I: Espionage, Diplomacy, and Survival.* Leiden: Brill, 2001.
Tyler, William H. *Flight of Diamonds: The Story of Broome's War and the Carnot Bay Diamonds.* Victoria Park: Hesperian Press, 1987.
Vandenbosch, Amry. *The Neutrality of the Netherlands during the World War.* Grand Rapids: Eerdmans, 1927.
Van der Meer, Harry. "Koolhovens Oceaanvliegboot." *Verenigde Vleugels* (Nov. 2007).
Vanwelkenhuyzen, Jean. *Le 10 janvier 1940 a Mechelen-sur-Meuse: le plan de Hitler aux mains des Belges.* Brussels: Goemaere, 1955.
Vašíček, Radko. "Fokker D.VII's and the Founding of the Czechoslovak Air Force." *Cross and Cockade Journal* 21, no. 3 (1980): 263-69.
Visser, Johan G. H. "Dutch Military Aircraft: 1910-1920." *Over the Front* 14, no. 4 (1999): 315-57.
Vredeling, Willem. *Fokker D.23.* Maarssen: Geromy, 2007.
Walaardt Sacré, H., W. P. van den Abeelen, and F. Spittel. *Vijf-en-Twintig Jaar Luchtvaart in Nederland.* Amsterdam: A. J. G. Strengholt, 1932.
Wenstedt, Joop. "Fokker's Paper Planes." *Aeroplane Monthly* (Feb. 1989): 121-24.
Wesselink, Theo J. M. "The Advancement of Dutch Civil Aviation by an American Millionaire: The Air Exploits of William van Lear Black." *American Aviation Historical Society Journal* 26, no. 2 (1981): 118-25.
——. "The B.A.T. FK23 'Bantam.'" *American Aviation Historical Society Journal* 22, no. 1 (1977): 26-27.
——. "The Fighter That Missed the War . . . The Last of the Koolhovens." *Air International* (Apr. 1976): 185-89, 198.
——. "The Saga of the T VIIIw." *Air Enthusiast* 20 (1982).
Wesselink, Theo, and Thijs Postma. *De Nederlandse vliegtuigen.* Haarlem: Romen, 1982.
——. *Koolhoven: Nederlands vliegtuigbouwer in de schaduw van Fokker.* Haarlem: Romen, 1981.
Westburg, Peter. "Deadly D-VIII: A Detailed Look at Tony Fokker's Ultimate Fighter . . . WWI's Best." *Wings* 9, no. 2 (1979).
——. "Fokker's Last Biplane Fight." *Air Classics* 1, no. 7 (1975): 60-73.
Weyl, A. R. *Fokker: The Creative Years.* London: Putnam, 1965.
Whiting, Charles. *Hunters from the Sky: The German Parachute Corps, 1940-1945.* New York: Stein and Day, 1974.
Wijdenbosch, R. Th. C. *Luchtvaartontwikkelingen in Suriname.* Paramaribo: Vaco N.V. Uitgeversmaatschappij, 1996.
Wilhelmina, H. R. H. *Lonely but Not Alone.* New York: McGraw-Hill, 1960.
Winter, R. de. *Hendrik Walaardt Sacré, 1873-1949: Leven voor de Luchtvaart.* The Hague: Sectie Luchtmachthistorie van de Luchtmachtstaf, 1992.
——. *Luchtmachtstructuren in Beweging: 80 Jaar Luchtmacht-organisatie.* The Hague: Sectie Luchtmachthistorie van de Luchtmachtstaf, 1994.
Wittert, René. *Het Vergeten Squadron.* Franeker: Uitgeverij T. Wever B.V., 1983.
Womack, Tom. *The Dutch Naval Air Force against Japan: The Defense of the Netherlands East Indies, 1941-1942.* Jefferson, NC: McFarland, 2006.

INDEX OF NAMES

INDEX OF AIRCRAFT

KONINKLIJKE LUCHTVAART MAATIJ
HN
ABE
HNABE
THE FLYING DUTCHMAN
GEEN LEGENDE MAAR WERKELIJKHEID

KONINKLIJKE LUCHTVAART
MAATSCHAPPIJ
KLM
H-
HNKLM
De Vliegende Hollander
Eéns LEGENDE-thans WERKELIJKHEID